The Cultural Mindset

To Sienna,
who effortlessly carries within her the many cultures that continue to shape her.

The Cultural Mindset

Managing People Across Cultures

Afsaneh Nahavandi
University of San Diego

Los Angeles | London | New Delhi
Singapore | Washington DC | Melbourne

FOR INFORMATION:

SAGE Publications, Inc.

2455 Teller Road

Thousand Oaks, California 91320

E-mail: order@sagepub.com

SAGE Publications Ltd.

1 Oliver's Yard

55 City Road

London EC1Y 1SP

United Kingdom

SAGE Publications India Pvt. Ltd.

B 1/I 1 Mohan Cooperative Industrial Area

Mathura Road, New Delhi 110 044

India

SAGE Publications Asia-Pacific Pte. Ltd.

18 Cross Street #10-10/11/12

China Square Central

Singapore 048423

ISBN: 978-1-5443-8150-3

Sponsoring Editor: Lauren Gobell

Editorial Assistant: Sarah Wilson

Production Editor: Preethi Agnes Thomas

Copy Editor: Christobel Colleen Hopman

Typesetter: TNQ Technologies

Proofreader: Benny Willy Stephen

Indexer: TNQ Technologies

Cover Designer: Ginkhan Siam

Marketing Manager: Jennifer Jones

21 22 23 24 25 10 9 8 7 6 5 4 3 2 1

BRIEF CONTENTS

DETAILED CONTENTS

PART III • KNOW—GROUP CULTURE AND DIVERSITY   183

CHAPTER 5 • Managing Diverse Groups   185

CHAPTER 11 • Managing Organizational Strategic Forces and Processes

PREFACE

Why I Wrote This Book

Culture is not a new topic. The world has not suddenly become more diverse; it has always been diverse. However, we are increasingly coming in contact with people who are different from us and realizing the importance of being able to interact successfully across cultures. Culture has become an ongoing challenge and an opportunity for many.

I often get asked the seemingly simple questions of "What is your cultural background? Where are you from?" And, I do not have a simple answer. I come from a multicultural background, while being ethnically Iranian. I grew up in Iran, but studied in a French school with kids from all different nationalities, speaking Persian as my native tongue and French as a first language, while also learning English and Spanish. I came to the US for university as a freshman, became a US citizen, and have lived in the US for many years. My citizenship is clear; but the answers to my cultural background and where I am from are not. My physical appearance and my accent do not provide clear clues to my cultural identities. The fact that I hold several cultural identities, Iranian by birth, US-American by citizenship, and French through my education, and find all of them equally attractive, desirable, and often completely contradictory, has fascinated and puzzled me for years. My Iranian, US, and French selves agree on some, but not many things; yet, they all live happily within me. I also have to consider how many other cultural factors, such as my gender and profession, just to name a few, further shape how I think. I have found that this complex sense of belonging to several cultures at once has provided me with the ability to move among different settings with ease, something that many others in this world, who are multicultural, also experience.

So, my academic interest in the role of culture in leadership and management stems from a very personal journey. When I started teaching various classes about culture and management, I had trouble finding textbooks and materials that fully explained and expressed culture, its complexity and impact. The books were almost always written from a Western perspective, or they were too prescriptive and "cookbooky," or too focused on skills, or just concerned with national culture, ignoring all other levels of culture such as gender and ethnicity. All this led me to develop and craft the concept of Cultural Mindset and its assessment, and the THINK–KNOW–DO roadmap, and to the writing of this book.

My Approach

This book offers a unique approach and several distinctive themes that differentiate it from others:

- *Culture is viewed from a cognitive perspective*, considering how culture, first and foremost, gives us the lens through which we see the world and therefore shapes how we think before it impacts our behavior, the way we run meetings, lead or greet one another. Culture is therefore something that we all have, not just something that "others" have.
- *Culture is addressed as the ever-present context* and background that impacts all that we do rather than something that just needs to be addressed in some situations. Culture is a meta-context (CMC). It is everywhere, and it guides our thinking and behavior.
- *Culture is considered from multiple levels*, not just nationality, allowing for a complex view of the topic. People are more than their country of citizenship; they are also part of regions and many other groups, including, but not limited to, gender, ethnicity, religion, and so forth.
- *Culture is considered from multiple perspectives* rather than comparing all cultures to that of the US or other Western countries.
- *Academic knowledge and practical examples* and applications are integrated throughout to take advantage of, and critically discuss, the extensive research about culture, while at the same time making that information accessible and useful to practitioners at all levels.

These unique and distinct elements make this a book that can be useful to anyone who works in multicultural settings and who is interested in being more effective when interacting across cultures.

Goals and Major Themes

In addition to my cultural background, I am an academic who strongly believes in putting good research and theory to work. Therefore, the book presents a blend and integration of theory and practice through:

- A research-based and empirically derived concept (Cultural Mindset—CM), roadmap (THINK–KNOW–DO—TKD), and self-assessment (Individual Cultural Mindset Inventory—ICMI) as the framework for the book

- Application of CM and the TKD roadmap to:
  (1) Increase the self-awareness of your own culture and its impact on your worldview
  (2) Expand your knowledge regarding culture and develop a vocabulary to help you understand, describe, and predict cultural differences
  (3) Grow your managerial and practical toolbox to become more effective in cross-cultural interactions
- Extensive and critical review of academic literature about culture from multiple disciplines including anthropology, sociology, psychology, and management
- A cognitive approach that recognizes how culture is ever-present and shapes everyone's thinking and behavior
- Repeated reminders about avoiding essentializing, overgeneralizing, and stereotyping others based on limited cultural characteristics or knowledge, while using cultural knowledge to understand, describe, and predict differences

Integration of Theory and Practice Through Pedagogical Features

In addition to discussion of theory and research related to cross-cultural management, examples from many different cultures, and inclusion of real-world examples that illustrate the concepts throughout the book, every chapter includes:

- An opening real-world *First Person* case
- *Window to the World* guide to doing business in specific countries
- *Applying What You Learned* section at the end of the chapter with specific guidelines on how to apply the material from the chapter
- *Managerial Challenge* section at the end of the chapter to help practice applying the concepts from the chapter
- Self-assessments that increase students' self-awareness
- Exercises that engage students and demonstrate how concepts can be applied
- Self-reflection questions that encourage meta-cognition, thoughtful application, and retention of the concepts
- A case at the end of each chapter to further apply the concepts and help wrap up the chapter

Target Audience

The Cultural Mindset is aimed at courses about managing across culture and cultural diversity in schools of business as well as public administration, nonprofit management, educational administration, and health-care management. It is oriented toward advanced undergraduates and master-level students. The book covers all the topics typically found in cross-cultural management courses, with the addition of extensive coverage of cultural diversity topics. The approach is highly applied and practical to prepare current and future managers in all sectors to work more effectively across cultures in increasingly diverse and global communities and organizations.

The material in this book is targeted to you if:

- You are a manager from any sector who works with others across national boundaries
- You are planning for or preparing to work or live outside your own country
- You work with diverse individuals and groups in your local organizations
- You interact with diverse people in your community
- You are simply curious to understand how and why people are so vastly different and want to learn more about the considerable richness of cultural differences

Teaching Resources

This text includes an array of instructor teaching materials designed to save you time and to help you keep students engaged. To learn more, visit sagepub.com or contact your SAGE representative at sagepub.com/findmyrep.

ACKNOWLEDGMENTS

This book would not have been possible without the critical and supportive feedback I received from Dr. Ali Malekzadeh, my husband and colleague, who patiently and enthusiastically reviewed many iterations of the chapters. I couldn't have found a tougher critic and more passionate and tireless cheerleader! Ms. Tuba Pagda has my special gratitude for her help in finding and preparing several of the cases. My colleagues at the University of San Diego, Drs. Juan Roche, Hans Schmitz, and Zeki Pagda, further assisted me with their feedback and input. The idea for this book took shape over several years through the many classes, workshops, and discussions with my students and colleagues at the University of San Diego and many other universities and organizations, and I am thankful for their insight and input and for contributing many examples of their own cross-cultural journeys that you can read throughout the chapters.

I would also like to thank the editorial team at SAGE, Lauren Gobell, Maggie Stanley, and Robert Farrell, for helping make this project a reality, and the following reviewers who provided valuable insight and critiques during the development of this text:

Bradford Frazier, *Belmont Abbey College*

Waheeda Lillevik, *The College of New Jersey*

Stacy Brecht, *University of La Verne*

Joy Schneer, *Rider University*

Burdin Hickok, *New York University*

Martha E. Maddox, *Tennessee Wesleyan University*

Archish Maharaja, *Point Park University*

Jennifer Huss Basquiat, *College of Southern Nevada*

Deborah Hagar, *University of La Verne*

Janie Harden Fritz, *Duquesne University*

Rod Carveth, *Towson University*

Robert Dibie, *Indiana University*

Ernesto Gonzalez, *Florida National University*

Alexander N. Chen, *University of Central Arkansas*

ABOUT THE AUTHOR

Afsaneh Nahavandi is professor of Management at the University of San Diego (USD) and Professor Emerita at Arizona State University (ASU). Prior to coming to USD in 2013, she taught at Arizona State University Business School and in the School of Public Administration. While at ASU she was director of the MBA program at ASU's West campus, director of University College, associate dean of University College and of the College of Public Programs. Prior to joining ASU, she was an assistant professor of Human Resources Management at Northeastern University in Boston. Most recently, she served as Chair of the Department of Leadership Studies at USD. She is the winner of several teaching awards, including ASU's 2004 Professor of the Year and the author of several other books, including *The Art and Science of Leadership*, currently in its 7th edition (2015), *Organizational Behavior (2014)*, *Ancient Leadership Wisdom* (2012), *Organizational Behavior: The Person-Organization Fit* (1999), and *Organizational Culture in the Management of Mergers* (1993), and numerous articles about leadership and culture.

PART ONE

INTRODUCTION

The first part of the book defines the concepts that are used throughout and introduces the unique themes that are implemented to managing people across cultures and to developing a Cultural Mindset. Specifically, Chapter 1 explains the importance and role of culture and the complexity and diversity of the concept and explains the key themes of Cultural Mindset, Culture-as-meta-context, and Culture-Just-Is, Chapter 2 further explores these themes and concepts and discusses the ten factors that make up Cultural Mindset and then introduces the THINK–KNOW–DO roadmap to being more effective across cultures.

CHAPTER ONE

THE IMPACT OF CULTURE ON MANAGING ORGANIZATIONS

FIRST PERSON

Culture Clash in a Joint Venture

I work for a US company that prides itself on having an informal and consultative culture. We discuss everything and have many informal and important information exchanges that occur during occasional chats when we stop by one another's offices or get together in small groups in the hallways. Our meetings rarely have a formal agenda and may appear confrontational to outsiders. People jump in regardless of their title, interrupt one another, forcefully argue, and disagree irrespective of who is talking. But, we all manage to get heard, make sound decisions, and come together when it is time to implement them. We recently started a joint venture (JV) with a Chinese supplier. The business case for the JV was strong, and there was no question that we could both benefit from our cooperation. Our managers had met face-to-face a number of times and worked out the overall plans, and it was now up to various groups to start the actual work. As we conducted our first meetings through video chats, things did not go as expected. While we made a conscious effort to tone down our usually unruly meetings, we got nothing but silence from our Chinese partners. They soon requested a formal detailed agenda at least twenty-four hours prior to our calls and inquired about an organizational chart that clarified our titles and roles, so that each person could work with their appropriate counterpart. One day after each of our meetings, our manager received a detailed summary of our discussions along with an outline of action plans and timelines. In some cases, we had already moved on the issues or even discarded them; in other cases, the items they listed had been points of discussion with no intention on our part to consider them

Learning Objectives

1.1 Explore how the complexity and diversity of today's world impact business and management.

1.2 Define the concept of culture and its characteristics.

1.3 Present the components and levels of culture.

1.4 Compare and contrast culture with other determinants of behavior.

1.5 Elaborate on the sources and purpose of culture.

1.6 Examine the critical challenges with the concept of culture.

1.7 Introduce the cognitive approach to cross-cultural management and explain the themes of culture-as-meta-context (CMC), culture-just-is (CJI), and the Cultural Mindset (CM).

further. It was clear that we simply worked very differently; our lack of structure and formal hierarchy frustrated them, and their need for order and formality annoyed us. Our cultures were clashing!

The *First Person* scenario provides an example of the challenges of managing people when working across cultures, a situation that is increasingly common in today's global world. The goal of this book is to prepare you to be more effective when working across cultures by understanding how culture impacts you and others and provide you with the necessary knowledge and tools to manage cross-cultural situations success-fully. This chapter provides the basic building blocks and defines culture and explores its characteristics, components, levels, sources, and functions. It further presents approaches to understanding culture and ends with the introduction of the three key themes of the book: culture-as-meta-context (CMC), culture-just-is (CJI), and the Cultural Mindset (CM).

We like to think that our modern world is uniquely complex, dynamic, and diverse. While the speed of change and increased ease of connecting with others are increasingly affecting how we manage our organizations, our world has always been complex, dynamic, and diverse. Human civilization is characterized by upheaval, complexity, and diversity. The ancient Egyptian, Persian, and Chinese empires underwent major changes and were made up of peoples and tribes with different traditions and languages who lived across vast geographical regions of the Asian, African, and European continents. Ancient African empires were collections of tribes with vastly different backgrounds. The early Greek democracy was a congregation of city states, each with its own unique practices. The Roman Empire imposed its Pax Romana over a third of the world and over an estimated 70 million people. These ancient governments and their leaders waged wars, resolved conflicts, and achieved peace and prosperity to expand their territories that included people with different religions, traditions, cultures, and languages. Throughout history, traders, who were the original global business people, built complicated networks that helped them move and exchange goods along the Ancient Silk Road, across the African continent, through the Roman roads, and sailed unknown oceans to explore new lands. They spoke multiple languages, made difficult managerial decisions under considerable uncertainty, and learned to negotiate and work with trade partners across many cultures. Complexity, dynamism, and diversity are not new; we have always lived and done business in a complicated, ever-changing, and culturally rich world where the ability to understand and to work with people who are different from us is indispensable and critical to success.

According to Nobel Laureate economist Herbert Simon (1979), people can make rational and accurate decisions in a predictable world where they have extensive knowledge of all relevant information, alternatives, and consequences, a situation that has been called "small world" (Savage, 1954, as cited in Gigerenzer & Gaissmaier, 2011). However, in a "large world" that is unpredictable and where some information is unknown and can only be inferred or guessed, the rules of decision-making change. As noted by another Nobel Laureate economist Joseph Stiglitz (2010), applying small world rules to a large world can have disastrous consequences. When we cross cultural boundaries, when we manage people who are different from us, when we conduct business with other cultures, we unavoidably move from our "small world" to a "large world." The rules change and we cannot apply the rules from one world and expect them to be effective in another. What works well for managers in one context does not necessarily work in another. *That is the cultural paradox and challenge that we address in this book* as we focus on helping managers be more effective when working across cultures.

1. A COMPLEX AND DIVERSE WORLD

LO 1.1 Explore how the complexity and diversity of today's world impacts business and management

Before we introduce the concept of culture and its impact on management, it is necessary to consider the complexity and diversity of the world we live in. Today's business leaders and managers are acutely aware of *globalization*, which is the extent to which cultures, societies, and economies are interconnected and integrated. In any business, your competitors, suppliers, manufacturers, and customers are likely to be global. They come from different parts of the world. If you work in government, education, a nonprofit, or health care, the same globalization impacts you through having to address the needs of people from different cultures, availability of services across the globe, and the constant information exchange. Access to global 24/7 news channels such as CNN, BBC, France 24, and Al Jazeera further reinforces the global interconnectedness which has been intensified by the widespread use of the internet that instantaneously connects people around the world. By some estimates, internet penetration is highest in North America and Europe with above 85% of the population having access to the web, 50% in Asia, and below 40% in Africa.

Globalization and working with diverse people are facts of life for today's managers. Our world is complex, diverse, and interconnected. Table 1.1 provides some key facts about this complexity and diversity.

1.1 Impact of Globalization on Management

Sophisticated technology, global trade, and migration link people more than ever before. Regardless of your profession, sector, or personal background, and whether

Table 1.1 A Complex and Diverse World

		Interesting Facts
World population	7.8 billion (as of March 2020)	Top five: China, India, United States, Indonesia, Pakistan
Number of languages in the world	Over 7,000	Top five languages: Mandarin, Spanish, English, Hindi, Arabic
Number of countries	195 recognized by the United Nations	Top five by area: Russia, Canada, United States, China, Brazil
Number of cultures	Approximately 10,000	Some countries have a few; some have hundreds, many associated with a distinct language
Number of religions	Estimated at 4,200	Major world religions (alphabetically): Baha'ism, Buddhism, Christianity, Confucianism, Hinduism, Islam, Jainism, Judaism, Shinto, Sikhism, Taoism, and Zoroastrianism Most practiced (in order): Christianity, Islam, nonsecular Hinduism, Buddhism
Growing international trade	World Bank data show the total merchandise export in 2019 at $19.5 trillion	The total world export was $122.9 billion in 1960
Top economies	2020 top five world economies based on GDP: US, China, Japan, Germany, UK	1960 top five world economies based on GDP: US, UK, France, China, Japan

you are a business leader, government official, entrepreneur, or a young employee starting out your career, you will be interacting with people from cultures other than your own. As a manager in any organization, it is inevitable that you will manage people who are culturally diverse. More than a third of the revenue of US-based S&P 500 companies is generated overseas (Ro, 2015), requiring managers and employees to work across many cultures. The number of minority students has already increased to over 50% in many schools in the United States ("Digest of Education Statistics," 2013), making it critical for teachers and school administrators to learn how to work with culturally diverse children. A look at the 100 top-ranked NGOs (nongovernmental organizations) around the world indicates that they operate widely in both their home countries and across the world (NGO Advisor, 2015), necessitating that their leaders, managers, and volunteers become culturally aware and competent. Scholars and practitioners in all areas recognize that to succeed in such an environment, people must know how to face the challenges of working effectively across cultures (e.g., Nahavandi, 2017; Ng, Van Dyne, & Ang, 2009).

Consider the deliciously ubiquitous Nutella, the hazelnut and cocoa paste originally created by Pietro Ferrero in the Piedmont region of Italy to address post–World War II cocoa shortages through the addition of hazelnuts. Nutella took its current form in 1964 and its supply chain is now global with ingredients from Turkey, Malaysia, Papua New Guinea, Brazil, the Ivory Coast, Nigeria, Ghana, Ecuador, several European countries, and the United States. It is sold in over 150 countries, claiming that over 30 million people worldwide enjoy it on a daily basis. Just think about the number of people a manager in the Luxemburg-based Ferroro Group that owns Nutella and employs 34,000 people across 53 countries with 20 production plants around the world ("About Nutella," 2019) interacts with. Nutella managers, like others around the world, work across cultures. The company bought Nestle's US confectionary business in 2018, further expanding its global reach. Nutella is not alone. The US fast food chains such as McDonalds (in over 115 countries) and KFC (118 countries, over 4,500 stores in China alone) reach across the globe. Seattle-based Starbucks coffee is sold in 23,000 locations in close to 80 countries with the now distinctive green Mermaid logo hanging over more than 3,600 stores in 150 Chinese cities alone (MacLellan, 2019). The Tata Group, a privately owned Indian conglomerate made up of 30 companies, employs 700,000 people in 100 countries across six continents with a 2017–2018 revenue of $110.7 billion. Tata makes, provides services, or sells anything from steel to cars (including Jaguar and Land Rover), chemicals, beverages, hotels, energy and power plants, and insurance, financial, and consulting services just to name a few (Tata Group Business Profile, 2019). The conglomerate prides itself on its culturally diverse workforce that hails from countries all over the world. The Chinese telecom giant Huawei with 180,000 employees reaches one-third of the world's population in over 170 countries ("#79 Huawei," 2018). The managers and employees in these companies know first-hand that their world is not small; it is complex and diverse.

1.2 Small World Rules in a Large World

As discussed in the introduction to this chapter, working across cultures presents a challenging paradox: the reliable rules that we develop and rely on in our own culture (our small world) do not necessarily apply in other contexts (larger worlds) that are unfamiliar. Consider the following example. A group of German business managers were considering a lucrative offer from an Indian partner. The Indian managers had prepared a presentation that detailed their company's past achievements around the world. The presentation included many anecdotes that highlighted their successes with a variety of foreign partners, but little information about the potential future benefits, sales, and profit projections of their deal. The Germans were frustrated by the lack of specific facts and information about the future cooperation. They could not under-stand the purpose of presenting information about what the Indians had done in other countries and with other partners. Instead, they wanted the details regarding their common future potential and goals.

In this example, both cultural groups are operating based on the rules of their own culture, their "small" world. As we will discuss in detail in later chapters, research has shown that Indians tend to value the past while Germans are more present and future oriented (e.g., Hofstede, Hofstede, & Minkow, 2010; House, Hanges, Javidan, Dorfman, & Gupta, 2004). As a result, the Indian managers are touting the past accom-plishments which they consider to be indicators of their capabilities. Conversely, Germans are seeking more specific information about the future performance of their cooperation and are less concerned about past accomplishments. In order for the parties to work together effectively, they need to understand how their culture may frame their perspective and provide them with rules that may not be appropriate for other contexts. Today's business organizations do not operate in a "small world." Managers and employees come in regular contact with people, products, and services that are global in one way or another.

Whether in the United States, Malaysia, India, Canada, or Tanzania that are culturally diverse, or in less diverse countries such as Japan and Korea, in order to be effective, today's managers must take a global and cultural perspective where they are aware of the their "small" world rules while also considering the "large world." While no one can possibly learn about over 10,000 cultures in the world, managers must be able to work with people who are different from them. They cannot be effective without having an awareness, understanding, and knowledge of culture and how it impacts them, others, and their organizations. They also need the skills and compe-tencies to be able to interact successfully across cultural boundaries; they need to have a *Cultural Mindset*.

2. DEFINITION OF CULTURE

LO 1.2 Define the concept of culture and its characteristics

The *First Person* example at the beginning of the chapter illustrates the challenge of working across cultures. The US organization has a distinct culture that is based on US-American cultural values of informality and egalitarianism where employees are comfortable with casual and direct communication, can disagree with their supervisors, and move fast on implementing decisions. Their Chinese partners, based on their cultural values, expect formality and respect of authority. Both organizations reflect their culture. But what is culture?

The word culture typically evokes art, music, and food; however, the definition is deeper. The origin of the word is the Latin word *cultura* which denotes growth and cultivation, referring to where one grows up. One of the first academic disciplines that studied culture also provides us with an early definition by British anthropologist Edward Tylor (2016). He defined culture as "… a complex whole which includes knowledge, belief, art, law, morals, custom, and any other capabilities and habits acquired by man as a member of society" (p. 1). Others have broadened the definition to include the concepts, summarized in Kroeber and Kluchhohn (1952), of social activity, collective symbols, values, and transmission of culture from one person or group to another. Culture is a social rather than genetic construct, as anthropologist Melville Herskovits (1948) suggests; it is man-made. Sociologist Ann Swidler (1986) considers culture to be a toolkit of strategies that helps people deal with their environment, a definition that is also echoed by international management expert Fons Trompenaars, who sees culture as a way in which people solve problems (Trompenaars & Hampden-Turner, 2012).

Management scholar Geert Hofstede provides another layer to the concept by defining culture as the mental programming or software shared by a group of people (Hofstede et al., 2010), emphasizing the cognitive aspect of culture and its power to shape how we think and act. In that sense, much the same way as a computer's software provides it with instructions on how to perform certain tasks, culture provides individuals with guidance, rules, and instructions regarding how to interpret the world, how to think, and what to do in different situations. Our genetic make-up is our hardware; our culture is part of our software. Hofstede's definition contains elements of anthropologist Clifford Geertz's (1973) definition which also emphasizes the role of culture as providing a set of control mechanisms. Luciara Nardon (2017), professor of international business, similarly considers culture to provide people with a logic of action or a mental model for doing things.

As you can see, there are numerous definitions of culture. For the purposes of this book, and taking into consideration the various definitions of the term, we define culture as:

A complex system of long-lasting and dynamic learned assumptions, beliefs, values, and behaviors shared by members of a group that makes the group unique and that is transmitted from one person to another, allows the group to interpret and make sense of the world, and guides its members' behaviors (see Table 1.2 for a summary of the characteristics of culture).

2.1 Culture as a System

Based on this definition, first and foremost, culture is a *system*. The various parts or components include assumptions, beliefs, values, and behaviors combined in a

Table 1.2 Characteristics of Culture

Characteristic	Description
An organized system	The various components fit together
Complex and multifaceted	Includes assumptions, beliefs, values, and behaviors
Unique to the group	Helps define a group's identity as separate from other groups
Stable and dynamic	Not only has staying power but also evolves in response to various challenges
Transmitted from one person to another	Formally and informally passed on to new and younger members
A tool to make sense of the world	Provides a framework for interpreting the world, events, and relationships
A guide to behavior	Provides protocol and direction regarding what is considered appropriate and desirable behavior

coherent, logical, and organized system where parts work together to meet the needs of the group. Because it is made up of different parts, levels, and elements that interact and function together, culture is *complex* and multifaceted. One cannot simply explain culture based on just one of its elements. For example, food or music are artifacts that provide a window into culture, but do not fully explain it. Therefore, fully understanding and knowing a culture would require deeper exploration of beliefs, values, and assumptions and their origins. Additionally, every culture is *unique* to a group of people. Several groups may share similar assumptions, values, beliefs, or behaviors, but each combination and its manifestation is unique. As such, this unique and organized system provides each group with a distinctive shared identity and worldview and sets it apart from other groups.

2.2 Culture as Stable and Dynamic

Culture presents an interesting contradiction. It is *stable and long-lasting* while also being adaptable and *dynamic*. In other words, a culture does not change rapidly, but it does shift and adapt over time. Consider how the culture in the United States has evolved since the 1950s as reflected in our business organizations. Even the most forward-looking and innovative organizations of the 1950s and 1960s, dramatically represented in the TV show *Mad Men*, included almost exclusively white men with few women or minorities. Men wore suits and ties and called their boss by his last name. Women wore dresses and typically worked in support roles and only until they were married and had children. Minorities were often consigned to blue-collar jobs with few in managerial ranks. Contrast those companies with today's organizations. There is considerable diversity at all levels, the dress code is more relaxed, and many of us call our boss or supervisor by his or her first name. The Civil Rights and Women's Liberation movements of the 1950s and 1960s changed some of the deeply held views regarding race and the role of women in society while many other values and beliefs, including culturally based racial and gender stereotypes, continue. Organizations have responded to those changes by implementing a variety of diversity and inclusion programs. All cultures evolve and change over time. While cultural change is often slow and evolutionary, rather than fast and revolutionary, it does take place. Cultures are dynamic while still being stable.

2.3 Transmitting Culture

Another characteristic of culture is that it is *transmitted* from one member to another; older and longer-tenured members teach their culture to younger newcomers, whether they are children or new immigrants. Culture is both actively taught and learned. Through direct teaching and communication or through subtler storytelling or role modeling, younger and newer members learn values and beliefs regarding what are considered desirable and appropriate behaviors. For example, as we will discuss in detail in Chapter 6, there are deeply rooted gender stereotypes that impact women's opportunities in organizations. Specifically, what has been called the "think manager–think male" belief represents automatically associating leadership and management with men rather than women. Children learn such expectations early in life. For example, after reviewing close to 6,000 children's books, Janice McCabe and her colleagues found that males were represented twice as often in their titles, and that almost 60% of the books had male central characters while only 31% depicted female central characters (McCabe, Fairchild, Grauerholz, Perscosolido, & Tope, 2011). They also found that even animal characters were more likely to be male.

Their findings indicate how cultural gender norms that impact our views of management are communicated to children through the literature they read. It is only recently that the media and parents are questioning these messages and the values they reinforce about girls being less important, helpless, and dependent by presenting powerful and independent female lead characters such as in *The Hunger Games*, in animated movies such as *Brave* and *Frozen*, or blockbuster movies such as *Wonder Woman*, *Rogue One*, *Black Panther*, and *Captain Marvel*. Similarly, through diversity and inclusion programs, organizations are attempting to relate and transmit gender egalitarian values to their employees and other stakeholders.

2.4 Culture as a Framework

Culture provides people with a framework and a way to interpret the world and make sense of the environment and events and people's behaviors. Culture is a key part of the software of our mind. Take a deceptively simple and humble head nod, which has many forms and meanings. What does shaking your head up and down or side to side mean? Well, it all depends on your culture. In North America, Australia, and some European countries, it is a sign of approval. But a very similar tilt back that may look like a nod means *no* in Greece and Iran. Go to Bulgaria and the nod clearly means *no*, while the side-to-side shake means *yes*. And then there is the famous Indian head shake or wiggle, wobble, waggle, or bobble, as it has been called, that looks like a smooth and continuous infinity sign (Ramadurai, 2018).

A multitude of articles and even videos demonstrate how to do it properly and explain what it actually means (The Indian Nod: Explained, n.d.). The simplest interpretation is that it is a sign of agreement, but most India experts, including Indians themselves, will tell you it really depends on the context. Priya Pathiyan, a Mumbai-based writer, says it usually indicates approval but "There is also an element of being friendly or being respectful, and it is difficult to say exactly which unless you know the situation" (Ramadurai, 2018). The wobble can also be a sign of exasperation, especially if it is done fast, or a polite way to not disagree when one actually disagrees. Pradeep Chakravarthy, a corporate consultant from Chennai, believes that in a country like India where respect for power and authority is high, the head wobble provides a way for an employee to respond politely to a challenging request from a boss or manager and it means: "I know I can't do it, but I can't say no either. So rather than outright refusal, I buy time by being deliberately vague" (Ramadurai, 2018). That is a lot of complexity packed in a simple movement of the head! It is, however, an excellent example of how culture provides the framework for interpreting events and behaviors. Without the framework or context that culture provides, the behavior would be difficult to interpret.

2.5 Culture as Guide to Behavior

Finally, culture guides behavior. How you address your boss and whether you make eye contact while you open doors for others, how often you interrupt your team members when they talk, when and what you eat, and whether you pursue higher education are just some of the many behaviors that have at least some cultural roots. Culture is not the only factor that impacts our beliefs, values, and behaviors; however, it is one of the significant determinants of human behavior.

Let's further unpack the definition of culture by considering some aspects of the US culture and its impact on behaviors. As we will discuss in later chapters (Chapters 7 and 8), there are well-researched and well-established beliefs and values associated with being a US-American—someone from the United States. Some of the dominant values are focus on the individual, performance orientation, short-term orientation, and relatively egalitarian views of power and gender. As the definition of culture suggests, these values are combined into a system that most, but not all, US-Americans share, and they are related to certain policies and behaviors. For example, the US Constitution and Bill of Rights reflect the focus on the individual and belief in some degree of egalitarianism. The latter also relates to a more relaxed and equal relationship between parents and children and between employees and supervisors. In the United States, children are generally not expected to obey their parents unconditionally and employees can disagree with their supervisors to some extent. As illustrated in the *First Person* example, many US firms demonstrate relatively egalitarian practices with employees calling their bosses by their first name and feeling comfortable expressing their opinion even when they disagree with them.

Additionally, while there are other cultures that tend to be individualistic, for example, Australia, the combination of various beliefs, values, and behaviors make US-Americans different from Australians. In both cases, their culture provides them with a unique character. In the United States, as is the case everywhere else in the world, children are taught cultural values formally and informally. US parents encourage their children to compete, value winning, sometimes over cooperation, and teach them to stand out through their individual achievements. These teachings reflect the cultural values of the importance of both individualism and performance. The value of performance and competition is further emphasized through the educational system and in the workplace where employees are recognized and rewarded for their individual performance through raises, promotions, and various awards.

WINDOW TO THE WORLD

Doing Business in the United States

The United States continues to be a highly attractive market for business opportunities. Stable growth, reliable legal and political systems, extensive resources, relatively few regulations along with leadership in many business and educational fields all make the country an appealing prospect. The US-Americans are proud of their country's achievement and power on the world stage. Their position as a top world power, the country's size and distance from other countries, along with the English language having become the universal language, allows many US-Americans to be relatively less knowledgeable regarding other countries and cultures. Here are some tips for doing business in the United States:

• Individual success and competition are highly valued and rewarded with the "American Dream" represented by people

(Continued)

succeeding based on their efforts, ingenuity, and performance.

- US-Americans are typically direct and short-term oriented. It is appropriate to get to the point and speak your mind and move quickly regarding business decisions.

- Business interactions tend to be informal. However, there are industry-specific expectations with younger and high-tech firms being less formal than older and more traditional businesses.

- There are specific ways of addressing race, gender, and diversity. Do your research regarding what is appropriate language and approach regarding these topics, which can be highly sensitive.

- US-Americans often talk about their family and personal life with ease. They share, sometimes overshare, personal information and form and disband relationships quickly.

- Women have been part of business organizations for many years, and they constitute at least half of mid-level managers in many organizations. While still less prevalent in the top leadership positions, there are no formal gender barriers and gender equality is considered an ideal, if not always a reality.

Because English is the international business language and because of the frequent presence and dominance of US films and other media around the world, it is easy for people from other countries to assume that they know the United States and its culture. However, the United States is diverse and complex, so while you may speak English and know the pop culture, you still need to do research to prepare yourself to do business in the United States.

3. COMPONENTS AND LEVELS OF CULTURE

LO 1.3 Present the components and levels of culture

Earlier in the chapter, we mentioned the various components that make up culture. Let's define and explain each in more detail. Culture is made up of four components (see Table 1.3 for summary descriptions):

- deep assumptions
- beliefs
- values
- behaviors

3.1 Deep Assumptions

The *deep assumptions* of culture are ingrained elements that are taken for granted and not questioned. For example, religious beliefs regarding the existence of a divine power are accepted by believers; they are a matter of faith and not questioned.

Table 1.3 Components of Culture

Component of Culture	Description and Example
Deep assumptions	Deeply ingrained assumptions that are accepted and taken for granted without the need for proof.
Beliefs	Convictions and ideas about what is true; *the way things are.*
Values	Long-lasting beliefs about what is important and what is right and wrong; *the way things should be.*
Behaviors and artifacts	Visible components; things we do; how we act and interact with others; visible elements of culture including art, music, food, and so forth.

Similarly, the assumptions regarding whether human beings are inherently good, bad, or somewhere in between vary across cultures. As we will describe in later chapters, cultures have different basic assumptions about such things as the nature of people, the relationship to nature and to time, and gender. These basic assumptions are the foundation of culture, and they are invisible to outsiders and sometimes even imperceptible to members of a cultural group. However, these deep assumptions are the source of many of our behaviors and practices in daily life and in organizations.

3.2 Values and Beliefs

Values and beliefs are the next components and are defined as convictions about what is true or false and right or wrong. *Beliefs* are convictions or ideas about what is true; they represent *the way things are.* Closely related to beliefs, *values* are stable, long-lasting beliefs and preferences about what is worthwhile and desirable; they reflect the way people think *things should be.* Beliefs often develop into values as people act on them and deepen their commitment to those beliefs. People hold two types of values. *Instrumental values* indicate *how* we believe we should go about doing things; *terminal values* indicate *what* we should be doing, meaning the goal (Anderson, 1997; Rokeach, 1973). So, believing that honesty, hard work, and self-sufficiency are important is an expression of instrumental values, whereas individual dignity, spiritual salvation, freedom, and happiness are terminal values or end states one believes are worth achieving. Beliefs and values are strongly influenced by culture, although many are based on other factors, such as experiences, family lore, education, and so forth; in other words, they can be both cultural and idiosyncratic. For example, you may believe that luck plays a big role in success and performance in your job. This belief may stem from your cultural background (we will explore this in later chapters), but may also be the result of personal experiences at work where your success or that of others appeared to be random, or it may stem from certain personality traits such as proactivity. How much one values financial achievement over spiritual salvation is to some extent a product of culture; these values then drive behavior and social policy. For example, while Western countries and many other industrialized nations value material wealth and measure their Gross National Product (GNP), the Bhutanese, people of a small South Asian country, calculate their Gross National Happiness (GNH), which they value as a holistic measure of the success of their culture (Bhutan's Gross National Happiness Index). The GNH measures factors such as psychological well-being, time use, community vitality, and ecological diversity and resilience—cultural values that have relatively less primary importance in many industrialized countries. In this case, what is valued drives economic and social policy.

3.3 Behaviors and Artifacts

The last component of culture includes *behaviors and artifacts*, which are how we interact with others, and other visible aspects of the environment, such as art, music, food, architecture, and social policy. For example, depending on your culture, you may greet people by shaking hands, hugging them, bowing to them, or any number of other forms of greetings. The Japanese and Indians bow, but not the same way; the Belgians and many other Europeans shake hands and often kiss each other on the cheek; South Americans may also kiss, but start on a different cheek, or they may offer a half hug; young Indians traditionally will briefly touch their elders feet as a sign of respect and subservience; the variations are endless.

Another example of culturally influenced behavior is the extent to which your speech is direct and to the point. A German manager is likely to provide negative feedback to her employees directly and bluntly, whereas a Thai manager would be much less direct and may even convey the negative information through a trusted third party. In our *First Person* example, the US-Americans were direct and confrontational, while their Chinese partners communicated through email and were not engaging in discussions. In other examples, the terminal value of wealth and material goods impacts beliefs about working hard, which leads to a positive view of work and contributes to actually working hard. The example of the United States fits well here. Material achievement, a terminal value, is generally considered worthwhile; there is shared belief that working hard is desirable and that belief translates into a positive view of long work hours, taking few vacations, and some suggest, resulting in a productive and entrepreneurial economy (see the case at the end of this chapter). These are visible actions that flow from assumptions, beliefs, and values. Clothing, art, architecture, food, music, and the many other artifacts that we typically associate with culture are part of this visible component of culture.

3.4 The Cultural Iceberg

The components of culture are represented through what is known as the *cultural iceberg* originally proposed by Edward Hall (1976). Just like a large part of an iceberg is hidden below the waterline, deep cultural assumptions and some values and beliefs are not visible to outsiders who can only see what people do (see Figure 1.1). The assumptions may even be invisible to members of the culture; they can be so deeply ingrained and taken for granted that people are not aware of them. Values and beliefs float just above or below the waterline. Some are visible to insiders and outsiders; some are invisible to both, and some are in between. As the iceberg analogy suggests, the aspects of culture that are hidden and invisible are much larger, and more fundamental and powerful than those that are easily accessible. Furthermore, just as an iceberg may present danger, culture and cultural interactions may be rife with conflict when the submerged and less visible layers are ignored.

Using the cultural iceberg as a visual representation of culture explains why tourists and visitors focus on the food, art, and architecture of a country they visit; these are the elements they can see and to which they have access. Many will prepare for their trip by learning some of the language and studying the customs and rituals. All of these are the visible and accessible aspects of culture. Through a visit or interaction with members of another culture, we can access the surface culture. While

Figure 1.1   The Cultural Iceberg

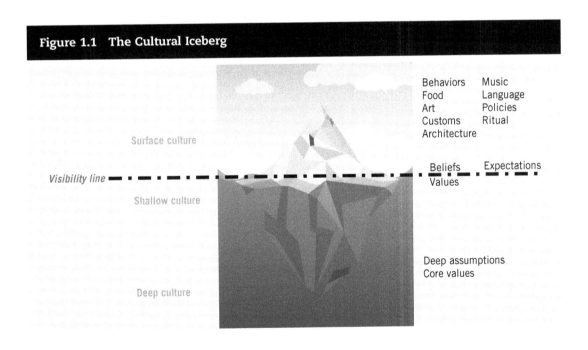

Surface culture

Behaviors   Music
Food   Language
Art   Policies
Customs   Ritual
Architecture

Visibility line

Beliefs   Expectations
Values

Shallow culture

Deep culture

Deep assumptions
Core values

these visible behaviors are interesting and a window into deeper values and assumptions, they are also superficial. For example, visitors to France marvel at the architecture, enjoy the food and art, and may complain about the curt and sometimes rude servers who refuse to bring salt or accommodate dietary restrictions. They can, but often do not, explore the cultural values, beliefs, and assumptions that drive those behaviors. They are likely therefore to attribute the refusal to change ingredients in a meal to accommodate dietary restrictions to rudeness, to the French people's sense of superiority, or to their dislike of tourists. However, these behaviors have deeper roots related to views of authority. The French believe that one does not question a Chef, who is an authority figure in the kitchen, and therefore one does not change his recipe. Interestingly, even the French themselves may not be aware that this belief stems from deeper assumptions about the importance of hierarchy and power which are deep-rooted in French history. Similarly, a Swede knows that cooperation is valuable, but that she can also question her boss's decisions—the Swedish culture values equal power. A Japanese expatriate working in Sweden also values cooperation, but may not be aware of Swedish values of egalitarianism. He therefore may hesitate to interrupt and challenge the boss as his Swedish coworkers do and may be frustrated by what he perceives to be their rudeness as they openly question their boss.

Knowing and understanding a culture, whether your own or the culture of others, means knowing behaviors and artifact and having access to the components that are below the visibility line. Members of a culture have access to their own beliefs and values. Although they may not be aware of the deep assumptions, they can access them and understand them when pressed and needed. However, outsiders to the culture do not have immediate access to the assumptions that are below the visibility line. They may like or dislike what is visible without fully knowing their roots. They will only understand them with more meaningful, sustained, and intentional interaction because without knowing the deep values and assumptions, cultural contact remains superficial.

3.5 Levels of Culture

Culture can be divided into three levels that often interact together (Figure 1.2):

1. National

2. Regional

3. Group

The first level is national culture, defined as the system of beliefs and values shared by people within a nation. Second, in addition to an overall national culture, many countries have regional differences that have geographic or historical origins.

Figure 1.2 Levels of Culture

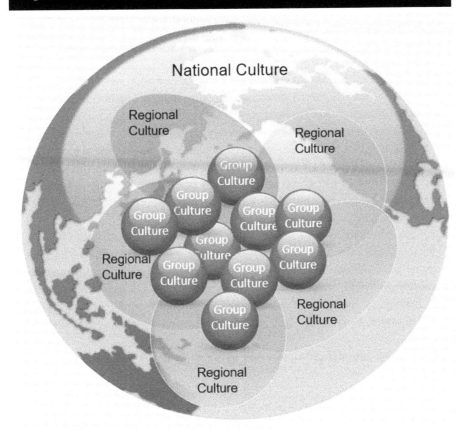

For example, in the United States, people refer to the South, which is located in the Southeastern (but not Southwestern) part of the country. The South is further defined by the Civil War and the history of slavery which fit into the third level of culture that relates to different groups, beyond regional differences. So, being a Southerner in the United States not only refers to a region of the country, it also refers to a cultural group. Race, gender, ethnicity, sexual orientation, religion, or socioeconomic factors are other cultural groups that fit into this third level of culture (we explore this level of culture in more detail in Chapters 5 and 6). Although these groups may share national cultural values, they have their own unique cultural traits based on membership in separate groups. Some countries, such as the United States, Tanzania, Canada, and Indonesia among others, include many regional and group cultures. Different cultural, ethnic, and religious groups are part of the overall culture of these countries and are spread out regionally. The third level of culture forms what is referred to as cultural diversity. *Diversity*, then, refers to the variety of human structures, beliefs systems, and strategies for adapting to situations that exist within different groups. The levels do not represent all possible levels which may also include organizational culture, which we discuss separately in Chapter 11.

3.5.1 Impact of Levels of Culture. Because national culture addresses many different aspects of life, it is likely to exert a strong and pervasive influence on people's behavior in everyday activities and in organizations. Whether regional or group cultures exert a stronger influence than national culture depends on the individual. For example, a person may believe that being a US-American is a key cultural identity factor or that being a Midwesterner in the United States is her primary culture, while someone else may believe that his gender or sexual orientation or religion is primary. From an organizational point of view, as you will see in later chapters, our cultural background impacts our views and expectations of leadership and management (House et al., 2004) and even the culture of an organization. Some researchers (e.g., Bartlett & Ghoshal, 1987) have suggested that a country's culture can have a significant influence on what they call its administrative heritage (further discussed in Chapter 11). Although differences distinguish one organization from another and one manager from another, national heritage can be noticeable and distinct so that, for example, French organizations are more hierarchical and status-oriented overall than their Swedish counterparts.

Now that we have defined culture and its components, let's explore the sources and purpose of culture.

4. CULTURE AND OTHER DETERMINANTS OF BEHAVIOR

LO 1.4 Compare and contrast culture with other determinants of behavior

Culture, nationality, ethnicity, and race are sometimes used interchangeably. Although they share some common elements and they all impact how people think and behave, they are not the same. Figure 1.3 differentiates among these concepts based on two dimensions of individual (idiosyncratic) versus group, and genetic or biological versus learned or acquired. On the left side of Figure 1.3 are drivers of behavior that are genetic or biological.

4.1 Race

Race, which refers to geographic, genetic, and biological groupings within a species (Gezen & Kottak, 2014), is a group-related concept. Because of human migration and extensive interbreeding, humans are highly similar to one another genetically. While race is widely used to classify people into various groups, there is no such thing as a White, Black, Asian, or any typically used racial categories. Research indicates that there is more genetic diversity within groups than between them and that race is generally not a biologically useful way to classify people (Feldman, Lewontin, & King, 2003). Instead, race is a socially constructed concept that is developed and used to describe differences in the physical appearance of people. The visible differences are superficial physical characteristics that manifest themselves in various groups ("AAA Statement on Race," 1998) and are genetically transmitted. These include, for example, skin color, height, eye color, and so forth. However, these do not reflect other genetic differences in the human race.

4.2 Personality and Ability

Two other key determinants of behavior are personality and ability or aptitude. *Personality* refers to a stable and consistent set of characteristics that make a person unique. While there is considerable debate regarding the extent to which personality is genetic and biologically based or something that develops early in life, there is agreement that personality is stable and consistent across time and situations. Additionally, research in brain and cognitive science is finding that some of what we consider willful individual actions is driven, at least to some extent, by biological factors. For example, some research suggests that broad personality dimensions such as extraversion or novelty seeking may relate to biological systems (Cloninger, Svarkic, & Prysbeck, 1993). *Ability*, or aptitude, is a natural talent for doing something mental or physical. Like personality, ability is somewhat stable over time and situations. While race is a group-related characteristic, personality and talent are individual-based.

4.3 Culture and Ethnicity

On the right side of Figure 1.3 are learned and acquired drivers of behavior, which include culture. Culture, ethnicity, and nationality are all group-based and learned or acquired. *Ethnicity* refers to the culture of a group within a particular geographic region. Like race, it is group-based, but it is learned. Individuals belong to a certain group with whom they share ancestral and cultural roots (Isajiw, 1993). Some ethnic groups are based on nationality and are therefore referred to as ethno-nationals (e.g., Turks or Japanese), while others are based on a common purpose or identity, for example, Asian Americans or Kurds, and are classified as pan-ethnic (Jiang, 2019). Also based on the group and an acquired characteristic, *nationality* is the simplest concept to define. It refers to the country of citizenship. Although several groups have a nationality without having a country (e.g., Palestinians and Kurds), nationality relates to being a citizen of a certain country and is often used as an approximation of culture.

Although race, ethnicity, and culture may overlap, they are not equivalent. For example, an Indian-American may be classified as a South Asian (a race or ethnicity), but not practice or share any of the values, beliefs, and customs of that group, instead considering himself to be culturally US-American. Similarly, Iranians come from many different ethnic and racial groups, but many would describe themselves as culturally Iranian. For some people, the question of "where are you from?" is simple. Their nationality, ethnicity, culture, and race all match. For example, a Japanese citizen whose ancestors have long lived in Japan, who was born in Japan, speaks Japanese, practices the Shinto religion, and is ethnically and culturally Japanese may simply say "I am Japanese." Her identity is Japanese. The answer may not be as simple for a first-generation Korean-Japanese born in the United States to a Japanese mother and a Korean father, who speaks only English and is an Evangelical Christian. What should his answer be to "where are you from?" Is he Japanese-Korean-Asian-American, or just American? The answer regarding his cultural and ethnic identity is primarily up to him. However, how he sees himself may not match how others see him. If he says "I'm Korean, or Japanese," more traditional Koreans or Japanese may not accept that description. If he says "I'm American," some may want to add the hyphenated "Asian" to his identity. Culture is not simple!

5. SOURCES AND PURPOSE OF CULTURE

LO 1.5 Elaborate on the sources and purpose of culture

Where does culture come from? Why do we have culture? What function does it serve? Why do we need culture? These may be questions you have asked yourself wondering if culture really matters and whether people can function without having culture. The answers are not simple, but they point to the essential role culture plays in our lives. All groups, communities, and societies have culture. It is an integral part of the human experience and therefore serves a clear and necessary purpose.

5.1 Sources of Culture: Environment and History

All groups and societies develop a pattern of assumptions, values, beliefs, and behaviors when solving environmental and social challenges it encounters. Those patterns become engrained and are the foundation of culture. One of the aspects of Icelandic culture presents a vivid example. Anna Möller, a German manager who was in Iceland to finalize a business deal, was getting increasingly nervous. Her host Margret had taken her on a tour of the popular Blue Lagoon in Grindavi when their car had broken down. They should have had plenty of time to be back for an important dinner but it had taken a while to find a tow truck that would come their way and they were still waiting. It was getting late, but Margret was cool as a cucumber. How could she be this relaxed when they were risking the whole deal? Seeing her guest's anxiety, Margret laughed and said "Well, 'Þetta reddast'—it will all turn out OK in the end. It's pronounced 'thet-ta red-ust' and it's like our national motto." She went on to explain that with such hostile and harsh climate and nature, unpredictable weather, with so many active volcanoes, and constant earthquakes, the island seems to be a living entity set on destroying its inhabitants. "We Icelanders have learned to go with the flow. We have seen many disasters that almost wiped us out. We know we'll figure out a way to make it right, we have always managed to do it." No matter how hard she tried, Anna did not feel "Þetta reddast" at all!

As exemplified in this example, the physical environment and history are closely intertwined with culture. Environmental factors such as geography and weather influence the creation of culture and the development of cultural values. Some research suggests that climate is a factor in economic development with colder climates being linked to higher productivity (Ingelhart & Welzel, 2005). Others (e.g., Berry et al., 1992) suggest that as people adapt to their particular environment, each group specializes or develops a certain culture based on the challenges that it faces. It is reasonable to assume that environment impacts culture as well. The Icelandic cultural trait of easy-going attitude and sense of humor in the face of challenges developed because of their environment. Similarly, Japan's small land mass, limited arable land, and its scarce natural resources may be factors in the value placed on long-term and careful planning. The Japanese saving rate is almost twice as much as that of the United States (Koll, 2018; Miller, 2018b). The relatively harsh environment with limited natural resources has taught the Japanese to be cautious. Additionally, without great expanses of space, the Japanese have developed very strict cultural codes in managing their privacy, ranging from discreet demeanor to flexible use of space in architecture.

Likewise, the relatively short history of the United States as a country is marked by key events including its beginning as a British colony, the American revolution, slavery, seemingly endless abundance of resources, and the expansion toward the Pacific Ocean undertaken by settlers. These events have marked the government, social policies, and culture of the country. The US Constitution and Bill of Rights focus on the individual and individual rights with an emphasis on balance of power and a healthy dose of skepticism toward government and centralized power. The apparent endless optimism that many perceive to be part of the American character (Keller, 2015) was mentioned by Alexis de Tocqueville in his 19th-century treatise *Democracy in America* (2000) and can be partly attributed to the ever-expanding opportunities that a rich continent offered the immigrants. The frontier appeared endless; resources were limitless; and opportunities boundless for those who took risks, set out on their own, and worked under harsh conditions. History and environment combine to impact the development of cultural assumptions, values, and beliefs.

5.2 Purpose of Culture

Given the pervasive presence of culture in every society and group, it is clear that it serves a necessary purpose. The definition of culture points to its purpose. Culture provides the basic assumptions, beliefs, and values that *allow us to understand and interpret* our environment and provides us with *guidelines to behavior*. For example, a US-American manager is likely to interpret an employee not showing up for work without a notice either as a sign that an emergency has occurred or that the employee has quit. In either case, after a few days of absence, the employee will be terminated. The same behavior in Mexico or the Philippines will be tolerated and treated more leniently because in both cultures, sudden absences due to family obligations are expected and understood.

Our culture guides our interpretation of events and our actions. In Turkey or Russia, the typical smile and chitchat with strangers that is so prevalent in the United States is likely to get you labeled as imbalanced. In those countries, you simply do not talk to or smile at people you do not know. If you are interviewing for a job in Spain, you would be wrong to interpret detailed questions into your family background as inappropriate and overly personal inquiries; they are normal for Spaniards who value family connections. What is appropriate depends on the culture. Without having some knowledge of the cultural context, it is hard to establish what is right or wrong, and what is appropriate or not.

5.3 Consequences of Absence of Culture

It is not every day that we find a group without culture. However, throughout history, we have witnessed instances of the devastating consequences on individuals and communities of the destruction of their culture. Particularly salient and vivid examples are the relatively recent treatment of native children and native communities in the United States, Canada, and Australia. The native cultures in these three countries were systematically destroyed and members were forced to give up their language, traditions, and beliefs while also being excluded from the culture of the dominant Europeans. These processes labeled *deculturation* or *marginalization* by scholars of culture (e.g., Berry, 1997; discussed in detail in Chapter 4) have harmful and destructive effects on individuals and their communities. Not having a culture leaves people without the context to interpret the world; they lose their basic assumptions, beliefs, and values and are left without a mechanism to fulfill the various functions of culture which we discussed earlier in this chapter. The absence of cultural norms, labeled *anomie* or *anomy* (Durkheim, 1893), engenders many social ills such as delinquency, crime and lawlessness, and personal distress and despair (Ritzer, 2007).

5.4 The Purpose of Culture in Organizations

The impact of culture on organizations and management is also pervasive. Organizational processes and managerial practices are widely different around the world. Extensive research shows that organizational policies are impacted by cultural values. For example, overall policies regarding employment, hiring and firing, as well as the number and frequency of vacations and sick days, vary across the world and reflect cultural norms. In countries that are more performance-oriented, such as Japan or the United States, organizations offer fewer vacation days, and employees take less time off. Similarly, what we expect of our leaders and what we consider to be effective leadership are different from one country and culture to another (House, Dorfman, Javidan, Hanges, & Sully de Luque, 2014).

Nonetheless, it is true that business has become global and many of the practices and values are shared across many countries. For example, research done with MBA students from the United States and several Central and South American countries has found that they share several key business values, championed by business education, related to social responsibility regardless of their country of origin (Roche, 2016). In some regard, their US-based education impacts them as much as their nationality. Even with globalization, and because of it, understanding culture continues to be an important factor in the success of today's managers. In spite of its importance, the concept of culture also presents some challenges.

6. CRITICAL CHALLENGES WITH THE CONCEPT OF CULTURE

LO 1.6 Examine the critical challenges with the concept of culture

The concept of culture is not without its shortcomings and serious critics. Many of the academic critiques come from the field of economics (e.g., Jones, 2006), where researchers suggest that because culture has so many different definitions, it is hard to measure and difficult to pinpoint, making it all but impossible to conduct serious research to establish its impact. They also point to many noncultural factors that drive human behavior.

6.1 Essentialism and Overgeneralization

We have been using broad generalizations of cultural differences based on nationality or other groupings throughout this chapter. For example, we have been discussing what US-Americans do and value, what the Japanese practice, what Turks prefer, and so forth. All of these examples are based on broad generalizations that group people based on one attribute, their nationality or culture, into the same category. We have, in effect, stereotyped them, using one characteristic and building groupings around it, as if it is the most important and unchanging part of who they are. This type of grouping also assumes that we can make predictions based on the one characteristic, the cultural group they belong to. This process *essentializes* cultural characteristics, assuming that we can narrow people or cultures down to their essence and use that essence to predict everything else. *Essentialism* assumes that the same characteristics are shared by all members of a group and that their essence can be captured by that characteristic. Such an approach has been strongly criticized when applied to ethnic groups and women in particular (Grosz, 1995).

The critique is legitimate. When you rely on one or a few characteristics to define a group of people, you will inevitably overgeneralize. Reducing a whole complex culture, group, or individuals to a few characteristics is clearly overly simplistic. Individuals who have been grouped together may not share the same characteristics because of many factors including their personality, personal preferences, or even inaccurate classification into the group. Osland and Bird (2000) suggest that our current approach to teaching and understanding culture relies on *sophisticated stereotypes* of various cultures which they define as generalizations based on research and theoretically sound concepts rather than limited personal experiences. While helpful and less inaccurate than the personal versions, the researchers indicate that these sophisticated stereotypes do not fully address the complexity of culture. Behavior is driven by many factors; not all Chinese, Italians, Vietnamese, or members of any cultural group or nation are alike, have the same assumptions and values, and act the same way. There is a danger in overgeneralization and oversimplification inevitably leading to mistakes.

6.2 Equating Country and Culture

A related challenge to the concept of culture is our tendency to equate country or nationality with culture. By the latest count, there are 195 countries in the world and an estimated 10,000 cultures; therefore, most countries host more than one culture. In examples throughout this chapter, we have mentioned how US-Americans, Germans, or Indians act. Clearly, not everyone in these countries share a culture or the same assumptions, values, and beliefs. While US-Americans are generally considered individualistic and present short-term oriented, many come from cultures, such as Mexico or the Philippines, where the collective is highly valued and the past considered important. Germany and India similarly include many cultural groups who may or may not share the same values. Not all German managers are direct; not all Indian employees value past accomplishments.

At the beginning of this chapter, we identified several countries that are some of the most culturally and linguistically diverse in the world, while others like Japan and the Korea include more homogeneous populations. For countries with more diversity, equating country and culture is even more problematic. For those with less diversity, some generalizations may appear more accurate. However, even then culture occurs at several levels (e.g., national, regional, and group) and each of these groups, not to mention each individual within the groups, is likely to have different assumptions, beliefs, and values. Equating country and culture is therefore problematic.

6.3 Reconciling the Challenges: Cultural Prototypes

International management expert Nancy Adler (Adler & Gundersen, 2008, p. 77) suggests that stereotypes can be helpful when

- They are applied to the group rather than the individual

- They are descriptive rather than evaluative

- They are accurate and based on research and data, i.e., sophisticated

- They are used as a first best guess

- They are flexible enough to be modified based on experience

It is imperative that, while we oversimplify cultures and essentialize them to a great extent in order to gain a basic understanding, such approach be just a first step. The research on various cultures allows us to rely on cultural *prototypes* that illustrate the typical qualities a group of people share. They provide general models and estimates that can be used for preparation and planning to ease initial interactions across cultures. A deeper understanding of culture and gaining access to the deep assumptions that underlie any culture require more than the use of such prototypes, but they can be a starting point. Culture is one of many factors that impact the behavior of individuals and groups in particular settings. Appreciating and considering the complexity of culture, groups, individuals, and organizations are essential.

The last section of this chapter will introduce three key concepts that are used throughout the book to help you become more effective at managing cross-cultural interactions.

7. A COGNITIVE APPROACH TO CROSS-CULTURAL MANAGEMENT: THE CULTURAL MINDSET

LO 1.7 Introduce the cognitive approach to cross-cultural management and explain the themes of culture-as-meta-context (CMC), culture-just-is (CJI), and the Cultural Mindset (CM)

Culture as a learned group-based characteristic can impact an individual's assumptions, beliefs, values, and behaviors. One of the most significant effects of culture is that it acts as a meta-context that provides the individual with a unique lens or perspective (Nahavandi, 2017). Each of us sees the world through our own cultural lens and acts accordingly. A person's culture provides the background, field, or context that helps construct various situations and presents a framework that integrates information logically.

7.1 The Cognitive Approach to Cross-Cultural Management

Cross-cultural management scholars and practitioners focus on the impact of culture on organizational practices and management. The goal is to understand, for example, how people from different cultures may have different leadership styles or be motivated by distinctive incentives. There is further interest in how a country or region's culture impacts business regulations, organizational systems, or human resources practices. Typically, detailed descriptions of the content of culture are not of interest unless they are applicable to business interactions, organizational settings, or managerial decision-making.

The *cognitive perspective* to cross-cultural management that is used in this book focuses on people as thinkers who seek to consistently make sense of their world. Culture, as presented in our definition, is the *software* and one of the key factors that impact how people think and behave. This approach to culture is distinctive in that it seeks first to understand how individuals' cultural backgrounds may shape their worldview and perspectives. In helping managers become more successful across cultures, one key goal of this book is to develop awareness of your own cultural assumptions, beliefs, and values and their role in how you think and how you can use that knowledge to be more effective when interacting across cultures.

7.2 Culture-as-Meta-Context

The word *context* comes from Latin meaning knit together or make a connection. The context allows us to link our observations, perspectives, and events into a coherent whole (Rousseau & Fried, 2001). Having context, thus being able to contextualize, is essential to an accurate understanding of what goes on around us. This is the idea behind *culture-as-meta-context* (CMC), which can be explained in two ways (see Figure 1.4):

- First, *meta* as an adjective indicates a higher-level context. As such, as meta-context, culture provides the background, the setting, and the situation in which events happen and help understand and interpret them.

- Second, *meta* as a noun refers to a post or column that framed a racetrack to mark the turning point and guide competitors in ancient Rome. Therefore, culture provides the guideline to actions and behaviors.

7.2.1 Culture-as-Meta-Context as Background. As we have presented in many examples throughout this chapter, without knowing the context, it is difficult to understand and explain events and behaviors correctly; culture provides that context. Managers rely on their own culture and the organization where they work to provide such a context and decide, for example, what goals and behaviors are appropriate and desirable and how

Figure 1.4   Culture-as-Meta-Context

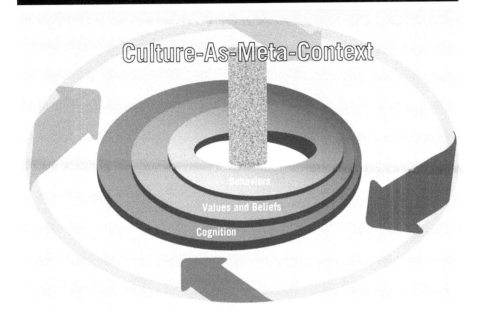

they should react to their employees' actions. Culture as a meta-context provides the background and shapes our cultural lens or perspective. We see the world through our CMC and we apply our CMC to various situations to make sense of them.

There are many contextual factors that we use in organizations to help explain events. For example, we consider the structure of an organization or the competitive environment. Culture-as-meta-context stands in the background behind the others and can be used to complement them or further refine them. Consider the situation where a supervisor sits down with an employee to provide guidance and coaching about a poorly handled customer experience. The organizational policies and procedures, the tenure and experience of both the manager and the employee, the customer's behavior, and many other organizational factors are part of the context the manager must consider. When they sit down to chat, the employee does not maintain eye contact with her supervisor and keeps her gaze to the floor. In the United States and some other countries, lack of eye contact is interpreted as cageyness and dishonesty, so a manager from one of these cultures may suspect that something is amiss and that the employee may be lying. However, the lack of eye contact may have a completely different meaning when contextualized. If the employee is a Navajo Native American or originally from India, their lack of eye contact may have a different explanation. In both of those cultures, a person who has less status shows respect to a supervisor, a person with higher status, by not making direct eye contact. The culture provides the meta-context, the higher-level context, that supplements organizational factors to understand the event.

7.2.2 Culture-as-Meta-Context as Guide. Culture-as-meta-context not only is the lens through which we see the world but also serves as a guide for our perceptions, cognition, perspectives, values, behaviors, and even emotions. In the example relating to meaning of eye contact, the manager is likely to be guided by culture for deciding on a course of action. Will the manager address the situation directly and provide the negative feedback to employee bluntly or gently remind the employee about the importance of treating customers well? Will the manager involve a third party to provide the feedback to avoid direct confrontation and loss of face? The selection of these options is guided by CMC.

Consider a Swedish manager in charge of organizing the international sales meeting for her company for the first time who was experiencing considerable frustration as many of the meetings and events were not going according to her plans. Some international participants were arriving late or skipping the key events altogether. Some wandered in and out of various talks, sometimes accompanied by spouses and children, talked loudly in small groups in the back of the rooms, or interrupted the presentations. Many complained about the high number of meetings and lack of time to socialize. The organizer was feeling considerable frustration at what she perceived to be some participants' rudeness and lack of civility. Before launching into her next event, she got advice from a seasoned conference organizer who reminded her about how people from different countries have different expectations when it comes to attendance and participation in sales meetings. Some see it as an opportunity for a mini-vacation or as a reward for hard work; others see it as an opportunity to network or learn new skills. With that advice in mind, the second time around, the manager sent out a program that started with the company mission and statement about its culture, including detailed goals for the meetings along with carefully worded expectations regarding attendance and professional conduct during sessions. She also built in frequent breaks, opportunities for informal gathering, as well as formal networking hours and provided planned activities for family members. Through these actions, she was able to address the different cultural expectations regarding professional and social interaction and make her sales meeting a resounding success.

In this example, the manager's CMC provides the context for her perceptions and reactions. Considering how others may have a different view and different CMC allows her to modify her program, still achieve her goals, and satisfy other participants' expectations. In summary, our culture as *CMC provides the background and context for our interactions and acts as a guide to our thinking and behavior.*

7.2.3 Omnipresent Culture-as-Meta-Context. CMC is always present (Nahavandi, 2017). Similar to other environmental and structural contextual variables, culture may not always be relevant and important; not every interaction has a cultural side, but culture is always in the background. Not being aware of the ever-present context or not understanding its potential role and impact hamper our abilities to work effectively. We need to know our own CMC and the lens and perspective it creates and understand that others have their own unique and equally powerful and relevant lens. Consequently, the term CMC will be used in the book when referring to an individual's culture, while the word culture will be used in more generic references such as Indian or Chinese culture.

7.3 Culture-Just-Is

At the core of understanding CMC is understanding and accepting the idea that culture is ever-present and exists for everyone. Humans are social and belong to various groups with whom they share basic assumptions, beliefs, and values; we all have culture. Culture is not just about ethnic minorities, a certain gender, or others; people are all cultural beings. One of the key goals of this book is to help you become aware of your own CMC and its potential impact on your thinking and behavior. Additionally, just as we are impacted by our CMC, others are equally impacted by theirs. While we have the tendency to value our own and often see it as superior to others, a topic we will explore in-depth in Chapter 4, all cultures simply exist to provide groups with assumptions, beliefs, and values and allow them to survive and thrive in their environment.

We call this idea that all cultures have equal value in their own context, *culture-just-is* (CJI; Nahavandi, 2017). One culture is not objectively better than another; they all exist and they all provide their members a meta-context that allows them to function. CJI is a descriptive rather than evaluative statement. The idea of considering all cultures as equal because they all form a meta-context for their group members may be uncomfortable and controversial. We can all think about cultural values or practices that we find personally objectional or even unethical or immoral. However, it is important to keep the following in mind:

- CJI does not suggest that an individual should be equally comfortable in all cultures or like all cultural values and practices equally.

- CJI does not deny or critique the importance and the role of having pride in one's culture.

- CJI does not deny that some cultures may have experienced more success than others at various times and therefore some cultures may have been better at addressing the environmental challenges the members faced.

- CJI does not negate the fact that everyone is likely to agree with some cultural assumptions, beliefs, and values and disagree, sometimes vehemently, with others.

- CJI does not reject or disallow individual preferences.

CJI merely implies that all groups, whether at the national, regional, group, or any other level, have a culture that provides them with a meta-context and impacts how they think and behave. In that regard, all cultures are equivalent; they all simply *are*. They all provide their members with a system of basic assumptions about the world. They all teach beliefs and values that lead to certain acceptable and unacceptable behaviors. They all evolve and change. The content of cultures is infinitely rich and varied; the fact that they all serve the same purpose and function to help explain the world and help individuals cope with it is universal. All cultures exist and have a critical function for their members. Understanding how your own culture-just-is and how others' cultures are also simply present is an important step in effective cultural interactions and successful cross-cultural management.

7.4 The Cultural Mindset

CMC and CJI, which are based on cognitive approach to cross-cultural management, are foundations to the key theme of this book, the *Cultural Mindset*. In order to be able to interact successfully and effectively across cultural boundaries we need to have a *Cultural Mindset* (CM; Nahavandi, 2017). CM is defined as:

> *A way of thinking and a frame of mind or reference that considers culture as a factor when assessing yourself and other people and situations, and when making decisions and acting on them. Having a CM means that you are aware of your own cultural backgrounds and the fact that culture-just-is and that it provides a meta-context.*

Having a CM involves the three following:

- Awareness of one's own CMC

- Knowing when to shift one's frame of reference because of crossing cultural boundaries

- Having the cultural knowledge, competencies, and skills to act accordingly

Understanding CMC and CJI allows you to have a CM as a way of thinking that goes beyond competencies and skills (Nahavandi, 2017).

7.4.1 CM and the Small World Paradox. Let's revisit the paradox we introduced at the beginning of this chapter: What works in one context does not necessarily work in another. Our worldview and our rules are generally effective for us within our own CMC. They allow us to function well in our "small" world for which they were developed and where we know and understand the rules. That same rules and perspective are not likely to work or be useful in another world (whether large or small) where the context is different (the culture is different) and the assumptions, values, beliefs, and rules for behavior are unfamiliar. The rules of one world do not apply to another. Having a CM is a way to solve this paradox and be able to be effective across cultures. The next chapter will examine in detail the roadmap to a CM, and the Think—Know—Do model and the tools you need to interact effectively across cultures.

FIRST PERSON REVISITED

As you have read in this chapter, culture plays a role in providing people with a framework and guide to behavior. Culture similarly impacts organizational cultures. Our assumptions about work and how we interact with others and how we make decisions are impacted by the cultures in which we grew up. In this case, the US-American companies reflect the values of informality and egalitarianism that are part of the US culture. People interact freely and informally, decisions are quick, and employees are not limited by their title. The Chinese company also reflects the country's culture with more emphasis on hierarchy and formality and more careful processes to reach decisions. Neither approach is better than the other. However, the differences can create challenges when people from two cultures interact and have to work together.

APPLYING WHAT YOU LEARNED: GETTING STARTED WITH THE IDEA OF CULTURE

You have learned the definition of culture and its potential impact on how people think and act. You have also read about the potential dangers of overgeneralizing. Here are some pointers as you start to apply the concept of culture in your personal and work life.

1. *Be prepared for mistakes and missteps*—Don't expect to get things right the first or second time, or even after many attempts. Mistakes are opportunities to learn and grow.

2. *Everyone has culture*—Culture is not something that applies just to minorities, women, or "other" people; everyone is part of one or more cultures. So, if you ask about it, ask everyone, not just the minorities or women in the group.

3. *Culture may be one, but not the only factor* that plays a role in any given situation. Think about the role it may play, but don't get obsessive about it. Culture impacts many things, but it does not explain everything.

4. *Culture is more than nationality and ethnicity*—there are many different levels and layers that play a role. Consider all the possible levels of culture.

5. *Practice asking questions* to find a respectful way to inquire about culture.

6. *Maintain a sense of humor*—laugh at your mistakes, forgive yourself for making them and keep going!

MANAGERIAL CHALLENGE: THE UNRESPONSIVE TEAM MEMBERS

You have been assigned as the formal team leader of a multicultural team of seven people. Two of the team members are Chinese, connecting with you mostly through video and email. Two are from your Middle East operation also connecting through video and email, and three are US-Americans on-site with you. You are the newest member but you come with extensive experience. Your team has a short deadline to resolve a critical supply chain challenge caused by a couple of your suppliers who are no longer able to deliver the key components for one of your products. Your first team meeting is set for early morning your time, to accommodate the time difference. The Chinese members happen to be in the Middle East and on the video chat together with your Middle Eastern colleagues; it's too early for you and too late for them, but you're all there. After spending what appears to be a long 20 minutes on introductions and social niceties, you present your ideas and possible solutions and then ask each member to give you their take and their ideas about how to address the challenge. You emphasize that time is of the essence and that you need a quick turnaround on this. The three US-American members jump right in and propose several alternatives. The others on video vigorously agree, but propose nothing different. You press them for their opinions, but they just repeat that what you suggest is great. You ask that they send you their thoughts within 24 hours, after they have a chance to think about other possible solutions and alternatives; you insist that you need their input because you don't know the region as well as they do. They enthusiastically agree to do as you have asked. Twenty-four hours pass with nothing from the overseas group. They respond as a group to your email reminding them to send their ideas with "What you proposed in the meeting was a great solution; we will continue working to see if we can add to that." Another day passes, and still nothing from the group.

1. What is your assessment of this situation?

2. What are some cultural factors that you may want to consider?

3. What should you do?

SELF-ASSESSMENT 1.1: CULTURE, ETHNICITY, RACE, AND NATIONALITY

You have now learned the differences between culture, ethnicity, race, and nationality. Using Figure 1.3 as a framework, identify your culture(s), ethnicity(ies), race(s), and nationality(ies), keeping in mind that many of us have more than one of each. As you work through the graph, include any key personalities, competencies, and skills.

1. How many factors could you identify in each quadrant?

2. Which ones are easier or harder to identify? Why?

3. How many cultures, ethnicities, races, and nationalities did you list?

4. How easy or hard was it to identify each?

5. How well do they all match?

6. Which one defines you best? Consider the other factors such as personality as well.

Figure 1.3   Culture and Other Determinants of Behavior

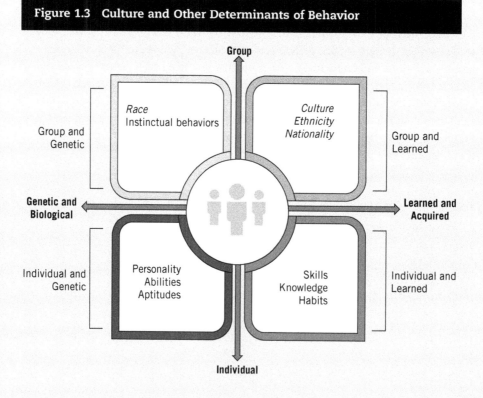

SELF-ASSESSMENT 1.2: YOUR VALUES

First, review the values listed below. Then rank each of the values in each category from 1 being most important to you to 5 being least important.

Rank	Instrumental Values	Rank	Terminal Values
_____	Ambition and hard work	_____	Contribution and a sense of accomplishment
_____	Honesty and integrity	_____	Happiness
_____	Love and affection	_____	Leisurely life
_____	Obedience and duty	_____	Wisdom and maturity
_____	Independence and self-sufficiency	_____	Individual dignity
_____	Humility	_____	Justice
_____	Doing good to others (Golden rule)	_____	Spiritual salvation
_____	Treating people fairly	_____	Financial success

Scoring:

The values that you rank highest in each group are the ones that are most important to you.

Interpretation:

Address the following questions.

1. Are there values that you consider to be universal?

2. Where and when do you think you acquired these values?

3. What role do you think culture plays in the development of these values?

EXERCISE 1.1: MAP OF THE WORLD

Objective: This exercise demonstrates how our culture shapes how we view the world. It addresses the cognitive factors in CM.

Directions:

Individual Work

From memory, draw a simple map of the world that includes the seven continents. You do not have to provide details; you can use rough geometric shapes if needed.

Group Work

Get together with at least one other student and compare your maps. Discuss the following:

- Where did you start (which continent and where on the paper)?
- What are the relative sizes of the continents?
- How does your map reflect your culture and the country you are from?

Review in Class

Your instructor will provide a map of the world to guide discussion of how your culture impacts your view of the world.

EXERCISE 1.2: THE WASHING MACHINE AD

Objective: This exercise demonstrates how culture shapes our interpretation of events. It addresses the cognitive factors in CM.

Directions: The image below is reproduction of an ad used by a US appliance manufacturer to market its washing machine in several Arab countries. The company's marketing director was aware of religious sensitivities about portraying women, who were their primary target market. She also did not want to simply translate their US ads into Arabic, worrying about confusing possible translation errors or missteps. After much research, she and her team decided that using simple images would be the best way to convey their message. So, they came up with the ad that is reproduced below (Figure 1.5).

Figure 1.5 Washing Machine Ad

Sources: istockphoto.com / omersukrugoksu; istockphoto.com / s-cphoto; istockphoto.com / Aslan Alphan.

Take a minute to review the image.

1. Describe what you see.

2. Would you consider this to be an effective ad?

3. Can you think of any cultural differences that may impact the ad's effectiveness and impact?

After deploying the ad, the company found out that it was not only ineffective, but also it seemed to be causing sales to drop.

1. What do you think went wrong?

CASE STUDY: TRUE AMERICAN VALUES?

"Why do we work so hard? For what?" is the starting question of a 2014 one-minute commercial, called *Poolside*, for the Cadillac ELR Coupe which first aired during the 2014 Winter Olympics and again during the Academy Awards that year (Poolside, 2014). The ad features actor Neal McDonough walking around, or some might say strutting, in an obviously expensive house, casually interacting with his family and touting the value of material goods, working hard and not taking too much time off. He then rattles off the names of famous US-American successful entrepreneurs and mentions the unique US achievement of landing on the moon as proof of the outcome of the work-hard-no-play approach. The commercial ends with McDonough getting into the Cadillac and saying: "...that's the upside of only taking two weeks off in August. N'est-ce-pas?"

The commercial oozes stereotypical US-American values, male bravado, and symbols of wealth. Craig Bierly, Cadillac's advertising director at that time, said the commercial intended to be "brand provocation," rather than a statement about American values (Voelcker, 2014). Uwe Ellinghaus, then Cadillac's global chief marketing officer, added that the company wanted to generate a buzz about the car (Colias, 2014). It certainly provoked a buzz! Some saw it as a representation of the "ugly American." One person who saw the ad thought it was insulting and embarrassing because of the way it portrays Americans (Voelcker, 2014). Others celebrated it as a representation of true American values and capitalism (Colias, 2014) and others as a shameless celebration of a work-hard-buy-more culture (Gregoire, 2014).

The *Poolside* commercial made it to the 2017 "Hall of Shame" of commercials that commit multicultural blunders for insulting just about everyone in the world, alienating its potential international markets, and demeaning a good segment of the US population by suggesting that those who can't afford the car are perhaps too lazy (Fromowitz, 2017). Meanwhile, some simply wondered whether such an ad can actually spur sales (Woodyard, 2014). Not to let a good crisis go to waste, Cadillac's competitor Ford used a parody of the *Poolside* commercial to tout another set of American values to sell one of its own cars. That commercial, featuring an African American woman, plugs being entrepreneurial, being green, caring about the environment, and wanting to make the world better as the key values of a new generation (Ford's Response, 2014). While seemingly presenting two opposing views of the US-American values and ideals and targeting two different markets, the two commercials tapped into an interesting representation of cultural values and maybe unintentionally presented the richness of a culture.

Watch the two commercials on YouTube:

Cadillac's Poolside: https://www.youtube.com/watch?time_continue=27&v=xNzXze5Yza8

Ford's commercial: https://www.youtube.com/watch?v=24VerifhVJk&feature=youtu.be&t=67

Questions

1. What are the values that are presented in each of the commercials?

2. To what extent are the values uniquely US-American?

3. Which commercial more accurately represents being US-American?

4. Can you think of some countries where the Cadillac ad may not play well? Why?

5. What is your reaction to the two companies using cultural values to sell their product?

Sources

Colias, M. (2014). Caddy CMO subbed in electric car to make ad 'more socially palatable'. *Ad Age*, March 6. Retrieved from https://adage.com/article/cmo-strategy/cadillac-put-electric-car-ad-make-ad-palatable/292010. Accessed on May 28, 2019.

Ford's Response. (2014). Retrieved from https://www.youtube.com/watch?v=24VerifhVJk&feature=youtu.be&t=67. Accessed on May 28, 2019.

Fromowitz, M. (2017). Hall of shame: More multicultural brand blunder. *US Campaign*, February 10. Retrieved from https://www.campaignlive.com/article/hall-shame-multicultural-brand-blunders/1423941. Accessed on May 28, 2019.

Gregoire, C. (2014). Cadillac made a commercial about the American dream, and it's a nightmare. *Huffington Post*, February 27. Retrieved from https://www.huffpost.com/entry/this-commercial-sums-up-e_n_4859040. Accessed on May 28, 2019.

Poolside. (2014). Retrieved from https://www.youtube.com/watch?time_continue=27&v=xNzXze5Yza8. Accessed on May 28, 2019.

Voelcker, J. (2014). Cadillac says viewers should calm down about its obnoxious electric car ad. *Business Insider*, March 6. Retrieved from https://www.businessinsider.com/cadillac-calm-down-about-car-ad-2014-3. Accessed on May 28.

Woodyard, C. (2014). Is Cadillac's ELR causing a rich-guy backlash? *USA Today*, March 3. Retrieved from https://www.usatoday.com/story/money/cars/2014/03/03/cadillac-elr-ad-poolside/5965439/. Accessed on May 28, 2019.

CHAPTER TWO

THE CULTURAL MINDSET

FIRST PERSON

The "Conquistadores" Mentality Persists

What do you do when a direct report looks down at you publicly because you come from a region that used to be a colony of his country? I was born and raised in Latin America and, as many people from that region, my ancestors came from different European countries. After working for an American multinational company in several countries in Latin America, I was promoted and appointed president of the European operation, based in Barcelona, Spain. I was thrilled to live and work in a country that I loved and considered an important part of my heritage, which should have made the cultural adaptation process smooth. Little did I know! In my very first day at work, I had a management meeting with all my direct reports with the objective of introducing ourselves and discussing the main issues and challenges we faced. When it was the turn of the vice president of operations, who reported directly to me, he said: "Why did the company appoint a *sudaca* (a highly derogatory term used in Spain to refer to Latin-Americans) to be our boss? Don't you know that Latin America was our colony? We have plenty of Europeans in the company to do the job!" At that moment I knew I had a problem. It was evident that he was expressing what many others might be thinking. I had to act, and quickly. To re-establish my authority, I fired the VP on the spot and then set out to change the culture from a Spaniard company to a multinational one.

–Juan Roche, PhD

As the title of this book indicates, the Cultural Mindset (CM) is the primary theme with the goal of helping you become more

Learning Objectives

2.1 Provide a detailed working definition of Cultural Mindset (CM) and elaborate on the ten factors that make up the CM.

2.2 Explain the details of the CM cognitive factors.

2.3 Present details of the CM personality factors.

2.4 Present details of the CM knowledge factors.

2.5 Elaborate on CM as a threshold and a continuum.

2.6 Compare CM to other approaches to cultural competence.

2.7 Detail the steps of the THINK–KNOW–DO roadmap to developing a CM.

effective at managing across cultures. The *First-Person* scenario illustrates how culture acts as a meta-context to shape people's view of the world. In this case, the V.P., who is a Spaniard, views the world from an old colonial perspective that he has acquired through his education and experience, where a Latin American is seen as inferior. That perspective influences his reactions and behaviors and has likely been effective. However, his worldview and reaction to his boss also lead to his firing. We again see the basic culture paradox at work: What works in one context does not necessarily work in another. All of us are shaped to varying degrees by our cultural background which provides us with sets of assumptions, values, beliefs, and rules for behavior. It shapes what we pay attention to, what we remember, how we react, and how we manage people. Awareness of our own culture is one of the first steps to developing a CM that will allow you to move from one world to another more effectively and be more adept at managing people across cultures. This chapter examines the concept of CM in detail, provides a tool to assess its ten factors, and presents the THINK–KNOW–DO model that offers a roadmap for managers to develop a CM.

1. THE CULTURAL MINDSET: A WORKING DEFINITION

LO 2.1 Provide a detailed working definition of Cultural Mindset (CM) and elaborate on the ten factors that make up the CM

In Chapter 1, we discussed how having a CM starts with an awareness of your own cultural backgrounds, the fact that culture-just-is (CJI) and that it provides a meta-context (CMC). We examine the CM in detail in the next section and present the ten factors that constitute the CM.

1.1 What's a Mindset?

First, let's explore the definition and meaning of the word *mindset*. The concept of mindset started being used in cognitive psychology in the early 20th century (Gollwitzer, 1990) and has been adopted since by a number of disciplines including organizational theory and management (e.g., Gupta & Govindarajan, 2002) and education (e.g., Dweck, 2016) to explore how what people think about a certain topic or situation shapes their actions (French, 2017; Gollwitzer, 2012). A *mindset* is defined as "the sum total of activated cognitive procedures" tied to a particular task (Gollwitzer & Bayer, 1999, p. 405) or "the general cognitive operation with distinct features that facilitate a given task" (Torelli & Kaikati, 2009, p. 232). It is a mental attitude or disposition that relates to certain inclinations. A mindset includes the following:

- A predisposition to see the world and simplify it in a particular way (Rhinesmith, 1992)

- A frame of reference (Benson & Dvesdow, 2003)

- A guide to how people interpret the world (Dweck, 2016)

- Cognitive filters that help us see the world (Gupta & Govindarajan, 2002) and

- A procedural tool kit that we use to structure our thinking (Oyserman, Sorensen, Reber, & Chen, 2009)

These definitions and characteristics of the concept of mindset indicate that we develop various mindsets related to specific situations to help us simplify a complex world and provide us with ways of interpreting it. Our mindsets shape what some scholars have called theories of action that give us guidelines for behavior (Argyris & Schon, 1974). They have been recommended as the basis for good management (Gosling & Mintzberg, 2003) and suggested to be the filters that we apply to make sense of the world (Gupta & Govindarajan, 2002; we explore these processes in detail in Chapter 3). In other words, *the beliefs that we hold, also hold us*, often without us being aware of their existence or their impact. The theories that we hold in our heads about various situations and how things are or should be shape our actions.

Consider the case of Min-Jun Kim, who after obtaining a business and engineering degree in South Korea finished his MBA with an emphasis in finance in a prestigious US university and is looking to do an internship for a year or two in the United States before returning to his home country. With several years of work experience in Korea and Singapore under his belt and outstanding grades, he was confident that he would have no trouble finding a position. As the summer months pass, Min-Jun is surprised that in spite of many interviews, he does not have a single offer or prospect while most of his classmates have found highly desirable positions. He had fully prepared for each interview, was very careful to show humility and proper respect, did not interrupt his interviewers, answered their questions clearly and thoughtfully, and did not brag about himself. He believed that his résumé spoke for itself. He had found the interviews childish and sometimes silly with interviewers joking too much and not appearing to take things seriously. The MBA's placement director was also surprised that Min-Jun was not getting offers, so she decided to check with the companies and see if she can get some feedback. The response was consistent: Min-Jun looked great on paper, but he was unfriendly, too serious, uptight, and appeared to lack initiative or even real interest in the jobs.

In this example, Min-Jun is behaving according to his own mindset regarding what is appropriate interview behavior: he is serious, respectful, and self-effacing, all of which are appropriate in the South Korean culture. His interviewers are disappointed that they are not seeing an aggressive and competitive go-getter that is consistent with a graduate of the top US MBA program. The parties are using different mindsets or frames of reference and seeing the world through their own lenses.

A particular application of mindset, then, is to culture. Our cultural assumptions, values, and beliefs all are part of our CM; they provide us with filters or lenses that influence how we perceive people and situations, tell us what is right and wrong, shape our theories of action, and guide our behaviors, all the while being almost invisible to us as a meta-context.

1.2 Cultural Mindset

We have defined a CM as follows:

CM is a way of thinking and a frame of mind or reference that considers culture as a factor when assessing yourself and other people and situations, and when making decisions and acting on them. Having a CM means that you are aware of your own cultural backgrounds and the fact that culture-just-is and that it provides a meta-context.

The concept of the CM provides a unique perspective on how one can be effective when working across cultures. The way we think about a situation, in this case the cultural lens or perspective, shapes what we believe and how we behave. Management scholars Jonathan Gosling and Henry Mintzberg (2003) suggested that managers' understanding and managing of context comes from paying attention to areas where various contexts intersect and being able to understand situations without imposing our own points of views.

When we are in our own culture (aka our "small world"), where we know and understand the context, we have *expert intuition* and we are mindlessly competent; we don't have to think hard about how to proceed because we understand the situation and know the rules. Therefore, we are able to be fast, efficient, and accurate in our perceptions, judgments, and decisions. We automatically know how to read the situation and how to behave; we do not need to think about culture because it is our own culture. However, when we cross cultural boundaries and enter novel cultural contexts (aka the "large world"), we no longer can or should rely on that fast information processing and automatic and associative memory and well-practiced cultural behavioral scripts that our mindset provides. We are literally in what Greek philosopher Plotlemy called *terra incognita*—parts unknown, referring to lands that were unknown and undiscovered. In these unknown parts, we do not have the appropriate context and narrative for other cultures. For example, in the United States and several other European countries when employees make a mistake or mishandle a situation, their managers will most likely address the situation directly and provide feedback to correct the behavior. They do not have to think twice about whether the employee may lose face or be embarrassed, as long as the correction is done in private. The same manager working in Thailand cannot operate automatically and will have to more carefully weigh how to best provide feedback and do so indirectly or even through a third person.

To avoid error and to be effective, we must first recognize and accept that the rules from our world may not apply, and then intentionally think about the cultural context and actively engage our CM in order to understand and interpret the situation. To do that, we have to know the content of our CM first and we have to become aware of our assumptions, beliefs, and values.

1.3 The Ten CM Factors

The CM is composed of a combination of ten factors that work in conjunction with one another (see Figure 2.1). These factors address who we are, how we think, and what we know and together influence what we do. Having a CM is, first and foremost, a way of thinking. Assessing people's CM therefore requires knowing first how they think, then some of their personality traits, and what they know. Accordingly, developing a CM requires that we first become aware of how our culture impacts our cognitive processes, how these processes operate, and then build our knowledge of culture and our cultural vocabulary. The large majority of existing cultural training addresses only developing cultural knowledge or literacy about other cultures. That knowledge is ***necessary, but not sufficient***. For example, when businesses send employees to work overseas, either temporarily or on a more long-term basis as expatriates, they provide them with language instruction and teach them about the culture of the country they will be visiting. The information is focused on knowledge about the others, with little attention to exploring the culture of the expats and the lens and perspective that their culture may provide. However, successful cross-cultural interaction requires understanding how culture operates as our software, how it shapes our own as well as others' thinking. The CM approach is unique in that it focuses on how people's cognitive processes operate and impact their assumptions, values, beliefs, and behaviors and how culture acts as a meta-context that both guides us and provides us with context to interpret our world.

1.4 The Cognitive, Personality, and Knowledge Components

Before you read on and explore each of the ten factors, complete the ICMI (Individual Cultural Mindset Inventory) using the code provided in your book and record your results in Self-Assessment 2.1 (for information on the development of the

Figure 2.1   Ten Cultural Mindset Factors

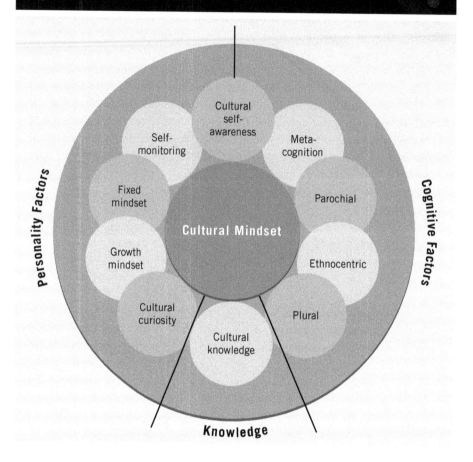

ICMI, see Appendix A). Table 2.1 presents the ten factors that make up the ICMI, which is an assessment of your CM. The ten factors are divided into three groups:

- *Cognitive factors* that are concerned with how we think. These include cultural self-awareness, meta-cognition, and views of culture (parochial, ethnocentric, and plural).

- *Personality-based* factors that stem from characteristics that people either inherit or develop early in life and are relatively stable over time. These include self-monitoring, curiosity, and fixed and growth mindsets.

- Knowledge factors address information we have about other cultures. These include various cultural knowledge we have.

Table 2.1 Factors in Cultural Mindset (CM)

CM Factors	Description
Cognition	
1. Cultural self-awareness	Having knowledge of your own culture(s), assumptions, values, and beliefs and their implications for how you think and behave.
2. Meta-cognition	Ability to think and reflect about one's own thinking; understanding one's own thinking, how it operates, and its impact.
3. Parochial	A narrow view of culture that only considers one's own culture, with little interest in other cultures and a belief that culture is not important.
4. Ethnocentric	A view of culture that considers one's own culture to be more important than and superior to others. It includes both a sense of pride and superiority.
5. Pluralistic	A view of culture that considers all cultures to be of equal value with a high interest in other cultures.
Personality	
6. Self-monitoring	Ability to read the cues from the environment and adjust behavior accordingly. May vary from one cultural context to another.
7. Cultural curiosity	Interest in learning about culture, one's own and that of others; seeking cultural experiences; willingness to engage with different cultures. May vary from one cultural context to another.
8. Fixed mindset	Belief that people have limited—or fixed—talents and abilities to learn and grow and are therefore unable to change substantially.
9. Growth mindset	Belief that people can change and grow, meaning that time and experience allows us to develop.
Knowledge	
10. Cultural knowledge	Having information about other cultures' values, history, organizational systems, etc.; knowledge of world events outside of one's culture and country. May vary from one cultural context to another.

2. COGNITIVE CM FACTORS

LO 2.2 Explain the details of the CM cognitive factors

As we have discussed, CM provides a cognitive perspective to cross-cultural management. The starting point is how a person perceives and interprets the situation and event's cognition. Culture shapes our cognition and provides a frame of reference and a lens through which we see the world.

2.1 Cultural Self-Awareness

Where are you from? What is your culture? We have asked these questions in Chapter 1 and will be returning to them throughout this book. Self-Assessment 1.1 started you on the path to answering them; Self-Assessment 2.2 continues to dig deeper. Your culture shapes your CMC and the lens through which you view and interpret the world and provides a guide for your behaviors. Knowing your own culture and its assumptions, values, and beliefs is the foundation of a CM. Most of us are part of more than one culture and our various cultures impact us to different degrees. The sense of belonging to different groups makes up one's *cultural identity*. Some of us are keenly aware of our identity and actively rely on it in our personal and organizational life; others barely think about their cultural identity. People in the first group are likely to provide a quick and possibly complex answer to the question of "what's your cultural background?" They may take some time to answer and provide details and examples. People in the second group may be puzzled at the questions, not quite know how to answer, or in some cases, even say that they don't really have a culture (Nahavandi, 2017).

Interestingly, in the United States, those who consider themselves white and European and part of the majority of the population are more likely to not be aware of their cultural identity and its impact. If you are part of that group, you are more likely to associate culture with minority groups or something about other people. Similarly, on the group level, gender as culture is often associated with women (Menendez, 2019). Conversely, those who belong to a minority group are more likely to identify their culture or cultures. A biracial woman or a new immigrant will have a quick and possibly detailed response to the culture question; a person considered an outsider or part of the minority will most likely have an answer as well. Anglo-European Americans who consider themselves part of the majority are more likely to respond with "well, I'm American."

2.1.1 The "Norm" and White Privilege. Having cultural self-awareness is an essential factor in CM. As we will discuss at length in Chapter 3, not being aware of your CMC means that you are not aware of how and when it impacts you. Lack of cultural self-awareness is also likely to lead to the automatic assumption that the way you perceive and interpret situations and events is simply objective and normal and the way things are. In other words, you are likely to believe that your lens is "the" lens. The much-debated issue of *white privilege* is partially related to this lack of cultural self awareness. Peggy McIntosh (1989) has called white privilege the "invisible knapsack." The dominant majority groups are considered the "norm" and do not think about their culture as often and as much as those who are members of less dominant cultural groups (Fabregat & Kperogi, 2019; Metzl, 2019; Morris, 2016). For example, we rarely use a white person's race as a descriptor because the "norm" is white, whereas other ethnic descriptors such as black, Hispanic, and Asian are often used (Chalabi, 2018). When your culture is invisible to you, you are not aware of its components and impact. Instead, you may simply assume that how you are is how things should be; that is the norm, that's average, typical, or standard. Whether caused by our drive for efficiency (as you will see in Chapter 3) or lack of knowledge, or a conscious motive to view one's culture differently than others, not having an awareness of one's culture and its assumptions, values, and beliefs makes it impossible to fully develop a CM. If you are not aware of your culture, its assumptions, values, and beliefs and associated rules and behaviors, you are likely to use the same CMC in every situation, assume that your CMC is "the" CMC, and manage every employee the same way regardless of the context or his or her cultural background.

2.2 Meta-Cognition

Another cognitive factor in the CM is being able to use meta-cognition when thinking about cultures. *Meta-cognition* is the ability to think about and reflect on one's thinking (Baker & Brown, 1984; Flavell, 1985) and on one's actions and situations. People who actively use meta-cognition plan and monitor their actions and reflect on their experiences and how they approach different situations. They also evaluate their own and other people's actions and ask questions regarding what they do, why they do it, and how they think, all of which have been found to be conducive to learning (Bransford, Brown, & Cocking, 2000). The ability to apply meta-cognition is essential in developing a CM and learning from cultural experiences. People who know how to use meta-cognition are able:

- To think critically, which means they consciously process and evaluate information about themselves, others, and events

- To plan their actions based on their evaluation

- To absorb information and knowledge that derives from their experiences, which means they learn from their experience and that knowledge shapes their future actions.

Meta-cognition facilitates and supports understanding of the CMC, cultural assumptions, values, and beliefs, and the lenses that one uses. Managers who rely on meta-cognition are aware and conscious of their actions. When they manage people across cultures or simply find themselves in different cultural contexts, they notice differences, evaluate their sources, plan and act accordingly. Additionally, they reflect on their actions and events and use the information they gather to learn and change their future actions.

2.3 Three Views of Culture

The next three cognitive factors in the CM relate to how one views one's own culture in relation to other cultures. Do you believe that culture is irrelevant and not a major factor in human interactions or that people are the same across the world regardless of their culture? Are you primarily interested in your own community and believe that your values and beliefs are superior to that of others? Do you consider all cultures, including your own, to be of equal value? The answers to these questions determine your view of culture.

1. *Parochialism* is the view that the world is narrow and limited to our own backyard. Someone with a parochial view does not believe that culture really matters and has little interest in their own or other people's culture. Their cultural view is focused on their immediate environment, which they assume is all there is. For them, culture does not matter. As a result, they are unconsciously going to assume that who they are is the norm and how everybody is or should be.

2. *Ethnocentrism* is the view that one's own culture is superior to that of others. It also involves a sense of pride of one's culture. People with this view know that there are many cultures, but they see their own as superior. Most of us have, and should have, some pride in our cultural background. However, having cultural pride does not necessarily mean that you devalue other cultures; you can be proud of who you are and still respect and appreciate others who are different.

3. *Multiculturalism and pluralism* are on the other end of the spectrum of parochialism and ethnocentrism. People who hold this view accept other cultures and value their uniqueness and hold a relativistic view that recognizes the impact of culture. They have an interest in culture and generally accept the idea of CJI. A plural view would lead to the belief that all cultures serve a purpose and function for their members, therefore all have equal value.

The worldview that a person has, the way they think about culture—their own and that of others—clearly impacts their interest in and interaction with their own and other people's culture and impacts their CM. We explore these worldviews in detail in Chapter 4. Cultural self-awareness, meta-cognition, and views of culture together form the cognitive aspect of CM.

3. PERSONALITY CM FACTORS

LO 2.3 Present details of the CM personality factors

In addition to how people think, several personality factors impact people's CM. *Personality* traits are defined as relatively permanent individual characteristics that develop early in life and are typically stable from one situation to another. While personality traits do not dictate behavior, they provide people with a range that makes certain behaviors easier or harder. For example, managers who have an extroverted personality draw their energy from other people, tend to be sociable and talkative, while introverted managers are more likely to be reserved and less likely to seek out social situations. However, in both cases, their personality does not entirely limit them. Each can behave in a manner typically associated with the other group, although they may find those behaviors more difficult or stressful.

3.1 Self-Monitoring

The first personality factor in the CM is the extent to which people are able to perceive, read, and use cues from the environment to adjust their behavior. The concept of *self-monitoring* was developed by social psychologist Mark Snyder (1974) to measure people's ability to manage their self-presentation. It addresses the degree to which people are capable of reading and using the cues from their environment to determine their behavior. Those who score high on the scale:

- Can read environmental and social cues regarding what is appropriate behavior

- Can use environmental cues to modify their behaviors

- Can adjust how they present themselves and manage impressions well (Turnley & Bolino, 2001)

- Can mirror and mimic others' behaviors better than low self-monitors (Estow, Jamieson, & Yates, 2007).

Conversely, those scoring lower on self-monitoring either do not perceive the cues, or choose not to read them, or do not use them to change their behavior. Given a higher ability to read the environment and adjust behaviors, it is reasonable to suggest that in situations that are ambiguous and difficult to read, such as in cross-cultural environments, those who score higher on self-monitoring are likely to be more effective. Additionally, being able to mimic others' behaviors and mannerisms allows a person to make connections with others, a factor that further can support effective cross-cultural interactions.

3.2 Fixed and Growth Mindsets

Carol Dweck (2016) popularized the idea of fixed and growth mindsets to look at how and why some students learn more effectively than others. The concepts address whether you see people and yourself as unchanging and unable to grow or as capable of learning, growing, and changing. On the one hand, a person with a *fixed mindset* is likely to believe that people do not change or learn much past a certain point; people are the way they are because of innate abilities and therefore unlikely to change. So, people with a fixed mindset may believe that they lack either the ability or the agency to effect change and are therefore likely to seek order and predictability. On the other hand, individuals with a *growth mindset* see challenges as opportunities to effect change, learn, and grow. They are more likely to be open to trying and failing, which they believe leads to opportunity, learning, and growth.

Research has linked these two mindsets to a number of organizational outcomes (e.g., O'Keefe, Dweck, & Walton, 2018). Having a fixed mindset poses a particular challenge when crossing cultural boundaries:

- If you tend to view people and yourself as unchanging and not capable of learning, you will have more difficulty with the lack of predictability that is inherent in cross-cultural encounters.

- You are also less likely to take the risks involved with cross-cultural encounters because you do not believe that you can learn from those experiences.

Conversely, having a growth mindset is likely to make it easier for people to develop their CM. Managers who believe that change and making mistakes provide an opportunity for learning and growth are more likely to encourage their employees to experiment. Similarly, because they are open to new challenges, they are more likely to engage in cross-cultural interactions that may appear daunting to those with a fixed mindset.

3.3 Cultural Curiosity

The fact that you are reading this book, either as part of a class that you have elected to take or on your own, indicates that you likely have some degree of curiosity about other cultures and cross-cultural management. That curiosity is another personality-based factor in the CM. Curiosity has been defined in two ways:

- First, it can be *state-based*, meaning that it is temporarily triggered by something novel

- Second, it can be *trait-based*, which means it involves personality and more intrinsic motivation to learn and seek new experiences.

More specifically, cultural curiosity involves motivation to learn about other cultures, their assumptions, values, beliefs, and appreciation of visible cultural elements such as food, music, and literature. Predictably, a person who has cultural curiosity is more likely to seek and acquire knowledge about other cultures, therefore having curiosity and seeking cultural experiences are factors that support a CM. For example, expat managers who work in countries other than their own who have cultural curiosity are more likely to inquire about culture and seek interactions with the local population and therefore more likely to be successful in their assignment than those who show no interest in the country and focus only on getting their job done.

4. CULTURAL KNOWLEDGE AS A CM FACTOR

LO 2.4 Present details of the CM knowledge factors

The last factor in CM is having knowledge of other cultures. Knowledge can include information about history, assumptions, values, and language, as well as more specific cross-cultural management experience regarding leadership styles, organizational structures, and legal frameworks in other countries. All are essential to successful cross-cultural interactions and to developing a CM. Developing of cultural knowledge has long been a cornerstone of many popular approaches to cultural competence and literacy training (e.g., Morrison & Conaway, 2006). There is no doubt that having knowledge about other cultures, at any level, is critical and essential to successful cross-cultural interactions. Preparations for cross-cultural interactions should involve learning about the other people's culture. However, there are limits to relying on cultural knowledge alone. Specifically,

- With over 10,000 cultures in the world, it is impossible to learn about all of them or predict with which culture you will be interacting.

- Knowledge of customs and learning to behave appropriately only addresses the visible aspects of culture and is likely to be superficial.

- There is the risk of overestimating how much one knows and thus have misplaced confidence, leading to overgeneralizing and making inaccurate judgments.

- Relying on stereotypes, even sophisticated ones based on research and knowledge, can lead to essentializing and overgeneralizations.

- Finally, focusing on cultural knowledge alone can lead to mislabeling and miscategorizing individuals into cultural groups; most people have complex cultural identities that are not always visible to others.

Consider the challenge of a manager who is preparing to go to the UAE for a business negotiation. Clearly, it would be appropriate for her to learn about the country's culture and traditions. However, given that a very large percentage of those living in the UAE are not native or considered citizens, which culture should she study? Should she read about Islam, tribal cultures, the various groups and generations in the UAE, the large expat and migrant community, or the UAE's short history? Additionally, armed with some knowledge, however accurate, the manager must also accurately identify which group the people she meets belong to. Having knowledge of other cultures is necessary, but not sufficient. For these reasons, while cultural knowledge is essential, it is only one of the ten factors that contributes to a CM.

The cognitive factors in CM such as having awareness of one's own culture and its role in CMC as both context and guide and having meta-cognition can help moderate lack of cultural knowledge. Specifically, if you are aware of the rules from your world and know that they may not apply in a new situation, you can slow down, use your meta-cognition, and approach the other world more prudently and thoughtfully. By not applying the rules of one world to another, you are likely to prevent mistakes. Notwithstanding, the more one knows about other cultures, the better, and such knowledge fully supports the development of a CM.

Developing a CM improves one's ability to understand where culture plays a role. It involves self-awareness of one's own culture and its role and impact as a meta-contextual factor, knowledge of cultural differences, and having the knowledge and skills to be able to slow down one's thinking to avoid error and systematic bias in cross-cultural situations. It involves knowing when the rules and assumptions of your world may not apply to another world. Absent the development of a CM and absent the ability to address cross-cultural situations at a cognitive level, learning new skills and competencies is likely to be ineffective and lack broad applicability.

5. CM AS A THRESHOLD AND A CONTINUUM

Developing a CM is akin to crossing a threshold into another world or dimension. The idea of crossing thresholds in learning was originally developed by Meyer and Land (2003, 2006), who identified certain topics as conceptual gateways that once crossed, open up new and previously inaccessible ways of thinking that can transform people and help them understand and interpret the world in radically different ways. Grasping the concept of CM is such a critical threshold (Nahavandi, 2017). When managers develop a CM, they are able to perceive and see events with a new perspective and are able to learn new skills which allow them to cross into a new world.

5.1 Characteristics of Thresholds

Four characteristics of thresholds are significant to understanding CM (see Table 2.2 for details):

1. Crossing a threshold is transformative.

2. Crossing a threshold is irreversible.

3. Crossing a threshold is integrative.

4. Crossing a threshold is troublesome.

Incorporating culture into your thinking, i.e., developing a CM which involves crossing a threshold, changes how you view yourself, many day-to-day interactions, and the world. For example, becoming aware of your cultural assumptions, values, and beliefs may help you understand the reason why you have a high degree of respect for authority and have trouble calling your boss by her first name. It also may help explain why you are punctual or why you connect closely with your family and community. All of these behaviors relate to cultural values we will discuss in detail in later chapters. Of course, your personality may play a role as well, but CMC is likely to have an impact. Taking a cultural view may further help explain why some of your colleagues or yourself have more or less trouble working in a team environment, why some people put competition ahead of group cohesion, or why some of us focus on facts and others rely more on emotions. Culture is not the only factor, but many situations have a cultural explanation, and once you start on the path of considering culture, it is hard to "unsee" it. Once a CM is developed, you are likely to see how culture is one of the foundations of social interaction and how it provides a meta-context in most situations.

Table 2.2 Characteristics of Cultural Mindset (CM) as a Threshold

Characteristics	Description
Transformative	Crossing critical thresholds leads people to experience a significant shift in perception, thinking, and appreciation of events and situations. *Developing a CM makes you see the world differently.*
Irreversible	Once crossed, the perspective cannot be undone—you cannot "unsee" what you have seen. *Once you develop a CM, it is hard to leave it behind and ignore culture.*
Integrative	Crossing thresholds brings together and integrates facts, information, and relationships that seemed previously unrelated. *CM helps integrate cross-cultural experiences.*
Troublesome	Because crossing a threshold provides new information that challenges prior knowledge, it often creates discomfort. *CM provides a new view of the world that may challenge existing views and be uncomfortable.*

Sources: Based on information in Meyer and Land (2003, 2006) and Nahavandi (2017).

Furthermore, relying on CM allows you to integrate elements that may have appeared disjointed and unconnected. For example, if, like many people, you come from more than one cultural background, the assumptions, values, and beliefs of those cultures may conflict. Your Mexican culture may push you to respect authority and focus on the group, while your US-American culture makes you individualistic, independent, and informal; the integrative theme that makes you unique is culture. Finally, developing a CM, seeing CMC, and accepting cultures as they are (CJI) can be challenging and troublesome. Having pride in your own cultures and valuing them while at the same time accepting that other cultures are equally valuable is not an easy process. Cross-cultural encounters often violate our expectations and perspectives and can create strain (Niwa & Maruno, 2010) as we are introduced to ideas and behaviors that may appear inappropriate or inconsistent and for which we have little or no context. Moving from our small world to another one is disconcerting and unsettling. We feel that we have lost our anchors and may lose confidence in our ability to make correct decisions. For these reasons, crossing the threshold to CM is bound to be troublesome.

For example, consider Paul Spencer, US manager who was assigned to work in the Brazilian subsidiary of his company in São Paulo. His years of experience and success in the United States have helped him develop an easy-going style of interacting with his supervisors and employees. He also is used to making many decisions related to his department and team on his own without checking the details with his superiors.

However, to be effective in Brazil requires him to cross a threshold that is likely to be uncomfortable and troublesome. Brazilian organizations are more bureaucratic and hierarchical, and the independent decision-making that was effective in the United States is likely to be met with considerable resistance. After several incidents where he is reminded to go through the channels, he finally accepts that although people are very friendly and appear very relaxed, one of the key characteristics of Brazilian organizations is their highly rule-bound and bureaucratic processes. Once he crosses that threshold, he begins to be more successful.

5.2 CM as a Continuum

CM presents a continuum ranging from no CM to a fully developed CM (Figure 2.2). At one end of the continuum, a low CM would mean that culture is a *subliminal* factor; it is not perceived or used. People in this range are generally not conscious of the presence of culture and have limited awareness of how culture impacts their own or others' behaviors. They also have limited knowledge of cultural differences. Culture is not an issue they think much about, and although they sometimes may know that culture impacts situations, they do not often change their actions based on that information. Furthermore, people with low CM may believe that "people are just people," that culture does not play a role, but rather what works for them is appropriate across all cultures. A person with low CM would not be conscious or mindful of culture and its impact, have little interest in the topic, and have little

Figure 2.2   The Cultural Mindset Continuum

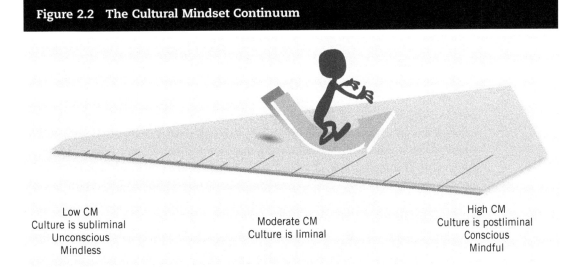

Low CM
Culture is subliminal
Unconscious
Mindless

Moderate CM
Culture is liminal

High CM
Culture is postliminal
Conscious
Mindful

knowledge, skills, or competencies related to culture. They are prone to relying on their automatic, tacit, and ritual knowledge that they mindlessly apply to all situations. For example, such a person would automatically assume that because he is proactive, highly competitive, and motivated by monetary achievements, that is the way everyone else is and should be; recognition and words are nice, but what matters is the bottom line. Therefore, as a manager, he may rely primarily or exclusively on monetary rewards for all his employees without regard for other factors that may motivate them.

In the middle of the continuum, where many of us fall, people either do not think about culture, only do so occasionally, or have limited cultural curiosity, knowledge, and competencies. Culture is *liminal*, barely perceptible. Someone in this range may be aware of some cultural differences, but may not have the knowledge and skills to use that awareness in a proactive manner. They may notice cultural differences, but because they do not have full information and knowledge on how to address them, they may see culture as troublesome and undesirable. At the other end of the continuum, having a high CM means that you consider culture when you enter a situation and engage with others. That is the *postliminal* stance. You are aware of the presence, manifestation, expression, and impact of culture in all aspects of your own life and those of others. You understand that culture, as CMC, is a constant factor that can impact your own and others' thinking and behavior. You have knowledge of cultural differences, the vocabulary, and skills to integrate culture into your decisions, and are able to use appropriate cultural information to address situational requirements. You often use culture as a factor in making personal or professional decisions and you also have the knowledge, ability, and skills to adjust your behavior. A person who has a fully developed CM unconsciously and automatically takes culture into consideration and has the interest, knowledge, competencies, and skills to interact effectively across cultures; that person is unconsciously mindful and culturally competent.

While some of the factors in CM such as fixed or growth mindset and self-monitoring are relatively stable, others, for example, self-awareness, meta-cognition, views of culture, level of curiosity, and knowledge, are more dynamic. Consider the example of a biracial African and Vietnamese American woman who, because she grew up with the African-American side of her family with little contact with the Vietnamese side, is aware of her African-American culture and connected with its assumptions, values, and beliefs. Additionally, her darker skin color makes that ethnic group salient to others, further reinforcing that aspect of her identity. Consequently, she is aware of some, but not all, of her roots. However, she is generally interested in learning about Asian, particularly Vietnamese, culture that she still considers to be part of herself, whereas she has little curiosity or interest in many other cultures that she may encounter.

CM, like culture itself, is neither genetic nor biological. Depending on the level of interest and motivation to learn and change, the level of CM can change. We can all learn about our own cultures and become more self-aware. We can work on nudging a fixed mindset toward a growth mindset. We can be exposed to different views of culture and change our approach. We can practice meta-cognition and learn to think and learn better. We can decide to seek cultural knowledge and practice new behaviors to gain more competence. The core of CM, as the definition implies, is consideration of culture when making decisions and being aware of culture as CMC; it's a way of thinking, something that we will explore in detail in the next two chapters. This focus on cognition makes CM distinct among various approaches to cultural competence, as we will discuss in a later section of this chapter.

5.3 Stages of the Development of CM

The goal of this book is to give you the knowledge and tools to develop your CM. Depending on where you start and the degree to which you already have a CM, you may go through the stages of CM development presented in Figure 2.3 in different ways. The first stage is becoming *aware* of culture and CM. Developing cultural self-awareness is the cornerstone; knowing that culture is not just about other people is key. By becoming aware of culture, you move past the subliminal stage; you start to

Figure 2.3   Stages of Cultural Mindset Development

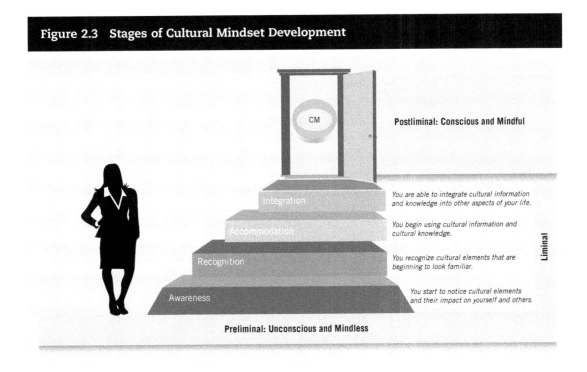

CM

Postliminal: Conscious and Mindful

Integration — You are able to integrate cultural information and knowledge into other aspects of your life.

Accommodation — You begin using cultural information and cultural knowledge.

Recognition — You recognize cultural elements that are beginning to look familiar.

Awareness — You start to notice cultural elements and their impact on yourself and others.

Liminal

Preliminal: Unconscious and Mindless

notice culture and its impact. Reading about the importance and impact of culture and the processes that shape your worldview and behavior contributes to the development of self-awareness. As with any learning, motivation to learn, regular exposure, and practice allow you to reach the second stage, which is *recognition*. As you increase your awareness and knowledge, you will gradually recognize cultural situations and challenges. Culture is now liminal; you are aware of it and start considering it. The next stage is being able to use new knowledge and skills to *accommodate* new situations. As you get more experience with including culture in new situations and expand your knowledge and cultural vocabulary, you will be able to *integrate* new information with your existing knowledge and develop new appropriate patterns until you proactively and automatically consider culture in your actions and decision-making. You are now at the postliminal stage and have crossed the cultural threshold.

Consider the example of two college first-year students and roommates. Alejandra is a management major who comes from a small rural community in the Central Valley of California, and her roommate Ségolène is an accounting major from Sacramento. Alejandra grew up in a majority Hispanic community where many, including her own family, are immigrants from Mexico and Central America. She speaks Spanish at home and has traveled throughout California and the Pacific Northwest and parts of the East Coast. Having grown up in a rural community, she has had limited interaction with other cultural groups. She is staying in the residence halls at San Diego State University. Like Alejandra, Ségolène's parents are immigrants, with her mother from Haiti and father from the Congo. She speaks fluent French and Haitian Créole and has traveled to her parents' home countries as well as several parts of Europe. While Alejandra gets along with her roommate and likes her, she becomes aware that they are very different: they eat different foods, some of which seem strange to her, listen to completely different music, enjoy different shows, and have widely differing social and political views. They are taking some basic business classes together, but they appear to be from different worlds. Alejandra is a practicing devout Catholic and somewhat conservative, values she had not really thought about, but now tend to stand out when compared to her roommate's views and the generally liberal college culture. Ségolène is also aware of their differences. She is liberal and politically active in the Black Lives Matter movement and environmental causes. She says she is spiritual and does not believe in organized religion and has crystals all over her side of the room. Ségolène has interacted with many people who are different from her on several dimensions, including many of her very conservative and religious family members. She thinks her roommate is sweet, but considers her unsophisticated and tends to look down on her rural roots. For Alejandra, many of Ségolène's actions and beliefs are unusual and they sometimes make her uncomfortable. The roommates sidestep many discussions on abortion, gun rights, and several other hot-button issues to avoid conflict, but they find common ground in immigration. Slowly, Alejandra gets to know many of Ségolène's friends and joins in on some of the lectures they attend, particularly those related to immigration and humanitarian crises around the world. Alejandra tries several of Haitian dishes—loves the fried pork—and goes to a Congolese party where she discovers a common appreciation for dancing and falls in love with the Congolese Coupé and Decalé and Makolongulu dances. Her fluent Spanish seems to make it easy for her to remember some French she had taken in high school, and she considers minoring in French or international business. During some of the debates she attends with Ségolène, she connects with several friends from back home who know her roommate and like her are active in various political movements. With some hesitancy, Alejandra invites Ségolène to go home with her one weekend and her family, as expected, welcomes them both with food and parties. Ségolène comes back from the weekend with a new appreciation for Alejandra and her family. Their tight family bonds, strong work ethic, and hospitality are in stark contrast with the cut-throat and competitive urban life. By the end of the year, Alejandra and Ségolène move seamlessly between their two worlds; they comfortably tease each other about their political differences and often argue and debate various topics with passion and while each holding their own positions. Their common immigrant roots and their shared experiences as minorities and many similar family values bridge the differences that they continue to have. Alejandra's cultural journey started with no thought or awareness of her own culture or that of others, and as she became aware of her own assumptions and learned about her roommate's, she integrated them to move toward a CM. In Ségolène's case, she was further along in her CM journey, having learned to accommodate and integrate other cultures with her own much earlier in life. However, she also further developed her CM as she learned about a culture she did not know or appreciate.

The stages of the development of a CM are not static and rigid; they point to a general progression from lack of awareness and knowledge to more thoughtful inclusion of culture in how a person thinks and acts. Many other models have looked at cultural competence; we consider them next.

6. CM AND OTHER APPROACHES TO CROSS-CULTURAL COMPETENCE

LO 2.6 Compare CM to other approaches to cultural competence

There is strong and growing interest in training people to work across cultures. A comprehensive review and evaluation of intercultural competence approaches and tools identified nineteen different terms used to describe the idea ranging from global, cultural, communicative, and international competence to ethno-relativity, global competitive intelligence, and intercultural sensitivity, to name just a few (Sincrope, Norris, & Watanabe, 2007). An extensive project conducted by Alvino Fantini and

Aqeel Tirmizi (2006) for *The Experiment in International Living Federation* found that the various tools and approaches focus on one or more of the following concepts or processes:

- Knowledge: Factual information about other cultures

- Attitude: How people feel about other cultures and cross-cultural situations

- Skills: Specific expertise related to culture or cultural situations (for example, language skills)

- Awareness: General understanding of differences among cultures

It is clear from the research that there is distinction between "knowing" and "doing," where approaches that focus on sensitivity, awareness, and knowledge of culture address what people know, while competence and literacy, in their many forms, relate to behavior.

6.1 How to Evaluate Approaches

It is important for students and practitioners interested in the area of cultural competence to appreciate the variances among the different approaches and tools. When organizations train their managers in cross-cultural management, they focus on one or more of the processes. Clearly, not all approaches are equally well designed and equally valid or equally comprehensive, making it challenging for organizations to decide on which approach may be more beneficial. Table 2.3 presents some of the key criteria that can be applied to compare the various approaches. Specifically managers should consider the theoretical and research foundations, the specific sector that is targeted, the general scope, the processes that are addressed, and the proposed outcomes. In other words, what will be the outcome of the program; is it based on valid and reliable research and how broadly does it apply to various sectors?

For example, the *Global Mindset* (Javidan & Walker, 2013), a widely used and extensively researched approach to cultural competence, focuses on the business and management sectors with the goal of training managers to improve their effectiveness in international business. The model addresses national culture, emphasizes knowledge, which it calls "Intellectual Capital," while also touching on passion for diversity, quest for adventure, and self-assurance (Psychological Capital), factors that relate to the personality factors of CM and some skills such as communication, negotiations, interpersonal interaction, and diplomacy (Social Capital). The theoretical and conceptual bases for the Global Mindset are the comprehensive GLOBE project which we will discuss in detail in Chapter 8. Another popular model used in management and business is *Cultural Intelligence—CQ*, developed by Christopher Earley and Soon Ang

Table 2.3 Criteria for Comparison of Cultural Competence Approaches/Models and Assessment Tools

Criteria	Description
Theoretical bases	What are the model's theoretical and conceptual frameworks? What are theories that were applied to develop the model?
Research and validation	Is there research and validation to support the model and its assessment tools?
Target sector	What is the target sector or audience (e.g., business, education, nonprofit)?
Scope	What level of culture does it address? Does it consider cross-national cultures or address diversity (e.g., national or group-level)?
Concepts and processes addressed	What processes are addressed? Does it address cognition, behaviors, skills, or other processes (e.g., awareness, knowledge, behaviors)?
Proposed outcome	What is the proposed outcome? What will you know or be able to do when you apply the model (e.g., better communication; global knowledge)?

(2003) and popularized by David Livermore (2011). CQ is focused on business and management and primarily national culture, although diversity issues are occasionally addressed. The model includes cognitive (meta-cognition), physical (ability to mimic), and emotional (motivation and curiosity) components (Earley & Mosakowski, 2016). It has strong research backing and addresses how an individual strategizes about culture (labeled meta-cognition in the CQ model); cognition or knowledge of and respect for other cultures; behavior or the willingness to change in novel situations; and motivation or the person's desire to interact interculturally.

Many other practitioner and case-based approaches are useful although their theoretical foundations and evaluation of the assessment tools are not always clear or they tend to be narrow in scope and focused on specific sectors such as business or education. Some, such as Adam Molinsky's *Global Dexterity* (2013), target teaching people how to adapt their behavior across cultures. Others, for example, Erin Meyer's *The Culture Map* (2014), target managerial skills that must be modified when working across cultures, focusing on some of the cultural values that we will present and evaluate in detail in Chapters 7 and 8. Both of these, like many others, target the business sector and concentrate on cross-national cultural interactions rather than group-level diversity. The highly popular Developmental Model of Intercultural Sensitivity (DMIS; Bennett, 1986, 1993) and its corresponding assessment tool the Intercultural Development Inventory emphasize personal growth and development in the area of culture. While reliable, the theoretical foundations are not clear and the model has focused on education in general and higher education in particular. Furthermore, other approaches with a narrower perspective on psychological and attitudinal processes and targeting specific sectors have advocated particular skills such as developing cultural humility (Foronda et al., 2016). The choices and options are extensive.

6.2 Beyond the "What": Learning "How"

The CM model used in this book has broad theoretical roots in cognitive and cross-cultural psychology, cross-cultural management and leadership, and in the field of education. A unique key characteristic of the CM model and its roadmap, THINK–KNOW–DO, that we discuss in the next section, is that they address the *how* as well as the *what* of learning about the culture, whereas other approaches focus primarily on the content (or the what). Focusing on *how* is what educators call *transformative learning* because it has the potential to fundamentally change how people think and their understanding of themselves, not just what they know (Kegan & Lahey, 2009; Mezirow, 2000). Approaching culture through CM and through the THINK–KNOW–DO roadmap has many of the aspects of transformative learning (Mezirow, 2000) including

- Encouraging self-examination and self-reflection

- Providing options for new behaviors

- Developing knowledge that can be used to undertake new actions

- Building confidence through the self-examination and knowledge development

- Planning a course of action

CM aims at making people aware of their frame of reference and changing it to include considerations of culture.

Additionally, as compared to other approaches that focus either on national culture or on cultural diversity, the CM model targets culture both at the national and group (diversity) levels and is applicable to any sector. It broadly addresses cognitive processes, the acquisition of knowledge, and the development and implementation of appropriate culture-responsive management practices. Finally, the ICMI, the corresponding assessment tool, has been validated and is reliable in measuring its target constructs. The CM model therefore provides a broadly applicable approach that encompasses many of the key elements of effective learning that is transformative as well as informative to make managers more effective at cross-cultural interactions. We next consider how to develop a CM through the THINK–KNOW–DO roadmap.

WINDOW TO THE WORLD

Doing Business in Singapore

Singapore is a multicultural city-state that heavily depends on foreign talent to fuel its stunning economic growth and prides itself as a bastion of cultural tolerance. The "Chinese, Malay, Indian, Other" or CMIO categorization is used to describe the city-state's diverse cultural landscape where each cultural group is encouraged to preserve its unique culture while also respecting others. The multiculturalism and aggressive competitive entrepreneurial spirit drive business in Singapore. Keep the following in mind when doing business in Singapore:

1. English is typical in business settings, but Chinese, Malay, and Tamil are official languages with "Singlish," a local English mixed with a combination of other dialects and slang are commonly used.

2. There are many rules and laws governing behavior in Singapore that are strictly enforced. Personal display of affection between the sexes along with many other behaviors including jaywalking, smoking in public, not flushing toilets, and chewing gum are all illegal. Learn about the many legal restrictions before you go to prevent serious faux pas and legal trouble.

3. Be on time; punctuality is important; they may be late, but you shouldn't.

4. Focus on people's accomplishments; they matter and they are a point of pride.

5. Take your time and don't rush—taking time to respond to requests, questions, and inquiries is a sign of respect that shows that you are giving important matters due consideration.

6. There are complex rituals that govern the exchange of business cards. Study them and respect them. Carelessly tossing a business card that is handed to you in your bag is the fastest way to lose your business partner's respect.

7. Singapore is community- and group-oriented where elder members are given considerable respect. Act accordingly and show deference to the person with the most tenure, including senior members of your own team.

8. People ask lots of very personal questions that may be inappropriate in many other cultures (e.g., regarding your income, your weight)! Don't get offended and think about gracious ways of not answering if that is what you choose to do. Do not reciprocate and delve into people's personal lives; stay professional.

9. Singapore is ranked among the least corrupt countries in the world. While exchanging small gifts such as pens or merchandise with company logo is expected, bribes or other gifts that may give the appearance of bribes are not appropriate.

10. Remember that Singapore is culturally and religiously diverse which means that there are different values that you need to consider. If and until you become an expert in the culture, keep it simple and being polite, discreet, modest, and formal is likely to help avoid many uncomfortable situations.

7. THINK–KNOW–DO: A ROADMAP TO DEVELOPING CM

How can managers develop their CM? CM relies on the cognitive approach to cross-cultural management and therefore aims to examine first how we think, then relies on acquisition of cultural knowledge used to provide skills and competencies, and finally leads to monitoring and changing behavior. Having a CM is first and foremost a way of *thinking* to help people understand that culture acts as a meta-context (CMC) for themselves and for others. Fundamental questions include:

- How do we perceive the world?

- What are the mental models that we use?

- How do we organize and interpret information?

This cognitive approach starts with self-examination and self-awareness of your own culture and how it acts as a frame of reference that guides how you interpret the world. The second component is developing *knowledge*. In order to be effective across cultures, you must have the knowledge, literacy, and competencies related to those cultures. Key knowledge questions include:

- What are key cultural values that people hold?

- What is diversity and its impact?

- How do gender and culture interact?

- How does culture impact leadership, management, and organizational processes?

Having accurate and reliable knowledge regarding culture is critical to guide our decisions and actions. Finally, a CM involves *acting* appropriately by applying the thinking and knowledge. Among many others, the types of questions that are addressed include:

- How should you greet people?

- What is the best way to communicate?

- What would be the most appropriate way to evaluate employees?

- What goals and rewards might work in different settings?

- What style of negotiation would be effective?

- What mission would be motivational?

- What would be the best time frame for goals?

Thinking, knowing, and doing are all three indispensable to interacting effectively across cultures.

7.1 Elements of the THINK–KNOW–DO Roadmap

The roadmap to developing a CM is the THINK–KNOW DO model presented in Figure 2.4. The cognitive-THINK, knowledge-KNOW, and behavioral-DO elements of the model are outlined, and the corresponding ICMI factors that address each are listed.

People with a CM are effective across cultures because they are aware of their own culture and how it creates a perspective and lens through which they see the world. They see how culture provides a meta-context (CMC) and how it simply is always present (CJI). Having this awareness allows people to recognize culture's impact and

Figure 2.4   A Roadmap to Cultural Mindset: Think–Know–Do

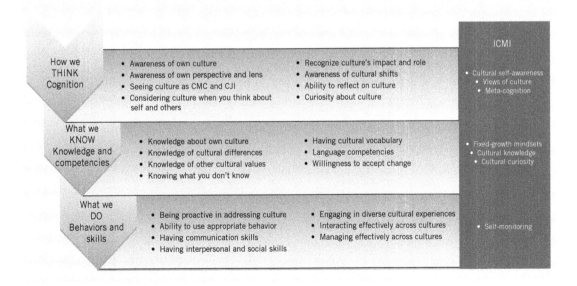

know when the cultural environment has shifted requiring a corresponding suspension of their own assumptions and a shift in their lens or perspective. They know when they are and when they are no longer in their "small" world and when they need to shift their frame of reference because they have crossed cultural boundaries. They also have the cultural knowledge, competencies, and vocabulary to act accordingly. Finally, they have the social, communication, and interpersonal skills to engage in diverse cultures effectively.

Consider the example of James, a US business executive who has traveled across the world both as a tourist and on business and speaks some Spanish and Chinese in addition to his native English. He enjoys the food and arts from many parts of the world, and his home is decorated with artifacts from countries he has visited. As a result of his MBA and his business experience, he is familiar with business legal frameworks in several countries including those where his company manufactures its products. When asked about culture, he is eager to discuss the interesting and sometimes strange traditions of people in other countries. When asked about his own culture, he responds: "Well, I'm not sure what you mean. I am American of course." He is very proud of the fact that his company has brought Western-style business and management practices and wealth to many people in developing countries. He likes to point out how his company has set up generous individual bonuses for performance, has clear goals and consistent policies, treats people fairly regardless of their ethnic background and social class, and that managers do their best to treat their overseas partners the same way they treat their US-based employees. He says that, as a result of his company's overseas operations, managers in other countries have learned to be objective and efficient, set clear policies and boundaries, and focus on facts and profit with monthly or quarterly goals to help them achieve efficiencies. While profits are high, he complains about two irritating problems. First, his company faces an extremely high turnover rate at both the managerial and employee levels in many of their overseas operations. He says:

> It's unbelievable! We pay better than local companies and have better benefits; our policies are fair and clear. The managers and workers just disappear; sometimes they come back and want their jobs back, which doesn't sit well with us at all. But we can't fill our positions fast enough, so we re-hire them. In some cases, we never see them again but they refer someone else who shows up because they know we have an opening. I don't get it.

His second complaint involves how much time it takes to get things done. He adds:

> Every time we have to make a decision, start a new project, change an operation, or implement any plan it ends up taking ten times longer than it should and much

longer than we had anticipated—it's really frustrating. We work with our local partners to set up specific timelines that they agree to so that we can get things done in a timely fashion, but it never works out as it should. We could all be making so much more money if we just moved things at the right pace.

Clearly this business executive has some information and knowledge of other cultures. He speaks a couple of languages and is well traveled. He also appreciates other cultures. To him, being American is well, simply "being American," while others have interesting cultural features. What he is lacking is a self-examination and self-awareness of his own culture and an understanding of how his cultural lens, worldview, and perspective and his company's practices are based on US cultural values of individualism and performance focus. While these may work well in most of the US cultural contexts, they may not be the most appropriate if their overseas operations are in countries with different values. Our business executive has some of the "KNOW" and some of the "DO" of a CM, but is evidently lacking the critical "THINK" element, which requires awareness regarding his own culture and how culture operates as a meta-context both for him and his company and for their overseas partners.

CM is not something you are born with. Although some personality traits such as self-monitoring and curiosity may make it easier to develop a CM, it is not a personality trait or an ability. CM can be developed. We can learn to think about culture, our own and that of others and how it provides and acts as a meta-context and "just is" a frame of reference. We can develop insight into cognitive processes and how they impact what we see and how we interpret the world. We can acquire knowledge about culture, and finally we can cultivate and practice the skills necessary to behave appropriately across cultures. Just like culture itself, ***a cultural mindset is learned.***

7.2 How Do We Get There?

The chapters in this book will guide you through the THINK–KNOW–DO roadmap, each building on one of its elements. Throughout, you will also work on expanding your cultural self-awareness to gain more in-depth knowledge and information about the cultural assumptions, values, and beliefs that guide your thinking and behavior and practice your meta-cognitive skills. The general outline for the roadmap is as follows.

7.2.1 THINK. Part II (Chapters 3 and 4) will closely examine the cognitive aspects of CM. Through the information in Chapters 3 and 4 you will:

- Engage in cultural self-examination to expand your cultural self-awareness

- Gain awareness of *how* you know what you know and the role culture plays in the process

- Gain knowledge about the perceptual processes that describe how you perceive the world

- Become aware of your views of culture and their impact

- Recognize your biases and the shortcuts that we all use and their origins so that you can avoid systematic errors

- Gain awareness of the lenses you may apply to your social interaction

- Improve the ability to identify and understand where and when culture plays a role

- Stop automatic responses and activate thoughtful judgment

- Avoid overconfidence

- Consciously activate different lenses and perspectives

The THINK part of the roadmap relies heavily on extensive research in cognitive and social psychology on the role, impact, and power of cognitive processes, biases, and heuristics in how we perceive the world. While these processes are an inherent and unavoidable part of how human beings think and function, awareness of how they operate and the role that cultural assumptions may play in shaping them goes a long way to provide us with the ability to slow down our unconscious and automatic systems and make us more methodical and deliberate thinkers. We will also draw on anthropology and cross-cultural psychology to examine views of culture and how cultures interact and how those may color your perspective.

7.2.2 KNOW. The focus of Part III and Part IV of this book is on acquiring cultural knowledge and a broad cultural vocabulary to be able to understand and explain cultural differences. Chapter 5 will elaborate on diversity; Chapter 6 will examine gender. Chapters 7 and 8 will present the national culture models that will expand your knowledge of cultural values and beliefs. Throughout, the information will also be relevant to further deepen your own cultural self-awareness. The goal of Parts III and IV is for you to:

- Know the facts regarding cultural diversity in the United States and other parts of the world and the opportunities and challenges it presents

- Gain knowledge about the impact of gender and group membership

- Acquire a vocabulary that will allow you to talk about and explain different cultures and cultural differences

- Apply various models of cultural values to understanding culture

The KNOW part of the roadmap provides you with the content of culture with knowledge based on research in a variety of disciplines including cross-cultural psychology and cross-cultural management and leadership. The rich information from these disciplines provides the vocabulary that you need to understand culture and develop competencies in cross-cultural interactions.

7.2.3 DO. The last part of the roadmap applies the information and knowledge you acquired to become more effective in managing and interacting across cultures. Chapters 9–11 present the tools of managing and leading multicultural organizations. The goal is for you to:

- Apply the concepts of leadership and management appropriately in different cultural settings

- Have the tools and skills to manage and lead multicultural teams

- Manage effectively organizational systems and processes across cultures

The last chapter integrates the knowledge you have acquired and provides summary guidelines on how to cross the cultural threshold and develop a CM. In an increasingly global and cultural world, you have fundamentally three options. You can

1. Ignore culture

2. Fight culture by arguing that it does not matter or that your viewpoint is the right one or

3. Develop and expand your CM so that you can effectively work across cultural boundaries

These are obviously false choices since success in organizations, and in any relationship in a diverse and global world, depends on understanding culture and cultural differences and on being able to navigate their complexities. Particularly, organizational leaders at all levels need to understand how culture impacts their own and others' thinking and behavior. CM provides you with a roadmap to reach that destination.

FIRST PERSON REVISITED

While working for a global company, it is clear that the V.P. has maintained a distinctively traditional Spaniard perspective that, in his case, includes a Conquistador sense of superiority toward former colonies and its people. His lack of awareness of his own CMC and lack of knowledge and understanding of other cultures lead to insulting his new boss, and losing his job as a result. While the Conquistador mentality may have been tolerated while he was working with others who shared his worldview, and had apparently not hampered his success in the firm, it clearly was not appropriate in a larger context. What worked for him in his small world did not work in a larger one. The need to understand the role and impact of culture and to have a CM to be able to succeed in a global and interconnected world is obvious.

APPLYING WHAT YOU LEARNED: RECOGNIZING AND CHANGING A FIXED MINDSET

There are many reasons we may have developed a fixed mindset that tells us that things are the way they are, that we really can't change ourselves or others, that we have reached our limits, or that there is no point in trying to do things differently. These are all parts of having a fixed mindset. There may also be some genetic or personality factors; however, we can learn to check the triggering of a fixed mindset that may hamper our learning and development. Here are some steps you can undertake:

1. Identify situations where your fixed mindset pops up most often. Are there some reliable patterns? For example, does it come up when you face competition at work, or when you are assigned big projects?

2. Identify factors that support your fixed mindset; for example, fear or risk-avoidance.

3. What are your typical reactions to your fixed mindset? How have they helped you? How can they hurt you?

4. Learn to recognize the fixed mindset "voice," what you typically tell yourself (e.g., I just can't do that, or I always mess these up, or this never works out for me, or it's all rigged so what's the point).

Once you have identified situations where your fixed mindset is activated and your fixed mindset "voice," explore alternative approaches. Particularly, identify substitute explanations, other scenarios, and people who can help you. Finally, develop a strategy and protocol for yourself, what is called a Plan–Do–Review, and include the following:

1. Practice using the simple and powerful word "Yet." For example, instead of "I don't know how to use flowcharts" say "I don't know how to use flowcharts, yet." A little word with a big punch.

2. Set stretch goals. Start with your regular and customary process, then review each goal and stretch each a little bit.

3. Identify things that you do not know how to do or goals you cannot achieve, yet, but would like to master. Reflect and plan while using "yet" and consciously blocking the fixed mindset "voice." It may appear as an overreaching exercise at first (that would be your fixed mindset voice talking); however, the consideration of new possibilities is the starting point.

4. While you can dream big, keep your goals small and simple; one step at a time and a few targets at a time.

5. Get help and support from friends, colleagues, and even your supervisor.

MANAGERIAL CHALLENGE: TO PASS OR NOT TO PASS?

You have a complex cultural background that includes Middle Eastern, North African, and European roots. You are most connected to the first two cultural groups and consider them to be who you really are. However, your physical appearance is European with light skin, green eyes, and brown hair, traits that you inherited from your Berber and Kurdish ancestors. Since you grew up in a suburb of Chicago, you have the typical Midwestern or Great Lakes accent that some consider the most "American." There is little in your appearance or behavior that indicates to you being a minority; yet that is who you are and how you see yourself. You frequently encounter touchy situations where people make comments about one or another minority group in your presence. You know they would not say those things if they knew your background. You also often get comments such as "Oh wow, you're African (or Middle Eastern) really? How is that?" or "How come you are so interested in minority issues? What's the catch?" It is offensive and frustrating and yet, being part of the cultural majority has its advantages…

1. How would you handle this situation?

2. What are the consequences of each of your alternatives for you personally and organizationally?

SELF-ASSESSMENT 2.1: THE ICMI

Please visit the following site, http://usd.qualtrics.com/jfe/form/SV_3pYOssk8k TwD6N7, and complete the ICMI—Individual Cultural Mindset Inventory. Once you complete the self-assessment, enter your score for each factor below and on the radar graph.

Work on growth mindset

	CM Factor	Score		CM Factor	Score
1.	Cultural Self-Awareness (CSA):	_____	6.	Plural (Pl):	_____
2.	Fixed Mindset (FM):	_____	7.	Meta Cognition (MC):	_____
3.	Growth Mindset (GM):	_____	8.	Cultural Knowledge (CK):	_____
4.	Parochial (Pa):	_____	9.	Cultural Curiosity (CC):	_____
5.	Ethnocentric (E):	_____	10.	Self-Monitoring (SM):	_____

Review your scores and consider the following questions:

1. What are your areas of strength?

2. Where can you improve?

3. Based on information from this chapter, what are some areas you can address?

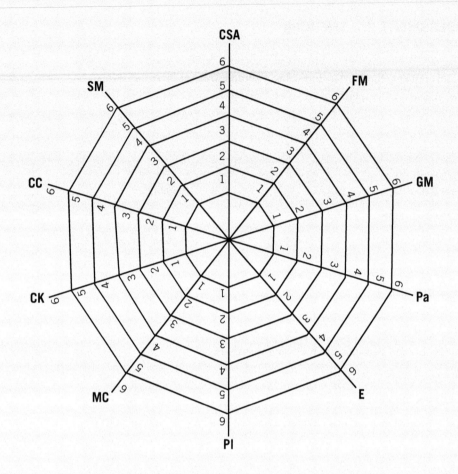

SELF-ASSESSMENT 2.2: WHAT IS YOUR CULTURAL BACKGROUND?

In Self-Assessment 1.1 from Chapter 1, you started the process of identifying various nationalities, races, and cultures that may be part of. Using the information from that self-assessment, make a list of the top five cultures that you consider to be part of your primary cultural background. You may identify only one or two or have more than 5. Keep in mind that nationality is only one level of culture: ethnicity, gender, professional background, disability, and many other group-level cultures can be part of a person's cultural identity.

1. _White american_
2. _Christian_
3. _____
4. _____
5. _____

1. You probably listed the cultures in order of their importance to you. If not, can you rank-order them? Which ones are more central to who you are than others? Why and how does that manifest in your thinking and behavior?

2. What do you think makes each culture unique? _– We are each unique_

3. What are some of its key teachings from your key cultures about what is important? What is right?

4. How did you learn these values?

5. How much do you agree with them? Why or why not?

6. How much of your behavior do you think is influenced by each culture?

EXERCISE 2.1: CULTURAL VALUES AND BELIEFS

Objective: This exercise addresses the cultural self-awareness and meta-cognition.

Instructions:

Individual Work

Make a list of the five values and five beliefs that you hold dear. In making your list, think about things that you have learned from your family or have valued and believed in for a while.

Remember that values are defined as

> *Long-lasting beliefs about what is important and what is right and wrong; the way things should be. These could be instrumental or terminal values (how to get things done and the goal).*

And beliefs are

Convictions and ideas about what is true; *the way things are*

	Values	Beliefs
1.		
2.		
3.		
4.		
5.		

Consider the following questions in preparation for the next step.

1. How important are these values and beliefs to you?

2. What are the origins of each? Where do they come from?

3. How do they reflect in your day-to-day life and interactions with others?

4. To what extent have these changed over your life?

5. How easy or hard would it be to give up or change these values and beliefs?

Group Work

Get together with at least one other student and share your list and share the answers to the questions that you have prepared. In addition, discuss the following:

1. To what extent do the similarities and/or differences surprise you?

2. What do you have in common? What is the source of the commonalities?

3. What are differences? What is their source?

4. What role does culture play in your values and beliefs?

EXERCISE 2.2: WHAT IS WHITE?

Objective: This exercise helps you develop your cultural self-awareness and your knowledge of cultures.

Instructions: Your instructor will share statistics, data, and readings regarding behaviors and preferences of white US Americans. After reviewing that information, in groups of 4–5 discuss the following:

1. What is your assessment of the information provided?

2. Based on the information provided and the collective knowledge in your group, what are they key elements of white US-American CMC? What are key assumptions, values, beliefs, and behaviors?

3. What criteria do you use to define "whiteness"? How does your group define "white"? In other words, who is part of the group in the United States and in the world?

4. There is a good chance the information created some discomfort for you. If so, discuss sources and reasons for the discomfort.

5. Discuss how taking a CM and CJI perspective can change the way this information is presented and perceived.

CASE STUDY: L'ORÉAL'S BRAND OF MULTICULTURALISM

L'Oréal, the world's largest cosmetic company with sales of €26.9 billion($29.9 billion) and 7.1% growth rate, is distinctly French and ubiquitously global. It was established in 1909 in France by Eugène Schueller, and it currently operates in 150 countries and employs over 86,000 people. Over the past more than 100 years, L'Oréal has built a unique portfolio of diverse and complementary brands including the French Lancôme, Cacharel and Yves Saint Laurent Beauté, US-American Maybelline, Ralph Lauren, Urban Decay, and Redken, Italian Giorgio Armani, Chinese Yue Sai and Magic, Brazilian Niely, British House 99, and Japanese Shu Uemura, just to name a few of its brands (Brands, 2019). Approximately half of the company's sales are from Western Europe and North America with the rest from Asia Pacific, Latin America, Eastern Europe, and Africa-Middle East (L'Oréal in figures, 2018). The company dominates most of the markets it enters and shows every sign of continuing its growth and dominance. It seems to have a knack for being in the right place at the right time and addressing local needs with a celebrated French flair that come with being part of L'Oréal.

Emerging markets provide companies of all sizes from every industry with unique opportunities to grow their revenue. These markets make up over half of the world population, and it is projected that the consumption of these markets will be $62 trillion by the year 2025 (MIRAE Assets, 2018). Many of L'Oréal's competitors, for example, Unilever, are actively targeting these emerging market (Chandrana, 2012). With all its global presence, L'Oréal's top management team has been strongly rooted in the French culture with few outsiders and non-French at the helm. Out of the only five CEOs since its creation, only one was not French, the Welsh Lindsay Owen-Jones who was CEO from 1988 to 2006 and is widely described as being *Français dans l'âme* (French in his soul). Other non-French managers insist on mentioning their long tenure with the company and their perfect French (Hong & Doz, 2016). The top leadership notwithstanding, the firm has struck a successful balance between having some uniformity and integration of activities across markets and responsiveness to local cultures and needs.

With research and innovation being central to the L'Oréal's strategy (Hall, 2018), the company has internationalized midlevel managers and product teams who provide needed local knowledge and are at the core of its success (Remon, 2019). The firm pointedly recruits managers and executives with mixed cultural backgrounds from its local subsidiaries, other global firms, and international business schools. For example, in the Latin American hair-care group, a Lebanese–Spanish–American manager in charge of hair color and a French–Irish–Cambodian who leads hair care share an office (Hong & Doz, 2013). Others include a Hong Kong–British–French project manager and an Indian–American–French project manager (Hong & Doz, 2016). Before being deployed throughout the world, the new members undergo an intensive 12-month training and executive education in France and around the world, then spend a couple of years in L'Oréal's Paris headquarters before returning to their home regions as brand directors and managers.

The strategy of hiring employees with a mixed cultural background is hardly random. L'Oréal is well aware that these individuals see connections and relationships that their unicultural colleagues may miss, can interpret complex knowledge better and be more innovative, and can form successful multicultural teams (Doz, 2013). For example, a French–Irish–Cambodian manager responsible for skin care realized that many face creams in the Asian market offer both tinted and lifting effects in the same product. However, face creams in Europe were used to provide these effects in separate products. Using his knowledge about the features of the beauty industry in two different markets, this manager and his team created a tinted cream with lifting effects for the French market and became very successful (Hong & Doz, 2013).

Mixed culture individuals and people who are called Third-Culture kids, based on having grown up in a culture that is different from that of their parents, have dealt with cultural challenges and integration of culture since childhood. Dealing with culture is part of who they are, they have always had to bridge cultural differences, so they do not have to be taught to be sensitive to them; it is who they are. One of L'Oréal's multicultural managers states:

> My French boss never starts meetings on time. So whenever we have a meeting planned with him, we can get frustrated if we are not flexible. If I am running behind myself, I make sure to tell my team members in advance why I am behind and ask them for their next availabilities. Conflicts may still exist in my team, but we handle them more tolerantly. (Hong & Doz, 2016, p. 44)

L'Oréal proudly remains a characteristically French company. However, it has also managed to embrace its global workforce and address the needs of its diverse markets.

Questions

1. Specify how L'Oréal addresses the challenges of central control and integration of local needs?

2. What are the benefits and disadvantages of drawing top managers from one culture?

3. How does L'Oréal address the global market needs?

4. What role does CM play at L'Oréal?

Sources

Brands. (2019). *L'Oréal*. Retrieved from https://www.loreal.com/brand. Accessed on December 17, 2019.

Chandrana, H. (2012). The consumer goods industry – succeeding in the emerging markets. *WIPRO*, November. Retrieved from https://www.wipro.com/en-US/blogs/hiral-chandrana/-the-consumer-goods-industry–succeeding-in-the-emerging-markets/. Accessed on December 17, 2019.

Doz, Y. (2013). The rise of multicultural managers. *Forbes*, August 1. Retrieved from https://www.forbes.com/sites/insead/2013/08/01/the-rise-of-multicultural-managers/#1260c3d43445. Accessed on December 17, 2019.

Emerging markets: Learn from the companies to get it right. (2018). *RWS*, October 9. Retrieved from https://www.rws.com/insights/rws-moravia-blog/emerging-markets-learn-from-the-companies-getting-it-right/. Accessed on December 17, 2019.

Hall, G. (2018). L'Oréal interview: Millennial attitudes makes people-based marketing a necessity. *Nielsen.com*, April 3. Retrieved from https://resources.marketingeffectiveness.nielsen.com/blog/loreal-expert-interview-why-millennial-attitudes-make-people-based-marketing-a-necessity. Accessed on December 17, 2019.

Hong, H. J., & Doz, Y. (2013). L'Oréal masters multiculturalism. Harvard Business Review, June. Retrieved from https://hbr.org/2013/06/loreal-masters-multiculturalism. Accessed on September 7, 2020.

Hong, H. J., & Doz, Y. L. (2016). L'Oréal masters multiculturalism. In *HBR's 10 must read on managing across cultures* (pp. 35–46). Boston, MA: Harvard Business Review Press.

L'Oréal in figures. (2018). *Annual report*. Retrieved from https://www.loreal-finance.com/en/annual-report-2018/key-figures-2-2/. Accessed on December 17, 2019.

Remon, P. (2019). How to manage cross-cultural teams effectively. *HRZone*, September 16. Retrieved from https://www.hrzone.com/community/blogs/peter-remon/how-to-manage-cross-cultural-teams-effectively. Accessed on December 17, 2019.

PART TWO

THINK—YOUR CULTURAL PERSPECTIVE

The second part of the book explores the THINK portion of the THINK–KNOW–DO roadmap (see Figure II.1) and details the importance of cognition in developing a Cultural Mindset. The next two chapters focus on how the way we think shapes our CMC and our interpretation of events. Specifically, Chapter 3 details the role of cognitive processes, heuristics, and biases in cross-cultural management, while Chapter 4 elaborates on the impact of views of culture on how we view ourselves and others.

Figure II.1   The Focus of Part II

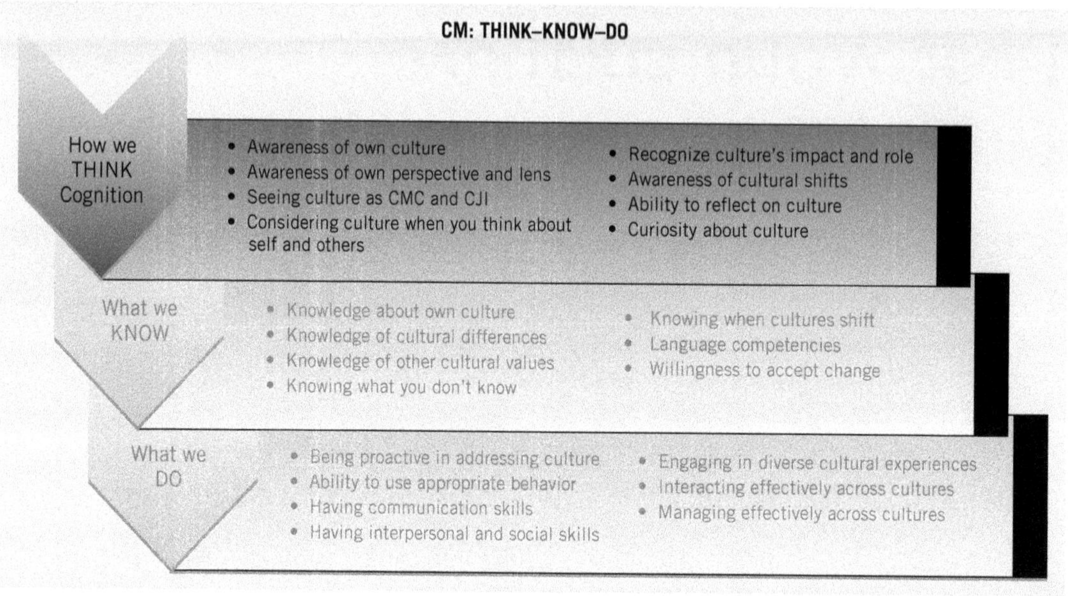

CM: THINK–KNOW–DO

How we
THINK
Cognition

- Awareness of own culture
- Awareness of own perspective and lens
- Seeing culture as CMC and CJI
- Considering culture when you think about self and others

- Recognize culture's impact and role
- Awareness of cultural shifts
- Ability to reflect on culture
- Curiosity about culture

What we
KNOW

- Knowledge about own culture
- Knowledge of cultural differences
- Knowledge of other cultural values
- Knowing what you don't know

- Knowing when cultures shift
- Language competencies
- Willingness to accept change

What we
DO

- Being proactive in addressing culture
- Ability to use appropriate behavior
- Having communication skills
- Having interpersonal and social skills

- Engaging in diverse cultural experiences
- Interacting effectively across cultures
- Managing effectively across cultures

CHAPTER THREE

THE ROLE OF COGNITIVE PROCESSES IN CROSS-CULTURAL MANAGEMENT

FIRST PERSON

Sit Quietly and Work on Spreadsheets

I am an organizational consultant in the United States whose work is heavily research-based. Most of my client projects involve considerable research and data analytics. While I enjoy statistical modeling and conducting research and do them well, my favorite part of any project is the opportunity to present the data to the client. I enjoy sharing findings with audiences, explaining what the data mean, engaging in question and answer sessions, and participating in discussions about the implications of the data and how to turn the information into future actions. Over the years, I have received many compliments about my presentation style and public speaking skills. While delivered with good intentions, a number of these compliments have included comments such as, "Usually the Indian guys just sit quietly and work on their spreadsheets all day. They can't ever clearly explain their work to other people. You were surprisingly good in your presentation, I wasn't expecting that!" These types of comments have made me aware of how people's expectations shape how they see me and how important it is for me to try to shape those expectations. I am therefore strategic about the types of roles I take on in my work and within a team. If I am not intentional with my approach and don't actively seek out to do what I do well, I may not get to participate in the type of work that I enjoy because it doesn't fit into the expectations or mental models many have of people who come from my culture.

–Bharat Mohan, PhD

Learning Objectives

3.1 Present the social perception process with its limited capacity and emphasis on efficiency.

3.2 Elaborate on the stages of social perception.

3.3 Detail the critical impact of heuristics and biases.

3.4 Contrast System I and System II and their link to CMC.

3.5 Explain the critical importance of cultural identity and its impact on CMC.

3.6 Provide guidelines for managing the social perception process.

The *First Person* anecdote illustrates how people's beliefs about others, in this case the consultant's national origin, can shape their expectations and the way they interact with them. In this chapter, we elaborate on the cognitive factors of CM and the THINK component of Think–Know–Do roadmap in depth by addressing:

- What we pay attention to

- How we gather and interpret information

- How we use information to make decisions

- The shortcuts we rely on and the biases that impact our perceptions

- How to avoid the negative impact of biases in management

Throughout the discussions, we detail the connection between these processes and CMC. Our discussions rely on cognitive psychology principles that explain how we perceive and construct the context in which we live and how, in seeking consistency and efficiency, we rely on shortcuts that are subject to errors and biases. Accordingly, we address the hardware (the way our brain and perceptual system work) and the software (our cultural perspective or CMC) that a person calls upon to make decisions. The goal of this chapter is to make you aware of your own cultural assumptions, values, and beliefs and how they operate as a unifying theme, background, or lens that colors your world and affects how you manage people. We first detail the cognitive processes, heuristics, and biases that operate in conjunction as a goal-oriented semi-automatic process, and then explore cultural identity and its role in those processes, ending with guidelines for managing social perception to avoid error.

1. THE SOCIAL PERCEPTION PROCESS

LO 3.1 Present the social perception process with its limited capacity and emphasis on efficiency

Consider this situation:

> *A surgeon and his son are in a terrible car accident. The father is killed.*
> *The boy is rushed to the hospital in critical condition. The best qualified ER surgeon is summoned and says:*
> *"I can't possibly operate on this boy – he is my son."*

The situation seems impossible: The father has been killed, so how is he in the ER refusing to operate? The answer is simple: The ER surgeon is the boy's mother. If you missed this, you are not alone. Your culturally based views of gender prevented you from assessing the situation; your CMC acted as a guide and interfered with your ability to be accurate. Similarly, managers are impacted by their often subconscious expectations and views regarding other people and the groups they belong to. They may assume that some people are better at leading while others are better team members; or that, as in the *First Person* example, some people are more skilled at technical work than others. All of us are impacted by our assumptions, values, and beliefs. However, being unaware of them and how they operate can have dire consequences on a manager's ability to manage effectively, especially in cross-cultural situations.

Social perception is the process of gathering, selecting, and interpreting information about others. In most cases, there is no objective way to clearly and conclusively perceive others; it is unavoidably a subjective process. The perception process is designed to be efficient and is fundamentally geared toward keeping us out of harm's way, but it does so often at the expense of being accurate.

1.1 Managers as Information Processors

Human beings are thinkers; they continuously and often subconsciously process information in order to make thousands of big and small decisions regarding themselves and others. Accordingly, we spend a considerable amount of time trying to understand ourselves, other people, and the social situations we encounter. Our goal is to assess every situation as accurately as possible before we move on to the next task. We rely heavily on our first impressions, ask a few questions, gather information, evaluate it, reflect a bit, and appraise the situation. The job of managers, especially when working across cultures, relies heavily on social perception as they perform tasks such as:

- Evaluating candidates for various positions and deciding who to hire

- Deciding who to assign to various tasks

- Providing feedback and conducting performance reviews

- Managing conflicts and negotiating agreements

All of the activities that managers perform involve gathering, selecting, and interpreting information about others. Most of us believe that we are reasonably good at these tasks, and we are surprised when we are off the mark by more than a bit; we typically consider serious errors in judgment to be rare. We believe that we can be objective and thorough when we try, and that we can avoid bias since we are not motivated to harm others. Unfortunately, reality does not match our beliefs and expectations in this regard.

Consider the example of a team leader who is working with a diverse group of team members from different nationalities, genders, ethnic backgrounds, and functional areas. Team members will have individual styles, approaches, needs, and expectations influenced by their personality and culture among other factors. The team leader must be able to quickly and continuously take in all that information and interact effectively with each person while also understanding the group processes and achieving the task goals. While this process may take place without a conscious effort, it is highly complex and involves taking in, organizing and interpreting information, and making instantaneous decisions based on that information. The research on social perception tells us that this process will inevitably be impacted by the manager's ability to process information and by his or her limited capacity and biases.

1.2 Limited Capacity

We are relentlessly bombarded with physical and social stimuli and cues from our environment. Considerable research shows that people are not capable of absorbing all these cues and stimuli. We do not record everything, instead selectively process information and we change the recording as it happens. In other words, instead of objectively logging in information, we contribute to reality (Fiske & Taylor, 2017). In addition to the very complex social interactions we face, sounds, smells, visual cues, and tactile sensations are ever-present. Take a moment to stop and pay attention to all the various stimuli in your environment. What do you hear? What do you smell? What do you see and feel on your skin? You have not been paying attention to all of these while you are reading this chapter; you cannot possibly pay attention to everything simultaneously. Our brain, the hardware, has evolved to systematically and automatically filter out some stimuli while paying attention to others.

Our culture, the software that helps us make sense of the world, acts as one of the filters that help us manage our limited capacity to process information. Our culture tells us what is important and needs our attention and what is not. Therefore, the world is not an objective reality, but a construction based on what you pay attention to and process. This is especially true in social situations.

When you interview a prospective new employee, within fractions of a second you automatically sift through a large amount of information about that person and decide quickly what is relevant and what is not. You will notice and remember if the person has a strong accent or if she is wearing something that is out of the ordinary while you are likely to ignore the same characteristics in your coworkers. Why do you notice the new person's idiosyncrasies and not those of others you know well? Does one set of information matter more or is one more relevant than the other? How did you make that decision? Because the stranger is unfamiliar, your brain that has biologically evolved to separate danger from safety, has to assess where the stranger fits: friend or foe? Friend is safe; foe could be dangerous. Doing this task instantaneously could be a matter of life and death, so your brain pays more attention to the stranger than your friend.

1.3 Efficiency Over Effectiveness

Human beings are what psychologists Susan Fiske and Shelley Taylor call *cognitive misers* (Fiske & Taylor, 2017). Because we are biologically limited in how much information we can process, we try to be as parsimonious and efficient as possible. As a result, the goal of our social perception process is to make an evaluation as quickly as possible with as little information as possible and move on to the next person or event that requires our attention. The attention to efficiency is the result of our biological evolution and our basic flight or fight instinct that allows us to assess complex and dangerous situations. We have evolved to decide quickly whether something needs our attention and what we need to do about it; careful deliberation is not the first option.

We form impressions within a few seconds, some research suggests even in a fraction of a second (Willis & Todorov, 2006) and organize it to make decisions. That is the basic social perception process that is driven by the need for efficiency, speed, and consistency in order to allow us to survive when we interact with our world. We process information efficiently and quickly, but we change it as we process it and as a result, introduce our biases and perspectives.[1] We automatically prioritize efficiency over accuracy. We are seldom cognizant of what information has influenced our decisions. We take many shortcuts to process that information, and we are subject to many biases that cause error in our assessments. Nowhere is that more prominent than in unfamiliar and novel settings such as during cross-cultural encounters where information is ambiguous and difficult to interpret, therefore increasing the likelihood of error. Our personal background and perspective and our culture act as a meta-context (CMC) and provide us with the lens that filters information and impacts how we perceive, gather, and evaluate information. Our CMC allows us to see the world through our own *cultural lens*. The lens functions as it should and unavoidably filters out information that is unfamiliar and it does not know how to process; that information often is left out of our perception of events.

1.4 Closure

As a result of our need to form quick impressions and conduct rapid assessments, we use a process called *closure* which refers to how we fill in missing information to understand a situation. Figure 3.1 illustrates this process. As you can see, although the pictures are incomplete, you are fully able to make sense of them and understand them; your mind immediately fills in the gaps. Many factors impact how quickly and accurately closure operates; culture is one such factor. Exercise 1.1 (Chapter 1) about the washing machine is an example of using culturally based closure to make sense of a picture, leading to an error. In that example, because your brain processes

---

1This view of perception is the core of Gestalt psychology introduced by Brunswick (1955) and Koffka (1935). Gestalt psychology argues that we actively construct and interpret social situations rather than simply process them objectively. Therefore, the context shapes what we see and understand.

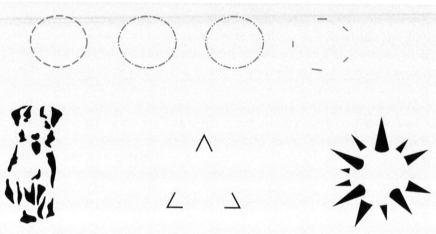

Figure 3.1 Closure

information by reading from left to right, you likely could not see the possible problem with the marketing pitch in cultures where people read from right to left.

Culturally determined illustrations of closure are presented in Figure 3.2. How you interpret these images depends on your culture. Is white the proper color for weddings or funerals? How about black? Does a spoon at a table setting mean that you will have soup? What if there is no knife and just a fork and spoon? Your cultural assumptions fuel the closure process and culture provides the meta-context that tells you immediately how to interpret the pictures. Hindus and Buddhists wear white to funerals; Europeans wear black. If you see a spoon in the place setting at the dinner table what do you assume? In many parts of the Middle East and North Africa, spoons in place settings are intended for eating rice, which is usually the main dish. Consider the case of the durian fruit. If you are from or have traveled to Southeast Asia, you are likely to know what it is, and unless you are part of one of the Southeast Asian cultures such as Malaysia, Thailand, Hong Kong, or Singapore, you are not likely to appreciate it. Durians have been banned from many public locations because of their smell, some would say indescribable stench (a combination of turpentine, onions, sewage, and gasoline). In Singapore, the fruit is formally banned from all forms of public transportation. However, it is considered a delicacy and much appreciated in some cultures. The fact that some people enjoy durians and others are repulsed by them is simply cultural; even our sense of smell and how we interpret the information it provides us is not objective. Many other examples of food further illustrate this point. What you are willing to eat and consider tasty or even a delicacy is very much a matter of your

Sources: a) istockphoto.com/Boogich; b) Shutterstock/Kzenon; c) istockphoto.com/Neosiam; d) Shutterstock/Gregory _m_photo.

cultural upbringing. Whether you eat and appreciate beef, snails, squirrels, tripe, dogs, fattened diseased goose liver (foie gras), fish eggs (caviar), horsemeat, manioc, or durian depends on your culture. A cricket is a pest in Western countries, a pet in China, and food in Thailand. Similarly, although globalization has reduced some of the differences, what we perceive as beauty is also culturally determined. While it may seem that our senses should provide us with objective and verifiable information, how we interpret the information that our senses receive is very much culture-dependent.

Similarly, what a manager may focus on when evaluating job candidates is likely to be influenced by culture (Hofstede et al., 2010; Trompenaars et al., 2012). A US manager will discuss job applicants' skills, abilities, and experience and how they can contribute. In France, candidates' educational credential related to which schools and universities they attended will be critical. In Lebanon and many other parts of the Middle East, the key information is who recommended the candidate and the community and social networks they belong to, factors that are irrelevant and even inappropriate to consider in the United States. The managers' CMC shapes their approach to gather and use information.

2. THREE STAGES OF PERCEPTION

LO 3.2 Elaborate on the stages of social perception

The multistage social perception process is presented in Figure 3.3. The three stages of attention, organization, and interpretation lead us to decisions or behaviors, and they are each impacted by a variety of biases and shortcuts we will discuss later in this chapter. CMC provides the background for social perception and has the potential to impact all of its elements and outcomes. If Figure 3.3 looks busy to you, it is intentional; our perceptual process is a busy place with many stimuli begging for our attention and numerous conscious and subconscious activities happening simultaneously.

Figure 3.3 The Social Perception Process

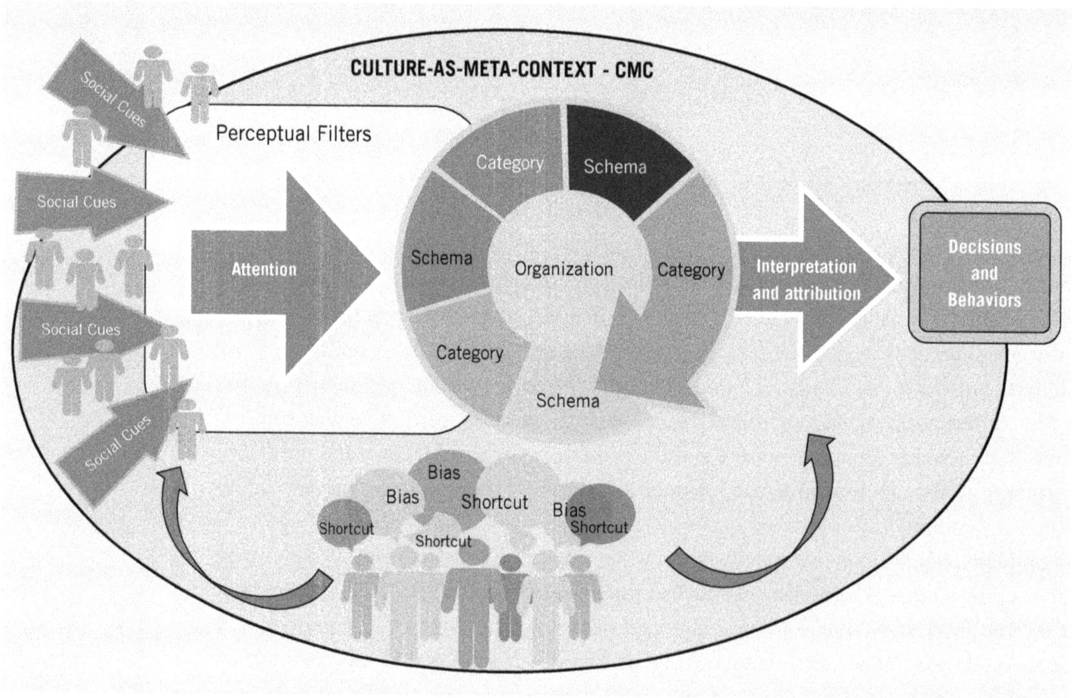

2.1 Attention

The first stage of social perception is *attention* where some cues catch your attention while others do not, since there is no way that we can pay attention to everything. Our brain automatically and spontaneously applies filters that decide what is important and relevant and what can be ignored. The filters operate subconsciously and involuntarily at a subliminal level to process social stimuli and then react to them. Some things make it through our filters and we pay attention to them; others are filtered out and never reach our consciousness. In the earlier example relating to a job interview, the information about the job candidate's accent and dress were considered important and allowed through the filter while the same information about coworkers went unnoticed. Research has shown that we pay particular attention to faces, especially to those who are looking at us (Macrae, Hook, Milne, Rowe, & Mason, 2002; Mason, Tatkow, & Macrae, 2005), and that we very quickly make strong trait inferences about those faces (Willis & Todorov, 2006). For example, psychologists have found that people associate black faces with criminality more often than white faces (Blair, Judd, & Chapleau, 2004; Eberhardt, Dasgupta, & Banaszynski, 2003).

Generally, anything or anyone that is *salient*, meaning is novel, unusual, or different, and stands out, passes through the filters, and gets our attention. For example, extensive research shows that our views of race and gender impact what we pay attention to and what inferences we make about people. For instance, the fact that ethnic minorities and women are still often "novel" in organizational settings makes them salient and deserving of our consideration; they pass through the filters and we become aware of them; they garner our attention. So, while the mistake or inappropriate comment of a white male employee, who still is more common and typical and therefore not likely to pass through a manager's perceptual filter, may go unnoticed, the same mistake from a Hispanic new employee with an accent will be noticed and remembered. One's culture impacts what is considered unusual, novel, or salient.

A woman wearing a professional sleeveless knee-length dress with her hair up in a pony tail in an Atlanta office is not likely to be considered unusual or garner any particular attention. The same person will stand out like a sore thumb in Saudi Arabia. Similarly, a woman in a hijab concealing her hair and fully covered by loose clothing is still novel enough in many Western countries and likely to draw attention, whereas she will simply not pass through people's filters in Muslim countries because her dress will be familiar and "normal" and not deserving of attention. Our culture acts as a CMC to influence what we pay attention to. Keep in mind that these processes are taking place in a fraction of a second. People and events that pass through our filters get our attention and become what we focus on and what we remember.

2.2 Organization

The next stage of the perception process is organizing what we paid attention to into categories and useful sets that are integrated and connected with other information we have stored, our assumptions, values, and beliefs. This organization is essential to allow us to later retrieve information. Keep in mind that we are driven by the need to have order and consistency so we organize the information into categories and groupings that provide that order, consistency, and predictability. In this stage of the process a useful tool is our *schemas* that are mental models and patterns about situations and events (Fiske & Taylor, 2017). Schemas provide the mental structures that bring together our expectations about situations and events. They help us fill in information using the closure process, as we organize what we have perceived. For example, we have schemas about what a job interview is and should be. We expect a certain level of friendliness and courtesy, anticipate some questions, and know what is inappropriate and we can predict certain outcomes. The more experience one has with interviews, the stronger and richer one's schema about them will be—a factor that produces some comfort and confidence. If you have limited experience with interviews, you have fewer categories to rely on for order and consistency and therefore you are more likely to be nervous and anxious regarding what to expect, and more hesitant in your reactions and responses. More experience means that you are likely to have well-developed schemas that help you process and remember information.

Our schemas make us efficient. They are influenced by our cultural background (Adair, Taylor, & Tinsley, 2009; DiMaggio, 1997) where both national and regional differences are likely to play a role. For example, in the Northeastern United States, such as in Boston or New York, interactions are typically rushed and somewhat curt. In Southern states or in the Midwest, people are more likely to take their time to socialize. A New Yorker in the South may feel that people are not moving fast enough and wasting time on social niceties; an Arkansan in Boston may deem people cold, dismissive, and even rude. How each will perceive and remember an interview is affected by the cultural schema. When they recount the event, the interactions and events that didn't fit their schema, that required them to stop and think will be front and center in their memory. The differences in schemas become even wider across national boundaries. For example, personal questions about marital status and family background that are illegal and inappropriate in the United States are perfectly normal and expected in many parts of the world. Interpersonal warmth expressed through smiling is expected in some cultures and frowned upon in others. Directness is desirable and expected in some cultures and considered rude in others. Our cultural schemas help us organize information and impact what we remember and how we remember it.

2.2.1 Dealing With Incongruent Information. There is another aspect to how we organize information. What happens when the information we receive is incongruent with our existing categories and schema? In these cases, not only do we notice the information because it is novel, we also cannot attach it to any category or schema that we already have. It simply does not fit what we know and, therefore, is likely to create discomfort. The options in that case are to (for some examples of research on these options see Brannon & Gawronski, 2018; Davis, 2018; De Brigard, Brady, Ruzic, & Schacter, 2016; Hunzaker, 2016):

- Ignore the information and not organize anywhere, which will lead to forgetting it

- Create a new category for this unusual and novel information so that we now have new grouping for future reference

- Change or distort the information to fit into existing groupings, so that what you remember is closer to your expectations

Consider how encountering individuals who do not fit racial stereotypes trigger these processes. If you have strong racial stereotypes against ethnic group X that includes believing that its members are lazy, unintelligent, poorly educated, and unmotivated, encountering a member of group X who violates that stereotype is likely to catch your attention. You will notice him or her and will spend some time trying to figure out why the person is different from what you expect. However, your organization system does not have a category or schema for "intelligent, educated, and motivated people from group X," so your options are to either classify the person as the exception to his or her group, change your view of group X, or after a while, forget that you ever encountered an intelligent member of group X and remember the person as having the characteristics consistent with your stereotype. If you encounter many members of group X who do not fit your categories and who are intelligent, educated, and motivated, you may create a new category or change your original one. In either case, your groupings help you process and remember information in an orderly and efficient manner that causes the least amount of disruption (Davis, 2018).

2.3 Interpretation and Attribution

In the final step in our perceptual process, we interpret the information we have paid attention to and organized and make inferences or attributions regarding people and events. We act as naïve scientists and sift through the information, more or less systematically and often subconsciously, to decide why people did what they did and we then use the information to infer the cause of behavior. What motivated your employee to disagree with you and the rest of the team and speak out in the meeting? Why does your coworker always come in late? Why did the new intern leave early? Why is the person you are negotiating with being stubborn and not giving an inch?

Why is your supervisor insisting on getting your input before a decision? The process of inferring the cause of behavior, meaning deciding why people act the way they do, is known as the *attribution* process and has long been the topic of extensive research in social psychology (Heider, 1958; Jones & Davis, 1965; Thibaut & Kelley, 1959). The basic options in attributing the cause of behavior are to infer that either something about the person or something about the situation determined behavior. For example, here are your options in the examples above:

- Your employee spoke out in the meeting because she is confident and assertive, or because she is having a bad day, or because her department had the most relevant information that she needed to share.

- Your coworker is chronically tardy because he is lazy, or because of a difficult commute and heavy traffic in the city.

- The intern left early because she is lazy and uninterested in her work, or because there is nothing to do in the office, or because of a family emergency.

- The stubbornness of the person you are negotiating with is due to his difficult personality, or because of instructions from his boss to be tough.

- Your supervisor always consults you because she has been trained to empower employees and she is a natural team builder, or because she lacks confidence and experience.

In all of these cases, you are trying to decide whether the person or the situation, or something that is stable (e.g., personality) or temporary (e.g., a bad day) are the cause of behavior. Not surprisingly, how we attribute the cause of behavior is, to some extent, impacted by culture including language. For example, English speakers will say "I broke the vase" focusing on the actor, whereas Spanish speakers will typically say "the vase broke or the vase broke itself," which focuses on the situation (Boroditsky, 2017). Similarly, in English people would say "I broke my arm," placing the responsibility of the break on the actor, whereas in Persian "my arm broke" is a construction that would, more accurately, remove the focus on the actor since people do not intentionally break their arm. Generally, cultures that are highly individualistic, such as the US, are more likely to lean toward placing causality in the person rather than the situation, whereas in collectivistic cultures such as Japan the situation is more the focus (Miyamoto & Kitayama, 2002). Some research further suggests that people from more collectivist cultures consider more information before assigning causality than those from individualistic cultures (Morling & Masuda, 2012; we discuss cultural dimensions in detail in Chapters 7 and 8).

Every step of the perceptual process takes place within a cultural context where culture provides the CMC. What we pay attention to, how we organize information into categories and schemas, and how we make inferences and attribution are impacted by our cultural assumptions, values, and beliefs. How you perceive and interpret the world is shaped by your CMC; others will be equally impacted by theirs. While in some cases, it may be possible to establish that one person's perception is more accurate than another's, in many other situations, both versions may be equally valid and accurate and depend on how the person views the world. Culture provides the meta-context that guides interpretation and reactions; culture provides us with our worldview and CJI. Using the language example, the English construction that puts the actor in charge of breaking her arm is no better or worse, or more or less accurate than Persian passive voice. They both simply reflect how the culture presents events. We next consider the various shortcuts and biases that impact our perception.

3. HEURISTICS AND BIASES

LO 3.3 Detail the critical impact of heuristics and biases

As we discussed earlier, we are cognitive misers who are biologically limited in how much information we can process and therefore try to be as parsimonious and efficient as possible. As a result, we look for and adopt strategies that simplify events and take shortcuts whenever and wherever we can. These strategies provide adequate outcomes, especially in familiar and routine situations, but do not always yield accurate or optimal solutions. So, it is important to note that our perceptual processes are driven by our inherent limitations, not necessarily our motivations and desires. In other words, most of us are not intentionally biased nor deliberately filter out information or activate certain categories consciously. These are the result of our hardware. Nonetheless, we can simultaneously act as *motivated tacticians* who are engaged thinkers who both consciously and subconsciously look for strategies to make sense of the world (Fiske & Taylor, 2017). Our cultural background is one of the factors that impact what strategies we use. Combined with our desire to be efficient, CMC guides and influences our views of the world.

3.1 Heuristics: The Shortcuts We Use

Because we face complex environments and many demands on our attention, we use shortcuts, also referred to as *heuristics*, to process information. Heuristics are defined as efficient shortcuts, methods, strategies, or rules of thumb that are used to derive a solution. They are "strategies that ignore information to make decisions faster, more frugally, and/or more accurately than more complex methods" (Gigerenzer & Gaissmaier, 2011, p. 454). When we use heuristics, we assess a situation by using rules that are easily accessible and available, but that may not really fit the situation at hand (Kahneman & Frederick, 2002). Heuristics simplify a situation, seek less information, reduce our effort, and allow us to reach a decision efficiently (Shah & Oppenheimer, 2008). They help us make sense of a complex world quickly and provide guidelines to action in specific situations. Our experiences teach us how to use them and when they apply.

Psychologists Amos Tversky and Daniel Kahneman (1974) conducted extensive research about the heuristics that are commonly used and can be effective in some situations and inaccurate in others (Kahneman, 2011). We use them because they often work, not because we are intentionally trying to be unfair. More specifically, they work in more routine situations where they allow us to simplify information. However, in unfamiliar situations where there is considerable complexity, the heuristics we use are more likely to lead to error. Just on the basis of the definition, it is clear that heuristics are linked to CMC as both are tools to make sense of the world and provide guides to action. In some ways, culture itself is a heuristic as it provides us with easily accessible rules to interpret events and make decisions. Whereas culture is broad and generic, heuristics inform specific situations or challenges we face. Table 3.1 presents a list and description of common heuristics.

The heuristics presented in Table 3.1 are some of the most common ones that relate to our CMC and cultural perspectives. People may have many other rules of thumb for making decisions in specific situations. When these rules are used often and are perceived to yield good results, they are likely to become automatic and intuitive. You can see from the examples in Table 3.1 that the heuristics rely on basic assumptions, values, and beliefs that often have cultural roots. For example, our views of leadership are frequently gender-based and are strongly influenced by our culture resulting in the "Think leader–think male" mentality. Cultural assumptions, values, and beliefs regarding gender (discussed at length in Chapter 6) impact whether women are provided with leadership opportunities.

3.2 Biases: Systematic Errors

When heuristics are used consistently and systematically lead to error, they can turn into biases (see Table 3.2 for a list and description of biases). *Biases* then are systematic and often subconscious errors in thinking. Using heuristics can further reinforce the many biases that we have in how we perceive and interpret social information. For example, hearing about terrorist attacks by Muslim extremists can trigger the availability heuristic and reinforce stereotypes (a bias) of Muslims. Many of the heuristics and biases are related and operate in conjunction with one another. For example, availability, theory-induced blindness, and representativeness can combine

Table 3.1 Some Common Heuristics

Heuristic	Description	Examples
Availability	Relying on immediate examples that are easily available "What you see is all there is" (WYSIATI) We use information that is accessible to make a decision rather than consider more complete information.	We may hesitate to fly immediately after hearing about a plane crash. We may fear all those we think are Muslim after a terrorist attack by Muslim extremists. When thinking about other cultures, we are likely to rely on information in the media, news, or movies that we have recently seen, incidents that are available in short-term memory, rather than gathering more information.
Representativeness	Tendency to use the most representative example of a group to generalize We have ideas about what and who represents a group and fit people and events in those groups rather than seek more information.	Because jurors have an image of what a guilty person looks like, they are more likely to convict a person who fits their image regardless of the facts of the case. If the accused is a good representative of criminals, then he must be one. There is a stereotypical image of what a leader looks like—often male, white, tall, with slightly graying hair and a deep voice. We consider those who fit that image to be good leaders while anyone who does not, minorities and women in particular are not considered to have leadership potential.
Framing	The context in which a decision is made impacts the decision. We use certain frames to define and limit how a decision is made.	Politicians frame immigration in extreme ways either in terms of immigrants being criminals and people who replace local workers or as a source of valuable labor. That framing impacts proposed policies and how their constituents perceive immigrants.
Theory-induced blindness	Difficulty to change one's mind or notice the flaws of a long-held theory We rely on our own theories to make decisions but do not seek or accept information that does not fit the theory.	You strongly believe that your culture is superior and have many examples to support your view. You ignore any information that does not support the view and provides negative information about your culture. We connect with social media that support our views while ignoring information that does not; this has been called the "echo chamber."

Sources: Based on Tversky and Kahneman (1974) and Kahneman (2011).

Table 3.2 Common Biases

Biases	Description	Examples
Commitment bias	The tendency to want to be consistent with past behaviors and attitudes leads us to commit to something even when we should not	If you voice an opinion or act in a certain manner publicly, you are likely to commit to it and not want to change in spite of contradictory evidence. Managers continue investing in a failed venture or bad decision because they have made a public announcement. This is known as escalation of commitment.
Confirmation bias	The tendency to seek information that confirms existing assumptions, values, and beliefs and disregard information that does not support them	You hold a stereotype that Asians are smart and better at math and science. You are likely to pay attention and remember examples that support your belief and disregard, explain away, and forget those that disconfirm it.
Stereotypes	Beliefs regarding people based on the group to which they belong and assuming that all members of the group are similar Some stereotypes are broad and culturally based, others are narrow and based on family or clan beliefs.	Millennials are entitled. African-Americans are athletic. Women are emotional. Asians are intelligent. Men are better leaders than women. New Yorkers are rude. Southerners are closed-minded.

Similar to me	People's tendency to disproportionally like and favor those who are similar to them and dislike those who are different, or not part of their immediate group	A French-Canadian supervisor favors French-speaking employees over English-speaking ones regardless of other relevant qualifications.

A Millennial supervisor hires and promotes other Millennials over qualified older-applicants. |
| Seeking a second opinion from similar person | The tendency to seek second opinion or advice from people who are similar to us

We do not seek help from people we do not like or do not trust and who are more likely to disagree with us. | A manager has a negative impression of a job candidate he has interviewed. He wants to be fair and asks the opinion of his colleague regarding the candidate. The colleague he seeks out is someone he likes and trusts, who shares his values and beliefs and is therefore highly unlikely to disagree with him. |
| Fundamental attribution error | The tendency to overestimate how much a person rather than situational factors is the cause of behavior

We are more likely to place the cause of behavior with the person than the situation. | A manager who is evaluating her employee's performance attributes his poor performance to the employee's lack of motivation or laziness rather than poor organizational support, a difficult territory, uncooperative coworkers, or her own poor management. |
| Dunning–Kruger effect | The tendency for those with the least knowledge or information to believe they know more than they do | Although people know very little about another culture, they assume that the story they heard or the movie they saw provides them with all the information they need and think they actually have sufficient information about that culture. |
| Halo/Horn effect | The tendency to let an overall positive or negative impression of a person influence more specific and unrelated decisions | You meet someone at a party and enjoy his company while you both have several drinks. A few days later you hear he has applied for a job in your company and you recommend him without reviewing his resume. |

(Continued)

Table 3.2 Common Biases *(Continued)*

Biases	Description	Examples
		A person driving ahead of you gets the last spot in your office parking lot and waves at you with what you think is a smirk as she leaves her car. You are irritated and late to your meeting. You find out that she is the supplier who is trying to get your business. You can't shake the negative impression you have of her.
Projection	The tendency to overestimate how much others agree with you and assume that what you believe or think is shared by others	You assume that your negative stereotypes of a certain group are widely held by others. A manager who is impressed with one of his employees can't understand why many others do not appreciate his talents.
Just world hypothesis	The tendency to believe that the world is fair and that good things happen to good people and bad things happen to bad people	We blame victims of accidents or crimes by seeking information regarding mistakes they may have made that contributed to their situation. The rape victim was drinking; the drive-by shooting victim was out late at night, etc. By blaming them, we feel that we are protected since the world is just and we do not engage in those types of behaviors.
Self-fulfilling prophecy or Pygmalion effect	The tendency to make our impressions become reality through our own actions	A manager who has a negative impression of an employee does not assign him any good projects, provides little feedback or coaching, limits her interaction with him, and does not give him a chance to show his potential. As a result, the employee does not perform well, confirming the manager's initial impression.
Primacy	The tendency to rely on early information and disregard or not seek more recent information	We form impressions of others within seconds, or even fractions of a second. Our first impressions are long-lasting and hard to change.

with confirmation bias, stereotypes, and commitment bias to enhance their effects; or stereotypes can combine with the similar-to-me bias and negatively impact those who are not part of a person's in-group.

It is important to keep in mind that heuristics and biases operate automatically and result from our innate tendency to seek efficiency over accuracy and from our desire to have consistency and order. They are the rules that we have consistently applied and used in our "small" world. We do not set out to use only easily available information, or rely only on our first impressions, or consciously frame things one way or another; these operate mostly subconsciously and automatically. While some people may be intentionally and consciously biased, most of us do not have hidden motives to use these heuristics and biases; we are simply cognitive misers trying to process complex information quickly. As a matter of fact, some research suggests that when stakes are high or when people become aware of the complexity of a situation or have experience with their failed heuristics, they become more deliberate in their thinking. In other words, when people are made conscious that the rules of their small world are either faulty or not applicable everywhere, they reconsider them. However, when we have little information about a group or a culture, we are more likely to rely on our biases to fill in information (Ellemers, 2018). These biases contribute to the filters that impact what we see and remember about other people (Amodio, 2014).

Heuristics and biases make some sense from an evolutionary perspective. At some point in our distant past, we had to take as few risks as possible and make quick life-and-death decisions. Additionally, we could only trust those we knew and those who were part of our family or clan. We are therefore instinctively comfortable with people who look like us and have similar background (Menon, 2018). However, what may have been legitimate fear of the unknown and of strangers in our evolutionary past is no longer valid. We live in a generally safe, orderly, and highly diverse world, which although still highly complex, provides us with many opportunities to be more deliberate in our thought processes.

4. AUTOMATIC OR DELIBERATE? SYSTEM I AND SYSTEM II

LO 3.4 Contrast System I and System II and their link to CMC

The way we perceive and organize our world ranges from a fully subconscious and automatic to a conscious and deliberate process (see Figure 3.4). The first impressions that form within fractions of a second are both automatic and subliminal. We rarely become aware of what has triggered them, and they form without us knowing that they are developing. For example, a manager's first impression of his negotiating partner as friendly is immediate. At the other end are conscious, deliberate decisions that are based on careful consideration and evaluation of information. After working with the partner, the manager's impression may change or get solidified based on the partner's

Figure 3.4 From Automatic to Deliberate

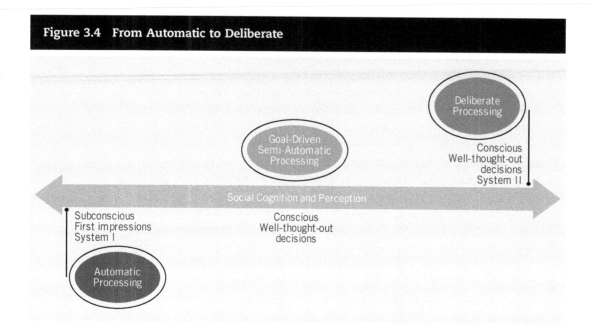

actions and words. Social and cognitive psychologists have devoted considerable research to understanding this dual-processing mode that ranges from automatic to deliberate (e.g., Chaiken & Trope, 1999) and have shown that we are capable of using both modes, and many others in between, and move among them with ease. The heuristics and biases we discussed earlier in this chapter are typically automatic and subconscious but can shift to the other end if we become aware of them and start reflecting on their operation and implications. We next consider the two systems of processing information and the role of culture in those processes.

4.1 System I and System II

Nobel Prize laureate Daniel Kahneman (2011), relying on extensive research with his colleague Amos Tversky, popularized the idea of the two systems of thinking, one fast and efficient (System I) and the other slow and deliberate (System II). Table 3.3 summarizes the characteristics of the two systems. System I operates automatically and is based on well-practiced and deeply ingrained assumptions, values, beliefs, and knowledge. It is effortless and allows us to respond quickly to familiar situations. It kicks in when we think we are facing situations we know well and allows us to respond almost reflexively based on habitual responses we have learned and have become second nature where we can rely on our expert intuition. These are the rules

Table 3.3 Key Characteristics of System I and System II

Automatic System I	Deliberate System II
Fast	Slow
Cannot be turned off	Must be consciously activated
Effortless	Effortful
Intuitive	Rational
Reflexive	Reflective
Habitual	Calculated
Subconscious and subliminal	Conscious and deliberate
Examples: Driving on a familiar road in broad daylight; solving 2×2; finishing familiar proverbs such as "Birds of a feather..."; responding to a greeting in your native language	**Examples**: Driving at night on dark streets looking for an address; solving 28×93; remembering lyrics of a song you have not heard in years; answering a question in a language you barely know

Sources: Fiske and Taylor (2017) and Kahneman (2011).

that regulate our "small" and predictable world. For example, you drive home every day taking the same route without having to think and, as a result, you barely remember what you see on the way. With some experience, many of the routine and day-to-day decisions managers make are part of their System I.

Conversely, System II involves deliberate and effortful processing of information. It does not operate thoughtlessly and unintentionally. For example, to solve 28×93 or answer a question in a language you barely speak, you have to slow down, think, and activate knowledge and skills that require effort. It is the processing that you need when you face unfamiliar and complex situations, such as when you are in a cross-cultural situation. Using System I when you should be using System II can be disastrous; using System II where System I would work is a waste of precious time and resources. In order to be effective in the "large" world, we have to consciously engage our System II thinking.

Let's take these two systems to a cultural context. When you are in your own CMC (your small world), one that is familiar and where you know the assumptions, beliefs, and values and corresponding behaviors and you have well-established categories and schemas for various situations, you can typically operate in System I efficiently and effectively. You know how to answer a greeting in your own language; you know whether to smile or not; you know how to address your boss; you know what is an inappropriate comment or joke; you know what topics of conversation are proper for casual, formal, business, or personal settings. You know how not to violate someone's personal space and whether you can hug them or not, or give them a pat on the shoulder. You can rely on the automatic System I to effortlessly respond for you. There may be situations where you make a mistake, but those mistakes will not be related to your misreading the cultural cues; they are likely to be more idiosyncratic to the person or situation. However, when you interact across cultures, particularly across ones you do not know well, you cannot rely on your System I; you must activate System II. You need to focus, think, and make conscious and careful decisions regarding most of your actions. You have to think about basic processes such as how to respond to greetings, whether to extend your hand or hug the person (or keep your distance); you must decide on the topic of conversation and how much and what information to share; whether to speak your language or venture into the other; every step needs to be governed by System II. If you simply rely on your System I and respond based on your own CMC, chances of errors and misunderstandings are high and you are not likely to be effective. Referring back to the paradox we introduced in Chapter 1, the rules that work well in one world do not necessarily apply in another.

Our cultural assumptions, values, and beliefs fit somewhere in between the two ends presented in Figure 3.4. Some are deeply ingrained and below the consciousness and visibility line and others are accessible and visible (see the iceberg in Figure 1.1 in Chapter 1). That in-between area where culture fits is called goal-dependent or goal-driven semi-automatic processing (see Figure 3.4; Fiske & Taylor, 2017).

4.2 Culture as a Goal-Driven Semi-Automatic Process

Our cultural assumptions, values, and beliefs guide our thinking, impact the heuristics we use, shape our biases, and guide our decisions and actions. They impact our cognitive processes. Susan Fiske and Shelley Taylor (2017) describe the *goal-driven automatic* process as:

> *automatic according to some of the criteria, such as lack of awareness of the process itself, not needing to monitor the process to completion, and lack of intending all the specific outcomes…. However, by definition, goal-dependent automaticity also varies by the perceiver's goals, so it is partially responsive to intentional control. Goal-dependent automaticity thus is not entirely automatic, in that it requires intentional processing and depends on the task undertaken. (p. 41)*

As the definition implies, the cognitive processes that are triggered based on our cultural assumptions operate automatically and while we are aware of some of the impact of our CMC and may intentionally rely on those values, others operate without our knowledge. The assumptions, values, and beliefs are the goals that drive us; they are the "goal" in the goal-driven semi-automatic processing.

Consider when a Japanese automaker builds a manufacturing plant in the United States. The Japanese plant manager will make decisions regarding the structure of work and reward system automatically based on his CMC and the corresponding cultural assumptions, values, and beliefs about what a well-run organization looks like. These may involve a formal work environment and extensive use of team work and team-based rewards that are typical in Japan. However, to be effective in the United States and to meet his production goals, he may need to stop those assumptions from operating and be more intentional about how he motivates the American employees. He may end up still relying on the same management systems, but he has to consider the implications of that decision before he does. Celebrating holidays is another good illustration of this goal-driven semi-automatic process. If you are US-American and celebrate Christmas, you have clear and automatic expectations about what should and will happen during the holiday ranging from the shopping and gift-giving, to get-togethers, meal preparation and sharing, office parties, and the expectations of joy and some stress. You are likely to fall into the CMC-based routine almost automatically, but you are also able to change this routine if you apply different intentions. Falling into the routine takes little thinking; intentionally changing it takes effort and is more deliberate. Consider what would happen if you are in a different country during Christmas where the holiday is not celebrated and where none of the automatic processes are in place or different events are taking place. In that situation, every step of your culturally based holiday schema would have to be deliberate.

As mentioned at the beginning of Chapter 1 and discussed here, we can make quick, rational, and accurate decisions in familiar settings where we have knowledge, experience, and information (Simon, 1979) and we can rely on System I. Although we never have perfect and complete information, our own cultural environments provide familiarity and knowledge of the situation; they are a "small" world that we know. Because we are experienced and skilled and successful, we can rely on our expert intuition and can therefore operate in the goal-driven semi-automatic mode. The biases and shortcuts we have developed throughout our lives have worked in the past and are likely to work again. Although they cause many mistakes due to stereotypes and biases, they still generally work. We have schemas that are functional and fit the environment.

4.3 When to Activate System II

When we cross cultural boundaries, we have to consciously place our System I on hold and switch on our deliberate System II. The challenge is two fold because, not only may it not be easy to switch on the System II processing, in some cases, we may not be aware that we have crossed cultural boundaries and that we need to actually slow down our System I and activate System II. For example, if you are in a business meeting, you may assume that at least based on their looks, everyone is from the same cultural background as you. However, as you have explored in the various self-assessments already, people may have many cultural backgrounds that are invisible to others.

When we cross cultural boundaries and find ourselves in new environments, in the "large" world where we do not know the rules of the game, our ability to be efficient and accurate by relying on our heuristics is considerably hampered. Many, if not all, of the processes that fit our culture and make us efficient may no longer apply. The automatic processing of System I is much less likely to be effective. A new cultural environment, or interactions across cultures, can, although not always, make you cross a threshold (see Chapter 2). You enter a different world where your old heuristics and experiences may not work. It is safer to assume they will not apply rather than jump in and let your assumptions run amuck. Therefore, we must activate System II in order to be effective.

Disregarding or ignoring culture can have dire consequences. However, we face several challenges before deliberately activating System II:

1. First, we must recognize that we have actually crossed cultural boundaries. Although it may seem easy, there are many situations where we may not be aware that we are in an unfamiliar cross-cultural environment. Either because of simple lack of awareness, or inattention, or even arrogance, we may not understand that we are in unfamiliar settings.

2. Second, we must acknowledge that when culture is in play, it is a game-changer or at least has the potential to be. Even if you are aware that the environment is unfamiliar and new, you may still assume that the new culture does not matter and decide to act based on your own assumptions.

3. Finally, we must have the knowledge and skills to address the situation. Awareness and recognition are a starting point, but you must also have the tools to deal with the new environment effectively.

These steps are part of the development of CM we discussed in Chapter 2 (see Figure 2.3). It is also important to note that assuming that culture is a factor when it is not can also create challenges such as offending the other person or wasting time and resources where they are not needed. A fundamental element is awareness of one's own cultural identity, a topic we discuss next. If the assumption is "people are people" (something we will discuss in the next chapter), then we will continue using our own CMC and its corresponding System I.

WINDOW TO THE WORLD

Doing Business in Mexico

Mexico is the United States' third largest trade partner after China and Canada, ahead of Germany, South Korea, and other EU countries, while the United States is Mexico's largest partner. If you live in one of the two most populous states in the United States, California and Texas, or other Southwestern states, you are even more likely to be working with Mexico. Additionally, more than sixty percent of the Hispanics in the United States are of Mexican origin. While there is considerable cultural diversity in Mexico, the emphasis on family, friendship, graciousness, and respect are dominant.

1. Take the time to build friendships and enjoy the process. Expect to share meals and develop relationships; rushing into business or pushing things will backfire.

2. While many business people speak English, Spanish is the official language; do not assume that meetings will be done in English. Spanish is a relatively easy language to learn, especially if you are in the United States, where Spanish language courses and Mexican cultural events are pervasive and easy to find. Otherwise, have an interpreter present.

3. Having knowledge about and showing interest in the history and culture of the country will be much appreciated. It will also help understand the context and manage your interaction more successfully.

4. The business culture values warmth, graciousness, formality, and indirectness. Be courteous, engage in small talk, be patient, and dress the part.

5. Status and rank are important, so make sure you send team members who have appropriate seniority and connect with those with equal rank and status.

6. While Mexicans are looser with the concept of time and they may be late to meetings, as a guest, it is always desirable to be punctual.

One of the fatal mistakes US-Americans make is to consider Mexico as somehow subservient to the United States. Mexico is a proud country with a long and rich history and culture. While the United States is a key business partner, establishing successful relationships requires treating your partners as equals.

5. UNDERSTANDING YOUR CULTURAL PERSPECTIVE: YOUR CULTURAL IDENTITY

LO 3.5 Explain the critical importance of cultural identity and its impact on CMC

Now that you have an understanding of the cognitive processes involved in social perception, it is essential that you gain awareness of your own cultural identity and its corresponding assumptions, values, and beliefs. Your cultural identity provides you with your CMC and some of the content that drives your System I. Your cultural assumptions, values, and beliefs shape the schemas and heuristics you use and the biases that may be influencing how you think, behave, and work. Some are related to your national culture; others are group-based; and some have roots in your nuclear or extended family.

5.1 Definition and Functions of Cultural Identity

Cultural identity provides part of the answer to the question "Who am I?" It refers to a person's sense of belonging to one or more groups and sharing characteristics with that group (Unger, 2011). Although it typically has racial, ethnic, or geographical origins, it can also be related to other factors including gender, sexual orientation, class, religion, or other groups that a person considers significant. Cultural identity is one aspect of our social identity which is more generally part of an individual's self-concept that is derived from group membership (Tajfel & Turner, 1986). As we have discussed in Chapter 2, a critical factor in CM is awareness of one's culture.

Both cultural and social identity play a key role in a person's self-esteem, and we derive positive outcomes from a sense of belonging to groups with whom we share some characteristics (Turner, Hogg, Oakes, Reicher, & Wetherell, 1987). People's identities provide a self-schema of sorts, an organized set of information that allows them to summarize and reduce complex information about themselves (Howard, 2000). For example, when someone identifies himself as Cuban-American, that label provides a short-hand for him and for others to describe who he is. Prototypically, being Cuban-American is associated with either being the child of Cuban emigres who fled the country after the Castro-led revolution of 1959, or an immigrant in the following years. Some other general characteristics associated with being Cuban-American include speaking Spanish, being from Florida, being politically conservative, and being Catholic. The cultural identity provides a short-hand to who a person is. Describing oneself with any cultural label has the same effect.

In addition to providing a self-schema, the purpose of cultural identity is to promote our sense of self and our self-esteem (Umaña-Taylor, 2011). By giving us reference points and validation through membership in certain groups, our cultural identity provides us with frameworks to interpret information, solve problems, and make decisions (Berzonsky, 2011). Consider the example of someone who is a recent convert to a religion. Faith and spirituality are likely to have been the motive for conversion; however, the religion also provides the person with moral, social, and behavioral codes and guidelines regarding what is appropriate and desirable and what is to be avoided, for instance the consumption of alcohol or direction regarding social and political decisions. These guidelines are particularly helpful on matters over which the person may not have a strong opinion. By identifying with the new religion, the convert satisfies her spiritual needs, has a sense of belonging and pride, and is armed with new guidelines regarding how to make some decisions.

Our cultural identity, our sense of belonging to one or more groups, allows us to see ourselves in a positive light and leads us to see those who are like us, the people in our cultural groups, in the same positive light. A strong cultural identity inevitably contributes to the creation of an in-group (those who are like me) and an out-group (those who are not like me; more on this in Chapter 4). This process has been found, in some cases, to lead to more favorable treatment of in-group members (e.g., Simon, Hastedt, & Aufderheide, 1997; the similar-to-me bias described in Table 3.2). For most people, cultural identity is made up of many intersecting groups. For example, we belong to groups based on nationality, ethnicity, as well as gender, class, age, sexuality, and many other factors. While every person prioritizes these groups differently, research has shown that some group memberships are more salient and stronger, both in terms of self-identification and in terms of how others see us.

It is no surprise that racial and ethnic identity is one such category (Howard, 2000), meaning they are more salient than other characteristics. These salient factors become *chronically accessible concepts* which are characteristics that are easily accessible, often triggered subconsciously, and often applied when assessing ourselves or others (Fiske & Taylor, 2017). What this means is that people will prioritize these accessible concepts more often when describing themselves, and others will prioritize them in describing them; they are codes that we use routinely and automatically (Higgins, King, & Mavin, 1982). For instance, skin color, often associated with race and ethnicity, and gender are both visible and chronically accessible. Both are categories that we use first and frequently when describing ourselves and others. Chapters 5 and 6 will explore these topics in more detail.

5.2 Awareness of Cultural Identity

Your cultural identity is both assigned and selected. This means that it is stable and fluid (Berzonsky, 2011). Your nationality, race, ethnicity, and gender, as well as other factors that make up your background are assigned to you by virtue of your birth, and more significantly, most people construct their cultural identity by selecting the groups to which they want to belong. This concept, called *self-categorization*, occurs when people identify themselves as belonging to particular groups (Hogg & Terry, 2000; Turner et al., 1987). Researchers suggest that historically and in simple societies and less complex settings, a person's identity was assigned (Howard, 2000). However, in increasingly diverse, complex, and dynamic societies many individuals select their identities. A familiar example of self-categorization is when teenagers start to pull away from the identities their parents and community have assigned to them and select new groups that provide them with a sense of belonging, self-esteem, and new perspectives on how to view the world and how to behave. Figure 3.5 presents a visualization of these intersecting identities using Venn diagrams. People will have more or fewer circles representing different cultural groups with which they identify, with the size of each circle representing the importance of that group to the individual.

Given that cultural self-awareness is a cornerstone of developing a cultural mindset, it is critical that you be aware of the various elements of your cultural identity. Each of the groups to which you belong contributes to your CMC and its associated assumptions, values, and beliefs. Some aspects of your cultural identity will be equally prominent to you and to others; other aspects may be central to you, but invisible to others; and yet other identities may be used by others to categorize you even though they are not central to you. Being conscious and mindful of the various aspects of your cultural identity and their corresponding elements allows you to determine some of the heuristics you may use, your biases, and the factors that may be chronically accessible to you and impact how you see others. Similarly, understanding which cultural identities others may assign to you can support more effective social interaction.

For example, when Natalia and her husband Raul started their business careers working for a company in the United States, they were often surprised at people's reactions and comments. They were both from prominent and wealthy Mexican

Figure 3.5   Intersecting Cultural Identities

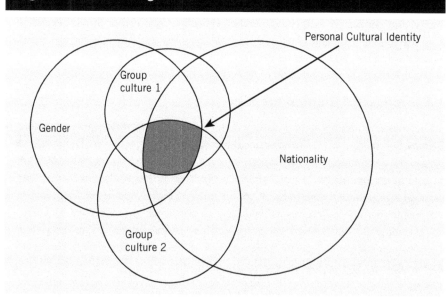

families and had completed their PhDs in a top school in the Eastern United States. Prior to coming to the United States, they had studied in France and had traveled extensively around the world. With Spanish surnames, they were automatically considered to be part of the Hispanic minority group by their coworkers and many of the people they met in their new city. Natalia was offended when several people commented that neither of them, and particularly she, whose family originated in France and moved to Mexico in the 1800s, looked very Mexican. They were both assigned projects that involved various Hispanic communities, and their boss suggested that they join the Hispanic Mentoring group in the company. Natalia and Raul were uncomfortable with these assignments and questions. They did not consider themselves to be a minority, had never been part of the minority group in their home country, and, except for language, had little in common with community members on the projects they worked on. Advocating for minority groups and serving Hispanic communities did not come easily to them. Their cultural identities, which included upper-class, highly educated Mexicans whose roots connected them with the Spanish and French colonial powers, simply did not match what people were assigning to them.

Unless you are aware of your cultural identity and its different aspects and components you cannot fully understand your assumptions, values, and beliefs and how they contribute to your CMC. Consequently, you may also be unaware of some of the cultural aspects of your System I and when it may be operating. In order to be effective at managing across cultures, managers must know their own cultural perspectives, the rules of their "small" world, so that they know when those rules may not apply.

6. MANAGING OUR SOCIAL PERCEPTUAL PROCESS: AVOIDING UNCONSCIOUS BIASES

LO 3.6 Provide guidelines for managing the social perception process

The cognitive processes that we have discussed in this chapter are at the core of how human beings think and process information. They have developed and evolved to allow us to function and survive. They are not easy to change. That said, there are many steps we can take to manage our social perception processes and to avoid inappropriately applying heuristics and relying on biases. While managing them may be important in our personal lives, in our roles as managers, it is critical to become aware of unconscious biases, their sources, and how they impact reactions and decisions. In a global environment, such awareness and knowledge are indispensable.

Therefore, the most important and critical step in managing biases is awareness and knowledge. Having learned about the social perception processes, how heuristics and biases operate, and some of the assumptions, values, and beliefs associated with your CMC can go a long way to help you know:

- What your "small" world rules are

- When these rules, meaning your automatic System I, are operating

- When you need to activate the more deliberate and thoughtful System II

The goal is not to eliminate all heuristics; they are useful rules of thumb to address a complex world. Similarly, our System I processes are needed and efficient and effective in many situations and context. The goal is to know when and how they operate and are effective and when and how we have to engage in more deliberate thinking. Managing across culture is clearly such a situation.

There is no panacea and no easy answers. The material in this book is aimed at building your self-awareness, helping you recognize the role and impact of CMC, and giving you the tools to make more deliberate and thoughtful decisions when needed. Consistent and continuous reminders, reflection (which encourages meta-cognition), and practice will allow you to make thoughtful choices while remaining efficient. This chapter has started the process of helping you understand cognitive processes and how we THINK and process information addressing the first set in the THINK–KNOW–DO model. CMC provides the background for this process. Your various cultural assumptions, values, and beliefs color and influence your biases; understanding them is necessary to develop a CM.

FIRST PERSON REVISITED

The organizational consultant in the *First Person* case is affected by his clients' use of heuristics and biases. They hold certain stereotypes about Indians and are surprised when he does not fit them. Whether these biases affect him negatively may depend on the situation. However, the fact that he is aware of them and how they operate allows him to manage the situation appropriately and prevents any possible negative impact. Similarly, any of us can get some control of situations by being aware of perceptual processes and their interaction with culture.

APPLYING WHAT YOU LEARNED: AVOIDING PERCEPTUAL ERRORS

There is no guaranteed way to reduce using heuristics inappropriately and prevent us from falling prey to biases. The human brain is built to be efficient, so we will always filter information, use various schemas, and rely on subconscious rules of thumb and biases. However, awareness and knowledge of these processes are the best tools you have. Here are some things you can do to help you make better judgments in cross-cultural situations:

1. Assume that you will be wrong, so go into the situation expecting that your first impression and judgment will be wrong and that you will need to be deliberate

2. Pay attention and be present—good advice in any setting, essential in cross-cultural interactions

3. Observe rather than make judgments—describe rather than evaluate

4. Take your time (count to ten or twenty if you need to!) before you respond to important questions or address key issues

5. Don't be shy to ask questions referring to your own lack of knowledge and cultural differences. For example, "In my culture, x would mean this. I wonder if it is the same for you?"

6. Show humility—for example, "I really don't know a lot about what this would mean here (or in your country), so please help me understand x"

7. Be careful about assigning culture to someone inaccurately. For example, don't assume that someone who looks different is from a different culture.

The key is to learn to suspend judgment and avoid reaching quick conclusions in unfamiliar settings. Your automatic system will do its job and operate in any setting; it is up to you to not trust it until you are able to gather more information and be more deliberate and thoughtful.

MANAGERIAL CHALLENGE: TO HIRE OR NOT TO HIRE?

You have had a key opening on your team for several months and have had difficulty finding the person with the right expertise, experience, and personality for the job. Your team is tight knit and the members have to be able to work well together. One of your fellow managers hands you the résumé of someone who used to work with her, who is now in another division and looking to move from his current position. His qualifications are a perfect match. You decide to call him in for an informal lunch with you and a couple of the senior members of the team. You are all impressed and are seriously considering him for the job as he indicates that he is interested and would like to apply as an internal candidate, a process that is relatively simple. Once he formally throws his name in the hat, you start hearing some rumors about him being difficult to work with. His current supervisor tells you everything is fine but that "he will be a much better fit for your team," without elaborating. One of your team members hears that being subject to recent sexual harassment may be the reason the candidate wants to move, but nothing is formal. You check with HR regarding his performance evaluations and see that he has been a consistent performer. Several of the team members express concerns about hiring him; others insist that he is perfect and it's time to fill the position.

1. What is your assessment of this situation?

2. What information should you consider in your decision process?

3. What should you do?

SELF-ASSESSMENT 3.1: YOUR CULTURAL IDENTITY

Using the information you developed in Self-Assessment 2.1 (Chapter 2) and the material you read in this chapter regarding cultural identity, draw a Venn diagram with each circle or oval representing one of your cultures and proportional to importance of that culture to you. Please refer to Figure 3.5 for an example with four cultural groups. You may have more or fewer.

Every person's Venn diagram will be unique and the intersection of all the circles is an individual's personal cultural identity. Even siblings of the same gender may have different identities as they may prioritize each culture differentially.

After reviewing your Venn diagram, reflect on the following questions.

1. How easy or hard was it to develop this diagram?

2. What does it tell you about your identity?

3. What is unique about your cultural identity?

4. Which one of the cultures are visible (e.g., skin color or gender)? Which ones are less visible? The invisible cultures could be anything including nationality, ethnicity, disability, socioeconomic status, or sexual orientation. These may be more or less visible for different individuals.

5. To what extent would someone you just met see you the same way you see yourself?

EXERCISE 3.1: THE MYSTERIOUS CASE OF THE COLLEGE EXAM

Objective: This exercise addresses the cognitive factors in CM.

Instructions:

Individually

Read the following short case carefully and as often as you think is necessary for full understanding. You will not be able to refer to it until the end of the exercise as instructed by your instructor.

> *A well-liked college instructor had just completed making up the final exam and had turned off the lights in the office. Just then, a tall, dark and broad figure appeared and demanded the exam. The professor opened the drawer. Everything in the drawer was picked up and the individual ran down the corridor. The dean was notified immediately.*

When you think you have a good grasp of the case answer the questions that your instructor provides without referring back to the case. For each question, T indicates that you feel the answer is true and correct; F indicates that the answer is false; and ? indicates that you either cannot tell or are not sure.

Still **without referring back to the case**, how many answers do you think you got correct?

_____ out of 10.

In a Group

Still **without looking at the case** and without changing your answers, compare your answers with other group members and discuss the reasoning behind your answers. The goal is not to reach a consensus, but to discuss how you came to your answers.

Now that you have discussed the case, how many answers do you think you got correct?

_____ out of 10.

Please wait for further instructions.

EXERCISE 3.2: HEURISTICS AT WORK

Objective: This exercise addresses the cognitive factors in CM.

Instructions:

Individual Work

Individually answer each of the following questions.

1. My friend is dating a really interesting guy. He is tall and wiry, has quite a few tattoos, is very quiet and introverted, teaches yoga as a hobby, has traveled extensively around the world, and plays several instruments. Can you guess what his major is?

    a. Psychology

    b. Chinese literature

    c. Business

    d. Philosophy

2. A new neighbor just moved in next door to me. She is very outgoing and has already thrown a few parties. She's very concerned about health and the environment and rides her bike to work most days. She has three cats and two dogs and plans to plant a vegetable garden in her backyard. I wonder what her profession is?

    a. Lawyer

    b. Librarian

    c. Personal care aid

    d. Retail salesperson

3. You have not been feeling well and after you see a doctor and she conducts some tests, she tells you that you may have an extremely rare disease that only 1 in 10,000 get. She also tells you that the tests she conducted, like most medical tests, have a 10% failure (or false positive) rate. How likely is it that you have the disease? Should you be worried?

4. If you were to look for words that include the letter "k" in a book, which words are you more likely to find?

    a. Words that start with the letter "k"?

    b. Or words that have "k" as their third letter?

5. Which of the following statements do you think is accurate?

   a. The world is more violent today than in the past 50–100 years.

   b. The majority of the world's population lives in middle-income countries.

   c. In the last 20 years, the proportion of the world population living in extreme poverty has almost halved.

   d. 80% of people around the world have some access to electricity.

   e. Only 20% of the world's 1-year-old children are getting vaccinated.

6. Maria just bought a $1,000 digital camera and needs a case for it. Which is she most likely to do?

   a. Buy the $50 case that is recommended when she is buying the camera

   b. Wait for a sale to buy a case for 20% less

7. You have just started your business and have several packages and options for your potential customers. You would obviously like to sell more of the expensive packages. What would be the best way to list them on your website?

   a. From least expensive to most expensive

   b. From most expensive to least expensive

   c. Alphabetically

   d. By color

8. You are a marketing manager for a health food chain and would like to encourage your customers to make better health choices by listing fat content on your products. Which would be a better option to use?

   a. This product is 90% lean

   b. This product contains only 10% fat

9. You are a salesperson for a solar company. Which of the approaches is most likely to help you make the sale?

   a. Going solar is going to help save money

   b. Not going solar is causing you to lose money

Group Work

In groups of 4–5 share and review your answers to each question.

1. What are the corresponding heuristics for each of the questions you answered?

2. How did they impact your response to each question?

CASE STUDY: JB'S TROUBLES

Jean Baptiste Honoré was very excited about his new job. After finishing his MS in accounting and graduating with honors, he had landed the perfect job in a small accounting firm just a few miles from his family home in Dorchester near Boston, Massachusetts. The pay was great, the benefits were excellent, and the firm was offering support for the CPA exam and a bonus and potential raise when he passed it. His supervisor, Dennis Hampton, told him that he would be working with several teams and departments on different projects so that he would have the opportunity to learn different areas of accounting. He could not ask for more!

Jean Baptiste's parents had immigrated to the United States after fleeing Haiti in the 1970s. They had faced considerable hardship, worked at many menial jobs to put their only son through college while also helping support a large extended family still in Haiti. Jean Baptiste felt the weight of his community and family on his shoulders as he started his new job. He was ecstatic that he would finally be able to fully contribute to the family. Life in the United States had not been easy for him or his family, but he knew that they would have faced a terrible situation back home. Jean Baptiste had often felt that he did not fit in, although they lived in a diverse neighborhood. College was not much better. He had joined the Black student association and an international student group where he got to speak French, a language he had learned at home, but neither felt quite right. The other students seemed too young and immature and too focused on partying. He had felt most at home with some of the other accounting "nerds," where his excellent study habits, his great accounting skills, and his quiet and serious personality made him a favorite teammate for class projects. He had high hopes for having a stronger sense of belonging in his new job.

Although Jean Baptiste was one of only a handful of minority employees at the company, he had felt welcome during the interviews and in the first few weeks in various orientation events. His boss and the senior partners seemed invested in his success. The other people all appeared to have a lot in common with him: Many were young, good at their jobs, dedicated accountants, and hard working. He was working with a group of five other new hires, three women and two other men. All three women and one of the men were Caucasian, and the other member of his team was Asian, part Vietnamese and part Chinese. They made a good team and were supportive of one another. For the first time in a while, he actually felt at home.

Right from the start, JB, as he came to be called—his name was too hard and too long Dennis told him—was put on several easy projects that were right up his alley. He appreciated starting with simple tasks so he could demonstrate how well prepared and competent he was. He was also happy that he was working with minority clients who quickly came to rely on him. Their business was pretty routine, but JB was glad to be able to contribute to people from his own neighborhood that he often got to visit since much of his work was done off-site with the clients. He was initially fine with the arrangement and he made sure not to bother Dennis while giving him regular updates. He did not hear much from Dennis, except for an occasional "great job" and "we are so glad you have joined us" in emails when he sent in reports. Everyone was friendly and nice, the atmosphere was relaxed, and few people wore suits or ties, something Jean Baptiste found a bit strange. He was used to dressing up formally and thought his colleagues looked a bit sloppy. As one of the few minorities in the firm, he certainly did not want to make a bad impression. He also knew that his clients expected him to look like the professional that he was.

After 4 months, the work was getting boring. Doing taxes, some HR work, and helping small business owners with their books was fine, but it got old fast. Jean Baptiste was applying what he had learned, but there was little challenge, and for the most part, he felt like he was a bookkeeper, not an accountant. And he was not learning much. However, he was very busy, and he noticed that he had more clients than his other team members, which did not leave him much time to study for the CPA exam. Some of his team members were getting together to study after work, seemed to know the senior partners well, and often chatted about office politics and gossip which he knew nothing about. Jean Baptiste was beginning to feel isolated.

He decided to ask Dennis for a lighter work load and new projects that would challenge him and keep him in the office more. He told him he needed time to study for the exam and to make sure he connects with others in the firm. Dennis replied that new projects would be coming soon, but that they needed him where he was. He also jokingly asked him: "So how can you handle new projects if you are already overwhelmed and don't have time to study? Which one is it? Too much or too little?" Jean Baptiste was taken aback; he had been very clear about the need for challenge. The rest of his team and several of the younger associates had already worked on multiple projects and two of them had already taken sections of their CPA exam. He knew that they had fewer clients than him. So, he pushed back, gently, and told Dennis that he was looking for new projects to broaden his experience, not more of the same. A few days later, Dennis sent him an email with "Congratulations JB!" in the subject line. He had assigned him to two new projects as he had asked and would be replacing a retiring partner on the board of two nonprofits that were important clients of the firm. Not exactly what Jean Baptiste had asked for, but he thought that it was a great honor to replace a partner, until he found out that both organizations were small minority-run community groups and part of the firm's community outreach.

Jean Baptiste's six-month review was "just fine." Dennis told him he was doing great and helping the firm with their presence in the minority community, something that they had been planning to do for a long time. He just needed to be patient and not push so hard; he needed to work on being a better team player. Not exactly what Jean Baptiste expected…Four out of the five other people who had started with him had passed their CPA exam and received a substantial bonus and raise. He did not see much hope. He was hesitant to chat with Dennis again and worried to seem pushy. Two weeks later, Jean Baptiste accepted a job with a large accounting firm and gave his notice. Dennis was very surprised and felt betrayed. He told one of the partners: "I gave him everything he asked for; I really counted on him and he clearly did not appreciate all that we did for him! It's a shame."

Questions

1. What role does social perception play in the case?

2. What biases and heuristics are impacting Jean Baptiste's perception of the situation?

3. What biases and heuristics are impacting Dennis' treatment of Jean Baptiste?

4. What are the elements of Jean Baptiste's cultural identity? What role do they play in the events of the case?

5. What do you think could have been done to prevent Jean Baptiste from resigning?

CHAPTER FOUR

VIEWS OF CULTURE AND ACCULTURATION

FIRST PERSON

I Became Just Zeki

After earning my MBA in the United States and working 7 years in different countries including the United States and Germany, I came back to my home country, Turkey, to work for Kimberly Clark, a large American multinational consumer goods company. My job was to establish the business for Kimberly Clark, launch their brands, and look for possible partnerships to grow their Turkish operation. Right away, the members of my team started calling me "Zeki Bey," as "Bey" is a term of respect in Turkish culture. It is standard in the Turkish culture to call people of higher rank by adding "Bey—for men" or "Hanim—for women" after their name. Enthusiastically, and with pride, I insisted that they be more informal and call me just "Zeki." I had learned through my MBA program and in my experience in my foreign assignments that informality and approachability are effective management styles, so I followed the same path here. I knew that it was difficult to implement this in the Turkish culture that is more hierarchical, but I was determined to help my team members learn and grow. They were hesitant and clearly uncomfortable, but I did not give up. It took some doing, but after a few months, I finally became just Zeki. Quickly after that, the team members appeared much more relaxed, started being increasingly informal, and acted as if we were friends and at the same managerial level. At first, I saw these behaviors as signs that my informal style was having the desired effect. However, I realized that the familiarity and removal of rank barriers had some unintended consequences: I had also lost my authority! They no longer took me seriously and they were not doing their work. Things were especially difficult when I was giving them feedback regarding low performance; they would get very upset since friends do not criticize friends. It was a disastrous experience for me, and I quickly came to regret what seemed to be a simple decision to have

Learning Objectives

4.1 Explore the presence and consequences of in-group and out-group and the "Us-vs-Them" mentality on management.

4.2 Define the three views of culture, parochialism, ethnocentrism, and pluralism, and elaborate on their impact and consequences on the Cultural Mindset (CM).

4.3 Detail the concept and process of acculturation and its impact on organizations.

4.4 Elaborate on key acculturation strategies and acculturative stress.

4.5 Discuss the case of expatriates and their adaptation to new cultures.

4.6 Appraise the role of views of culture in developing a CM.

them call me by my first name. Performance was declining and I had lost the authority and clout to do much about it. I realized that what I had learned in the United States and had worked for me abroad was just not working at home. My only option was a painful restructuring in my team with a heavy cost to my company and a big lesson for me.

–Zeki Pagda, PhD

The *First Person* anecdote illustrates how rules that work in one context do not necessarily work in another. In this case, the tried-and-true informal management style that is natural and often expected in the United States and some other countries backfires in the Turkish context. Does this indicate that one approach is better than the other? In a US-based organization, should US management wisdom be imposed or should the Turkish practices prevail? These are topics we address in this chapter by considering how we view our own culture in relation to others and how we resolve the many small and large conflicts that inevitably arise when we come in contact with people who have different values and views related to how the world works and should work. At the core of these discussions are issues related to whether you consider culture to be a critical factor in determining thinking and behavior, and how you view the relative position of your culture and its associated assumptions, values, and beliefs when compared to others. Are you proud of your culture? Do you think it is superior to others at least on some dimensions? Should others do what you do? Do you believe that all cultures have equal value? When you interact with diverse groups, how do you determine whose cultural norms should prevail? When individuals from different cultures interact, how do they adapt to one another's cultures? These are important matters for managers to be aware of and address since they speak to the core of whose rules and management systems should be implemented in today's multicultural organizations. How managers solve these questions depends on their cultural software and the culture-as-meta-context (CMC) that they bring to any situation.

In this chapter, we will explore the processes and consequences of belonging to various groups and cultures and forming in-groups, elaborate on how we view our own culture in relation to others, a key factor in the Cultural Mindset (CM), and discuss the various options for interacting with other cultures, including the case of expatriates who live and work in cultures other than their own.

1. IN-GROUPS AND OUT-GROUPS

LO 4.1 Explore the presence and consequences of in-group and out-group and the "Us-vs-Them" mentality on management

American *Exceptionalism*; China as the Middle Kingdom (*Zhonggo*); Iranians as the only holders of true art; the uniqueness of Japan (*Nihonjinron*); French cultural superiority;

Britain's superior legal system; the Argentine sense of being better than other South Americans.... These are all examples of how members of different cultures view themselves as unique, and maybe a little bit better than others. There is no cultural group that does not have some sense of being special and extraordinary:

- American Exceptionalism refers to the country being distinctive among all others in history (Tyrrell, 2016).

- The Mandarin name for China is *Zhongguo*, which translates into middle or central kingdom or country, reflecting the Chinese belief that their country is the center of the world, geographically and culturally.

- Iranians often refer to a popular poem by Ferdowsi, a 10th-century poet, that states that they are the *only* ones who have true art.

- *Nihonjinron* refers to the uniqueness of the Japanese identity that includes, among other characteristics, association with the collective, closeness to nature, and a belief in having an unparalleled language (Befu, 2001).

- The French are known to believe in their cultural and intellectual preeminence (Hazareesingh, 2015).

- The British consider themselves superior to most other nations, certainly to other continental Europeans (O'Reilley, 2017).

- Argentines think themselves more European than other Central and South American countries, and therefore superior to them (Romero & Gilbert, 2014).

The list is long and further includes other examples such as the Danes, who although often humble regarding their place in the world, have considerable pride in their unique practice of coziness (Hygge; Altman, 2016). Similarly, the Swedes tout their appreciation for balance and moderation as being "perfect-simple" (Langom; Hart, 2017) and the Dutch are proud of their ability to do nothing (Niksen; Spector, 2019). Whether it is because of wealth, ancient history, political or legal systems, ethnicity, food, art, living standards, or any other dimensions, every cultural group demonstrates cultural pride and sees itself as separate and distinct and values its own culture and traditions. This sense of being special is inherent in cultural pride and identity and, when accompanied by disdain for others, can cause members of any culture to be accused of having a sense of superiority.

The underlying reasons and consequences for the sense of self-importance are diverse, but they almost always contain pride in your group and your culture with a concomitant belief about being better than others. This belief often engenders a dualistic view of an in-group vs. out-group, and sometimes, an "Us-vs-Them" attitude. The stronger the identification with one group, the stronger the potential for such an attitude. While the presence of in-groups and out-groups provides individuals and groups with certain benefits, it also creates distinct challenges, particularly when working and managing in cross-cultural environments.

1.1 Characteristics of In- and Out-Groups

Having a cultural identity inevitably means that you belong to some groups and not to others (Abrams & Hogg, 2006; Tajfel & Turner, 1986). As we have explored in previous chapters, some of us belong to several groups while others may claim membership in one or a few. *In-groups* are the group to which we belong, with members who are similar to us and whose welfare concerns us. *Out-groups* include those we perceive as different and distant from us. In Chapter 3, we discussed that belonging to a group is an essential and beneficial aspect of our cultural identity. That group membership further provides a point of reference and the ability to validate who we are, how we view the world, and how we manage and lead in organizations; it is the context in CMC.

1.1.1 In-Groups and Cultural Identity. As illustrated in the *First Person* example, cultural identity can be both based on nationality and other factors. The Turkish manager was defining himself as part of the US managerial culture as well as a Turk. The US-American part of his identity called for different behaviors than his employees' Turkish culture. Similarly, consider the example of a female Japanese-American manager working in the financial industry. Her behavior at work and her style as a manager will be influenced by her complex cultural identities, which are based on her US nationality, her Japanese ethnic group membership, and her professional group identity, as well as her own personality. At various points, she may have to decide which cultural norms are more important to her and which group is her in-group and which are her out-groups? Should she be direct and to the point, as her national and professional cultures prescribe, or more indirect and subdued as her ethnic cultural identity might recommend? How does she craft her managerial style based on membership in these various groups?

1.1.2 Features of In- and Out-Groups. We define ourselves based on our membership and belonging to various groups. Table 4.1 summarizes the characteristics and features of in- and out-groups. The in-group members are familiar and safe; people in the out-group can be perceived either as simply different, as inferior, or even as a threat because of their differences. Furthermore, humans have evolved to trust members of their in-group (Romano, Balliet, Yamagishi, & Liu, 2017). We expect greater cooperation from them and are more concerned about our reputation among them (Yamagishi, Jin, & Kiyonari, 1999). We are also more likely to trust those who belong to our in-group and

Table 4.1 In- and Out-Groups

Members of the In-Group—Us	Members of the Out-Group—Them
Familiar	Unfamiliar; strangers
Similar to me	Different from me
Safe	Threatening; dangerous
Trustworthy	Shifty
Normal; how things are supposed to be	Unusual; outside the norm
Friends	Adversaries; enemies
Even exchange and reciprocity	Transactional interactions
Validate our perspective	Challenge our perspective
Sense of obligation to treat people fairly	Willingness to lie to and cheat out-group members
Assumptions, values, beliefs, and rituals taken for granted	Assumptions, values, beliefs, and rituals closely examined
Predictable	Surprising

lie more easily to members of the out-groups (Mealy, Stephan, & Urrutia, 2007). We share a common CMC with members of our in-group; we have similar assumptions, values, beliefs, and behaviors that we consider natural and normal. Members of various out-groups have different assumptions, values, beliefs, and behaviors that may challenge our perspectives and appear to be outside the norm. Some out-groups may be perceived as very distant while others may seem close to us. For example, American Europeans are likely to see other Europeans as out-groups with whom they share many cultural characteristics, while individuals from Asia or the Middle East may be perceived as out-groups that are more distant and dissimilar. Likewise, to a Mexican-American, other Latin Americans may be part of out-groups, but less distant than Eastern Europeans.

1.2 Sources of In- and Out-Groups

How people are classified as in- or out-groups who are either close or distant is complex and multifaceted. The Turkish manager in our *First Person* example and our Japanese-American manager both had to decide who their in- and out-groups were.

Throughout history, neighboring countries, regions, and tribes have seen the "other" as different and often inferior in some way. These views of cultures sometimes have long historical or religious origins, such as in Ireland between Catholics and Protestants, the Chinese and the Japanese, the Southern and Northern Indians, or the French and Germans. In other cases, they are based on social class and economic differences or ethnicity and race. Upper classes (the 1% as they have been recently called) have disdain for those with less means (the "moochers"); the natives or those who have immigrated in earlier times consider new immigrants as less worthy; different ethnic groups see one another negatively, and so forth. In yet other situations, the in- and out-groups are based on artificial and arbitrary differences, such as the deadly conflict between Hutus and Tutsis in Rwanda in 1994 that led to the slaughter of an estimated 500,000 to 1 million people. In that case, the differences between the Hutus, who were farmers, and the Tutsis, who were livestock herders, were intentionally amplified by the colonial powers that ruled the region until they reached the explosive genocidal end.

Research has shown that this "Us-vs-them" feeling can form very quickly when different groups interact. The origin can even be superficial, arbitrary, and completely insignificant differences. For example, in the classic Robbers Cave experiment, the random assignment of boys to competing teams during a summer camp led to the formation of strong bonds within their groups and negative stereotypes of the other group and resulted in verbal and physical aggression (Sherif, Harvey, White, Hood, & Sherif, 1961). Similarly, when third-grade teacher Jane Elliot whose goal was to demonstrate the effect of racism assigned children to a superior and inferior group based on eye color, the children quickly adopted strong stereotypes of the other group and mistreated the "inferior" group (A class divided, 1985). It does not take much to create this Us-vs-Them feeling among different groups. National, ethnic, and group cultures are one of the primary sources of this attitude as we identify with our own group and consider others as outsiders. But its origin can be much simpler and more superficial.

Robert Kovach, director of *Leader Success* for Cisco corporation, observed the impact of color group assignment in the London marathon:

> *The competitive nature of some participants is so high that this random color assigned is enough to evoke an* identity. *We essentially become red, blue, or green* tribes *and, when meeting a group of the other color, we are encountering members of one of the other tribes. (Kovach, 2017)*

Similar processes occur when people join competing business organizations and form strong allegiances to them. Several legendary business rivalries such as Coke vs. Pepsi, Ford vs. GM, Microsoft vs. Apple, or more recently iPhone vs. Android engage employees and customers into identifying with a product or company and create a dualistic approach that triggers strong feelings. In the case of the first two examples, the Us-vs-Them rivalry prevented those companies and their managers from perceiving the competitive threats coming from Red Bull and Toyota (Fortune Editors, 2013).

1.3 Consequences and "Us-vs-Them"

As our discussion above indicates, the sense of in-group and out-group exists because it provides many benefits to the members of the in-group. The sense of belonging, the validation, the cohesion, and trust can provide a comfortable and supportive environment and a sense of physical and psychological safety. The in-group's norms can further provide guidelines to behavior. However, it can also present serious challenges. With a strong and beneficial sense of "we" and group-based identity comes an equally strong, and sometimes harmful, sense of "they" that can lead to negative views of the "other" and the development of the "Us-vs-Them" attitude. For example, a feeling of animosity toward another country can impact consumers' choices where they show less inclination to purchase goods from a country they do not favor (Klein, 2002). Moreover, it can just as easily operate at the group level and between and within organizations with additional practical implications. Management vs. labor, doctors vs. nurses, sales vs. manufacturing, knowledge workers vs. production workers, Baby Boomers vs. Millennials, and faculty vs. administration are all instances of identifying with one group and seeing the other groups as inferior and as potential threats. We like those in our group, show them favoritism, treat them better while we are less positive toward those who are not part of our group.

In other instances, a strong dualistic view is blamed for lack of engagement and motivation in organizations (Haken, 2018; Reiger, 2011). Employees from one organization, referring to management, stated: "They said they had an open-door policy. But the door was never open. We didn't dare even come into the office unless we were invited" a factor that prevented them from sharing their ideas (Fotsch & Case, 2016). In yet another example where the success of a merger between direct-marketing company Draft and Foote Cone & Belding (FCB) was threatened, Marty Stock, one of the heads of advertising at FCB, stated: "The differences drove an 'us' and 'them' mentality which was never really resolved, and which made integration unbelievably difficult" (Fondrevay, 2018). In the London marathon example, cited earlier, the creation of arbitrary color-based tribes led to booing those who were not part of each competing group's *tribe* (Kovach, 2017).

Figure 4.1 presents some of the consequences of the Us-vs-Them mentality. Some suggest that the "Us-vs-Them" approach causes fear and closed-mindedness and can not only hurt when applied within organizations but also do damage even when working across organizations (Blomstrom, 2019). If assumptions, values, and beliefs of your in-group are the norm, meaning they define what is normal, and the standard by which behaviors should be evaluated, the culture of the out-group can

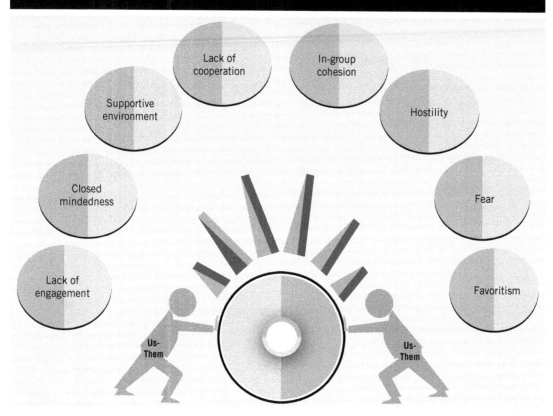

Figure 4.1 Consequences of Us-vs-Them

then be perceived as abnormal and deviant, justifying potential hostility toward members of that out-group (De, Gelfand, Nau, & Roos, 2015). In other words, when your culture or your group becomes *the* culture or group, you are more likely to engage in an "Us-vs-Them" mentality. For example, recent research about the impact of having strong political affiliations in the United States indicates that this "Us-vs-Them" approach isolates members of each of the groups and increases the likelihood of them misperceiving members of the other group (Ahler & Sood, 2018). Specifically, according to this research, Republicans think that 32% of Democrats are members of the LGBTQ community (6% is the actual number), and Democrats believe that 38% of Republicans earn over $250,000 a year (2% is the correct percentage; Ahler & Sood, 2018).

Based on the information we just presented, we can draw some conclusions regarding identification with in-groups and out-groups:

- The presence of different groups is a fact of life; we live in a complex and culturally diverse world.

- Belonging to one or more groups and having a cultural identity are necessary, desirable, and unavoidable.

- The presence of in- and out-groups has both positive and negative consequences.

- Having an "Us-vs-Them" mentality is the most negative consequence of having in- and out-groups.

- Having an "US-vs-Them" mentality that sees the other as a threat is preventable while maintaining the benefits of in-groups.

The extent to which we have a strong sense of in-group and out-group and an Us-vs-Them attitude toward other cultures is reflected in our views of culture and our expectations regarding cultural interactions. These views are part of our CMC and impact the CM. There are a variety of options for how one views and interacts with other cultures; we consider them next.

2. THREE VIEWS OF CULTURE

LO 4.2 Define the three views of culture, parochialism, ethnocentrism, and pluralism, and elaborate on their impact and consequences on the Cultural Mindset (CM)

We have a wide range of options regarding how we view our in-groups and our own cultures in relation to others. We can consider people who are not part of our groups as inferior, hostile, and abnormal or simply as people who are different from us. We can have a strong cultural identity and considerable cultural pride with or without a sense of superiority.

2.1 Definitions and Overlapping Views

Figure 4.2 presents a visual of those options with the three general views of culture as separate, but related and overlapping. *Parochialism* is defined as having a strong attraction to one's in-group and being centered on one's own community, region, religion, or culture (and even organization). *Ethnocentrism* is defined as the belief that one's country, culture, ethnic group, tribe, or way of life (and even organization) is unique, predominant, and superior to others (Levine & Campbell, 1972).

Figure 4.2   Views of Culture

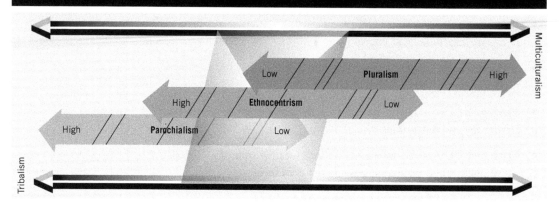

Pluralism is defined as the view that all cultures have equal value and should all be respected and appropriately represented.

We will discuss each view of culture in detail next, but first consider the representation in Figure 4.2. The three views of culture are presented each on a separate continuum with different polarities, stacked on top of one another, indicating a possible progression from one to the other. This representation indicates that each is a different, multifaceted, and independent view of culture, rather than ends of a continuum. Individuals can be anywhere on each of the continua simultaneously. At one extreme, a person who has a high parochial view is not likely to agree with any aspect of a pluralistic view of culture. That view involves a tribal approach where *tribalism* is defined as loyalty to one's in-group or tribe with a strong sense of superiority; it is associated with a strong Us-vs-Them attitude where the out-group is seen as a threat and treated with hostility. For example, a manager may believe that the formal and top-down approach to management he has learned through his experience is appropriate in all settings regardless of the makeup of his team. He may then see any of his younger team members' request for participation and openness as inappropriate, offensive, and a challenge to his authority.

At another extreme is multiculturalism where someone with a high pluralistic view is similarly not likely to agree with any aspect of the parochial view. *Multiculturalism* is defined as the coexistence of equal and diverse cultures where cultures are assumed to contribute equivalent value. In the middle of Figure 4.2 are various combinations of the three views where one may believe in pluralism, and be both ethnocentric and parochial to some extent. In other words, although there is a progression of sorts from believing that only your in-group and culture matter and have value to fully valuing all groups and cultures equally, the fact that we all have distinctive cultural identities that we hold with varying degrees of pride and affection, and therefore belong to some groups and not others, causes most of us to hold some elements of all three views of culture. For example, while most managers are likely to habitually fall back on and prefer management styles they have learned through experience or as part of their culturally based education, they may become more accepting of other approaches when they encounter employees who are culturally diverse and who would perform best when managed differently. We define and explore each view of culture in detail next and consider their possible interaction and impact on the CM and managing across cultures. Table 4.2 presents a summary of the characteristics of parochial, ethnocentric, and plural views.

2.2 Parochialism: "My World Is the Only World"

Parochialism implies a local and narrow focus, seeing only one side of things, and deriving one's identity from one's in-group (Hofstede, Hofstede, & Minkow, 2010). For a person with a parochial view, their "small" world is the *only* world with the assumption

Table 4.2 Comparison of Three Views of Culture		
Parochialism *"My world is the only one"*	**Ethnocentrism** *"My world is the best one"*	**Pluralism** *"My world is one of many"*
Synonyms: provincial, insular	*Synonyms: chauvinistic, intolerant*	*Synonyms: multicultural, polycentric*
• Lack of awareness of presence or impact of cultures • "People are people" mentality • Intuitive attachment and pride in own way of life • Lack of interest in others • Mindless in-group favoritism • Subconscious assumption that one's views are the norm • Unaware of biases • Operate in automatic System I—unaware of need to slow down	• Awareness of presence of other cultures • Recognition of cultural differences • Conscious attachment and pride in own culture • Conscious sense of superiority • Deliberate in-group favoritism • Conscious view of own culture as the norm and the "best way" • Active use of biases to support own view • Operate in System I—unwilling to slow down	• Awareness of presence and impact of cultures • Recognition of cultural differences and their impact on people • Conscious attachment and pride in own culture • Cultural relativism • Belief in equality and value of all cultures • Appreciation for own and other cultures • Deliberate neutrality—CJI • Aware of biases and active attempts to try to counteract • Operate in System I and able to activate System II when needed

that the rules from that world automatically apply in all other settings. Words such as provincial (having a limited outlook) or insular are sometimes used as synonyms to parochialism. Others (e.g., Bennett, 1986, 1993) have called this approach a denial of culture. Whereas being provincial and insular have derogatory connotations, parochialism can be relatively neutral. Some have even suggested that it can offer potential benefits (Tomaney, 2012). For example, research shows that people draw many benefits from focusing on their in-group (Fessler et al., 2015; Yamagishi, Jin, & Kiyonari, 1999), and that a parochial approach supports cooperation and the development of a sense of reciprocity within a group (Yamagishi & Mifune, 2008). The desire to belong to a group and attachment to a place, which are further aspects of parochialism, are suggested to be inherent to the human experience (Tuan, 1977). American writer Lucy Lippard (1998) has proposed that the "lure of the local" which attaches us to a place is a powerful and spiritual force for human beings. Therefore, some degree of parochialism appears to be part of our human experience.

2.2.1 Elements of Parochialism. Parochialism has several key elements:

- First, it involves *not recognizing culture's impact* on people and organizations (Adler & Gundersen, 2008) and a corresponding lack of awareness of other cultures and perspectives (Gelfand, Leslie, & Fehr, 2008). For example, a manager with a parochial view would believe that "people are people" and that there is no need to consider cultural differences or modify her approach when leading team members with different cultural backgrounds.

- Second, because of the lack of recognition of culture, people with a parochial view are *unaware* that their own perspective and behaviors are determined by culture. Therefore, they are likely to assume that their assumptions, values, and beliefs and practices are simply the norm. A manager would assume the same motivation approach, the one that works for him, will work for everyone regardless of culture or the context. The belief is therefore that there is a right and a wrong way no matter the situation and context, and that the right way or the norm is based on one's own worldview.

- Third, parochialism is often accompanied by a *lack of interest in and/or knowledge* of other cultures and cultural perspectives. Managers with a parochial view may be ignorant of the world outside their area and show little interest in learning about what is not in their immediate surrounding.

Ruchita Chandrashekar, an Indian immigrant to the United States, recalls various comments she regularly hears including repeated referral to the movie *Slumdog Millionaire*, and expressing surprise that she speaks fluent English, that she was not a child-bride, and that her parents could afford to educate her (Chandrashekar, 2017).

2.2.2 Parochialism in All Cultures. Parochial views of culture are by no means unique to people in the United States. In China, the idea of parochialism or closed-mindedness, called *xiao nong* or petty peasant mentality, has long been used to explain lack of creativity and unwillingness to accept new ideas (Feng, Liu, & Jians, 2019). Recent research suggests that the pervasive parochial view held by some Chinese managers may be an obstacle to the global growth of Chinese businesses (Feng et al., 2019). Similarly, parochial views in Russia (Anders, 2013), Spain (The perils of parochialism, 2008), Japan (Dujarric, 2015), South Africa (Corrigan, 2019), and many other countries are blamed for closed-mindedness, lack of cooperation, and other negative outcomes. Researchers have noted that favoring one's in-group, something that has been called *altruistic parochialism*, can make cordial intergroup relations challenging (Halevy, Bornstein, & Sagiv, 2000). Additionally, calls for decolonizing knowledge (Fanon, 1952; Smith, 2018), which involves taking broader perspectives that go beyond Western cultures (i.e., the researchers' in-group) and integrating information from many different cultures, have been made in many disciplines, including management, psychology, international relations, and sociology, just to name a few.

2.2.3 Consequences of Parochialism. Extensive theory and research tell us that seeing the world from just one perspective, our own, can be unproductive. However, the difficulty may be that having a parochial mindset involves a lack of awareness of the impact of culture and its role in the biases we hold. It therefore entails overrelying on System I thinking (see Chapter 3). If we do not recognize that there are many different cultural contexts, we do not know that our worldview is not the only one. We therefore continue to depend on the fast and automatic thinking that works in our own culture, even when we cross cultural boundaries and the context changes; in other words, we do not know what we do not know. Consequently, we will not try to stop our automatic thinking to activate our deliberate System II that is essential in unfamiliar situations. We continue to operate as if every situation is the same as our own "small" world and continue to apply one set of rules to all situations.

Attachment to one's own culture, absence of awareness of the role of culture, ignoring its impact, lack of cultural knowledge, holding negative or hostile views toward other groups, and operating based on our automatic assumptions are all part and parcel of parochialism.

2.3 Ethnocentrism: "My World Is the Best World"

Similar to parochialism, ethnocentrism seems to be a natural part of the human experience. It involves pride in one's culture along with a sense of independence from others. As opposed to people with a parochial view, those with an ethnocentric view do not assume that people are the same everywhere. They are aware that there are many different cultures that can impact how people think and behave. However, they think that their own culture and its assumptions, values, beliefs, and practices are superior to others. For them, their culture provides the ideal norm that is more appropriate and desirable than others.

2.3.1 Elements of Ethnocentrism. Ethnocentrism and parochialism are sometimes used interchangeably. For example, Bennett (1986, 1993) considers denial of other cultures to be a stage of ethnocentrism with other stages including sense of superiority and trivialization of differences. However, ethnocentrism presents some differences with parochialism (see Table 4.2 for a comparison). The distinguishing characteristics of ethnocentrism are:

- *Deliberate pride and superiority* (Hammond & Axelrod, 2006) rather than the more unaware and uninformed attitudes that characterize parochialism. As opposed to parochialism, which often is mindless and intuitive, ethnocentrism involves a more conscious and mindful approach.

- *Awareness of the presence of other cultures* where the person with an ethnocentric view knows that his or her culture is not the only one.

- *A conscious preference for one's own* and demonstration of a clear sense of superiority with methodical favoritism toward their in-group. Whereas a manager with a parochial view is not likely to expect challenges when crossing cultural boundaries because she does not think that culture matters, a manager with an ethnocentric view would anticipate cultural shock when interacting with another culture since he believes that others have different approaches that are less desirable than his own. However, because of an ethnocentric view, the person would intentionally apply his own rules to people from other cultures.

- *Some awareness of one's own biases*, likely accompanied with belief that they are correct and should be used to support one's view. So, people are aware of their beliefs and the fact that others may disagree with them, but still believe that they are accurate and based on factual and legitimate information.

2.3.2 Consequences of Ethnocentrism. The case of Renee Bach who, at the age 19, went to Uganda to set up a charity she called "Serving His Children" to help malnourished children provides a dramatic example of the negative consequences of ethnocentrism (Aizenman & Gharib, 2019). Bach's nutrition center took in and "treated" 949 children between 2010 and 2015 without having a medical license or any medical personnel on staff. One hundred and five of the children died, a death rate that is much higher than other facilities in the country. With many good intentions, a strong religious faith that her work was God's plan, but no medical training, Bach believed that the poor Ugandan children did not have a better place to go, so she provided care for many who needed intensive medical attention. In one case, documented in her own blog, she refers to seeking advice on Google to make medical decisions (Aizenman & Gharib, 2019). Bach is being sued by the Ugandan government for practicing medicine without a license. Lawrence Gostin, the head of the Center on National and Global Health Law at Georgetown University, calls Bach's actions and attitude arrogance where "The American cultural narrative is that these countries are basket cases," resulting in "college kids to credentialed doctors routinely parachute [ing] into poor countries for medical missions that completely disregard local laws and conditions" (Aizenman & Gharib, 2019).

Business examples rarely have such serious consequences; nonetheless, ethnocentric attitudes affect business and management. For example, multinational companies that operate in a variety of countries focus on adapting the products and services that are developed in the West for distribution in local markets (Radjou, 2009) or send managers from the home country to various locations. In these cases, the focus is the home country and the exchange is unilateral. Many other multinational organizations have diversity in their managerial ranks but continue to appoint their top leaders from their home country. A case in point is Nintendo, the Japanese video game company, which in spite of its extensive global presence, has had only Japanese men in the top leadership position since its creation in 1889.

Because ethnocentrism involves a conscious sense of superiority and belief in the supremacy of one's culture and practices, individuals with such a view do not see a need to change. They often will overrely on System I thinking with no attempt at slowing down in different situations. People with ethnocentric views will see their "small" world not as the only world, but as the best world and therefore see no need to activate System II to be more deliberate and thoughtful in other cultural contexts.

The concept of ethnocentrism is widely used in business and international management. The popular press, training programs, and academic research have focused on the negative impact of ethnocentrism in a global and interconnected world. There is no country or cultural group, at any level, that does not demonstrate some degree of ethnocentrism. Having a cultural identity automatically leads to having pride in that identity and a preference for that identity, culture, and way of life over others. That pride is both desirable and can have positive effects on group cohesion and support for in-group members. However, pride does not need to be associated with a sense of superiority. The attitude that one's cultural assumptions, values, beliefs, and practices are superior to all others is the negative aspect of ethnocentrism and is problematic in a global and multicultural world (e.g., Benmamoun, Kalliny, Chun, & Kim, 2018). If everyone believes that their culture is not only good and worthy but also better than others and therefore should be dominant, cooperation and productive cross-cultural interactions become difficult, if not impossible.

2.4 Pluralism: "My World Is One of Many"

Because of an awareness that some aspects of parochialism and ethnocentrism are obstacles to effective interaction in a culturally diverse context, the concept of pluralism has gained considerable traction in management. Some have used the term *ethnorelativism* (Bennett, 1986, 1993) to indicate an approach that is accepting and welcoming to other cultures. In philosophy, the idea of pluralism suggests that there is more than one way of approaching the truth and accessing knowledge (Spencer, 2012). Pluralism is further akin to the concept of *cosmopolitanism*, which recognizes that human beings are different and can learn from one another's differences and recommends an openness to the world (Appiah, 2006). A pluralistic view is further associated with the idea of *cultural relativism* (Brown, 2008; Dall & Boas, 1887) that suggests that although truth exists, many values are relative to a cultural context (Booth, 2001).

2.4.1 Elements of Pluralism. Pluralism suggests that:

- All cultures are *valuable* and appropriate in their own right with each culture making unique contributions.

- *All cultures should be evaluated and assessed within their own context* rather than based on absolute standards. In other words, while the ethnocentric view would suggest that one group's assumptions and values are the norm and the right and best way by which other cultures should be evaluated, pluralism and cultural relativism assert that there are multiple norms, that what is right depends on the cultural context, and that any culture should be considered in its own right rather than compared to others—culture-just-is (CJI).

- Pluralism is associated with *respect for all cultures and cultural pride in one's own* culture. While parochialism involves automatic and mindless favoritism toward one's own group, and ethnocentrism is a conscious and deliberate view of one's culture as being superior, pluralism implies a conscious and deliberate choice to view cultures as neutral and equal.

Pluralism, multiculturalism, and relativism are the building blocks of CMC, CJI, and the CM that are central themes of this book. They are also inherent in the cultural diversity and inclusion approaches that have become commonplace in US organizations and many other parts of the world (we will elaborate on cultural diversity and inclusion in detail in Chapter 5).

2.4.2 Consequences of Pluralism. As we discussed in Chapter 3, people operate under the need to be efficient; our heuristics and biases drive our thinking. Having a plural view of culture does not change those processes. However, being aware of the presence and impact of culture and making a conscious decision to respect differences can help individuals become aware of the need to slow down their automatic System I thinking and activate their deliberate and thoughtful System II. Related to a pluralistic view, scholars and practitioners in international business and management have advocated for a *polycentric* orientation to managing across cultures (Amin, 2000). This orientation encourages managers to consider the uniqueness of each country and culture and to implement country and culture specific business and management practices in different settings. The polycentric business practices are part of many multinational companies where they have more than one center, employ different marketing and HR strategies (e.g., Thite, Wilkinson, & Shah, 2011), and even apply different criteria to strategic and ethical decisions (e.g., Jackson, 2000) in different countries and cultures.

For example, Nestlé, the world's largest food company that employs over 300,000 people in 447 factories in 189 countries, implements a polycentric approach in its human resources and marketing practices (https://www.nestle.com). In each country, local managers run various divisions and market products that address local tastes. Similarly, McDonald's provides considerable flexibility to its global restaurants so they offer different menu items including gazpacho in Spain, shrimp burgers in Korea, tzatziki wraps in Croatia, poutine in Canada, McPaneer Royale in India, chicken veggie burgers in Japan, and wine and macarons in France (Schlossberg, 2015). MTV International has also adopted a comparable polycentric approach by partnering with local companies through joint ventures to deliver programming in over 160 countries and 32 different languages. MTV UK head Kerry Taylor says: "People these days want to be local, but they see themselves as global citizens and we weren't making the most of the fact that we got this amazing global creative community" (Szalai, 2015).

2.4.3 Critiques of Pluralism. The ideas of pluralism and cultural relativism, and the corresponding cultural diversity practices in organizations, have become hallmarks of progressive and antidiscriminatory practices in society. They have also been widely discussed in philosophy where some have suggested all cultures share some common minimal standards such as love, truth, and respect for life (Bok, 2002). However, these views are not without detractors and controversy (for an example see Malik, 2007). Critics have used examples of political correctness, claims that pluralism does not allow for cultural pride, and suggestions that heinous crimes such as genocide would be justified under cultural relativism as arguments that pluralism and multiculturalism are unacceptable (for a review see Booth, 2001). Many of these discussions have strong political undertones and implications and are beyond the scope of this book (for example, see United Nations documents about universality and diversity at https://www.ohchr.org/EN/NewsEvents/Pages/UniversalityReport.aspx or Galston, 2018). However, these debates have made their way to corporations and have implications for how we address and implement pluralism and cultural diversity practices in our organizations. For example, a Google employee's lengthy antidiversity manifesto that suggested that diversity efforts work against gender biological differences went viral in 2017 and was quickly condemned by many in the company (Liptak, 2017). Likewise, universities have come under attack for practicing "reverse discrimination" in the name of multiculturalism, diversity, and inclusion (Newkirk, 2017).

Some have also suggested that pluralism and multiculturalism create divisions rather than allow for better understanding among groups. For example, former British prime minister, David Cameron, in a speech about Islamist extremism in 2011 stated that the practice of multiculturalism has:

> ...encouraged different cultures to live separate lives, apart from each other and apart from the mainstream. We've failed to provide a vision of society to which they feel they want to belong. We've even tolerated these segregated communities behaving in ways that run completely counter to our values. (Cameron, 2011)

Others, such as Trevor Phillips, chairman of the UK Commission for Racial Equality, have stated that multiculturalism is out of date because it encourages separation of cultural groups (Multiculturalism, 2011).

These critiques can be addressed to some extent by exploring approaches to how cultures interact, a topic we discuss in the next section. People's views of culture shape their CMC and impact how they see their own culture and that of others. It also impacts the degree to which they have a CM. Depending on where your views are, you are more or less likely to be conscious of culture, your own and that of others, and its impact. You are also more or less likely to accept others as equal to you. We next discuss the various ways in which people adapt to their contact and interaction with other cultures.

3. ACCULTURATION: CULTURAL CONTACT AND ADAPTATION

LO 4.3 Detail the concept and process of acculturation and its impact on organizations

What happens when we move from one culture to another, come in contact with people who are in our out-groups, or interact with people from different cultures for extended periods of time? How do we resolve the challenges posed by facing

WINDOW TO THE WORLD

Doing Business in the United Arab Emirates

The United Arab Emirates (UAE) is one of the world's newest and richest countries, having been founded in 1971 as a federation of seven emirates that include Abu Dhabi, Dubai, Sharjah, Ajman, Umm Al Quwain Fujairah, and Ras al Khaimah. Its population of close to 10 million is made up of only 11.5% Emirati citizens with the remaining 88% made up of expatriates, which include many laborers from the Indian subcontinent as well as business people from around the world. The official language is Arabic. Most business travelers or tourists are likely familiar with Dubai, which has become a favorite destination, as a sunny, ultramodern, and flashy playground, financial center, and gateway to many other Middle Eastern, African, and Asian countries and markets. While both modern and highly Westernized on many levels, travelers must keep in mind that the UAE, including Dubai, has deep conservative Muslim roots that still govern formal and informal interactions and relationships. Here are some key factors to keep in mind:

- Dress and act modestly and conservatively. Formal business attire is typical for meetings, and while foreign women are not expected to cover up, as they are in Saudi Arabia or some other Muslim countries, they should be mindful of the local customs. Public displays of affection and loud and boisterous behaviors in public are not appropriate and will be met with swift official action.

- Hospitality, courtesy, and respect are the rule. Follow rules of etiquette and treat people with kindness, politeness, and respect and they are likely to fully reciprocate. These are tribal cultures with deep roots of desert hospitality; they highly value their guests.

- Invest in relationships and respect authority. As is the case in a large majority of the world, family, relationships, and community are primary, so establishing a connection before rushing into business is important, as is being mindful of the hierarchy and status of those you work with.

- Time is flexible and thinking is nonlinear. Be prepared for nothing being on time or going as planned. Conversations may appear chaotic and activities poorly organized; these are all part of the culture and not an indication of lack of competence or respect for you, so stay calm and go with the flow.

- Avoid discussions of politics, religion, and social issues. While this is always good advice for guests, unless you have expertise or are clearly called upon to contribute to such discussions, as a guest, it is best to avoid these topics.

Many, particularly business people, in the UAE have extensive experience with the West and speak English. However, the UAE is an Arab country that, although young with a short history, has strong cultural traditions. Take the time to do your research and prepare before you interact with people and before you travel.

differences in assumptions, values, beliefs, and practices and realizing that our rules may not work or apply? Acculturation addresses these challenges.

3.1 Definition of Acculturation

Acculturation is defined as the process by which two cultural groups that have come in continuous and direct contact resolve the inevitable conflicts and challenges that arise from their contact resulting in changes in one or both groups (Redfield, Linton, & Herkovitz, 1936). It involves a psychological and cultural change in the individual and the group due to sustained contact with another culture (Berry, 2005). It addresses the interaction among cultures and how they combine their various elements and how individuals who come in contact with another culture relate to it. Acculturation can take place both at the individual level or group levels where a person or a group undergo psychological changes in assumptions, values, beliefs, or behaviors after contact and interaction with other cultures (Berry, 1997). When people come in contact with other cultures, they react in a variety of ways. Some ignore the other culture and avoid further contact while others learn each other's languages, share cultural elements, or adopt and modify each other's values and practices.

It is important to note that acculturation addresses sustained or continuous interaction rather than short-term contact such as during tourism or one-time negotiations. Many of our business interactions and encounters fall in this sustained category. We work with team members and managers who come from different cultures for extended periods of time; we build long-term relationships with our suppliers; we establish enduring ties with partners in other regions and countries; and we send expatriates (expats) and their families to live and work abroad for significant periods of time. All of these interactions are long term and involve acculturation. In anthropology and cross-cultural psychology, acculturation focuses on how colonial or dominant cultures interact with the less dominant or immigrant populations, often considering the role of power in these relationships (e.g., Berry, 1997). However, the process of acculturation has also been applied to many other types of interactions where cultures come into contact with one another including understanding how organizational cultures interact in mergers and acquisitions (Nahavandi & Malekzadeh, 1988), during intercultural training (Bhawuk, Landis, & Lo, 2016), or how first-year students with disability adapt to college (Whitaker, 2018).

In a general sense, understanding the acculturation process can explain how we expect different cultural groups to interact. Should one group dominate the other? Should all cultures be preserved? Should they combine their cultural elements or each remain separate? The views of culture that we reviewed in the first part of this chapter play a role in how we engage in these challenges.

3.2 Examples of Different Types of Acculturation

Consider the following examples that all involve two or more cultures coming in contact and resolving how they will adapt to each other.

- Google in Nigeria is providing their google map app narrated in a Nigerian-accented English along with the British accent.

- Every major city in the United States has cultural enclaves such as China Town, Little Italy, Little Korea, or Little Havana where specific ethnic groups along with their culture, language, food, and art are dominant.

- Businesses offer formal interest groups for women and members of under-represented groups to provide mentoring and support their success; these groups coexist in conjunction with other onboarding and talent development programs.

- In many countries, radio and TV stations and news outlets in different languages serve various cultural groups alongside media in the dominant language.

- Immigrant families name their children using names from their new country, sometimes along with their own cultural names.

- The "English Only" movement in the United States advocates making English the only and official language in government operations while some states provide official documents in multiple languages corresponding to several large immigrant populations in those states or cities. For example, Los Angeles County prints election ballots in at least nine languages including the recent addition of Punjabi, Hmong, Syriac, Armenian, Persian, and Arabic.

- German, French, and Italian are the official governmental languages in Switzerland, and each region in the country, known as a canton, has the authority to establish its own language.

- There has been a continued struggle in Canada to establish the extent to which English and French, and their corresponding cultural elements, are the two official languages of the country.

- The *melting pot*, a metaphor for all cultures blending together, has been used as a descriptor of the immigrant assimilation practice in the United States.

- The *salad bowl* or *cultural mosaic* are the metaphors commonly used to describe immigration in Canada, and more recently also used by some in the United States.

- German was the second most commonly spoken language in the United States from the 17th to the beginning of the 20th century with many German schools and a thriving press. The language saw a steep decline during World War I.

- Immigrant families celebrate holidays from their home country together with those of their newly adopted country. For example, in the United States, Indian Hindus, Jains, and Sikhs celebrate Diwali (the Festival of Lights) or Iranians celebrate Nowruz (the Persian new year) while also celebrating Thanksgiving, the New Year on January 1, and Independence Day.

- Indian Residential Schools established in the United States during the 19th century, with the last one closing in the 1970s, removed Native children from their families and forced them to give up their language and culture with the goal of assimilating them. Similar schools operated in Canada, Australia, the Soviet Union, and other countries, all with the goal of erasing cultural elements through education.

These are all examples of how cultural groups acculturate to another culture. Every time two cultural groups come in contact, the differences in their assumptions, values, beliefs, and practices require a decision, sometimes minor and sometimes major, sometimes conscious sometimes subconscious, regarding how they will interact and whose rules will be applied to understand and interpret the world.

3.3 The Acculturation Process

Regardless of the circumstances, the acculturation process ensues when two different cultures, as a group or an individual, interact while bringing their own assumptions, values, beliefs, and practices, and their own CMC. In all cases, the typical acculturation process occurs in three steps (see Figure 4.3).

3.3.1 Contact. The first step of acculturation occurs when individuals and groups from different cultures come in contact. The contact and exchange may start with brief encounters that eventually are sustained or take place over a period of time. For example, an expat manager may have had many shorter contacts with business partners from a certain country while still at home or during short business trips, but eventually the contact will become more extensive when he moves to the host country, at which point the length and depth of contact with coworkers in organizational settings, and with others in that community increase. In the case of expats, a very large majority moves with family members who interact with local communities and people in more diverse settings than the expat manager.

3.3.2 Conflict. Conflict is likely to occur when disagreements between members of two cultures over assumptions, values, beliefs, practices, and so forth occur. Conflict is

Figure 4.3   Steps in Acculturation

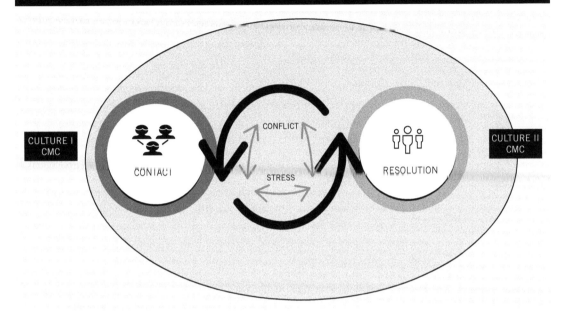

CULTURE I CMC

CONTACT

CONFLICT

STRESS

RESOLUTION

CULTURE II CMC

expected and does not mean winners or losers; it simply means that there is disagreement. Whether small or large or significant or trivial, disagreements over many different elements are inevitable. Some of the conflict may be over central norms and fundamental assumptions; others may be over minor and more peripheral issues. For example, a manager from a culture where there are strict gender norms and where few women play significant roles in the workplace may have difficulty interacting with women who are his colleagues or his superiors during his assignment in a country like Sweden or the United States. The conflict in this case is caused by differences in two cultures' assumptions regarding gender roles. Sarah O'Meara, who moved from the United Kingdom to Shanghai, states a conflict similarly related to basic assumptions: "The parameters governing everyday life in China are arbitrary and the final judgment comes from the most powerful person in the room" (Roberts, 2015). In other instances, there may be disagreement over more surface level differences such as use of teams, or a highly centralized organizational structure where the manager has to approve all processes before decisions can be implemented. It may also be over something that may appear trivial, such as the length of a lunch break. In the case of an expat family, such big and small cultural clashes they experience are cited as one of the primary reasons expat assignments fail and they request to return home (Vlachos, 2017).

The conflict that results in the sustained contact between two cultural groups often results in *acculturative stress*, which is the physiological, psychological, and behavioral reactions to the conflict (Berry, Kim, Minde, & Mok, 1987). Such conflicts are inevitable, and there must be some sort of resolution or adaptation which closes the loop of the acculturation process. However, the cycle is likely to continue as each contact and conflict may be different.

3.3.3 Resolution/Adaptation. The resolution of the conflict is the third step in acculturation (see Figure 4.3). In this step the two cultural groups or individuals reach some decision regarding how the conflict is resolved and how their cultural differences should be handled. There are two key questions that guide how a group decides to resolve the conflict (Berry, 1997, 2005):

1. To what extent do members of each group want to maintain their cultural elements? In other words, how much are they willing to change and adapt? They have to consciously and subconsciously decide which of their assumptions, values, beliefs, and practices they want to keep and which ones they may give up.

2. To what extent do they want to adopt assumptions, values, beliefs, and practices of the other culture? In other words, how attracted are they to what the other group has to offer? They have to consciously and subconsciously decide which of the assumptions, values, beliefs, and practices of the other group they may be willing to integrate into their own culture.

Each person and each cultural group makes a different decision regarding these two questions. For example, consider that globalization and increased contact among cultures has led to the adoption of new foods. You can find Chinese food and Sushi in most countries; Mexican food is popular worldwide; French pastries and Italian dishes are ubiquitous almost in every major city around the world. Middle Eastern hummus is sold in many grocery stores. These are just surface behaviors, but at some point, cultural groups have made a decision to integrate the foods of other groups and have changed some of their eating habits as a result.

Gender equality provides another example of how groups that come into contact resolve their differences. Women's right to vote and work and other laws establishing gender equality have been part of some, but not all, cultures for more than a century. Increased direct contact between cultures around the globe, through business inter-actions, political and diplomatic exchanges, and students studying in universities outside their country, all create conflict regarding gender equality. Global contacts have encouraged adoption and adaptation of some gender equality practices in cultures where they were not the norm, slowly changing values, beliefs, and practices regarding gender differences. Businesses, even in many countries where gender equality is not a dominant cultural norm, for example in the Middle East and South and Central America, increasingly take steps to hire and promote women to managerial and leadership ranks (Labor Force, Female, 2019).

In another example of acculturation in business, the use of teams, which was part of the business culture in Sweden and Japan for many years and supported by both countries' collectivistic cultural values, has become the norm in many other more individualistic countries such as the United States. The US basic assumptions regarding the preeminence of the individual, something we will discuss in detail in Chapters 7 and 8, have not changed, but organizational practices have adapted to teamwork as a result of sustained contact with other successful managerial practices. The *First Person* account at the beginning of this chapter further shows how a Turkish expat acculturated to the US MBA culture and the global business context by adopting the informal business practices valued in those contexts. He then faced another acculturative challenge and conflict when returning home. These changes are the product of acculturation where cultures change and adapt as a result of contact with others. The process of resolution and adaptation is the heart of acculturation, and we will consider different strategies and their connection to views of culture next.

4. ACCULTURATION STRATEGIES FOR ADAPTATION

LO 4.4 Elaborate on key acculturation strategies and acculturative stress

The answer to the two questions outlined above (What do we maintain and what do we adopt) are the basis for strategies related to how we interact with and acculturate to other cultures. Although people do not ask these questions consciously, they are at the heart of challenges we face when we come in sustained contact with other cultural groups. The combined answer to these questions yields four options presented in Figure 4.4. The four options are:

- Assimilation

- Integration

- Separation

- Marginalization

Table 4.3 provides a summary description of the four strategies for acculturation with each representing a different way of interacting with and acculturating to other cultures with many gradients in between. Keep in mind that each of the two groups

Figure 4.4 Four Acculturation Strategies

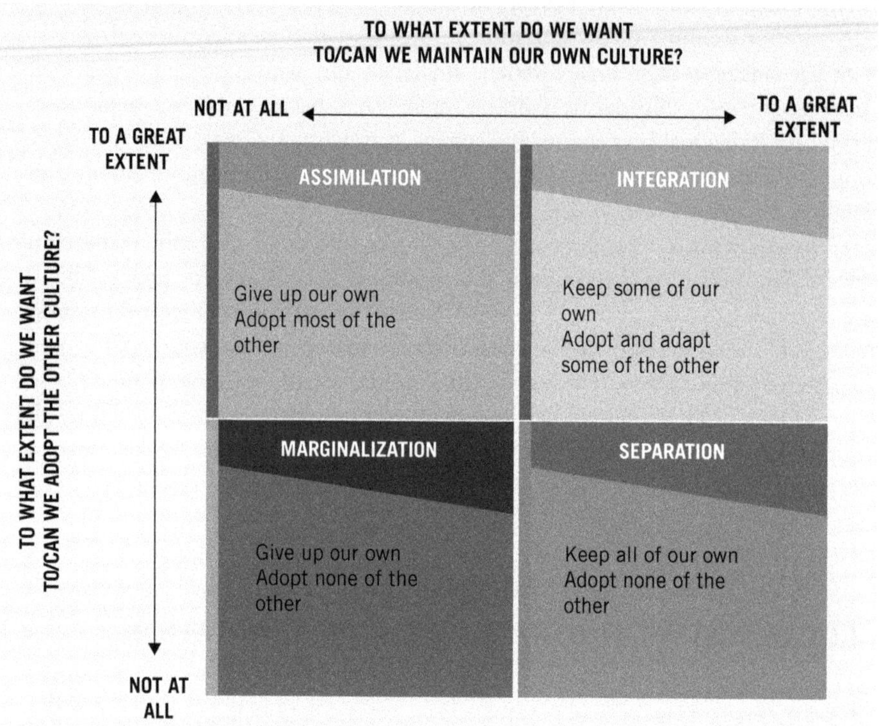

TO WHAT EXTENT DO WE WANT TO/CAN WE MAINTAIN OUR OWN CULTURE?

NOT AT ALL ←————————————————————————→ TO A GREAT EXTENT

Vertical axis: **TO WHAT EXTENT DO WE WANT TO/CAN WE ADOPT THE OTHER CULTURE?** (TO A GREAT EXTENT ↑ / NOT AT ALL ↓)

ASSIMILATION Give up our own Adopt most of the other	**INTEGRATION** Keep some of our own Adopt and adapt some of the other
MARGINALIZATION Give up our own Adopt none of the other	**SEPARATION** Keep all of our own Adopt none of the other

who are in contact may have a different answer to the questions and therefore the two groups may not agree on the outcome of their contact. For example, one group may want to maintain its cultural elements and not interact with the other group (separation), while the other may want them to give up their own practices and adopt new ones (assimilation). Whether the resolution is positive or negative for one or both groups depends on the degree to which the groups agree on how they should come together. The higher the degree of agreement regarding the strategy for acculturation, the less the conflict.

4.1 Assimilation

Assimilation, also called accommodation, occurs when one group gives up most of its cultural elements and adopts the assumptions, values, beliefs, and practices of the other (see Figure 4.4 and Table 4.3). The most common example of assimilation is the

Table 4.3 Description of Strategies for Acculturation

Acculturation Strategy	Description
Assimilation or accommodation	• One group (usually smaller or less dominant) gives up most of its cultural elements and adopts the culture of the other group (usually larger and more dominant) • The process is voluntary • The larger group welcomes the smaller group • One-way exchange • Involves a parochial or ethnocentric view of culture from both groups *Example: Melting Pot immigration*
Integration or synergy	• Both groups keep most of their cultural elements and adopt and adapt some of the other group's culture • The process is voluntary • Both groups welcome the cultural exchange • Can involve development of new joint cultural elements • Involves cultural pride and a plural or multicultural view of culture from both groups *Example: The salad or mosaic approach to immigration*
Separation or dominance	• One group keeps most of its cultural elements without adopting any of the other group's culture • The process can be voluntary with both groups agreeing to the situation leading to "peaceful coexistence" • When it is forced it becomes segregation • There is no cultural exchange • Involves a parochial or ethnocentric view of culture from both groups with an Us vs. Them attitude *Example: Cultural enclaves in major cities; apartheid in South Africa*
Deculturation or marginalization	• One group loses its cultural identity without replacing it with any other • The process is involuntary and forced on members of the less dominant group • There is no cultural exchange and one culture is destroyed • Involves strong sense of superiority and extreme Us vs. Them mentality and hostility toward the less dominant group *Example: Treatment of Native and Indigenous populations in the United States and Australia*

melting pot analogy that used to be the ideal for immigrants in the United States. The expectation was that once they come into the United States, immigrants would give up their own culture and become Americans, as indicated in a 1919 speech by US President Theodore Roosevelt where he stated:

If the immigrant who comes here in good faith becomes an American and assimilates himself to us he shall be treated on an exact equality with everyone else. But this equality is predicated on the man's becoming in very fact an American and nothing but an American. There can be no divided allegiance here. Any man who says he is an American but something else also, isn't an American at all.

The idea of assimilation is sometimes used, inaccurately, as a synonym for acculturation with assumptions that the only option is for a smaller and less dominant group to give up its culture, blend into the other more dominant culture, and become indistinguishable from all others. This is the strategy that Rakuten, a Japan-based global e-commerce company, selected in bringing together its many different cultural groups. The company used to be multilingual with employees in different countries using their own language to communicate and translators supporting cross-cultural communications. In 2010, CEO Hiroshi Mikitani decided that everyone communicating in English would better support their success through a global work orientation (Neeley, 2017). Not surprisingly, this assimilation into one language caused challenges for many. The Japanese employees, whose many cultural elements such as *kaizen* (continuous improvement) and *omotenashi* (hospitality) were practiced throughout the firm, struggled with learning English while the US-Americans had trouble with directives and expectations coming from Japan. Interestingly, Rakuten's non-Japanese- and non-English-speaking employees in countries such as Brazil, France, and Thailand were the ones who adapted most easily (Neeley, 2017).

If both groups agree on the choice of assimilation, it can be a relatively simple resolution to the acculturation conflict. Referring back to the examples at the beginning of our discussion of acculturation, the "English Only" movement is an attempt at assimilation that has been met with considerable resistance. A more positive assimilation is illustrated by the decline of German schools and other cultural elements during World War I, although brought about by pressure from the outside, was undertaken by German-Americans. As can be seen from these examples, assimilation typically also entails either a parochial or ethnocentric approach where one culture and its elements are assumed to be better than the other. The challenge of course is that not every group is willing to give up its cultural elements.

4.2 Integration

In 2017, while reflecting on the unique culture of Singapore and its blend of Chinese, Malay, Indian, and Eurasian cultures, Prime Minister Lee Hsien Loong of Singapore stated:

Singapore is not a melting pot, but a society where each race is encouraged to preserve its unique culture and traditions, and appreciate and respect that of others...No race or culture is coerced into conforming with other identities, let alone that of the majority... Being Singaporean has never been a matter of subtraction, but of addition; not of becoming less, but more; not of limitation and contraction, but of openness and expansion. (Lee, 2017)

Lee's description of his country's stated ideal cultural policies explains integration as a strategy for acculturation. *Integration* occurs when both groups want to maintain their cultural elements and are also motivated to interact and are interested in adopting some of each other's assumptions, values, beliefs, and practices (see Figure 4.4 and Table 4.3). It is also called *synergy* because the interaction and cooperation between the cultures often creates a new culture, or at least generates new elements that are combination of the two—what Lee described as addition rather than subtraction. People who refer to themselves as bicultural are relying on integration as their strategy for acculturating their two cultures. The challenge with integration is that cultural groups involved must agree to maintain some of their own and adopt some of the other. Such an approach requires a pluralistic and multicultural view of culture where all cultures are assumed to have some, if not equal, value. Several of the examples at the beginning of this section represent instances of integration including having media in multiple languages, businesses encouraging support groups for women and minorities while maintaining other corporate programs, immigrants using names from their own culture along with those from their newly adopted country, celebrations of many different holidays, and the language policies in Switzerland. Similarly, when Google managers in Nigeria found that using the British-accented pronunciation of many street names was confusing Nigerian drivers whose English reflected a multitude of local accents, they hired Kola Tubosun, a speech linguist, to help them create narration in a generic Nigerian-English accent as an option for its map narrator (Werman, 2019). Their decision to adopt both accents provided a better product to their customers in that region, Google integrated a new norm into its business practices, and the Nigerian customers got some version of their own accent.

Integration requires a give-and-take and exchange, something that has been the immigration approach in Canada and is referred to as the cultural mosaic or the salad. Each culture preserves many of its cultural elements while each also adopting elements of others. As a result, cities like Toronto pride themselves on being highly multicultural with over 200 distinct ethnic groups and 180 languages and dialects. Torontonians on the *Narcity* website state: "We have the privilege to learn and get an inside scoop into people's traditions, languages and overall lucky enough to appreciate the differences in others. To be a Torontonian is to be accepting and proud of who you are, with the willingness to share it with others"; and "We don't want people just to come here and claim themselves Canadian, but we want them to embrace their cultural differences as well—because that's truly Canadian and especially Torontonian" (Fajardo, 2017). Achieving integration can be challenging and requires continuous explicit and implicit negotiations about how the two cultures come together. However, research has found that integration can reduce the acculturative stress associated with the unavoidable conflict that occurs when cultures come in contact (Berry, 2005; Krishnan & Berry, 1992).

While the purpose and goal of multicultural efforts is to integrate cultures, there is often the perception that it leads to separation, the next strategy we discuss.

4.3 Separation

Separation, also called *dominance* because one culture dominates, involves a group keeping most of its cultural elements without adopting any of the other culture's (see Figure 4.4 and Table 4.3). It does not involve cultural exchange or any change for either cultural group. In an ideal form, separation can involve peaceful and separate coexistence. The various national enclaves in several cities, such as China Town or Little Havana, represent such an approach. For the most part, although these enclaves are, for example in San Francisco or Miami, one is unlikely to hear or see signs in English, see US-American newspapers or any evidence of being in the United States. Many who live in those communities function without interacting with other cultures. As is the case with the other strategies, the two groups agreeing on how they want to acculturate is key. Disagreements increase the conflict. For example, the continued struggle of integrating French and English and their corresponding cultures in Canada comes from the fear of reviving a strong historical desire for the French-speaking province of Québec to become independent—using separation as a strategy—from Canada in spite of the majority of Quebecers no longer supporting sovereignty for their province (Presse Canadienne, 2019). The struggle is between what is perceived as a desire for separation while others would like Québec to either assimilate or integrate with the rest of Canada.

Much of the fear of and backlash against multiculturalism and pluralism are actually based of worries about separatism without understanding the difference between separation, assimilation, and integration. Just as assimilation is used as a generic term for acculturation by some, separation is used as the example of acculturation gone awry by others. A case in point is the 2011 speech of UK Prime Minister David Cameron's and Trevor Phillips's reaction (both cited earlier in this chapter). They expressed concerns about multiculturalism leading to segregated communities in the United Kingdom. However, the examples they were using of communities living apart illustrate separation rather than multiculturalism, which is best represented by integration.

Examples of using separation as a strategy for acculturation can be found in some corporate acquisitions where the acquiring company specifically agrees to leave its acquisition separate and allow it to keep its culture and practices. When British-Dutch consumer giant Unilever acquired the highly distinctive Vermont-based ice cream manufacturer Ben & Jerry's in 2001, the two companies agreed that the latter would keep many of its unique features, including its commitment to left-leaning social causes and playful ice cream names such as Karamel Sutra and Chocolate Therapy and (Caligiuri, 2012). Yves Couette, the CEO (that is Chief Euphoria Officer for Ben and Jerry's) that Unilever appointed, showed particular skills in adopting and preserving the ice cream maker's culture while imposing some financial controls. Couette believes "the best way to spread Ben & Jerry's enlightened ethic throughout the business world was to make the company successful" (Caligiuri, 2012). Microsoft and LinkedIn made a similar agreement to keep the two entities separate when Microsoft bought LinkedIn for $26.2 billion in 2016. The terms of their deal allowed LinkedIn to keep its "distinct brand, culture, and independence" (Tweedie, 2016). Longtime LinkedIn CEO Jeff Weiner says: "Microsoft hasn't really intervened that much, considering the vast scope and price tag of this integration" ("How's Microsoft's marriage with LinkedIn working out?", 2018).

Separation is a conscious and voluntary decision by one group to keep its culture intact and stay separate from the other group. As is the case with the other two strategies, it can only work if both groups agree that separation should be the strategy for acculturation. When separation is forced on one group, such as during apartheid in South Africa, it becomes segregation. Similarly, if one group, typically the smaller group, decides to remain separate while the other, the larger more dominant one, pushes for another strategy, conflict is likely to ensue, and in the worst case, may lead to the least desirable type of acculturation, deculturation.

4.4 Deculturation

Deculturation, also called *marginalization*, occurs when one culture gives up its cultural elements without adopting any of the other group's culture (see Figure 4.4 and Table 4.3). Deculturation is always forced on a group where members are pressed into abandoning their culture all the while not being allowed to assimilate or integrate into the other culture. The example of Indian Residential Schools in the United States and similar operations in Canada, Australia, and in other countries such as the Soviet Union are drastic examples of forced deculturation. Members of Native cultures, in this case children, were removed from their cultural context, and prevented from practicing any of their cultural elements such as language or religion. While the stated goal was assimilation into the dominant culture, because of racism and discrimination, they were not allowed to join the dominant cultural group and remained at the margin of that society. As opposed to some immigrant groups, for example Germans who also were pushed toward giving up some elements of their cultural elements after World War I and were welcomed into the dominant culture, members of these Native cultures were prevented from fully joining the dominant cultural group.

Deculturation leads to cultural destruction and provides examples of anomie, which we discussed in Chapter 1. Not having a cultural identity can have devastating effects on individuals and groups. Using deculturation as a strategy involves a strong sense of superiority and destructive ethnocentrism along with a considerable negative view of the "other." It is obviously highly devastating and leads to considerable acculturative stress with corresponding individual psychological distress, physical ailments, and social ills (Berry, 2005).

A substantially less drastic example of deculturation can occur in organizations during acquisition of one firm by another (Nahavandi & Malekzadeh, 1988). During some acquisitions or hostile takeovers, the acquired company is dismantled and liquidated, leading to the elimination of its corporate culture. While clearly not on the scale of the examples of Native cultures, the hostile corporate takeover process creates considerable distress for employees of the targeted firm. They experience loss of jobs and income and often mourn the dismantling of their social networks.

4.5 An Example of Acculturation Strategies in Practice: Hong Kong

Hong Kong provides examples of several of the strategies of acculturation. Starting in the summer of 2019, the island was rocked with increasingly violent protests over the expansion of China's power and authority, indicating a trend toward less independence for Hong Kong and a shift in how the two cultures resolve their contact and conflict. In 1997 the British, who had ruled Hong Kong since 1841, returned it to China. During the 150-year British colonial rule and after the Chinese communist takeover in 1949, Hong Kong developed its own distinctive culture and became a capitalist symbol of financial wealth and a refuge and playground for many from mainland China and other countries. The 1997 agreement that handed Hong Kong back to China allowed the island some political and social autonomy through a "one country, two systems" policy that is set to expire in 2047 (Blakemore, 2019). This agreement set up something between separation and integration as a way to acculturate the two groups. They would open up to each other but each maintains separate systems.

When the initial agreement was first made in 1997, Hong Kong's GDP was 20% the size of the mainland's economy providing the island with some power and influence in determining its own fate. That percentage had dropped to 3% in 2017 (HK vs. China GDP, 2017) as China has become a global economic powerhouse that has less reliance on Hong Kong's economic contributions. That change in economic wealth creates a shift in power; Hong Kong is now clearly the less dominant party and is pushing China to fully assimilate the island, contrary to the desires of Hong Kong residents for either integration or separation. These two cultures that share the same ethnic background and long history will continue to explore options on how their contact progresses. Understanding how two groups decide to resolve the inevitable tensions, conflicts, and stress that arise when they come in contact and which strategies they choose to acculturate to each other is essential to being able to be effective when crossing cultural boundaries.

4.6 Acculturative Stress

We have mentioned how various strategies to acculturate can involve more or less acculturative stress. *Acculturative stress* is a physiological, psychological, and behavioral response resulting from the process of acculturation when individuals cannot easily adjust to the other culture they encounter (Berry et al., 1987). The contact and unresolved conflict are the primary causes of the stress. While similar to *culture shock* (Ward, Bochner, & Furnham, 2001), which refers to distress experienced in an unfamiliar cultural setting, the two are different on several dimensions:

- Acculturative stress is the result of sustained intercultural contact (Berry, 1997) rather than short-term reaction to one culture that leads to culture shock.

- Acculturative stress, like acculturation itself, is a more sustained and long-term process than culture shock.

- Culture shock involves distress and is always negative; acculturative stress can have both positive and negative outcomes. For example, students who study abroad for short periods of time, or tourists who visit an unfamiliar country may experience culture shock in the unfamiliar settings; the differences and novel settings are uncomfortable and may upset them; but they go back home.

- Acculturative stress is a more complex process than culture shock. It is not just related to cultural differences, but rather to how the person interacts with two different cultures (Berry, 1997; Berry et al., 1987).

4.6.1 Acculturative Stress and Acculturation Strategies. As long as members of the two cultures agree on how acculturation should take place and how they should interact with one another, the level of conflict and stress remains relatively low (see Figure 4.5). Particularly, integration into pluralistic societies has been found to engender the least amount of conflict and stress (Berry et al., 1987). New immigrants to a country may be eager to join their new country and willing to give up many of their cultural elements and integrate, particularly if they are welcomed by members of the dominant culture. They will experience challenges, culture shock, and some stress, but not necessarily feel distress. Similarly, assimilation and separation can ideally present relatively moderate to low conflict. Research shows that

Figure 4.5 Acculturation, Conflict and Stress

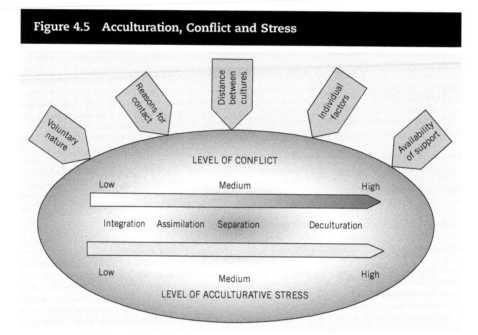

while the process of interacting and adapting to a new culture is always stressful, many groups experience relatively moderate levels of stress and positive outcomes (Vega & Rumbaut, 1991). The exception is, of course, deculturation.

Table 4.4 describes the factors that impact the level of conflict and acculturative stress people may experience. Entering long-term cross-cultural contacts voluntarily, for example when we join an organization with a diverse workforce, or eagerly accept a foreign assignment to expand our experience base, or work on a venture with an overseas business partner, is likely to mitigate the levels of acculturative stress. However, the same expats who enter the cross-cultural contact with the goal of profitable and successful business relationships may be pulled in other directions with their families not having the same motivation and expressing a desire to return home. Additionally, the more different the two cultures are, meaning the more distant from one another, the more challenging acculturation will be. For example, we tend to feel less stress when we speak the same language, or have common cultural or regional roots even when we travel to another country.

4.6.2 Acculturative Stress, Views of Culture, and CM. One of the key factors in determining the level of conflict and stress are the individual's cultural views that we discussed earlier in this chapter and the level of a person's CM. Extensive research in

Table 4.4 Factors That Impact Conflict and Acculturative Stress

Factor	Description
Voluntary nature	Is the long-term cross-cultural interaction forced on the person or is it something he/she has opted to do? *Examples of voluntary*: Immigrants; business relationships *Examples of forced*: Refugees; employees in a hostile takeover
Reasons for contact	Why are the two cultures interacting? What is the goal for each? What are potential benefits or disadvantages for each? *Examples*: Immigrants are motivated to build a new life and integrate or assimilate; expats want to be successful in their assignment but may have challenges with their families.
Distance between cultures	How similar are the two cultures? The more similar they are, the less conflict and the lower the likelihood of acculturative stress. *Example*: US-Americans perceive that working with Brits or Australians is easier than with many other countries because of language and cultural similarities.
Individual factors: View of culture and CM	Having parochial, ethnocentric, or plural views of culture impact preferences for acculturation. A stronger CM can support resolution of conflict. *Example:* A person with an ethnocentric view of culture is likely to consider others assimilating as the only acceptable strategy for acculturation; whereas someone with a well-developed CM will be more accepting of other cultures.
Availability of support systems and tools	Having access to resources and support networks, as well as formal training tools, can help reduce the acculturative stress. *Example*: Expats and their families receive training before going on assignment and are provided with cultural mentors in their host country.

Sources: Partially based on information in Berry (1997), Berry et al. (1987), and Berry (2005).

cross-cultural psychology has shown that pluralistic cultures more easily interact with other cultures and therefore acculturating with them causes less friction for individuals and groups (for a review see Berry, 2005). For example, Malaysia, Indonesia, Singapore, Canada, and the United States, which are all multicultural and plural to varying degrees, have continued to welcome and integrate new cultural groups to a much higher extent than Japan or Korea, which are less diverse and more culturally homogeneous. On an individual level, how people view culture, whether they have a parochial, ethnocentric, or plural view of culture, will impact their CM and how they choose to approach cross-cultural contact, what they expect others to do, and the resolution of the conflict and disagreement that are bound to occur. Specifically, people with parochial or ethnocentric views are much less likely to engage in a mutual cultural exchange or accept that others may want to maintain their own cultural elements. They are therefore less likely to rely on integration strategies, instead pressuring the other group to select assimilation, separation (or segregation), or even deculturation.

Finally, the level of acculturative stress will be impacted by the availability of support systems and resources to the individuals and the groups involved. Extensive research has shown that individuals and groups who have strong social support networks have better mental outcomes when acculturating to new contexts (e.g., Puyat, 2013). Multinational organizations are fully aware of the role of such support in the success of expats as we discuss next.

5. THE CULTURAL ADAPTATION OF EXPATRIATES

LO 4.5 Discuss the case of expatriates and their adaptation to new cultures

Sending employees and managers to live and work in a country other than their own for a few months to a few years to conduct business is a common and growing practice for many businesses (Mossman, 2016). We have mentioned these expatriates, or expats, in a variety of examples throughout this chapter because they provide excellent examples of acculturation. They interact with other cultures in a sustained manner and have to acculturate not only when they go abroad, but again when they come back home, as illustrated in the *First Person* example in this chapter. They face many challenges that by some estimates cause 50% of them to not complete their assignment, at an estimated loss of $2 billion for US companies alone (Steinlauf, 2019).

5.1 Success Factors

There is considerable research about factors that make expats successful and how to support them when they go abroad and when they come back (for a review see Holopainen & Björkman, 2005). The following are key:

- *Send the right people for the right reasons* specifically for generating knowledge and developing global leaders, rather than rewarding an employee or getting them out of the way (Black & Gregersen, 2016).

- *Consider culture* since cultural factors are often at the forefront of both success and failure since expats face serious acculturative challenges.

- *Consider families* who often encounter many problems. While the expats are on familiar ground to some extent at least in their work environment, where there is structure and familiarity, the family members often enter an unstructured world where they have to build new networks for every aspect of their lives.

- *Plan for the long term* both abroad and back home since expats and their families have to acculturate when they go abroad and when they come and they need time to adjust.

Businesses invest considerable resources in sending an employee abroad. By one estimate, the cost of a 3-year international assignment can exceed $3 million (Managing International Assignments, 2017). Table 4.5 presents a summary of the specific tools that can be used to help expats.

Table 4.5 Tools to Support Expats

Tools	Description
Selection of expats	Selecting individuals with certain characteristics that allow for easier adaptation and acculturation including consideration of views of culture
Preparation through practical, tactical, and cultural training and education	Formal training and education about the expat experience and host country culture for expat and family members
Language instruction	Language instruction prior to leaving and during stay for expat and family members
On-site family support	Formal and information support mechanisms for family members including connecting with local families and other expats
Mentor	Local cultural mentor to help with understanding of culture, or other expats who know the host country and the challenges of being an expat
Regular home visits	Frequent and regular home visits for expat and family members to stay connected to home and avoid a sense of isolation
Postassignment support	Formal programs to support expat and family after they return home

Sources: Partially based on information in Black and Gregersen (2016), Managing International Assignments (2017), and Steinlauf (2019).

5.1.1 Selection. The first step is the selection of people who are more likely to succeed. In addition to the right business experience, self-monitoring, which is one of the ten CM factors (Caligiuri & Day, 2000; Harrison, Chadwick, & Scales, 1996), and other variables such as communication ability (Holopainen & Björkman, 2005) have been shown to be good selection criteria. Another factor to consider is the expat's view of culture, another CM factor. Simply having international experience does not guarantee a plural or multicultural view. The less parochial and the less ethnocentric and the more plural the expat is, the more likely he or she is to be able to successfully interact with partners in the host country. Noch Noch Li, who was moved multiple times by her employer, states:

> *Many expatriate executives make the mistake of arrogance: they land in the new city, new office, with new colleagues, and brutally want to show them how "it's supposed to be done." They mock the local culture for inefficiencies and are determined to change it within the two years they are posted there. Most of them leave defeated, and brand the local host country as "hopeless." (Li, 2012)*

Her observation echoes what research recommends: respecting culture is essential; having a parochial or an ethnocentric view makes the interaction and experience more challenging and more likely to fail.

5.1.2 Education and Training. All forms of education, training, and support for the expats and their family are essential (for a review see Littrell, Salas, & Hess, 2006). While expats need such training to be effective in their job, since family's lack of adjustment is one of the primary reasons they leave their assignment early, providing similar preparation to family members is equally important. Connecting all of them with locals or experienced other expats who can serve as resources and support them are further steps that help make a foreign assignment successful. Manfred Kets De Vries, professor of leadership and organizational change at INSEAD, recommends:

> *Global companies need to ensure that cross-cultural coaching is available in every international posting. Enlisting such people can powerfully and effectively assist expatriates and their families in dealing with the many challenges that emerge during the course of an expatriate assignment. (Steinlauf, 2019)*

A final factor in success is helping the expats and their families both move to a foreign country and then reenter their home country. Next, we will discuss acculturation strategies for expats as well as how to prepare them for returning home and to reacculturate.

5.2 Acculturation Strategies for Expats

Having a plural mindset that entails accepting and respecting other cultures is essential for an expat to be successful. Consciously and deliberately selecting the right acculturation strategy is also necessary. Considering the two key acculturation questions of maintaining one's own culture and adopting other cultures (see Figure 4.4), it is likely that expats want to maintain their own cultural elements, both in terms of national and group culture and in terms of the organizational culture. After all, they are sent abroad to represent their company and their country and are often seen by people in the host country as representatives of their country, culture, and company. The two acculturation strategies that are available to them are therefore integration and separation.

5.2.1 Integration for Expats. In integration, the expat learns as much as possible about the host country, studies the language, and immerses himself or herself in the culture, adopting many of the practices, if not some of the values and beliefs. Similarly, the expat family can send their kids to a local school and live closer to the host community than to the expat community. Integration would be possible if the host country welcomes them. This strategy is one that is often recommended for success, particularly when the assignment is relatively long term. For example, business executive Randy Steinlauf (2019) recounts how his decision to avoid being a "corporate tourist" (someone who just pops in and out) and stay in Tokyo through the last business day before holidays was appreciated by his Japanese colleague who said: "I've worked at this company for more than 10 years. You're the first expat I've met who is staying with us to work through year-end. That means a lot to me." Others recommend befriending locals and avoiding living in the expat bubble.

Consider the example of a woman expat from the United States or Canada moving to a European Union country. The EU countries are multicultural, accepting of newcomers, and used to women working in professional capacities. The expat would have no trouble integrating if she chooses to do so. She could live anywhere she desires, travel freely, join any activity, interact with local communities as little or as much as she decides, and socialize with and date whomever she wants. Even if she does not know the language, she is likely to encounter many familiar cultural elements. In spite of some differences, many aspects of the political systems, social norms, values, and beliefs will be recognizable to her. If she has a family or partner, they can choose which schools to attend, relatively easily get work permits, and also select how they want to interact with people in the host country. She can therefore integrate into the host country culture to learn and share cultural and business practices.

5.2.2 Separation for Expats. Staying isolated and not making any efforts at integration would entail using separation as a mode of acculturation. This can occur for two reasons. Either the expat may not want to mingle with the local community or the local community may not welcome the expat. The example of the same US or Canadian expat in Saudi Arabia illustrates the points. With over 32 million population, Saudi Arabia is estimated to have upward of 10 million expats, many of whom are manual laborers along with numerous business people. Most Saudi cultural practices, beliefs, values, and assumptions are different from what a US American or Canadian is used to. The segregation of gender, strict dress codes, the highly restrictive rules about consumption of alcohol and social interaction, censure of the internet and the press, along with highly centralized and intrusive government control of most activities and social life provide considerable challenge.

Almost all expats in Saudi Arabia, particularly managers and other executives, live in compounds, surrounded by high walls with tight security, that mimic life in Western countries, but constrain contact with local Saudi communities (Tony, 2018). Expats are therefore practically segregated from the local community. If our manager is married (living with a partner, but not married would not be an option), her spouse would have a hard time getting a visa and their children will only be able to attend an international school. Even if the expat tries to integrate with the Saudi culture, she is unlikely to be able to do so; separation is her only available strategy for acculturation. This separation, or segregation, is one of the contributing factors to the well-documented difficulty expats have in Saudi Arabia (e.g., Naithani & Jha, 2010). For most Westerners, the cultural distance is great and the host country is not interested in a cultural exchange.

5.2.3 Acculturation When Returning Home. Expats face yet one more challenge when they return home. If they have acculturated through integration and adopted new cultural assumptions, values, beliefs, or practices, they are likely to experience some difficulty returning home. Their expectations are that home will be easy and comfortable. However, sustained contact with another culture, particularly if they have integrated successfully, will be challenging. They will have changed as a result of acculturating to a new culture; home will have changed as well. Therefore, they will face challenges fitting back into their own culture when they repatriate (for a review see Szkudlarek, 2010). Recognizing these challenges, the US State Department offers resources to their returning diplomats on what it calls reverse culture shock (https://2009-2017.state.gov/m/fsi/tc/c56075.htm).

Whether it involves interacting with a new culture or getting reacquainted with a familiar one, the process involves acculturative stress. Therefore, many business organizations and nonprofits provide training and support to ease the acculturation of their expats back into their own culture. While the challenges are not likely to be as great as those faced when they went abroad, the fact that most expats do not expect to have any difficulty makes the process challenging. Even though acculturation almost always creates some level of stress, as stated earlier, most of the challenges related to acculturative stress do resolve themselves with time. Awareness, preparation, and deliberate choices can help ease the process.

6. VIEWS OF CULTURE, ACCULTURATION, AND THE CULTURAL MINDSET

LO 4.6 Appraise the role of views of culture in developing a Cultural Mindset (CM)

In Chapter 2 we defined the CM as a way of thinking and a frame of mind or reference that considers culture as a factor when assessing yourself and other people and situations, and when making decisions and acting on them. Having a CM means that you are aware of your own cultural backgrounds and the fact that CJI and that it provides a meta-context (CMC). We also presented the ten factors that make up the CM (see Figure 2.1 and Table 2.1). Several of the CM cognitive factors are directly addressed in our discussions of in- and out-groups, Us-vs-Them mentality, and views of culture in this chapter.

6.1 View of Culture and the CM

How you view your culture in relation to others, meaning whether you have a parochial, ethnocentric, or plural view, is part of your CM. Knowing the elements of your cultural identity and how they might frame how you interact with people in your in-group and those in your out-group are part of the essential cultural self-awareness that support the development of a CM. Whether you are unaware of culture—a parochial view, or see your own as superior—an ethnocentric view, or strive to value and respect all cultures—a plural view, directly influences whether you include culture in your deliberations and decisions.

The plural view of culture is in line with accepting cultures as they are (CJI), as metacontextual variables that play a key role in shaping our worldview and guiding our behavior. However, given that the three views of culture overlap and are intersecting (see Figure 4.2 and corresponding discussion earlier in this chapter), having a plural view does not prevent valuing one's own culture and having cultural pride. The different viewpoints are one of the paths toward developing a CM, as expanding one's view of culture, moving from parochial or ethnocentric toward a plural view, helps one become aware of the existence and impact of culture on oneself and on others. In relation to views of culture, having a CM means that:

- You are moving from not considering culture, and automatically and mindlessly making decisions without considering the context, toward more deliberate process where you know when and if you need to consider culture.

6.2 Acculturation and the CM

The acculturation strategies that you engage in are not solely under your control since the other group's preferences also determine the course of acculturation. However, awareness of your identity, your own views of culture, and the acculturation options allows you to better navigate the many long-term cross-cultural interactions you will face in your personal and professional life. Successful sustained cross-cultural interaction requires a CM, which involves an awareness of your view of culture and how it impacts the way you interact with others and how you expect them to interact with you. Cross-cultural relationships are about two, or more, groups coming together. The approach and viewpoint of just one group is not sufficient to determine how the interaction will occur. For successful interaction, all groups need to be in general agreement about how they will acculturate and be ready to address inevitable conflict and acculturative stress.

Sustained exchanges with another culture will always pose challenges. How we view cultures, the level of CM, and how we undertake acculturation can be key factors in the success of our cross-cultural interactions. Acculturation is concerned with resolving cultural differences during such continued and long-term interactions.

FIRST PERSON REVISITED

The manager in the *First Person* anecdote experienced the challenges of acculturation when returning home and trying to decide which cultural rules to apply to managing his team. Having learned and practiced management techniques and approaches in the United States and Germany, he adopted some of their cultural norms which have been integrated in his professional cultural identity. He returns home and implements them in a context that he automatically assumes he understands. He relies on what has become automatic System I knowledge developed from working in other countries, to guide his decisions in his home culture, instead of taking the time to slow down and more carefully evaluate the context and his actions. He is eventually able to correct course, reacculturate to his own culture, and integrate more culturally appropriate approaches in how he manages his team. Part of Zeki's challenge is familiar to many expats who adapt to a foreign culture well and then experience culture shock when returning home. While there is often some support when going abroad, returning home is expected to be easy and simple. The example illustrates the inherent challenges of moving from one culture to another and trying to adapt.

APPLYING WHAT YOU LEARN: THE HOST–GUEST FRAMEWORK—SHORT-TERM CULTURAL INTERACTION

"They have come here, why can't they just learn our language and how we do things?" "We have our own way; I don't need to do things the way you do!"

"You are here now, so just do it our way."

"I like to eat my own food, why can't I get what I like here?"

"Why is service so bad?"

"Why are people rude here?"

We have all heard, or maybe made, comments like these. They address our frustrations and discomfort when facing different cultural practices. The acculturation processes and strategies we discussed in this chapter provide long-term and complex solutions. But how do we deal with the short-term interactions? Using the Host–Guest framework provides a simple and practical analogy for short-term cross-cultural interactions. The Host–Guest framework acknowledges that neither the host nor the guest have a motivation or reason to change; they both just want to spend a peaceful and enjoyable few hours, or few days, together. Consider the two lists below; they are based on a combination of advice given in various websites and family magazines about being a good host and a good guest.

Good Host	Good Guest
• Make it about your guests, not about you	• Arrive on time
• Address your guests' needs	• Bring a gift
• Make as many accommodations as you can	• Ask about the house rules
• Show sincere interest in your guests	• Be kind and courteous
• Be clear about house rules	• Lend a hand when necessary
• Be prepared and ready to improvise	• Respect your host's personal space
• Ensure everyone is comfortable	• Clean up after yourself
• Don't make friends feel like intruders	• Leave things as you found them
• Make your home visitor friendly	• Know when to leave
• Be a good listener	• Send a thank you note

Sources: Adapted from Fusaro (2009), Mayne (2019), and Rox (2011).

ETIQUETTE RULES FOR HOSTS AND GUESTS

Whether you are the host or the guest in a cross-cultural interaction these rules of social interaction, which involve politeness, graciousness, and thinking about others rather than how to advance your own needs, can go a long way to start the encounter on a positive note. You may know little about the culture and assumptions, beliefs, values, and practices of your host or your guest, and may not care or not have time to learn about them. The goal of any host is to make guests feel welcome to enjoy the visit together; the goal of any guest is to be courteous, not impose on the host, and enjoy the visit together. On the one hand, good hosts go out of their way to accommodate their guests rather than expect their guests to adhere to strict rules they may not know. Good hosts provide their guests what they need, and take their need into consideration. They also let them know gently if something is not right. On the other hand, good guests show gratitude to their host, respect their host's home, are not demanding, and leave things as they found them. The Host–Guest framework is applicable to short-term cross-cultural interaction. Without even knowing anything about culture or cross-cultural interactions, this framework can help you start on the right foot.

MANAGERIAL CHALLENGE: THEY WANT NOTHING TO DO WITH US...

You are an expat manager in the UAE leading a diverse department that includes several other expats from Europe, and India, and the Middle East and two local engineers. The department is productive and people generally get along. You joined them a couple of months ago and enjoy your assignment. One of your goals is to create a strong sense of cohesion that you think will make the group more productive and support a more innovative and risk-taking corporate culture. To that end, you create various opportunities for your department to socialize, engage in sports activities together, and join in cultural events and include their families. Everyone attends almost all of the events, except for the two local engineers. For five gatherings now, they RSVP-ed that they will attend and bring their wife and kids, but they did not show up. Since these are social events, you cannot require them to attend, but their absence is affecting your plans to create a tight-knit social group and your department could really benefit from their local perspective. You have approached each of the two with gentle questions about their lack of attendance, and they have responded with vague comments about family responsibilities and emergencies preventing them from attending. It does seem that they really don't want to have anything to do with you or the team outside of work....

1. What is your assessment of the situation?

2. What are the cultural factors that may be operating?

3. What can you do? What should you do?

SELF-ASSESSMENT 4.1: REVIEWING YOUR ICMI RESULTS

The goal of this self-assessment is to make you aware of your views of culture and two personality factors related to your CM. You have taken the ICMI as part of Chapter 2. Several of the factor scores that comprise your CM are relevant for discussions in this chapter. Consider your scores in the following factors:

Parochialism: _____ Ethnocentrism: _____ Pluralism: _____

Using the figure below, place yourself on each of the factors based on your score.

Additionally, consider your scores in the following two factors:

Self-monitoring: _____ Cultural curiosity: _____

1. How do your scores regarding your views of culture help or hinder your cultural interactions?

2. How do your scores in self-monitoring and cultural curiosity help or hinder your cultural interactions?

3. What are areas that you can address?

4. Can you think of specific examples where your cultural views regarding parochialism, ethnocentrism, or pluralism helped or hindered your work progress?

SELF-ASSESSMENT 4.2: PREFERRED STRATEGY FOR ACCULTURATION

The goal of this self-assessment is to increase your self-awareness and knowledge regarding acculturation strategies and their impact. Consider various sustained cross-cultural interactions you have had. This may have been while living in another country, working with a multicultural group for a period of time on a class project, getting to know new friends who are from a different culture, connecting with someone in another community, or during a volunteer experience. Although face-to-face interactions provide more details, you may have also had such encounters through online contact with virtual teams. The key criteria for selecting an interaction is that it should be sustained and over a period of time, not just one or two encounters. Consider the following questions:

1. What are the cultures involved (yours and the other one, or there may have been more than one)?

2. How did you acculturate with the other cultural groups? Which strategy do you think you used? Use the figure below to answer this question.

3. How did members of the other groups acculturate? (you can use the figure to answer this question)

4. What were the factors that encouraged you to use the acculturation strategy you used?

5. What role did acculturative stress play in your interactions? How high was the level of conflict? Why?

6. To what extent was the acculturation strategy you used effective? How about their strategy?

7. Now that you've read this chapter, which other acculturation strategies could you have used? Why?

EXERCISE 4.1: AFRICA WON THE WORLD CUP!

Objective: *This exercise addresses the cognitive factors in CM.*

Instructions: Read the following prompt and letter, then watch the short clip before completing the individual and group work exercises.

On July 15, 2018, France won the FIFA World Cup final becoming the football (or soccer for US readers) champion of the world. Out of 24 players, the French team's roster included 12 players of African origin. Following that victory, on July 18, comedian Trevor Noah congratulated both France and Africa for winning the world cup, triggering an angry reaction from many in France and a protest letter from the French Ambassador to the United States. The transcript of the letter, as read by Noah on his show, is below:

> *Sir I watched with great attention your July 17th show when you spoke of the victory of the French team at the 2018 FIFA World Cup Russia final which took place last Sunday. I heard your words about an African victory, nothing could be less true. As many of the players have already stated themselves, their parents may have come from another country but a great majority of them—all but two out of 23 were born in France. They were educated in France, they learned to play soccer in France, they are French citizens. They are proud of their country, France. The rich and various backgrounds of these players is a reflection of France's diversity. France is indeed a cosmopolitan country but every citizen is part of the French identity and together they belong to the nation of France. Unlike in the United States of America, France does not refer to its citizens based on their race, religion or origin. To us, there is no hyphenated identity. Roots are an individual reality, by calling them an African team it seems like you're denying their Frenchness. This, even in jest, legitimizes the ideology which claims whiteness as the only definition of being French. (https://www.youtube.com/watch?v=COD9hcTpGWQ)*

After reading the letter on the air, with the appropriate French accent, Noah proceeded to highlight how the presence of African players was related to France's colonial past rather than random immigration. He reported that these players are often verbally abused by some fans with racial taunts and slurs, denying their French citizenship. Noah highlighted how people from Africa all over the world celebrated the performance of these athletes and that they should not have to deny their African roots to be considered French. He further mentioned that the US approach to allow for a dual (or more) identity, rather than forcing a choice of one or other ethnicity, is what makes for cultural diversity. He pointed that when African migrants commit crimes or are considered somehow "unsavory" they are called African, but when they do acts of heroism or win the World Cup, they become French. He further highlighted the importance of context and his ability to comment on the matters such as these because of his race and dual identity as an African-American from South Africa, something that may be considered otherwise racist.

Watch the *Daily Show* episode from July 18, 2018 at https://www.youtube.com/watch?v=COD9hcTpGWQ.

Individual Work

Prepare a one-paragraph summary of the segment, then develop brief answers to the following questions:

1. What are the cultural identities that Trevor Noah discusses?

2. What are the acculturation strategies that the French Ambassador highlights in his letter?

3. What are the acculturation strategies that Trevor Noah addresses?

4. What are the implications of each of the strategies?

Group Work and Debate

1. Discuss your answers to the questions.

2. Your instructor will assign you to one of the acculturation strategies discussed in the video segment.

3. Prepare your arguments to support that strategy in a debate.

EXERCISE 4.2: US-VS-THEM

Objective: This exercise addresses the cognitive factors in CM.

The goal of this exercise is to explore the factors that lead to the development of in- and out-groups and an Us-vs-Them duality and the power and impact of this duality in shaping perceptions and behavior.

Instructions:

Group Discussion

Watch the Frontline documentary *Class Divided* at https://www.pbs.org/video/frontline-class-divided/

Discuss the following questions in your group:

1. How did the in- and out-group form?

2. Why did the children accept the groups? Consider some of the benefits they derived from their membership.

3. When and how did the Us-vs-Them attitude start?

4. What could have been done to avoid that attitude?

5. What are some applications of this experiment to situations you face? Provide specific examples.

Presentation

Prepare a 5–10-minute group presentation that includes examples of the situations you faced and how an Us-vs-Them attitude can be avoided while keeping the benefits of a strong cultural identity.

CASE STUDY: IKEA'S FIRST STORE IN INDIA

The research and first draft for this case was prepared by Tuba Pagda

Visit an IKEA store almost anywhere in the world and you may feel a bit like you are in Sweden. The stores' exteriors are painted in the blue and yellow colors of the Swedish flag; you will find Swedish meatballs, marinated salmon plate, and Swedish apple cake on the restaurant's menu and you will have to struggle to pronounce product names that are a tongue twister for non-Swedish speakers. You will also experience the pared-down industrial or country style that is uniquely Scandinavian. The global furniture retailer empire, which was founded by Ingvar Kamprad in 1943 and now operates more than 300 stores around the world, displays its cultural roots proudly.

In August of 2018 IKEA opened its first store in India in the southern city of Hyderabad in a district known at Hitec City. This is just the first foray into the world's second-most populous nation where a young and growing middle class buys $30 billion of furniture and other household items a year (Goel, 2018). IKEA's challenge is to attract and keep a good portion of these valuable customers as it plans further expansion in the country, with 25 more outlets projected by 2025 (Iyengar, 2018).

The retail giant has been very methodical about approaching the Indian market. Given the congestion and difficult traffic for which Indian cities are notorious, IKEA is planning on smaller urban stores so that its potential customers can avoid the longer drive to a large suburban store (Chaudhuri & Abrams, 2018). It also took 6 years of careful research to gain insight into the complex dynamics of the Indian market and lifestyle (Chaudhuri & Abrams, 2018). IKEA researchers gathered information regarding anything from purchasing patterns, to family structure, sleeping habits, food preferences, and entertaining and house-cleaning practices by visiting more than 1,000 homes all over India to assure that its products and services appeal to their estimated 7 million new yearly customers. As a result, the Hyderabad IKEA is still a bit of Sweden and also uniquely Indian.

To start, IKEA-Hyderabad has the same flow and general structure, but cabinets and counters are installed lower to accommodate the Indian customers who, on average, are shorter than Europeans. The displays for many of the master bedrooms include a child's bed, as typically Indian children sleep in their parents' room until they reach elementary school age (Goel, 2018). IKEA researchers found that Indian families spend considerable amount of time socializing with family and friends with many short as well as overnight often unplanned visits. So, IKEA added folding chairs and stools, mattresses made of coconut fiber, and colorful floor pillows to their product line. The doormats spell "welcome" in different Indian languages and pans are designed to make

Indian flatbread (Chaudhuri & Abrams, 2018; Iyengar, 2018). Instead of the typically European eating utensil set that include a fork, a knife, and a spoon, many sets, especially those for children, include a set of spoons instead, since Indians use them primarily as eating utensils (Goel, 2018). To address the cleaning practices of washing out the floors with water, IKEA designers created waterproof risers for the metal or wood furniture (Goel, 2018). Meanwhile, in order to attract lower-income customers and match the purchasing power of the Indian consumers, many low-price products are offered along with lower prices of other merchandise (Iyengar, 2018). IKEA further took advantage of the huge and cheap Indian labor market to offer carpenters and installers to their middle-class customers who were not about to build their own furniture, especially given the availability of relatively low-cost labor (Chaudhuri & Abrams, 2018). The ubiquitous IKEA cafeteria seats 1,000 people in Hyderabad, the largest of any IKEA store, and but still offers a taste of Sweden. However, the meatballs are made of chicken or vegetables rather than the beef and pork that are not part of the diet of the majority of Indians, and biryani and samosas cater to the tastes of the local population who eats in a much more leisurely fashion than the typical Western customer who runs in and out (Goel, 2018; Iyengar, 2018).

While it is still early to fully gauge the success of the research-based marketing strategies and products, with such a large potential market, IKEA has taken the time to integrate Indian cultural practices into its new operation—still a little bit of Sweden, but with distinctly Indian texture and flavor.

Questions

1. Summarize the steps IKEA took to address the cultural characteristics of its newest store?

2. How would you characterize IKEA's approach based on:
   a. The views of culture you read about in this chapter
   b. The acculturation strategies you read about in this chapter

3. What are the strengths and weaknesses of IKEA's approach? To what extent do you think it would work for other organizations?

Sources

Chaudhuri, S., & Abrams, C. (2018). IKEA's strategy in India: If we build it, they will come. *The Wall Street Journal*, July 23. Retrieved from https://www.wsj.com/articles/ikea-lets-some-take-diy-off-the-table-1532338200. Accessed on January 4, 2020.

Goel, V. (2018). IKEA opens first India store, tweaking products but not the vibe. *The New York Times*, August 7. Retrieved from https://www.nytimes.com/2018/08/07/business/ikea-first-india-store.html. Accessed on January 4, 2020.

Iyengar, R. (2018). IKEA's first India store opens to customers. *CNN*, August 9. Retrieved from https://money.cnn.com/2018/08/08/news/companies/ikea-in-india-hyderabad/index.html. Accessed on January 4, 2020.

PART THREE

KNOW—GROUP CULTURE AND DIVERSITY

Previous chapters addressed how we THINK and were aimed at expanding self-awareness by explaining cognitive processes and how culture-as-meta-context (CMC) provides us with the lenses and perspectives we use to view and interpret the world. The two chapters in Part III focus on building knowledge of cultural values and differences at the group level and present information that can help you manage more effectively in different cultural groups within a national context. The attention is on the KNOW part of the THINK–KNOW–DO roadmap (see Figure III.1). The topics we tackle in the next two chapters typically fall under the label of diversity and inclusion. We will be discussing issues related to various group-level differences and their implications for cross-cultural interactions and organizational processes.

Figure III.1   The Focus of Part III

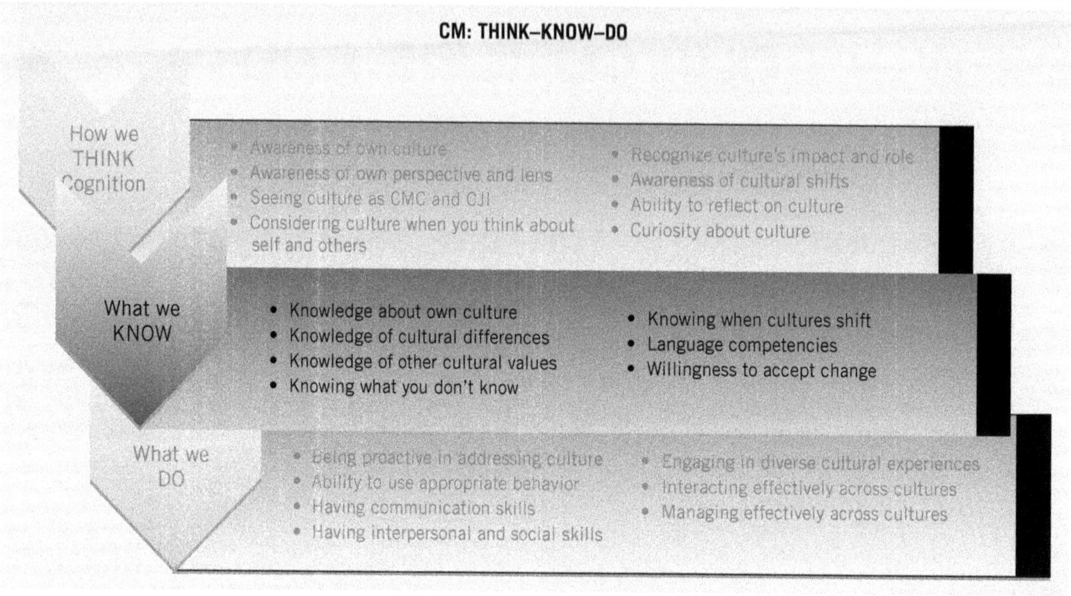

CM: THINK–KNOW–DO

How we THINK Cognition	• Awareness of own culture • Awareness of own perspective and lens • Seeing culture as CMC and CJI • Considering culture when you think about self and others	• Recognize culture's impact and role • Awareness of cultural shifts • Ability to reflect on culture • Curiosity about culture
What we KNOW	• Knowledge about own culture • Knowledge of cultural differences • Knowledge of other cultural values • Knowing what you don't know	• Knowing when cultures shift • Language competencies • Willingness to accept change
What we DO	• Being proactive in addressing culture • Ability to use appropriate behavior • Having communication skills • Having interpersonal and social skills	• Engaging in diverse cultural experiences • Interacting effectively across cultures • Managing effectively across cultures

CHAPTER FIVE

MANAGING DIVERSE GROUPS

FIRST PERSON

Can You Please Get Me Some Cream?

I have been in sales for quite a few years. I attend my share of social events and conventions across the United States and really enjoy the opportunity to network with potential customers and partners, and even with my many competitors. I have stopped counting how many times, while I am getting coffee, drinks, snacks, or what not at the buffet table or going into the planned lunches and dinners, one of the other participants has turned to me and asked me if I could get some cream, coffee, ice, napkins…you name it, obviously mistaking me for the wait staff! I also get occasional surprised looks when I settle at one of the typical round dinner or lunch tables, as if people are wondering why I am joining them. I am at a loss about what to do about this. I am a sharp dresser, quite fancy actually; I am an old hand at these meetings and feel right at home there. Often, I have a name tag around my neck, identifying me as a participant in the event. The problem, at least for some people, seems to be that they just don't see any of these and just focus on my face. I am first-generation Mexican-American, and I fully look, well, stereotypically Mexican—dark hair, olive skin, dark eyes; and that seems to be all that matters. It's funny because the conventions and meetings are not the only time this happens. I have similar experiences when I work on my front yard, which looks amazing by the way because of my efforts, in our upscale neighborhood. I've had several people stop and ask me how much I charge for gardening services. My son tells me I should stop wearing the big straw hat or just stop doing the work myself, something he would love since he is required to help me. Still don't quite know how to deal with this…

–Anonymous

Learning Objectives

5.1 Define diversity and review the challenges and opportunities it offers today's organizations.

5.2 Elaborate on the research about the impact of diversity on groups and organizational performance.

5.3 Present data regarding diversity in the United States and other countries.

5.4 Compare approaches to diversity around the world.

5.5 Consider the historical context of diversity through the lens of colonialism, immigration, and slavery.

5.6 Discuss prejudice and discrimination and their impact on individuals and organizations.

5.7 Detail organizational responses to diversity.

The *First Person* anecdote exemplifies the impact of stereotypes on how we perceive and react to other people. The Mexican-American salesperson is assigned certain roles simply based on his group membership. Expectations and stereotypes are part of our Culture-as-Meta-Context (CMC); they stem from the cultural assumptions, values, and beliefs we grow up with and are therefore often engrained in our thinking and our behavior. In some cases, we may not even be aware that we are relying on them; in other cases, we may actively use these mental models to make decisions. These expectations and stereotypes can be based on different national cultures or on groups within countries or regions. This chapter considers group-level culture, aka diversity, and its implications to provide you with knowledge to build effective organizations that can take advantage of diversity. We will define diversity and its related concepts, review the benefits and challenges it engenders, and appraise how organizations address diversity and inclusion (D&I). In doing so, we consider colonialism, immigration, and slavery as key factors in today's cultural diversity; outline the social and demographic trends that drive it; and look at prejudice and discrimination and their role in diversity efforts.

1. DIVERSITY: COMPLEX DEFINITIONS, CHALLENGES, AND OPPORTUNITIES

LO 5.1 Define diversity and review the challenges and opportunities it offers today's organizations

Some countries, for example the United States, Canada, Indonesia, Tanzania, or Papua New Guinea, are culturally diverse and others less so (e.g., Japan and Korea). However, even countries that are homogeneous on some dimensions, for example ethnicity or religion, include groups that have distinctive identities and characteristics based on other dimensions such as gender, generation, or many other factors. People have dissimilar cultural identities even when they share a nationality, ethnicity, or language. As we discussed in Chapter 1, cultural diversity is neither new nor a debatable topic; it is a simple fact of human existence. Increased globalization and interconnectedness have not made the world any more homogeneous than it was in the past. If anything, by increasing contact among people, globalization is highlighting how diverse people are and how cultures around the world address the unique challenges various people encounter. As discussed in Chapter 4, we know that we use many factors to define in- and out-groups, so that nationality and ethnicity are only two of many other dimensions we rely on. People's identity and needs are complex and include national-, regional-, and group-level cultural factors. We have to be able to address this diversity to help societies and organizations thrive.

Consider the case of The Virgin Group, a family-owned multinational company that includes over 60 businesses from multiple industries including airlines, hotels, media companies, retail stores, and even a commercial space venture. It claims 53 million customers worldwide, 69,000 employees in 35 countries, with a 2019 revenue of £1.6 billion (Virgin-About Us, 2019). The founder is the colorful entrepreneur Sir Richard Branson, who started the company in 1970 in the United Kingdom with Virgin Records and now claims one of the most recognizable brands in the world with a reputation for forward-looking business and managerial practices that address profit, people, and the planet. In addition to having to tackle cross-national cultural differences, Virgin has a particular focus on diversity. Branson says: "People tend to hire those who are most like themselves, and we don't want to have a company in which everyone looks and thinks alike" (Virgin-About Us, 2019). He adds that in order to be successful a company must:

> *Embrace diversity, starting with the choices you make for your first hires. An entrepreneur who hires a lot of people who are just like her and have had the same experiences will find that she's leading a team that is less creative and helpful to customers, and ultimately produces lower profits. Plus you'd have a lot less fun! (Ferrel, 2014)*

Branson is expressing what many other managers are finding out. To be effective and creative, they need diverse talent and they must help those talented individuals thrive.

1.1 Definition and Dimensions of Diversity

The definition of culture is the same at the national, regional, or group levels. Culture is the complex system of long-lasting and dynamic learned assumptions, beliefs, values, and behaviors shared by members of a group. It is what makes that group unique and allows it to make sense of its environment. This definition applies to ethnic groups, gender, religion, and many other group-level cultures.

1.1.1 Definitions of Diversity and Its Related Concepts. Cultural diversity refers to presence of people with distinctly different group affiliations and who hold significantly different cultural identities (Cox, 2000). One could use the term cultural diversity to address differences between nations, but the term typically refers to differences between groups within a country. The importance of addressing cultural diversity dates back to the 1960s and 1970s with the Civil Rights movement and legislations that we detail later in this chapter. Accordingly, business organizations started actively including diversity training, first to comply with legislation, then to improve work relations, and finally to leverage its potential power to support organizational effectiveness and productivity (Anand & Winters, 2008). With over 50 years of diversity focus, the concept is still hotly debated and in spite of the fact that discussions of cultural diversity have become commonplace in many settings, research indicates that there is little agreement on its definition (Anand & Winters, 2008).

The large majority of organizations in the United States and many other countries address cultural diversity to some extent and currently, the expression *diversity and inclusion* or *D&I* is more often used to refer to an organization's vision and practices regarding cultural diversity in the workplace. The use of both terms is significant for the following reasons:

- Diversity is relatively objective, observable, and measurable and focuses on differences.

- Managers can quantify diversity, and organizations have devised a number of metrics to measure it. The metrics can be as simple as statistics on the number of women and minorities who are recruited, retained, or promoted and their average salaries.

- Through measures of diversity, organizations aim to demonstrate that they have a diverse workforce that includes people who are representative of different communities.

For example, when the UK's Lloyd's Banking Group put D&I at the core of its operations, it set targets to have 40% women in senior roles by 2020 (Bourke, van Berkel, Garr, & Wong, 2017). Considerable research on cultural diversity focuses on gathering and analyzing these types of data. The numbers that indicate diversity matter. The US Bureau of Labor Statistics regularly measures and reports on various dimensions of cultural diversity; we rely on several of their findings in this chapter.

As opposed to diversity, *inclusion* is a subjective feeling that employees have of belonging and being accepted in an organization. It differs from diversity in that:

- Inclusion addresses an organization's efforts to generate and encourage those feelings.

- It takes into account that, although there may be diverse groups and individuals in an organization, they may not feel welcome, accepted, or engaged.

- Using both D&I is an attempt to address not only the objective count but also whether the organization is actually embracing the diverse employees and whether they feel valued and engaged.

Lloyd's of London also made inclusion and particularly gender equality a core value and changed many of its recruiting practices. Similarly, the North American bank BMO when targeting D&I, not only put in place metrics and new diversity focused measures of success, it also implemented training programs that addressed biases and prepared managers to have tough conversations and codevelop solutions (Bourke et al., 2017).

A more recent trend goes even further and considers the importance of *belonging* defined as

> *...the feeling of security and support when there is a sense of acceptance, inclusion, and identity for a member of a certain group or place, and as the basic fundamental drive to form and maintain lasting, positive, and significant relationships with others. (Agarwal, 2019)*

Belonging moves beyond diversity or D&I and aims at normalizing differences to allow people to address them and helps organizations address cultural diversity more effectively.

1.1.2 Dimensions of Diversity. Diversity can be based on many different factors. Figure 5.1 presents the primary and secondary dimensions that are typically included

Figure 5.1   Primary and Secondary Dimensions of Diversity

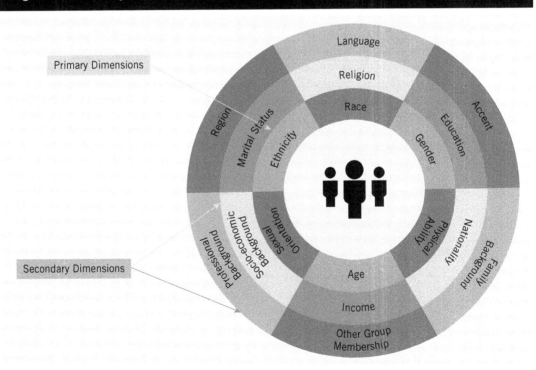

when considering cultural diversity. The distinction between primary and secondary dimensions was first proposed by Marilyn Loden in 1996. The primary dimensions (sometimes called endowed traits—those depicted closest to the individuals in Figure 5.1) are those that are typically visible and less subject to change. They include race, ethnicity, gender, sexual orientation, age, and physical ability. These will be the primary focus of our discussions here and in the next chapter.

The secondary dimensions (sometimes called acquired traits—those depicted further from the individuals in Figure 5.1) are those that can usually be changed and include factors such as nationality, religion, income, education, marital status, as well as several others. Some primary and secondary dimensions will be relevant for some individuals and groups but not for others. For example, your age and the generation you belong to may be a central part of your identity, while for another person, race and sexual orientation may be central. Additionally, each of these dimensions may be more or less visible. For instance, physical abilities may be invisible to others, as may be race or ethnicity or sexual orientation. Similarly, secondary dimensions such as one's religion may be highly visible, such as for Muslim women who wear a hijab or Christians who wear a prominent cross, or they may be undetectable such as when a married person does not wear a wedding ring or band, or when people's nationality is not discernable from their physical characteristics or accent. As we will discuss later in this chapter, some of the dimensions of diversity, particularly those that are visible and prominent, can become a focal point for individuals themselves and for those around them.

1.1.3 Legally Protected Classes in the United States. While organizations may rely on various dimensions of diversity, in the United States, there are a limited number of categories that are considered legally protected (Protected class, 2020). These are:

- Race
- Color
- Religion or creed
- National origin or ancestry
- Sex, including sexual orientation
- Age
- Physical or mental ability
- Veteran status
- Genetic information
- Citizenship

People who belong to any of the above categories are federally and legally protected from employment discrimination on the basis of that characteristic. Many US states have created additional categories, for example protection for LBGTQ individuals. Additionally, each of these categories may include various other factors, such that, for example, sexual harassment falls under sex discrimination. While organizations are legally mandated to not discriminate based on these groupings, they can choose to either strictly comply with the law or expand their own definition and practice of diversity (we discuss this at the end of the chapter).

1.2 Why Does Diversity Matter?

Why should we address diversity in organizations? Wouldn't treating everybody the same way be enough as long as managers are fair? Why do we have to consider individual cultural identities or build diverse teams? In the next section, we will review the research on the specific benefits and challenges to having diverse groups. Here, we address some of the basic social and business reasons why addressing diversity matters. Two fundamental reasons for addressing diversity are social justice and the overall benefits to organizations. Specifically:

- In a fair and just society where there is social justice, there is a moral obligation to treat all individuals with the same respect and provide everyone the same opportunities to perform and succeed. Focusing on diversity aims to achieve this fundamental ideal of social justice.

- Associated with the ideal of social justice is the concept of corporate social responsibility that states businesses can and must be a force for good and take actions that can improve society and the communities in which they operate. Addressing diversity is one such action. In August of 2019, JP Morgan CEO Jamie Dimon, the chair of the US Business Roundtable, speaking on behalf of the group that includes CEOs of several major companies including Amazon and American Airlines, stated: "Major employers are investing in their workers and communities because they know it is the only way to be successful over the long term" (Dilts, 2019).

- A more pragmatic reason for implementing diversity programs is that doing so is a legal requirement. For example, businesses must have regulatory compliance with laws that prevent discrimination based on the protected classes we discussed earlier.

- Diversity is good for business in that it improves performance as measured by financial outcomes, innovation, or employee engagement and satisfaction and allows businesses to access a broader customer base, as demonstrated by a number of research studies.

- Finally, talent is precious and hard to find, culture neutral, and the workforce no longer homogeneous. Managers consistently state that one of their major HR challenges is attracting and retaining high-quality employees (Starner, 2019). If they want to address that challenge successfully, they must be able to address the needs of many diverse employees, not just those who are similar to them or have traditionally been dominant in the workplace.

Today's workforce does not look like the workforce of the 20th century. It is complex and diverse. The reasons society and organizations need to address diversity are complex and a combination of these factors. Regardless, cultural diversity is a fact of life and culture matters and cannot be ignored. Diversity is not decreasing, and it is clear that, by and large, businesses have embraced it as a basic element of success in a global environment.

1.3 Challenges and Controversy

In spite of the social and business case for addressing diversity, the topic is not without challenges and controversy. While most of us are comfortable discussing cross-national cultural differences, handling group culture and diversity often presents a challenge. Talking about culture when we contrast Americans, Canadians, Chinese, Germans, Indians … and so forth, is easy. We can admit that we don't know certain things, we are comfortable asking questions and making comparisons, and we can even keep our sense of humor during such discussions. Members of cross-national teams have no trouble referring to their cultural differences. However, group cultures involve a very different dynamic.

1.3.1 Difficulty in Addressing Diversity. Conversations that involve race, ethnicity, gender, sexual orientation or identity, religion, or other group-based factors are emotionally charged and hard to undertake. As a result, we often avoid them and pretend to ignore key dimensions of one another's complex cultural identities. However, the problem is that because of demographic changes, increased contact, and public scrutiny (e.g., the #metoo movement and lack of diversity in Silicon Valley tech companies) learning to address group-level diversity constructively is more essential than ever.

Consider how comfortable you would be asking people about the dimensions of cultural diversity in Figure 5.1. Would you ask your coworkers sitting next to you in a meeting or at lunch what their race or ethnic background is, how old they are, or what their sexual orientation is? How easy would it be to ask about their income and socioeconomic status, religion, marital status, or the origin of their accent? Alternatively, how comfortable would you be to share that information about yourself?

Table 5.1 Reasons for the Difficulty in Addressing Diversity in the Workplace

For Managers	For One-on-One Interactions
• They may have a parochial view of culture and simply assume that everyone in their organization is the same.	• The diversity dimensions of culture are more personal and potentially more revealing of a person's identity than nationality. They are therefore likely to be a more significant and meaningful part of our cultural identity.
• They may focus on being fair and treating everyone the same.	• Because they are more personal, they may appear inappropriate as a topic of conversation, particularly in work settings.
• They may not have the knowledge and tools to address diversity constructively.	• Some of the dimensions of diversity have deep social, cultural, and historical antecedents and implications that are significant and consequential.
• They may get defensive about addressing cultural issues that appear more personal than cross-national cultures.	• Because of their deep roots, they are often the basis of many stereotypes and biases that people hold and may be unwilling to expose.

The traditional power differential among groups is a key factor. Additionally, in work settings, legal restrictions and organizational policies make these questions sensitive and sometimes illegal.

Your likely discomfort is not unexpected. It is representative of the challenge we face in addressing cultural diversity in all its complex dimensions. The mention of cultural diversity in an organization engenders emotional responses ranging from "Yes; we need to talk about this! It's about time." To "Oh, no; not again…" Why are these areas so hard to address? At some basic level, they are simply another level of culture, another dimension of our cultural identity. The several possible reasons why we are often reluctant to address culture at this level are summarized in Table 5.1.

In their official capacity, managers may believe that everyone is basically the same and therefore, all employees should be treated the same. Highlighting differences or providing something different to one group may appear unfair. For example, a manager may resist requests from a parent who has young children for a flexible schedule or modified work hours because he may feel that doing so would show preferential treatment. Lack of knowledge and skills regarding culture and diversity management can also be a factor. Other challenges further arise during one-on-one interactions at work. Dimensions of diversity can be deeply personal and revealing, making them difficult to address. They also may be the basis of stereotypes and prejudices that we, or others, hold and worry about exposing during such discussions. Group diversity is associated with traditionally unequal power among groups, making the topic hard to address. Finally, because of employment and antidiscrimination laws and regulations, it may be impossible to address some of these diversity issues directly. For example, asking a coworker or employee how old they are and when they may want to retire, even in a casual conversation, may become problematic if the person is let go during layoffs soon after.

There are many good reasons why we may shy away from discussing the dimensions of cultural diversity at work or even in our personal relationships: Too personal, too private, too difficult, and certainly illegal in some cases. However, given that effectively motivating and managing people to help them be engaged and productive means matching individual needs and organizational goals, considering and addressing the cultural diversity dimensions are relevant and essential. Additionally, if discussions of cultural diversity make people uncomfortable because they are personal and meaningful for most of us, that is precisely why we must learn how to address them *appropriately* in organizational settings and in our roles as managers. Finally, if the discomfort is related to blatant or implicit prejudice and biases related to views of in- and out-groups, then addressing them becomes particularly important as they may impact work-related decisions. If these dimensions matter to us and if they are a significant and meaningful part of who we are, we cannot simply ignore them.

1.3.2 Controversy and Challenges. To make matters even more challenging, issues related to the management of a diverse workforce have become both political and controversial, triggering a diversity backlash (Eli Inc., 2020). Critiques range from complaining that the concept is poorly defined, to diversity being overused, to having philosophical arguments related to questioning the need for such programs (for a review see, Berrey, 2015). Specifically:

- The definition of diversity can be as simple as what was presented earlier in this chapter. But it can also include other factors, such as racial inequality, gender discrimination, the relative power and positioning of various ethnic groups, often in comparison to white males, or the issue of white privilege (Holmes, 2015). It is not easy to define what a diversity program is supposed to address.

- Diversity and how it is applied is further interpreted differently depending on group membership. For example, for African Americans, diverse or integrated neighborhoods mean a 50/50 split between whites and minorities, whereas for Whites, the distribution is less equal (e.g., Farley, 2018). Determining the desired outcome of diversity programs is therefore challenging.

- The prevalence of the term diversity in various organizations along with various definitions and different interpretations often creates confusion and some suggest that it has become an empty buzzword (Demby, 2015; Sanneh, 2017).

- Finally, some critiques of the concept of diversity suggest that in their search for social justice and equality, diversity programs create a new type of unfairness and discrimination that targets the majority white population (for a review see Dover, Major, & Kaiser, 2016).

This final point is the most controversial and emotionally charged critique of diversity. Accusations of "reverse discrimination" that have led to lawsuits, most notably against college admission processes (e.g., the lawsuit against Harvard University in 2019; Hartocollis, 2019), are associated with this position. On the one hand, some argue that by addressing diversity, organizations show favoritism to some groups over others. As a result, such programs alienate and anger some groups (Dover et al., 2016) and may lead to people questioning the qualifications and competence of diverse employees and managers (Lawrence, n.d.). On the other hand, proponents of diversity state that by not addressing diversity, organizations ignore the long-standing and residual impact of social, racial, and gender injustice. Debating such issues is beyond the scope of this chapter or book. However, it is essential that managers be aware that what may be a relatively straightforward and simple matter to some will undoubtedly look very different to others.

Whether one agrees with how organizations have approached diversity or not, there is no denying that people have different cultural identities that influence their assumptions, values, beliefs, and behaviors and how they see and interpret their environment; diversity (in its simplest definition) is a fact of life. Therefore, insisting that one approach to management should and must work for everyone is, at best, unproductive. Effective managers who have a Cultural Mindset (CM), are aware of their culture and its impact, and take culture into consideration when managing others. The approach in this book is to focus on CMC that shapes everyone's assumptions, values, beliefs, and behaviors, rather than culture being something about "others," meaning minorities, or blaming one group or another. Further, the concept of culture-just-is (CJI) as a factor that should be understood and taken into consideration, rather than evaluated, help managers address culture and support their employees, and organizations can be more effective, while avoiding some of the more controversial aspects of diversity discussion.

2. RESEARCH ON THE IMPACT OF DIVERSITY

LO 5.2 Elaborate on the research about the impact of diversity on groups and organizational performance

One way to answer the question of why companies should aim to be diverse and inclusive is to review the research on the impact of diversity on individual and group performance and on overall firm performance. How and to what extent does diversity in membership impact groups and organizations?

2.1 Diversity in Groups

Do groups with diverse or heterogeneous members have an advantage? Research on the composition of groups shows it can have an impact on how a group functions and the type of decisions it makes (Moreland, Levine, & Wingert, 2009; van Dijk, Meyer, van Engen, & Loyd, 2017; Yam et al., 2018). Strong evidence suggests that groups with members who have similar backgrounds and orientations achieve higher cohesion (e.g., Dunlop & Beauchamp, 2011); those members often like one another more (Glaman, Jones, & Rozelle, 1996); they experience less conflict (Moreland et al., 2009); they reach decisions more quickly (Civettini, 2007); and they have lower turnover (O'Reilly, Caldwell, & Barnett, 1989). It is clear that similarity of group members helps the internal functioning of a group, provides validation to the members and, by reducing conflict, provides a comfortable environment for its members.

However, having diverse groups offers many benefits as well (Moreland et al., 2009; Nahavandi & Aranda, 1994). Diverse groups generate more alternatives and conduct a more thorough evaluation of those alternatives than homogeneous ones (e.g., Finkelstein & Hambrick, 1996). They also consider the ethical and moral consequences of their decisions more fully (Kujala & Pietilainen, 2007) and support members in integrating information that can improve their decision-making (Rink & Ellemers, 2010). Studies indicate that a diverse group with lesser ability members performs better in problem-solving than a group of similar high-ability individuals (Hong & Page, 2004), and groups with gender diversity have been shown to be more effective in tasks requiring complex information management and processing (Fenwick & Neal, 2002). Some research further suggests that being around a diverse group of people can lead group members to be more critical thinkers, reexamine facts, remain more objective, and make fewer factual errors (Rock & Grant, 2016). Furthermore, diverse perspectives are particularly needed when groups face complex situations (Mello & Ruckes, 2006), and such diversity is one of the elements that can prevent the poor decision-making that results from groupthink (Dumphy, 2004; Esser, 1998; Janis, 1971; Morehead, Neck, & West, 1998). In their comprehensive analysis of the impact of various types of heterogeneity on top management teams (TMTs) of organizations, Hambrick, Cho, and Chen (1996) conclude that heterogeneity is generally associated with performance improvement.

Overall, diversity in group membership appears to improve some outcomes such as productivity and innovation and negatively impacts process issues such as conflict (for a review see Stahl, Maznevski, Voigt, & Jonsen, 2010). The benefits of diversity appear to be most evident in complex, turbulent, and changing environments and situations where multiple perspectives can contribute to group performance. Harvard Business School Professor Francesca Gino suggests that a diverse group can help reduce the impact of biases:

> *That our decisions get sidetracked by biases is now well established. While it is hard to change how our brains are wired, it's possible to change the context of decisions by architecting the composition of decision-making teams for more diverse perspectives.* (Larson, 2017)

Her views are supported by many other researchers. Katherine Phillips, Professor of leadership and ethics at the Columbia Business School, says: "Simply interacting with individuals who are different forces group members to prepare better, to anticipate alternative viewpoints and to expect that reaching consensus will take effort" (Phillips, 2014).

These research findings have been part of the impetus for recommendations to increase diversity in organizations (Cox, 2000; Fitzsimmons, 2013), and especially to increase diversity in the leadership of public and business organizations (Combs & Luthans, 2007).

2.2 Diversity and Organizational Performance

In addition to the social justice argument, research indicates that diverse groups, including diverse leadership teams, can make better decisions particularly in complex environments, but does that translate into better organizational performance? In other words, does having a diverse workforce provide a competitive advantage, increase profits, or create value? Is there a business case to be made for D&I? An extensive study by McKinsey & Co provides clear answers regarding the impact of gender and ethnic diversity on firm financial performance by looking at over 1,000 companies in several industry groups across different countries (Hunt, Prince, Dixon-Fyle, & Yee, 2018). The research finds that more gender-diverse companies are 21% more likely to have better financial performance and better value creation (as measured by their profit margin). Likewise, ethnic diversity in the organizations is associated with 33% higher likelihood of better profits. These findings are further mirrored for diversity in the TMT and on the board of directors (Barta, Kleiner, & Neuman, 2012; Hunt, Layton, & Prince, 2015; Torchia, Calabró, & Morner, 2015). Interestingly, the researchers also find what they call a "penalty for low diversity" where companies with a less diverse workforce are more likely to underperform (Hunt et al., 2018). The link between diversity and financial performance has even been found in venture capital companies that are notoriously nondiverse, where the more similar the partners, the lower their investments' performance (Gompers & Kovvali, 2018).

Extensive research further shows that diversity at all levels is associated with more innovative strategies and more innovation (e.g., Jg et al., 2017). A survey of 321 executives conducted by *Forbes* indicates that they value diversity as an engine of innovation (Global Diversity and Inclusion, 2011). Companies with diverse management introduce more product innovations and are better able to serve global markets (Nathan & Lee, 2015), and countries where there are many different value orientations are better innovators (Ramasamy & Yeung, 2016). The large majority of these studies have been across different industries and conducted in the United States as well as other countries. For example, a survey of 1,700 companies across eight countries shows that there is a significant correlation between diversity and innovation, and the more the companies included different dimensions of diversity, the stronger their innovation (as measured by the freshness of their revenue mix; Lorenzo & Reeves, 2018). The study's authors state:

> *Diversity has sometimes been critiqued as a culturally normative concept. Our results show that diversity can drive innovation performance in countries as different as Germany and India, however. Moreover, they imply that it can so do in a variety of ways. (Lorenzo & Reeves, 2018)*

2.3 The Bottom Line

The evidence of the overall positive impact of diversity on performance of groups and organizations is consistent: diversity enhances innovation, decision-making, and the financial bottom line. These effects are due to several potential reasons. Companies that have diverse leadership and a diverse workforce:

- Project a positive image in an increasingly global and diverse world

- Can attract a wider and deeper talent pool

- Can access a broader group of consumers

- Are able to engage their diverse employees and motivate them better

- Have access to diverse perspectives and approaches when facing complex situations that are the norm in today's global and turbulent environments

Lisa Wardell, the CEO of Adtalem Global Education, a Fortune 1000 company with over 18,000 employees, who has been highly successful in building diversity at all levels of her organization, says: "I believe that by broadening the talent pool, we've been able to recruit the leadership needed to focus on student outcomes and improvements, increase performance, drive growth, and meet the strategic objectives of our diverse board" (Wardell, 2018a, 2018b).

3. THE DIVERSITY LANDSCAPE

We know from extensive research that having a diverse workforce that is engaged and contributes to the organization, while sometimes challenging, can help an organization be more innovative and effective, particularly in a complex environment. That in and of itself should be reason enough for organizations to aim to have a diverse workforce. However, there is also the simpler matter of the changing demographic landscape both within countries and across the world. The workforce and consumers are not the homogenous groups that some managers remember them to be; the world has changed.

3.1 Changes That Drive Diversity

People from many different backgrounds who embrace their diverse cultural identities are an increasingly large part of the workforce and a powerful segment of consumers. While these diverse groups have always existed, many were not welcome in business organizations, and when they were present, they either were expected to fully assimilate to how the majority acted, were relegated to low-level positions, or simply ignored and dismissed. The 1950s and 1960s organization so dramatically represented in popular media by programs such as *Mad Men* was populated and run by Anglo-European men. Minorities were a rare sight, and women, as long as they were not married, typically held low-level and support jobs. That cultural context no longer exists. Whether it is based on ethnic differences, gender, or generational changes, the population and the workforce are not homogeneous.

3.1.1 Cultural and Social Changes. Various events in the 1960s created major cultural and social shifts that affected the society and changed the face of the workforce. By the end of the 1970s an increasing number of women were using the pill (Goldin & Katz, 2002), freeing them from unwanted pregnancies and allowing them to enter and stay in the workforce in record numbers (18 million in 1950 to 66 million in 2000; Toossi, 2002). By pushing for antidiscrimination laws and numerous other equality-driven practices, the Civil Rights movement in the United States during the same period lowered barriers in education, housing, social programs, and other areas and allowed a large number of minorities to more easily enter various organizations. While previous generations of these diverse groups, when they were allowed into the workplace, had little power and were expected to assimilate fully and be satisfied with their lower status and pay and limited opportunities, with increasing numbers driven by legislation and social change, the new participants started demanding equal rights, equal pay, and the ability to be themselves and contribute in their own right. Continued demographic shifts further contributed to pressures for change.

3.1.2 Demographic Changes. Organizations simply have to respond to the needs of diverse groups if they want to attract and retain the best talent and continue to be able to sell their products and services. Figures 5.2 and 5.3 represent the cultural diversity in the United States. A variety of demographic trends and projections, some of which are presented in Table 5.2, further show that the workforce is changing in the United States and around the world. Organizations simply cannot expect to continue attracting the type of employees or customers they have been relying on; they must learn to work with diverse audiences.

The demographic changes and trends in the United States and around the world are drastic and clear. The number of Anglo-European men who have been dominant in business and were the majority in most organizations is decreasing while women, various minorities, and younger generations are entering the workforce at higher numbers. Cultural diversity is also driven by migration (the movement of people around the world) and immigration (relocation to specific countries), as businesses in the United States and other countries rely heavily on new immigrants as workers and consumers (Aguilar, 2013).

3.1.3 Migration and Immigration. In the United States, continued immigration from around the world, and more specifically from Central and South America and Asia, is

Figure 5.2 US Demographic Makeup

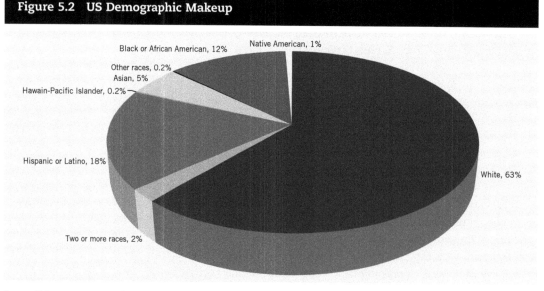

Black or African American, 12%
Native American, 1%
Other races, 0.2%
Asian, 5%
Hawain-Pacific Islander, 0.2%
Hispanic or Latino, 18%
Two or more races, 2%
White, 63%

Source: U.S. Census – American Fact Finder 2017.

Figure 5.3 Changes in Diversity in the United States by Age Group

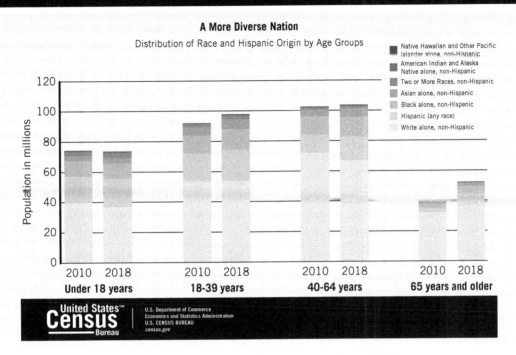

A More Diverse Nation

Distribution of Race and Hispanic Origin by Age Groups

Legend:
- Native Hawaiian and Other Pacific Islander alone, non-Hispanic
- American Indian and Alaska Native alone, non-Hispanic
- Two or More Races, non-Hispanic
- Asian alone, non-Hispanic
- Black alone, non-Hispanic
- Hispanic (any race)
- White alone, non-Hispanic

United States™ Census Bureau
U.S. Department of Commerce
Economics and Statistics Administration
U.S. CENSUS BUREAU
census.gov

Source: Vintage 2018 Population Estimates www.census.gov/programs-surveys/popest.html

increasing the diversity of the workforce, where Hispanics and Asians are the two fastest growing groups in the labor force (Toossi, 2002). Economics Professor Sari Pekkala Kerr believes that with an aging workforce around the world "immigration is a powerful way for countries to continue economic development and growth" (Blanding, 2018). As exemplified by the number of businesses they start and many success stories, immigrants are highly entrepreneurial and a source of economic vitality. In the United States many new immigrants including cofounder of Sun Microsystems Vinod Khosla from India, Arianna Huffington from Greece cofounder of Huffington Post, Chinese-born Weli Dai cofounder of Marvel Technologies, South-African Peter Thiel cofounder of PayPal, Canadian-South African, Elon Musk of Tesla, and Gisele Bundchen from Brazil founder of Sejaa Skincare are among the top entrepreneurs. Numerous second-generation (born in the United States to immigrant parents) immigrants including Steve Jobs, founder of Apple, Jeff Bezos, founder of Amazon, and others such as founders of EBay, Kraft Food, Google, Yahoo, and Panda Express are among the top entrepreneurs in the United States. By some estimate, 40% of Fortune 500 companies are founded by immigrants or their children (Aguilar, 2013).

Worldwide, migration and an aging population in many countries are further creating demographic shifts. In Japan and Western and Northern European countries, there simply will not be enough "native" people to work to support the economy and

Table 5.2   Some Demographic Trends

- By 2050, Caucasian or white Americans will no longer constitute the majority of the US population.

- By 2050, the total US population will increase by 36% to reach 441 million, with immigrants and their children making up 88% of the increase.

- Hispanics are projected to be the largest minority group of voters in the 2020 US election.

- By 2055, Asians, who made up less than 6% of population in 2018, are estimated to surpass Hispanics as the largest foreign-born group in the United States.

- Women are expected to see their numbers in the labor force grow slowly, but their growth rate will still be faster than that of men, leading to an increase from 46.8% in 2014 to 47.2% in 2024.

- The number of women in workforce was 18 million in 1950 and 66 million in 2000 (growing approximately 2.4% a year).

- Men's share of the labor force is expected to decrease from 53.2% in 2014 to 52.8% in 2024, a rate that has been declining steadily since the end of the 1940s (growing only 0.6% a year).

- By 2024, Hispanics are projected to be nearly one-fifth of the labor force.

- Black men have a lower labor participation rate than men from other race and ethnic groups. Black women have had the highest labor participation rate, compared with women of other race and ethnic groups.

- Millennials may be the largest generational cohort in history—79.8 million in 2016.

- Immigrants to the United States started one out of four venture-backed public companies between 1990 and 2005.

- More than 40% of new businesses in New York and California are started by new immigrants.

- The number of consumers within the American population is growing less than 1% annually.

- There are more than 250 million migrants worldwide (2018).

- By the end of the 21st century, there will be more Muslims than Christians in the world; and 10% of all Europeans will be Muslims.

- The number of young and working-age people is projected to decline by 10% in China, 25% in Europe, 30% in South Korea, and more than 40% in Japan.

- By the mid-2050s, a third or more of the population in Europe and East Asia will be over 65 years.

- The United Nations estimates that 2 million people a year will move from poorer to developed nations over the next 40 years.

Sources: Based on information in Blanding (2018), Cilluffo and Cohn (2019), Danzinger (2018), Kotkin (2010), and Labor Projections to 2024 (2015).

the social systems. Germany became aware of this challenge earlier than most other countries during its post–World War II economic boom. When recruitment from Southern Europe did not fulfill the country's need, Germany's big businesses pressured their government to turn to its former ally Turkey, and invited Turks between the ages of 18 and 45 years to be *Gastarbeiter*, or guest workers (Reay, 2017). While they were supposed to stay for short periods of time, by 1973, 700,000 Turks were living in Germany and although under German law they could not become citizens, their children and grandchildren did. There are now approximately 4 million people of Turkish descent living in Germany (Reay, 2017). Studies indicate that they are poorer, less educated, underpaid, and less well integrated into German society than other immigrant groups (Bartsch, Brandt, & Steinvorth, 2010). They are, however, essential to the economy, while Germany, like many other European countries, is struggling to integrate diverse people it desperately needs for its economy to continue to flourish.

3.2 Diversity in Organizations

Many companies have had some sort of program to increase workforce diversity since at least the 1970s and several boast about extensive recruitment efforts and organizational changes that have attracted diverse individuals (Dobbin & Kalev, 2016). According to the Bureau of Labor Statistics, the overall US workforce roughly mirrors the country's demographic makeup with labor participation approximately 60% across all ethnic groups (BLS Reports, 2018). All groups, including women, are working more or less to the same extent. However, some striking disparities and gaps emerge.

3.2.1 Disparities in Pay. First, there are earning gaps among all the groups and between men and women that hold across all major occupational groups (see Table 5.3). Asians fare better than other ethnic groups in the income area, but they still face challenges. Because they have both more education and higher average income than others, they are often overlooked in diversity discussions and sometimes even included with whites in various diversity measures (McGirt, 2018). Buck Gee and Denise Peck, two former Silicon Valley executives who looked into the challenges that Asians face in organizations, state: "Because Asian Americans are not considered an underrepresented minority, they are given little priority or attention in diversity programs" (McGirt, 2018).

3.2.2 Lack of Diversity in Leadership. In 2018, the BBC created a composite image of the top 100 US Fortune 500 CEOs to produce the average face of a CEO and, not surprisingly, it was a white male (What the average American CEO looks like, 2018). The numbers in Table 5.3 regarding leadership of Fortune 500 companies fluctuate as CEOs retire and are replaced, but the overall trends are not changing.

Table 5.3 Labor Statistics by Ethnicity[a] and Gender

	Whites	Blacks	Hispanics	Asians
Percentage of the US workforce[b]	78%	13%	17%	6%
Earning/week	Men: $971 Women: $795	Men: $710 Women: $657	Men: $695 Women: $603	Men: $1,207 Women: $903
Number of leadership positions in Fortune 500[c]	Men: 456 Women: 23	Men: 3 Women: 0	Men: 11 Women: 0	Men: 5 (4 Indians; 1 Chinese) Women: 2 (1 Indian; 1 Chinese)

[a]BLS does not provide data for other ethnic groups.
[b]89% of Hispanics are classified as White—the total adds up to more than 100%.
[c]These numbers change regularly—these are best ones available as of August 2019.
Sources: BLS Reports (2018) and Donnelly (2018).

The shocking 2015 *New York Times* headline "Fewer Women Run Big Companies Than Men Named John" dramatically illustrates the gender gap in the leadership of big US companies (Wolfers, 2015). There has been some progress in corporate boards, but the top leadership is still strikingly white and male, all the while the labor force no longer is. An Ernst and Young study showed that for every one woman, there were more Jameses, Roberts, Johns, and Williams—combined—serving on the boards of S&P 1,500 companies (McGregor, 2015). A recent study shows that women and members of underrepresented groups occupy 38.6% of board seats of Fortune 100 companies (Olson, 2019).

However, when it comes to top leadership, minorities, and particularly women of color, are practically absent. It is clear that minorities face a considerable, and sometimes insurmountable, challenge when trying to reach top leadership roles. Many minorities have voiced how lonely and stressful it can be to be one of the few people of color in still white higher organizational levels. The feeling of being on the spot and under a microscope, having to carefully monitor one's behavior, and having to judiciously craft an appropriate and acceptable professional identity can be taxing and difficult to manage for women of all races, ethnic minorities, and members of the LGBTQ community. Devon Carbado and Mitu Gulati (2013), authors of the book *Acting White?*, suggest that members of minority groups have to be careful to not too closely fit the stereotypes others have of their group, in other words "be black, but not too black." We discussed some of the challenges created by such perceptual biases in Chapter 3, and we will revisit them later in this chapter.

US companies are not alone in the lack of diversity in their leadership. For example, a 2019 report by Deloitte indicates that while minorities make up 23% of Canada's population, they only hold 4% of corporate board positions (Canada at 175, 2019). Additionally, the report indicates that members of underrepresented groups, including many LGBTQ individuals, continue to witness or face discrimination. A 2017 survey in the United Kingdom found that there were only 36 ethnic minorities and women among the top 1,000 most powerful leaders in a variety of sectors (Duncan & Holder, 2017). France has only one top female CEO (Engie's Isabelle Kocher); women lead only 3% of the 145 large Nordic companies. Referring to the gender gap Karen Frøsig, who is the CEO of Denmark's Sydbank, says: "At the executive level the cork is still in the bottle" (Zander, 2014). To address this gap, Norway has a formal 40% quota for women on company boards, Finland has a softer quota, and the EU is looking at imposing similar rules. However, even with the required quota in Norway, there was no female CEO in the top 32 companies in that country (Zander, 2014).

The demographic changes are evident and undeniable. The social and historical contexts that shape them and triggered the social movements of the 1960s and 1970s and underlie the diversity debate are more complex.

4. APPROACHES TO DIVERSITY AROUND THE WORLD

LO 5.4 Compare approaches to diversity around the world

The dimensions and definitions of cultural diversity are not the same across all countries. While in the United States diversity means cultural diversity and refers to the dimensions presented in Figure 5.1, in Europe the focus is more often on language and nationality. In other countries such as Mexico or China the word diversity evokes biological diversity (Mor Barak, 2014). All countries do not have similar assumptions regarding how diversity should be addressed, or if it should be addressed at all. Table 5.4 presents a checklist of the presence of diversity-related laws in the world's top five economies. It is important to note that the simple existence or absence of legislation does not necessarily indicate cultural diversity practices, lack of discrimination, or inclusive organizations. However, as you can see from the information in Table 5.4, all of the countries in this list have some legislations or policies aimed at some aspect of diversity. Although there are differences in whether and how countries address diversity, a global survey conducted by the accounting firm Deloitte shows that close to 70% of executives rate D&I as an important issue (Bourke et al., 2017). The same research also shows that progress is not fast enough and that many companies and executives could be doing more.

Table 5.4 Diversity Legislation in the World's Top Five Economies

Country	Race/Ethnicity	Gender	Sexual Orientation	Ability	Age	Religion
USA	x	x	x	x	x	x
China	–	x	–	x	–	–
Japan	–	x	x	x	x	x
Germany	x	x	x	x	x	x
UK	x	x	x	x	x	x

Sources: Adapted from information in Human Rights Watch-World Reports (2019) and Mor Barak (2014).

4.1 Two Different Philosophical Approaches to Diversity: France and the United States

Comparing France and the United States illustrates two of the philosophies related to addressing diversity. While both countries are Western democracies and include many culturally diverse individuals and groups, they approach diversity in dissimilar ways.

4.1.1 Liberté, Egalité, Fraternité. The French constitution's first article states that the country is an "indivisible, secular, democratic and social republic. It ensures the equality of all citizens before the law, without distinction of origin, race or religion" (McGonagle, 2017). France's constitution is based on the principles of secularism and universalism where everyone is the same. By focusing on this sameness, the French ideal is to treat everyone fairly by *erasing*, rather than celebrating, their differences. As a result, the country does not collect data related to race or ethnicity or other group-related differences or institute policies, laws, and regulations that in any way may highlight differences. It is estimated that 85% are white Europeans with other groups from many of France's former colonies in sub-Saharan Africa, and an estimated 10% are Muslims. One aspect of France's approach to cultural diversity which is in line with the country's identity as a secular nation is the ban on the conspicuous display of obvious religious symbols, such as a yarmulke, a veil, a turban, or a cross in public settings such as schools. UCLA professor Laure Murat, a French immigrant to the United States, states:

> *The legacy of secularism in France, promoting the idea of a "neutral" and "universal" citizen regardless of his or her race, religion, sexual orientation, and so on, leads to a politics that is the reverse of American multiculturalism… On the*

one hand, you have a utopia that would like to erase all kinds of differences and posit a neutral Republic, on the other, a society that pays lots of attention to identity differences, focusing on the rights of minorities and promoting "inclusiveness." (Murat & Perreau, 2016)

France's approach to diversity is based on an admirable ideal that aims to treat everyone equally by removing differences and their impact. However, a negative outcome of this approach is that when you disregard cultural differences, you simply do not address them or the challenges and problems that they create in organizations and in society. Referring back to acculturation strategies we reviewed in Chapter 4, by relying on the assumption that there are no cultural differences based on ethnicity or race, and that therefore, there is no need to preserve them, everyone in France is supposed to assimilate and simply become French. Addressing this challenge and how ethnic groups are treated, Bruno Perreau, an MIT professor, states: "They are asked to abandon who they are and what they think and to prove they can act, talk, and function like the majority. But they are permanently called out in the name of their identities and practices" (Murat & Perreau, 2016). In other words, assimilation is the only option that is considered; however, because of obvious and clearly visible differences in physical characteristics, religion, language, and accents, in-groups and out-groups still exist and various groups are seen as different and are not allowed to fully assimilate. The riots in 2005 and 2017 in several areas of France have been partly attributed to segregated housing, discrimination in employment and education, police brutality targeting ethnic minorities, and overall lack of economic opportunity for ethnic groups. Nadira Achab, whose grandparents were Algerian, but whose family has lived in France, echoed the perception of many minorities in the country: "People here just want to be treated like normal citizens, not second-class citizens. It's sad that we're still not…I'm French, my parents are French, we've been French for two generations, yet I'm still constantly being asked: 'Are you French?'" (Chrisafis, 2015).

4.1.2 A Nation of Immigrants. The approach to multiculturalism in the United States is drastically different than that of France.

Given the history of immigration in the United States, the presence of different groups is fully recognized. Although the various groups have not been treated equally, the ideals and goals in the United States are no longer to erase differences but instead to acknowledge and respect them. The melting pot which favored assimilation has given way to the salad or mosaic. Without debating which of the two approaches is more effective, they are both the product of different approaches and assumptions related to cultural differences. Each is the result of the CMC in which it was developed and they simple are—CJI. Nonetheless, the French are often shocked at the extent to which Americans focus on race and talk about ethnic differences. Americans, for their part, are puzzled by how the French do not allow for personal expressions of differences and focus on sameness instead.

The United States has been at the forefront of both the social movement toward cultural diversity and some, but not all, of the legislation that protects various minority groups. Other countries have made more progress regarding some aspects of both gender and LGBTQ rights; nonetheless, topics related to D&I appear to be more in the fabric of many US companies than other countries. In the United States, the Title VII of the Civil Rights Act of 1964 gives the Federal government broad powers to fight discrimination through the Equal Employment Opportunity Commission (EEOC; see Appendix B for a timeline). Several other legislations have further built on the 1964 Act to provide protection based on a number of categories, called protected classes. Specifically, in the United States, employers may not legally make employment decisions based on a person's race, color, religion, sex (including pregnancy, gender identity, and sexual orientation), national origin, age (40 years or older), marital status, disability, or genetic information (EEOC—https://www.eeoc.gov/employees/). These laws address several forms of discrimination including sexual harassment and hostile work environments. While providing equal opportunity as a principle is not controversial, affirmative action, that aims at correcting historical discrimination particularly against African Americans, by providing them with additional opportunities, has been hotly debated and labeled as "reverse discrimination" by some. Even with affirmative action, the United States does not have any quotas regarding women or minorities, as is the case in Mexico for political parties or some other countries such as Norway regarding percentage of women on company boards.

While all organizations claim to comply with diversity-related laws, the many complaints and lawsuits brought on by employees indicate that even basic legal compliance is far from simple or fully implemented. In 2018, the EEOC received 76,418 charges of workplace discrimination related to retaliation, sex, disability, race, age, and national origin as the top causes, and secured $505 million for victims in private sector, state and local government, and federal workplaces (EEOC, 2019). These do not include the many other complaints that are addressed internally and through civil lawsuits that are brought or settled. Nonetheless, the ideals and principles of diversity have taken hold in the large majority of US companies as represented by the focus on D&I.

4.2 Mexico: Legislating Gender Parity

Similar to France, Mexico does not keep official statistics on ethnicity. Statistics available through other organizations estimate that 60% of the country's population is Mexican Mestizo from the intermarriage of indigenous people and Europeans, with 30% Amerindians or mostly Amerindians who are the indigenous people of the country and another 10% Europeans who are primarily the direct descendants of the Spanish who conquered Mexico in the 16th century (World Atlas-Mexico, 2019). Mexico recognizes 62 ethnic and 68 linguistic groups (Herrera, 2015). Commenting on race and appearance is much more tolerated than in the United States, and Mexicans tend to focus more on social class and socioeconomic background as the source of inequality and discrimination rather than on race or ethnicity. Additionally, slang labels based on skin color are common as those who have light skin, whether they are Mexican or foreigners, are openly called "güero(a)." A particular area of challenge for Mexico has been gender inequality in a highly masculine culture (more about this in Chapters 7 and 8). Glaring and persistent gender inequality continues to exist in areas of economic participation, health, employment, and education (The Global Gender Gap Report, 2018).

Mexico's approach to diversity has been top-down through changes in legislation rather than slower, voluntary actions. In the mid-1990s the country officially and legally recognized its multicultural character (Herrera, 2015), and a 2014 landmark constitutional reform now mandates that political parties enforce gender parity in their selection of candidates, so that women must make up 50% of those on any party's ballot. As a result, in 2018, women won close to 50% of the seats in the Lower House of Congress and Senate, placing Mexico in the top five countries for gender equity in political representation (Mlambo-Ngcuka, 2018). The new mayor of Mexico City, Claudia Sheinbaum, states: "Gender equality has to be a part of the national project. It can't just be women in elected posts, and that's it. The country is going to have to change dramatically, with more rights and more representation for women" (Whelan, 2018). It will take some time to see whether this legislated gender parity will lead to cultural changes regarding gender in other areas. However, the Mexican case provides an experiment for other countries to see whether legislating equality and diversity can be effective.

4.3 Japan: Slow Entry Into Cultural Diversity

Japan, which is a liberal democracy and the world's third largest economy, is often cited as one of the most culturally homogeneous countries in the world. Ninety-eight percent of the country's residents identify themselves as Yamato, a dynasty that has ruled Japan since its birth in the 7th century BC (World Atlas-Japan, 2019). There are few regional differences and even fewer immigrants. In modern history, Koreans, who are the largest group of immigrants in Japan, came after Japan colonized Korea and in the aftermath of the Korean War between the North and the South in the 1950s. They have not been particularly welcome and have never fully integrated into the mainstream. Since there are no birthright citizenship laws in Japan, Korean immigrants and their children who are born in Japan do not have permanent status and have remained on the fringes of society (Smith, 2019). Gender equity is a further challenge. Japan's constitution has recognized equal rights for women since the end of World War II, but it has one of the worst records among industrialized countries regarding gender equity (ranked 110 among 149 countries; Global Gender Gap Report, 2018) with three quarters of Japanese companies reporting no female senior executives. Japanese women still face a stark choice between staying single and working or getting married and having children. Women work in high numbers, but they often do so in part-time and low-paid jobs and quit to get married and start a family. In a recent scandal where academic records were altered to give male medical students preferential admission over more qualified women, Tetsuo Yukioka, a university administrator, admitted: "I suspect that there was a lack of sensitivity to the rules of modern society" (Larmer, 2018). The reason for denying women admission was the age-old assumption that they will waste their education since they will quit once they have children.

Japan is facing demographic-driven economic challenges. Its population is aging and the birth rates are low, factors that have contributed to the impetus for the beginning of a diversity movement. The country has recently granted over 300,000 visas to workers primarily from China, Vietnam, and the Philippines for the care-giving, food, farming, and a number of other industries (Yamawaki, 2019). These newcomers are not expected to stay long, and many are not allowed to bring their family members. Similarly, economic needs have been the cause of a movement labeled "womenomics" originated by Kathy Matsui, the Japanese-American vice chair of Goldman Sachs Japan, and adopted by former Prime minister Shinzo Abe who stated that his aim is to create "a society where women can shine" (Larmer, 2018).

The idea of multiculturalism is new to Japan, and it is driven by labor shortages and economic needs rather than social justice or human right principles. Regardless of the motive, like many other parts of the world, there is a recognition that the talent needed to feed the economic engine is diverse. As a result, the government has stated that it aims to create a "vibrant cohesive society that respects diverse cultures" (Yamawaki, 2019).

4.4 India: Social Class as a Dimension of Diversity

India is not as ethnically diverse as many other countries (72% Indo Aryans, 25% Dravidians, and 3% other ethnicities; CIA World Factbook-India, 2019), but the country offers cultural diversity on other dimensions. By some estimates, there are over 200 dialects and languages spoken in India, 22 of them officially recognized, with Hindi as the most dominant (41% of the population), followed by Bengali (8.1%), Telugu (7.2%), Marathi (7%), Tamil (6%), and many others, and English serving as the official and business language (World Atlas-India, 2019). There is also consider-able religious diversity with a majority of Hindus (80%) and a number of other groups (Muslims [14.25%], Christians [2.3%], Sikhs [1.7%], and 2% other religions (CIA World Factbook-India, 2019). Legislation in 2019 that banned new Muslim migrants from the country gave rise to accusations of racism and considerable social unrest that illustrate India's ongoing challenges regarding religious diversity. Additionally, many regional differences are reflected in rivalries between groups such as Southern and Northern Indians, and Punjabis and Madrassis or Tamilians.

A significant diversity dimension that is rather unique to India is the ancient caste system that provides a rigid social hierarchy and divides Hindus into four categories (Brahmins, Kshatriyas, Vaishyas, and Shudras) and the outcaste or untouchable. The main casts are further divided into thousands of subcastes based on occupations, or Jatis (Meena, 2015; "What is India's caste system," 2019). The caste system, which was reinforced by the British during their occupation of the country to segregate Indians, is no longer legal or officially recognized. Although there is mobility among the castes, a whole group, not individuals move up, so the system continues to create sharp dividing lines in India. As a result, since the 1950s, many laws, similar to affirmative action laws in the United States, have aimed to stop caste discrimination and correct its impact through quotas in government and education ("What is India's caste system," 2019). While the country is changing, the fact that only 5.8% of Indian marriages are between people from different castes, a percentage that has changed little in 4 decades (Ray, Chaudhuri, & Sahai, 2017), indicates that the laws have not erased the deep cultural assumptions, values, beliefs, and behaviors. A recent murder of a young man who married a woman from a higher caste further demonstrates the staying power of old stereotypes (Slater, 2019).

Deep cultural assumptions change slowly, but India's booming economy and business organizations are taking advantage of the country's diversity. Studies indicate that linguistic, religious, and regional diversity are increasing in many organizations, and gender diversity is particularly prominent in the powerful software industry (Meena, 2015). Additionally, 2014 laws have aimed to end discrimination against transgender individuals by recognizing a third gender, taking a step toward changing deep stigma associated with the LGBTQ community. Furthermore, several other new policies governing maternity benefits and reporting requirements to prevent sexual harassment support gender diversity (Wijekoon, Sutton, Alvi, & Gopalikrishnan, 2018). Finally, the many powerful and successful global and multinational corporations such as the Tata Group (https://www.tata.com/newsroom/diversity-is-good-for-business-tcs), Café Coffee Day (https://www.cafecoffeeday.com/awards), the Godrej Group (https://www.godrej.com/who-we-are.html), and other more local companies have made D&I a cornerstone of their mission and corporate culture. Vidur Gupta, director of the staffing firm Spectrum Talent Management, states: "A lot of our clients, which are global multinationals, give us an extra or added incentive—up to 25% of our fee—to help recruit female candidates" (Sushma, 2018).

4.5 The European Union: Ideals of Equality and Uneven Application

The European Charter of Fundamental Rights Title III-Article 21 broadly supports diversity and states:

Any discrimination based on any ground such as sex, race, colour, ethnic or social origin, genetic features, language, religion or belief, political or any other opinion, membership of a national minority, property, birth, disability, age or sexual orientation shall be prohibited. (https://eur-lex.europa.eu/legal-content/EN/TXT/?uri=CELEX:12012P/TXT)

While the EU can be considered as a collective, there are many differences among the various countries. Attitudes and legislation regarding immigration vary from one country to another, as do issues of gender parity and LGBTQ rights. For example, only half of the 28 EU countries have legalized same-sex marriage as of 2019. Based on the Global Gender Gap Report (2018), many, but not all, of the countries rank in the top 50 regarding women's economic participation, educational and health attainments, and political empowerment. Countries such as Hungary, Cyprus, Malta, the Czech Republic, Greece, and Italy fare less well on addressing the gender gap. Additionally, while the laws provide equality and protection to ethnic minorities, the practice is less consistent, as described in the example of France.

More recently, the number of Muslims who made up 4.9% of the EU population in 2016 (Hackett, Conner, & Stonawski, 2017) saw a dramatic rise as a result of the Syrian civil war and other conflicts in the Middle East and Africa. In spite of pro-diversity leaders such German Chancellor Angela Merkel who stated "It is beyond question that our country was historically formed by Christianity and Judaism. But it's also the case that with 4.5 million Muslims living with us, their religion, Islam, has also become a part of Germany," and liberal and humanitarian laws, the integration of Muslims has been challenging in many parts of the EU (Frum, 2018). White nationalists have called the newcomers invaders, and the intolerance has engendered violence against the Muslim and Jewish populations with bombings of mosques and synagogues (Beckett, 2019).

Different definitions and conceptions of diversity and different legal frameworks have led to widely different results in how diversity is addressed around the world. It is essential to not approach diversity with a parochial or ethnocentric view; diversity does not mean the same thing in all countries. The dimensions that need to be addressed are not the same. We therefore must recognize the *diversity within diversity* and acknowledge the importance of societal contexts. What is clear is that, at least in theory, the large majority of countries recognize the importance of addressing some form of cultural diversity, whether it's language, religion, gender, ethnicity, sexual orientation, social class, or other dimensions. Similarly, businesses have, to a large extent, tried to capitalize on the cultural diversity of their workforce and their customers and have implemented a variety of programs to be more inclusive.

5. THE SOCIAL AND HISTORICAL CONTEXTS

> **LO 5.5** Consider the historical context of diversity through the lens of colonialism, immigration, and slavery

Understanding the deep social and historical roots of diversity in the United States and around the world is beyond the scope of this book. However, it is essential that managers understand some of the roots and the social and historical factors that drive the movement to diversify organizations and the accompanying debates and controversies. Worldwide, colonialism and its lingering effects shape many of the diversity discussions. In the United States, slavery and immigration are key factors. Whether these are part of one's personal experiences or not, and whether we are aware of them or not, they are a factor in everyone's CMC. These historical events have left their indelible imprint on how people perceive their world and how they think; they are part of and inform the culture and diversity discussions.

Colonialism and slavery are not proud elements of our cultural heritage; nonetheless, their presence and impact have to be acknowledged and their legacy has to be taken into account. We will present the key issues in this next section, with the recognition that an in-depth and exhaustive discussion is beyond the focus of this book.

5.1 Colonialism

Colonialism, defined as one country fully or partially controlling others, has existed since the dawn of history. In the more recent past, European colonialism started in the 15th century with Spanish and Portuguese explorers and reached its peak with the dominance of Northern European powers around the end of the 19th to the middle of the 20th century. Similarly, Japanese imperialism was focused on Asia, stretching to some parts of Russia. In one way or another, colonialism has involved the dispossession of indigenous populations of their land and other resources and an accompanying narrative of "civilizing" them (Jazeel, 2012). The concept of *postcolonialism* recognizes the continued impact of colonialism on the groups who were colonized and on the relationship between them and the colonizers (Jazeel, 2012; McClintock, 1992; Nash, 2002). The groundbreaking work of Edward Said (1978) suggests that our very conceptions of the East (Orient) and West (Occident) are in and of themselves based on seeing one as the starting point, and are therefore artificial and socially constructed points of views. The "Far-East" is only far from a Western perspective; for the Chinese it is the middle kingdom. How we view the world and its history is inherently a cultural perspective.

5.1.1 The Lasting Impact of Colonial Views on Culture and Organizations. For our purposes, one of the lasting impacts of colonialism is ethnocentric views with a strong sense of superiority and a clear Us-vs-Them attitude that see the other as "less than," hostile, and dangerous. Additionally, colonialism has relied on deculturation, sometimes presented as assimilation, as the imposed strategy for acculturation for the colonized groups who were, in all cases, seen as inferior and expected to give up their culture. Such discussions may appear to be beyond the scope of a managerially oriented text about culture; however, colonialism has impacted not only those directly involved, but it has also shaped the global economy. Institutions such as the East India Company (or its Dutch equivalent, the Dutch East India company), which was created in the 1600s to control the trade between England and India, imposed the English culture on the colonies and laid the foundation for future international trade. It was a business organization that became a political power house. In his book *The Corporation That Changed the World* (2006), historian Nick Robins argues that the East India Company was the foundation of modern multinational business by its focus on profits, pioneering the shareholder model and the excesses and ethical scandals of its executives. The American Revolution was precipitated by imposition of new tax laws from Great Britain. Trade, economic development, and business are closely intertwined with colonialism.

It is essential that we acknowledge the sometimes direct and sometimes indirect residual impact of colonialism in our worldviews and perspectives. For example, as stated earlier in this chapter recent data from the United Kingdom show that 97% of key decision-makers in the country are white (Duncan & Holder, 2017). Specifically, in a country with a strong and recent colonial past, and with now decades of anti-discrimination laws that have governed all aspects of society, including education, and where 13% of the population is considered to be ethnic minorities, still only 36 out of the 1,000 most powerful political, financial, judicial, cultural, and security leaders are from ethnic minorities and only seven are Black or ethnic minority women (Duncan & Holder, 2017). There are clearly many reasons why this power imbalance exists; however, the impact of parochial and ethnocentric views that shape people's CMC cannot be overlooked. Edmond Burke, a member of parliament stated in a 1783 speech: "Every rupee of profit made by an Englishman is lost forever to India" (St. John, 2012, p. 76). This legacy continues to impact the United Kingdom and other colonial powers and the many countries that they colonized.

5.1.2 Colonialism and Diversity. Similar factors play a part in diversity discussions and challenges in all Western European countries as immigrants from their former colonies, along with many others, make up the cultural diversity of their population. By some estimates, close to 45% of immigrants to France are from Northern and Sub-Saharan Africa, many from previous French colonies with immigrants from other EU and European countries coming second with around 32% (Elkins & Bisson, 2019).

The *First Person* account by Dr. Juan Roche (Chapter 2) shows the continued impact of Spanish colonialism in the relationships with its former colonies. In 2007, the King of Spain bluntly told the Venezuelan president to "Shut up," as he was using Spain as a foil for his attacks on the West. This insult was taken by many as a further indication that Spain still treats its former colonies as children (Romero, 2007). The several hundred year-long relationship between Spain and its former Latin American colonies has resulted in extensive migration from those countries to Spain with many migrants complaining of xenophobic treatment and even violence in Spain (Romero, 2007).

Parochialism, ethnocentrism, the Us-vs-Them attitude, and seeing people from the out-group as inferior and less worthy are part and parcel of the colonial history of the world. Whether we are aware of it or not, they are a factor in our CMC. As we are increasingly recognizing the benefits and challenges of diversity, we do so with these attitudes coloring many of our views and actions.

5.2 Immigration and Slavery in the United States

It may be no surprise that US organizations and human resource practices are at the forefront of many current D&I efforts. The United States has a deep and troubled connection with diversity through immigration and slavery. Many have suggested that unequal treatment based on race and ethnicity is deeply ingrained in US-American culture and institutional practices (e.g., James Baldwin and Ta-Nehisi Coates).

5.2.1 Immigration to the United States. While many in the United States have the view that immigration is the heart of the country and highly desirable and cite the Emma Lazarus 1883 sonnet on the Statue of Liberty, *Give me your tired, your poor, your huddled masses yearning to breathe free*, as the symbol of the American ideal, the country has a mixed record regarding immigration. Ian Haney Lopez, Professor of Public Law at the University of California in Berkeley, suggests that the United States has dual and contradicting traditions: one that welcomes immigration as the life blood of the country, and another that stems from nativism and racism and favors Europeans, particularly Northern Europeans, as superior and desirable (Vega, 2019).

Appendix B presents some examples of the anti-immigrant side of this duality. There are many legislations and policies that have favored "white," defined in a variety of ways (Smith, 2002a, 2002b). What is clear is that being white continued for many years to be the dominant criteria for granting citizenship and led to systematic discrimination against other groups. While these legislations were abolished in 1965, the more recent populist, nationalist, and anti-immigration movements indicate continued strong parochialism, ethnocentrism, and an Us-vs-Them attitude and hostility toward people of color. These are part of the US-American cultural context, and it is within that CMC that organizations implement the D&I practices. The *First*

Person account at the beginning of this chapter presents one example of the continued views of the limited roles assigned to immigrants of color.

5.2.2 The Legacy of Slavery and Segregation. There is no way to overstate the dark legacy and continued impact of slavery and racial segregation in the United States. A recent issue of the *New York Times Magazine* entitled The 1619 Project (the year the first African slaves were sold in the American British colony; https://www.nytimes.com/interactive/2019/08/14/magazine/1619-america-slavery.html) paints a bleak and horrifying picture of slavery and its lasting impact in the United States. While, the short presentation here will not do the topic justice, it aims at highlighting key points as one of the main impetuses behind the diversity movement. (Appendix C presents a summary timeline of key events related to the enslavement of an estimated 10 million Africans and milestones of the Civil Rights movement in the United States).

Slavery goes far beyond ethnocentrism and simple hostile attitudes which are at the root of seeing the "other" as less than, and inferior. In 2006, Ron Law and 18 others filed a complaint of workplace discrimination with the US Equal Employment Opportunity Commission against the Austral USA, a defense contractor commercial ship builder in Alabama. They had found nooses hanging from the ceiling in the breakroom, racist graffiti in the bathroom, Ku Klux Klan references, slurs etched into the ships they were building, and images of hanging men at the job site, had been subject to direct threats from other employees, and had overheard their managers referring to black employees in highly derogatory terms (Jameel & Yerardi, 2019). These incidents are but one example of the lasting legacy of slavery. Many other instances of racism and discrimination ranging from police brutality, to healthcare and housing disparities, to criminal justice and educational inequalities, and job discrimination just to name a few continue to impact African Americans and other ethnic minorities in the United States. The formal and institutional vestiges of slavery were not dismantled that long ago and their impact has not disappeared.

When slavery was legally abolished in 1865, various forms of legal and informal segregation laws and practices replaced it, from Jim Crow laws to redlining in housing (see Appendix C for key points). As a result, many other forms of racism and discrimination impacting all aspects of social and organizational life remain. While there are numerous examples of positive changes, old cultural assumptions and corresponding behaviors still persist. The recency of these historical events suggests that major cultural changes, particularly those related to deep assumptions, values, and beliefs regarding race in the United States are still very much a work in progress. The CMC does not simply change because of legal changes. In addition to policies favoring white immigrants and the lasting legacy of slavery, numerous other instances of racism and discrimination are easy to find. In the United States, the decimation of native people and their cultures including the creation of reservations and forced boarding of children in Indian Schools (the last one closed in 1970s in the United States), the internment of Japanese-Americans during World War II, and the recent immigrant family separation policies are just some of the most dramatic examples.

5.3 Continued Impact

As the United States moves forward on achieving its ideals of an equal and just society, hate crimes against racial, ethnic, and religious minorities; LGBTQ individuals; women; and many others who are perceived or labeled as outsiders have been on the rise. FBI reports indicate a 17% rise of hate crimes from 2016 to 2017 with 3 out of 5 motivated by race or ethnicity (Eligon, 2018). Verbal and physical attacks on Asian Americans increased in the wake of the COVID-19 epidemic of 2020 with many, including government officials, inaccurately calling the virus "Chinese or Wuhan virus" further fanning the flame of ethnic divisions.

The stabbing of five people during a Hanukkah celebration in December 2019 in Monsey, New York, had anti-Semite motives; mass shootings in El Paso, Texas, in August of 2019 that killed 22 people targeted Mexican immigrants; 11 worshippers were killed in the Tree of Life Synagogue in Pittsburgh, Pennsylvania, by a man yelling anti-Semitic slogans in 2018; the massacre of 49 people in a Latino gay nightclub in Orlando, Florida, in 2016 was motivated by hate; the killing of 9 people inside a historically Black church in Charleston, South Carolina, in 2015 was racially motivated (Faupel, Scheuerman, Parris, & Werum, 2019).

Similarly, around the world, demonstrations and violence by white nationalists and neo-Nazi groups, with extreme and hostile views of the "other," targeting individuals who are members of what is considered diverse groups, are occurring with more frequency. Fifty-one people were killed in a Mosque in Christchurch in New Zealand in March of 2018; six Muslim worshippers were killed in Quebec City in 2017; twelve people were injured in the United Kingdom by a van driven by a man motivated by anti-Muslim hatred; a British member of parliament was stabbed to death by an avowed white supremacist for her liberal views in 2016; a rapper and antifascist activist was stabbed to death in Greece in 2013; 77 people were killed by a shooter in Norway who wanted to prevent a "Muslim invasion" (Beckett, 2019). Blatant and unconcealed racism and discrimination may not be the norm in many societies and organizations, but incidents that indicate persistent parochialism, ethnocentrism, and the Us-vs-Them attitude are not hard to find. Such attitudes are not limited to ethnic groups. Many other primary and secondary dimensions of diversity, specifically gender and sexual orientation and identity, are the basis of bias and discrimination in many countries and organizational settings.

While these examples may appear somewhat disconnected from cross-cultural management, they are a fundamental and inherent part of the cultural assumptions, values, beliefs, and practices that form the meta-context of group-level culture. They are at the heart of cultural diversity movements. It is essential for managers to be aware of how and when these factors in CMC may influence their own and others' decisions and actions.

6. CHALLENGES: PREJUDICE AND DISCRIMINATION

LO 5.6 Discuss prejudice and discrimination and their impact on individuals and organizations

While some may argue that the United States and other parts of the world have overcome their past history and are now postracial where prejudice and discrimination are no longer serious or significant issues, researchers have by and large debunked such assertions (e.g., Coates, 2015; Hannah-Jones, 2016). Accordingly, examples of both blatant and subtle prejudice and discrimination and hatred and violence motivated by racism are on the rise.

6.1 Examples of Prejudice and Discrimination

The legacy of colonialism and slavery may appear to be part of the distant past and many who are not part of various minority groups may rarely if ever witness or experience any instance of prejudice or discrimination. However, both continue to impact many around the world.

- In the wake of the COVID-19 epidemic, on March 9, 2020 in Los Angeles, Yuanyuan Zhu, who had moved to the United States in 2015, was going to her gym when a man shouted at the bus driving past her to "Run them over." He then approached her and spit in her face (Tavernise & Oppel, 2020).

- A black female executive in her 60s who was boarding a plane during priority first-class seating was told by fellow passengers that she is in the wrong line.

- In March of 2020, an Asian American family in Fresno contacted police after they found graffiti on their SUV spelling out a hateful message mentioning COVID-19 (Martinez, 2020).

- Jimmy Kennedy, who had earned $13 million during his National Football League career, was repeatedly denied a coveted "private client" status at JPMorgan Chase, and after repeated attempts, was finally told bluntly that being Black and of large stature was a factor in the denial (Flitter, 2019).

- "I am a German when we win, but I am an immigrant when we lose. I am still not accepted into society" are the words of Mesut Özil, German-born soccer superstar, when he quit the German national team citing racism as a primary reason (Smith & Eckardt, 2018).

- On April 12, 2018, Donte Robinson and Rashon Nelson were waiting to meet a business associate at a Starbucks in Philadelphia when the café manager called the police reporting that they were in the café without ordering anything leading to their arrest. Their arrest touched off a national furor over racial profiling and prompted Starbucks to take the unprecedented action of closing all its 8,000 US stores for 1 day to provide racial bias training to all its employees (Starbucks stories, 2018). The two men eventually settled their lawsuit with the city of Philadelphia for a symbolic $1 each and a promise from officials to set up a $200,000 program for young entrepreneurs (Whack, 2018).

- Ariana Miyamoto, a biracial beauty queen who was crowned Miss Universe Japan in 2015, and half Indian Priyanka Yoshikawa who became Miss World Japan in 2016 were both attacked in Japanese social media for not being Japanese enough (Miss Japan, 2016).

- Blacks are systematically undertreated for pain, and some healthcare professionals hold medically false beliefs, such as black skin being thicker or blacks aging more slowly than whites, that contribute to disparities in healthcare delivery (Hoffman, Trawalter, Axt, & Oliver, 2016) and lower life expectancies for black Americans, who face greater risk of developing a variety of health problems and not receiving equal attention and care (Schwartz & Dawes, 2020).

- Asians are more likely to be hired than other groups, but they are less likely to be promoted into management and therefore less likely to lead organizations (McGirt, 2018).

- Minority job applicants who "whiten" their résumés by changing references to their race double their chances of getting interviews and jobs even in companies with diversity programs (Kang, DeCelles, Tilcsik, & Jun, 2016).

- A black female dean does not wear jeans or dress casually, even on weekends, because campus police has stopped her repeatedly, even though she has worked in that university for over 20 years.

6.2 Stereotypes, Accessibility, and Primary Dimensions of Diversity

Beliefs and expectations about who others are and should be have real and significant consequences. We discussed various biases, including *stereotypes*, which are

Figure 5.4   From Stereotypes to Discrimination

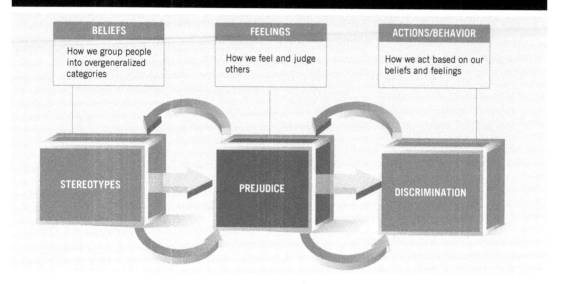

beliefs regarding people based on the group to which they belong, in Chapter 3. Although *blatant* stereotypes that are deliberate and unconcealed are not as common as they used to be, *subtle* and *unconscious* biases continue to impact how we perceive others and how we act (Amodio, 2014; Fiske & Taylor, 2017).

6.2.1 Definitions. Stereotypes are the basis of *prejudice*, which is an emotional response to and judgment of a social group and its members based on stereotypes and other preconceptions. Prejudice can lead to *discrimination*, which refers to unfair and differential behaviors and actions (see Figure 5.4). As we discussed earlier in this chapter, the roots of stereotypes, prejudice, and discrimination are historical and social; they stem from our culture. The primary goal of D&I efforts is to prevent, reduce, or eliminate the impact of these processes to assure that all members of an organization have the same opportunity to contribute and to perform.

The various biases and stereotypes that we hold are rooted in our cultural assumptions; they are part of our CMC. Our stereotypes become the basis for what has been called a *master status* and lead to *chronic accessibility* of certain traits or categories. Master status refers to social positions that are the primary identifying characteristic of an individual (Van den Scott & Van den Hoonard, 2016). These characteristics become chronically accessible, meaning that they are the ones that we notice and use to categorize others (Fiske & Taylor, 2017). The visible primary dimensions of diversity are frequently used as master status and are chronically available to us. They become what is available and easy to access and what we use to decide who others are, or should be. The more we use them, the more engrained they become, causing us to use them even more often.

The *First Person* scenario illustrated how physical characteristics and assumed ethnicity were used as the basis of assessing who the person is and making assumptions regarding what he should be doing. Research shows that the first things we notice about others is their skin color (often used as a proxy for ethnicity) and their gender; both are visible and help us to quickly categorize people. Both are also the basis of many stereotypes and prejudice that are then applied to those individuals. Our evaluation of, our decisions regarding how we treat them, are based on that one visible and accessible master status. In Chapter 3, we discussed in detail how our cognitive processes help us simplify events and allow us to be efficient while often causing us to be ineffective.

6.2.2 Implicit Biases in Management and Organizations. These processes are at the heart of our *unconscious* or *implicit biases*. They are activated without our conscious knowledge and operate automatically and outside of our control before we become aware of them. While they have been the subject of cognitive psychology research for many years, it is only recently that they have been applied to managerial settings. For example, in addition to using the concept in D&I initiatives, researchers have started looking at how these biases have made their way into technology and the algorithms that are triggered in our web searches. Consider that until recently, typing "CEO" in your message box on a mobile phone would have brought up the emoji of a man in a suit; you are now likely to get both a man and a woman, but they are still both blond and obviously white. Similarly, the default for all emojis where skin color is represented is white. Subtle messages such as these reinforce stereotypes and implicit biases. More significantly, recent studies show that various algorithms used in hiring can replicate institutional and historical biases against women and minorities (Bogen, 2019).

For example, Facebook ads for cashiers were shown primarily to women (85%) and jobs at taxi companies were shown disproportionately to black users (75%). These programs are designed to learn and replicate patterns of behaviors; it is therefore not a surprise that they learn and replicate our biases. In 2018, Amazon scrapped its Artificial Intelligence (AI)-based recruiting tool because it was found to show a bias against women. The reason was that the system was built on patterns of résumés submitted to the company over a 10-year period, most of which came from male candidates, so it learned that males were what it should look for (Dastin, 2018).

The biases in our modern technologies are a contemporary example of *institutional biases*, which refers to biases based on race or sex or other dimensions that are embedded in the fabric of our society and that systematically disadvantage certain groups. Just as our personal biases are subconscious and automatic, institutional biases often operate below the radar and can go unnoticed for periods of time (Dobbin & Kalev, 2016). Racial and ethnic disparities in the healthcare and criminal justice systems, racial profiling, systems for school funding and governmental housing, and financial policies that favored whites and wealthier individuals and communities are societal examples of institutional biases (Jana & Diaz Mejias, 2018). Organizational practices such as regularly moving employees to different locations, evaluation and promotion criteria that are written based on stereotypically male characteristics, or the school system schedules and hours that are built on outdated gender roles are other examples. All of these practices move stereotypes and prejudice into actions and behaviors that lead to discrimination.

6.3 Discrimination

Our stereotypes and biases can translate into prejudice, and then discrimination. What you think about a group of people (your stereotypes) may create strong negative feelings, opinions, and judgments (prejudice) that can then translate into discriminatory policies, and behaviors (see Figure 5.4). The small number of minorities and women in top leadership positions is, at least partially, caused by subtle or even blatant discrimination. The many formal and informal complaints and grievances based on racial, ethnic, gender, and other forms of discrimination suggest that prejudice and discrimination impact many. Consider the following cases:

- In 2010, 60 African American workers filed a suit against GE after their supervisor called them the N-word, lazy blacks, and other derogatory terms, and denied them bathroom breaks and medical attention. The company was also sued in 2005 for wage and promotion discrimination (Nittle, 2019).

- In 2018 the Big 5 corporation paid a management trainee Robert Sanders $165,000 because the store manager subjected him to ongoing racial harassment, calling him derogatory names, telling him he had the face of a janitor, and making death threats against him (https://www1.eeoc.gov/eeoc/newsroom/release/9-18-18.cfm).

- Clothing retailer Abercrombie & Fitch settled a lawsuit for $50 million brought against it by Black, Asian, and Latino employees who were not allowed to work on the sales floor because they did not look "classically American" (Nittle, 2019).

- Over the past 40 years, data from the Harvard Business School indicate that 40% of non–African American Harvard MBAs reach top ranks in organizations as compared to only 13% of black female Harvard MBAs (McGregor, 2018).

- In 2019, Dante Trice and Angela Washington sued the Pearland Independent School District in Texas for humiliating their son after a teacher used a sharpie marker to color his fade haircut (where the sides and back are cut very close to the head giving the appearance of lighter color), although it did not depict any inappropriate symbols disallowed by the school's dress code policy.

Blatant discrimination is not rare and neither are its subtler forms. A recent study shows the negative reaction of white male executives when a woman or minority is appointed as a leader of their organization. Researchers Michael McDonald, Gareth Keeves, and Jim Westphal (2018) looked at the aftermath of the appointment of 1,000 female or minority executives in various companies. They found that white males' negative biases of their new CEOs negatively affected their identification and engagement with the company and reduced their willingness to help and support other minorities in their organization. Westphal only could provide one explanation: "I think it is part of a biased reaction to a minority assuming a very high-status position in the organization" (McGregor & Siegel, 2018).

6.3.1 Impact of Discrimination. Some of the effects of prejudice and discrimination are measurable and obvious, as in the cases described above: people lose their job, are denied promotions, get less pay, and are humiliated. Other effects are subtler. Many women and minorities feel that they have to be constantly on guard to avoid potential bias and discrimination. Georgetown University Professor Laura Roberts says: "Much of the advice that minorities are often given around advancing and succeeding emphasizes the ways in which they may need to conform or assimilate—to see who's in power and emulate those models of power;" while they are constantly in the spotlight, every misstep is magnified and they are not allowed to be themselves (McGregor, 2018). Research cited earlier in this chapter about trying not to be "too black" further echoes the effect of subtle discrimination.

Many members of nontraditional groups have learned to "code switch" and act "white" in order to get and keep their jobs and be successful. Moses Monterroza (2017) says: "For us, code-switching is a tool that allows us to circumvent those uncomfortable situations, to put on a mask so as not to confuse people with our 'otherness'." Another person describes her experience: "You feel like you're losing a part of yourself, and you feel like you have to blend in this new predicament or situation" (Monterroza, 2017). These responses to perceived prejudice and discrimination place an emotional tax on many members of underrepresented groups, preventing them from putting all of their energy and effort into simply doing their job and helping the organization achieve higher levels of success. While individuals attempt to prevent discrimination through their own actions, organizations have the responsibility, power, and resources to affect major change.

WINDOW TO THE WORLD

Doing Business in India

With considerable natural resources, as the world's second most populous and diverse nation, largest democracy, and one of the oldest civilizations, India has become a vibrant and dynamic powerhouse that has undergone considerable change while presenting many stark contrasts and paradoxes. The vestiges of the British rule continue to impact the country that is now a high-tech mecca while it continues to retain deep religious and traditional roots. Understanding India is certainly not easy, so no easy guide could do it justice.

- Maybe to a greater extent than many other countries, the long and rich history of India plays a significant role even today. Read and learn about it before you go.

- Religious, linguistic, and regional diversity is considerable, so it is important that you know the background of the individuals and groups you will be interacting with. The caste system is no longer legal, but still practically in effect. There are many divisions and deeply ingrained inequalities in the country that may be hard to accept. CJI! As a visitor, try not to make assumptions and keep your judgments to yourself.

- The culture is collectivistic with deep respect for elders, one's family and clan, and those who have power. Establishing relationships is therefore essential.

- There is a strong sense of fatalism that translates into letting things happen and not having high anxiety about time and getting things done, while there is also a strong entrepreneurial spirit. People will be late, appointments may not be kept, plans will change often. Being patient and flexible and going with the flow will help you succeed.

- Direct confrontation, especially blunt refusals, is not desirable. Practice getting to your point more circuitously and allow your partners the time and space to get to their point as well.

- Because of the cultural diversity, how you greet people, what you eat, who you can interact with, what gifts to bring, and so forth will vary greatly. Do your research about your primary partners ahead of time, so that you can avoid faux pas.

While English is one of the over 20 official languages in India, do not assume that you can get by without help. Get a guide or cultural mentor who can help you navigate this rich and complex culture that provides immense possibility for success and quick and serious mistakes.

7. ORGANIZATIONAL RESPONSES TO DIVERSITY: REACH AND LIMITATIONS

LO 5.7 Detail organizational responses to diversity

Notwithstanding the different definitions of diversity or national variations in approaches to cultural diversity, organizations around the world have a range of options on how they address and manage diversity from ignoring it and not addressing it to fully implementing D&I practices.

7.1 Stages of D&I

Few organizations are homogeneous or completely ignore diversity. Even in countries where the labor force is ethnically homogeneous such as in Japan or Saudi Arabia, other diversity dimensions including gender or age require addressing the needs of diverse people. D&I is therefore not an "all or none" proposition; organizations can undertake a variety of efforts. Figure 5.5 presents various stages of addressing D&I, which range from:

- *Doing nothing*: The organization makes no effort to address diversity. Such uniform organizations are increasingly rare, at least in the United States, most industrialized countries, and many other countries in the world.

- *Compliance with legal requirements*: The organization conforms with the letter of the law without showing further commitment beyond avoiding legal jeopardy.

- *Valuing cultural diversity*: The organization may try to mimic the cultural diversity of its community in its employees and managers by hiring people who represent various groups or by concentrating on the needs of their community. It would provide visible artifacts to represent diversity, for example different interest groups and ethnic celebrations, and track its diversity efforts through performance measures such as percentage of minorities and women, who gets promoted, and so forth. A firm operating in a Hispanic community may, for instance, recruit new employees at universities that have a large Hispanic student body, hire and promote Hispanic managers, provide various documents and services in Spanish, and devise a Spanish language marketing campaign. In this stage, the focus is often on pointing to the business benefits of diversity.

- *Systematic and Deliberate D&I*: The final stage in response to diversity is both quantitatively and qualitatively different so that the organization not only has

Figure 5.5 Range of Responses to Diversity

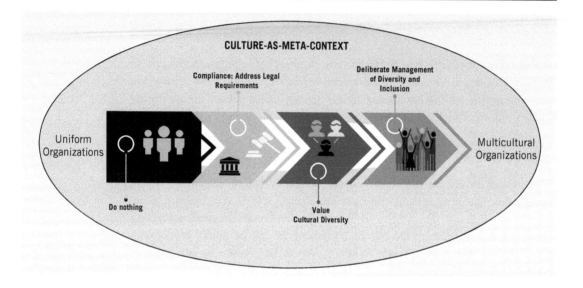

more processes to value diversity, it further addresses cultural diversity in more complex ways by integrating it in the mission and working on changing its culture. It is currently upheld as the model for D&I. Organizations in this stage address both diversity and inclusion, where diverse groups feel welcome and accepted.

Examples of organizations that systematically and deliberately address diversity include P&G. The company has spent over $2 billion annually over the past 7 years to build a diverse supplier group that includes 1,500 women and minority-owned businesses (P&G Diversity, 2015). It further has an extensive leader development strategy that supports diversity; has focused on multiple dimensions of diversity including physical ability; and holds managers and executives accountable by tying part of their compensation to achieving diversity goals (Burke, 2017). Other firms, such as Dow Inc., Comcast Corp, and Salesforce.com, are showing their commitment to D&I by having top executives in the C-suite, rather than in Human Resource departments only, responsible for diversity efforts (Holger, 2019).

The stated desire and goal to be both diverse and inclusive are based not only on the simple fact that the workforce and consumers are changing but also because of many of the well-documented benefits of diversity. Part V of the book will focus specifically on ways in which individuals and organizations can be effective in cross- and multicultural environments, which include group-level culture. Here we will look at the areas an organization that aims to be inclusive can address. What can be done and what are the limits?

7.2 Organizational Options

Figure 5.6 presents a typology of prejudice and discrimination to help guide an organization's actions. On one dimension, individuals—or groups and even organizations—may range from having prejudice and strong negative *feelings* toward members of other groups, to having no negative or positive feelings. On the other dimension, they may or may not *act* on their feelings and judgments. As a result, people are likely to have four generic approaches to how they view and react to diversity:

- Those in the upper-right quadrant (nonprejudiced and nondiscriminatory, NP-ND), are open-minded, tolerant, and appreciate and seek multiculturalism. They have few prejudices and do not act in a discriminatory manner toward others. These are the allies and diversity advocates. They are already on board with D&I.

- On the opposite quadrant, at the bottom-left (prejudiced and discriminatory, P-D), are individuals who openly show their prejudice toward different

Figure 5.6 Framework for Organizational Programs

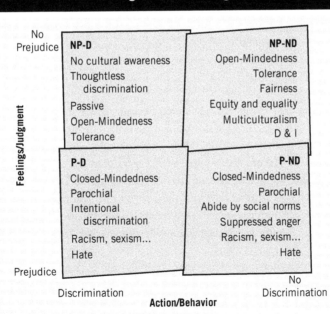

groups and are willing to act on them. These are individuals who are most likely set in their belief system and unwilling to consider alternatives and prone to openly resisting D&I efforts. James Damore, a Google engineer who wrote a lengthy memo called *Google Ideological Echo Chamber* expressing his traditional views of women that were in sharp contrast with the company's D&I mission, would fall in this category (Wakabayashi, 2017).

- On the upper-left side (NP-D) are individuals who do not have strong prejudicial feelings but may inadvertently discriminate or passively tolerate discrimination. They are generally unaware of cultural issues and may have an open mind, but either because of lack of knowledge or interest in learning about cultural factors, or simply because they act out of habit or follow others, they may discriminate against some groups.

- At the lower-right side are individuals with strong prejudicial convictions who do not act on them (P-ND). They may abide by perceived social norms, bow down to peer pressure, or abide by organizational directives regarding nondiscrimination, all the while their personal beliefs and feelings remain intolerant of out-groups. For example, business owners who continue to serve diverse customers and immigrants while still holding prejudicial feelings toward them would fall in this category. They suppress their feelings and their judgments of the "other" and behave in socially acceptable or financially beneficial ways.

Individuals in each of these quadrants have different CMCs and operate based on different assumptions, values, and beliefs. Therefore, they are likely to respond very differently to an organization's effort to create or maintain a diverse workforce and would require a different program: there is no "one-size-fits-all" approach to implementing D&I programs.

7.2.1 Implementing D&I Programs. The classification depicted in Figure 5.6 can be used to catalog organizations as well and can provide a framework for D&I. For example, organizations that are simply complying with legal and regulatory pressures, without a mission or culture that supports diversity, may fall into the lower-right quadrant. Those that are champions of diversity and integrate D&I in their culture, strategies, and processes would place into the upper-right quadrant. Many organizations fall in the middle with careless and inadvertent discrimination because, although they may have good intentions, they have not fully aligned their values and beliefs with their processes, mission, and culture.

For example, consider a university that abides by the Federal Title IX mandates that require it to address diversity issues as they relate to their students and includes the appropriate language in their documents. Accordingly, all faculty, staff, and students are required to complete a yearly diversity-related training. However, the university does not collect data beyond what is required for student issues, does not provide support to address faculty and staff diversity challenges, and has few systems in place to address discrimination for employee. As a result, although it aims to support diversity, it lacks some of the systems it needs to address any issues that may arise.

So, whom should organizations target? Where would resources be most effectively and efficiently expended? Each group in Figure 5.6 needs a different type of support and training; there is no one-size-fits-all solution. As social science research has well established, changing behaviors is much easier than changing feelings and attitudes. Additionally, actual behaviors are, by and large, appropriate areas to address in work settings, whereas feelings are not. Organizations can expect their employees not to discriminate, but cannot require them not to have prejudices. While we may hope to also change employees' and managers' beliefs and feelings, organizations cannot address them directly.

Those who are in the NP-ND group do not need basic training and information about the importance of diversity; rather they need resources and support to expand the D&I focus. They are ready to be the change champions and allies and likely willing to mentor others and take on leadership and advocacy roles in the D&I process. British consultant Sheree Atcheson (2018), who specializes in D&I, defines *allies* as "any person that actively promotes and aspires to advance the culture of inclusion through intentional, positive and conscious efforts that benefit people as a whole." On the opposite end of the spectrum are those who are in the P-D group and who are likely to be unwilling to learn and change. They are a poor fit for organizations that are diverse and aim to be inclusive. James Damore, the Google engineer, was eventually fired from Google (Wakabayashi, 2017). The NP-D group is an excellent target for growth and development. People in this group are generally not prejudiced and not likely to hold strong stereotypes and may have an open mind. However, they lack awareness, knowledge, and information. Training and development can help them recognize the power and impact of their action. Finally, the P-ND group can be a challenge. Their feelings and judgments may be well hidden and they may abide by organizational policies and act in a nondiscriminatory manner. Changing their deep-seated assumptions may not be possible.

The classifications presented in Figure 5.6 are not just for nondiverse individuals; everyone operates with a CMC. Members of diverse groups also can be found in different quadrants. We all have culture and a cultural identity that shape our perspectives. Everyone's CMC acts as a context and as a guide. Culture is not about just diverse people. Gaining awareness of our own cultural assumptions, values, beliefs, and behaviors is a necessary starting point for everyone. Additionally, we all have explicit and implicit biases. Therefore, training and development and participation in various programs should not target just one group. Furthermore, it is important to focus on broad diversity factors rather than making a program just about a minority group. Learning about unconscious biases, the processes that they engender, and how to address them benefits all members of an organization in their interactions with diverse groups.

7.2.2 Focused Targeting of D&I Programs. Going back to the basic question at the beginning of this chapter: How do we address diversity? There is, of course, no simple answer. There is considerable evidence that shows that many programs that target only one group (often white males) fail and may create a backlash (e.g., Dobbin & Kalev, 2016; Rampen, 2019; Weber, 2018). Creating guilt and shame is not effective in any type of learning and equally ineffective in business settings. Given the disagreements, controversies, and diversity in the definition of diversity, it is clear that there is not one program that works for everyone. People have different views of culture and its role and different CMCs. Managers can disagree with and debate the benefits and consequences of various diversity programs and how they are implemented.

What is not debatable, and is increasingly critical, in the global business environment is understanding the fact that people's cultural identities are diverse and that they have different CMCs. We simply cannot manage everyone the same way, or assume that our own CMC and its corresponding assumptions, values, beliefs, and practices are the norm and will or should work for everyone. There are no right or wrong cultural values; CJI. Therefore, managers in today's global environment must learn how to develop a CM that allows them to address the needs of their diverse employees. Being aware of your CMC and how it acts as a background and a guide is essential. Your own culture and your biases and how they operate (THINK) is the starting point. Having knowledge about diversity, its historical and social roots, and its challenges and benefits, the topics we have addressed in this chapter, provides the KNOW and some tools to start the difficult conversations.

FIRST PERSON REVISITED

The salesperson in the opening anecdote is experiencing the impact of stereotypes. His Mexican origin, its corresponding physical characteristics, and the stereotypes they trigger are used as a master status that creates certain expectations regarding who he is and what he should be doing. Those expectations are the first thing people access when they see him and cause them to disregard relevant and factual information about who he is and his role in those settings. While for some, these biases may be intentional and even malicious, in many other cases, they are simply implicit and subconscious and rooted in people's CMC. Changing them starts with awareness and then knowledge and information.

APPLYING WHAT YOU LEARNED: HOW TO BECOME AN ALLY

A diversity ally is someone who is committed to D&I and actively promotes equality, equity, and fairness through words and actions to benefit all members of an organization. Based on material you have read in this chapter, you know that to be an ally you must both not hold strong stereotypes (both positive and negative) of others and not discriminate against others. An ally does not need to be a member of a specific group since many of us have multiple cultural identities. Here are some steps you can take:

1. Work on self-assessment through reflection and feedback. You must become aware of your own explicit and implicit biases and their impact on your thinking and actions.

2. Connect with diverse individuals and groups in your organization and develop strong relationships.

3. Be open to learning; ask questions when you don't know.

4. Practice what you preach—your actions are stronger than your words.

5. Listen and trust others—you may not understand or have direct experience with what they are experiencing and describing; you have to be willing to trust and empathize.

6. Focus on lifting others—all others, regardless of the group they belong to.

7. Call out inappropriate behaviors when you see and hear them.

8. Use inclusive language.

9. Be humble and an active listener; learn to ask questions.

10. Finally, remember that others must see you as an ally; it is not something that you can declare for yourself and it is not about you!

MANAGERIAL CHALLENGE: OFF-COLOR COMMENTS

One of your highly productive team members who has been with the organization the longest has made slightly off-color comments that border on inappropriate. Recently, she commented on how cute one of your new clients is and was wondering if he may be gay because he is so well put together and always smells so nice. She is a bit too friendly with him, but he seems to respond well to her. On another occasion, she made a joke about not being able to make sense of a colleague's memo and how it seemed to be written in Arabic (the colleague is Egyptian). These are not common occurrences, but they come up. Aside from these comments, this productive team member is extremely helpful and goes out of her way to support others, mentor new people, and is generally cheerful and positive. She really contributes to the team and to the organization. You have noticed that others sometimes cringe at her jokes and comments, but no one has complained.

1. What is your assessment of the situation?

2. What can you do? What should you do?

3. What are the implications of your actions?

SELF-ASSESSMENT 5.1: THE IMPLICIT BIAS TEST

We have talked about biases in Chapter 3 and revisited the topic in this chapter. We know that our brain has developed to process information quickly and efficiently. The need for efficiency along with our desire to be consistent make all of us subject to biases. The first step in being able to address our biases is to be aware that we have them and use them. While we can identify some of our biases with reflection and self-observation, others are deeply engrained, implicit, and hidden.

The *Project Implicit* at Harvard University provides a broad range of test of implicit bias. You can take as many of the self-assessments as you would like at https://implicit.harvard.edu/implicit/takeatest.html.

Consider the following questions after you complete the self-assessments you selected.

1. Why did you take the assessments you did?

2. To what extent did the result surprise you?

3. What did you learn about yourself?

4. How can you use this information in the future?

SELF-ASSESSMENT 5.2: THE STEREOTYPES I HOLD

All of us hold stereotypes about various groups. We acquire them from our family and community and through our own experiences. While some may appear to have some basis in fact, stereotypes always overgeneralize people based on the group to which we think they belong and therefore are likely to lead us to either oversimply or make mistakes regarding others. The first and most significant step to prevent mistakes is self-awareness.

1 Identification

Using the grid below, identify several stereotypes that you hold about different groups, exploring the sources and listing personal experiences related to them. An example is provided. This is a self-assessment to allow you to reflect and grow, not a class exercise. The more honest you are, the more you will benefit.

Stereotype	Source	Personal Experience
Example: Asians are good team members but not leaders.	• My grandfather always said that. • I learned about Asians being team players and conformists. • I have read about Japanese baseball and how they are good at teams.	• My Chinese team member last semester was very quiet. • Asian students in class rarely talk.

2 Looking for Disconfirmation

For each of the stereotypes you listed above, reflect on events or evidence that you have either directly or indirectly that contradicts the stereotype and may disconfirm it. Finding or remembering disconfirming information may be difficult since our cognitive processes and biases may interfere with that process. An example is provided.

Stereotype	Disconfirming Information
Example: Asians are good team members but not leaders.	• The Japanese, Chinese, Indians, and Koreans are leading the world in many areas of business. • There are many Asian leaders in high-tech firms. • The Japanese are courageous military leaders.

3 Review and Plan

Now that you have some awareness of a few of the stereotypes you hold, consider the following:

- How often have you relied on these stereotypes?

- What have been the outcomes?

- What changes can you make?

- How will you go about making those changes?

EXERCISE 5.1: EQUALITY AND EQUITY

Objective: *This exercise addresses the cognitive factors in CM.*

Instructions:

Consider the image below:

Source: Illustrating "Equality VS Equity" by IISC. January 13, 2016.

Group Work

In your group discuss the following questions.

1. What does each panel present? What approach does each represent? What is the key message?

2. What are some examples of each approach in society and in organizations?

3. How would each approach translate to organizations? How would managerial and organizational practices differ under each approach?

4. What are the implications of each?

Debate

Your instructor will assign you to one of two groups: Equality vs. Equity. Prepare persuasive arguments for the approach you have been assigned to make the case that it is the best approach to addressing diversity in organizations.

EXERCISE 5.2: STATEMENTS ON D&I

Objective: This exercise builds your knowledge of diversity.

Instructions: Read the prompt before completing the individual and group exercises below.

Most companies have some statement regarding D&I posted prominently on their website. Here are some examples:

P&G (https://us.pg.com/diversity-and-inclusion/)

A commitment we take pride in

The people who use our products every day are as diverse as our world. The more we reflect them, the better we can understand their needs. That's simply meeting expectations.

Inclusivity is where we go beyond them. Our employees are encouraged to bring their unique selves to work every day, and bring out the best in each other. Because when every skill is used and every voice heard, positive change can happen.

McDonalds (https://corporate.mcdonalds.com/corpmcd/about-us/diversity-and-inclusion.html)

McDonald's has potentially created more economic impact for diverse communities than any other company in the world. Our belief is rooted in **"Diversity IS Inclusion"**, a bold and seismic value proposition where **EVERY** individual feels their culture, identity, and experiences are valued and respected. We know that listening to and participating in knowledge-sharing and eclectic insights has helped make us the organization we are today—from our crew members to our board members. From our suppliers to our customers to our community partners.

By aligning our **"Diversity IS Inclusion"** proposition with our culture pillars of **Customer Obsessed**, **Better Together**, and **Committed to Lead**, we are affecting the business in a positive way.

Google (https://diversity.google/)

Making progress on diversity, equity, and inclusion

Google's mission is to organize the world's information and make it universally accessible and useful. When we say we want to build for everyone, we mean everyone. To do that well, we need a workforce that's more representative of the users we serve.

Google is committed to creating a diverse and inclusive workforce. Our employees thrive when we get this right. We aim to create a workplace that celebrates the diversity of our employees, customers, and users. We endeavor to build products that work for everyone by including perspectives from backgrounds that vary by race, ethnicity, social background, religion, gender, age, disability, sexual orientation, veteran status, and national origin

Individual Work

Search for two other statements on D&I in other organizations (business, nonprofit, health care, education, or government).

1. How are they similar or different?

2. What are common themes?

3. What makes some more powerful than others?

Group Work

1. Review the D&I statements that each of your group members have found.

2. Identify the common themes.

3. As a group, develop a D&I statement for one of your member's companies or for your university, school, or college.

4. Prepare a 5-minute presentation to pitch your D&I statement.

CASE STUDY: PERSONAL TRAGEDIES

George Williams

George Williams has been working for his company for over 20 years. He knows almost everyone and has good relationships with his coworkers. He occasionally goes out to lunch with coworkers and regularly attends company picnics and other annual events with his wife and family, when they are invited. Their home is relatively far from work, and he spends his evenings and weekends with his family and friends, who are almost all from his community rather than from work.

Last year, George's wife, Elizabeth, developed a serious illness that required extensive hospitalization and outpatient care and sadly passed away after a few months. While she was ill and needing care at home, George used some of his many accumulated sick days and vacation days to attend to her, while their several grown children who live close by all pitched in. When Elizabeth passed away on a Friday afternoon, George was understandably devastated. He spent the weekend with his children making the funeral arrangement, which was set for the following Thursday in the afternoon. On the Monday following his wife's death and the rest of that week, George went to work. He did not tell anyone about his wife; no one even knew that she was sick. He took Thursday afternoon and the following Friday off to attend the funeral and went back to work on Monday.

One of George's coworkers who lives in the same community as him found out about Elizabeth's death and told their boss on the Monday after the funeral. George's boss got him a condolence card and sent flowers on behalf of the company; coworkers awkwardly stopped by to tell George how sorry they were. He stoically accepted his coworkers' sympathy. Life at work went back to normal.

Grace Santos

Grace Santos was born in the United States, the only daughter of Filipino immigrant parents. Her father passed away when she was in college and her mother Joyce, and one of her three brothers, Joseph, decided to return to the Philippines a few years ago to be closer to the large extended family. The other two brothers and Grace built successful business careers in the United States. Grace has been working for 12 years for the same company since she graduated with her accountancy masters and has done very well. She is a well-respected and well-liked manager and has been promoted several times and is being considered for a top leadership position.

Grace's mother, Joyce, who lives in the Philippines developed a serious illness that required extensive hospitalization and outpatient care. Her son Joseph, her sisters, and brothers and cousins all took turns to care for her, but Grace had to travel to Manila to help her mother. Her boss was understanding as Grace took time off using her many days of accumulated sick leave and some vacation days. He suggested that Grace take family leave but she decided against that option and volunteered to do work remotely while with her mother in Manila. Although she managed to get a lot of work done and kept up with all the demands and deadlines, many of her coworkers have made comments about her absence.

Over a 1-year period, although Grace's mother was stable, she was not really improving, so Grace made two extended trips to be with her. Unfortunately, Joyce passed away while Grace was back in the United States. Grace was devastated. She told her boss that she was traveling back to Manila but did not have a return date planned because she had to take care of her mother's house and support her family. She used the 2-day bereavement leave and since she had only a few days of sick leave and vacation left, asked her boss to support her with some flexible work options again.

The company allowed employees to donate sick days to other employees and Grace got a few days from several of her closest associates. They also sent flowers and a card. Although Grace was one of his best employees and she managed to still get her job done remotely, her boss was irritated and wondering if Grace is really committed to her job, a feeling that was shared by several others in the company. He was reconsidering whether she really is leadership material.

Questions

1. What is your reaction to how George and Grace each handled the challenges posed by a sick family member?

2. What is your evaluation of the behavior of each of their bosses and coworkers?

3. In your opinion, were the situations handled properly?

4. What role do you think George and Grace's culture plays in this situation?

5. What role do you think your culture plays in your assessment of the situation?

6. How should managers handle these types of situations?

CHAPTER SIX

GENDER IN ORGANIZATIONS

FIRST PERSON

Invisible

I, along with two other coworkers, had recently been promoted to our positions, and we were in a meeting with five other mid-level managers. We were brainstorming on ways to improve communication regarding various resources available to our employees. With a background in communication and PR, I was really interested in this topic and eager to contribute some of my ideas. The meeting was pretty informal and everyone was jumping into the conversation without taking turns. After listening for a bit, I made my first suggestion. They all looked at me, smiled, nodded their heads, and continued the discussion, ignoring my comments. I was a bit taken aback, but I didn't give up. A few minutes later, I tried again and got the same results. After a few rounds, one of my coworkers who had been promoted with me restated my idea almost word for word, without giving me any credit. The group loved it... I could not believe it! It was clearly my idea—the one that was completely ignored; and now he was simply restating and getting full credit for it! The same thing happened once more during this 90-minute meeting. I was getting nods and smiles, but no one was really listening to me. I started noticing the only other female manager who was actually one of the most senior members of the group. She didn't say much, but every time she started talking, she was interrupted; she didn't get to finish a single one of her ideas during the meeting. Our coworkers were simply talking over her and me. We were in the meeting, at the decision-making table, but we were clearly invisible. As we were walking out, one of the other managers smiled at me and said "nice job in there." After he had completely ignored me, it was so condescending! This group had a couple of other meetings in the weeks following. I am not proud of myself, but even though I had much to contribute,

Learning Objectives

6.1 Present a brief historical overview and modern definitions related to gender.

6.2 Review the status of women in society and organizations in the United States and around the world.

6.3 Elaborate on the role of culture in views of gender.

6.4 Identify and explain the causes of lack of gender parity in organizations.

6.5 Clarify the role and importance of the double bind women face.

6.6 Review successful social policies, organizational practices, and personal strategies to address gender effectively.

I stayed pretty quiet. I keep replaying the meetings in my head over and over and asking myself what I did wrong and what I should have done differently. I started thinking that maybe the promotion was too early and I was not really ready and even whether I really belonged in the company. I still don't have any answers. What's worse, although I really like my job, I am increasingly dreading our team meetings and losing my self-confidence.

–Anonymous

Almost every woman who has worked in a group setting where men were present has experienced what the manager describes in the *First Person* anecdote. Even in the 21st century, women's experiences at work are often considerably different than men's. Throughout history and in most civilizations, women have held limited leadership roles, and although there have been many changes, socially and in regards to leadership in society and in organizations, we are far from men and women being treated equally or having achieved parity.

As we discussed in Chapter 5, there are many dimensions of diversity that are key to people's cultural identity; we will be focusing on primary dimensions and address gender in this chapter as it is one of the visible primary dimensions that is used as a master status to categorize people. We review the status of women in organizations and in leadership roles, consider our culturally based gender stereotypes and their impact on organizations and their leadership, explore the myths and realities about causes of gender inequality and inequity in organizations, and end the chapter with consideration of personal and organizational solutions to gender inequity. Through these discussions, we continue to focus on the KNOW aspect of the roadmap to Cultural Mindset (CM; see Figure 5.1), with the goal of building your knowledge of gender-related concepts to allow you to address them better.

1. A BRIEF HISTORY, MODERN DEFINITIONS, AND CURRENT STATE

LO 6.1 Present a brief historical overview and modern definitions related to gender

The movement toward gender equity is relatively recent in the thousands of years of human history. While women have always worked both inside and outside the home to contribute to their family and society in a variety of ways, it is only in the 19th century that they started demanding recognition and formal power to accompany their unacknowledged and unpaid labor. The US National Museum of American History recently presented an exhibit entitled "All work, no pay" that documented the extensive unpaid and invisible work women have done and continue to do. Professor Kathleen Franz, chair and curator of the exhibit, states: "There is a historical relationship between unpaid work and the lower wages that women often receive in the workplace," highlighting both the roots and the impact of gender roles ("Women's Invisible Labor," 2019).

1.1 Women Leaders in History

While there are historical examples of female leaders with formal titles and authority, for example, Egypt's Cleopatra (1st century BC), Queen Zenobia of Palmyrene (modern-day Syria, 2nd century), China's Empress Wu Zetian of the Tang Dynasty (7th century), England's Queen Elizabeth 1st (16th century), Lakshmibai, India's Rani of Jhansi (19th century), and the United Kingdom's Queen Victoria (19th century), they are not the norm. Women have also had proximal power and considerable influence through their association with powerful men, husbands, or sons and, in a few cases, have been recognized for their impact, for example, Empress Theodora, wife of Byzantine Emperor Justinian (6th century) or China's Empress Dowager Cixi (19th century). Others, such as Joan of Arc (France, 15th century), have led without the benefit of formal titles.

Undoubtedly, there have been many more women who have led their communities and organizations and have had considerable influence, without ever receiving any recognition. By some account, the French revolution of 1789 was started by women who were hungry and marched on the palace of Versailles demanding bread and thereby triggering the revolution; however, they are rarely mentioned in history books. There are likely countless others; yet we have no record of their accomplishments. Formal written history, the one that children learn in school and that contributes to their views of leadership, is still the story of male leaders.

Women make up roughly half of the world's population, but except in a very few areas and in rare countries, they still do not hold social or economic power commensurate with their numbers and their ability to contribute to society. The United Nations and other world bodies have consistently recognized that world economic development and the well-being of communities are closely tied to the empowerment, education, and active participation of women—half the world's population—in social, business, and political life (UN Women, 2018a). The 20th century has seen many changes. We have had female heads of states in some countries; women have gained economic power and social rights around the world; and, female CEOs, although they are not the norm, are no longer considered an anomaly. Women have made considerable gains in all areas of social, political, educational, and business life. But we are far from having parity between men and women in regard to income, power, and social standing.

1.2 Definitions, Binary Gender, and Intersectionality

Until a few years ago, there was little discussion regarding gender and the definition of the term. In most of the world, gender was and still is simply binary: people are either male or female. Views and definitions of gender have become considerably more complex as we have also expanded our study of gender and its role in society and organizations.

1.2.1 Definitions. Although gender and sex are sometimes used interchangeably, the two are not the same. Sex refers to biological differences, whereas gender is socially and culturally constructed (Fixmer-Oraiz & Wood, 2019). The World Health Organization defines *gender* as "...the socially constructed characteristics of women and men, such as norms, roles, and relationships of and between groups of women and men. It varies from society to society and can be changed" (WHO, 2020). Additionally, gender identities and gender expressions are even more complex and impacted by culture.

GLAAD (formerly the Gay and Lesbian Alliance Against Defamation) defines gender identity as: "One's internal, personal sense of being a man or woman. For transgender people, their own internal gender identity does not match the sex they were assigned at birth" and gender expression as an "external manifestation of gender, expressed through one's name, pronouns, clothing, haircut, behavior, voice, or body characteristics. Society identifies these cues as masculine and feminine, although what is considered masculine or feminine changes over time and varies by culture" (GLAAD, 2020). These more complex approaches to gender are increasingly accepted and used, although research about their link to organizational behavior is still scarce. It is clear that much of what society assigns to gender differences are expressions of culture, rather than biological differences.

1.2.2 Binary and Non-Binary Gender. Recent years have seen considerable evolution in the concept of gender, expanding from the traditional binary male–female view to considering sex and genders to be on a continuum that allows for multiple options and changes over time. Although such nonbinary views are new to many Western countries, they have historically been part of other cultures including indigenous cultures in Central and North American and several parts of Asia. For example, many Native tribes of the North American continent traditionally believed in "Two Spirits" that combine in more than two genders, in some cases, up to five (Krempholtz, 2019). European settlers' imposition of Judeo-Christian beliefs forced them to adopt the strict two gender conception (Davis-Young, 2019).

In the past few years, LGBTQ movements around the world have been the impetus for nonbinary definitions of gender. However, as stated above, as of yet, these conceptions of gender are not yet widely applied in business and management and in the research about gender in management and leadership, making it challenging to fully consider a nonbinary perspective in discussions of gender. However, at least, we do have considerable research on traditional gender differences with a specific focus on women in management and leadership and gender parity in organizations.

1.2.3 Intersectionality. Another further indication of the complex and rich nature of gender and culture is the concept of *intersectionality*, first coined in 1989 by lawyer and civil rights activist Kimberlé Crenshaw (1989). She suggests that simply looking at gender fails to consider the many other essential layers and factors such as race, class, and sexual orientation, as well as other group-culture factors including age or disability. The intersection and connection of all these factors more fully explain and predict bias, discrimination, inequity, and oppression. Some of these factors are presented in Chapter 5; others will be discussed here and in other chapters.

It is beyond the goal of this chapter and book to explore the intricacies and complexities of the topics of binary or nonbinary gender and intersectionality. While nonbinary individuals and women who are also members of a number of other cultural groups are likely to experience many of what we discuss in this chapter, they also face unique obstacles that are not separately addressed here. The focus of this chapter, as the rest of the book, remains on culture-as-meta-context (CMC) and on developing a CM which emphasizes the importance of awareness of culture, its many layers and levels, and how it may impact the way we think and behave. Although still not encompassing many other dimensions of diversity, many of the processes related to in- and out-groups, issues of diversity we covered in Chapter 5, together with the research and information related to women in organizations can provide a starting point for understanding and exploration of nonbinary groups in organizations.

Additionally, while it would be easy to dismiss information about genders discrimination or more broadly the challenges of diversity as related to only women or members of the other under represented groups, as you will read in this chapter, research shows that gender disparities affect everyone negatively, and that creating inclusive organizations that practice gender parity benefits all employees and engender positive organizational outcomes.

1.3 Challenge of Essentializing and Overgeneralization

Throughout this chapter, we will be referring to women and men in broad terms. The challenge of essentializing what we discussed in Chapter 1 and that applies to any aspect of culture is also clearly present when discussing gender. It is obvious that not all women or all men behave the same way (Wood, 2009). There are no essential qualities that define either men or women that all members of these groups possess. As is the case with other aspects of culture, we are using generalizations that refer to prototypes. Additionally, any of the prototypes we may refer to are based on research rather than personal opinion or experiences, isolated anecdotes, or stereotypes. As a matter of fact, as we will review research on gender stereotypes later in this chapter, it will become evident that much of what societies and cultural groups, as well as some individuals, believe to be essential qualities of women and men, are in fact, stereotypes.

2. WOMEN IN TODAY'S ORGANIZATIONS

LO 6.2 Review the status of women in society and organizations in the United States and around the world

Women make up approximately 50% of the world's population. As you will see in the following section, their role and power in society and organizations are far from approaching parity commensurate with their numbers. However, since the 20th century, there has been considerable progress in many aspects of social, political, and organizational life.

2.1 Women in the Workforce

As compared to 1955, when approximately 35% of women worked outside the home in the United States, the latest data indicate that close to 60% do now, compared to over 70% for men. At least in most industrialized countries, they are also close to 50% of the workforce (see Table 6.1 for a summary). Women working outside the

Table 6.1 Women in the Workforce (Countries Included Are Those Listed in Table 1.1)

Percent (%) of Women Who Work (2017 Data)*	Percent (%) of Workforce That Is Female (2018 Data)**
Brazil: 55.4 (2016)	Brazil: 43.4
Canada: 61.3	Canada: 47.3
China: 64.0 (2010)	China: 43.6
Germany: 55.6	Germany: 46.5
India: 27.3 (2012)	India: 22.1
Indonesia: n/a	Indonesia: 38.9
Japan: 50.4	Japan: 43.6
Pakistan: n/a	Pakistan: 21.9
Russia: 63.8	Russia: 48.3
United Kingdom: 58	United Kingdom: 46.7
United States: 57	United States: 46
	By Region
	Euro area: 45.9
	Latin America and Caribbean: 41.2
	Middle East and North Africa: 20
	Sub-Saharan Africa: 46.4

Sources: *Ortiz-Ospina and Tzvetkova (2017) and **Labor Force (2019).

home have not been a novelty for at least 50 years. As a matter of fact, the latest data indicate that women outnumber men in the US paid workforce by a small margin (50.04%–49.99%; Seigel, 2020). The lowest rates of women in the workforce are in the Middle East and North Africa with some of the lowest in Yemen (8%), Qatar (14%), Iraq (14.5%), the UAE (15%), and Saudi Arabia (17%) and the highest in several African countries (e.g., Burundi at 52%; Sierra Leone at 51%; Angola at 50%). Simply looking at these percentages provides some indication that culture plays a key role in women at work. Countries with the lowest participation of women in the workforce have cultural religious traditions of gender segregation that keep women out of public life.

New York Times reporters Susan Chira and Brianna Milord (2017) asked women to share their experiences in the workplace; more than 1,000 responded. Readers recounted instances similar to the *First Person* account at the beginning of this chapter. Attorneys were being told to calm down and take a Midol (an over-the-counter medication marketed for menstrual cramps); managers heard that they are too masculine when they voiced their opinions; other women were told that they didn't get a raise because they were not the head of the household; clients asked women if there was a man who could help them; still others reported being ignored when complaining about blatant sexism; while some shared stories of inclusion and being valued for their contributions (Chira & Milord, 2017).

Anecdotal accounts such as these as well as formal research show that in spite of increasing numbers of women in the workplace, they still face considerable challenges and obstacles that are related to the cultural assumptions, values, and beliefs that make up people's CMC and guide behavior.

2.2 Women in Management and Leadership

As women have been systematically part of the workforce in many parts of the world for many years, they have also been increasingly holding managerial positions (see Table 6.2 for a summary).

2.2.1 Women in Middle Management. Data from *Catalyst* indicate that 75% of businesses globally have at least one woman in senior leadership and that approximately one-third to half of managerial positions in industrialized countries are held by women (Quick Take-Global, 2018). A study by the *Center for American Progress* reports US census data that indicate that women hold 52% of management and professional jobs, a number that shows gender parity at mid-organizational levels (Warner et al., 2018). In the political sector, the US elections of 2018 were record-breaking for women and people of color with a large number of candidates running and winning offices at all levels of government; women are, and have been for many years, present in mid-level managerial and leadership positions.

Table 6.2 Women in Management and Leadership Positions (2018)

Senior Leadership Positions Held by Women

Corporate CEOs
- 5% in Fortune 500
- 7% in Fortune 100
- 10% in S&P 1500

Corporate Boards
- 25% of Fortune 100 seats
- 34% of Fortune 500 seats
- 19% of S&P 1500 seats

Financial Services
- 61% of accountants and 53% of financial managers
- 12% of CFOs in Fortune 500

Global Development
- 20% of NGOs' single highest paid employees
- 10% of thinktanks' highest paid employees
- 30% of foundations' highest paid employees
- 2% of mediators, 8% of negotiators, 5% of witnesses and signatories to major global peace processes

Global Politics (149 Countries)
- 17 women as heads of state
- 18% of ministries
- 24% of parliamentary seats

Hollywood
- 4% of directors across 1,200 movies
- 17% of top executive positions
- 18% of producers

US Politics
- 18% of governors
- 23% of mayors of 100 largest US cities

Academia
- 52% of assistant professors; 40% of associate professors; 32% of full professors
- 30% of college presidents

Legal Profession
- 45% of associates
- 23% of partners
- 19% of equity partners

Medicine
- 40% of all physicians and surgeons
- 16% of medical school deans

Sources: ABD (2018); Desilver (2018); Kenny and Jaluka (2018); Olson (2019); *The Global Gender Gap Report* (2018); UN Women (2018b); Warner, Ellmann, and Boesch (2018); and Women and Hollywood (2019).

2.2.2 Women in Leadership. The data are not as encouraging when looking at top leadership positions in all sectors (see Table 6.2). The number of women CEOs in Fortune 500 and Fortune 100 or S&P 1500 is disheartening. Even more disheartening is the very slow or complete lack of progress. For example, the highest number ever of female CEOs in Fortune 500 companies was 32 in 2017; it dropped 25% to 24 in 2018 with many retirements and sudden exits including Denise Morrison of Campbell Soup, Meg Whitman of Hewlett Packard, Irene Rosenfeld of Mondelez, Shari Goodman of Staples, and Sheri McCoy of Avon (Zarya, 2018). A study by the Pew Research Center (Desilver, 2018) not only finds that women hold barely 5% of CEO positions but also that they only fill about 12% of the executive positions just below that level. This is significant because these would be the people who are in the pool of future top executives.

The same study finds that women lag in corporate leadership across industries with a slightly higher percentage in utilities, consumer goods, and healthcare. A 2017 study of European companies by McKinsey & Co (Devillard, de Zelicourt, Kossoff, & Sancier-Sultan, 2017) found that a mere 7% ranked diversity among their top priorities and that many employees and managers within those companies do not think that diversity and gender-related policies are taken seriously. The World Economic Forum's (WFE) report on the gender gap estimates that at this pace, it will take more than 200 years to reach parity in many areas (*The Global Gender Gap Report*, 2018). Klaus Schwab, executive chair of the WEF, states: "The equal contribution of women and men in this process of deep economic and societal transformation is critical. More than ever, societies cannot afford to lose out on the skills, ideas and perspectives of half of humanity."

The situation for women of color is even less encouraging. For example, as of January 2020, there was only one female CEO of color (0.2%) among Fortune 500 companies, Joey Wat of Yum China (Rabouin, 2019); there were only 2 women of color for several years prior to that date (Donnelly, 2018). Women of color only represent 2% of governors and 10% of mayors. Indra Nooyi, former PepsiCo CEO who was born in Chennai, India, believes one reason is work–life balance:

> *As you get to middle management, women rise to those positions, and then that's the childbearing years. And when they have children, it's difficult to balance having children, your career, your marriage, and be a high potential outperformer who's going to grow in the company, in an organization that is a pyramid. It starts to thin out as you move up. We have to solve that. (McGregor & Siegel, 2018)*

Others blame the traditional image of leaders being mostly white males as the primary reason. If we expect and believe that leaders should fit a certain image, women clearly will not fit and therefore are not considered legitimate (Vial, Napier, & Brescoll, 2016); women of color even less so. Professor Katherine Phillips of Columbia Business School states: "If you boil it down to who people are expecting to see as a potential leader, there still is a very sticky prototype of a leader being tall, white and male" (McGregor & Siegel, 2018).

2.3 The Glass Ceiling and Glass Cliff

As they increasingly join middle-management ranks, women face what has been labeled the *Glass Ceiling*—the invisible barrier that holds them back. They reach certain levels, but cannot go any higher. Some who shatter the glass ceiling have encountered a *Glass Cliff* where women are picked for leadership roles that have a high risk of failure (Ryan & Haslam, 2007). The prime example is the former UK prime minister, Theresa May, who, while many in her party had leadership ambitions, was picked for the impossible task of orchestrating Brexit, where, as the outcome shows, chances for success were slim to none. Other examples are Mary Bara, the first woman promoted to be CEO of General Motors, Harriet Green appointed as CEO of Thomas Cook, and Jill Soltau CEO of JC Penney. In Bara's case, GM was in the midst of a 2.5 million car recall and lawsuits involving the deaths of several people because of defective ignition systems; Thomas Cook selected Green during a time when many feared it would not survive; and JC Penney had been struggling for many years when it appointed Soltau as its first female CEO.

The Glass Cliff is attributed to gender stereotypes that expect women to be able to take care of problems partly because they offer something new and because as Anna Beninger, senior director of research and corporate engagement partner at Catalyst, says: "They're effectively handed the mess to clear up" (Steward, 2018). Carol Bartz, who ran Autodesk and Yahoo, in a recent interview asserts: "Listen, it is absolutely true that women have a better chance to get a directorship, or a senior position if there's trouble" (Dubner, 2018). In addition to these individual cases, research supports the perception that women are likely to do better when the situation is difficult and requires cooperation and caring for others (Cook & Glass, 2013). Furthermore, because women have fewer opportunities, they are more likely to be willing to accept risky positions.

2.3.1 Challenge Without Reward. Interestingly, as they are pushed into challenging leadership roles, women are not often rewarded for taking such risks. Activist investors have been found to be more likely to target women CEOs to be fired, and when women do not succeed, they are not provided as many chances as men; their lack of success is used to further reinforce the stereotype that women cannot be effective leaders. Carol Bartz says:

> It's not that all of a sudden the boards wake up and say, "Oh, there should be a female here." They do that sometimes, because it's easier to hide behind, "Well, of course. Of course, that failed, because it was female." What could we have been thinking? (Steward, 2018)

Researchers Alison Cook and Christy Glass (2013) further find that when women CEOs do not perform as expected in their risky assignments, they are more often than not replaced by a man, who is seen as the savior. Our views and expectations of men and women and their roles and strengths have impacted how many women are in leadership positions. The same culturally based expectations are a factor in how we compensate people for their work.

2.4 The Pay Gap

One of the major areas of disparity between men and women in society and in organizations is in their pay. The *pay gap* refers to a differential between the pay of men and women in similar jobs. The average pay gap in the United States is approximately 80%, with women making 20% less than men for similar jobs ("The Simple Truth," 2018). Table 6.3 summarizes some of the key facts. As you can see, ethnicity and location both impact the extent of the pay gap, as does the type of occupation. The smallest pay gaps are in the retail and food industries with several jobs in financial services being at the bottom for pay parity. Interestingly, in spite of consistent and overwhelming evidence regarding the existence of the pay gap, some still consider it a myth with studies of professionals showing that close to 20% of women and 40% of men do not believe that it exists (Ellevest Team, 2018).

2.4.1 Factors in the US Pay Gap. While there are always individual differences, having higher levels of education does not always equalize pay. For example, while a smaller pay gap exists for minimum wage food preparers and workers (99%–87% depending on the data), female surgeons earn 71% of what male surgeons earn in the same specialty (Salam, 2019). Statistics from the US census further show that education only closes the wage gap by a few percentage points (Day, 2019). When looking at two-income families, a Pew Center survey finds that, across two-parent households where both parents are employed at least part time, the father earns more than the mother in close to 60% of the cases with only in 17% mothers earning more and 23% being equal ("Raising Kids," 2015).

Interestingly, some research has found that husbands are least distressed when their wives earn 40% of the household income; anything much higher or lower tends to be associated with higher stress for men, a pattern that is not replicated for women (Syrda, 2019). Furthermore, women are overrepresented in the most low-wage

Table 6.3   US Pay Gap Quick Facts

- Overall in the United States = 80%
- Asian = 85%
- White = 77%
- Native Hawaiian and Pacific Islander = 62%
- Black or African American = 61%
- American Indian or Alaska Native = 58%
- Hispanic or Latina = 53%
- Women aged 25–34 = 88%
- Women aged 55–64 = 77%

- State with lowest gap: California at 89%
- State with the highest gap: Louisiana at 69%
- Five best occupations: Buyers (109%); advertising (100%); HR specialists (100); chemists (96%); pharmacists (91%)
- Five worst occupations: Financial specialists (66%); podiatrists (67%); brokerage clerks (71%); physicians and surgeons (71%); pilots (71%)

Sources: Miller (2014) and The Simple Truth (2018).

occupations such as childcare (95% women) and home health aides (89% women), while at the same time, they are underrepresented in top income groups (Ortiz-Ospina & Roser, 2018). The pay gap further gets worse with age. While younger workers who are entering the workforce are closing the pay gap to some extent, older workers experience even a wider gap ("The Simple Truth," 2018). Additionally, women provide an overwhelming share of unpaid and volunteer work in society further reducing their pay (Folbre, 2012).

2.4.2 The Global Pay Gap. The US pay gap is better than the global average, which stands at 63% according to the World Economic Forum (WEF) *Global Gender Gap Report* (2018; see Table 6.4). Various surveys and indices consider other aspects of the gender gap that relate to income and economic power, for example, land ownership, control over financial decisions, and inheritance (Ortiz-Ospina & Roser, 2018). In all dimensions, women rank lower than men. While some countries are closer to parity than others, and the rankings vary depending on how compensation is measured and which countries are included, women are not paid more than men anywhere in the world (see Table 6.4 for summary of global rankings). Another troubling trend is that even in top levels of organizations, only 11% of top earners of S&P 500 companies are women (Pyramid, 2019). According to a recent survey, only 4 out of 25 of the highest paid US CEOs were women, with men holding the top 10 ranks (Suneson, 2018). Not a single one of the top 15 highest paid CEOs worldwide is female (Zambas, 2018). Studies by the Economic Policy Institute show that progress regarding gender parity in economic power and pay has stalled and will take many years to fix. The most recent World Economic Forum report projects that, at the current rate, pay equality is likely to be achieved by year 2277 (Jackson, 2019).

2.4.3 Explaining the Pay Gap. The pay gap is not a myth; it is real and it is not closing. Saadia Zahidi, the WEF's head of social and economic agenda, states: "The overall picture is that gender equality has stalled. The future of our labor market may not be

---

Table 6.4 Global Pay Gap: Quick Facts[a]

Smallest Pay Gap	Largest Pay Gap
• Laos (92%) • Barbados (87%) • Bahamas (86%) • Benin (85%) • Burundi (84%)	• Iraq (26%) • Syria (27%) • Yemen (30%) • Pakistan (32%) • Saudi Arabia (34%)

[a]The percentage indicates how much women make compared to men—a higher number indicates a smaller gap.

Source: Global Gender Gap Report (2018).

as equal as the trajectory we thought we were on" (Neate, 2018). To address the problem, more than 100 companies, including AT&T, Gap, Mastercard, and Target, have pledged to review their salaries annually to close the existing pay gaps (Cowley, 2018). Many signed the Equal Pay Pledge in 2016, a pledge that was triggered by Lilly Ledbetter's lawsuit against her company and led to the signing of the Fair Pay Act in 2009. Ledbetter stated: "Unequal pay hurts women. It hurts their families. And it hurts us all" (Salam, 2019).

It is clear that no single factor can explain the pay gap. Among the many reasons mentioned are the motherhood penalty, women's inability to negotiate higher salaries, the double bind regarding what is appropriate and expected, and simple bias and discrimination. Referring to women taking time to raise their children, Olivia Mitchell, professor of business economics and public policy at the Wharton Business School, suggests: "There's an opportunity cost of staying home. Time out of the labor force is a penalty" (Farber, 2017). Women end up paying a "motherhood penalty" where their pay and promotion opportunities are reduced with every child they have. Claudia Goldin (2014), professor of economics at Harvard, further suggests that one possible explanation is the structure of our organizations. Her research shows that organizations disproportionally reward people who can work continuous long hours, a schedule typical in high-paying jobs such as finance and law. This structure reduces flexibility and comes at a high price for women who often have family responsibilities. All these reasons, which we discuss throughout this chapter, have cultural roots. Our culturally based beliefs and expectations of men and women (i.e., our CMC), their appropriate place and role in society and in organizations, all have consequences, including leading to a pay differential between what men and women earn.

WINDOW TO THE WORLD

Gender Discrimination in Hiring in China

Many industrialized countries have specific laws that prohibit discrimination based on gender. China is no exception, where both labor and advertising laws ban gender discrimination. The economic growth of the country has created considerable opportunities for women; 64% of women work and they are close to being half of the workforce (43%; see Table 6.1). However, it is not unusual for job ads to clearly and plainly discriminate against women. A job ad for an information feed reviewer at Baidu, a multinational technology firm, on the company's website lists the job requirements as: "Associate degree or above, *men*, any major, have relevant job experience." A review of national civil service job lists in 2017 and 2018 shows that 13% and 19% list "men only" or "men preferred" or "suitable for men." Other ads focus on women's physical characteristics. For example, a job ad for a train conductor starts off with "fashionable and beautiful high-speed train conductors."

Source: Stauffer (2018).

3. CULTURE AND GENDER

LO 6.3 Elaborate on the role of culture in views of gender

As we have already presented in this chapter, there are numerous instances of gender differences in organizations and most often reflect lack of parity between men and women in regard to issues such as opportunities, power, and salary. While women have made headway everywhere in the world, they are still at a disadvantage. What explains this lack of parity? Are there biological differences between the sexes or genders or do other factors, particularly cultural values, explain the different outcomes?

3.1 Nurture Over Nature

Increasingly, advances in biology, brain research, and cognitive science are debunking the beliefs that biological, physiological, or evolutionary factors explain gender differences and the lack of gender parity (e.g., Fine, 2013). Scientists have not found clear connections between biological factors such as hormones and behavior (e.g., van Honk, Terburg, & Bos, 2011) indicating that despite commonly held beliefs, our gendered behaviors are essentially not determined by our biology and physiology or whether we have more testosterone or more estrogen (Dabbs & Dabbs, 2000). Additionally, evidence about activities in traditional hunter-gatherer communities indicates that gender egalitarianism may have been more prevalent than is often assumed (Dyble et al., 2015).

In a comprehensive 2014 review of gender differences and similarities, Janet Shibley Hyde finds few significant differences between the genders in terms of cognitive performance, personality, or social behaviors (Hyde, 2014). For example, her review suggests that while a few differences in math performance favoring men are found and men may perform better in some spatial skills, "…more recent data indicate that, in general, females have reached parity with males in math performance" (Hyde, 2014, p. 381). She also does not find significant differences when it comes to being emotional or in the widely held view that men are more aggressive (Eagly & Steffen, 1986; Hyde, 2014; Richardson & Hammock, 2007).

Social psychologist Naomi Ellemers (2018) states: "Research indicates that gender differences develop over the life span, due to the way boys and girls are raised and educated." The gender differences we observe in society and in our organizations in terms of career choices, how much people progress, how they lead, and how well they perform are about how society, both men *and* women, constructs gender roles. The differences and disparities that are common and typical around the world stem from the assumptions that people hold about the role and position of gender in society, their beliefs and values related to gender roles, and systemic actions and policies that flow from those assumptions, beliefs, and values. Just as blatant and subtle racial biases have become entrenched in our institutions (see Chapter 5), gender biases have created *institutional sexism*, which refers to gender inequity and discrimination and are ingrained in the policies and practices of institutions and organizations.

Our culture-based views regarding people from different genders translate into how we think they should behave (Prentice & Carranza, 2002) and the opportunities that we make available to them; they are the source of gender stereotypes.

3.2 Gender Stereotypes

Cultural assumptions about the nature of women and men in society are a key component of any culture. These cultural assumptions operate both at the national and group levels and are the source of *gender stereotypes*, which are beliefs regarding people based on their assigned gender. In most societies, gender-based assumptions or stereotypes involve a hierarchical view of genders with men being dominant, strong, and independent and women being perceived as subservient, weak, and in need of protection. The deep assumptions, of which many people are barely conscious, lead to specific values and beliefs regarding the role of men and women in society and in our organizations. A review of gender stereotypes by social psychologist Naomi Ellemers (2018) indicates that gender stereotypes not only describe our expectations but also prescribe our behaviors; so they are both descriptive and normative. While stereotypes allow us to be efficient and make quick decisions, as discussed in Chapter 3, they also prevent us from gathering additional information and are therefore likely to lead to errors.

3.2.1 Typical Stereotypes. Figure 6.1 presents the list of typical characteristics associated with men and women. While these stereotypes or their occurrence and strength may differ from one culture to another, some are prevalent in most cultures. A review of the lists presented in Figure 6.1 indicates that, not surprisingly, men are seen as powerful agents who have the ability and the right to be strong, independent, action-oriented, and in charge. Women, on the other hand, are stereotypically seen as vulnerable, focused on relationships, dependent, and more likely to follow than lead. Even the symbols used to refer to the two genders, used in Figure 6.1, reflect these themes. The male symbol represents a shield and sword; the female symbol is that of a mirror with a handle. Males are powerful warriors and outward looking; females are inactive, passive, and reflective.

Research shows that men estimate their own intelligence to be higher than women's (Bennett, 1996) and their father's intelligence to be higher than their mother's (Hogan, 1978). Women are supposed to be nicer and kinder than men and more caring and communal (Cuddy, Fiske, & Glick, 2004). Few people, at least in most industrialized countries, will directly voice such highly traditional gender

Figure 6.1 Stereotypical Gender Characteristics

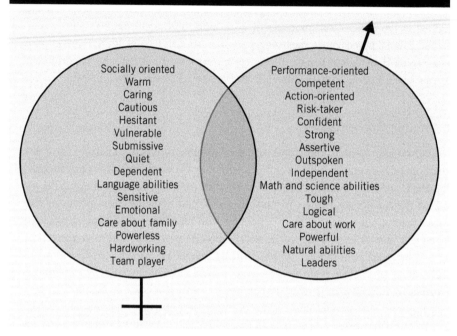

Socially oriented	Performance-oriented
Warm	Competent
Caring	Action-oriented
Cautious	Risk-taker
Hesitant	Confident
Vulnerable	Strong
Submissive	Assertive
Quiet	Outspoken
Dependent	Independent
Language abilities	Math and science abilities
Sensitive	Tough
Emotional	Logical
Care about family	Care about work
Powerless	Powerful
Hardworking	Natural abilities
Team player	Leaders

Sources: Based on Ellemers (2018); Hyde (2014); Schmader et al. (2007).

stereotypes. However, studies on implicit bias show that we are influenced by our past experiences in ways that we may not be aware of. For example, a series of studies show that even in the 21st century in the United States, housework is considered women's work and women are judged more harshly than men when the space they occupy is messy (Miller, 2019). The culture-based gender stereotypes impact women's perception of themselves and their behavior (Caprino, 2015). A study by Thomas Buser, Niederle, and Oosterbeek (2014) shows that while girls and boys have the same level of academic ability, boys select prestigious careers involving science and math to a great extent because of their competitiveness (Buser et al., 2014).

3.2.2 Benevolent Sexism. Many of these characteristics presented in Figure 6.1 are subtle and implicit. Indeed, few of us are aware that we see genders as having different strengths or abilities; even fewer of us can point to the deep assumptions about the inequality of men and women that underlie our beliefs. In some cases, beliefs that males are and should be dominant—something that tends to create hostility toward women—is replaced by what is called *benevolent sexism*, which is characterized by putting women on a pedestal along with a desire to protect them (Glick et al., 2000).

This benevolent sexism is kind and views women as nicer and more caring than men; however, it still propagates the view that women, because of their kindness, are in need of protection. Benevolent sexism, therefore, also contributes to gender disparities and inequality. Whether explicit or implicit, or hostile or benevolent, the belief that men and women have different characteristics is persistent and impactful.

3.3 Early Development of Gender Expectations

A comprehensive 2017 research project called the Global Early Adolescent Study (GEAS) involved a series of cross-cultural studies in several countries including the United States, China, India, Belgium, Egypt, Kenya, and Nigeria designed to explore gender role development and its impact on adolescents. The project helps shed some light onto when and how gender roles and expectations develop and are reinforced. Elizabeth Saewyc, one of the senior researchers on the project, suggests that in spite of considerable change, the world is still a highly gendered place and culturally based gender expectations profoundly affect women's experiences throughout their lives (Saewyc, 2017). Kristin Mmari, faculty at the Johns Hopkins University who also worked on the project, referring to gender disparities, states: "We were actually anticipating more differences than similarities, and one of the big findings is that there are still consistent forms of patriarchy around the world" (Dastagir, 2017).

3.3.1 Consistent Stereotypes. GEAS researchers found widely held assumptions and beliefs about girls being vulnerable and dependent, while boys are considered to be strong and independent. These assumptions translate into clearly gendered values that drive parents to try to protect girls, something they label the *hegemonic myth*, by limiting their behaviors and ability to explore their environment (Blum, Mmari, & Moreau, 2017).

The cultural values are passed on from one generation to another reinforcing the message that women's primary asset is their body and that they must guard and protect it or face dire consequences. For example, research about identity development in adolescents shows that in India and China, mothers play a strong role in guiding boys and girls toward adopting traditional gender roles and behaviors passing on the norms they grew up with to their offspring (Basu, Zuo, Lou, Acharya, & Lundgren, 2017). As a result, girls learn to restrict their environment, be cautious and fearful, and avoid standing out. These gender norms affect both boys and girls. Robert Blum, one of the researchers on the project, says: "If you're a girl, you're on guard. If you're a boy you learn that you're an aggressor. It's like a self-fulfilling prophecy" (Peck, 2017). The findings point to some flexibility with stereotypical norms for girls, but less so for boys. Girls are allowed to act more masculine and show power typically associated with the male gender, whereas boys have less leeway to display the lower prestige behaviors associated with the female gender (Yu et al., 2017). The results of GEAS studies indicate that regardless of the country, when girls reach puberty, they are pushed out of some aspects of public life and face more limited choices than boys. One girl in Egypt said: "Now I look at myself in the mirror and I say, 'Yeah, I've grown. I can't go out anymore'" (Peck, 2017).

3.3.2 Social and Cultural Nature of Stereotypes. The GEAS project's findings are consistent with those of many other studies regarding gender beliefs and expectations: what we consider gender differences are to a very large extent assumptions and beliefs that are socially and culturally constructed and reinforced. Kristin Mmari concludes: "How you perceive girls and boys is socially driven. It's not biologically driven" (Dastagir, 2017). Our culturally based assumptions have deep historical roots and significant staying power, and they are actively and subconsciously transmitted from one generation to the next. They have become the basis of persistent stereotypes and discrimination and therefore have a sizable impact on our individual behaviors, social and institutional policies and structures, and our organizational practices and processes.

3.4 The Consequences of Stereotypes

A particularly interesting finding regarding gender stereotypes is that while many of the stereotypes and expectations we have about various groups, for example, a stereotype you may have about artists or accountants, tend to be fluid and change from one situation to another, gender and racial stereotypes are stable and act as a primary feature of how we perceive others (Bennett et al., 2000; Ito & Urland, 2003).

3.4.1 Gender as Master Status. In other words, much like skin color, gender provides a master status that leads to chronic accessibility (see Chapters 3 and 5). Our views of gender dominate our perceptions of others and are effortlessly and often subconsciously available and therefore used frequently. Gender is one of the first things we notice about others; it triggers many biases that quickly, automatically, and subconsciously become the basis of beliefs and judgments and guides behaviors.

In a dramatic illustration of the power of gender stereotypes, a 2018 training program at the accounting giant Ernst & Young stated that women's brain makes it hard for them to focus, instructed women how to dress in flattering ways, act nicely around their male colleague (Peck, 2019). In other examples, women in Japan and Korea have been loudly protesting against rules for dress and makeup, such as requiring high heels and makeup and forbidding wearing glasses, that apply only to women and, in many cases, impose a heavy burden on them (Berger, 2019). Current organizational practices still value a work model based on a good mother *or* a good worker model that reinforces traditional gender stereotypes (Williams, Berdahl, & Vandello, 2016), further restricting women's career choices.

3.4.2 Gender Stereotypes and Career Options. Because stereotypes are both descriptive (how we are) and prescriptive (how we should be), they guide the life and career choices of both men and women. In 2012, Anne Marie Slaughter, current CEO of New America, former dean of the Princeton Woodrow Wilson School of Public and International Affairs and Director of Policy and Planning in the State Department under Secretary Hillary Clinton, triggered an ongoing debate about whether women can achieve the same success as men. In her article *"Why women still can't have it all,"* she made the point that, because of the structure of US society and economy, it is much harder for women than for men to have a career while also having a family (Slaughter, 2012). Her words have been echoed by many others and reflect the impact of culture in social policies, organizational practices, and individual behaviors.

Surveys in 30 industrialized countries indicate that men and women continue to work in different occupations with men in typically male professions and women in typically female ones (Jarman, Blackburn, & Racko, 2012). Nordic women who have achieved some of the highest level of gender parity in the world are still disproportionately present in public sector careers that provide better work–life balance but less growth and income (Zander, 2014). Even when both genders are engaged in acts of helping others or heroism, men are found to engage in more active and dangerous roles (e.g., saving lives), whereas women engage in helping in communal ways (e.g., volunteering for the Peace Corp; Becker & Eagly, 2004).

In her extensive 2014 review of the research on gender differences, psychologist Janet Shibley Hyde concludes that countries that have greater gender equity show smaller gaps between men and women in a variety of areas (Hyde, 2014, p. 392). In other words, when culture, society, and organizations support equality and the success of women in education and the workplace through various policies and strategies, gender disparities start to disappear and women, like men, have a better chance at "having it all."

For example, as we will consider in more detail, Nordic and Scandinavian countries have some of the best records regarding gender parity in the workplace, public or private; those are driven by those countries' cultural views and corresponding policies regarding gender, not by biological differences; Nordic women are not different than women in other parts of the world. The gender-based cultural assumptions and beliefs of those countries have led to egalitarian public policy and organizational practices that have allowed women to maintain a career and still have a family.

3.5 Gender and the Cultural Mindset

Gender inequality and disparities exist because of our cultural *software*, the way we have been programmed, not because of the *hardware* of human beings. The programming of our mind is what drives us to expect and accept gender differences.

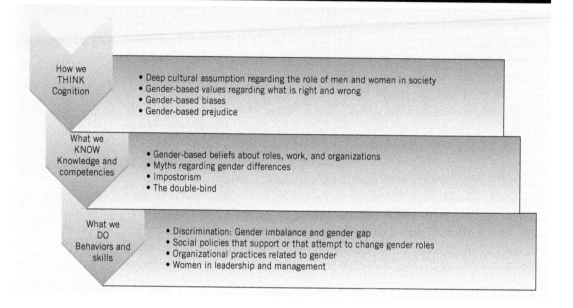

Figure 6.2 Gender and the Cultural Mindset

How we THINK Cognition	• Deep cultural assumption regarding the role of men and women in society • Gender-based values regarding what is right and wrong • Gender-based biases • Gender-based prejudice
What we KNOW Knowledge and competencies	• Gender-based beliefs about roles, work, and organizations • Myths regarding gender differences • Impostorism • The double-bind
What we DO Behaviors and skills	• Discrimination: Gender imbalance and gender gap • Social policies that support or that attempt to change gender roles • Organizational practices related to gender • Women in leadership and management

They exist because we assume they are appropriate and because we have not taken actions to change them. As they are part of the culture and the software of our mind, our assumptions, values, beliefs, and practices, they form our CMC. Using the THINK–KNOW–DO roadmap to developing a CM, Figure 6.2 illustrates that how we THINK (our cultural assumptions and biases) drives what we KNOW (our beliefs) and then what we DO (policies, practices, and individual behavior).

In addition to shaping our CMC, our views of gender have considerable impact in organizations. As managers, our views shape how we manage our employees and who we decide to interview, hire, promote, or reward. There are additional and related causes for lack of gender parity in organizations; we review those next.

4. CAUSES OF LACK OF GENDER PARITY IN ORGANIZATIONS: MYTHS AND REALITY

LO 6.4 Identify and explain the causes of lack of gender parity in organizations

Why, in the 21st century, after over 100 years of legislation, social policies, and organizational efforts, is there not parity between the genders in organizations?

Table 6.5   Most Cited Reasons for Lack of Gender Parity in Organizations

- Gender differences in abilities or leadership style
- Gender differences in experience level
- Gender differences in educational level
- Women face work–life balance challenges
- Gender-based discrimination in society and in organizations

Do women lead and manage differently? Are they not educated and experienced enough or are there social and organizational obstacles that block their success? Table 6.5 summarizes the most-often cited reasons for the lack of gender parity. Although not supported by research, the most persistent, enduring, and simplest explanation for lack of parity is that they are caused by actual differences in abilities or style, otherwise referred to as "a kernel of truth hypothesis." In other words, men and women are different and what women bring to organizations either does not fit organizational needs or is not appreciated.

Popular books such as *Men Are from Mars, Women Are from Venus* (Gray, 2004) reinforce both the stereotypes and the message that they have a genetic or biological basis. It is clear that many of us believe that men and women think and behave differently, and many discuss gender differences in ways that seem to indicate that they have biological bases. For example, Christine Laguarde, President of the European Central Bank, who was the former French finance minister and later head of the International Monetary Fund (IMF), referring to the 2008 financial crisis said: "If Lehman Brothers had been 'Lehman Sisters,' today's economic crisis clearly would look quite different" (LaGuarde, 2010).

Our culturally based views of gender may not have biological bases, but they have a real impact on social interactions and in organizational life and real consequences. They create substantial barriers for women in organizational settings (Koening, Eagly, Mitchell, & Ristikari, 2011).

4.1 Gender Differences in Leadership

Research has also extensively explored whether there are gender differences in leadership styles, and if so, whether some styles are less effective than others.

4.1.1 Some Differences. Studies support commonly held beliefs that there are some gender differences in terms of some of the leadership behaviors or styles between men and women. For example, women tend be more cooperative, team-oriented, and change-oriented (Eagly, Johannesen-Schmidt, & van Engen, 2003). British businesswoman Stephanie Shirley, who was one of the first women to start a software company in the 1960s, says: "All the talk was about money, profits, cash flow, whereas I was much more interested in team work, innovation, excellence, quality assurance—some things that people consider the softer things of management" (NPR Staff, 2013). Carol Smith, vice president for Conde Nast's Bon Appetit and Gourmet Group, believes that women's ability to connect with people makes them better managers: "In my experience, female bosses tend to be better managers, better advisers, mentors, rational thinkers. Men love to hear themselves talk." She further believes that men are better at letting things roll off their back while women rethink and replay events (Bryant, 2009).

Such assertions are supported by some research that indicates that women value maintenance of relationship to a greater extent than men (Gino & Wood Brooks, 2015) and collaborate more (Cullinan, 2018), while men initiate negotiations to a higher extent (Bowles, Babcock, & Lai, 2007). Other research by Herminio Ibarra and Otilio Obodaru (2009) suggests that female leaders outshine men in many dimensions in 360-degree assessments. However, these differences are not significant when it comes to leadership.

4.1.2 Insignificant Impact. Overall, when considering leadership style, extensive research related to gender does not show significant differences between men and women (Eagly et al., 2003; Eagly, Karau, & Makhijani, 1995). Interestingly, while it commonly and persistently believed that women lack confidence (e.g., Katty & Shipman, 2014; Zenger, 2018) and suffer from what is called the *impostor syndrome*, or impostorism (Clance & Imes, 1978; Sakulku, 2011), even that gap tends to be situational and in response to specific contexts, as we explore later in this chapter.

More significantly, where there might be some differences in management and leadership styles between men and women, such differences, if anything, should help women rather than hurt them (Amanatullah & Morris, 2010; Su, Rounds, & Armstrong, 2009; Tannen, 1993; Wittenberg-Cox, 2014). Specifically, many current leadership theories emphasize teamwork, cooperation, and power sharing rather than competitiveness and aggression, areas where women are supposed to have the upper hand. This finding would suggest that, if the even gender differences in leadership style are present, they should make women more effective and thereby translating into more women in leadership positions, something that we know is not the case (see Table 6.2) anywhere in the world.

4.2 Experience and Education

It would be tempting to attribute the lower number of women in leadership positions and the pay gap to women's lower levels of education and experience. However, data do not support this explanation.

4.2.1 Experience. The number of women in middle management positions has been climbing steadily since the 1970s. According to the *Women's Bureau of the US Department of Labor* ("Women in the Labor Force," 2010), women account for close to 52% of workers in high-paying management and other professional occupations such as financial managers (53.2%), public relations managers (60%), accountants and auditors (60.1%), and education administrators (63%). Research by the global nonprofit organization *Catalyst* shows that more than half of the management occupations in Fortune 500 companies are held by women (Quick Take-US, 2018). There are therefore many women with the appropriate experience to head our organizations.

4.2.2 Education. Data regarding education are even more enlightening. The US census data for 2017 ("Educational Attainment in the US," 2017) indicate that for people over 25, a higher percentage of women than men have earned a bachelor's or master's degree, a trend that started in 1978 (Dishman, 2017). Data from the *National Center for Education Statistics* (IES-NCES, 2017) further document that close to 200,000 more women than men earned a university degree in 2015–2016, while men continue to have an edge in the STEM fields. The first time more women than men earned doctorates in the United States was in 2005–2006, with close to 10,000 more women earning doctorates in 2015–2016 ("Digest of Education Statistics," 2017).

Some data reveal that slightly fewer women are earning their MBAs as compared with men (57% vs. 60%), a fact that has been attributed to women having a hard time getting loans partly due to the pay gap that they are anticipating when they graduate (Dishman, 2017). Nonetheless, many top MBA programs around the world have seen a steady increase of women applicants and students for many years now with some achieving parity between the number of male and female students (Six top online MBA programs, 2018). Susan Kulp, professor of accounting at George Washington University, attributes this trend to strong diversity efforts: "We become seen as a place committed to fostering diversity, and as a result we attract more women" (C.S-W, 2017)—all factors that are possible partly because of education.

Although there may be individual cases that can be held up as an example of how lack of education or experience explains lack of parity, overall, it is clear that neither explains why fewer women are leading our organizations or why they are paid less than their male counterparts.

4.3 Work–Life Balance

Work–life balance or imbalance has been found to be a key contributor to gender disparities in organizations. Because of culturally based gender stereotypes and expectations regarding how to be a good mother, wife, and daughter, women continue to contribute more significant time than their male partners to household work.

They come back from a full day at the office and try to fulfill expectations of a full-time stay-at-home mom. Cinta Putra, CEO of National Notification Network, believes: "The greatest challenge has been balancing all the demand of being a woman, a parent, a wife, a sister, a daughter, a friend *and* a CEO" (Bisoux, 2008). Studies show that women carry these expectations to the office and engage in low promotability activities such as volunteering for various tasks more often than men (Babcock, Recalde, Vesterlund, & Weingard, 2017). Interestingly, the social distancing and lockdowns that drove many to work from home during the COVID-19 pandemic further intensified this imbalance with women spending even more time on both childcare and education and other household duties (Fenson, 2020).

4.3.1 Unequal Time. Women spend more time on household activities, including childcare, and increasingly caring for aging parents, than men do, regardless of their employment status (Miller, 2019). The American Time Use Survey (2017) by the US Bureau of Labor Statistics indicates that 49% of women and 19% of men did some housework on an average day and that in households with children under 6, men spent 1.3 hours a day on household activities compared with women's 2.4 hours. The more recent Time Use Survey shows that women who work continue to spend more time on housework and childcare and less time on leisure activities than men who work (Harrison & Oh, 2019). A survey in the United Kingdom shows an even greater disparity with women spending twice as much time than their live-in male partners even when both work outside the home, although the proportion for younger Millennials, as compared to Baby Boomers, is more balanced (Stern, 2018). A Pew Research Center study further finds that although women carry a heavier burden of household work, dads are much more likely than moms to believe that they share equally in the work ("Raising Kids," 2015). Significantly, twice as many working mothers, as compared to fathers, report feeling that responsibilities with family and household affect their career negatively.

An increasingly aging population is presenting a new challenge for many women who, in accordance with expectations of being a "good" daughter, are part of what is called the sandwich generation who is caring for both young children and aging parents. Angelina Grigoryeva, a researcher at Princeton University, finds that women step up to care for aging parents twice as often as men and experience the physical, psychological, and financial stress of doing so with 43% of people who are caring for their aging parents saying that it has affected their professional career (Diab, 2016; Graves, 2014). Further demonstrating the impact of gender stereotypes, a fascinating research by Bittman and his colleagues (2003) shows that when women earn more money than their husband, they actually increase, rather than decrease, the amount of time they invest in household work. The authors suggest that they do so to compensate for having violated the traditional views of division of labor when their income surpasses that of their husbands.

4.3.2 Consequences. The challenge of balancing work and life has clear consequences for women. Amy Barnes, who is a working mother, says:

> *You basically just always feel like you're doing a horrible job at everything. You're not spending as much time with your baby as you want, you're not doing the job you want to be doing at work, you're not seeing your friends hardly ever. (Miller, 2015)*

Fathers are not immune to these pressures; however, the Pew survey shows that they are clearer about work–life balance and less conflicted about the priority they place on their work ("Raising Kids," 2015). Thinking about her baby and the work–life balance, Amy Barnes adds:

> *Especially now because he's still below school age, I feel very torn about having a full-time job and basically missing out on all of that time. Either it's the undercurrent of how I feel every day for the next few years, or I figure out a way to work a little bit less. (Miller, 2015)*

The consequence of this imbalance in work and life is that mothers in general are less employed and have lower pay than other women, whereas fathers work more than other men. Women being hit with what has been labeled a "mommy tax" is one of the explanations for the pay gap we discussed earlier in this chapter. While men and women may start with similar salaries, as women become mothers, they increasingly spend more time on their family responsibilities and less time at work further worsening the gender pay gap (Miller, 2017). This starts a vicious cycle where as women earn less, they do more at home; they then have less time to devote to their career, which further reinforces the pay gap and the traditional views of the role of women (see Figure 6.3). Research has shown that while working parents in general are seen as less committed, mothers pay a particular price as they do not fit the image of what an ideal worker should be (Fuegen, Biernat, Haines, & Deaux, 2004).

The roots of the work–life imbalance that women experience are the widely held cultural gender stereotypes about the role of men and women in society and in organizations. Both men and women hold traditional gender-based expectations about what each should and must do and what is appropriate and desirable. These expectations play a key role in burdening working women with challenges related to their work–life balance and impact their career success. Our culturally based stereotypes are clearly one of the main reasons why women do not enter the workforce, do not achieve as much as men, and do not earn as much as men. A cursory look at the countries where women have the lowest participation in the workforce indicates the common theme of cultural traditions that have segregated women in public life and until recently kept them from education and any major role in public life. Conversely, in countries where cultural values are more gender egalitarian, women have fared considerably better.

Figure 6.3   The Work–Life Balance Vicious Circle Cycle

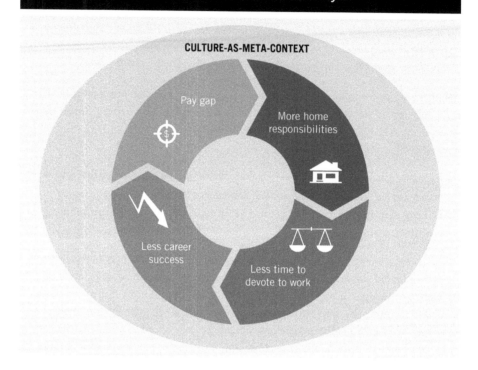

4.4 Workplace Discrimination

A 2018 lawsuit claims that Nike "intentionally and willfully discriminated against women with respect to pay, promotions, and conditions of employment" (Golden, 2018). Former employees Kelly Cahill and Sara Johnson accuse the company of hiring women at lower salaries, marginalizing and demeaning them, passing them over for promotions, and judging them more harshly than men, leading to lower compensation (Hsu, 2018). The suit claims that: "For many women at Nike, the company hierarchy is an unclimbable pyramid, the more senior the job title, the smaller the percentage of women." Just prior to the lawsuit, female employees, fed up with the situation, conducted their own survey regarding sexual harassment and gender discrimination and delivered the results to CEO Mark Parker (Creswell, Draper, & Abrams, 2018). The company responded by announcing the retirement of then-president Trevor Edwards, who had been blamed for creating a hostile work environment for women (Golden, 2018), raising the wages for more than 7,000 employees (10% of its workforce), and reviewing its overall training and compensation policies (Cowley, 2018). The pattern of discrimination had been going on for years and had caused many to leave Nike, including the head of diversity and inclusion (Creswell et al., 2018). Francesca Krane, another employee who left in 2016, said: "I came to the realization that I, as a female, would not grow in that company."

Nike is not alone. Even companies that are lauded for being progressive and claim significant commitment to inclusivity and gender equity are not immune. In 2018, Elizabeth Rose filed a pay discrimination suit against Vice Media after she found out that a male subordinate she had hired made $25,000 more than her. He was promoted to be her boss because he was a "good personality fit" for male clients she was told (Miller, 2018a). A *New York Times* report further found numerous accusations of blatant sexual harassment that had been settled out of court (Steel, 2017). Kayla Ruble, who worked at Vice Media from 2014 to 2018, states: "The misogyny might look different than you would have expected it to in the 1950s, but it was still there, it was still ingrained" (Steel, 2017). Similar allegations and others related to workplace discrimination based on gender are the basis for thousands of complaints filed with the Equal Opportunity Commission (Jameel & Yerardi, 2019). From politics to business, to daily life, our gender expectations impact how we treat women in the workplace.

4.4.1 Areas of Discrimination. Women face considerable discrimination in selection and hiring, promotion, and other employment-related matters because of gender stereotypes (for a review, see Bishu & Alkadry, 2017). Figure 6.4 summarizes the areas of discrimination. Such discrimination provides a reliable explanation for the lack of gender parity in organization. Researchers have found that men are given preference when attributes such as academic brilliance are considered important to the job, reinforcing the stereotype that men have more intellectual abilities than women (Leslie, Cimpian, Meyer, & Freeland, 2015), an assumption that is not supported by the fact that higher number of women are earning university degrees, including advanced degrees. Men and women both also are more likely to select a male for a task that involves mathematical skills partly because, as some research shows, men tend to inflate their abilities while women tend to downplay theirs (Reuben, Sapienza, & Zingales, 2014).

Studies consistently find that when reviewing résumés, people favor candidates they think are men (Gonzàles & Cortina, 2019; Proudfoot, Kay, & Koval, 2015), and that they offer men and women different and unequal training and educational opportunities (Witte, Stratton, & Nora, 2006). Similar findings, where men are preferred to women for long-term employment, show up in research in other countries (Petit, 2007). It appears that we are particularly uncomfortable when people violate gender norms, so women are rated even more harshly when they are perceived as acting forcefully and independently (Rudman & Glick, 2002) or when they violate traditional stereotypes of motherhood (Verniers & Vala, 2018). Furthermore, our

Figure 6.4 Areas of Gender Discrimination

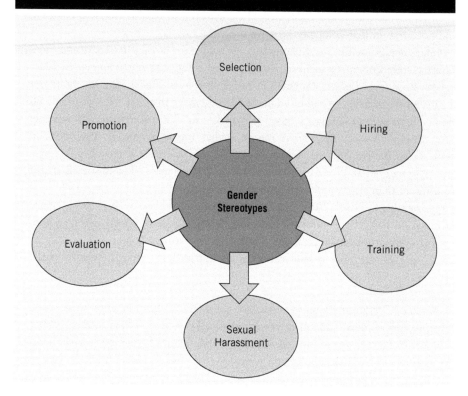

views of what is appropriate affect how people rate performance of men and women (e.g., MacNell, Driscoll, & Hunt, 2015; Treviño, Gomez-Mejia, Balkin, & Mixon, 2015), and the work women do is often devalued in spite of objective criteria (Dutt, Pfaff, Bernstein, Dillard, & Block, 2016; Joshi, Son, & Roh, 2015).

It is clear that discrimination in various areas of employment is one of the major factors that prevent women from success in organizations and contributes to lack of gender parity. Sexual harassment, although technically classified as workplace discrimination, is another form of workplace discrimination that deserves a separate discussion.

4.5 Sexual Harassment

Sexual harassment has garnered considerable attention with the #MeToo movement that has led many coming forward to share their stories on social media.

Sexual harassment is classified as a form of workplace discrimination and it is defined by the US Equal Employment Opportunity Commission (EEOC, 2019) as

> *Unwelcome sexual advances, requests for sexual favors, and other verbal or physical conduct of a sexual nature constitute sexual harassment when this conduct explicitly or implicitly affects an individual's employment, unreasonably interferes with an individual's work performance, or creates an intimidating, hostile, or offensive work environment.*

4.5.1 Incidents of Sexual Harassment. People of all genders can be both victims and harassers, and harassment can come from supervisors, coworkers, other employees, as well as clients or customers. A Pew Research Center report indicates that 59% of women and 27% of men they surveyed have experienced some form of sexual harassment with more people being concerned with unreported cases and harassers getting away with the behavior than with false reporting (Graf, 2018). Reports of harassment have become common place: from well-publicized cases of FoxNews' Bill O'Reilly and Roger Ailes, to Kevin Spacey and Harvey Weinstein, to Ani Chopourian winning a $168 million judgment against Catholic Health Care West, Browne Sander's case against Isiah Thomas and the NY Knicks, and a clinic CEO in Billings, Montana, being ousted after being accused of making jokes about sexual acts, crude remarks, and inappropriate gestures on a daily basis (Rappleye, 2019). It is clear that harassment is not a rare occurrence, and it has serious personal and organizational consequences.

4.5.2 Impact of Sexual Harassment. Depending on the length and severity, it can cause lack of motivation, feelings of embarrassment, shame, guilt, anxiety, depression, and PTSD, as well as many other stress-related symptoms ranging from sleep problems to more serious cardiac episodes. Negative health effects are reported for both men and women who experience mistreatment (Harnois & Bastos, 2018). Psychologist Nekeshia Hammond has found that: "Sometimes sexual harassment registers as a trauma, and it's difficult for the [patient] to deal with it, so what literally happens is the body starts to become overwhelmed" (Spector, 2017).

In addition to these serious consequences for the individual, overall morale for other employees can be affected, as was the case in Nike, and company performance is likely to suffer. Nannima Angioni, an attorney who works on sexual harassment cases, suggests that it can be like a: "slithering snake that ripples its way through a work environment causing disastrous results" (Spector, 2017). Sexual harassment is *not* about sex or attraction, it is related to the unequal power that is based on societal gender norms. Our expectations about who belongs in the workplace and who does not and the roles we expect people to play are key drivers. Discussing causes of sexual harassment, Amanda Lenhart, deputy director of New America's Better Life Lab and coauthor of a report on sexual harassment, suggests: "it's really about power" (Nania, 2018). She adds: "myths and narratives that we tell about who does what kind of work and what are appropriate roles for people of different genders" contributes to gender-based harassment. These "myths we tell ourselves" are also what's helped shield "the creative genius" or the "rainmaker" from consequences for inappropriate actions (Nania, 2018). The celebrities who have been accused of harassment all took advantage of their power. While women are the most common victims, anyone who does not conform to traditional gender norms and is therefore perceived as powerless, including members of the LGBTQ community, is more likely to be targeted.

Our cultural values regarding gender are part of our CMC. They provide the context and background and they guide behaviors and social policy. They impact both men and women's views of appropriate gender roles, their expectations, their stereotypes, and their actions. Given the dearth of evidence as to actual gender differences or research findings regarding the fact that women are less effective than men, these differences do not provide an explanation for why we have disparities in the number of women in leadership positions, why they are paid less, or why they are less successful in being promoted in organizations. If anything, research shows that when the culture and context even out the playing field, such as has been done in Scandinavian countries, many of the disparities and differences fade (Hyde, 2014). In many cases, these cultural expectations and gender stereotypes set up a double bind for women, a key factor that limits their choices and behaviors.

5. THE DOUBLE BIND: ROLE INCONGRUITY AND NARROW PATHWAYS

LO 6.5 Clarify the role and importance of the double bind women face

Close your eyes for a second and imagine what a CEO looks like. What image popped in your mind? Chances are that it is a tall white man, with slightly graying hair, and a deep resonant voice; if so, you are not alone. Not only do we hold gender stereotypes, but also those stereotypes impact our views of leadership. The stereotypically male characteristics (see Figure 6.1), including competence, action orientation, confidence, and strength, among many others, are those that are typically associated with leadership. Conversely, the content of stereotypes of women, including vulnerability, submissiveness, dependence, and powerless, is clearly not how one would describe a leader.

5.1 Think Leader–Think Male

"Think leader or manager–think male" is the belief and expectation that leadership and management by and large equate with male, often white male, stereotypes (see Figure 6.1). As a result, being male is the default for leadership (de Pillis et al., 2008; Koening et al., 2011). In most cultures, authority and femininity are contradictory. As long as being a leader is equated with these male stereotypes, women will never fit.

5.1.1 The Double Bind. The *double bind* refers to an impossible situation where no matter what women do, they are not considered leadership material (see Figure 6.5). On the one hand, when women act in accordance with what is expected of them as women, meaning if they are caring, vulnerable, submissive, quiet, and sensitive, they will not be considered leadership material, and they will not succeed in many competitive environments. On the other hand, however, if they act in stereotypically male ways by being assertive, independent, and outspoken, they will be violating cultural gender expectations and roles, and therefore, they will not be liked and still

Figure 6.5   The Gender Double Bind

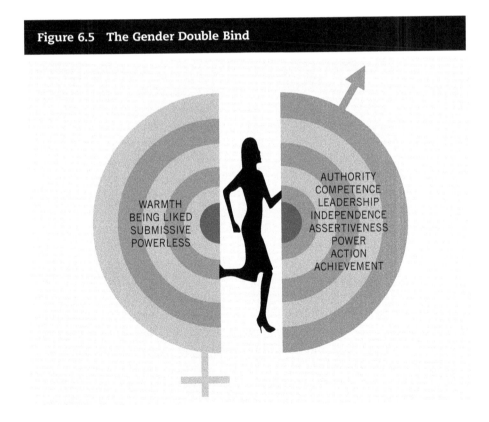

considered unfit and inappropriate for leadership. When people disconfirm our expectations, we judge then harshly and devalue them.

This double bind sets up a "Damned if you do; doomed if you don't" scenario (Catalyst-Double-Bind, 2018) that leaves women with tough choices:

- Do they choose to be competent performers and leaders and risk being disliked?

- Do they act in ways that will make others like them, perform less well, and have no chance at being perceived as a competent leader?

- Do they remain invisible by complying with female gender stereotypes?

- Do they act outside of those stereotypes and face disapproval?

The 2020 US female presidential candidates, similar to many business leaders, experienced this double bind directly and repeatedly. Questions about their "likability" were common, something that few if any male politician had to answer. When they had a reputation for toughness, they were perceived as too being too tough, and their "electability" questioned; however, if they did not show toughness, they were considered not strong enough for the job. Slow speech is attributed to lack of confidence for women candidates and thoughtfulness for men candidates; men are perceived as assertive and women are bossy; if women cry, they are showing their softer side, when men do, they are passionate (Sclafani, 2019).

The US Women's soccer team, four-time World Cup champion and four-time Olympic gold medalist, has faced all aspects of gender stereotypes, the pay gap, and a striking example of the double bind in the 2019 World Cup. In June 2019, the team did what it was supposed to do and won big, scoring 13 goals against the Thai team. Instead of focusing on their stunning accomplishments, the players were chided by some in the media for being unsportsmanlike, gloating, and celebrating too much. The *Atlantic* headline was telling: "They gave America 13 goals and got a lecture in return" (Hill, 2019). The focus was not on the win, or on the players' athletic abilities, or their unquestionable dominance in the sport—all clearly demonstrated as the 13 goals for this one game was more than the US men's team total number of goals in World Cup games since 2006. Instead, the focus was on how the manner in which they celebrated their hard-earned success was not kind to the other team. Olympic Gold medalist and professional soccer player Sydney Leroux Dwyer wrote: "You spend your entire life trying to get to a World Cup, and you get there and you're supposed to tone it down and make people more comfortable?" The US soccer team's 13-goal win came in the context of a gender discrimination lawsuit they filed against US Soccer Federation on International Women's Day 2019 (Das, 2019). The women's team charged the Federation with pay inequity (they make less than 40% of what men do) and unequal working conditions, including the number of games, coaching and medical care, and travel arrangements, all the while they have continued to generate considerable revenue ($23 million in 2015 alone; Golshan, 2019). Other female athletes, including Serena Williams, have been subjected to similar double standards when they have been criticized and penalized for behaviors that were accepted from male athletes.

5.1.2 Immediate Consequences. The double bind contributes to women having to prove themselves over and over again because most of what they do is not recognized, rewarded, or perceived as "leader-like." Whether in the soccer field, tennis court, politics, or corporate life, the double bind and double standard deal women tough choices. Women who are masculine are often not liked and considered ineffective (Powell, Butterfield, & Parent, 2002). Men particularly expect women to act in ways that are stereotypically feminine and evaluate them poorly when they show the more masculine characteristics typically associated with leadership. In some cases, evidence suggests that even women do not support other women in getting leadership positions (Andrews, 2020), and men are given more credit than women when they support diversity efforts in their organizations (Hekman et al., 2017). Furthermore, women who actively seek leadership and show a desire to direct others are not well accepted (Carli, 1999).

5.2 Role Incongruity

The double bind is partly explained by what researchers Alice Eagly and Steven Karau (2002) call role incongruity. In most cultures, the role of being dominant or being a leader is inconsistent or incongruent with being female, whereas it is consistent and congruent with being male. On the one hand, when you behave in role, as others expect you to behave, you are liked, accepted, and viewed positively; on the other hand, when you behave out of your assigned role, you are disliked and negatively evaluated (Badgett & Folbre, 2003; Fiske & Taylor, 2017). The result of this stereotype-based role incongruity is that in our CMC we believe men should lead and women should not, or at least that men are likely to be better leaders.

5.2.1 The Power Double Bind. Columbia Professor Adam Galinsky further uses the concept of the double bind to connect gender stereotypes to his extensive research on power and its effects (Galinsky, 2017, 2018). Galinsky's research shows that people who have power have a wide latitude as to what they can do; they are expected and allowed to assert themselves. Those with less power have less room to maneuver; they have limited options both in terms of what they are allowed to do and what they are willing to take on. As men typically have power and women less so, this differential creates a *power double bind* for women. When they assert power, they are unsuccessful because they are stepping outside of the acceptable and expected range for women. When they do not assert power, they are ignored and often unable to lead in organizational settings.

5.3 Self-Perception and Self-Advocacy

The double bind not only affects what others expect but also our self-perception and what we allow ourselves to do. It limits the range others give us and what we give ourselves. Megan Karsh who teaches negotiation at Stanford Law School says:

> …*women are told in so many ways to be smaller, take up less space, deprive themselves. Don't eat this, don't take credit for that, don't cause a scene no matter how uncomfortable someone else made you. We've linked it to how women should act. What are your internal narratives about size and taking up space, and what do you metaphorically tell yourself about what you have a right to? (Zalis, 2018)*

This process seems to start very early because even in preschool, girls and boys change their vocal pitches to match expectations, with girls speaking at a higher pitch and boys at a lower pitch than their natural range (Eckert & McConnell-Ginet, 2003). Women, as compared to men, learn not to ask and not to advocate for themselves, often perceiving self-promotion and negotiation as a chore (Babcock & Laschever, 2003; de Janasz & Cabrera, 2018), which translates into unwillingness and inability to negotiate well. Interestingly, while many women do not negotiate forcefully for themselves, they are able to advocate well for others, something that fits with gender stereotypes of being caretakers.

5.4 Narrow Paths to Organizational Success

The overall impact of the double bind is to limit what women can and are allowed to do. We have already discussed how gender expectations lead adolescent women to limit their physical presence in public spaces in many countries. The double bind acts similarly as a psychological limit. While men have a wide path to walk and many options to consider, women have to precariously navigate a narrow track with strict parameters and often no desirable choices regarding how to behave at work and how to manage others.

Learning to lead and manage takes practice. Becoming skilled at anything takes work, experimenting, and failure. Because of culturally based societal expectations and stereotypes, men have a much wider latitude in what they are allowed to do than women. They have more choices; they can experiment and are allowed to fail. When they do, they are not blamed for it and are given more opportunities. The gender stereotypes that set up a double bind strongly limit what women do and what they allow themselves to do; they walk on a narrow path. When women cannot fully practice their craft and use a full range of behaviors and skills, their personal career suffers, but so do organizations that fail to fully benefit from the potential of close to half their workforce.

5.4.1 The Impostor Syndrome. As a result of the double bind, women get an inconsistent message regarding who they should and can be. Being stereotypically female is increasingly not acceptable; however, being stereotypically male is not either. Because, no matter which path they choose, they are not likely to succeed or feel that they are accepted and liked, they end up doubting themselves and feeling that they are *impostors*, unable to internalize and accept credit for their accomplishments. They attribute their success to anything but their own abilities and skills.

The various culturally based stereotypes we reviewed in earlier parts of the chapter all give women the not-so-subtle message that their strengths and characteristics are not what is needed in the workplace; they reinforce the message that they are indeed impostors. Brittany Berger, the founder of WorkBrighter.co, a digital media company, states:

> *For me, impostor syndrome looks like not going for opportunities because I feel like I'm not experienced enough, keeping my prices low for products and services and going too long without increasing them, and setting ridiculously high expectations for myself, so that, of course, I'll fall short. (Ambrose, 2019)*

Tara Bhargava, a marketer and strategist, further says that for her the impostor syndrome involved "…internalized fear, self-doubt, and playing down my accomplishments" (Ambrose, 2019). Valerie Young, author of *Secret Thoughts of Successful Women*, suggests that not having more role models can exacerbate this feeling: "The more people who look or sound like you, the more confident you feel. And conversely, the fewer people who look or sound like you, it can and does for many people impact their confidence" (Abrams, 2018).

Because of culture-based gender stereotypes and related presence of organizational and social obstacles, we have not been able to achieve gender parity in organizations. The causes are as complex as the possible solutions.

6. ADDRESSING GENDER DISPARITIES

LO 6.6 Review successful social policies, organizational practices, and personal strategies to address gender effectively

Gender disparities are the results of complex cultural assumptions, values, and beliefs resulting in social policies and organizational practices. Fully addressing them is

Figure 6.6 Addressing Gender Disparities

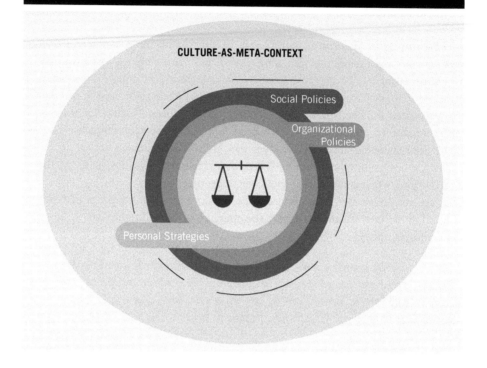

CULTURE-AS-META-CONTEXT

Social Policies

Organizational Policies

Personal Strategies

therefore a cultural endeavor combined with changes in social policy, targeted and supportive organizational processes, and individual strategies (see Figure 6.6).

6.1 Social Policies

Women's participation in social and political life and the number of women in leadership of various organizations is systematically higher in some countries than others. Review of the policies and practices in those countries provides a roadmap regarding how to address gender disparities on a social level. The United States, along with many industrialized countries, has antigender discrimination laws that aim to address disparity and discrimination. However, many of these laws such as the Equal Pay Act and Title VII of the Civil Rights Act are not easy to enforce. However, various legislations that results in social policy can play a key role in supporting gender parity.

6.1.1 Family Friendly Policies. Imbalance in work and life and the heavy burden of managing work and family is one of the primary reasons women are not able to fully pursue their career, leading to lower salaries and lower advancement. Social policies that support families in general and gender parity in particular can address some of these challenges. They include policies and practices such as

- Paid family leave

- Affordable and accessible child care

- Medical and vacation leave

- Support for elder care

Consider that Swedish parents of all genders are eligible for 16 months of paid leave and have access to subsidized and fully regulated childcare that allows early drop-off and late pick-up. Similar family friendly policies are in effect in other Nordic countries and others including France, Canada, Iceland, Portugal, Turkey, and Mexico (Cohn, 2014; Ruhm, 2011). As a Swedish parent puts it:

We don't mind paying high taxes as we and our children benefit. We would not want to live in a country where taxes may be lower but the benefits are less and you don't get to spend time with your children when they are young. (Cohn, 2014)

Conversely, inflexible work hours and hard-to-find and highly regimented and regulated childcare are primary factors preventing Japanese mothers from fully engaging in their work (Boykoff, 2019). Research finds that both support for and the health of the elderly in the United States are behind that of other industrialized countries (Fisher, 2013; Seegert, 2017), putting an extra burden on family members, particularly women, as they struggle to take care of their aging parents.

Having family-friendly policies may be related to cultural values and difficult to implement in some countries. However, in spite of much talk of the importance of family, the United States is the only industrialized nation that does not yet guarantee paid leave for new parents, with only 12 weeks of unpaid leave as a federal requirement. Addressing the lack of family-friendly policies in the United States, Dorothy Roberts of University of Pennsylvania states: "There's a basic inconsistency in saying we support families, we have family-friendly policies, when in fact we have the worst family policies of any developed high-income democracy. We don't have family-friendly policies at all" (Badger & Miller, 2018).

6.2 Organizational Practices

While social policy may be overall more impactful in the long run in addressing deep assumptions and changing values and may provide long-term solutions to achieving gender parity and equality, organizations have the power and ability to

Table 6.6 Organizational Practices to Support Gender Equality

Practices	Description
Pay equity and transparency	Address the pay gap with frequent audits and transparent wage policies and practices
Organizational policies targeting discrimination	Training and processes to address all forms of discrimination including sexual harassment
Leadership and development training and mentoring	Specific programs targeting women including mentoring opportunities
Stable work schedules	Provide stable work schedules and predictable travel schedules
Good benefits including sick and vacation leave	A good benefit package that includes insurance and flexible sick and vacation leave to address family needs
Flexible hours and creative job options	Allow variations in schedules and times; provide options such as job sharing, flextime, and telework
Transparency	Sharing information about pay, access to resources, availability of resources, and so forth openly
Role modeling	"Walking-the-talk" to provide appropriate examples of behaviors
Family leave	Extend the legal requirements of 6 weeks unpaid leave to longer paid leave periods
Onboarding after family leave	Provide support for onboarding following family leave

address many of the areas that cause gender inequality with potentially significant results. From addressing the pay gap to focusing on eliminating discrimination in other areas, to offering family and work–life balance friendly benefits, to leadership training and development, to processes that address workplace discrimination, and role modeling by leaders, organizations can do much to address the issues we have discussed in this chapter (see Table 6.6 for a summary).

6.2.1 Examples of Impactful Organizational Practices. Some organizations have led the way in addressing various aspects of gender parity. Marc Beniof, CEO of Sales-Force, has found himself in the spotlight and has become a celebrity as an advocate for equal pay, helping his company land a series of awards. In 2015, Cindy Robbins, SalesForce's chief personnel officer, first raised the pay gap issue with her boss. Beniof's first reaction was: "That's not possible here because we have a great culture and we don't do that—it's impossible; it's crazy" (60 Minutes). The company was already rated as top place to work and it had a commitment to gender equality.

However, when Robbins' audit found a $3 million pay gap, with disparities throughout the company at every level, Beniof was quick to respond and correct the gap. Two years later, the same audit showed again a $3 million gap, partly the result of acquisitions; again, it was addressed. What SalesForce has discovered and Beniof often states is: "There is no finish line when it comes to equality," addressing inequality is an ongoing process ("SalesForce CEO on Equality," 2017). Beniof also squarely puts the burden of addressing this problem with the leadership: "CEOs, with one button on one computer, can pay every man and every woman equally," he adds. "We have the data. We know what everyone makes. There's no excuse" (Schwantes, 2018). Beniof is not only changing policies, he is also role-modeling appropriate expectations and behaviors.

In 2019, Francis Collins, the director of the National Institutes of Health, the US' powerful biomedical institution with a close to $40 billion budget, announced that he would no longer speak on all-male science panels. As Beniof did, Collins challenged others to follow his lead and stated: "it is time to end the tradition in science of all-male speaking panels, sometimes wryly referred to as 'manels'," adding that if "attention to inclusiveness is not evident in the agenda, I will decline to take part" (Bernstein, 2019). Collins further recognized the role that he and other scientists must play in battling the sexual harassment that limits women's advancement.

These CEOs have both role-modeled and set policies that support equity and transparency. Ray Dalio, founder of Bridgewater Associates, the world's largest hedge fund firm, has advocated transparent processes, including openly sharing salary information, as a way to not only address disparities but also to build a strong organization: "Continuous growth requires deeper conversations and when I see leaders embrace radical transparency it can unleash new energy into the culture" (Hammet, 2018). Beniof's, Collins's, and Dalio's actions demonstrate the crucial role of top leaders in addressing gender issues in the workplace. They have considerable power through their actions—walking-the-talk, in addition to the organizational policies they implement, to effect change.

6.2.2 Broad Impact Beyond Gender Parity. Many organizations have become aware that inequities and discrimination hurt all employees, not just minorities and women; and that policies that help women and minorities help everyone in the long run. They have also realized that they do not need to wait for legal action or public policy to implement change. For example, asking about salary history has been shown to reinforce the pay gap and is now illegal in some states such as California. However, some employers, including Amazon, Wells Fargo, Cisco, Google, and American Express, have implemented the practice of not asking applicants about their salary history (Noguchi, 2018). These employers have found that eliminating the past salary question has allowed them to recruit and hire a more diverse pool of candidates giving them broader access to the talent they need.

A McKinsey & Co report on gender equity finds that companies that have comprehensive programs to address gender equity that are fully implemented show positive results (Devillard et al., 2017). While some of these practices are targeting women and gender equity, any practice that provides equity, flexibility, and is focused on employee needs, not only benefits women or minorities but also improves the overall culture of an organization. For example, sound practices regarding onboarding of new employees can help returning new parents or employees coming back from any extended leave or expats coming home after time working abroad. One mother returning to work stated: "Returning after maternity leave didn't feel like coming back to my old job. It felt like starting a new one. Everything from the company's internal comms to my team structure had changed while I was away" (Blight, 2019). As a result of her experience, she proposed new processes including resource groups, lunches, specialized management training, and parent cohort groups that were adopted in her company successfully.

Other options that provide flexibility in work schedule involve a variety of work accommodations such as flextime, arriving late, leaving early, unlimited days off, and job sharing. For example, several firms such as MindTools and some departments of The Gap have shifted their focus to results and contributions, rather than actual work hours, a process known as ROWE-Results Only Work Environment. Instead of counting work hours, they focus on goals and what employees deliver and produce. Another company, MammothHQ, offers unlimited vacations or days off focusing not on the days employees work but on their actual contribution and the results they deliver (Diab, 2016). While these novel options may not work for all jobs and all individuals, any flexibility is often welcome. As a matter of fact, a report in Bloomberg shows that: "When workers have control over their own schedules, it results in lower levels of stress, psychological distress, burnout, and higher job satisfaction" (Greenfield, 2016). Control of work hours can benefit everyone, not just parents or women.

While waiting for social policies and laws to change, organizations and their leaders have considerable leeway and power in implementing practices that support equity and eliminate discrimination. As is the case with social policies, organizational practices mostly target behaviors. However, behavior changes are likely to, over time, create attitude change and eventually support cultural changes. Just as people first were shocked by seeing women and minorities where only white men had worked, and eventually the practice became commonplace and expected, implementing practices that eliminate gender disparities is likely to eventually become the norm.

6.3 Personal Strategies

In addition to social policy and organizational practices that address specific actions and behaviors, several personal strategies can help women address culturally based gender imbalances. Some of these strategies, such as increased education, networking, building support groups, advocacy, and managing stress, are typical good career advice and undoubtedly necessary and helpful. However, the key is to address women's own assumptions, expectations, and stereotypes regarding how they should behave and the perception of their power; they have to consider their own CMC and adopt a CM that targets gender-based issues.

6.3.1 Changing Cognition. By focusing on changing how they think and what they believe, women can then expand their range of behaviors and skills. They can therefore address all levels of their CM TKD roadmap as it relates to gender (see Figure 6.1). Sheryl Sandberg, COO of Facebook, garnered much attention, and no small dose of controversy, by telling women that part of the problems they face is due to their own lack of initiative and unwillingness to step up (Sandberg, 2013). While the idea seems to be past its prime, especially after Michelle Obama bluntly said: "I tell women, that whole 'you can have it all'—nope, not at the same time; that's a lie. It's not always enough to lean in, because that s— doesn't work all the time" (Singletary, 2018), women do have a role in gender disparity.

Women share in culture's deep assumptions about gender roles and most have grown up in a gendered world where they have internalized the impostorism and experienced the double bind and lack of power in a variety of ways throughout their lives. So, part of the solution is for women to consider their gender expectations in their CMC and to change their mindset along with the social and organizational structures that reinforce gender inequity. For example, Brittany Berger of founder of WorkBrighter.co, mentioned earlier in this chapter, has found that adjusting how she thinks about herself has helped:

> *Another thing I've found really helpful is taking things my impostor syndrome tells me and adding the word 'yet' to turn it into a goal-setting prompt. So I haven't written for [dream publication]' turns into 'I haven't written for this publication yet. What can I do to change that? (Ambrose, 2019)*

Harvard professor Amy Cuddy, who has one of the most watched TED talks about how physical posture can change your level of confidence, has done considerable research about the negative impact of powerlessness and the positive impact of self-affirmation, in changing how we think and behave. She advocates what she calls "fake it till you believe it" (Cuddy, 2015). In her book *Presence*, Cuddy (2015) emphasizes the importance of becoming aware and trusting your own story and being able to express your thoughts and feelings with confidence and passion. She also addresses how not having power, particularly personal power over yourself and your own fate, can lead to dire psychological and physical consequences. While her work does not focus on gender differences, others, such as Deborah Tannen (1986), have looked at gender differences in communication and how women through their speech patterns that include frequent apologies and discounting of their own strengths send a message of submissiveness and powerlessness.

6.3.2 Changing Behavior. Changing cognition and established thinking patterns is not easy and may take extensive practice. However, considerable research supports the fact that targeting behaviors is an effective starting point. In other words, we can change attitudes by first changing behaviors. By making small alterations, something that has been called "nudging" (Thaler & Sunstein, 2009), we can slowly achieve desired outcomes and effect attitude change. For example, as Deborah Tannen's (1986) work has demonstrated, women often use speech patterns that signal that they are submissive. Monitoring and reducing how often they apologize or how often they thank others unnecessarily can be a starting point for projecting power and feeling confident. Similarly, Amy Cuddy's (2015) research has shown that using a power posture, what she calls the Wonder Woman or Starfish pose, can have an impact on feelings of confidence and actual performance. Small changes in behavior lead to deeper changes in thinking.

The exercises and self-assessments at the end of this chapter provide an opportunity to identify areas where small changes can be made, slowly building up to larger impact.

The material in this chapter is aimed at building your knowledge (KNOW) of gender, which is a group-level cultural element. Knowledge of the current status of women in organizations, culturally based stereotypes, their development, and their impact, the causes of lack of gender parity in organizations and social, organizational, and personal actions that may help address them provide you with essential information to address your own biases and plan personal and organizational actions that can address gender more effectively. As outlined by the TKD roadmap to developing a CM (see Figures 1.5 and 6.2), the starting point is awareness, recognition, and understanding of beliefs and values that may be impacting behavior; from there, targeting behaviors helps the process of changing beliefs and then values.

FIRST PERSON REVISITED

The First Person account at the beginning of this chapter represents a simple and common example of gender stereotypes at work. The manager feels invisible because her contributions are not recognized. Her male colleagues do not appear to have negative intentions, but culturally based gender stereotypes lead them to ignore both her and her female colleague. Being ignored leads to a reduction in contributions, feelings of inadequacy, and lack of motivation, all of which not only affect the individuals involved but also prevent the firm from benefiting from everyone's creativity and contributions. Solutions to such situations cannot rest only on the women. Instead, this must be addressed with both personal and organizations strategies.

APPLYING WHAT YOU LEARNED: NAVIGATING THE DOUBLE BIND

Almost any woman who has some work experience can give examples of how her actions are interpreted differently from men. Men can bring their kids to work and they are seen as great fathers; women who do the same are perceived as not caring about their work. Men get angry and they are seen as assertive; women raise their voice and they are considered overly aggressive. Men can negotiate forcefully and win; women speak up and are disliked, and so forth. While these biases must be addressed, what can you do if you face this in the here and now?

1. *Be aware and name it*: Know when it's happening, take note, and keep track.

2. *Don't personalize*: Realize that while it impacts you directly and personally, it is not about you; it is a systemic issue.

3. *Collect data*: Take notes, have your examples, dates, and times ready.

4. *Talk to your supervisor*: Your boss can be an ally; provide him/her with data and examples and seek help.

5. *Point it out*: When you face this, point it out and describe it objectively; just the facts.

6. *Advocate for others*: It is easier to address when you are not involved, so help colleagues and make your point.

7. *Bring together your colleagues*: Chances are that you are not alone. Talk to others and address the issue as a group.

8. *Get others to advocate for you*: Rely on, and *ask*, your friends and colleagues to advocate for you.

9. *Use humor*: While not always effective, humor can be a powerful tool, especially if it comes naturally.

10. *Seek HR help*: If possible, seek advice and help from HR. Some of what you face may be illegal and actionable; some may not be. In either case, HR can address the systemic issue with training and workshops.

Whatever you do, don't suffer in silence! Act; if not for your own sake, for the sake of others who will follow your footsteps.

MANAGERIAL CHALLENGE: WHO SHOULD GO?

You are managing a team that is charged with marketing a new product to the Middle East. This is a great opportunity for growth and an excellent career opportunity for you and your team; doing well would be great for all of you. Your job is to develop a plan to work with partners in the UAE and Saudi Arabia to launch this product. Your boss has told you, and you agree, that you should start with visits to your partners and should assign a couple of your team members as key liaisons ready to travel back and forth while others work more from the home base. Your team is made up of three more senior women and two more junior men. If this was in the United States or Europe or Asia, you would not hesitate and send two of the women to start the process. They have the knowledge, skills, and experience and are ready to go. But, these are two Arab countries and while the UAE may be easier, Saudi Arabia does present challenges. You worry about the whole thing falling through, and you worry about being accused of sexism if you don't send the two experienced women.

1. What factors should you consider in making your decision?

2. What will you do?

3. How will you implement your decision to assure the best chance of success?

SELF-ASSESSMENT 6.1: IMPOSTOR PHENOMENON

Please go to http://impostortest.nickol.as to take the Clance Impostor Phenomenon test.

What is your score: _____?

1. What does your score tell you about yourself? How well does it represent how you react?

2. What are the areas where you scored high and those where you scored low? For example, school vs. work, or accepting credit vs. fear of failure.

3. To what extent could your response be different for different settings? For example, would you score differently if you focused on your work, or your volunteer activities, or your family?

4. What are some key takeaways for you? How can you use this information?

EXERCISE 6.1: GENDER STEREOTYPES AT WORK

Objective: This exercise builds your knowledge and self-awareness regarding gender.

Instructions: Read the following prompt before completing the individual and group work below.

In 1992, Barbra Streisand delivered a "Women in Film" speech that perfectly captured the essence of the double bind many women face. Here's a short version of her comments:

A man is commanding—a woman is demanding.

A man is forceful—a woman is pushy.

He's assertive—she's aggressive.

He shows leadership—she's controlling.

He's committed—she's obsessed.

He's persevering—she's relentless.

He sticks to his guns—she's stubborn.

If a man wants to get it right, he's looked up to and respected.

If a woman wants to get it right, she's difficult and impossible.

Source: Barbra Streisand: Library Archives. (1992).

Individual Work

1. Thinking about gender stereotypes you have used or heard, add several to Barbra Streisand's list.

2. What is the context in which these comments were used? How much do you agree or disagree with them?

Group Work

Review and discuss Streisand's list and the ones added by the group members using the following questions:

1. What is the impact of these statements on the individual?

2. How do such statements impact how we work?

3. What are some actions that can be taken to reduce the use of these stereotypes and their impact on individuals and organizations?

EXERCISE 6.2: THE CLANCE IMPOSTOR PHENOMENON TEST

Objective: This exercise builds your knowledge regarding gender.

Instructions:

Individual Work

Complete the Clance Impostor Phenomenon Test in Self-Assessment 6.1 and record your score.

Group Work

Your instructor will team you up with several other students in the class.

1. Share your score with your group.

2. What are some patterns of differences? For example, are there any gender, age, experience, or other cultural differences?

3. In the group, discuss any themes from your scores.

4. Prepare a list of "nudge" strategies that you think you could implement to address a strong feeling of impostorism. Consider personal, interpersonal, and organizational strategies.

REFLECTION QUESTION 6.1: WHAT GENDER STEREOTYPES DO YOU HOLD?

Think about past family experiences you have had where gender stereotypes have come into play. For example, it may be a family discussion with an older member about women working or something your parents may have told you would or would not be appropriate for a girl or a boy.

Keeping those in mind, describe your family and your cultural views and expectations of women in regard to the following areas (please add other areas that you think are important).

Area	Family View	My View
Relationships		
Power		
Work		
Marriage		
Children		
Other: _____		

Review your responses and reflect on the following:

1. To what extent do you agree with your family's views?

2. How do you think your family has shaped your views of women?

3. How do you think your views reflect themselves in the workplace?

4. What are some steps you would like to take in the future to either reinforce or change your views?

REFLECTION QUESTION 6.2: WHAT DOES IT FEEL LIKE?

Think about a situation where you have felt in control and powerful. The situation does not necessarily need to be the one where you had social or organizational power; it should be one where you felt that you had personal power or control over yourself and your fate.

1. Describe the situation?

2. Describe how you felt and how you behaved?

3. Describe how it was different from other situations where you may not have felt powerful?

4. Is there a different way of looking at the situation?

5. How can you transfer some of those feelings and behaviors of power to other situations?

CASE STUDY: HOW DO I GET BACK ON TRACK?

Elena Novak is a highly successful woman who speaks three languages and earned her master's degree in international management from a top-rated school graduating at the top of her class at the age of 26. She easily found her dream job with a great salary and benefits in marketing in a high-tech firm. Within 6 months, she was identified as a high potential employee and selected for several coaching and training programs, all of which she completed successfully. The long hours, extensive travel, and two relocations all fit her life, and she put in what was needed to succeed leading to several substantial raises and a couple of promotions. When she was 30, she married Keith, a senior executive in another division of her company and they soon decided that they wanted to start their family. By then she was in her early thirties and he in his early forties. When their son, Eduard was born, Elena took advantage of the generous family-leave policy and stayed at home with him for 3 months. Keith also took 3 weeks of paternity leave, but broke his up into two periods when Elena was ready to go back to work. With a few glitches and a bit of bumpy transition that took a couple of months to resolve, Elena was able to pick up where she left off and came back to work when Eduard was 3 months old, and she felt that her career was back on track.

Although, the couple was able to hire a day nanny who came from 7 to 5 to take care of their son, and while Keith was an involved dad, Elena was the primary caretaker for Eduard. The nanny was a life-saver but she also had a family and she could only work for so many hours. Elena soon found that the typical 10-hour workdays that she used to put in were much harder to handle. With less sleep and the lack of flexibility to stay late or to travel on a dime to see a client or start a new project, or difficulty to work on weekends as needed, she was feeling the strain of trying to balance everything. She asked her boss for a more flexible schedule and requested some telework days; her boss was understanding and made several accommodations for her. She constantly felt guilty about either not spending time with her son or not working as hard as some of her coworkers. When opportunities for additional development and new projects came up, she reluctantly passed them up, not wanting to add to her busy life. Meanwhile, Keith was also feeling the strain from having a new baby at home, lack of sleep, and their family life having changed. Life was much more hectic. While he did help, he did not feel that he could do as much for Eduard at this early age. For one thing, Elena was breastfeeding Eduard; for another, she seemed so much better at taking care of their son than he was.

Keith's career stayed on track and he got a couple of big promotions which nearly doubled his salary. Elena's career meanwhile was secure; she was doing well but she was aware that she had slowed down. She simply did not have the energy to put in what she needed to push forward as she had in the early days. When Eduard went to day care at two and half, Elena and Keith, who had always wanted two kids, decided to have their second one. Their daughter Agatha was born when Eduard was almost 4. Again, Elena took the generous three-month family leave that was available; Keith took 1 month this time. With two kids at home, life was hectic for the family. They were lucky that, in addition to having a nanny for Agatha, Elena's mom, Ivona, who had been widowed several years ago, started a 5-year phased retirement and was able to help some of the time. Keith took Eduard to day care, either Ivona or the nanny picked him up at 5. Elena came home before 6 to feed and bathe the kids. Keith rarely came home before 7 and often picked up dinner on the way. He also traveled frequently with his new promotion.

Elena and Keith's life was falling into a routine that they were managing with Ivona's help. Unfortunately, Ivona was diagnosed with a neurological disorder which made it impossible for her to drive; she retired earlier than expected. Keith and Elena offered to have her move in with them; they had a big house and she could spend time and help with the kids. While that presented a good solution, Ivona needed some help herself. Elena now was taking care of two young kids and her mother. The cost of day care was building up on top of a part-time nanny to pick up the kids and stay with them until the parents came home. Increasingly, she worried about leaving her mother alone all day; Ivona was independent, but didn't have good balance and, not being able to drive, she was home by herself for long hours.

After long discussion, Elena and Keith decided that the best course was for Elena, who was now 38, to take a couple of years off and stay home with the kids and her aging mom. Keith was making enough money to support them, and they saw this path as a way of getting their life back. Elena resigned from her job and became a stay-at-home mom. Their life became much more peaceful. Elena barely had a minute to spare but was grateful to have time with her kids and with her mom. Elena looked for part-time job opportunities to work, but all she could find was retail or substitute teaching jobs. She tried those, but did not find them satisfying or financially worthwhile. She started a side consulting business and picked up several contracts doing independent marketing for several companies, enough to keep up her network and her skills. When Eduard started middle school and Agatha was in primary school, Ivona passed away. Elena was facing another transition point. With a good network of moms, neighbors, and a couple of reliable teenagers to pick up the kids, Elena, now just barely 40, was ready to go back to work. Keith's career was slowing down, and he was considering a lucrative early retirement package and starting a consulting business with some friends. The economy was in an upswing; Elena had much to offer; and she was ready to dive back in.

A year later, Elena had not been able to find anything that remotely looked like her previous position. She was amazed that being away for less than 10 years to raise a family and take care of her mom seem to have made her "unhirable." How could she get back on track?

Questions

1. What are the challenges that Elena and Keith are facing?

2. What are the causes of the challenges?

3. What could they have done differently?

4. How could the company have supported them better?

5. What should Elena do now?

PART FOUR

KNOW—MODELS OF NATIONAL CULTURE

Part IV, which includes Chapters 7 and 8, aims at developing your knowledge of models of national cultures that can be applied to understand differences across countries. As was the case with Chapters 5 and 6 in Part III, the attention is on the KNOW part of the THINK–KNOW–DO roadmap (see Figure IV.1). However, instead of considering group-level cultures, the topics we address in the next two chapters focus on national culture and cross-cultural management. The information allows you to develop or enhance a vocabulary that can be applied to describe differences among cultures at a broader national level. This chapter details Hall's framework of high- and low-context styles of communication, and the Kluckhohn and Strodtbeck value orientation model, which are the basis of many other frameworks for understanding cultural differences. Chapter 8 elaborates on models that were specifically developed to address managerial differences across cultures with a discussion of

Figure IV.1   The Focus of Part IV

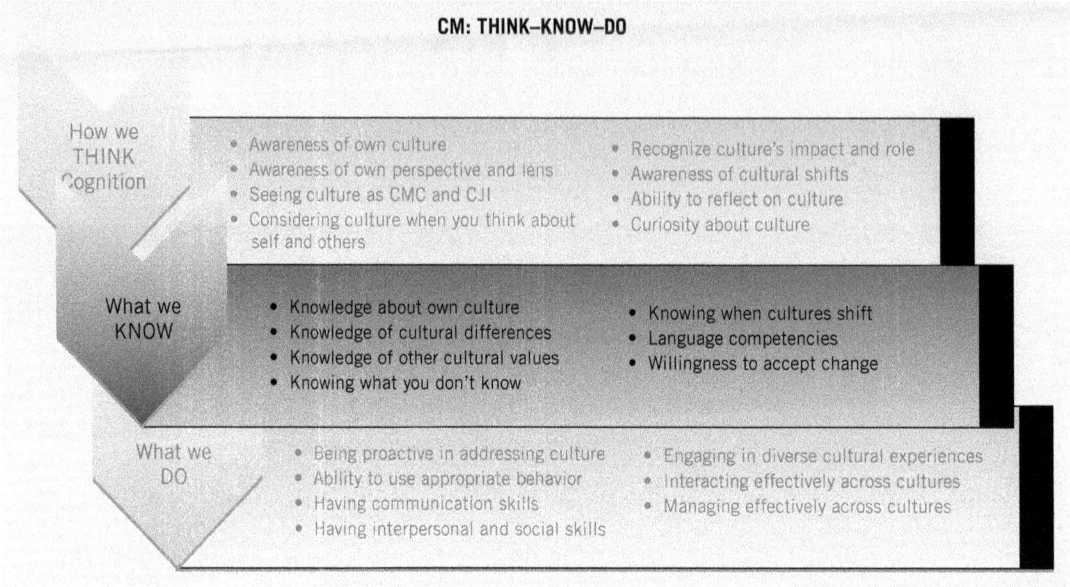

CM: THINK–KNOW–DO

How we
THINK
Cognition

- Awareness of own culture
- Awareness of own perspective and lens
- Seeing culture as CMC and CJI
- Considering culture when you think about self and others

- Recognize culture's impact and role
- Awareness of cultural shifts
- Ability to reflect on culture
- Curiosity about culture

What we
KNOW

- Knowledge about own culture
- Knowledge of cultural differences
- Knowledge of other cultural values
- Knowing what you don't know

- Knowing when cultures shift
- Language competencies
- Willingness to accept change

What we
DO

- Being proactive in addressing culture
- Ability to use appropriate behavior
- Having communication skills
- Having interpersonal and social skills

- Engaging in diverse cultural experiences
- Interacting effectively across cultures
- Managing effectively across cultures

CHAPTER SEVEN

CULTURE AS VALUE ORIENTATION

FIRST PERSON

Socialization First, Business Next

As the new head of an American multinational corporation for the Middle East, I was responsible for establishing a joint venture with a Saudi company. The investment was important for both parties and the timing for implementation was short given the dynamic and competitive nature of the market. The business plan was sound, the implementation well structured and carefully planned, most of the personnel was on board, and the financing set. It should have been easy. Well, not so fast! I had to make three trips to Saudi Arabia, where social events and conversations about family, politics, and world affairs were the only topics of discussion. It was as if any talk of business was systematically and intentionally avoided. I got to know more about these business partners than any of my other ones; and I probably shared more information with them about my family and background, going back several generations, than I have with any other business acquaintance. When we finally got to actually talk about the partnership, I was focused on how to make it work for the next 12 months; they were looking much further down the line at the next 100 years. I needed to nail down the details, and they were looking at the big picture. I spent more time than I think was reasonable gaining their trust, but once that was established, the execution was flawless and fast.

–Juan Roche, PhD

Few people would question the requirement of doing business globally. We cannot avoid interacting with people from around the world as we market products globally, rely on global supply chains, and work with diverse people in our communities. Accordingly,

Learning Objectives

7.1 Discuss how research-based frameworks of cultural differences can be used to understand, describe, and predict behavior across cultures.

7.2 Detail the elements and predictions of Hall's communication context framework of culture.

7.3 Elaborate on the different communication styles across cultures.

7.4 Discuss Kluckhohn and Strodtbeck's value orientation theory.

7.5 Evaluate the strengths and weaknesses of the frameworks and their application to management.

Dr. Roche in our *First Person* anecdote has to work across national boundaries to help his firm achieve its goals. Like many other executives and managers, he knows that the success and prosperity of his business depend on managing relationships expertly at home and on a global level. As stated by cross-cultural management expert, professor André Laurent (1983) of INSEAD, all managers have some implicit management gospel in their heads that is, to a great extent, based on their culture. This gospel is one part of what we have been calling the CMC (culture-as-meta-context) that provides the context through which we interpret events and people and manage our workforce. Our CMC tells us what is good, or at least better, and what is desirable and appropriate. As illustrated in the *First Person* example, people from two cultural groups approach situations differently. Each person enters the interaction with their own CMC and being able to effectively work together requires understanding of the cultural context and working on an approach that is acceptable to all individuals involved.

In this chapter, we review two approaches to national culture that provide you with the knowledge to understand, describe, and predict cross-cultural differences. We begin by reviewing the communication cultural context framework proposed by Edward T. Hall, consider the particular differences of communication styles across cultures, and then detail how cultural values can be used to classify and categorize cultures based on the work of Florence Kluckhohn and Fred Strodtbeck which lays the foundation for many of our current approaches to differentiating cultural groups. The chapter ends with a discussion of the strengths and weaknesses of the frameworks and their applications to management.

1. USING FRAMEWORKS TO UNDERSTAND CULTURE

LO 7.1 Discuss how research-based frameworks of cultural differences can be used to understand, describe, and predict behavior across cultures

We know that culture impacts how people think, interpret the world, and act. We are able to understand and predict how people from our own cultural groups behave, but how do we gain access to information about other cultures in order to be able to interact effectively across cultures? How can managers understand, explain, and predict how their culturally diverse employees will react and behave, so that they can manage them effectively? We already know that given the diversity of cultures, it is impossible for any one person to simply learn about the cultural assumptions, values, beliefs, and practices of all the various people he or she may encounter.

Consider the case of Stefan, a German manager who has worked for Henkel AG, the giant German chemical and consumer goods company, headquartered in Düsseldorf, for several years (Pagda, 2019). After delivering consistently strong results throughout the 5 years in his position, the company promoted Stefan to be general manager of one of its operations in Egypt. Before taking over the position, he had been to Egypt several times for business. He knew most of the managers, many of the employees, and the office setting. He also had spent a good amount of time in Cairo, so he was confident that he would not have any problems adjusting to his new position. When the head of human resources in Düsseldorf asked him whether he was ready to take on this challenge, he confidently told her that he was. As he settled into his new office in Cairo, he became increasingly frustrated. Many of his employees came to work around 10 or 11 a.m., a couple of hours after the official start time. They turned in their reports late, and when asked for estimates regarding needed resources to accomplish a task or project, they either did not provide a clear answer or were off by a considerable amount.

Every time Stefan requested specific information, he got vague responses. When he asked about how he could help them overcome problems and complications, they smiled and told him that there were none and everything was fine. When Lars, his boss in Germany asked him casually how well he had adapted to the Egyptian way, Stefan strongly affirmed: "Lars, I will not adapt to this culture; they are the ones who need to adapt to our better culture of doing business. I will change the people here so that we can successfully perform as a team." Accordingly, Stefan set out to make things right. He started scheduling important meetings first thing in the morning, became very clear about deadlines, and confronted everyone when things were late or when the information was not clear. He wrote detailed instructions and asked his reports to repeat them before they left his office. Yet, nothing seemed to work. His team members started avoiding him, they appeared demotivated, frustrated, and stressed out, and productivity went down (Pagda, 2019).

Stefan is experiencing challenges related to cultural differences. How he thinks the job should be done and what he values as manager are guided by his CMC. The challenge is that his values do not match the way his Egyptian colleagues work and what they think is important. They are operating based on their own CMC. Both Stefan and his employees believe that their approach is better and are frustrated with the other party. Short of learning about every culture in the world and immersing ourselves in them, an obviously impossible task, how can we understand, describe, and predict cultural differences without depreciating or disparaging them? What vocabulary do we use? How do we differentiate among cultures without stereotyping them?

1.1 A New Vocabulary Based on Frameworks and Models

To answer these questions, we need valid and reliable knowledge that arms us with a language and vocabulary to communicate cultural differences in a consistent, systematic, and objective way. We need this vocabulary to

- Understand

- Describe, and

- Predict cultural differences.

The focus on understanding and description that arms us with knowledge to predict differences is critical to avoid the tendency to evaluate. In this chapter and the next, we explore the details of frameworks or models of culture that offer consistent and reliable ways to achieve these goals. They have been developed to understand national and broad regional differences among cultural groups and provide the basic structure that can guide our understanding of cultures, our own, and that of others.

1.2 Inside and Outside Views: Benefits and Disadvantages of Using Frameworks

Frameworks provide theoretical and research-based description of cultures based on common dimensions; they therefore address group and national cultures. They are intended to be used to describe rather than evaluate cultures by relying on well-developed knowledge that can allow managers to reliably address cultural differences.

1.2.1 Emic vs. Etic. Social scientists have used two approaches to understanding culture, labeled emic and etic. These two terms were first proposed by linguist Kenneth Pike and later adopted and further developed by anthropologist Marvin Harris (Headland, Pike, & Harris, 1990).

- The *emic* approach takes the internal perspective and relies on the description of the culture provided by members of that culture (Kottak, 2006). It is an inside-out approach. For example, members of a culture would describe what they consider effective leadership and how power is applied in their organizations, using their own terms.

- The *etic* approach relies on outsiders' description of a culture, using information gathered by outsiders who observe the culture and collect data through various means (Kottak, 2006). It is an outside-in approach. For example, consultants would use questionnaires and surveys to assess ideals of leadership and application of power in a culture.

Each approach has advantages and disadvantages. On the one hand, insiders have access to rich and detailed information about their own culture that is not available to outsiders. They can therefore provide a unique perspective on their own assumptions, values, beliefs, and practices. However, they also have biases that may make them interpret information in a subjective manner, or in some cases even ignore some key information. On the other hand, outsiders have a more objective view, but are likely to lack the depth and richness that comes from personal knowledge of a culture.

1.2.2 Frameworks. Social scientists and organizational researchers have relied on the etic and emic approaches, as well as a combination of both, to understand culture and its impact on people. For example, to understand differences in management styles across cultures, researchers might interview a few members of the certain culture, asking them to describe management processes in their organization or how their manager interacts with them (emic). They then conduct research through observation and deploy a survey that includes some of that information provided by insiders, along with questions based on theoretical frameworks, to gather more extensive data from a larger group in order to fully understand the management style within that culture (etic). Finally, they may use all the information they have gathered to develop a framework that both describes and predicts management within that cultural setting. That framework can be communicated to others to help them understand the culture in question.

1.3 Applying Frameworks

As you become familiar with various cultural frameworks, you will find them to be useful tools that can help you understand, describe, and predict cultural differences. You will acquire knowledge (KNOW in the THINK–KNOW–DO) that offers you a new vocabulary to talk about cross-cultural differences in a consistent manner. You can also use frameworks related to cultural differences to adjust the rules that you apply to different cross-cultural situations and modify your own behavior accordingly. However, you must be mindful of the risks and challenges we discussed in Chapter 1:

- When we categorize people and cultures, even when relying on well-researched frameworks, sophisticated stereotypes, or prototypes based on reliable research, we run the risk of overgeneralizing and essentializing. So, for example, you may have information about the Mexican culture based on various cultural models, but you cannot assume that every Mexican employee of your organization will behave according to the dimensions presented in those models; every individual is likely to be unique.

- Frameworks and models do not replace the in-depth knowledge of cultures that can result from immersion, detailed study, and extended interactions. However, they provide accurate general descriptions and prototypes of cultural groups.

- Frameworks are an excellent starting point for understanding cultural similarities and differences. For example, as organizations provide cultural training to their expat managers and their families, they provide them with knowledge of various models before they go abroad. This type of information starts highlighting the fact that rules from one culture may not apply to another and sensitizes the expats to suspend or slow down their System I when they are abroad.

This chapter presents two frameworks that have been widely adopted and applied to the business contexts. One uses the communication context as a framework; the other relies on values as a framework to understand culture.

2. HALL'S COMMUNICATION CONTEXT FRAMEWORK

LO 7.2 Detail the elements and predictions of Hall's communication context framework of culture

"One of the functions of culture is to provide a highly selective screen between man and the outside world. In its many forms, culture therefore designates what we pay attention to and what we ignore" (Hall, 1976, p. 85). This quote from anthropologist Edward T. Hall introduces the framework that he developed to explain how people use information and rely on the context to communicate with one another. Hall suggests that people rely on preprogrammed information to interpret events and create meaning. His framework specifically focuses on cross-cultural communication because, according to Hall (1992): "We believed that culture is communication and no communication by humans can be divorced from culture" (p. 212).

Hall divides cultures into two broad groups: those that are *high context (HC)* and those that are *low context (LC)*, based on the extent to which people rely on either the context and information that they have internalized or on specific language and clear external codes to make sense of their communications and interaction (Hall, 1976). Table 7.1 presents a summary of the differences between high- and low-context cultures. One way to contrast the two groups is to consider the cultural iceberg presented in Chapter 1 (see Figure 1.1). HC cultures tend to function more below the visible waterline where shared values and assumptions are unstated and implicit. LC cultures focus on elements that are above the waterline with clearly stated norms and behaviors.

2.1 High-Context (HC) Cultures

In order to communicate, people from *high-context cultures* (HC) pay attention to and use information that they have either internalized or is present in the environment around them (see Table 7.1 for a summary). They rely on nonverbal cues such as tone of voice and body posture to express themselves or interpret others' communication. In HC cultures, contextual factors, for example a person's title and status, provide meaningful information that is the basis of how people interpret various situations. They have internalized many social norms that regulate their actions if the environment does not provide clear direction. For example, employees in these cultures would pay attention to who enters meeting rooms first, where people sit, and who speaks first as cues they use to understand the power hierarchy.

Table 7.1 Characteristics of High-and Low-Context Cultures

High-Context Cultures (HC)	Low-Context Cultures (LC)
• Rely on nonverbal cues (tone of voice, body posture, facial expressions) • Value traditions • Slowly build long-term relationships • Decisions and activities based on trust • Indirect and conflict avoidant • Polychromatic and nonlinear time—many things happening at once (P-time) • Close identification with group or clan • Clear boundaries between in- and out-groups • Formal with strangers until close relationships are formed	• Rely on specific verbal or written messages • Value clarity and the here and now • Quickly build short-term relationships • Decisions and activities based on formal agreements • Direct and confrontational • Monochromatic and linear time—tangible and sequential activities (M-time) • Reliance on self • Rule and task-oriented • Many wide networks of relationships • Generally informal in interactions

Source: Based on information in Hall (1976).

In HC cultures, relationships are often based on family ties, with clear distinctions between in- and out-groups, and it takes time to develop relationships with those outside of the in-group (Hall, 1976). People are nonconfrontational and less direct, especially with members of their in-groups. They are also more communal, interacting with many individuals and groups at once and taking time to form deep and long-lasting relationships. Trust develops slowly and is essential to being able to work in organizations where having trust is considered to be on par with written communication or legal contracts, so that business can be done on a handshake or based on verbal agreement. The Saudis in our *First Person* example are typically classified as an HC culture; their insistence on developing a relationship is one aspect of their HC culture.

The two HC and LC groups are further characterized by their conception and use of time and space. According to Hall (1976), HC cultures are polychronic (P-Time) where time is perceived as flexible, many actions happen at once, and events and activities are not ordered in a linear fashion. In HC cultures, the need to be on time is less urgent. For example, in Mexico or Brazil, being late for a meeting or a business appointment is tolerated and even expected. Additionally, given that time is flexible, there is no need to end an ongoing activity to start another previously scheduled one. The approach is that things will get done when they get done, so visitors may be left waiting beyond their appointment time while another meeting is still in course.

2.2 Low-Context (LC) Cultures

As opposed to HC cultures, people from LC cultures focus on explicit and specific verbal and written messages to understand people and situations and to communicate with others (Hall, 1976). The written message, whether it is letter, email, or contract is taken seriously and therefore must be clear and precise. For example, in most North American or European cultures, businesses rely on detailed contracts to regulate relationships with customers and suppliers; doing business based on a simple verbal agreement would be highly unlikely. People in LC cultures are less bound by conformity to social norms and tend to behave according to their own rules and decisions, particularly if direction is not clearly and specifically provided through verbal or written communication.

Relationships are formed quickly, can be short term, and members of LC cultures are comfortable with direct confrontation and disagreement (Hall, 1976). Because of self-reliance and less community orientation, individuals may not have highly distinct in- and out-groups and many of their interactions occur through networks that form and dissolve quickly, or in one-on-one relationships based on specific tasks (Hall, 1976). For example, people in the United States who move more often based on their jobs quickly form friendships with their neighbors or through church or their children's school. They repeat this process when they are transferred for a job again. As opposed to HC cultures, time in LC cultures is monochromatic (M-Time) and linear (Hall, 1976). Events do not happen simultaneously, but rather in clear and manageable sequences. Time is considered tangible, finite, measurable, and valuable. The US, British, or German insistence on clear schedules and punctuality is partially the result of this LC monochromatic view of time.

Any Western and Northern European or North American business person who has tried to schedule meetings and set deadlines or has attempted to rush a project in the Middle East, Latin America, Africa, or Asia has had a first-hand experience with these differences. While the latter are LC and on M-time, focus on managing, saving, making up, and not running out of time, the former, who are HC and on P-time, manage multiple things, do not adhere to schedules, and take nonlinear routes to get to their goals. They look at their M-time colleagues with consternation for setting what they consider to be artificial and arbitrary limits on time, space, and activities. The *First Person* anecdote and Stefan's experience in Egypt are both a case in point.

2.3 The High- and Low-Context Continuum

High and low context fall within a continuum so that whether a culture is considered higher or lower is relative to others. For example, US Americans are generally considered LC and M-time when compared to Latin Americans or many Asian or African cultures. However, when compared to Germany and some other Northern European cultures, the United States is less LC. In the *First Person* anecdote the author Dr. Roche and his

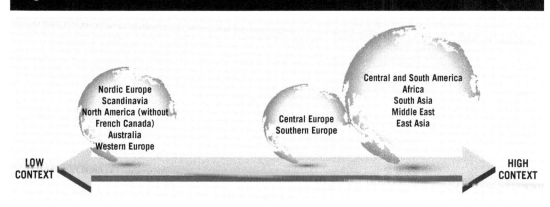

Figure 7.1 Countries on the Context Continuum

Nordic Europe
Scandinavia
North America (without French Canada)
Australia
Western Europe

Central Europe
Southern Europe

Central and South America
Africa
South Asia
Middle East
East Asia

LOW CONTEXT

HIGH CONTEXT

partners are both from HC cultures, but his Saudi partners are more HC than he is. Furthermore, having worked in Western companies, Roche is accustomed to a more LC approach to communication. Similarly, Stefan, the German manager in Egypt, is operating under his own LC CMC in a country where people are more HC.

The differences between HC and LC can explain many cross-cultural communication problems that managers face when they work with people from a culture that is at the opposite end of the HC–LC continuum. The LC European and North American managers might get frustrated working with followers from HC Asian or Middle Eastern cultures because the LC managers focus on specific instructions while the HC followers aim to develop relationships and trust. Similarly, HC managers might be offended by their LC followers' directness, which they may interpret as rudeness, lack of respect, or a challenge to their authority.

Figure 7.1 presents an approximate placement of country groupings along the context continuum. These placements are based on anecdotal accounts rather than rigorous research, as Hall or other researchers have not provided a comprehensive and consistent classification of countries (Kittler, Rygl, & Mackinnon, 2011).

2.4 Applying the Cultural Context Framework

The placement and groupings in Figure 7.1 provide a broad categorization that illustrates several points.

- First, Hall (1976) estimated that close to 70% of people in the world are HC rather than LC. So, considering the large population of East and South Asia, together with Africa, the Middle East, and parts of Europe, the large majority of cultures in the world tend to be more HC than LC.

- Second, the classifications of HC and LC paint a very broad picture that does not represent finer differences. For example, English-speaking Canada is generally considered LC, but French-speaking Canada is often grouped with France, which places in the middle of the continuum. Similarly, Finland is often excluded from the Scandinavian countries.

- Finally, the country classifications are not based on formal and reliable research. Rather, these classifications are the results of anecdotes and case studies.

For example, within Europe, Germans (an LC culture) often complain about people from almost all other parts of Europe being imprecise; the French and Italians, who fall in the middle of the HC–LC continuum, criticize the Germans for insulting them by providing too much irrelevant directions. North American expats in Central and South America often gripe about the lack of promptness; while Central and South Americans see their northern neighbors as unnecessarily obsessed with time. For those who travel and do business around the world, these anecdotes ring true; they have experienced many similar ones. They therefore are likely to find Hall's cultural context framework descriptive and accurate.

Additionally, it is typical for people to feel more comfortable with what is familiar to them and prefer the communication context that is part of their culture. The comfort with the familiar notwithstanding, culture-just-is, CJI. Hall never claimed that either approach is necessarily better than the other. Each has some strengths and some weaknesses. HC and LC are simply different modes and methods of communication, each having developed as a result of cultural groups' interaction with and adaptation to their environment (Hall, 1976). Having the vocabulary to describe cultural differences allows managers to describe rather than evaluate or denigrate differences.

3. COMMUNICATION STYLES ACROSS CULTURES

LO 7.3 Elaborate on the different communication styles across cultures

Hall's concept of HC–LC addresses the extent to which people use the context to communicate. Embedded, but not specifically and directly mentioned in the HC–LC concept, is the idea of cross-cultural communication styles. Whether you use the context or internal cues and norms does not fully address how you convey information. Do you simply say what you mean clearly and directly or take a circuitous and roundabout way with many deviations and diversions? Do you provide concrete examples or talk in theoretical terms? These address the *style of communication* rather than content; how you communicate rather than what you communicate (Liu, 2016). The differences in communication style are one of the most evident and visible differences in cultures.

3.1 Areas of Communication Impacted by Culture

The style of communication is addressed in one way or another in all the frameworks we present, but because of its importance in cross-cultural interaction, we discuss it in detail here. Table 7.2 summarizes the areas covered by communication style. It is important to note that

- Each area presents on a continuum or spectrum so that there are, for example, degrees of directness or circularity, rather than a simple either-or style.

- While individuals or cultural groups may have a preference for one approach over another, and therefore perceive some to be more desirable than others,

Table 7.2 Areas of Communication Style	
Areas and Approaches	**Description**
Direct to Indirect	From blunt, clear, specific, and explicit *to* subtle, vague, general, and implicit A ➡ B A ┈┈➤ B
Linear to Circular	From making a straight connection between points *to* starting at one point, taking a detour, then going back A ➡ B A 〜〜➤ B
Abstract to Concrete	From communicating through data, concepts, and theories *to* through examples, stories, and metaphors
Task to People	From expressing ideas by focusing on ideas, outcomes, and results *to* on people and relationships
Intellectual to Emotional	From sticking to objective and logical arguments to conveying feelings, emotions, and subjective impressions as part of the message

these are meant to be descriptive rather than evaluative. In other words, relying on a linear style is not better or worse than a circular one, or a preference for an emotional approach is not superior or inferior to an intellectual one; CJI.

- The context, whether it's the culture or the organizational context, makes one approach more desirable or more effective. The style that you prefer and fall back on is part of your CMC, and like all other cultural elements it simply "just is."

3.2 Directness

How directly a person communicates is one of the most significant differences in cross-cultural communication. Germans, Scandinavians, and North Americans are notoriously direct when compared to many other people from Latin America, Africa, the Middle East, and Asia (e.g., Lim & Urakami, 2019). German, Swedish, or US-American managers are comfortable providing straight and candid feedback to their employees regarding performance. Their actions are based on the deep cultural assumptions that honesty is an indispensable component of proper social order. Arab, Thai, or Japanese managers will convey the same information, particularly if it is negative, more subtly and may even use a third party to communicate the negative feedback to assure that all parties save face.

3.2.1 Saving Face. Saving face refers to a desire and a strategy to avoid embarrassment and humiliation, and maintain one's own and others' dignity and reputation (Brill, 2010; Eriksson, Mao, & Villeval, 2017). In many cultures, the goal is to conduct social interactions in a way to maintain *everybody's face*. In China, for example, respecting someone is called "giving face" (Hofstede & Bond, 1988). Face saving may even come at the cost of sacrificing honest feedback where maintaining face is more valued than simple frankness. Face saving is less important in North American and Northern and Western European cultures where directness is highly prized (Naffsinger, 1995), where people may devise strategies to avoid embarrassment and keep their own reputation intact, but are less concerned with protecting the reputation of others (Eriksson et al., 2017).

3.2.2 The Purpose of Saving Face. In Asian, African, and Middle Eastern cultures, where reputation and how one is perceived by others is fundamental to social order, saving face is directed at self and at others and it aims to sustain essential social obligations and order. In these cultures, one protects one's own face, but also that of others. Managers who publicly criticize their employees can cause both themselves and the persons who are targeted to be embarrassed and humiliated. Such direct confrontation threatens the social order and the group identity, and therefore is to be avoided. Similarly, employees would be considered rude and inappropriate if they directly, even if honestly, state that they cannot or will not complete a task, the reason. Such straight refusal reflects badly on them and on their manage everyone to lose face.

Stefan's frustration with his employees, not telling him about their cha the example at the beginning of this chapter, is an illustration of how Egypt save face for themselves and their manager. Telling Stefan that they have and cannot accomplish their task would not only be humiliating for thei reflect badly on his competence as a manager. Similarly, outsiders who complain about local conditions or criticize how things are done when working abroad or visiting a country where saving face is important bring shame to their hosts and to themselves. Being aware of your own culturally based directness and that of those you interact with is critical when communicating across cultures, so that you can use the appropriate rules to interpret and react.

3.3 Linear vs. Circular

Another key communication style is the degree of linearity as opposed to more circular communication. Linear styles, often used by Europeans and North Americans, involve moving from point A to point B through straight and explicit communication. Conversely, people with circular styles meander and take detours and express ideas in subtle ways. They may digress to tell a tangentially related story, move to a different loosely connected topic, and then return to their original communication, often frustrating and irritating those who have a more linear style of communication.

The long-winded storytelling often observed in Middle Eastern and African cultures partially relates to a circular style of communication. For example, a negotiating partner from those cultures may mention what appears to be unrelated facts and observations while negotiating. Individuals from cultures with a more linear style are more likely to stay on one topic, complete it, then move to another.

3.4 Abstraction, Task Orientation, and Intellectual Styles

As presented in Table 7.2, there are several other additional potential communication style differences across cultures. Those using abstract styles rely on data, concepts, and theory (again more common in Northern Europe), while concrete communicators (more Asian, African, and Middle Eastern) include metaphors, stories, and anecdotes that illustrate an idea or concept rather than simply stating it. Negotiating partners from these two different types of cultures are likely to be both puzzled and exasperated by their different styles of communication. The abstract people will present data, use as few words as possible, and submit concise conceptual arguments to make their case. The concrete partners will inject seemingly irrelevant anecdotes of other events, tell stories, cite proverbs, refer to ideals, and mention historical figures without asking specific questions or providing clear answers.

Additionally, cultures differ in the degree to which they focus on either the task or people when communicating and how much they rely on intellectual rather than emotional arguments. Those who are more task-oriented (e.g., Germans and US-Americans) will focus on the task and outcome in arguing their case, whereas the more people-oriented cultures will use human stories and anecdotes. Often related to the task–person distinction is the intellectual rather than emotional focus of the communication which refers to the use and demonstration of emotions. For example, Brazilians, who tend to be more emotional in their style of communication, may be unconvinced when their Japanese partners remain calm and collected when making their sales pitch.

3.5 Communication Styles in a Culturally Diverse World

Consider the following dialogue between a US-American and Mexican manager during negotiations:

American manager: *We are eager to do business with you and reach an agreement as soon as possible. We think that we are great partners as you can see from the chart that shows the synergies we can each attain. The handout presents our pricing and the timeline and what we need to do to reach a healthy profit margin. We have also figured out how much both our companies can make with several scenarios. It all is clearly laid out; so, do you have any questions? Where do we go from here? Let's look at our next steps.*

Mexican manager: *We are enchanted to be discussing this with you. We have a long and proud history of working with our friends across the border. Even in times of disagreement and conflict that go back a hundred years, we have managed to keep our cooperation going. The province and its governor have met with many people from your state government and are now talking about even more cooperation at their levels. There is much we can do to both prosper and build long-term relationships. I know that your family often spends time in our beautiful beach resorts and several of us have children who go to school in the US. They would be very proud of our achievements. So, we would both be fortunate to do more business and build our relationships.*

American manager: *Great, so let's go over the numbers.*

Mexican manager: *There will be plenty of time for that. We can study these at some point together. We would like to show you the community where our partnership will have the most impact. I think you will be impressed by the dedication of the local government and the workers. They are really impressive and very enthusiastic. So many of them have built their lives in such difficult situations that seeing them so eager to welcome our partnership is wonderful. A great opportunity.*

American manager: *Of course; we have data that show how much our partnership can benefit the communities on both sides of the border.*

Mexican manager: *I'm so glad we agree on these principles! That is very encouraging and a clear sign of our long-term friendship.*

American manager: *I'm not sure what we have agreed on, so let's look at the various points to hash out the areas of agreement and identify things we still need to work on.*

Mexican manager: *Well of course! We have so much to talk about, so many details to work out. The other day, I was talking to one of the company managers and he was telling me about the differences in our HR policies. We are all abiding by our own laws and it's sometimes hard for our workers to adjust. I am sure we can work those out. We have to look at the big picture and make sure our bosses are all in agreement as well.*

American managers: *The existing plants are part of prior agreements, not related to our discussions today. I'm sure we are abiding to all the agreements we made, but I will be happy to bring up any issues with my managers and have them address anything they can; but those are not the topic here. So, let's look at page 3 of the handout where some details of the new agreement regarding HR are spelled out…*

Mexican manager: *Yes of course, but we really need to look at the big picture….*

These managers are using two different styles of communication: The US-American manager is direct, linear, abstract, task-focused, and intellectual. The Mexican manager is indirect, circular, concrete, people-focused, and more emotional. Neither style is right or wrong or more or less effective in and of itself; rather, each reflects the person's CMC. The managers are behaving in ways that address and satisfy their assumptions and values about what is right and wrong and what constitute good communication. However, the two styles do not match, and the differences are likely to frustrate both parties where neither seems to be achieving their goals.

Difference in styles of communication can create confusion and challenges in global corporations and international teams where the culture and communication style of the parent company may be different from that of its many employees. For example, the French cosmetic giant L'Oréal relies on open confrontation as a path to creativity. An Indonesian employee of the company observes "To an Indonesian person, confrontation in a group setting is extremely negative, because it makes the other person lose face. So it's something that we try strongly to avoid in any open manner." This view is echoed by a Mexican employee: "In Mexican culture, open disagreement is considered rude, disrespectful, and too aggressive" (Meyer, 2014).

In another example, Bill McDermott, the American CEO of the German multinational company SAP, recalls his early career with Xerox when he worked in Asia: "I needed to work more slowly, to get to know customers and focus on the

, not the transaction" (McDermott, 2016). Another American manager ⎥ in Japan and was too direct and confrontational found herself physically ⎝m the group, although no one ever verbally confronted her:

⸱rally put my office in a storage room, where I had desks stacked from floor to ⸱⸱d I was the only person there. So they totally isolated me, which was a pretty ⎝al to me that I was not a part of the inside circle and that they would communicate with me only as needed. (Brett, Behfar, & Kern, 2006)

These employees' culturally based communication styles run counter to their coworkers' and company's style. What works in their "small" world and culture is not effective in other worlds and cultures.

3.6 HC and LC and Communication Styles

As you review the areas in Table 7.2, it should be clear that the first set in each area resembles the LC cultures described by Hall (1976), whereas the second set is closer to HC cultures. For example, being indirect and circular in communication is typically associated with people from HC cultures, whereas being direct, linear, and task-focused is typically LC. By providing more specific categories through communication styles, the concepts of HC–LC can be further clarified. For example, France is usually ranked as more HC than the United States. However, the French use a very direct communication style, particularly in work settings. French managers provide direct negative feedback to their employees in a fact-based and unemotional way, whereas most managers in the United States shy away from such direct communication or sandwich negative information between two positive statements.

Additionally, considerable research in cross-cultural communication has focused on communication styles, allowing for description and prediction of various cultures in each of the areas (e.g., Holtbrügge & Berning, 2017; Park & Kim, 2008). For example, some research shows that HC style of communication may be less effective in web design than the more direct and simple LC styles (Usinier & Roulin, 2010). Germans and Scandinavians are notoriously direct (e.g., Lim & Urakami, 2019), linear, unemotional, and abstract. US-Americans are further known for being blunt and often perceived as uncaring and rude by people from cultures where being indirect and relationship-oriented are prized. People from these cultures are more likely to say what they mean and mean what they say. The US-American saying of "Tell it like it is" is much valued by members of that culture, yet appears thoughtless and insensitive to a Japanese or an Indian. The famous Indian head wobble (see Chapter 1) is one indicator of indirect nonverbal communication. Similarly, in many cultures, directly saying yes or no is considered inappropriate and the tone of voice or nonverbals when the words are spoken may change their meaning. Such intricacies are impossible to describe using simple labels; understanding them requires people to slow down and carefully collect and evaluate information. In other words, it requires suspension of the automatic and efficient System I thinking and activation of the more deliberate System II processes.

Considering communication style provides a more specific description to add to the general communication context presented by Hall. How and what we communicate is based on our assumptions, values, and beliefs and part of our CMC. Therefore, in order to be effective, managers must choose to develop their CM, which involves having self-awareness and knowledge of our own and others' communication context and communication style.

WINDOW TO THE WORLD

Doing Business in Russia

As the world's largest country with boundless natural resources and a tumultuous recent history, Russia provides many opportunities and challenges. The country spans 11 time zones and presents a mixture of old traditions, high-risk entrepreneurship, and soviet-style bureaucracy. Words used to describe prototypical Russians include: action-oriented, emotional, loyal, pessimistic, patriotic and suspicious of outsiders, and direct. Here are some tips:

- *Blat*, which is Russian for connection is everything; take the time to establish relationships before you go and work at maintaining them. Doing favors and loyalty to people is deeply engrained and you should cultivate those exchanges.

- Russians are more group-oriented than individualistic and highly hierarchical. The collective (family, community, etc.) takes precedence over individuals, and those with higher rank and status are respected and obeyed.

- Few decisions are made quickly or on the fly, so be patient and persistent.

- Russians are direct and can be confrontational and challenge you. Stay calm and be as direct as they are. Compromise is likely to be seen as a sign of weakness. You may hear a lot of "nos," a response that is not likely to be final; be persistent.

- Stay formal and use full names and titles, dress formally, and be on time.

Although there are many ethnic and religious minorities in the country, the strong emphasis is on being Russian and discussions of minority groups and their rights are topics that should be avoided. While sometimes stern, Russians are hospitable and highly sociable with a strong tradition of drinking and toasting, particularly during business meetings and when with valued guests. There are many verbal and nonverbal pitfalls to watch out for and, as always, extensive research is essential. To start, keep in mind that shaking hands across doorways is considered bad luck and likely to engender much discomfort.

₁CKHOHN AND STRODTBECK'S VALUE ₁ENTATION THEORY

vvnether working within our own "small world" and culture or in a larger context across different cultures, one of the key challenges we face is how to explain, describe, and predict behavior. Researchers have started to link biology and behavior, but such an approach is not feasible in the workplace. We also have access to many personality measures, some more reliable than others, with a few traits, for example conscientiousness having some correlation to job performance (e.g., Anderson, Spataro, & Flynn, 2008). However, many robust personality traits, such as emotional stability, are not clearly related to work behaviors, and few apply equally across all cultures. Additionally, personality traits focus on individuals rather than groups.

However, rather than relying on biological differences or personality traits, social scientists have, for many years, found that values can be a strong predictor of behavior (see the early work of Vernon and Allport (1931) and Parsons and Shils (1951)). In other words what you think is right or wrong and desirable can predict how you will act.

4.1 Values and Culture

As we defined in Chapter 1, *values* are stable, long-lasting beliefs and preferences about what is worthwhile and desirable. They reflect the way people think the world should be and are connected with beliefs that, in turn, often develop into values as people act on them and deepen their commitment to those beliefs. Earlier in the book, we identified two types of values. *Instrumental values* indicate *how* we believe we should go about doing things; *terminal values* indicate *what* we should be doing, meaning the goal (Anderson, 1997; Rokeach, 1973). Both types of values are strong and reliable predictors of behavior. Knowing what people value provides a reasonably clear window into what they may do.

Values are a core component of the culture (see Table 1.3 in Chapter 1). We know from considerable research in anthropology and cross-cultural psychology that people in different cultures find different things desirable and worthwhile (see frameworks in this chapter and the next). For example, being independent from others, including one's family, is considered desirable, worthwhile, and a sign of a healthy adult in the United States. Being dutiful, respectful, and a contributing member of a family or clan is desirable and worthwhile in Pakistan (we will explore these in detail in Chapter 8). These are different values regarding how people should relate to one another. Comparably, in some cultures where hierarchy is valued and considered desirable, supervisors are afforded a wider latitude of power and employees will show respect for authority and comply with orders from their manager. In other cultures, egalitarianism may be valued leading to more equal power distribution in organizations and to employees challenging their boss or questioning their directions. These values can help predict how managers in different countries lead and how organizations structure their activities.

4.2 Shared Human Challenges

Given the power of values in predicting behavior and their link to culture, it is no surprise that researchers have used values as a way of describing different cultures and have used them as the basis of frameworks to explain culture. One of the earliest approaches to using values to understand culture was proposed by anthropologists Florence Kluckhohn and Fred Strodtbeck (1961) in a framework that is known as the Values Orientation Theory. Their theory is also the basis for many of the other management and organizationally oriented models of culture we discuss in the next chapter.

4.2.1 Three Assumptions. The Kluckhohn and Strodtbeck (K&S) (1961) framework starts with three assumptions about people and culture:

1. There are a limited number of common challenges or problems that every group or society faces.

2. There are a limited number of solutions and answers to these challenges.

3. All solutions and answers are available to all groups, but each group selects some, but not other solutions, resulting in unique combinations that create differences in cultures.

4.2.2 Six Human Challenges. Kluckhohn and Strodtbeck then identified six basic challenges or problems that groups and societies face (see Figure 7.2). Each of these challenges presents fundamental issues regarding how we interact with the world and with one another, and various groups respond to these in unique ways. The challenges include

- How we view human nature

- How we relate to time

- Our relationship with our natural environment

Figure 7.2   Six Challenges Humans Face

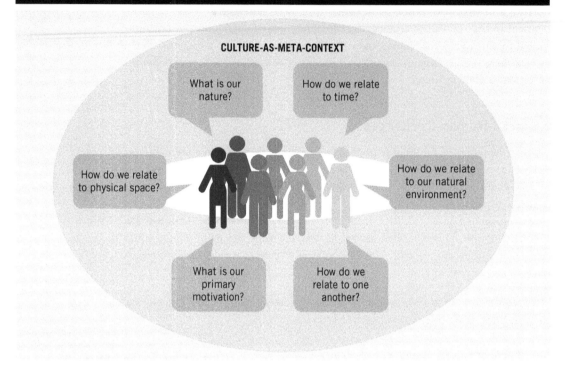

CULTURE-AS-META-CONTEXT

What is our nature?

How do we relate to time?

How do we relate to physical space?

How do we relate to our natural environment?

What is our primary motivation?

How do we relate to one another?

- Our relationship to other people

- The motivation behind our actions

- Our relationship to physical space

Different cultural groups have adopted different answers and solutions to each of these six challenges (see Table 7.3), leading different cultural groups to have unique identities that reflect and represent their cultural value orientations. These value orientations impact the social structures and processes and the way people work and manage organizations.

4.3 Challenge 1: What Is Our Nature?

Midway during his flight from Singapore to Vancouver, a Canadian businessman noticed that his wallet containing a sizable amount of cash, his identification, and several credit cards was missing. He cancelled his cards as soon as he landed and had

Table 7.3   Alternative Answers to Six Universal Challenges: The Value Dimensions

Universal Challenge	Alternative Answers
What is our nature?	• *Good*: Human beings are good. • *Mixed/Neutral*: Human beings are neither all good or all bad; or human beings are both good and bad. • *Bad*: Human beings are evil.
How do we relate to time?	• *Past*: We value the past, traditions, and history and want to preserve them. • *Present*: We focus on the here and now and adjust the past to fit the present. • *Future*: We focus on the future and plan ahead to replace the old with the new as needed.
How do we relate to our natural environment?	• *Mastery*: We exercise control over the environment. • *Harmony*: We manage the environment and live in balance with nature. • *Submission*: The environment and natural forces control us.
How do we relate to one another?	• *Hierarchy*: Some of us have more power, and we defer to them. • *Group*: We are all equals, and we aim for consensus. • *Individualism*: Individuals are independent and do what is best for them.
What is our primary motivation or mode of activity?	• *Being*: Internal motivation; we do what is best in the moment. • *Striving*: We focus on personal development. • *Doing*: External motivation; we do what is approved by others.
How do we relate to physical space?	• *Private:* Property and object belong to individuals and groups. • *Mixed:* Some things are owned by individuals, some are public. • *Public:* Physical space is owned by no one/everyone.

Sources: Adapted from information in Hills (2002) and Kluckhohn and Strodtbeck (1961).

given up on ever seeing the cash when a couple days after his arrival, he got a surprise call from the security office at Singapore's Changi airport. A cab driver had turned in his wallet, and it would be mailed to the address listed on his driver's license shortly. The surprise was even more pleasant when the wallet showed up with all the cash intact. The Canadian's expectation of never seeing his wallet or money again was based on a more negative view of human nature, where people are expected to cheat and take advantage of others.

4.3.1 From Good to Evil. "Who are we, what is our nature and can we change and improve" are basic and fundamental questions for all human beings. How people answer these questions is partly related to culture, and it impacts our social interactions and how we manage people. In the United States, people generally have a mixed view of human nature and believe that improvement and growth are achievable, but that people can also be untrustworthy. The Hindu caste system represents another perspective where individual change is not possible, but rather change only occurs when a whole group achieves a new state. The Confucian traditions of China and other Asian countries lean toward a positive view of human beings where trust in others is expected and practiced, as the Canadian businessman in our example experienced.

In most countries, urban cultures have developed a relatively negative view of human nature while rural communities have more positive views as evidenced by unlocked doors and cars, reliance on neighbors, and openness toward community members (e.g., Svendsen & Svendsen, 2016). Consider the example of the Tata group in India. To staff its luxury hotels in India, the global conglomerate focuses its recruiting efforts in villages rather than urban centers, to find employees who hold traditional values of service and hospitality, which the company then reinforces with training programs and reward systems (Deshpandé & Raina, 2011).

4.3.2 In- and Out-Groups. Interestingly, we often ascribe a different nature to people based on whether we consider them part of our in- or our out-group, and how strongly we differentiate between the two. We tend to see those close to us as good and trustworthy (a proxy for a positive view of human nature) and those who are not so close, or who are different from us, as less honorable or virtuous. Additionally, many recent cases and stories point to an increasingly negative view of others in the information age.

A 2018 report in *The Atlantic* states that the US population is the least trusting among the 28 other countries surveyed, just below South Africa (Friedman, 2018). The report suggests that political conflict, strife, and economic conditions all play a part in how people view each other and their social institutions. The more contentious the climate, the less positive people's views of one another while a growing economy and positive climate engenders a more trusting and positive view. Furthermore, a 2019 Pew Research Center survey indicates that the majority of younger US-Americans (those between 18 and 29 years) see others as selfish, exploitative, and untrustworthy (Gramlich, 2019).

The 2020 COVID-19 worldwide epidemic provided a dramatic example of the differences in trust across cultures and the impact it can have. For example, countries where there is higher trust generally fared better than those, like the United States, where trust is low (Fukuyama, 2020). Specifically, Germany, where trust in government is high and where people followed directions closely, had one of the lowest death rates in the world (Benhold, 2020).

4.3.3 Consequences for Management and Organizations. Clearly, our culturally based views of human nature are an important factor in understanding ourselves and others and how we structure and manage our organizations. Knowing how you and others around you would address this question can provide some information regarding their motives and the causes of their decisions and behaviors. Your negotiating partner may be a suspicious person or acting based on his cultural belief that people tend to cheat and are not honest. Table 7.4 presents some examples of statements associated with each of the challenges and value dimensions.

The impact of views of human nature can be seen in how organizations treat their employees. Many organizations provide their employees with some degree of autonomy and invest in training and development to help them learn and grow while still monitoring them. On the one hand, if a manager believes that people are inherently evil and cannot change, she is likely to monitor employees closely and invest little in training and development focusing instead on hiring people she can trust. On the other hand, a manager who believes that people are good and can change is more likely to be trusting and help employees grow and develop. Although these two extremes may be rare, cultures around the world answer these questions in different ways.

The belief that people can change based on a relatively neutral view of human nature also characterizes the United States. The history and diversity of the United States offers a mixed picture of how human nature is perceived. On the one hand, individuals and corporations invest considerable resources in education and training programs that they trust will improve their capabilities and effectiveness. By one estimate provided by the Training Industry Report (2017, 2018), US companies spent over $90 billion on training and development programs in 2017 and over $87 billion in 2018. Another study estimates that employees spend approximately 50 hours a year in training in 2018 (Hours of Training, 2019). Undoubtedly these numbers indicate that businesses believe that people can change. On the other hand, the strong Puritan influence with a negative view of humans shaped the founding fathers' goals of controlling and remedying people's darker motives through institutional checks and balances. The cultural diversity brought on by immigration further introduces different views of human nature in the United States.

4.4 Challenge 2: How Do We Relate to Time?

How do you view time? Are you focused on the past, the present, or the future? Do you make long-term plans or live in the moment? Do you value tradition and look to the past for guidance or concentrate on the future benefits of your decisions? While the answers to these questions may be driven by personality differences, they are also a reflection of your culture (see Table 7.4 for examples). Some cultures are more short-term-oriented while others take a longer-term view; some value the past while others look to the future (Kluckhohn & Strodtbeck, 1961). The relationship to time is reflected in how managers and organizations plan and how they measure performance and the factors that drive vision, mission, and goals.

		Example of Statements
		People will generally try to do their best. People want to contribute to the best of their ability.
	Mixed	People can be both good and bad and can change depending on the situation. They need both opportunity and some monitoring.
	Evil-Bad	We should be suspicious of others. People will take advantage of others if they get a chance, so they should be watched closely.
Relationship to Time	Past	It is important to maintain and respect traditions. The past is an excellent guide to the future. We can find answers by looking at past performance of our organization.
	Present	We need to pay attention to the here and now.
	Future	We should save for the future. The best way to judge an action is to look at its future impact. We need to think how our organization is impacting the future.
Relationship to the environment	Mastery	We should take advantage of all of the resources available to us. We can shape nature to serve our needs.
	Harmony	All things in nature deserve care. We should respect nature and balance our needs with it. Our organization should try to be fully sustainable.
	Submission	People can't really change nature. It is best to let problems solve themselves. We should let things run their course.
Relationship to others	Hierarchy	People should listen to those in higher levels and with more status and power.
	Group	People should sacrifice their own goals for the good of the group. Conforming to the group is important. Teamwork is the best way to perform.
	Individual	People should think first of themselves. People should be encouraged to show their uniqueness. We should encourage individual competition.

(Continued)

Table 7.4   Examples of Statement for Each Value Dimension (Continued)

Value Dimensions		Example of Statements
Motivation and activity mode	Being	We should take time to enjoy life. Life is too short to focus only on work.
	Striving	We should try to improve. Organizations must help people reach their potential.
	Doing	Actions speak louder than words. Accomplishments are the best measure of a person.
Relationship to physical space	Private	A man's home is his castle. Those who have more power deserve more privacy and resources.
	Mixed	We should balance public and private resources.
	Public	Natural resources belong to everyone. We should all have access to what we need.

Sources: Based on Kluckhohn and Strodtbeck (1961) and Maznevski, DiStefano, Gomez, Noorderhaven, and Wu (2002).

4.4.1 Consequences for Management and Organizations. Consider the diffference between the United States, which is more short-term-oriented and focused on the future, and China or Japan, countries that both have a longer-term orientation and value past traditions. US companies pay considerable attention to quarterly, and in some cases daily, measures of performance and do not look to the past to determine their future. They also do not commit to their employees for the long term, and employees do not expect to stay with a firm more than a few years. HR practices are geared toward short-term performance. For example, probation periods for new employees rarely extend beyond 3 months.

In long-term-oriented cultures such as Japan, and even in Europe, probationary periods can extend to 12 months (for example, in Belgium and Ireland) with 6 months being the norm (Employment, 2020). Similarly, how much notice employers and employees give before firing or leaving a job are much longer than in the United States, with many countries using a sliding scale that may require employers to give an extended period of notice for more long-term employees. Japan offers a drastic example of such long-term orientation where companies hire college graduates with expectations that they will stay until retirement (Krook, n.d.). Employees, at least male employees, have similar expectations. Although economic conditions have somewhat tempered these practices, the sense of long-term loyalty is still highly valued in Japan.

Another example of this long-term orientation is the span of strategic planning. In the United States, a long-term plan typically addresses a 3- to 5-year window. Masayoshi Son, founder and CEO of Japanese holding company SoftBank, recently told a group of reporters that his vision for the company spanned 300 years (Bajarin, 2019). Likewise, China's government and businesses have been developing long-term global plans and initiatives for infrastructure and high-tech projects such as the Belt and Road Initiative that will impact 62% of the world's population for the next decades or longer (China Power Project, 2019).

4.5 Challenge 3: How Do We Relate to Our Natural Environment?

Do you believe you can master or at least impact nature and the physical environment or are you at their mercy? Can you manage them and live in harmony and peaceful coexistence? Human beings have tried to change and manage their physical environments to different degrees, but how that is done and what their goals and ideals are differ. For example, native cultures in the United States and Canada value living in harmony with nature. The environmental writer William MacLeish (1995) notes that although the Iroquois were skilled hunters, they also respected their prey and avoided overhunting. A report by the National Institutes of Health further points to Native American healing systems where the ideal state is living in health through harmony with the environment (Koithan & Farrell, 2010).

The ancient Chinese practice of *feng shui* is based on a similar value of harmonizing individuals with their environment to take advantage of natural energy forces. The Japanese aim for harmony in social life and try to appreciate and coexist with nature in all its forms. The concept of *ikigai* refers to creating balance between what you love, what you are good at, and what the world needs (Mitsuhashi, 2017). The ideal of harmony does not necessarily mean that these cultural groups manage the environment better than other groups, rather valuing harmony is how things should be, an ideal and a goal.

4.5.1 Consequences for Management and Organizations. Living in harmony with the physical environment is contrasted with a mastery or domination approach where people believe that they can and should actively change the environment to fit their goals and needs. The US and Brazil's active exploitation of their natural resources are examples of this approach as are major dam projects such as the Three Gorges dam in China, the Bhakra in India, the Aswan dam in Egypt, or the Kariba in South Africa. Christian beliefs of having dominion over the earth and animals (Genesis 1:26) are a further representation of a mastery approach. At the other end of the continuum is the view that humans are controlled by nature and they can neither master nor manage it; all they can do is submit to their environment. Subsistence farming represents submission where farmers hope or pray for rain rather than actively manage their crops through irrigation.

People's relationship with their environment plays a role in how they run organizations. The view that nature can be mastered is partially reflected in a highly proactive and entrepreneurial approach. From early in its history, people in the United States (excluding members of the native cultures) have actively changed the environment to fit their goals and needs, in some cases leading to high productivity and progress, in others leading to environmental damage. The example of China provides an interesting case that shows both a traditional desire for harmony and a more recent and modern mastery approach.

4.6 Challenge 4: How Do We Relate to One Another?

Are individuals or groups more important? Do we consider all people within our family, clan, or society to be more or less equal or is there some hierarchy among them? These options relate to how we view ourselves in society and are core to social interactions (see examples in Table 7.4). As you will see in many other examples in the rest of the book, our relationship to others is one of the key cultural values that differentiates among cultures.

The value orientation related to relationships with others has been discussed in a number of disciplines going back several centuries. Confucius addressed the importance of both the common good, duty, and social order, as well as personal development and direct honesty. Greek philosophers debated the duality of individualism-collectivism with sophists leaning to the individualistic approach, and Plato and Socrates advocating for the common good. Eighteenth-century French philosopher Jean Jacques Rousseau similarly was a proponent of the general will, while John Locke supported a more individualistic view, which came to be associated with the American Revolution with the writings of de Tocqueville (2000).

4.6.1 Individuals and Groups. The differences between Japanese and American baseball provide a striking example of different values related to individuals and groups. The sport is highly popular in both countries, and the basic rules are fundamentally the same. However, there are telling differences that illustrate the divergent cultural values in the two countries. Japanese baseball players are not represented by agents and rarely change teams; as is the case with all employment in Japan. Players stay with the same organization throughout their careers, and the stars do not demand or command outlandish salaries. The loyalty goes both ways as teams rarely trade the players they carefully groom throughout their career (Bagarino, 2018). Players live together in dormitories during the season with highly regulated group activities and practice schedules. Such practices would be unimaginable to US baseball players, many of whom earn astronomical salaries and pride themselves on standing out from their team. Fans behavior is also drastically different. US fans relish in booing calls and taunting and heckling the other side, practices that some would consider part of the fun of the game. In Japan, seating in the stadium is segregated by team so that each team's supporters and fans sit together in the same area to cheer for their team with highly organized chants and songs. There is, however, no jeering of the other team, something that is common in American baseball. The thought of not declaring a winner would be unthinkable to American fans; however, in Japan, tied games are declared a draw after 12-innings in regular and 15-innings in postseason matches (Bagarino, 2018). It is common to see Japanese referees huddle and deliberate before rendering a decision, rather than the absolute power granted to the American umpire. The power and preeminence of the collective is clearly reflected in how the Japanese play this quintessential American sport.

In individualistic cultures such as the United States, Australia, and many Western European countries, people draw their identity from their own accomplishments and consider the individual to be relatively more important than the collective. In collectivistic cultures, such as all Asian, Middle Eastern, many African, and many Central and South American countries, people draw their identity from their group, and the collective's needs and goals supersede that of any individual.

4.6.2 Consequences for Management and Organizations. In individualistic cultures, organizations hire and reward employees based on their performance, encourage competition among them, and see conflict as productive. In collectivistic cultures, relationships and group membership play a more significant role in hiring decisions, and rewards are more often based on team or organizational performance. Additionally, cooperation and harmony are expected and valued. Whether the culture is individualistic or collectivistic, people may have either a hierarchical or an egalitarian view of groups and society. In more egalitarian cultures, such as Nordic countries, there is less of a formal and rigid hierarchy, whereas in India or Mexico, those with power are afforded more latitude and authority than other group members.

Considering that it has been central to many philosophical debates and the subject of social science research, the individual–collective dimension is clearly an important dimension for understanding human behavior. Accordingly, it is central to all models of national culture and we will further discuss it in detail in the next chapter.

4.7 Challenge 5: What Is Our Primary Motivation?

"Americans live to work; Europeans work to live" is commonly heard when comparing the two cultural groups. Europeans perceive US-Americans as being obsessed with achievement and work while they characterize themselves as having a more balanced approach to work and life, as, for example, represented by the Italian concept of the *dolce vita* (a life based on indulgence, luxury, and enjoyment).

4.7.1 Consequences for Management and Organizations. The case at the end of Chapter 1 puts the differences in what motivates people in focus. The many anecdotes and statistics that show US workers not taking vacations, by some estimates foregoing millions of days, and Europeans organizing their life around their much longer vacations, point to the differences between *being* and *doing* (Harrington, 2019). Public and organizational policies regarding the number of vacation days in the United States where there are no policies or regulations, and many European countries, where 20 to 30 paid days is typical and mandated, further reinforce these views (Guzman, 2018). In *being* cultures, people focus on what feels right in the moment; in *doing* cultures, the focus is on achievement and external measures of success; *striving* cultures emphasize growth. As is the case with all the dimensions we have discussed, few people and cultures represent the extremes and countries fall on a continuum such that the United States may be closer to *doing* end than Europeans, but Northern Europeans are still in the *doing* group when compared to other countries such as Egypt or Italy. Each type is reflected in how people work and live and how organizations and managers set goals and measure success and effectiveness.

Doing cultures seek measurable and objective goals and standards by which they can evaluate their work and life. Their organizations focus on pay, promotion, and bonuses to engage employees and measure success. *Being* cultures are more "in the moment" with an emphasis on letting things happen in due time and less push to perform and achieve specific measurable outcomes. The United States and many Europeans are once again grouped together in the *doing* group, as are Koreans and the Japanese. Many African, Middle Eastern, and Central and South American countries fall on the *being* side of the spectrum. Leisurely lunches and dinners to get to know your colleagues and business partners, shorter work hours, taking time off to be with family members, less planning, and overall less focus on work are all part of the *being* cultures.

4.8 Challenge 6: How Do We Relate to Physical Space?

The last dimension of the K&S framework relates to how people view physical space and includes notions of ownership and private property. Do individuals or groups own objects and space? How public or private is your office, the work room, your yard, etc...? Are people allowed to walk into each other's "space"? These questions all relate to how we perceive and use space. For someone from a private property–oriented culture such as the United States these questions may seem unsettling. In the United States, people have private homes and offices; they own objects and land. Conversely, many indigenous cultures, although they have many diverse cultures and values, do not see the value in private ownership of land. As one member of the Tsq'escenemc people of the Northwestern North American continent states: "For indigenous people, land and water are regarded as sacred, living relatives, ancestors, places of origin or any combination of the above" rather than property (NoiseCat, 2017). The ongoing protests by the Standing Rock community over the Dakota Access Pipeline in the United States are not just an environmental movement with concerns over pollution, they represent cultural traditions that consider the river and the landscape as sacred components of the universe, rather than private property to be exploited (Campbell, 2017).

4.8.1 Consequences for Management and Organizations. The private–public dimension does not fall as neatly into an "East–West" divide as do several of the other dimensions. Asian, Middle Eastern, and European countries all have clearly delineated private and public spaces and private property. However, the use of space may be more mixed in some cultures than others. For example, private offices are more common in North America, Europe, and the Middle East and less so in Japan where they are rare even for executives, and desks are simply all placed in a common room with no walls or cubicles. Many other office practices in Japan indicate the mixed use of space, ranging from taking naps in public during the lunch break, to regular reshuffling of employees from one office to another (called *jinji ido*), to communal greetings, exercises, and speeches (Wilson, 2016). These practices further have deep roots in the collectivistic values of Japanese culture where the collective takes priority over the individual.

4.9 Profiles and Patterns Rather Than Single Values

We have been presenting each of the value dimensions separately to help you grasp their content and meaning. However, they are not intended to be applied separately. Some cultures are similar on some of the dimensions but not others. The possible patterns and visual profiles of three countries are presented in Figure 7.3 to illustrate this point. As presented in Figure 7.3, each culture is classified in one category or another, which are assumed to be independent (Kluckhohn & Strodtbeck, 1961). For example, the US and Japanese cultures are classified as *doing* rather than *being*, but they differ on

Figure 7.3 Comparing Cultures Using the K&S Model

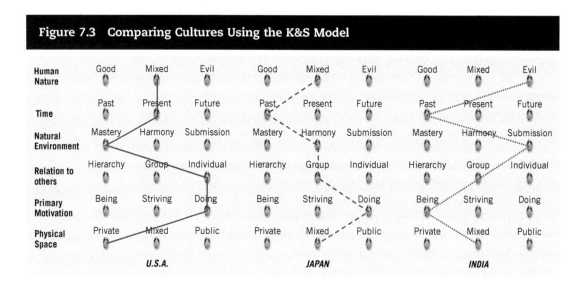

most other value dimensions. Clearly, the two cultures are more dissimilar than similar, pointing to the importance of looking at cultural profiles and patterns formed by a combination of the values rather than one or a few of the dimensions.

Therefore, in order to understand, describe, and predict people's behavior, applying the K&S framework requires looking for profiles that combine the various values to get a holistic view, rather than using a single value. Just knowing that a culture values private property, or is past-oriented, or hierarchical, or focuses on *doing* does not provide a complete picture.

5. CRITIQUES AND CONTRIBUTIONS

LO 7.5 Evaluate the strengths and weaknesses of the frameworks and their application to management

The frameworks we presented in this chapter provide managers with knowledge to better understand, describe, and predict cultural differences. They are intended for application to national and broad regional cultures. Both models were developed by cultural anthropologists relying on interviews and observations with limited groups. Several other studies have further refined and operationalized the dimensions and supported some of the country classifications (e.g., Maznevski et al., 2002) and linked the values to work behaviors (DiStefano & Maznevski, 2000). However, neither has benefitted from extensive research (for reviews see Cardon, 2008; Hart, 1999; Hills, 2002). Nonetheless, both constitute some of the earliest knowledge of cultural differences that has been applied to management and organizations and have been highly influential in a variety of ways, although not without critiques and shortcomings.

5.1 Critiques and Shortcomings

While useful as a beginning foray into understanding cultural differences, both models share some challenges. Specifically:

- Much of the research about the models has been done in anthropology using qualitative case studies that provide rich data, but where results are hard to generalize.

- Extensive testing has been lacking for both models, although anecdotal evidence is widely available (Kittler et al., 2011).

- Partly related to the lack of extensive research, the dimensions for both models are too broad and not clearly defined (for a review see Cardon, 2008) and inconsistently applied in different studies (Maznevski et al., 2002).

- There is a danger of overgeneralizing and essentializing based on narrow dimensions that inaccurately paint individuals and cultural groups with a broad brush culture (Chuang, 2003; see Chapter 1 for a detailed discussion).

- Using nationality as a proxy for culture without regard for the many diverse subcultures within a country is problematic (Craig & Douglas, 2006; Gerhart, 2008; Henderson, 2005).

In addition to these general shortcomings, each framework presents additional challenges.

5.1.1 Hall's Communication Context Framework. The HC–LC concept is too simplistic to address the depth and complexity of cultures. Two dimensions (LC–HC and P-time–M-time) cannot fully describe differences among cultures. Because the HC and LC groups include many different elements, for example individualism vs. group-orientation (which we discuss later in this chapter and in Chapter 8), as well as views of time, and formality of interactions, they lack clarity and predictive validity. For example, East Asian countries (e.g., China and Japan) are often cited for being very HC cultures, as are Middle Eastern and Africans countries. While they may share some characteristics that broadly make people in these countries more mindful of the context and reliant on internalized assumptions, they are also distinctly different on many other dimensions such as how they relate to power and their reliance on order and rules.

5.1.2 Kluckhohn and Strodtbeck's Value Orientation. In addition to the general critiques listed above, K&S's framework presents some unique challenges:

- The dimensions are too broad and not consistently defined.

- It is also not clear whether the various value dimensions are independent or on a continuum. For example, can a culture be hierarchal, collectivist, and individualistic at the same time, or does it fall in one or the other category?

- For some of the dimensions, there seems to be a mid-point (mixed in the case of human nature and relation to physical space); for others, each point appears to be a separate category.

These inconsistencies and overall lack of clarity regarding the value dimensions make it hard to consistently classify and compare cultures. Additionally, while some surveys have been developed to measure some of the dimensions, the measures are still based on interviews making them less practical for large-scale use, and creating challenges when generalizing across countries.

5.2 Contributions and Lasting Impact

In spite of these serious shortcomings, as the first models that provided a means to describe, classify, and categorize different cultures both frameworks have been applied widely in many settings.

5.2.1 Hall's Communication Context Framework. Hall's framework is the only one that specifically focuses on communication, an important and visible aspect of cross-cultural interaction. As a cultural framework, Hall provides a simple vocabulary and appealing short-hand to understand, describe, and predict behavior in different cultures. For that reason, it continues to be used when preparing people to work or travel across cultures. The HC–LC concept offers a good start for managers to think about how culture affects them and their employees. The relative simplicity of the framework, with only two key dimensions, has contributed to its popularity and use in cross-cultural training in many settings including business organizations. The HC–LC concept has further been applied to research about cross-cultural comparisons including recent studies looking at web design (Würtz, 2017), communication patterns in various countries (e.g., Zaharna, 1995), and how HC and LC affect uncertainty reduction and assumptions about strangers (Gudykunst, 2009) among other applications.

5.2.2 Kluckhohn and Strodtbeck's Value Orientation. K&S's framework's major contribution has been to provide us with a vocabulary to address basic cultural values. Their value orientation dimensions have become the basis for many of the other models such as Schwartz (1992), Hofstede (2002), and Trompenaars (Trompenaars & Hampden-Turner, 2012) and therefore have had a long-lasting impact on how we describe cultural differences. Particularly, the values related to time, how we relate to one another, and people's motivations (doing vs. being) have become essential elements of how cultures are described. Researchers have therefore built on these dimensions and value orientations to devise more complex models and frameworks for understanding culture.

5.3 Final Words

As is the case with any framework, overreliance on any concept as the only way to describe and understand cultures will inevitably lead to error. Cultures are complex and require a complex set of concepts to fully describe them. When used as a managerial tool, any single framework needs to be supplemented with additional models and frameworks that may provide finer details. Both models detailed in this chapter provide knowledge that helps us understand our CMC and that of others. This knowledge is a critical component in the KNOW part of the THINK–KNOW–DO roadmap. It provides a vocabulary to describe the cultural differences that you have learned to be aware of.

FIRST PERSON REVISITED

The executive in our *First Person* scenario is engaged with Saudi partners who have different cultural values than he does. Saudi Arabia is generally considered to be HC, collectivistic, long-term oriented, and a *being* culture. Knowing these Saudi prototypes can help manage negotiations and long-term relationships by adjusting expectations. Instead of pushing for quick decisions or suspecting that the slow process means lack of interest, the more judicious and effective approach that our executive adopts is to take time to develop relationships without assigning negative motives to his Saudi partners.

APPLYING WHAT YOU LEARNED: USING KNOWLEDGE OF THE COMMUNICATION CONTEXT

We have been working through the TKD roadmap and this chapter provides more specific knowledge that you can apply to become more effective in cross-cultural interactions. Hall's concept of HC–LC is an excellent starting point. As you read through the material about the concept, and complete the self-assessments take the following steps:

1. *Identify* what your cultural communication context is—do not simply rely on nationality.

2. *Reflect* on what impact your cultural context has had on how you communicate; think about specific instances of success and failure.

3. When you interact with other people, *do not assume* that they are either similar or different from you—take time to listen to what and how they are communicating.

4. *Describe, do not evaluate*—this may be your biggest challenge: Hold your judgment!

5. Given that the goal of any communication is accurate transmission and reception of a message, once you have a sense of how the person is using information, consider how you can *adjust your style* to be more effective.

6. Don't hesitate to ask questions to assure that you understand the other person and that they understand you.

7. Stay humble and keep your sense of humor.

MANAGERIAL CHALLENGE: SORRY, IT'S AUGUST...

You are part of a multicultural team made up of a German, a Dane, a Spaniard, a Chinese, a Kuwaiti, a Filipino, a Mexican, a Canadian, and a US-American. The team has worked well together, often remotely, and has been productive. Your manager, who is Canadian and located in Vancouver, has a project the team needs to complete. The deadline is tight, and she has made it clear that this is an important project. It is late July, and the team has just a couple of weeks to deliver the first part with the final product due in mid-September. As you come together to plan the project, there is strong disagreement among team members about how important and urgent this really is. The Europeans and the Kuwaiti are clearly not happy about the time frame. One says: "This is just impossible; it's August after all." Another chimes in: "This won't work; it is vacation time. It will simply have to wait." They all agree that the team can take this up in September and get it done then and maybe some team members who are around can get the project started, but they are adamant that it will have to wait. The Filipino, Chinese, and Mexican team members can't believe that that there is even a discussion; the boss wants this done; it will have to get done. The Canadian and American agree and focus on how doing well on this project can make everyone look great and may help everyone's year-end bonus. The team has never been this divided, and it appears that there is no solution.

1. What is driving everyone's behavior? Consider the cultural models you have read in this chapter.

2. What is the best course of action?

SELF-ASSESSMENT 7.1: COMMUNICATION STYLES

For each of the following statements, indicate whether it describes how you communicate to identify your style of communication.

Directness

I tend to say things as they are.	Yes	No
I prefer to address tough topics head on.	Yes	No
I believe that honesty is the best policy in every situation.	Yes	No

Indirectness

I am careful to communicate unpleasant information as softly as possible.	Yes	No
It is OK to not share all the information in some situations.	Yes	No
I feel uncomfortable with direct confrontation.	Yes	No

Linear

I like to follow a clear step-by-step process to explain things.	Yes	No
When I communicate, I rarely get off track.	Yes	No
There is no reason to add extra information when simple will do.	Yes	No

Circular

I like to embellish my communication with stories that may be off topic but are interesting.	Yes	No
I take my time to communicate my ideas.	Yes	No
I often jump from one topic to another when I communicate.	Yes	No

Abstract

I prefer using facts and data to make my point.	Yes	No
Just the facts—please.	Yes	No
I enjoy intellectual debates to explore all sides of issues.	Yes	No

(Continued)

Concrete

I prefer to use examples and stories to make my point.	Yes	No
I believe it is important to provide the context to any communication.	Yes	No
I like to provide specific detailed information.	Yes	No

Task

Getting things done is important to me.	Yes	No
I like to show the future outcome and result of ideas when I communicate.	Yes	No
I can separate logic and feelings.	Yes	No

People

I like to show how decisions impact people.	Yes	No
It is important to consider how people feel before making a decision.	Yes	No
Decisions are often more subjective than they seem.	Yes	No

Intellectual

I prefer to keep my voice steady and flat when I communicate.	Yes	No
Good ideas are the best way to persuade people.	Yes	No
I like to present my ideas in a logical way.	Yes	No

Emotional

I am very animated when I communicate.	Yes	No
Appealing to emotions is the way to persuade people.	Yes	No
I tend to be passionate when I try to persuade someone.	Yes	No

Scoring

Give yourself 1 point for every Yes answer. The highest for each category is 3 or −3.

- To calculate your Direct-Indirect score, subtract your total on Directness from your total on Indirectness. The higher your positive score, the more direct you are; the higher your negative score, the more indirect you are.

  (D:__3__) − (I: __0__) = __3__

- To calculate how Linear-Circular you are, subtract your total on Linear from your total on Circular. The higher your positive score, the more linear you are; the higher your negative score, the more circular you are.

  (L:__3__) − (C: __2__) = __1__

- To calculate how Abstract-Concrete you are, subtract your total on Abstract from your total on Concrete. The higher your positive score, the more abstract you are; the higher your negative score, the more concrete you are.

  (A:__2__) − (C: __3__) = __−1__

- To calculate how Task-People you are, subtract your total on Task from your total on People. The higher your positive score, the more task-focused you are; the higher your negative score, the more people-focused you are.

  (T:__2__) − (P: __3__) = __−1__

- To calculate how Intellectual-Emotional you are, subtract your total on Intellectual from your total on Emotional. The higher your positive score, the more intellectual you are; the higher your negative score the more emotional you are.

  (I:__2__) − (E: __3__) = __−1__

Review

Consider each element of your communication style.

1. To what extent do you think your style is related to your cultural identity? (consider various cultures that you may be part of)

2. When is the style most effective for you?

3. When has it not been effective?

SELF-ASSESSMENT 7.2: VALUE ORIENTATIONS

Consider each of the questions below. There are three possible answers to each; please consider each and circle the one that you most agree with or best fits you. There is no right or wrong answer.

1. When we make decisions in a group, it is best

    a to have everyone participate and discuss until there is a consensus

    b to leave the decision to those who have the most power and authority

    c to vote and let the majority decide

2. To stay healthy

    a I rely on modern medicine and medical professionals

    b I live properly to prevent getting sick

    c I do what I want since there is not much I can do about getting sick

3. When it comes to ethical and legal activities, most people are likely to

    a do something wrong if they think they can get away with it

    b change what they do based on circumstances

    c try to do the right thing no matter what

4. I believe our society should spend resources to

    a assure a better life for the next generation

    b take care of the problems we have now

    c maintain what we have and preserve the past

5. It is most important for society to

    a assure that private property is respected and maintained

    b balance the right of individuals with those of society as a whole

    c focus on the common good first

6. When it comes to work and success it is important

    a to be able to show your success with objective and tangible measures and indicators

    b to learn and grow

    c to put things in perspective and create a balance

Scoring

Each of the questions above addresses one of the Kluckhohn and Strodtbecks value orientation options. By reviewing your answers using the information below, you can assess your value orientation.

Question 1: Relationship to Others

When we make decisions in a group, it is best:

To have everyone participate and discuss until there is a consensus	➡	Group orientation—the group is more important than individuals; to achieve consensus is important
To leave the decision to those who have the most power and authority	➡	Hierarchy orientation—it is ok for people with power to have more privileges and to make more of the decisions
To vote and let the majority decide	➡	Individual orientation—the focus should be on the individual and their rights

Question 2: Relationship to Natural Environment

To stay healthy:

I rely on modern medicine and medical professionals	➡	Mastery—nature and its resources should be harnessed and used to improve life
I live properly to prevent getting sick	➡	Harmony—nature can be managed and balance can be achieved
I do what I want since there is not much I can do about getting sick	➡	Submission—there is not much we can do to change or manage natural events

Question 3: Human Nature

When it comes to ethical and legal activities, most people are likely to:

Do something wrong if they think they can get away with it	⟶	Evil—human beings are naturally bad unless they are controlled
Change what they do based on circumstances	⟶	Mixed—human beings are both good and bad and respond to the context
Try to do the right thing no matter what	⟶	Good—human beings are naturally good

Question 4: Time Orientation

I believe our society should spend resources to:

Assure a better life for the next generation	⟶	Future—we need to look at the future for results
Take care of the problems we have now	⟶	Present—the here and now is what counts
Maintain what we have and preserve the past	⟶	Past—traditions and history are most important

Question 5: Relation to Physical Space

It is most important for society to:

Assure that private property is respected and maintained	⟶	Private—private ownership of resources is appropriate
Balance the right of individuals with those of society as a whole	⟶	Mixed—there needs to be a balance between private and public ownership
Focus on the common good first	⟶	Public—resources should be available for everyone to use

Question 6: Primary Motivation

When it comes to work and success it is important:

To be able to assess your success with objective and tangible measures and indicators	➡	Doing—activity and objective results are what matters
To learn and grow	➡	Striving—development and continuous improvement is the key
To put things in perspective and look at the long-term big picture	➡	Being—work and material achievement are not the only things that matter

Questions

1. Is your assessment consistent with how you view yourself and the world? If not, what areas do not fit well?

2. What are some other personal examples of each value orientation?

Sources: Based on information in Kluckhohn and Strodtbeck (1961) and Hills (2002).

EXERCISE 7.1: SOFTWARE JOINT VENTURE NEGOTIATION

Objective: This exercise helps you apply your knowledge of cultural differences.

Instructions: Your instructor will assign you to one of two groups; read instruction for your group only.

You will be talking to another person and role-playing the following negotiation:

Situation

> You are representing two small software companies that have developed new phone apps that are highly complementary and if combined could be much more successful. You are hoping to work with them on a joint venture to get a combined product out to market before a competitor does. Both companies would very much like to come to an agreement to launch the joint venture. This is your first meeting.

Instructions

In preparing for your role-play, you can decide whether you are the owner or a manager. You can use your own name and make up any of the other information you would like. For example, you can come up with a company name, how long you have been in operation, whether you are the owner, developer, sales and marketing manager, etc.

Start the discussion by introducing yourself and explaining to the other person any information you have made up about your company.

Your role-play should take 5–10 minutes.

After completing the negotiation

First, individually, consider the following questions when you have completed your role-play.

1. How comfortable were you within your role?

2. What are the factors that made you either comfortable or uncomfortable?

3. To what extent does your behavior and level of comfort relate to your CMC?

4. What was most evident about the other person's behavior and style?

5. How effective do you think you were? What contributed to your level of effectiveness?

6. How effective was your partner?

7. What could you have done differently?

Review and compare your experience with your negotiating partners.

Instructions for each group

Please read only the information for the group to which you are assigned.

If you are in the LC group:

- Jump right into the topic.

- Rely on your verbal message; use your words clearly.

- Do not show emotion; stay neutral.

- Avoid using too many nonverbals.

- Refer back to previous agreements and contracts.

- Cut the other person off when they meander and go off topic.

- Challenge the other person when you think they are wrong.

- Stay focused on the task.

- Answer specific questions.

- Push for a quick agreement.

- Time is short and you are in hurry to get this done. There is a risk that a competitor could get to market before you; yet, you are confident that your product is better and taking time to work things out is risky.

If you are in the HC group:

- Take your time and ask social questions for as long as you can at the beginning and throughout.

- Actively use nonverbals (body language, tone of voice, eye contact).

- Stay silent for extended periods of time while looking like you are thinking.

- Use head nods and other signs of agreement; but do not verbally agree; just show that you are listening.

- Go off topic with stories that are tangential, but not directly related.

- Gently ignore the other person's confrontations; smile, shake your head, divert.

- Don't answer direct questions–divert.

- Don't ask specific questions—stay general.

- Stay focused on the big picture.

- Delay final agreement.

- Although time is short and there is a risk that a competitor could get to market before you, you are confident that your product is better and taking time to work things out is worth the risk.

EXERCISE 7.2: IDEAL VALUE ORIENTATION

Objective: *This exercise helps you apply your knowledge of cultural differences.*

Instructions:

Group Work

After completing Self-Assessment 7.2, form groups of 4 to 5 and discuss the following:

1. Share your results and examples of cultural values orientation.

2. Discuss how different value orientations may lead to differences in regards to

   a. How you manage people

   b. Organizational processes (e.g., planning, HR, supervision).

3. Based on your group discussion, develop your group's "ideal" cultural values orientation using each of the dimensions.

Presentation

Prepare a 5-minute presentation that outlines your group's ideal culture and its impact on management and organizational processes.

CASE STUDY: WALMART IN GERMANY

The research and first draft of this case were conducted by Tuba Pagda

Walmart is the largest retail company and largest private employer in the world with 2.2 million employees and $500 billion revenue in 2019. Founded by Sam Walton in 1962 with a single store in Bentonville, Arkansas, with the simple idea of selling more for less, the company now operates a chain of 11,200 stores, clubs, hypermarkets, discount department stores, and grocery stores in 27 countries and eCommerce websites in 10 countries (Walmart, 2019).

In 1997, as part of its international expansion strategy, Walmart acquired German retailer Wertkauf GmbH with its 21 hypermarket outlets, followed a year later by acquiring 74 hypermarkets from Germany's Spar Handels AG (Beck, 1998). Entering Germany, the largest and the most affluent market in Europe, was Walmart's first foray into Europe. The potential for creating efficiencies in the stodgier German operations through modernization and implementing Walmart's legendary efficient processes seemed endless.

Two years later, the acquisitions had not lived up to expectations with estimated losses of $120 million (129.5 million in euros) in 1999 (Boston & Zimmerman, 2000). Yet, Walmart persisted with a new 5-year plan. All of the market savvy and complex processes of the world's biggest retailer did not prevail and finally, in 2006 Walmart admitted defeat and sold the shares of its German operations to rival retailer Metro AG (Zimmerman & Nelson, 2006).

The retailer's success formula at home—low prices, successfully managed inventory control, and a large body of merchandise, along with its marketing techniques and HR and customer interface, which Walmart exported wholesale to Germany simply did not work with the realities of the German market (Landler & Barbaro, 2006).

The apparently idle employees standing at the door irritated German shoppers (Shurrab, 2014). The smiling cashier and cheerful Walmart greeter who were asked to chitchat with total strangers were viewed with distrust and suspected of flirting with customers (Landler & Barbaro, 2006; Pearson, 2018). The group activities, stretching exercises, and chants of "Walmart!" while in formation at the start of every day annoyed the employees (Christopherson, 2007; Macaray, 2011). The Walmart code of ethics that includes a "no dating" policy and a telephone hotline for employees to inform their employers if the rules are broken and report any misconduct were flagged by the powerful German union and ruled illegal by German courts (Macaray, 2011; Pearson, 2018; Schaefer, 2006). It did not help that the American CEO in Germany did not speak a word of German (Shurrab, 2014) and that English was the official corporate language for managers, especially when many of the older experienced managers from the acquired German retailers did not speak English (Knorr & Arndt, 2003). Walmart eventually gave up on many of its practices including requiring sales clerks to smile. Hans-Martin Psochmann, a manager with the Verdi union that represents Walmart employees, said: "People found these things strange; Germans just don't behave that way" (Landler & Barbaro, 2006).

In addition to disagreement regarding human resource policies, Walmart's business model went against traditional Germans' shopping habits of daily visits to local specialty stores that offer personalized service. The German habit of "Basket splitting," which involves shopping in different stores based on price further kept customers out (Landler & Barbaro, 2006), not to mention the lack of attention to European sizes for items such as bedding which left Walmart with a high inventory of pillowcases that did not fit German pillows (Schaefer, 2006).

In spite of its low-price reputation, Walmart faced stiff competition from German hard discounters such as Aldi and Netto with wide access to the German market and ability to sell their own top quality and well-established brands at low prices (Landler & Barbaro, 2006; Zimmerman & Nelson, 2006). The week Walmart opened its store in Berlin, a loaf of bread was priced $1.13, whereas the Aldi across the street was selling the same loaf of bread at $0.34. The well-practiced "Everyday low prices" Walmart tag line was clearly not ringing true in the German market (Christopherson, 2007).

A decade later, Walmart not only did not succeed in Germany, it also gave up on Japan and Korea, sold its controlling interest in the UK Asda grocery chain, and looked to leave Brazil as well (Shoulberg, 2018). Some have blamed the failure on Walmart's hubris. Beth Keck, an international spokesperson for Walmart, admits that it has been a good lesson on how not to manage global expansions: "Germany was an example of that naïveté. We literally bought the two chains and said 'Hey, we are in Germany, isn't it great?'" (Landler & Barbaro, 2006). The company is not alone in its inability to expand in the global arena. Home Depot and Best Buy have failed in China. Target tried and failed in Canada. Although American retailers are not alone in their struggle to globalize—Tesco and Marks & Spencer, both UK brands, have done poorly outside of Europe, Walmart's experience is telling. While the rest of the world may be attracted to the image of the United States, as one commentator suggested, there just may not be a good fit between the supersized US lifestyle and how the rest of the world lives (Shoulberg, 2018). Nonetheless, Walmart has also had successes in the international marketplace specifically by partnering with local retailers, often keeping the name of those companies. It has also had success in Central and South America, where it paid particular attention to local tastes and shopping styles.

Questions

1. Using the two models discussed in this chapter, identify the differences between US and Germany's culture.

2. What are the primary reasons for Walmart's failure?

3. To what extent are the causes cultural?

4. Why do you think retail, particularly groceries, may be a hard industry when it comes to global expansion?

5. Apply the TKD roadmap to the case and consider

   a. What areas of the TKD did Walmart lack?

   b. What aspects of having a CM could have helped the company?

Sources

Beck, E. (1998). Wal-Mart stores acquires 74 German hypermarkets. *The Wall Street Journal*, December 10. Retrieved from https://www.wsj.com/articles/SB913209813 116475000. Accessed on September 19, 2019.

Boston, W., & Zimmerman, A. (2000). Wal-Mart to continue expanding in Germany, adding 50 new stores. *The Wall Street Journal*, July 20. Retrieved from https://www.wsj.com/articles/SB964041717975999184. Accessed on September 19, 2019.

Christopherson, S. (2007). Barriers to 'US style' lean retailing: The case of Wal-Mart's failure in Germany. *Journal of Economic Geography*, 7(4), 451–469.

Knorr, A., & Arndt, A. (2003). Why did Wal-Mart fail in Germany? *IWIM*. Retrieved from https://thetimchannel.files.wordpress.com/2012/11/w024.pdf. Accessed on September 19, 2019.

Landler, M., & Barbaro, M. (2006). Wal-Mart finds that its formula doesn't fit every culture. *The New York Times*, August 2. Retrieved from https://www.nytimes.com/2006/08/02/business/worldbusiness/02walmart.html. Accessed on September 19, 2019.

Macaray, D. (2011). Why did Walmart leave Germany? *HuffPost*, August, 29. Retrieved from https://www.huffpost.com/entry/why-did-walmart-leave-ger_b_940542?guccounter=1&guce_referrer=aHR0cHM6Ly93d3cuZ29vZ2xlLmNvbS8&guce_referrer_sig=AQAAAH0J3naW9VkavNqT-TYgcUwOn3-R_wymiKCRZ1npvb0 TcA6QBY4MtVGZfqiK5T0umRaoepdlLVqvCO0btYTR_uLVM521fX-5C4Gyfu 0A1eyn8lUl4d3io_lULp1ICWXMTYy5W6wGyt4BpkbBe2JHCLTNyojJxgJVVm7-FpGMbs8. Accessed on September 19, 2019.

Pearson, B. (2018). German lessons: What Walmart could have learned from Lidl and vice versa. *Forbes*, February 5. Retrieved from https://www.forbes.com/sites/

bryanpearson/2018/02/05/german-lessons-what-walmart-could-have-learned-from-lidl-and-vice-versa/#736b7c45138c. Accessed on September 19, 2019.

Schaefer, L. (2006). World's biggest retailer Wal-Mart closes up shop in Germany. *Deutsche Welle*, June 27. Retrieved from https://www.dw.com/en/worlds-biggest-retailer-wal-mart-closes-up-shop-in-germany/a-2112746-0. Accessed on September 19, 2019.

Shoulberg, W. (2018). Lost in translation: Why Walmart and so many other U.S. retailers fail overseas. *Forbes*, May 4. Retrieved from https://www.forbes.com/sites/warrenshoulberg/2018/05/04/lost-in-translation-why-walmart-and-so-many-other-u-s-retailers-fail-when-they-go-overseas/#4af8fa7811ee. Accessed on September 19, 2019.

Shurrab, H. (2014). *Wal-Mart's German misadventure* (p. 6). Sweden: Mälalarden University.

Walmart. (2019). *Our Business*. Retrieved from https://corporate.walmart.com/our-story/our-business. Accessed on September 19, 2019.

Zimmerman, A., & Nelson, E. (2006). With profits elusive, Wal-Mart to exit Germany. *The Wall Street Journal*, July 29. Retrieved from https://www.wsj.com/articles/SB115407238850420246. Accessed on September 19, 2019.

CHAPTER EIGHT

CULTURAL DIMENSIONS IN MANAGEMENT AND LEADERSHIP

FIRST PERSON

Dig Deep Into My Cultural Roots

I am an Iraqi Christian who came to the United States as a child. I have built a successful business career and now work for a company that does a lot of business globally. Several members of my team are in India and we regularly do phone-video conferences. The time that works best for everyone is evening for me which is early morning for my Indian partners. Our first meetings were frustrating for everyone. Given the time, I was tired, done for the day, and ready to go back to my family, so I was eager to get down to business quickly. My Indian partners were just starting out. They were socializing, exchanging pleasantries, and avoiding any serious talks for a good part of our scheduled time, leaving me aggravated and even more tired. It was me against a group of four to five! I could feel my frustration grow and see that they were not happy either. Our exchanges were short and not productive at all. I had to find a solution. I dug deep into my own cultural roots. I thought about my interactions with the older members of my family, who, just like my Indian coworkers, took their time before discussing anything serious. I had to let go of my need to get things done quickly, control my fatigue at the end of the long work day, and let the socializing end naturally before we got down to business. So, I let them chat and joined in the conversation. I got to know them a whole lot better in the process; and, my strategy worked. We now have a happy medium and we do a little of both, socialize a bit and get to work, and we are quite effective. I know this is what I need to do to allow our team to be productive, but I still have to keep my frustration in check on occasion.

–Alen Glina

Learning Objectives

8.1 Detail Hofstede's cultural dimensions.

8.2 Explore the tight-loose dimension factors associated with individualism and collectivism.

8.3 Elaborate on the link between horizontal and vertical dimensions and individualism and collectivism.

8.4 Discuss Trompenaars's framework for understanding cross-cultural organizational differences.

8.5 Present GLOBE and its key findings.

8.6 Recognize the contributions and challenges associated with models of national culture.

8.7 Explore how to integrate knowledge of cultural frameworks to help managers be more effective across cultures.

In the *First Person* example, Alen Glina's multicultural background and identity allow him to recognize important cultural differences and draw on his CMC to adjust his behavior in order to be effective. Not all of us have multicultural backgrounds, and certainly none of us will always know what may be driving the behavior of those who come from different cultures. People are complex and diverse, and we cannot expect to know all the cultures that we may come in contact with; indeed, some suggest that we can never really understand other cultures. Even if we could understand other cultures, as presented in Chapter 1, with over 10,000 cultures in the world, there will always be a lot that we don't know.

However, what we can do is make a conscious choice to develop a CM to ensure that we consider culture when we make decisions. So, although we cannot know every culture, its assumptions, values, beliefs, and practices, if we are aware of the role culture can play, we can rely on research-based knowledge to guide our interpretations and our actions. In other words, we rely on the TKD roadmap. In Chapter 7, we introduced two models of national culture that provide knowledge regarding cultural differences. This chapter further focuses on the KNOW part of the TKD roadmap as we elaborate on frameworks that extend and enhance your knowledge and vocabulary of cultural differences specifically as they relate to organizational behavior and managerial applications. We start with Gert Hofstede's dimensions, followed by two concepts that refine the individualism and collectivism dimension, and then present a framework proposed by Fons Trompenaars, ending with the findings of the Global Leadership and Organizational Behavior Effectiveness (GLOBE) project. Together these models build on the knowledge you acquired in the previous chapter and provide a comprehensive and rich vocabulary to allow you to understand, describe, and predict cross-cultural differences. All three models rely on the concept of values and therefore extend the work of Kluckhohn and Strodtbeck.

1. HOFSTEDE'S DIMENSIONS

LO 8.1 Detail Hofstede's cultural dimensions

Around the world, companies that are aware of the importance of culture use their knowledge of essential cultural values to assure that their distinctive message reaches their target audience. McDonald's has a global reach and operates in over 100 countries. It appropriately not only changes its menu to fit local tastes but also presents a different web design in each country or region where it operates to assure that its marketing is effective. In Malaysia where power and hierarchy are important and respected, the company's web interface is clearly structured, hierarchical, and vertically scrollable with limited options and a prominent display of credentials and certificates regarding its restaurants' food (https://www.mcdonalds.com.my/; Klement, 2018).

In Sweden, where the culture is egalitarian, McDonald's website scrolls sideways and provides many opportunities for choices and feedback (https://www.mcdonalds.com/se/sv-se.html; Klement, 2018).

In other instances, web designers are mindful of culture and include individual-oriented pictures and graphics and use of pronouns such as "you" for countries such as the United States that are more individualistic. Conversely, in more collectivistic India, websites typically include many pictures of groups, whereas in the United Kingdom, where subtlety is valued, the designs are minimal and pricing less prominent (Tsai, 2016). Knowledge of cultural differences is indispensable for companies whose managers are aware of the role of culture to make appropriate decisions. One of the key sources of that knowledge are cultural frameworks models that, based on research, classify cultures using various dimensions.

1.1 Development of the Framework

One of the most well-known and most used frameworks for classifying cultural differences was developed by Dutch researcher Geert Hofstede. His framework, known as Hofstede's dimensions, is based on original research with IBM employees in 40 countries and was eventually extended to include over 110,000 surveys in 70 countries (Hofstede, 2002; Hofstede, Hofstede, & Minkow, 2010). Similar to Kluckhohn and Strodtbeck's Value Orientation, and in agreement with much research in social sciences, Hofstede considers values to be the core of culture (Hofstede et al., 2010).

Hofstede used the results of his surveys to develop basic cultural dimensions along which cultures differ: individualism-collectivism (IND-COL), power distance (PD), uncertainty avoidance (UA), and masculinity-femininity (M-F) (see Table 8.1 for a summary). In subsequent research, he added a dimension that addresses time and one that refers to the extent to which people in different cultures either seek and allow gratification of their needs or delay and curb them (Hofstede et al., 2010). We focus here on the most commonly used four dimensions and briefly discuss the additional ones separately.

1.2 Basic Four Cultural Dimensions

According to Hofstede, the variation in and combination of cultural dimensions lend each national culture its distinctiveness and unique character. Some of these dimensions should look familiar to you after reading Chapter 7. For example, the IND-COL and time orientation are revisited and expanded in Hofstede's approach. Additionally, the hierarchy value orientation is reinterpreted here as power distance (see Table 8.1 for a summary).

Table 8.1 Hofstede's Basic Cultural Dimensions

Dimension	Description
Individualism-collectivism	The extent to which individuals, or a closely knit social structure, such as the extended family, is the basis for social systems. Individualism leads to reliance on self and focus on individual achievement; collectivism leads to deriving one's identity from the group and looking after the collective.
Power distance	The extent to which people accept and expect unequal distribution of power. In higher power distance cultures, there is a wider gap between the powerful and the powerless.
Uncertainty avoidance	The extent to which people feel threatened by ambiguous situations. High uncertainty avoidance leads to low tolerance for uncertainty and an attempt to avoid ambiguity.
Masculinity-femininity	The extent to which assertiveness and independence from others is valued. Masculinity leads to high gender role differentiation, focus on independence, ambition, and material goods; femininity is focused on caring for others and quality of life.

Sources: Based on information in Hofstede (2002); Hofstede and Bond (1984); and Hofstede et al. (2010).

1.3 Individualism-Collectivism

According to Hofstede, the large majority of cultures around the world are collectivistic where people place the interests of the group ahead of the interests of individuals. There are therefore more collectivist cultures than individualistic cultures, although some recent research indicates economic development may be the driver behind increases in individualism in many countries (Santos, Varnum, & Grossman, 2017). Table 8.2 presents the ranking for several countries selected based on having the largest population, the largest area, and the highest GDP (see Table 1.1 in Chapter 1), along with the top and bottom ranked country in each dimension.

1.3.1 Collectivism. In collectivistic cultures such as Indonesia, Pakistan, Portugal, or Mexico, the group, whether it is the family, clan, or society, is the source of identity; "we" is more important than "I." In collectivistic cultures (Hofstede, 2002; Hofstede et al., 2010):

- The emphasize is on the needs and goals of the in-group over that of the individual (Triandis, 1995)

- High value is placed on obedience and respect of parents

- People are close to their in-group members with a strong sense of cohesion

Table 8.2 Sample of Countries Ranked for Individualism-Collectivism

Country	Ranking Among 76 Countries[a]
USA	1
Great Britain	3
Canada	4–6
Germany	19
India	33
Japan	35–37
Russia	39–40
Brazil	40–42
China	58–63
Indonesia	70–71
Pakistan	70–71
Guatemala	76

[a]A range indicates a tie among several countries. Countries ranked higher are more individualistic.
Source: Based on information in Hofstede et al. (2010)

- People are expected to take care of members of their group

- People have strong obligation toward members of their in-group

- Friendships tend to be based on family and group membership

- There is high conformity to in-group norms

- People spend a lot of time with family and in-group members

- Open disagreement and confrontation are considered rude and inappropriate

- Saving face is a major consideration

- Forgiveness is aimed at relationship harmony (Joo, Terzina, Cross, Yamaguchi, & Ohbuchi, 2019)

- People are more likely to rely on the situation as the cause of behavior and make external attributions (Triandis, 2004).

Additionally, collectivists tend to pay more attention to the context than the content of communication, meaning how a message is communicated, not what is communicated, making them more high context (Triandis, 2004).

1.3.2 Individualism. Conversely, in individualistic cultures such as the United States and Northern and Western European countries, people's identity is separate from others, and "I" takes precedence over "we" (Hofstede, 2002; Hofstede et al., 2010):

- Independence from others is not only valued, but considered a sign of maturity and mental health.

- Individuals are not responsible for or obligated to others.

- Friendships are not tied to family, but rather determined by other factors such as work or residence.

- Speaking one's mind is considered a virtue, and honesty takes precedence over protecting others' feelings. For example, some research shows that Canadians, who are individualists (IND) when compared to the Taiwanese, who are collectivistic (COL) are more likely to voice their disagreement in group contexts (Saad, Cleveland, & Ho, 2015).

- Forgiveness is aimed at self-enhancement (Joo et al., 2019).

- People are more likely to focus on the individual, rather than the situation, as the cause of behavior and make internal rather than external attributions (Triandis, 2004).

Hofstede further relates individualism with direct communication, which equates to Hall's low context. So, the German directness that we have discussed in previous chapters can be attributed to the strong value placed on individualism in that culture.

1.3.3 Managerial Implications. The implications for management and organizations are clear. People in individualistic cultures are mobile, value personal achievement and education as a means to advancement, and personnel decisions are expected to be based on individual performance, skills, and clear and objective criteria. In order to motivate and engage employees, managers in IND cultures must find a fit between the employees' personal needs and interests and the goals of the organization and provide personal incentives and bonuses (Hofstede et al., 2010). Self-actualization means reaching one's potential, and creativity is assumed to be based on individuals.

This individualistic approach is reflected in many US businesses. Specifically, US companies heavily invest in helping their employees and managers develop their creativity through workshops and training. For example, at Etsy, monthly meetings offer individual employees an opportunity to perform and shine (Abbott, 2018).

Other companies further focus on providing individual rewards to encourage creativity. Westin Hotels rewards individual employees with an all-expense-paid vacation if they suggest a good idea; others hold competitions and tournaments to encourage employees to come up with the best ideas (Craig, 2018). Some research suggests that individualistic values may enhance creativity (Goncalo & Staw, 2006), while a research comparing Canadians (who rank 4–6 on individualism) and Taiwanese (who rank 66) shows that although the former come up with more ideas, the quality of ideas from the Taiwanese is marginally better (Saad et al., 2015).

Organizations in collectivistic countries focus on capitalizing on relationships and group cohesion. Studies show that people from collectivistic cultures prioritize job security, equality in reward allocation, and dislike test-based hiring and merit-based hiring and promotions (Ramamoorthy & Carroll, 1998). Personnel decisions in COL cultures can be based on group membership and family connections, and a manager's relationship with employees parallels family structures with long-term loyalty and obligations from both sides. Rather than fitting a person to the organization, managers rely on group membership to create and maintain engagement with rewards based, at least to some great extent, on group or team performance. In COL cultures, self-actualization is achieved through the group rather than the individual.

As mentioned in Chapter 7, the IND-COL dimension is central to understanding differences in cultures and therefore has been used extensively in a number of fields and disciplines as a key concept to explore how individuals relate to groups and to society. We consider other aspects of IND-COL further later in this chapter.

1.4 Power Distance

Power distance (PD) refers to the extent a culture accepts and expects a hierarchy that creates inequality (Hofstede et al., 2010). In large PD cultures such as Malaysia, Russia, or Mexico, the difference between those with more and those with less power is greater than in small PD cultures (see Table 8.3 for country rankings).

1.4.1 Comparing High and Low Power Distance. In large PD cultures, "might makes right," inequality between people and dependence of those with less power on those with power is the norm. Children are expected to obey and respect their parents, and the youngest and oldest members of a family are treated with greatest care and warmth. In small PD cultures, such as Luxembourg, the Netherlands, or Costa Rica, power must be seen as legitimate and justified before people accept it, there is more equality between those with more and less power, and people are more independent from those who have power. Children are treated as equals as early as possible, and parents or elders do not get extensive preferential treatment.

1.4.2 Managerial Implications. When translated to management and organizations, small PD leads to looser and more dynamic hierarchies based on expertise and

Table 8.3 Sample of Countries Ranked for Power Distance (PD)

Country	Ranking Among 76 Countries[a]
Malaysia	1–2
Slovakia	1–2
Russia	6
China	12–14
Indonesia	15–16
India	17–18
Brazil	26
Pakistan	48
Japan	49–50
USA	59–61
Canada	62
Germany	65–67
Great Britain	65–67
Austria	76

[a]A range indicates a tie among several countries. Countries ranked higher have more PD.

Source: Based on information in Hofstede et al. (2010).

convenience so that consultation and participation are more common, and experience and expertise lend people power. In large PD cultures, organizational hierarchies are more formal, with centralized decision-making, less consultation, and many privileges accorded to those in higher positions.

Consider the case of the Austrian consultant, Matthias, who is meeting with a group of three Chinese managers to discuss providing their company with strategic planning and marketing services. He has extensive experience in international deals and considerable expertise in both strategic management and marketing. He is traveling to Shanghai with one assistant who is fluent in Mandarin. Matthias is armed with the title of senior manager of client development, and he has been in touch with the Chinese company for several months. During their first face-to-face meeting, after proper exchange of business cards, they chat pleasantly, and after what seems to be an appropriate length of time, Matthias presents his proposal, which is based on extensive research about China. He also provides a side-by-side comparison with several other consulting firms, two of which have worked with the Chinese company, showing the superiority of his company's services. The three managers, who are all young and educated in the United States and Europe and fluent in English, which ends up being the language spoken during the meeting, ask many questions and seem very enthusiastic about the Matthias proposal. The same group meets once more before Matthias and his assistant return to Vienna, with assurances from the Chinese managers that they will soon be in touch. A few weeks pass by without any contact. Matthias's assistant reaches out without getting a response; Matthias sends a couple of emails; no response. Matthias's boss, Johanna, the company's co-owner and senior vice president, decides to reach out to her counterpart in Shanghai, Mr. Wang. Within a few hours, she gets a very cordial response suggesting that they meet the following week when Wang is traveling to London. Johanna and Matthias meet Mr. Wang, who is accompanied by one of the managers Matthias had met. The manager is quiet during the whole meeting, and there is no mention of the earlier proposal at all. Johanna, who has sent the proposal to Mr. Wang through email, presents a few of the details to him and there appears to be good momentum for reaching an agreement.

Matthias's case shows the importance of titles and perceived authority in a large PD culture such as China. He did not have the right title to elicit a serious response and, as a result, was paired with managers who themselves had no power to make decisions. For the Chinese, an important decision must be made by people with power and cannot be left to lower level employees, no matter their expertise. For the small PD Austrians, the best expert has the right power; however, when working with a large PD culture, the deal cannot be completed until it comes from a person with a higher level of power and authority.

1.5 Uncertainty Avoidance

UA, or tolerance for ambiguity, refers to the degree to which people feel threatened or are uncomfortable in ambiguous or unknown situations (Hofstede et al., 2010). Change and unfamiliar situations create some level of stress for everyone. However, in high UA cultures, such as Greece, Uruguay, or Poland, where ambiguity is not well tolerated, the level of anxiety and discomfort when facing unfamiliar and unpredictable situations and events is higher than in low UA cultures, such as Singapore, Ireland, or Vietnam (see country rankings in Table 8.4).

1.5.1 Comparing High and Low Uncertainty Avoidance. In high UA cultures, a number of activities and policies aim to reduce or manage ambiguity. As a result, people in high UA cultures want to avoid uncertainty and implement extensive rules and planning aimed at codifying activities to reduce uncertainty and unpredictability. Generally, in these cultures, events and circumstances that are perceived as different

Table 8.4 Sample of Countries Ranked for Uncertainty Avoidance

Country	Ranking Among 76 Countries[a]
Greece	1
Russia	7
Japan	11–13
Brazil	31–32
Pakistan	35–38
Germany	43–44
Canada	62–62
Indonesia	62–63
USA	64
India	66
Great Britain	68–69
China	70–71
Singapore	76

[a]A range indicates a tie among several countries. Countries ranked higher are more uncertainty avoidant.

Source: Based on information in Hofstede et al. (2010).

are considered dangerous. By contrast, cultures that score low on UA tolerate more ambiguity, tend to be more lenient on rules, and may experience less anxiety and stress (Hofstede et al., 2010).

1.5.2 Managerial Implications. Regarding work-related behaviors, people from cultures that avoid uncertainty (high UA, such as Portugal, El Salvador, or Romania) stay longer with the same employer, seek and accept rules and regulations at work, and focus on tighter controls. Those from lower UA cultures (e.g., Hong Kong or New Zealand) have shorter tenure, as we see in the United States and many Western and Northern European countries. The long tenure and job stability in Japan are partly explained by the high UA, as is the practice of long-term planning (sometimes up to 100–200 years) that helps provide a sense of stability and predictability.

1.6 Masculinity-Femininity

Society is called masculine when emotional gender roles are clearly distinct: men are supposed to be assertive, tough and focused on material success, whereas women are supposed to be more modest, tender, and concerned with the quality of life. A society is called feminine when emotional gender roles overlap: both men and women are supposed to be modest, tender, and concerned with quality of life. (Hofstede et al., 2010, p. 140)

The gender reference in the name of this dimension has caused some confusion, and researchers have opted for focusing on the underlying concepts of the dimension, which are issues of competitiveness, cooperation, assertiveness, and quality of life (see Table 8.5 for country rankings).

Table 8.5 Sample of Countries Ranked for Masculinity-Femininity (M-F)	
Country	**Ranking Among 76 Countries[a]**
Slovakia	1
Japan	2
China	11–13
Germany	11–13
Great Britain	11–13
USA	19
India	28–29
Canada	33
Pakistan	34–36
Brazil	37
Indonesia	41–42
Russia	63
Sweden	76

[a]A range indicates a tie among several countries; higher ranking indicates more masculine culture.

Source: Based on information in Hofstede et al. (2010).

1.6.1 Comparing Masculinity and Femininity Cultures. In highly masculine cultures such as Slovakia, Austria, or Mexico (Hofstede et al., 2010),

- Earnings and achievements are important

- Gender roles are traditionally and clearly delineated with men being the breadwinner and more powerful

- The emphasis is on competition and toughness

- Men are expected to show little tenderness

- Aggression is more accepted, and

- Children's performance in school matters.

Conversely, in high femininity cultures (such as Sweden, Costa Rica, or Thailand; Hofstede et al., 2010),

- Relationships and the quality of life are important

- Gender roles are blurred, with men and women expected to contribute equally to income and family responsibilities

- Tenderness and caring are the expected norm for all genders, and

- Cooperation, enjoyment of life, and balance are encouraged.

The M-F dimension has some resemblance to Kluckhohn and Strodtbeck's *being-doing* value orientation, with M cultures' stronger focus on *doing*, accomplishments, and objective performance and F cultures' emphasis on *being* and balancing work and life.

1.6.2 Managerial Implications. The degree to which a culture is feminine or masculine is reflected in organizational and managerial processes with masculinity emphasizing decisiveness, win-lose, live to work, financial rewards, and a generally competitive workplace. Conversely, feminine cultures stress equal rewards, work–life balance, and consensus building. As the name of the dimension implies, cultures with a more feminine orientation present more gender egalitarian characteristics that translates into more women in positions of power and leadership. Some interesting research by Anne McDaniel (2008) shows that in more gender egalitarian cultures such as Sweden, men and women have equally strong attitudes toward egalitarianism, whereas in more masculine cultures such as Egypt or Pakistan, women more than men lean toward gender egalitarian attitudes.

The four dimensions presented above are the core of Hofstede's model. They are also the clearest and most used in both research and organizational settings.

1.7 Additional Dimensions

In further attempting to refine his framework, Hofstede and his colleagues developed two additional dimensions. The first one relates to time and has some resemblance to Kluckhohn and Strodtbeck's discussion of how people relate to time; the second one concerns whether people satisfy their needs (Hofstede et al., 2010).

1.7.1 Time Orientation. Hofstede and his colleagues (Hofstede & Bond, 1988) included the time dimension after research conducted in both English and Chinese (Hofstede, 2002). They first labeled the dimension Confucian Work Dynamism and later renamed it *long-term orientation (LTO)*. On the long-term end, this dimension is defined as "the fostering of virtues oriented toward future rewards—in particular, perseverance and thrift" (Hofstede et al., 2010, p. 239). Specifically, it refers to (Hofstede, 2002, p. 354):

- A dynamic and future-oriented approach

- Persistence

- Ordering relationships by status

- Thrift

- Having a sense of shame

The short-term orientation is defined as "the fostering of virtues related to the past and present—in particular respect for tradition, preservation of 'face', and fulfilling social obligation" (Hofstede et al., 2010). It is characterized by (Hofstede, 2002, p. 354):

- Relying on the past and on tradition

- Personal steadiness and stability

- Protecting your "face"

- Respect for tradition

- Reciprocation of greetings, favors, and gifts

As you read the definitions and consider country classifications, it is clear that, as compared to the other four dimensions, LTO is somewhat murky with various definitions that include a large number of elements that are not consistently connected. Accordingly, South Korea, China, and Japan are ranked in the top five among 93 countries in long-term orientation and are considered to value persistence and thrift with a sense of shame. Conversely, the United States, which ranks 69–71 with Iraq and

Mexico, is short-term-oriented with respect for tradition and protecting "face." While the short-term vs. long-term orientation of the dimension is clear, many of its other elements are not, making its application challenging.

1.7.2 Indulgence-Restraint. The newest addition to the Hofstede framework is the *indulgence-restraint* dimension. It focuses on whether (Hofstede et al., 2010)

- People satisfy their needs and prioritize enjoyment of life or

- They delay gratification through strict rules, and controls was introduced.

The dimension addresses broad issues such as happiness and subjective well-being and value placed on leisure, life control, enjoyment of life, and importance of having friends. Specifically, indulgence is defined as "a tendency to allow relatively free gratification of basic and natural human desires related to enjoying life and having fun" (Hofstede et al., 2010, p. 281). At the opposite end, restraint is "a conviction that such gratification needs to be curbed and regulated by strict social norms" (Hofstede, 2010, p. 281). Countries that rank high (out of 93 countries) on indulgence include Mexico, Nigeria, Sweden, and the United States. Among those that rank high on restraint are Pakistan, Egypt, Russia, China, and several Eastern European countries (Hofstede et al., 2010).

These two additional dimensions together seem to address a combination of the Kluckhohn and Strodtbeck time orientation and the doing-being orientation. The latter are considered to value leisure time, value the bottom line, have concern for the truth, be uncomfortable with conflict, and use analytical thinking with a dualistic orientation toward good and evil (Hofstede et al., 2010, p. 251). Conversely, the LTO cultures downplay leisure, are market-driven, value networks and common sense, and are comfortable with conflict. Many of the characteristics of the two dimensions seem to overlap. Their various elements do not provide much clarity, and the two dimensions appear to include many seemingly unrelated factors. Additionally, in the case of indulgence-restraint, little research is available regarding its managerial application; it therefore requires considerable clarification and development.

2. REFINING INDIVIDUALISM-COLLECTIVISM: TIGHT AND LOOSE CULTURES

LO 8.2 Explore the tight-loose dimensions factors associated with individualism and collectivism

As we have stated earlier, the individual-collective dimension of culture is one of the most powerful and significant value differences among cultures. Accordingly, it is widely considered fundamental to understanding and describing cultural differences. Because of its importance researchers have focused on refining and expanding that dimension by identifying factors that define and moderate how IND-COL manifests in individual and group behaviors across cultures.

Prominent cross-cultural psychologist Harry Triandis suggests that IND-COL is defined by many different attributes and that, when combined, lead to different types of individualist and collectivist cultures (Triandis, 1989, 1995; Triandis & Gelfand, 1998). The addition of other attributes to the IND-COL dimension is meant to complement and enrich the construct, not replace it. Furthermore, Triandis (1998, 2004) notes that in both IND and COL cultures, there are individuals who are *allocentric*, meaning they think and behave like people from collectivistic cultures, and people who are *idiocentric* and are more individualistic. In other words, there are US-Americans who are collectivistic and Japanese who are individualistic. What makes a culture more individualistic or collectivistic is the balance of the two groups within it; more allocentric people in COL cultures and more idiocentric people in IND cultures.

2.1 Unexplained Differences

The COVID-19 epidemic challenged almost all aspects of our lives. It also provided stark examples of cultural differences in how people and institutions react to the various challenges. As countries implemented rules and regulations to regulate social interactions, people's reactions were widely different. Some countries, such as South Korea, approached the crisis with discipline, strict restrictions on individual movement, and careful monitoring and tracking of people, actions that would make people in other countries, such as the United States, highly uncomfortable (Cha, 2020). Where some Americans panicked and hoarded groceries and toilet paper, and some even demonstrated against any social restriction, South Koreans appeared to have calmly followed instructions without any lockdowns (Kim & Kim, 2020). Similarly, Germany which had some of the lowest death rates in the world, particularly when compared to its Southern neighbor Italy that had some of the highest, approached the epidemic with strict early controls that were by-and-large accepted by its population (Bostock, 2020).

There will undoubtedly be considerable research about the effectiveness of the various country responses to COVID-19. However, many observers and social scientists have already considered the role of culture in these differences. Culture partially determined how each country and its population dealt with the pandemic. Specifically, it appears that some cultural groups follow rules more willingly than others. The dimensions that we have considered so far do not fully explain the difference. For example, Italy, Germany, and the United States are all individualistic cultures, yet responses were very different.

In other examples, even the casual traveler to Japan, Singapore, Israel, and Brazil, which are all collectivistic countries, can attest that there are noticeable differences among them. Most notably, in Japan and Singapore, people follow rules, norms, and standards closely and many aspects of their behaviors are regulated. For example, Singapore regulates the sale of gum, jaywalking, littering, not flushing toilets, not to mention more serious crimes such as vandalism and use of drugs. These laws which are aimed at protecting the group from unruly individuals and maintaining social order are consistently enforced with serious punishment for violators. Telling a Brazilian or an Israeli, who are also collectivistic, where they can cross the street and they will be punished if they do not flush a toilet is likely to trigger uproarious laughter and a few choice insults. In Israel and Brazil, there is much more tolerance, some would say an insistence, for violating rules, and behavioral norms are less enforced.

The Chinese practice of assigning social credit scores to citizens has the tag line "keeping trust is glorious and breaking trust is disgraceful" (Ma, 2018). This program, officially starting in 2020, gives people scores for being conforming citizens and publicly shames and punishes those with low scores. Those found to break the social trust, by, for example, having bad credit, spending too much time on video games or social media, or wasting money, face punishment such as bans on flying or taking trains, reduced access to high speed internet or the best jobs, having their children banned from attending good schools, or having their dog taken away (Ma, 2018).

While sharing some cultural values, most particularly those of collectivism, these cultures, however, do differ on one other significant dimension: how tight or loose they are.

2.2 Defining the Tight-Loose Dimension

Anthropologist Pertti Pelto (1968) proposed the concept of *tight-loose*, later elaborated upon by others (Triandis, 1989, 1995; Triandis & Gelfand, 1998; Witkin & Berry, 1975) to describe the degree to which people enforce and abide by norms and the level of tolerance and acceptance of deviation from those norms. In *tight cultures* such as Indonesia, China, Singapore, or Egypt (see Figure 8.1 for list of countries)

- Many norms and rules regulate people's behavior.

- People rely on established norms and social convention to evaluate situations and to make decisions.

- People self-monitor and self-regulate to assure that they follow the rules and expect others to do the same.

Figure 8.1 Countries With Tight and Loose Cultures

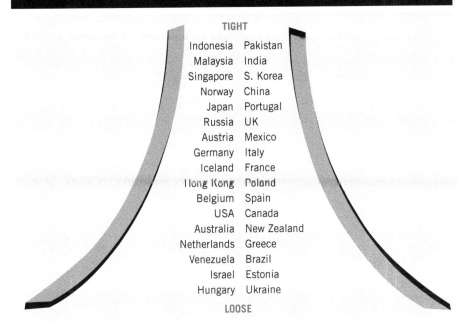

TIGHT

Indonesia	Pakistan
Malaysia	India
Singapore	S. Korea
Norway	China
Japan	Portugal
Russia	UK
Austria	Mexico
Germany	Italy
Iceland	France
Hong Kong	Poland
Belgium	Spain
USA	Canada
Australia	New Zealand
Netherlands	Greece
Venezuela	Brazil
Israel	Estonia
Hungary	Ukraine

LOOSE

- Various formal and informal social mechanisms are in place to enforce the norms.

- Violating norms is not tolerated and is criticized and punished.

Conversely in *loose* cultures such as Canada, Thailand, or Brazil, although rules exist, violating them is often overlooked and people are allowed considerably more leeway regarding what is expected and how they must behave. Whichever type of culture an individual belongs to will clearly feels like the "right" one. A Swede, US-American, or Canadian is likely to see the Chinese social credit policy as inappropriate and intrusive. Many US cities experienced demonstrations during the COVID-19 epidemic where protestors demanded a loosening of social and business restrictions often seeing them as a threat to individual liberty and civil rights, in spite of the fact that the United States was already much less restrictive than other countries (Rattansi, 2020).

Each of these cultural groups is likely to consider their practices as more appropriate. For example, a Singaporean is likely to consider large Western cities, where people have considerable latitude regarding their conduct, as unruly and decaying, while the many rules that Singapore imposes on its citizens and visitors are seen as overly restrictive by outsiders. However, in all cases, culture-just-is (CJI). Each cultural group has developed assumptions, values, beliefs, and norms that act as a CMC and work in its environment.

2.3 Factors Associated With the Tight-Loose Dimensions

Researchers have suggested that T-L is associated with (Gelfand et al., 2011; Triandis, 1995, 2004):

- The degree of homogeneity or diversity of a culture

- The extent of contact and interaction with other cultures

- Degree of collectivism

- Isolation from other cultures

- Population density

- Resource scarcity

- Sense of danger and perceived threat

Specifically, more homogeneous cultures, such as South Korea, enforce their norms to a higher degree than more diverse cultures (Triandis, 1995; Uz, 2014). Furthermore, Triandis (2004) proposes that because isolation is related to tighter cultures, globalization and increased contact are likely to increase the occurrence of looser cultures. For example, he places the United States in the moderate T-L category and shows that the US culture has increasingly moved toward becoming looser and more tolerant over the past 50 years. He further observes that T-L is related to UA as the tight social norms allow people to reduce the discomfort they experience when facing uncertainty (Triandis, 2004).

Others have found collectivism to be correlated with tight cultures such that the more collective cultures are generally tighter (Carpenter, 2000; Triandis, 2004). A 33-country study by Michelle Gelfand et al. (2011) indicates that high population density, resource scarcity, danger of natural disasters, and territorial threats are all associated with tighter cultures. Gelfand states:

> When people perceive threat—whether real or imagined, they want strong rules and autocratic leaders to help them survive. My research has found that within minutes of exposing study participants to false information about terrorist incidents, overpopulation, pathogen outbreaks, and natural disasters, their minds tightened. They wanted stronger rules and punishments. (Nussbaum, 2019)

2.4 Tight-Loose and Regional Cultures

The T-L concept has also been applied to regional cultures within the United States and results indicate that Northeastern, Western, and Mountain states have looser cultures, whereas Southern and Midwestern states have tighter cultures where there is more social stability and sense of order, but lower creativity and lower happiness (Harrington & Gelfand, 2014). The concept has further been applied to organizational cultures, for example, in the case of the merger between Amazon and Whole Foods, where Amazon has a tight culture when compared to Whole Foods' looser one (Gelfand, Gordon, Li, Choi, & Prokopowicz, 2018). Although T-L has not yet been as extensively researched as other dimensions, the studies that have been conducted to date have shown strong and reliable results related to the measurement of the concept and its antecedents (Gelfand, 2018) and relatively consistent country rankings.

2.5 Managerial Implications

As with other dimensions of culture, T-L has broad managerial and business implications. In tight cultures, employees are likely to want structure and predictability and follow the rules by behaving as they are expected. They will anticipate that their managers provide clear goals and guidelines; and managers will assume that their employees will follow directions. In organizations in loose cultures, such as in the Netherlands, there is little expectation that everyone will dress the same, behave the same, or closely follow every rule. Employees can ignore authority if they have a good reason. Supervisors are not considered omniscient, and rules are disputable because they are in place to help ease the work and assumed to be flexible; they therefore can be challenged when necessary.

Consider the example of Ian, the US-American intern in Dubai who is excited about having a well-paid year-long internship in a global financial institution. His manager, Mr. Khaled Halabi, is an Emirati educated in the West. He is kind and supportive, but not once has he asked Ian about his career goals and future plans. He provides very clear directions and keeps a close eye on his reports. When Ian asks about getting involved in various projects and learning new skill sets, Mr. Halabi refers him to HR for their intern training programs. As Ian's internship approaches the 6-month mark, he hopes to have a review where he gets a chance to ask for more targeted projects and get detailed developmental feedback. Instead, he receives a letter that is complimentary but vague. When he approaches Mr. Halabi one more time, he is told: "You are doing well; just do what we are asking and follow the path that we have laid out. All of our interns do that and they all receive good recommendations. That is what we expect of you." It is clear that Ian and Mr. Halabi have different assumptions about work. Ian, coming from a loose culture, expects to have an individual path that he can shape to his needs; Mr. Halabi is trusting the well-set program that is detailed and the same for all interns.

3. REFINING INDIVIDUALISM-COLLECTIVISM: VERTICAL-HORIZONTAL CULTURES

LO 8.3 Elaborate on the link between horizontal and vertical dimensions and individualism and collectivism

Another attribute that allows further refinement of the IND-COL dimension and a better understanding of complex cultural differences is the concept of vertical and horizontal. *Vertical* (V) cultures focus on hierarchy where people are not considered equal; *horizontal* (H) cultures emphasize equality with little hierarchy or power differentials (Triandis et al., 2001). The V-H dimensions addresses

- Whether individuals are seen as uniquely different from others
- Whether individuals are seen as superior or equal to others
- How much hierarchy and power differential there are
- The degree of individual self-reliance and self-direction

3.1 Combining Vertical-Horizontal With Individualism-Collectivism

The combination with IND-COL yields four distinct types of culture (see Figure 8.2). For example, although Sweden and the United States are both individualist cultures, they are different on the V-H dimension. Swedes are horizontal individualists (HI) and see individuals as unique but equal to others, whereas US-Americans are vertical individualist (VI), where the individual is viewed not only as unique but also superior to others. Similarly, in a horizontal collectivistic (HC) culture, such as Israel, all members of the group are seen as equal, whereas in vertical collectivistic cultures (VC), such as Japan and South Korea, authority is important and individuals must sacrifice themselves for the good of the group.

Scandinavian countries provide good examples of HI cultures (Nelson & Shavitt, 2002). Specifically, the concept of *Janteloven* (law of Jante) that can be found in Norway and Sweden involves a disdain for standing out and an aversion for self-promotion and conspicuous wealth while promoting self-reliance and independence. Some of the laws of *Jante* include: "Do not think you are anything special" and

Figure 8.2 Vertical and Horizontal Individualism-Collectivism

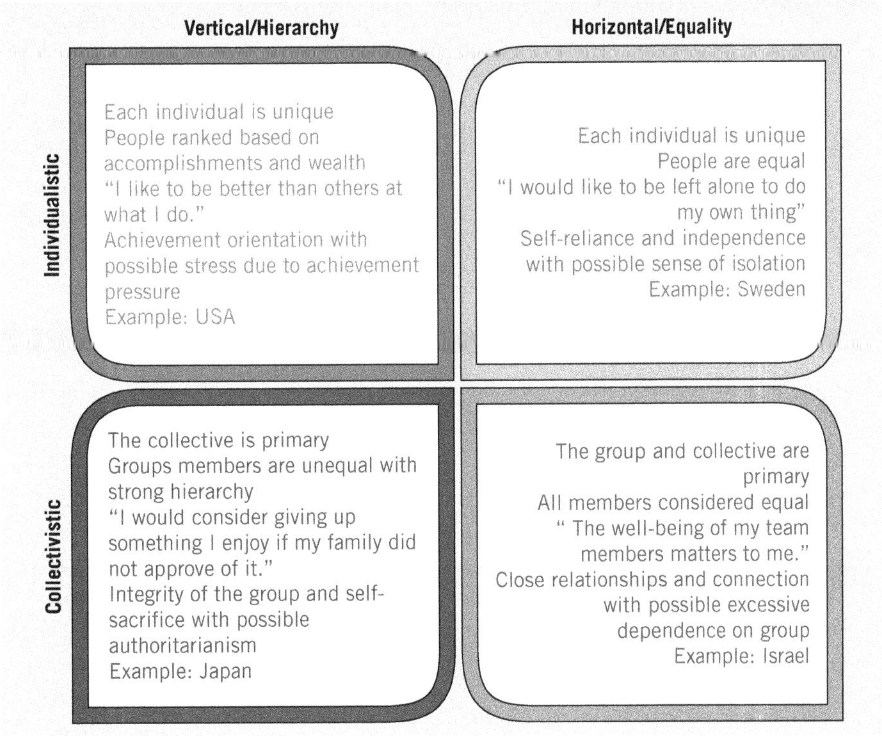

	Vertical/Hierarchy	Horizontal/Equality
Individualistic	Each individual is unique People ranked based on accomplishments and wealth "I like to be better than others at what I do." Achievement orientation with possible stress due to achievement pressure Example: USA	Each individual is unique People are equal "I would like to be left alone to do my own thing" Self-reliance and independence with possible sense of isolation Example: Sweden
Collectivistic	The collective is primary Groups members are unequal with strong hierarchy "I would consider giving up something I enjoy if my family did not approve of it." Integrity of the group and self-sacrifice with possible authoritarianism Example: Japan	The group and collective are primary All members considered equal "The well-being of my team members matters to me." Close relationships and connection with possible excessive dependence on group Example: Israel

"Do not think you are more important than we are" (Norman, 2018). Australians, who are classified with the United States on many cultural dimensions, including IND, are considerably more horizontal with a distinct disdain for showing off and a tendency to disparage and discredit those who try too hard or achieve too much, something referred to as "cutting down the tall poppy" (Luby, 2017). In the more vertical culture of the United States or France, competition and winning are highly valued and displaying wealth and establishing superiority to others are appropriate.

The American obsession with "being number 1," "being the best," and fondness for the rags-to-riches stories are indicators of vertical individualism. A story often told about the difference between a Brit and an American goes as follows:

American: I hear that you play tennis. We should play one of these days.

Brit: We should; that would be great fun.

American: To be fair, I have to warn you I'm an excellent player. I was ranked as the top player in my school and considered going pro *(he played on the varsity team in high-school)*.

Brit: I have played a bit, but it has been a while *(he played in Wimbledon a number of times)*.

As a VI culture, the United States places high value on achievement, competition, and self-reliance while considering each individual independent and uniquely superior to others. Standing out and being better than others are paramount. Consider that the United States and Japan tend to be on opposite ends of many cultural value dimensions; however, they are both vertical cultures and share similarities when it comes to valuing competition (Oyserman, Sorensen, Reber, & Chen, 2002). As a VC culture, Japan, like South Korea, Russia, and Poland that fall in the same category, places a high value on self-reliance, achievement, and competition as well as duty and self-sacrifice to the group (either family or society). Rank, hierarchy, and obedience to authority and to the group are highly prized, and inequalities within the collective are expected and accepted (Singelis, Triandis, Bhawuk, & Gelfand, 1995).

Some researchers suggest that vertical cultures, particularly vertical individualistic (VI) cultures, are most amenable to accepting authoritarianism (Triandis & Gelfand, 1998). Finally, similar to VC cultures, the HC cultures are communal with a focus on the group and where the self is merged with the group. However, because they are more egalitarian, the ideas of self-sacrifice or the obedience to the group or to authority are not prevalent. The Israeli kibbutz culture where cooperation and taking care of in-group members is highly prized is an example of HC (Triandis, 1995); China with an emphasis on egalitarian and group-centered values is another (Sivadas et al., 2008).

3.2 Benefit of Implementing the Vertical-Horizontal Dimension

The V-H dimension adds considerable richness to the IND-COL dimension allowing for more precise description and understanding of cultural differences. Given the larger number of cultures that are collectivistic as compared with individualistic, any finer distinction helps prevent grouping a large number of individuals and cultures into an undifferentiated group (Noordin, 2018). While the dimension has some similarities to PD, as they both relate to equality and hierarchy, V-H is broader and includes issues such as achievement, conformity, self-direction, and benevolence (Shavitt et al., 2011a, 2011b). As with the T-L dimension, the research on V-H has been consistent and highly promising with researchers systematically testing and extending its use (e.g., Cozma, 2011; Lee & Choi, 2005; Oyserman et al., 2009; Sivadas, Bruvold, & Nelson, 2008). For example, the concept has been applied in marketing to improve how advertising is targeted (e.g., Shavitt et al., 2006; Shavitt, Johnson, & Zhang, 2011b).

3.3 Managerial Implications

Managers can use knowledge of V-H to address different cultures within their team or their organization. It is particularly important to apply the concept to differentiate between people who are assumed to share the same cultural value. For example, managers should consider the degree to which their team members value informality and equality rather than hierarchy. In more horizontal cultures, hierarchy and status are less likely to matter and group members will expect to have equal opportunities for participation. In more vertical cultures, individuals with more seniority or more expertise will both expect and be expected to show leadership. In more horizontal cultures, group members will interact more as equals, feel more comfortable contributing equally, and are less likely to defer to those with more tenure or who have different status. Being aware of these differences allows managers to address individual needs and manage possible conflicts.

Adding tight-loose and vertical-horizontal to IND-COL refines our understanding of what being an individualistic or collectivistic culture means. Using IND-COL is not enough to explain all cross-cultural differences. With every dimension that is proposed and carefully tested, we increase our ability to use cultural prototypes to be more effective in our cross-cultural interactions. It is essential to emphasize yet again that overgeneralization is risky and likely to lead to error. As suggested by Triandis (2004), both individualistic and collectivistic cultures include some percentage of individuals who may hold values more consistent with those of the other group. Nonetheless, the T-L and H-V provide valuable knowledge to increase our self-awareness and build the KNOW component of our THINK–KNOW–DO roadmap.

WINDOW TO THE WORLD

Doing Business in Australia

The Australian culture, at least the European-Australian culture, is similar to the United States on individualism, masculinity, and UA, but it is lower on power distance, meaning that Australians tend to be more egalitarian and less vertical than their US cousins. The business culture is characterized by informality, egalitarianism, directness, and modesty.

Showing off and bragging about your accomplishments are not appreciated. Here are some pointers:

- You can be informal and easy-going, but make sure you dress appropriately and are on time. Just because they love the beach does not mean you can show up late and in flip-flops.

- Expect directness and some profanity; Australians are direct and straightforward.

- Decision-making is slower than in the United States as the culture leans toward *being* to some extent.

- Business relationships develop fast (and fail quickly as well) based on common interests rather than relationships.

- The egalitarian and informal values favor consultation and empowerment in decision-making, so making top-down decisions is not desirable or appreciated.

- Australians refer to cultural differences and diversity in open and sometimes playful ways, especially when talking about themselves.

- Socializing after hours is common and often involves alcohol.

- There are many policies, rules, and regulations and a large bureaucracy that governs business and the workplace.

- New Zealand is no more part of Australia than Canada is part of the United States!

If you are from the United States or another English-speaking country, do not assume that the same language means the same culture. Australia shares several cultural values and some common history with the United States and Canada; however, it has its own unique culture. It may appear easier to interact with Australians than people who do not share some of your language and values, but you are still in a different culture, people have a different CMC, and it is not your "small" world.

4. TROMPENAARS'S DIMENSIONS OF CULTURE

LO 8.4 Discuss Trompenaars's framework for understanding cross-cultural organizational differences

International consultant Fons Trompenaars and his colleague Charles Hampden-Turner (2012) have built on the work of others such as Kluckhohn and Strodtbeck and Hofstede to propose a framework of seven dimensions along which people from different cultures can be categorized. One of the unique features of their framework is its strong managerial and business orientation. They start with the question: "Why is it that many management processes lose effectiveness when cultural borders are crossed?" (p. 6) and with the assumption that one can never fully understand other people's culture. They recognize the power of culture to shape thinking and behavior (CMC) and set out to show how culture impacts management and organizations. Their framework is based on data gathered from more than 100,000 people from

60 cultures who participated in their surveys and workshops and the many anecdotes and cases they collected over 25 years.

4.1 The Seven Dimensions

Trompenaars starts with the three challenges that all human beings face, identifying them as:

1. How do we relate to one another?

2. How do we relate to time?

3. How do we relate to our environment?

The questions should be familiar to you by now, and the dimensions that we describe next also bear some resemblance to the other models that we have already discussed. They do however provide some unique elements and managerial applications that are worth considering. We will detail the dimensions that are unique to this framework, namely universalism-particularism, neutral-affective, specific-diffuse, and achievement-ascription (Table 8.6). The individual-communitarian dimension is similar to IND-COL we have extensively discussed; the time and environment dimensions focus on similar dimensions as the ones presented in Chapter 7.

4.2 Managerial and Organizational Implications

One of the most unique aspects of the Trompenaars framework is its direct managerial and organizational applications. The dimensions are presented in terms of how organizations and people within them interact and differ across cultures. Trompenaars classifies cultures along these dimensions by asking a series of questions. For example, for the universal-particular dimension he asks managers whether they would lie to protect a friend who was at fault in a car accident. People from particular cultures are more likely to be willing to lie to protect their friend, indicating that rules are applied differently based on relationships. People from emotional cultures say that they would show their emotions openly at work and are likely to make emotional presentations and more likely to storm off when they disagree during a negotiation. Employees in diffuse cultures more often agree to help paint their manager's house because a manager is perceived as having the same power outside of work and the status extends, or is diffused, to other settings. In specific cultures, a manager's title at work is not relevant to other situations outside of work, while in diffuse cultures, someone's work title is mentioned in social situations. Finally, organizations in achievement-oriented cultures base their hiring and promotion decisions on their employees' achievement and performance, whereas in ascription cultures who you know and your personal background is more likely to play a role.

Table 8.6 Trompenaar's Seven Dimensions of Culture

How Do We Relate to One Another?

Universal	*Particular*
There are universal principles and truths	Truth is relative
Rules and norms apply to everyone equally	Rules and norms change depending on
Impersonal and business-oriented interaction	who they are applied to
Successful business depends on clear contracts	Personal interactions
Countries: North American and Northern and	Business relationships are fluid and contracts
Western European countries	are a starting point that can be modified
	Countries: Venezuela, Russia, China,
	India, Mexico, Japan, Nigeria
Neutral	*Affective*
Non emotional interactions	Emotions are expressed freely
Focus on tasks	Heated discussions
Avoid emotional expressions	Passionate presentations and discussions
Countries: Ethiopia, Japan, New Zealand, China,	*Countries*: Kuwait, Egypt, Philippines,
New Zealand	Russia, France, Italy
Specific	*Diffuse*
Similar to low context	Similar to high context
Direct and purposeful relationships	Indirect and evasive
Quick and to the point	Slow interaction
Focus on performance	Respect for age and status
Direct confrontation	Saving face
Countries: Sweden, the Netherlands, UK, France,	*Countries*: China, Nigeria, Venezuela, Indonesia
Germany	
Achievement	*Ascription*
Similar to Doing cultures	Similar to Being cultures
Status and respect based on personal	Status and respect ascribed to people based on
achievement	their social class, age, gender, etc.
Informal organizations	Formal organizations
Promotions and supervision based on expertise	Supervisors have high power
Challenge of authority allowed	Little challenge of those in authority
Countries: Norway, USA, Australia, Canada, UK,	*Countries*: Egypt, Uruguay, Cuba, Romania,
Ireland, Sweden	South Korea, Indonesia, Japan, China, Brazil
Individualism	*Communitarianism*
Same dimension as IND	Same dimension as COL

How do we relate to time?

Similar to the time dimension in Kluckhohn and Strodtbeck and Hofstede

How do we relate to our environment?

Similar to the time dimension in Kluckhohn and Strodtbeck and Hofstede

Source: Based on information in Trompenaars and Hampden-Turner (2012).

5. GLOBE—GLOBAL LEADERSHIP AND ORGANIZATIONAL BEHAVIOR EFFECTIVENESS

The Global Leadership and Organizational Behavior Effectiveness—GLOBE—is the most recent addition to the collection of frameworks for understanding cross-cultural differences. The project was started with a clear goal: "... to increase available knowledge that is relevant to cross-cultural interactions" (House, Hanges, Javidan, Dorfman, & Gupta, 2004, p. 3). It is the most extensive research about cross-cultural differences and their impact on organizational behavior ever conducted with over 200 researchers in 62 countries contributing to the project (for detailed descriptions of the project, see Chhokar, Brodbeck, & House, 2007; House et al., 2004).

In addition to identifying nine cultural dimensions we review next and rich information related to ideals of leadership across cultures, the GLOBE findings clearly indicate that managerial practices reflect the cultural values of the country in which they operate, reinforcing the important role of culture as CMC in impacting individual and organizational behavior. Additionally, the research looks at the link between cultural dimensions and various indices of economic prosperity and measures of psychological well-being. We present the cultural dimensions and their impact on economic and social well-being next and review the findings related to organizational culture and leadership in next chapters.

5.1 GLOBE's Nine Cultural Dimensions

One of the major contributions of the GLOBE project is to clarify and refine cultural dimensions that can help differentiate among cultures. Based on extensive theoretical, statistical, and qualitative evidence, GLOBE suggests nine cultural dimensions, some of which are similar to those found in other frameworks we reviewed in this and the previous chapters (see Table 8.7). The nine dimensions help clarify and refine existing dimensions.

The first four GLOBE dimensions are closest to Hofstede's dimensions of PD, UA, and IND-COL. Through GLOBE, UA is more clearly defined and focused on how people address uncertainty. IND-COL is more precisely expressed by differentiating between institutional collectivism, which is based on social institutions and collective rewards and collective action (e.g., Japan), and group collectivism where the primary loyalty is to smaller groups such as one's family or organization (e.g., Malaysia). The latter is closer to Hofstede's IND-COL, and the former is a relatively distinct and new dimension (House & Javidan, 2004). Hosftede's M-F dimension is elucidated and enhanced by having a specific dimension related to gender

Table 8.7 Nine GLOBE Cultural Dimensions

1. *Power distance:* The degree to which power is distributed equally, concentrated, or decentralized
   Sample question: Followers are (should be) expected to obey their leaders without question.

2. *Uncertainty avoidance:* The extent to which a culture relies on social norms and rules to reduce unpredictability; avoiding uncertainty is associated with formal interactions and reliance on rules and contracts
   Sample question: Most people lead (should lead) highly structured lives with few unexpected events.

3. *Institutional collectivism:* The degree to which a culture values and practices collective action and collective distribution of resources
   Sample question: Leaders encourage (should encourage) group loyalty even if individual goals suffer.

4. *In-group collectivism:* The degree to which individuals express pride in and cohesion with their family or organizations
   Sample question: Employees feel (should feel) great loyalty toward this organization.

5. *Gender egalitarianism:* The extent of gender role differentiation and promotion of gender equity
   Sample question: Boys are (should be) encouraged more than girls to attain higher education.

6. *Assertiveness:* The degree to which individuals are assertive, direct, and confrontational
   Sample question: People are (should be) generally dominant in their relationships with each other.

7. *Humane orientation:* The degree to which a culture values fairness, generosity, kindness, and caring for others
   Sample question: People are (should be) generally very tolerant of mistakes.

8. *Future orientation:* The extent to which people invest in the future and engage in future-oriented behaviors and are willing to delay gratification
   Sample question: More people live (should live) for the present rather than the future.

9. *Performance orientation:* The degree to which a culture values and encourages performance and excellence
   Sample question: Students are (should be) encouraged to strive for continuously improved performance.

Sources: Based on information in Dorfman et al. (2012); House et al. (2004).

egalitarianism and one that addresses directness and assertiveness. Kluckhohn and Strodtbeck's value related to human nature is the basis of the humane orientation and the value related to perception of time is represented in the GLOBE future orientation dimension that considers whether people are past, present, or future oriented. Finally, performance orientation encompasses ideas of achievement orientation and valuing performance.

Information about these nine dimensions was collected through original scales that inquired both about values—what should be, and practices—what is being practiced. GLOBE data show that in some cases, the managers they surveyed said that what they value and what they do match; in other cases, it does not (House et al., 2004). For example, for many managers across different cultures, actual PD in their organization was higher than what they would value, indicating that in most cases managers would like more empowerment and flexibility than what their organization provides (House et al., 2004).

5.2 Country Clusters

Based on their findings, GLOBE researchers considered how countries may form clusters that share similar cultural characteristics. Their research yielded 10 country clusters. These, along with the key high and low cultural values associated with each of the clusters, are depicted in Figure 8.3.

In reviewing Figure 8.3, you can see, for example, that countries in the Anglo cluster such as the United States, Canada, and England place a high value on performance orientation and low value on in-group collectivism. Those in the Confucian cluster, for example, China and South Korea, value performance and both types of collectivism and are not low on any of the other cultural values. Similarly, people in

Figure 8.3 Country Clusters Based on GLOBE

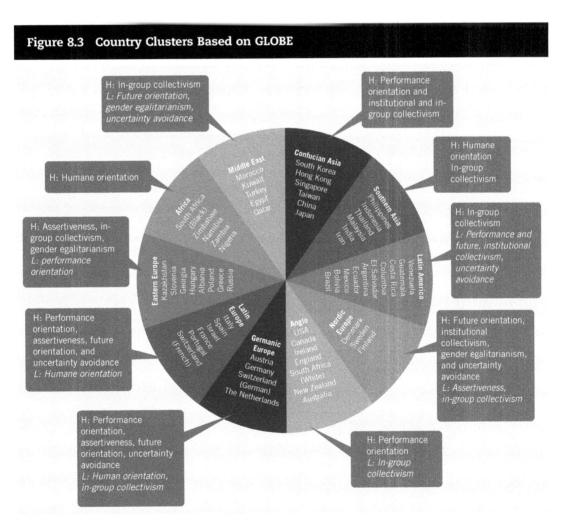

Source: Based on information in House et al. (2004).

the African cluster, when compared to other cultures, only rank humane orientation high. The Latin American cluster is high on in-group collectivism, but low on institutional collectivism, performance, and future orientation, and has a low tolerance for uncertainty. Further clarification of the clusters and the countries within them provides more details. For instance, in countries with high power distance, such as Thailand and Russia, communication is often directed one way, from the leader to followers, with little expectation of feedback. Finally, in cultures that value kindness and generosity, such as the Philippines or Egypt, leaders are likely to avoid conflict and act in a caring but paternalistic manner (Javidan, House, & Dorfman, 2004). Having information about these country clusters provides a regional profile as well as a more complete picture for different countries based on the combination of the nine dimensions. These clusters add one more layer to understanding cross-cultural differences and can be applied to being more effective when working across cultures.

5.3 Impact of Cultural Values on Economic Development and Well-Being

The GLOBE project studied the relationship between cultural dimensions, societal attitudes (both measured through GLOBE surveys), and several aspects of societal and economic health by including data from the United Nations and other global databases. These data included information about economic prosperity, global competitiveness, ecology, education, family, health indicators, religion, and many other factors. Below is a sampling of some of their key findings (Javidan, House, & Dorfman, 2004; Javidan & Hauser, 2004):

- Gender egalitarianism, assertiveness, and humane orientation practices are not related either positively or negatively to any of the economic prosperity or competitiveness measures.

- Economic prosperity and competitiveness are associated with cultural practice of performance and future orientation, UA, and institutional collectivism.

- Practices of in-group collectivism and power distance are negatively related to economic prosperity, competitiveness, societal health, and general satisfaction meaning the higher the in-group collectivism and the higher the PD, the less positive the outcomes.

- Performance and future orientation and UA practices are positively related to societal health and satisfaction.

- Human Development Index and life expectancy are positively correlated with gender egalitarianism, but negatively correlated with in-group collectivism, power distance, future orientation, and UA.

The GLOBE results linking cultural practices, but not values, with several economic and social outcomes are complex and multidimensional; however, they do point to the importance of culture in impacting social and economic outcomes. Overall, GLOBE provides a complex and rich vocabulary that allows managers to understand, describe, and predict cross-cultural differences and their impact on organizations. In addition to the cultural dimensions, country clusters, and research linking cultural practices with economic and social outcomes presented here, GLOBE focuses on understanding leadership differences across cultures. The findings regarding leadership is covered in detail in Chapter 9.

6. CONTRIBUTIONS AND CRITIQUES

LO 8.6 Recognize the contributions and challenges associated with models of national culture

The frameworks we have discussed in this chapter provide a research-based shorthand to understand, describe, and predict cultural differences. Each has strengths and weaknesses, and each has made contributions to our understanding of culture. Before we present each model's contributions and shortcomings, it is important to consider the overall challenges of using frameworks and prototypes yet again.

6.1 Word of Caution

The use of frameworks to understand, describe, and predict culture suffers from some shortcomings, regardless of the model you apply.

- Anytime you apply a framework to cultural differences, you are using an etic approach that takes an outside-in approach to culture. As we discussed in Chapter 7, the etic approach allows for a broad perspective but imposes an outsider's view. It therefore might lead to misinterpretation of many cultural elements or even completely disregarding important factors.

- All the frameworks we have discussed consistently confound country and culture with limited attention to subgroups and the cultural diversity that characterizes most countries. The few subgroups that are recognized include those in Canada (total vs. French-speaking Québec), Belgium (French vs. Flemish), Switzerland (German vs. French), and South Africa (White vs. Black). There are undoubtedly countless other groups within each country that are not considered. Ignoring the within-country differences is therefore problematic.

- When relying on frameworks, there is a strong tendency to overgeneralize and essentialize culture and people. Although the dimensions have descriptive, explanatory, and predictive power, one cannot rely exclusively on them when trying to understand culture. Every individual is, to some extent, unique and, as we discussed above, people may not fit the cultural prototype presented by the frameworks we presented.

Notwithstanding these potential shortcomings, the cultural frameworks we presented in this chapter have all made considerable contributions to cross-cultural management by providing managers with tools that allow them to be more effective when working across cultures. Their use can be particularly appropriate if managers take care not to overgeneralize and stereotype. Additionally, when trying to create a cultural profile, it is critical that many dimensions be included rather than using each individually. For example, although IND-COL is a powerful dimension of culture, relying on it alone is not desirable. We consider the shortcomings and unique contributions of each of the models next.

6.2 Hofstede's Framework: Contributions and Shortcomings

Hofstede's cultural dimensions are undoubtedly one of the most recognized and most used classifications of culture. They are widely applied in a number of disciplines and industries, including international and cross-cultural management, and at least the first four dimensions have been extensively researched (for details on the development and testing of the dimensions, see Hofstede, 2002; for a recent example, see Minkov et al., 2017).

Hofstede's work is responsible for popularizing the concept of culture in business and management and bringing attention to the topic when working across cultural boundaries. The extensive database of over 110,000 surveys provides a rich source of information for understanding cultural differences and has been the basis for pervasive training and consulting.

Nonetheless, the model also presents some unique shortcomings:

- While overgeneralization is a problem across the board, Hofstede's framework has a particular tendency to overgeneralize the use of the dimensions. For example, the 2010 presentation of the framework connects each of the dimensions to anything from style of government to income differentials, economic development, participation in religion, managerial practices, the style of teaching in schools, availability of health care, dating habits, and child-rearing practices just to name a few.

- The country classifications in each dimension shift from one study to another. While countries at the top (or bottom) of each dimension may not move to the opposite end, there is disagreement regarding where some countries fall on some of the dimensions, and the classifications change from one survey to another. For example, in one study, Indian MBA students were ranked higher in individualism than the United States and Irish groups (Ramamoorthy, Gupta, Sardessai, & Flood, 2007). In another, contrary to Hofstede's classifications, Anne McDaniel (2008) finds Indonesia to be low on gender egalitarianism and several eastern European countries to be high on that dimension indicating a more gender egalitarian attitude. The changes in a country's ranking may be related to cultural evolution, or different samples and methods, but the movement is problematic, nonetheless.

- Finally, methodological problems exist. The original data were collected in the 1960s from managers from different countries who all worked for one company, IBM, a company known for its strong corporate culture. The age of the data and the sample being from one company make generalization difficult. Additionally, there has been surprisingly little stringent research to examine, clarify, and replicate the value dimensions, which are not always clear. Studies that have attempted to address these methodological shortcomings and test the dimensions and their measurement (e.g., Orr & Hauser, 2008; SØndergaard, 1994) have not fully supported the model.

In spite of the shortcomings listed above, Hofstede's contribution to our knowledge and understanding of cross-cultural differences and our ability to have a vocabulary to talk about culture has been invaluable. This vocabulary allows us to describe our own and other people's CMC using research-based prototypes rather than personal experiences, stereotypes, and anecdotes. Knowledge of the dimensions further builds the KNOW of the TKD roadmap. Finally, Hofstede's work, much like Kluckhohn and Strodtbeck's, has directly or indirectly been the basis for other models we discuss in this chapter.

6.3 Tromprenaars's Contributions and Shortcomings

The Trompenaars framework has a strong managerial focus and provides extensive advice to managers regarding how to work and interact in different cultures. The managerial focus and the highly approachable presentation of the framework have made it very popular among business practitioners. The approach strongly reinforces the CJI concept. It relies on anecdotal evidence of how management styles and employee expectations differ across cultures and the idea that what works in managing organizations in one culture is not better or worse, but it simply may not work in other cultures. That is a powerful and important message which the authors also mention applies to other levels of culture such as regional or group, diversity-related cultures, although their research is less extensive in diversity-related areas. Other aspects of the framework that focus on classifying national organizational cultures and structures which we cover in Chapter 11 highlight the role of culture in management and organizations.

The book *Riding the Waves of Culture* by Trompenaars and Hampden-Turner (2012) provides many anecdotes and cases that illustrate the dimensions well. The very large data set upon which the concepts are based further lends it credence. However, in spite of the large number of surveys and cases that are used to illustrate the framework, the sample and methods with the managerial focus which are its strength are also its major shortcomings. There has been little reliable and valid research done to test and clarify the theoretical foundations and replicate the proposed dimensions (for a critique see Hofstede, 1996). The issue of confounding country and culture which is present in other models must also be considered for the Trompenaars framework, although there is some mention of other levels of culture and applications to group-level cultural differences.

6.4 GLOBE: Contributions and Shortcomings

GLOBE is an ongoing and unprecedented endeavor to map and test cultural differences with a focus on organizational behavior and leadership. GLOBE 2020 (https://globeproject.com/publications) summarizes the goals of the project, provides information about the contributing researchers, and lists the hundreds of publications about the various aspects and dimensions of GLOBE. The project and the considerable research it has generated make it a powerful and reliable framework for understanding culture and particularly understanding leadership across cultures. Because of the extensive nature of the project and the detailed and careful methodology used

- GLOBE is one of the strongest and best-supported models currently available.

- It is the only framework that provides a view into a large number of countries and cultures including many, such as African countries, that are typically ignored in other studies.

- Researchers associated with GLOBE and those who work independently from the project (e.g., Brewer & Venaik, 2011; Pagda, 2019; Warner-Søderholm, 2012) have endeavored to address many of the concerns and criticisms as the framework continues to improve.

- The dimensions and the measures that were developed and extensively tested are reliable and valid and provide a solid tool for describing and predicting cultural differences.

- The focus on leadership (examined in detail in Chapter 9) is unique and provides a useful organizational view of cross-cultural differences.

In spite of its strengths and contributions, GLOBE has not been without critics (for example, see Graen, 2006; Maseland & van Hoorn, 2010). For researchers and students of culture, GLOBE provides a wealth of data and many new questions to explore. For practitioners, however, that richness and complexity can be challenging as the findings are not easily accessible to them. This is a complicated project about a complicated topic that has yielded complex results. In spite of the clear links to economic development, well-being, and leadership and with the laudable goal of maintaining scientific rigor and understanding the framework, its findings and recommendations are often difficult to understand, creating a gap between their findings and managers' ability to implement them. The GLOBE researchers have produced many academic and practitioner-oriented reports in an attempt to bridge that gap, but the challenge of bridging the gap between research and practice still exists. Additionally, GLOBE is focused on national culture and has not addressed other levels of culture. The problem of equating country and culture that is present in the other models is also an issue for GLOBE.

Because of the large number of countries included in the studies and the extensive research that has been conducted, GLOBE provides a comprehensive model for understanding cultural differences as they relate to a number of business and management relevant outcomes. Knowing the cultural values within each country cluster and those held by people in each country can be of considerable value when working across cultures.

7. FRAMEWORKS AS TOOLS FOR CULTURAL KNOWLEDGE

LO 8.7 Explore how to integrate knowledge of cultural frameworks to help managers be more effective across cultures

In this and the last chapter we have reviewed six different frameworks that provide knowledge and a vocabulary to understand, describe, and predict cultural differences. They all address the KNOW part of the THINK–KNOW–DO roadmap. Although the frameworks were developed in different disciplines, for example, anthropology in the case of Hall and Kluckhohn and Strodtbeck, cross-cultural psychology in the case of tight-loose and horizontal-vertical, business and management for the others, either directly or indirectly, they build on one another. While academics delight in discussing their differences and pointing out shortcomings of each, as we have briefly presented in the critiques for each framework, students and practitioners are often left with the difficult task of trying to sift through the various models to ascertain which would be most useful to them. However, some legitimate questions remain. Why do we need to know all of these? Which model is better? Are some dimensions more critical than others? Which dimensions would be most helpful? How do I decide which one to use? Do I have to pick just one?

7.1 Integrating Your Knowledge

Fundamentally, all of the frameworks address the knowledge factor in CM and build the KNOW element of the TKD roadmap; they all provide valuable knowledge and vocabulary that can be used to increase your awareness of your own cultural values and practices. They can all serve as a first step in describing and understanding culture, allowing you to be more effective in your cross-cultural interactions. By providing that knowledge, they paint a picture of people's CMC and allow others to gain some insight into that CMC. All of the frameworks, especially the more recent ones, make the case for CJI. In other words, some cultures are not better than others; they each represent the way a group of people address sometimes successfully, sometimes unsuccessfully, the challenges that they face. They also point to the importance of understanding that the rules of one "small" world do not apply to other larger or smaller worlds.

7.1.1 Comparing the Frameworks. Figure 8.4 summarizes and integrates the dimensions proposed by the frameworks we have reviewed in Chapters 7 and 8: the rows are the general dimensions or values, the columns are the six models. The one concept that is not included is Kluckhohn and Strodtbeck's use of space, as it is not addressed by any of the other models.

As you can see from reviewing Figure 8.4, some dimensions clearly fit into the rows where they are (e.g., IND-COL); others such as Kluckhohn and Strodtbeck's hierarchy in the power dimension, or Trompenaars's specific-diffuse, which is included in the communication dimension, are not a perfect match. In several cases, the dimensions may address more than one concept. For example, GLOBE's future orientation also addresses performance. Figure 8.4 provides a visual comparison of the models to help you ascertain their contributions. You can also see their similarities and differences. Part V of the book will rely on these dimensions and the knowledge you have acquired to address the challenges of leading in multicultural settings.

7.1.2 Key Dimensions. The other key question is whether some dimensions are more important or more predictive than other. In other words, can we use a few dimensions rather than having to apply all of them every time we come across a new culture?

	Hall	Klockhohn and Strodtbeck	Hofstede	Tight-Loose vert-Hori	Trompenaars	GLOBE
Individualism Collectivism	--	Group Individualism	IND-COL	V-H	Individualism Communi-tarianism	1. In-group Col. 2. Institutional Col.
Power	--	Hierarchy	PD	T-L	--	Power distance
Tolerance for Ambiguity	--	--	UA	T-L	Universalism Particularism	Uncertainty avoidance
Gender	--	--	M-F	--	--	1. Gender Egal. 2. Assertiveness
Performance	--	Doing Being	Indulgence Restraint*	--	Achievement Ascription	Performance orientation
Emotion	--	--	--	--	Neutral Affective	--
Human Nature	--	Good, neutral evil	PD	--	--	Humane orientation
Time	M-time P-time	Past, present future	LTO*	--	Past, present future	Future orientation
Communication	High context Low context	--	--	--	Specific Diffuse	--
Environment	--	Mastery, Harmony Submission	--	--	--	--

There is wide agreement among scholars and practitioners that the IND-COL dimension, which addresses how people relate to one another, is a crucial and strongly predictive factor when trying to understand cultural differences. Having information about whether a culture is individualistic or collectivistic provides you important knowledge. It provides information regarding how people view themselves in relation to others, meaning it sheds a light on fundamental social interactions and structures.

A second critical dimension is the issue of hierarchy and respect for authority, which also addresses fundamental social structures and how people interact. The communication context and style of communication, which includes how people use information, how they convey it, and what they respond to, is another critical factor. The challenge is that depending on the situation, any of the dimensions you have learned about may become critical. For example, when looking at goal setting and planning, perceptions of time and tolerance for ambiguity may be more important than IND-COL or how directly people communicate with one another. Similarly, when working with people from different genders, which is increasingly a given rather than the exception, understanding cultural values related to gender is necessary. Effective managers who choose to develop and use their CM understand that culture is complex and that it cannot be accessed through simple and quick approaches.

7.2 The Cultural Prototype

The challenges of stereotyping and equating country and culture should not be taken lightly. The knowledge you acquire here allows you to have an estimate of what a prototypical person from a certain country is likely to be. Figure 8.5 provides a graphic depiction of where people might fit regarding various dimensions.

As depicted in Figure 8.5, while the average and highest number of people from one culture may fit at one end of one dimension (D1) and others from another culture may be more typically described at the other end of the dimension (D2), there are individuals from each culture that are outside of the average range; for example, individualistic Japanese, gender-egalitarian Saudis, hierarchical and status-oriented Danes, or direct Thais. Although such individuals may not fit their culture's prototype on some dimensions, they may do so for other dimensions.

Figure 8.5 The Typical Individual

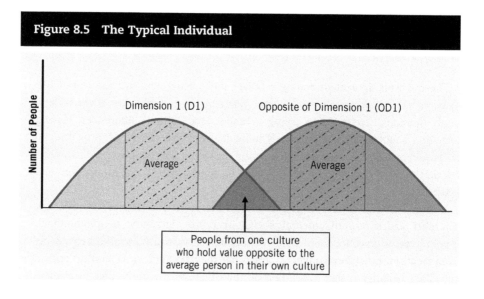

7.3 Frameworks as Tools

With these points in mind, the most productive approach is to consider each of the frameworks as a tool that may help you solve a particular challenge. The more tools you have in your cultural toolbox, the more knowledge you have, the better equipped you will be to cross cultural thresholds. A significant issue is not only getting "how-to" quick instructions on using these tools, but rather having knowledge of their origins and purpose. The deeper knowledge of cultural frameworks and prototypes you have acquired in Chapter 7 and here makes you a better consumer of the information and allows you to make educated decisions regarding what tools you should use and the benefits and disadvantages of each. You also know where to look for more detailed information if and when you need it.

It should be no surprise that you will find some of the tools (frameworks) more difficult to master and are likely to lean toward those that are simpler and more easily accessible, but may provide you with less reliable and less sophisticated understanding. The issue of accessibility partly explains why Hall's cultural context is popular; it is easy to implement and paints cultural differences using one broad concept with two sides. GLOBE, on the other hand, is considerably more complex. The most accessible and user-friendly answers may not always be the best ones, but it may be all that you can use in some situations.

Your goal as a manager should be to implement the frameworks to increase your self-awareness of your own culture or cultures so that you are cognizant of how your culture-as-meta-context (CMC) operates. You also can use the models and the cultural prototypes that derive from them as a starting point in your cross-cultural interactions.

FIRST PERSON REVISITED

Alan Glina in the *First Person* anecdote is able to develop a successful approach to the interaction with his Indian colleagues by relying on his awareness and knowledge of cultural differences. Having multicultural roots, he is able to temper his task-focused approach and harmonize with the group's need for attending to interpersonal interaction. All parties were acting based on their own CMC, but creating a workable approach that addresses everyone's values to some extent involves both awareness of differences and willingness and ability to adopt different behaviors. Alan activated his CM and took culture into consideration to decide what needs to be done. Having knowledge of key values that differentiate among cultures is part of this CM and helped him navigate the situation effectively.

APPLYING WHAT YOU LEARNED: MANAGING ACROSS CULTURES

You now have a lot of information regarding how to differentiate among different cultures based on values. Keep in mind that while these were developed to address cultural differences among people in different countries, they can also be applied to regional or group differences, although there is far less data available at that level. Some pointers on how to apply the different values follow, but first, some words of caution which should be familiar by now:

- Do not automatically assume the people fit into certain cultural groups—do some fact-finding first.

- Do not overgeneralize; the dimensions we have discussed are based on research and may represent typical qualities, but, nonetheless, they are still prototypes that describe the average or typical person.

With those in mind, nothing replaces getting to know people, spending time with them, and learning first-hand who they are and what their values are.

1. *First, look for clues regarding individualism-collectivism and power distance.* These dimensions apply across most cultures and are central. Try to figure out to what extent your partners see the individual as primary and how much they value the group over the individual. Then assess how they view power. Do they value hierarchy and accept inequality or are they more egalitarian? These two key values are excellent and essential starting points. You can achieve this by early preparation and reading, talking to others who may know them, or looking for patterns in their behavior and speech that may provide clues. Do they refer to the team a lot? Do they use "I" more than "we"? How do they address the person with the most power in the room? Can you even tell who has the most power?

2. *Second, pay attention to communication patterns and context.* To what extent are your partners subtle, direct, assertive, linear, emotional, etc.? Communication style can be based on culture or individual personality. Either way, letting them take the lead and adjusting your style to fit your audience will be a quick and effective way to establish rapport and trust.

3. *Third, try to ascertain how much clarity and structure they prefer.* Are your partners comfortable with ambiguity? Do they want clear answers that are black and white? Are they seeking structure and clarity?

As you are trying to figure other people out, don't forget that you must first "know thyself!" Before you do anything else, become aware of your own cultural values and which ones are most important to you. The three general steps above do not replace in-depth knowledge, but they are relatively easy first steps to help avoid major errors.

MANAGERIAL CHALLENGE: THE PERFECT CANDIDATE

Your company has recently transferred you to manage a plant in Mexico. As you get settled in, one of your first decisions is to hire someone to fill the assistant manager position that has been vacant for a while. Miguel, your very efficient office manager who has been extremely helpful to you and has been with the company a long time, quickly suggests one of his cousins, Francisco. According to Miguel, Francisco is the perfect person for the job; he is highly educated, has the right experience, happens to have just moved back in the area from Mexico City to be closer to his aging parents and is looking for a job, and, most importantly, is trustworthy, reliable, and loyal. Francisco's résumé happens to be on top of Miguel's desk, and indeed he does look like a perfect candidate. Miguel tells you that Francisco is coming over to have lunch with him and he can meet with you right away so that you don't have to waste your time and go through the inconvenience of interviewing and checking references of strangers.

1. How do you interpret and explain the office manager's offer?

2. What factors do you need to consider before you make your decision?

3. Will you hire Francisco?

4. What are the consequences of your decision?

5. How does culture factor into your decision?

SELF-ASSESSMENT 8.1: INTEGRATING CULTURAL VALUES

The goal of this self-assessment is to bring together the KNOW and the THINK components of the THINK–KNOW–DO roadmap. Using the knowledge you have acquired in the last two chapters, you can increase your self-awareness and gain further insight into your CMC and how it impacts how you think and behave.

Based on self-assessments you have completed in earlier chapters, select your one/two primary cultures (you may just have one or more than two; select the one or two that are primary to your cultural identity):

1. _____

2. _____

For each of the two cultures you have selected, indicate the corresponding cultural values. Provide one example for each. There is no right or wrong answer; CJI. Keep in mind that for most of the values, the answer is not "either-or" but rather the extent to which one side fits better than another.

For example: If your primary culture is Japanese and you closely identify with that culture, it is likely that you will prefer communication to be less direct; "we" would be more important than "I"; your in-group would be the larger society, etc.

Cultural Value	My #1 culture	My #2 culture
Communication context (high to low) *The extent to which communication should be direct and specific.*		
Individualism-collectivism 1 *The extent to which "I" is more important than "we." The extent to which I am independent from others.*		
Individualism 2 *Who do I consider to be the group to which I have loyalty? My family, my community, my organization, or the larger society?*		
Power distance *The extent to which inequality between those with and without power is acceptable.*		

Cultural Value	My #1 culture	My #2 culture
Tolerance for ambiguity *The extent to which I am comfortable with ambiguity and uncertainty.*		
Performance *The extent to which my identity is determined by what I do and how much I achieve.*		
Emotion *The extent to which I believe showing emotion is appropriate.*		
Human nature *The extent to which I believe people are fundamentally good or evil.*		
Time 1 *The extent to which I am short- or long-term focused.*		
Time 2 *The extent to which I focus on past traditions, the present, or the future.*		
Environment *The extent to which I believe people should use the environment for their benefit, live in harmony with it, or submit to mother nature.*		

Interpretation and Reflection

This self-assessment is designed to help you identify your cultural values. CJI and one set of values is not objectively better than another. However, you may have some preferences regarding which values fit you better. For example, your culture may be highly individualistic, but you, because of many factors including your personality or life experiences, could prefer a more collectivistic approach (this is what Triandis called being allocentric). Additionally, for many people who belong to more than one culture, the cultural values may contradict one another. In that case, you can live with the conflict and act differently in different situations or lean more toward one side or another. For example, your Mexican culture may be high context and subtle, but because you grew up in an individualistic culture such as the United States, you may be more direct (and likely to be told by your grandmother or aunt that you are too direct or even rude!).

SELF-ASSESSMENT 8.2: TIGHT AND LOOSE

The goal of this self-assessment is to further elaborate on the individualism-collectivism dimension and provide you with deeper knowledge regarding your cultural values.

Indicate the degree to which you agree with each of the following statements by circling the appropriate number (1 = strongly disagree, 2 = disagree, 3 = agree, 4 = strongly agree).

		Strongly Disagree	Disagree	Agree	Strongly Agree
1.	It is important for everyone to follow the same rules.	1	2	3	4
2.	People should not get away with breaking the rules.	1	2	3	4
3.	There are often different ways to do things.	1	2	3	4
4.	For groups to be successful, it is important for all members to get on the same page.	1	2	3	4
5.	People who do not follow established norms should face negative consequences.	1	2	3	4
6.	Those who have different views in a team should be encouraged to express them.	1	2	3	4
7.	The cohesion of a group can be threatened when people voice different opinions.	1	2	3	4
8.	Having too many norms and rules prevents people from being creative.	1	2	3	4
9.	It is important for groups to clearly state what the norms for behavior are.	1	2	3	4
10.	For society to function well, everyone must be subject to the same rules.	1	2	3	4
11.	Having clear rules allows people to figure out what they should do.	1	2	3	4
12.	Group members should self-regulate to assure that they follow the rules.	1	2	3	4

Scoring

Reverse your score for items 3, 6, and 8 (1 = 4, 2 = 3, 3 = 2, 4 = 1).

Then add up your scores for the ten questions.

Total: _____

The maximum score is 48, the minimum is 12 (midpoint is 24). A higher score indicates belief in tight rather than loose values.

Interpretation

A higher score indicates that you value rules and norms and believe that everyone must follow them in order for a group to function well (tight). A lower score indicates that you value looser norms and likely tolerate deviation from norms. Consider your score on this self-assessment along with your value of individualism and collectivism.

Sources: Based on information in Triandis (1995, 2004) and Uz (2014).

SELF-ASSESSMENT 8.3: HORIZONTAL AND VERTICAL

The goal of this self-assessment is to further elaborate on the individualism-collectivism dimension and provide you with deeper knowledge regarding your cultural values.

Indicate the degree to which you agree with each of the following statements by circling the appropriate number (1 = strongly disagree, 2 = disagree, 3 = agree, 4 = strongly agree).

		Strongly Disagree	Disagree	Agree	Strongly Agree
1.	I often do my own thing.	1	2	3	4
2.	My happiness depends very much on the happiness of those around me.	1	2	3	4
3.	It is important to me that I respect the decision made by my group.	1	2	3	4
4.	It is important for me to do my job better than others.	1	2	3	4
5.	I enjoy being unique and different from the others in many ways.	1	2	3	4
6.	Winning is everything.	1	2	3	4
7.	If a coworker gets a prize, I would feel proud.	1	2	3	4
8.	I am a unique individual.	1	2	3	4
9.	I feel good when I cooperate with others.	1	2	3	4
10.	I would sacrifice an activity that I enjoy very much if my family did not approve of it.	1	2	3	4
11.	Competition is law of nature.	1	2	3	4
12.	It is my duty to take care of my family, even when I have to sacrifice what I want.	1	2	3	4
13.	The well-being of my coworkers is important to me.	1	2	3	4
14.	Family members should stick together, no matter what sacrifices are required.	1	2	3	4
15.	I'd rather depend on myself than others.	1	2	3	4
16.	When another person does better than I do, I get tense and irritated.	1	2	3	4

Scoring

Horizontal Individualist:

Add up your score for Items 1, 5, 8, and 15: _____

Vertical Individualist:

Add up your score for Items 4, 6, 11, and 16: _____

Horizontal Collectivist:

Add up your score for Items 2, 7, 9, and 13: _____

Vertical Collectivist.

Add up your score for Items 3, 10, 12, and 14: _____

Interpretation

This self-assessment provides you with information regarding the extent to which your values match each of the following groups: HI, VI, HC, and VC. You may fit in more than one category. There is no right or wrong answers. To interpret your scores, consider whether you lean more toward horizontal or vertical and more toward individualist or collectivist.

Additionally, referring back to the information in this chapter about the H-C dimension, assess how well you fit in with each of the values and consider the source of that cultural value. You should also consider whether you have different cultural identities that may fit into different categories.

Sources: Adapted from questionnaires developed by Singelis et al. (1995) and Triandis and Gelfand (1998).

EXERCISE 8.1: CULTURAL BLUNDER

Objective: This exercise helps you apply the knowledge you have acquired.

Instructions:

Individual Work

Think of a cross-cultural situation that you believe you did not handle well. This could be related to national, regional, or group culture (including gender). Sketch out the details of the situation (e.g., who did what, what went wrong) and be ready to share with your group.

Group Work

In groups of 3–4 people, share the situations you outlined. For each person, the group needs to address the following questions?

1. What role did differences in cultural values play in the situations?

2. Which one of the dimensions or models that you have learned about in the last two chapters fits best to explain the situation? For example, the differences may have been based on the two people having different conceptions of gender roles, or different styles of communication, or different perceptions of power distance. The goal is to focus on cultural rather than personality factors (which may also be contributing to the situations).

3. What could have been done differently?

After each person's example is analyzed, the group must select one to present to the class.

Presentation

The presentation should be 5–8 minutes and address the following:

1. Briefly describe the situation

2. Explain which cultural dimensions or model helps explain the situation

3. Propose alternatives

EXERCISE 8.2: WHAT WOULD YOU DO?

Objective: This exercise helps you apply the knowledge you have acquired and develop your cross-cultural self-awareness

Instructions: In your group of 4–5 people, discuss the following scenarios and questions.

1. You are in a car driven by one of your friends when s/he hits a pedestrian. Your friend was driving approximately 10 miles over the speed limit. You are the only witness to the accident. As the police is arriving at the scene, your friend asks you to confirm that s/he was driving at the speed limit.

   Would you lie for your friend? Why or why not? What factors would impact your decision?

2. Because of one person's error in your team, the paper that you handed out for your class project includes a section that is plagiarized. Your instructor has called the team to her/his office to discuss the situation.

   Would you identify and blame the person who made the error or face the situation as a team? What factors would impact your decision?

3. Your boss has a teenager in high school who just tried out for the basketball team but did not make it. S/he finds out that your mother/father is the coach of the basketball team in that high school. Your boss asks you to do her/him a favor to ask your mother/father to give the kid a second chance.

   Does your boss have the right to ask this of you? Would you agree to do the favor? What factors would impact your decision?

Once you have discussed the questions, please wait for further instructions.

Source: Some questions in this exercise are based on the work of Trompenaars and Hampden-Turner (2012).

CASE STUDY: THE CANADIAN IN AUSTRALIA

Marie Bouchard is a 36-year-old French-Canadian manager working in Australia. She grew up in Montreal, has traveled throughout Canada, studied in the United States, Canada, and France, and has worked with diverse groups in Canada. Marie is deeply rooted in her French-Canadian identity, is a practicing Catholic, and is strongly dedicated to her career. In addition to her MBA from McGill University, she has completed certificate programs from Harvard and INSEAD and has been on the fast-track as a high-potential manager in her company. She has carefully selected several high-powered mentors who have guided and mentored her. Marie has developed an easy-going management style where she consults with her colleagues and direct reports while keeping some distance. She has found that she is not comfortable with too much familiarity, and that particularly as a woman, she needs to maintain some formality for people to respect her. She has consistently received high marks for her management skills and her technical expertise, making her one of the up-and-coming stars in her company.

Marie has completed several short-term stints with her company throughout the world, and this assignment in Sidney is a perfect step for her to build her international portfolio as she prepares for top executive positions. Her team members in Sydney include four European-Australians, Charlotte, Oliver, Lucas, and Jackson, and four Asians, Kiyoshi from Japan, Gan from Thailand, and Ashraf and Jihan from Malaysia. Marie hits the ground running and dives right into the work. She is the newest member, although Gan, Ashraf, and Jihan have not been in Australia long and Kiyoshi and Gan only recently moved to Sydney. Marie is replacing a much-beloved Australian manager who just retired after many years with the company. Her team is working well together, there are no major challenges and all the group members are well-trained and hard working.

The four Australians, believing that they should help the team feel welcome and show them some true Australian hospitality, are hard at work getting the group together for social events. They organize beach outings and after-work drinks. All team members have welcomed the socializing and even Ashraf, who is a practicing Muslim and doesn't drink alcohol, has eagerly joined in. Marie attended the first after-work social hour and treated everyone, but has not attended any of the other events. One of the Australian managers on another team who has run into Marie at the gym has encouraged her to hang out with the group, but Marie has kept her distance, instead choosing to socialize with managers at her level. She has, however, offered to pick up the tab for some of the social events and has encouraged them to continue getting together.

A couple of months after she starts, Gan, who is one of the top performers and always very discreet, requests to meet with her privately. After much hesitation, he asks her for advice on how to deal with Kiyoshi. Gan says Kiyoshi, who is one of the older members of the team, is micro-managing their project and pushing the other members too hard without providing much support. Gan says:

Kiyoshi is working very hard, like we all are. It's just that sometimes he really focuses on details and procedures that may not be so important. It makes it a bit hard to focus on what really matters. Of course, it just may be that I am not used to his work style.

Gan mentions that Jihan has also been upset, but did not want to bother her. He adds that they are effective, but they seem to be having difficulty working together. Marie asks Gan how serious the problem is. Gan tells her it's not a big deal, and that he just wanted to bring it up. Marie talks to other group members about the possible conflict and whether it has affected their work. Jihan states: "Yes, there have been some challenges and we have had words. But we will work it out. We get our work done; you don't need to concern yourself." Ashraf said all was well and that she was very happy with the work and her colleagues. Charlotte, the only Australian woman in the team, brushes it all off saying: "Kiyoshi is just being a guy. What do you expect? He likes to be in charge and likes everything done just so. It's no big deal." The other Australians on the team, Oliver, Lucas, and Jackson, shrug it off and say they had not noticed anything. Marie concludes that the problem is minor and decides to let them work it out, as she continues to monitor the situation.

In spite of the earlier complaint from Gan, the team seems to be very productive. They are exceeding all their targets and deadlines and have had great feedback from customers. As part of her responsibilities to help each team member with their development, after 3 months of working with them, Marie sets up brief discussions with each as a check-in. She encourages Ashraf to speak out more at meetings because they really need her considerable IT expertise. Ashraf responds:

You are right. I tend to be quiet; I know I should jump in, but it's hard. Everyone is so loud and I am still getting used to the rough language our Australian colleagues use. It's still a shock, but they are so nice. I will try my best and welcome your mentoring on how to get better.

Marie tells her to just jump in next time and not let them intimidate her. She chats with Kiyoshi about the team and asks him how things are going. He initially says all is well but after she presses him he hesitantly responds:

All is well of course; we are doing fine. I am doing my best to contribute and provide my experience to the team whenever I can. Sometimes the younger people can be impatient; that is normal. We just need to give them time.

During the meeting with Charlotte, she reiterates her earlier comments about "boys will be boys." She particularly mentions Kiyoshi and Lucas being too macho and trying to take over things when the team works together, but she says she is used to them and can handle it. Oliver and Jackson both are happy and productive. Marie particularly appreciates how easy it is to manage them; they do their work well and never ask for anything. Lucas, who together with Kiyoshi is one of the more senior members, gives her a run-down of his opinion of the more junior members and their performance and offers his help to supervise them more closely if needed. He also brings up how close-knit the group has become as a result of their social gatherings and mentions how many of the other managers have been dropping by with their team members: "We often have 15–20 people all hanging out; it's been great." During her meeting with Gan, Marie expects him to bring out his earlier concerns, but to her surprise, he does not. He tells her all is well.

Based on company HR procedure, all new managers get an informal review that includes feedback from several people at their level across the company and their direct reports. Marie's boss, Lachlan, is generally happy with her performance and believes she is on track. She gets a strong positive review. He also informs her that Gan has requested a transfer to another team in order to expand his experience base. The company typically approves these requests, but Gan's departure would leave Marie's team without an international marketing expert. Lachlan asks her to give it some thought and let him know about her decision. Meanwhile, he recommends that she takes some of the comments from colleagues into consideration, as she plans her next couple of years in Australia. Below are some of the comments that Lachlan shares with Marie.

Very efficient. Seems to have a lot of pride in her work.

She is nice and cares about the work. She does appear aloof. It's hard to talk to her about things.

Always willing to listen to concerns.

Great work ethic. Likes to keep to herself. Hard to get to know her.

She's all about the work and good at it.

Excellent technical expertise. Very goal-focused. Needs no help on anything.

Seems to have some trouble adjusting to life in Australia.

Marie is somewhat puzzled. It is clear that she is doing her job well. Gan's resignation has taken her by surprise, but people leave, so she can handle that. Mostly, she is not sure what she needs to take into consideration … she loves her work and is very happy in Sydney…; the review is very positive. What's there to consider?

Questions

1. What are the challenges that Marie needs to address?

2. Using concepts from this chapter, what is your analysis of the case?

3. What are your recommendations to Marie?

PART FIVE

DO—LEADING MULTICULTURAL ORGANIZATIONS

The fifth part of this book integrates the knowledge and skills you have acquired in the previous chapters with theories and practical information about organizational processes for leading and managing multicultural organizations. Now that you have a solid understanding of culture and knowledge regarding how to describe and predict cultural differences, we examine how these concepts can be applied to lead and manage better in global and multicultural contexts. The attention is on the DO part of the THINK–KNOW–DO roadmap. Chapter 9 explores leadership in a cultural context. Chapter 10 considers the challenges and opportunities of motivating employees and leading teams across cultures. Chapter 11 discusses organizational processes. Finally, Chapter 12 reviews and integrates the information and knowledge you have acquired to highlight how to successfully cross cultural thresholds and develop a cultural mindset (see Figure V.1).

Figure V.1   The Focus of Part V

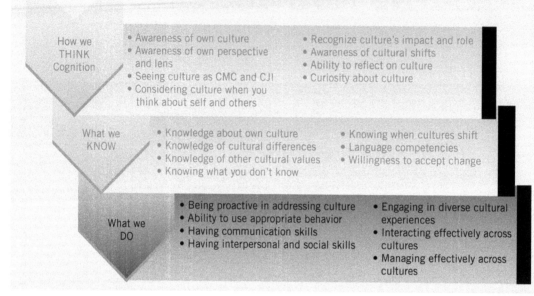

CM: THINK–KNOW–DO

How we THINK Cognition
- Awareness of own culture
- Awareness of own perspective and lens
- Seeing culture as CMC and CJI
- Considering culture when you think about self and others
- Recognize culture's impact and role
- Awareness of cultural shifts
- Ability to reflect on culture
- Curiosity about culture

What we KNOW
- Knowledge about own culture
- Knowledge of cultural differences
- Knowledge of other cultural values
- Knowing what you don't know
- Knowing when cultures shift
- Language competencies
- Willingness to accept change

What we DO
- Being proactive in addressing culture
- Ability to use appropriate behavior
- Having communication skills
- Having interpersonal and social skills
- Engaging in diverse cultural experiences
- Interacting effectively across cultures
- Managing effectively across cultures

CHAPTER NINE

FIRST PERSON

He's the Boss. Doesn't He Know What to Do?

I had been assigned as the director of my company's operations in the Middle East and was enthusiastic and ready to take on the challenge. I speak Arabic reasonably well and had traveled throughout most of the region multiple times. All of the team members who reported directly to me were from the region, all educated in a mix of local and Western universities. They were young, eager to learn, and responsive. One of our first challenges was to manage the integration of a new company that we had just acquired, a complex situation that had many different pieces and required broad expertise. I had successfully handled these types of integrations in the United States and in Europe, but I was aware that this one was particularly thorny because of several regional conflicts that made interactions especially difficult. I knew I would need the team's expertise and best ideas to make it work, so I was not shy about asking. I was upfront and told them about my extensive experience and success with these types of complex problems, then sought their help. I told them how difficult this merger was and that we had to be creative and use all of our resources, especially their expertise and experience, to make it a success. They all agreed and indicated that they were confident about our success. We had lunch catered to continue our first planning meeting and everyone seemed to be on-board. A few months into the implementation of our merger, things were not going well. I was facing all the challenges I had expected, and some I had not. And, I was getting no help from the team; no initiative, no suggestions, no ideas, no creative solutions; no push-back on any of my plans. They implemented faithfully and precisely everything I came up with, and that was sometimes the problem because I made mistakes that they didn't point out or try to correct. Pressure was mounting, and so was my frustration. One afternoon, I was early and about to walk into one

Learning Objectives

9.1 Review the definitions of leadership in a cultural context.

9.2 Summarize key leadership theories from the trait, behavior, and contingency eras.

9.3 Detail current neo-charismatic theories of leadership and their link to culture.

9.4 Appraise the global and worldly leadership approaches.

9.5 Elaborate on the leadership attributes proposed by GLOBE and different cultures' ideals of leadership.

9.6 Examine three non-Western leadership approaches.

of our weekly team meetings. The door of the conference room was ajar; I overheard my name in a hushed voice: "Why did they sent him? He seems to know nothing. Why does he keep asking for our help? He's the boss; doesn't he know what to do?" I was so surprised! This is not what I had expected. None of them had ever indicated that they questioned my abilities in any way. If anything, they seemed to support me more than is typical...

–Anonymous

The *First Person* anecdote illustrates an age-old leadership challenge that is compounded by differences in culture. What people expect of their leaders and what makes leaders effective depend on many situational factors, and of course, culture is one such complex situational factor. Leading people effectively has been a challenge, an opportunity, and a tremendous responsibility throughout human history. While the application of scientific methods to the study of leadership is relatively new, the interest in the topic is not. Philosophers, theologians, and historians have addressed and discussed leaders and leadership for millennia. From ancient Chinese, Persians, and Indians to classic Greek and Renaissance-era European philosophers to modern-day social scientists, the quest for answers to the deceptively simple riddles of leadership is ongoing. Who will be a good leader? What should leaders do? How do we prepare leaders? What does it mean to be an effective leader? There are many answers to these questions, and introducing culture only makes those answers more complex and multifaceted.

As you will see in this chapter, considerable research has been directed at understanding the circumstances and effects of culture on leadership. We present a definition of leadership within a cultural context, review several leadership theories and their cross-cultural applications, and present the concepts of global and worldly leadership. We then examine the extensive GLOBE research that considers the impact of culture on leadership and close this chapter with consideration of several non-Western views of leadership.

1. DEFINING LEADERSHIP IN A CULTURAL CONTEXT

LO 9.1 Review the definitions of leadership in a cultural context

In 2000, two US American and one British executives of a US technology company in Singapore decided to recognize and motivate their workforce using the occasion of the Chinese New Year. They believed that they were taking Chinese culture into consideration by offering their employees red envelopes containing four Singapore dollars (Pyrillis, 2011). The employees were confused and offended by the gift since the number four denotes death in many Asian cultures. The company leaders quickly reacted and decided to correct the situation by reissuing the envelopes with eight Singapore dollars this time. Unfortunately, the second time around, the amount included symbolized "double death." A gesture that was meant to show appreciation while taking into consideration the cultural context and increase morale negatively impacted motivation and engagement.

The many examples of success and failure of companies that operate in countries and cultures other than their own are more often than not related to leadership decisions that are made either without consideration of culture or with inaccurate or limited knowledge of cultural differences:

- Groupon was not able to replicate its considerable success in China because managers did not consider the tastes and habits of Chinese customers.

- Mattel, the giant toy maker, closed its 36,000-square-foot, six-story Barbie store in Shanghai only 2 years after it opened because managers made poor decisions regarding how to market a relatively unfamiliar product.

- Starbucks has successfully expanded across the globe, but faced considerable challenges in Australia and Israel because managers did not understand the coffee culture in those countries.

- McDonald's managers struggled to make the hamburgers successful in India, where calling their Big Mac the Maharaja Mac did not seem to help. It took them years to fully take culture into consideration and realize that the large majority of Indians do not eat beef.

1.1 Leaders and Leadership

After learning about cultural differences related to how we view relationships, power, time, and many other factors, it is no surprise that culture affects leaders and leadership. After all, leadership is a social phenomenon that involves people interacting, therefore, it unavoidably involves culture. As presented in the *First Person* anecdote and the examples above, who we expect our leaders to be and what we want them to do varies across cultures.

We know bad leadership when we see it. Bad leaders are abusive, self-centered, dishonest, and uncommunicative. But simply doing the opposite of what is bad is not enough to make a leader effective. There are many people who are kind and honest and communicate well, and yet they are not considered leaders and if they are, they are not necessarily effective. Defining effective leadership is challenging.

There are numerous definitions, each emphasizing different elements of leadership (for an extensive review and discussion of the various definitions, see Bass, 1990b):

- Dictionaries define *leading* as "guiding and directing others on a course."

- Researchers have defined leadership as an integral part of the group process (Krech & Crutchfield, 1948).

- Leadership as an influence process (Bass, 1960; Cartwright, 1965; Katz & Kahn, 1966).

- Leadership as the initiation of structure (Homans, 1950) and the instrument of goal achievement, just to mention a few.

Some have considered leaders to be servants of their followers (Greenleaf, 1998), and many recent approaches have emphasized the importance of emotional connection and inspiration (Bass & Avolio, 1990). Before we define our concepts, let's clarify the difference between *leaders who are people*, and *leadership, which is a process*. We often use the terms interchangeably, as we assume that the people who lead exercise leadership, but the two can be distinct. A person can be designated to be a leader, but not be able to actually lead effectively, and leadership can occur outside of a single individual.

1.2 Definition of Leadership and Effectiveness

The majority of the definitions of leadership share the following interrelated themes (Nahavandi, 2015):

- First, leadership is a *group and social phenomenon*; there can be no leaders without followers.

- Second, leadership involves some form of interpersonal *influence* or *persuasion*. Leaders interact with other people to guide them in certain directions.

- Third, leadership is *goal directed* and *action oriented*; leaders use their influence to guide others through a certain course of action or toward the achievement of certain goals.

- Fourth, the presence of leaders necessarily assumes some form of *hierarchy within a group*.

When combined, these four themes yield the following definition of a leader:

A leader is any person who influences individuals and groups within an organization, helps them establish goals, and guides them toward achievement of those goals, thereby allowing them to be effective. (Nahavandi, 2015, p. 3)

Furthermore, leadership effectiveness generally involves three dimensions. First is achievement of goals (whatever those goals are), second is internal maintenance or cohesion of the group, and finally some ability to adapt to change. Putting these three together:

Leaders are effective when their group achieves their goals, the group is cohesive, and they are able to adapt to change.

In other words, goal achievement is not the only measure of being an effective leader. Taking care of people and helping the group adapt to change are also key (Nahavandi, 2015). A leader who achieves his goals and keeps the group together but is not able to help them address the next challenge or adapt to change has limited effectiveness. Similarly, the leader who pushes through changes, but her group disintegrates as a result, or there is considerable internal conflict, she is only partially effective.

1.3 Leadership and Cultural Dimensions

Every element of the definition of leadership and leadership effectiveness and the themes that underlie them are affected by culture. As depicted in Figure 9.1, leadership is a social phenomenon that occurs within a cultural context. Who and what we consider good leaders and leadership is, to a great extent, determined by our CMC and the cultural dimensions that we have discussed in previous chapters (see Figure 9.1). From the power and importance of the group or collective, to what is considered appropriate communication style to influence and persuade, to how we view nature and time, to considerations of hierarchy and equality, all are culture-specific.

1.3.1 Cultural Values. For example, how much a leader should rely on the group and how she can and should use the group effectively depends on the CMC of both the leader and her followers (as illustrated in our *First Person* example). In individualistic cultures, group members are likely to jump in with their ideas, and depending on whether they are vertical or horizontal (e.g., Sweden vs. the United States), they may or may not accept unilateral decisions from their bosses.

In collectivistic cultures, reliance on the group and building consensus may be expected of the leader, yet the horizontal vs. vertical nature of the culture may impact whether group members will defer to the leader or expect equal participation. Similarly, persuasion and building consensus in a high-context and indirect culture that is more emotional than rational (e.g., Mexico) would require a passionate message filled

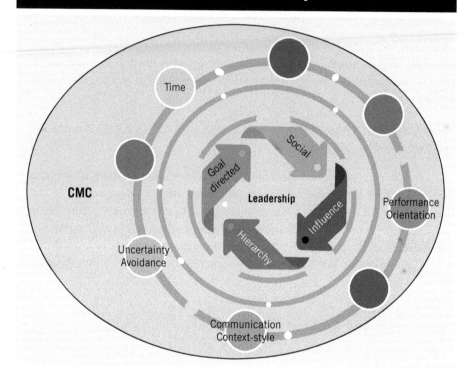

Figure 9.1   Cultural Dimensions and Leadership

with symbolism, whereas persuading followers who are low-context, are direct and assertive, and value rationality over emotions (e.g., Germany) necessitates a direct and simple message based on facts.

Which goals are valued and their time orientation are further impacted by culture. Should goals be based on specific outcomes and tasks to be accomplished and results to be delivered or be based on the well-being of the group or society? Should they be short-term-oriented or aim for long-term accomplishments? The answers depend on the time perspective and performance orientation of the leader and followers. In Japan and China, the time orientation will be much longer than in Australia or the Netherlands.

How much power the leader has, how formal that power is, and how approachable the leader should be again will depend on the CMC and cultural values, specifically regarding power distance. What may be considered cohesiveness and lack of conflict is partially impacted by culture. To a Swede, arguments within a group and with the leader are normal; the same level of disagreement to a group of Thais may be intolerable. How much the group expects to change may depend on cultural values and so forth.

1.3.2 Who Gets to Lead. More fundamentally, who gets to lead and how the leader is selected vary based on various dimensions of culture. In ascriptive cultures, who your family is will play a higher role in determining whether you get selected as a leader than in achievement-oriented cultures. For example, a leader's personal family background and caste will be critical in India where the culture is ascriptive, whereas in achievement-oriented cultures such as Canada or the United States, the selection criteria for leadership will most likely emphasize personal expertise and accomplishments. Similarly, women will have a better chance of reaching leadership positions and being successful in more gender egalitarian cultures such as Finland and Israel than more masculine cultures such as Japan, Mexico, or China. Considering all these factors, it is hard to separate leaders from the CMC in which they operate.

1.4 Is Leadership Universal?

We have been discussing the ways in which leadership may be affected by culture but there is an even more basic consideration:

Does the word, and the concepts it evokes for those of us who speak English, even exist in other languages and cultures?

The idea of someone in charge with a title and role within a formal hierarchy, such as the concept of ruler, boss, chief, supervisor, director, and so forth, is present in all cultures. The word leader, however, is not universal. The words in the previous sentence suggest the idea of a formal hierarchy and formal title. However, the other elements that we associate with leaders or leadership as a process of persuasion and guidance that is independent from the hierarchy of a group or an organization appear to be themselves culturally contingent, present in some, but not in all cultures.

1.4.1 Does Leadership Exist When There Is No Word for It? Consider that in Japanese, French, Italian, Russian, and Spanish, as well as many other languages, there is no direct translation for the words leaders and leadership. Instead, the word *leader* is used in various phonetic forms, for example, *líder* in Spanish. In Farsi, the closest translation of the word is *rahbar* which, because it has strong religious and political connotations, cannot be used in management. *Fürher* in German and *önder* in Turkish are similarly not appropriate for organizational settings.

If there is no word for a concept, does it still exist? The answer is not simple. There are people "in charge" in all cultures. The processes involved in getting people to achieve goals exist in all societies. However, who gets to lead, what makes them legitimate and effective, what followers expect, and so forth are culture-specific. For example, Doris Schedlitzki's (2012) research about language and leadership has shown that for Germans, leadership is achieved through technical expertise and competence, whereas in the United Kingdom, nontechnical attributes related to leading change are more relevant.

1.4.2 Current Ideas of Leadership Are WEIRD. Our current ideas regarding leadership and the corresponding research are, to some extent, the by-product of highly individualistic and leader-focused cultures. Many leadership researchers have lamented the excessive leader-centric approach that concentrates on the person of the leader (Antonakis, Day, & Schyns, 2012; Bryman, 2011; Nahavandi & Corbett, 2018) and disregards the complex ecosystem surrounding leadership that involves all other individuals and processes required to achieving goals (Mintzberg & Caldwell, 2017).

Social scientists and cross-cultural psychologists have used the acronym WEIRD—Western, Educated, Industrialized, Rich, and Democratic (Henrich, Heine, & Norenzayan, 2010)—to relate the narrow base and reach of many of our theories. Given that the majority of our research is done in this "WEIRD" context and that the large majority of people in the world do not fit in these groups, it is critical that we consider culture when applying our theories to other contexts. For example, in some cultures, leaders are more transitory and impermanent and specific to situations so that leadership is shared and there are different leaders for different tasks and goals. For example, Native cultures in the United States have a tradition where leadership is distributed and where being a leader is project- and situation-based (Becker, 1997). The Ojibwe word for leader is *ogimauh*, which translates roughly as the foremost person for the one project (Johnston, 1995). As situations change, the person leading changes as well. Similarly, in Japan, with no Japanese word for leader, the person in charge is a role model and one who facilitates and coordinates group processes (Buckenmeyer, 2009).

As we review leadership research and theory in the remainder of this chapter, keep these caveats in mind. We are applying a concept that is, in-and-of-itself, culture-specific. Although the world is global and business cultures in particular are heavily influenced by European and North American approaches, cultures are still distinct and people have different CMCs. What is developed in one cultural context does not automatically and necessarily transfer to another.

2. EARLY APPROACHES TO LEADERSHIP: TRAIT, BEHAVIOR, AND CONTINGENCY

LO 9.2 Summarize key leadership theories from the trait, behavior, and contingency eras

The modern scientific study of leadership started with the Western Industrial Revolution around the end of the 19th century when social scientists, instead of relying on intuition and a description of common practices, applied scientific methods and principles to measure, understand, and predict leadership effectiveness. The field of leadership is divided into four general approaches or eras: trait, behavior, contingency, and neo-charismatic (Nahavandi, 2015). Each approach has made significant contributions to our understanding of leadership and each presents some challenges (see Table 9.1 for a summary). It is important to note that the very large majority of the theory and research, and certainly all of the early work that we discuss in this section, has been done in Europe and North America, in countries that fit into GLOBE's Anglo and Germanic country clusters. As you are now aware, the researchers' CMCs have inevitably guided their perspective. Although many of the concepts are used to teach leadership across the world, their cultural applicability is not well established.

2.1 The Trait Era

Do you believe that some people have certain innate characteristics and traits that make them born leaders? Is leadership something we do or something we are? Is effective leadership the same across all situations? Are leaders born or made? These are all fundamental questions that theories of leadership have addressed.

The earliest formal research about leadership was dominated by the belief that leaders are born rather than made. Thomas Carlyle's book *Heroes and Hero Worship* (1907), William James's writings (1880) about the great men of history, and Galton's study (1869) of the role of heredity mark this trait era with the basic assumption that innate biological attributes determine human personality and behavior. Accordingly, researchers believed that their birth endowed certain people with special qualities that made it possible for them to become leaders. Based on these innate characteristics, some people were presumed to be leaders regardless of the situation or context: they were born leaders. The social structures and context in that period that afforded highly limited opportunities to common people, all but assured that only those born in certain upper strata of society were bound to become leaders of industry, further reinforcing these beliefs. The conviction that personality and other innate characteristics are determinants of leadership sent researchers on a massive hunt for leadership traits. The contemporaneous development of a variety of ability and personality assessments such as the IQ test made their research possible.

2.1.1 Some Leadership Traits. Researchers collected extensive demographic and personality data from existing leaders and followers and identified some attributes of leaders (for a thorough review of the literature, see Bass, 1990b). Specifically, the traits associated with leadership most consistently were:

- Sociability

- Aggression

- Motivation to take charge and lead

- Willingness to accept responsibility

Table 9.1 Early Theories of Leadership

Approach/Era	Assumptions and Description	Key Findings and Contributions	Weaknesses	Cultural Application
Trait Era Late 1800s to mid-1940s	• Leaders are born • There are a set of traits or attributes that make a person a leader • The difference between leaders and followers are their traits	• Identification of some traits and attributes related to leadership • No single trait or group of traits define or predict leadership	• Overly simplistic • Lack of consideration of the context or situation	• Based on European and North American CMC • Some research on traits or attributes has been done across cultures • More research is needed
Behavior Era Mid-1940s to late 1970s	• Effective leaders display certain behaviors	• Task (structuring) and relationships consideration are the two major categories of leader • Both types of behaviors can be effective • Behaviors can be measured and taught	• Overly simplistic • Lack of consideration of the context or situation	• Based on European and North American CMC • The two general categories of behavior are present in other cultures, but they may not be as distinct and separate • More research is needed
Contingency Era Early 1960s to present	• To understand and predict leadership we must consider both the leader and the situation	• Different leadership traits, attributes, styles, or behaviors work in different situations • The context of leadership includes followers, task, and power • What works depends on the situation	• Different theories and models have presented different problems • Too focused on supervisory and midlevel managers • Does not address change • Too much focus on transaction	• Based on European and North American CMC • Some of the models have been tested in other cultures • Results are mixed • More research is needed

- Being popular

- Having a sense of humor.

However, the differences between leaders and followers in these regards were not significant or consistent.

2.1.2 End of the Trait Era. As a result, more than 40 years of leadership trait research provided little evidence to support that leaders are born and that leadership can be explained or predicted through one or more traits. In other words, one trait or a combination of traits does not either guarantee being or becoming a leader or ensure that the person will be effective. However, the trait approach has contributed to our understanding of leaders by establishing that traits may play a role in leadership. Current interest in emotional intelligence and other traits has also yielded new research on the leader's individual characteristics suggesting that leaders' personality, by limiting their behavioral range or by making it more or less difficult to learn certain behaviors or undertake some actions, plays a key role in their effectiveness. None-theless, it is by no means the only or even the dominant factor in effective leadership.

2.2 The Behavior Era

As it became evident that the trait approach was too simplistic and could not explain or predict leadership, the advent of World War II created an urgent need to identify and train leaders. Partially driven by the dominance of behaviorist theories during this period, particularly in the United States and Great Britain, instead of identifying *who* would be an effective leader, leadership researchers focused on *what* leaders did. Focusing on behaviors provides several advantages over a trait approach:

- First, behaviors can be observed readily and reliably

- Second, they can be measured consistently

- Finally, teaching behaviors is much easier and more feasible than changing personality traits.

These factors provided a clear benefit to the military and various other organizations with a practical interest in leadership. Instead of identifying leaders who had particular personality traits, they could focus on training people to perform effective leadership behaviors. The early work of Lewin and his associates (Lewin & Lippit, 1938; Lewin, Lippit, & White, 1939) concerning democratic, autocratic, and laissez-faire leadership laid the foundation for the behavior approach to leadership and several major research projects identified key leadership behaviors (Fleishman, 1953; Halpin & Winer, 1957; Hemphill & Coons, 1957).

2.2.1 Two Major Leadership Behaviors. As a result, a clear and consistent list of *task* (also referred to as structuring) and *relationship* (or consideration) behaviors were identified as central to the work of leaders. Task/structuring behaviors include actions such as:

- Setting goals

- Setting timelines and deadlines

- Clarifying expectations and assigning tasks

Relationship/consideration behaviors include

- Showing empathy and understanding

- Being friendly

- Encouraging participation and nurturing followers.

The behavior approach established that in order for leaders to be effective they must attend to the task and to relationships and their followers' needs. Being considerate and supportive engenders higher follower satisfaction, loyalty, and trust, whereas structuring behaviors are more closely related to job performance (for a review, see Judge, Piccolo, & Ilies, 2004).

2.2.2 The End of the Behavior Era. Similar to the trait approach, the behavior approach to leadership, by concentrating only on behaviors and disregarding powerful situational elements, provides a relatively simplistic view of a highly complex process and, therefore, fails to provide a thorough understanding of the leadership phenomenon. Yet, *the two general categories of task and relationship behaviors are well established as the primary leadership behaviors.* Researchers and practitioners continue to discuss what leaders do in these general terms. However, this dichotomy between task and relationship does not describe leader's behavior adequately for cultures where values may be less individualistic and people may have different ideals of leadership (Ayman & Chemers, 1983; Chemers, 1969; Misumi & Peterson, 1985). The behavior research was further not able to establish which of these two sets of behaviors are more effective.

2.3 The Contingency Era

The next era of leadership theories considered both the leader and some aspects of the situation or context with the assumption that there is not one best way to lead. In other words, this contingency approach does not assume that one set of traits or behaviors will be effective in all situations, rather, what works depends or is contingent upon the situation. The concept of contingency or the situational nature of leadership and the fact that the same style or behavior does not work in all settings is well established and continues to be part of current thinking in leadership.

2.3.1 Major Contingency Theories. The most well-established and researched model among these approaches is Fred Fiedler's Contingency Theory (Fiedler, 1967; Fiedler & Chemers, 1974), which found that leaders' effectiveness is a function of the match between the leaders' style (task or relationship) and the situation as defined by the relationship between the leader and followers, the degree of structure of the task, and the leader's position power. Other contingency approaches include the Normative Decision that proposes that leaders must consider a variety of situational factors when selecting among decisional styles ranging from autocratic to consultative to delegation to the group (Vroom & Yago, 1988) and the Path–Goal Theory that proposes that the leader's main function is to use different behaviors to remove obstacles in the subordinates' path to allow them to perform their jobs and to be motivated and satisfied (House, 1971). Hershey and Blanchard's Situational Leadership model, although often used in organizational settings, has received highly limited research support, but similarly suggests that different leadership styles or behaviors are effective in different situations.

2.3.2 Continued Impact of Contingency Views of Leadership. The contingency view provides room for consideration of culture as one of the contextual or situational factors that may impact leadership. Although there has been some cross-cultural research with contingency theories (most notably with Fiedler's model), the cross-cultural applications are lacking and further research is needed (for a review see Ayman & Korabik, 2010).

The contingency models of leadership presented here are the foundation of current theory in leadership and continue to dominate the field of leadership. The beginning of the next era of leadership is marked with the Leader–Member–Exchange (LMX) model of leadership that shifts attention away from the transactional contingency models to consider the relationship between leaders and their followers. LMX suggests that leaders establish dyadic relationships with their followers and create in- and out-groups who then have different experiences related to leadership (Graen & Uhl-Bien, 1995). The in-group members consider their leaders to be inspirational and view them more favorably, while those in the out-group experience a transactional relationship that is less positive. Although the model has received strong support (for a review see Ilies, Nahrgang, & Morgeson, 2007), there is little research done, or support for the model across cultures or even with diverse dyads suggesting a need for more research.

3. CURRENT APPROACHES TO LEADERSHIP: NEO-CHARISMATIC AND VALUE-BASED ERA

LO 9.3 Detail current neo-charismatic theories of leadership and their link to culture

The current dominant approaches to leadership are neo-charismatic and value-based with theories such as charismatic, authentic, and servant leadership. These approaches share the following characteristics (see Table 9.2):

- They are based on an emotional connection between leaders and followers

- They focus on inspiration

- They are often aimed at leading large-scale change in organizations

- They have generally moved away from the principles of contingency and appear to adhere to the "one best" approach to leading others.

Table 9.2 summarizes the current approaches and their contributions. In the 1920s, sociologist Max Weber introduced the concept of charisma, which was integrated into social historian James McGregor Burns's (1978) presentation of transformational

Table 9.2 Current Theories of Leadership

Approach/ Era	Assumptions and Description	Key Findings and Contributions	Weaknesses	Cultural Application
Neo-charismatic Era 1980s to present	• The leaders' emotional connection to followers and ability to inspire are crucial • The link between leadership and change is key	• Transactional leadership is not enough • Connection to followers is important • Concepts address leadership at all levels	• Does not fully consider the leadership context and suggests a "one best way to lead" • Concepts are too broad and poorly defined	• Based on European and North American CMC • Charismatic and transformational leadership concepts have been tested in other cultural setting • More research is needed

leadership. Leadership scholar Bernard Bass built on Burns's work to propose a business-oriented version of transformational leadership, launching decades of empirical-based investigations (Bass, 1997). Since then, researchers have applied charisma to organizational contexts and proposed models of leadership that emphasize vision and large-scale change in organizations. The focus on values and a more spiritual aspect of leadership was also introduced in the 1970s with Greenleaf's (1998) work and has extended to authentic and spiritual leadership approaches. The newest developments borrow from positive psychology (Seligman, 2002), a concept with roots in the humanistic approach of the 1960s, and expand its application to organizational behavior (Cameron, Dutton, & Quinn, 2003) and positive leadership (Cameron, 2008).

3.1 Charismatic Leadership

The word *charisma* means a gift from the gods indicating that those who have that gift are endowed with grace and charm. For many people in the United States and some other countries, charisma is a requirement for being a leader. The ability to connect with followers and inspire them fulfills what many are expecting of their leaders. We often describe leaders we admire as charismatic (e.g., Mahatma Gandhi, John F. Kennedy, Nelson Mandela, Ronald Regan, Barak Obama, Oprah Winfrey). They inspire us and have followers who are loyal and devoted to them and their vision.

3.1.1 Elements of Charismatic Leadership. Figure 9.2 presents the three elements of charismatic leadership. While we tend to focus on the leader characteristics, their energy, self-confidence, and expressiveness, followers and the context play a key role in the advent and success of charismatic leaders. Charismatic leaders do not exist without devoted followers and rarely rise without some sense of crisis. In other words, although we tend to focus on personal characteristics of charismatic leaders, their followers and the situation play a key role in the rise and effectiveness of charismatic leaders.

Charismatic leaders are described as people with high confidence and energy and strong convictions regarding their beliefs (Bass, 1985; Bono & Ilies, 2006; Sashkin, 2004). They are often highly expressive and able to communicate well with their followers. These types of leaders actively use various symbols and tools to build and maintain their image (Conger & Kanungo, 1998) and to become a role model for their followers (House & Shamir, 1993). However, there are no charismatic leaders without their followers who often feel an intense emotional bond and a high degree of respect and affection for their leader. They are loyal, sometimes to the point of blind obedience, and expect their leaders to implement major change (for a review see Conger & Kanungo, 1998). Research has shown that charismatic leaders are most likely to emerge in times of real or perceived crisis, where followers feel a need for change or salvation (Davis & Gardner, 2012; Shamir & Howell, 1999).

Figure 9.2 Elements of Charismatic Leadership

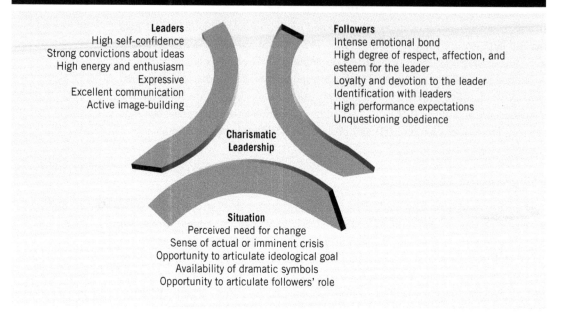

Leaders
High self-confidence
Strong convictions about ideas
High energy and enthusiasm
Expressive
Excellent communication
Active image-building

Followers
Intense emotional bond
High degree of respect, affection, and esteem for the leader
Loyalty and devotion to the leader
Identification with leaders
High performance expectations
Unquestioning obedience

Charismatic Leadership

Situation
Perceived need for change
Sense of actual or imminent crisis
Opportunity to articulate ideological goal
Availability of dramatic symbols
Opportunity to articulate followers' role

The political arena presents many examples of charismatic leaders and their followers. From Gandhi in India to Gamal Abdul Nasser in Egypt, Nelson Mandela in South Africa, and Barak Obama in the United States, these leaders generate intense emotions in their followers, and their detractors, and inspire them to change situations that they consider unacceptable. They all have particularly strong communication skills that appeal to what their followers hope can be achieved.

These elements of charismatic leadership (see Figure 9.2) also partially explain the possible negative impact of charismatic leadership (Samnani & Singh, 2013). A sense of crisis and blind obedience can be exploited by unethical charismatic leaders to advance their personal rather than their followers', organization's, or even country's goals and agenda (Howell, 1988; Howell & Avolio, 1992). The intense bond between charismatic leaders and their followers can lead to extraordinarily positive or negative outcomes.

3.1.2 Charismatic Leadership and Culture. As you review the elements presented in Figure 9.1, it should be evident that many of the leader and follower characteristics have cultural components. Cultural dimensions such as appropriateness of using emotions, uncertainty avoidance, and power distance, as well as the degree of horizontal vs. vertical individualism-collectivism all have the potential to impact whether leaders and followers find charismatic leadership desirable. Cultures with a strong tradition of prophetic salvation, in particular, are more amenable to charismatic leadership. For example, the Judeo-Christian beliefs in the coming of the savior create fertile ground for charismatic leaders to emerge and be accepted in a variety of settings.

Prophets by definition are charismatic saviors. Israel, for example, has this type of strong tradition. In cultures that rely less on such prophetic traditions, charismatic figures are less likely to emerge. For example, although China has experienced periods of crisis and change which would set the stage for charismatic leadership, the relationship between leader and followers is based more on the social hierarchy and need for order, as is prescribed in the Confucian tradition, rather than on the intense emotional charismatic bonds that exist in Judeo-Christian religions.

The GLOBE studies have further found that charisma is not a desirable leadership attribute in all cultures and how it is expressed may differ greatly in different cultural contexts (House, Hanges, Javidan, Dorfman, & Gupta, 2004). We will review these findings in detail later in this chapter. However, even when charismatic leaders are considered desirable, the factors that create the charismatic relationship may differ from one culture to another. The rise of a charismatic relationship in a culture such as Japan relies on the leader's development of an image of competence and moral courage, and the securing of respect from followers (Tsurumi, 1982). By contrast, in India, charismatic leadership is associated with a religious, almost supernatural, state (Singer, 1969). In the United States, charisma is assertive and direct, whereas in other cultures it may be quieter and nonassertive (Scandura & Dorfman, 2004). While charisma has become a dominant concept in current leadership theories, research clearly indicates that the leaders, and followers' CMC matters.

3.2 Transactional and Transformational Leadership

The majority of early leadership theories deal with a basic exchange or transaction between leaders and followers, where followers get certain rewards and outcomes in exchange for their performance—therefore called transactional leadership (Bass & Avolio, 1993). These theories do not address large-scale change or transformation in organizations. Prominent leadership researcher Bernard Bass suggested that although transactional leadership can be effective and is necessary in some settings, many organizations require transformational leadership that a transactional style of leadership cannot deliver (Bass, 1990a).

Transformational leadership (first proposed by McGregor Burns in 1978) has become the current dominant leadership approach, partially because of a perceived need for large-scale change in many organizations.

3.2.1 Elements of Transformational Leadership. Transformational leaders are those who go beyond simple transaction of setting goals and contingent rewards and inspire ers and enable them to enact large-scale change. They rely on charisma and ration, intellectual stimulation, and individual consideration to move their fol- rs and organizations to accomplish their goals (see Figure 9.3). Transformational rs use their charisma to inspire followers and to create a bond with them that them overcome their resistance to change (Bass & Avolio, 1993). They then motivate and empower followers by challenging them intellectually to question the status quo and look for new answers (Boerner et al., 2007). Finally, individual consideration based on personal relationships with followers, combined with the emotional connection formed by the charismatic relationship, motivates followers to sustain the change and deliver high performance and allow the leader to undertake necessary changes in the organization (see Figure 9.3).

3.2.2 Transformational Leadership and Culture. As the dominant theory in leadership, transformational leadership has been the subject of many studies that show it can lead to positive outcomes such as increased employee proactivity (Strauss, Griffin, & Rafferty, 2009), commitment (Braun, Peus, Weisweiler, & Frey, 2013), engagement (Tims, Bakker, & Xanthopoulou, 2011), and positive emotions (Liang & Chi, 2013), as well as

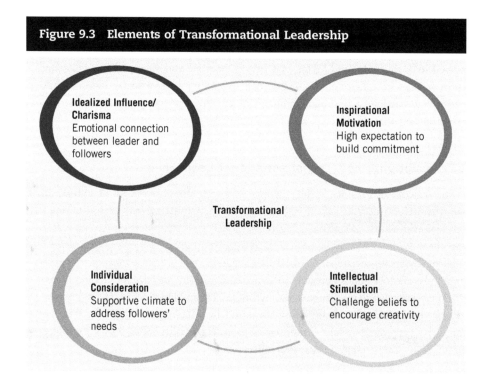

Figure 9.3   Elements of Transformational Leadership

Idealized Influence/ Charisma
Emotional connection between leader and followers

Inspirational Motivation
High expectation to build commitment

Transformational Leadership

Individual Consideration
Supportive climate to address followers' needs

Intellectual Stimulation
Challenge beliefs to encourage creativity

organizational innovation (Eisenbeiss, van Knippenberg, & Boerner, 2008). Researchers have also considered the potential impact of culture on transformational leadership.

Some have suggested that women leaders may exhibit more transformational attributes (e.g., Yammarino, Dubinsky, Comer, & Jolson, 1997), while others propose that that ideal leadership characteristics across many countries—such as Canada, South Africa, Israel, Mexico, Sweden, and Singapore—include some transformational leadership elements (Bass, 1997). The approach has also been studied in a number of countries such as Israel (Dunn, Dastoor, & Sims, 2012), Pakistan (Tipu, Ryan, & Fantazy, 2012), and Turkey (Karakitapoğlu-Aygün & Gumusluoglu, 2012) where researchers have found that transformational leadership exists in different cultures (Den Hartog, House, Hanges, Ruiz-Quintanilla, & Dorfman, 1999). Some research indicates that the approach may provide support for implementation of diversity initiatives (Ashikali & Groenveld, 2013). However, Bass has suggested that different cultures may respond differently to some of the transformational behaviors (Bass, 1997). For example, considering the role of cultural dimensions, individuals from collectivistic cultures may be more receptive to transformational leadership (Walumbwa & Lawler, 2003; Walumbwa, Lawler, & Avolio, 2007).

In spite of its popularity, transformational leadership presents serious shortcomings that have led some to suggest that the concept and label be abandoned in favor of a clearer and better-defined concept (for an extensive review see van Knippenberg & Sitkin, 2013). Specifically, transformational leadership is poorly defined, with each study using different definitions that overlap with concepts such as charismatic or authentic leadership. In other words, because it is defined in a number of different ways, it is not clear that various studies are looking at the same concept, thus making it difficult to generalize findings. Additionally, the theory and research do not fully explain why transformational leadership includes factors such as charisma, inspiration, or intellectual stimulation, and how each impacts effectiveness. Finally, transformational leadership is often presented as the best way to lead and a panacea to all organizational problems without consideration of the context, including culture. For example, not all organizations need transformation and not all cultures welcome change to the same extent. There is little research about how transformational leadership may fare in those settings.

3.3 Authentic and Positive Leadership

Two of the newer leadership theories that also rely on the relationship of the leader with followers are authentic and positive leadership.

3.3.1 Authentic Leadership. Authentic leadership highlights the leader's self-awareness and consistent values as key to effective leadership. Authentic leaders are those who have self-knowledge, accurately present themselves, and act according to their clearly stated values (Avolio & Gardner, 2005). Unbiased information processing and relational transparency are two other attributes of authentic leaders. Although there is a need for continued research to clarify how these attributes contribute to authenticity, some have suggested that authentic leadership is the cornerstone of charismatic and transformational leadership.

The approach has gained popularity with some evidence that it can have positive organizational outcomes (see Gardner, Coglier, Davis, & Dickens, 2011 for a review). However, as of yet, there is little research on its cross-cultural application. A few of the available studies point to the idea of authenticity being appealing in many cultures; however, as with other concepts, it may take different forms. For example, in more collectivistic and high-power distance cultures, knowledge of self may be less important than having the sense of the group and actions that may reduce the actual or perception of control of the leaders. Additionally, having too much transparency or providing too much positive feedback may be less desirable in some cultures (Saracer, Karacy-Aydin, Asarkaya, & Kabasakal, 2012).

3.3.2 Positive Leadership. The extensive work of psychologist Martin Seligman and his colleagues (Seligman & Csikszentmihalyi, 2000; Snyder, Lopez, & Pedrotti, 2011) has contributed to a growing interest in positive leadership (Cameron, 2008). *Positive leadership* emphasizes individual strengths in helping people achieve their highest potential, and what some researchers have called the psychological capital (PsyCap). *PsyCap* involves positive psychological states, confidence, positive attributions, perseverance, and resilience (Youssef-Morgan & Luthans, 2013).

The various characteristics of positive leaders which include focusing on strength, resilience, affirmative bias, confidence, optimism, and perseverance are suggested to operate together to allow leaders to function in their optimal range, something that is referred to as flourishing (Youssef & Luthans, 2012). Positive leadership, similar to authentic leadership, has gained popularity especially with the development of related tools such as Gallup's strength finder.

3.3.3 Cross-cultural Applications. Both authentic and positive leadership approaches belong and fit with Euro-centric (WEIRD) individualistic cultures where individual self-development is the primary focus and transparency is valued. Cross-cultural application of both authentic and positive leadership needs considerable further development. Applying these two approaches to cultures where there are different views of human nature, the individual is less relevant than the collective, and openly sharing feelings and values may be less desirable, is likely to be challenging. Consider the following exchange during a performance review between a European–US manager and her Indian-born report:

Manager: You have had a very strong 6 months. You have hit all of your performance targets and have exceeded them in two key areas. Your contribution to the department has been great.

Report: I am so happy that I have been able to contribute to the team. This means so much to me.

Manager: Your team members feel that they can count on you and you come through every time. Again, a clear area of strength. Work is done on time and you support your team.

Report: Thank you. I always strive to do my best to support the department.

Manager: There are, of course, always some areas that need improvement.

Report: I am so sorry; did I do something wrong?

Manager: No, you didn't do anything wrong. There are some things to address though. Your team members feel that you don't often tell them what you need and that you don't share feedback openly. They don't know where you stand and sometimes think that you may not be happy with their contributions.

Report: I assure you that all is well. They don't need to worry.

Manager: I am not worried. We work in a pretty high-pressure environment and we all need to be very honest and be able to blow off steam to assure that we communicate openly. If things are not going well, or if you are upset at something, you need to share that with the team members so they can support you.

Report: I'm not sure I understand. You want me to tell them that I'm upset? I don't get upset too much and when I do, it's never a big deal. Why would I tell my reports about how I feel and burden them with personal things that I can work out?

Manager: It's not a burden. It's being open and honest and sharing feedback.

Report: I always provide feedback to people who report to me; they know what they don't do well and I help them fix whatever is wrong. I wouldn't let one of my group member's mistakes affect the rest of the team. I work hard on predicting everything that can go wrong so that it doesn't happen again.

Manager: Yes, you do actually. You may want to focus on a more positive approach to build your team members' strengths. You really do worry too much; we have a great team and we are ahead of our competition.

Report: Of course, I will try. But you know that we face so many challenges. I can stay ahead of them by thinking about the worst case and making sure the team is aware of all the possible problems we could face...

The exchange between these two people can be seen as a simple disagreement regarding how to approach managing a team. There is also the potential layer of different CMCs. The manager is approaching her work from an optimistic perspective, with focus on transparency, and sharing, which are all part of both authentic and positive leadership and fit her CMC. The report's reactions are also based on his CMC, which guides him toward keeping feelings to himself, correcting subordinates' mistakes, and having a more pessimistic view of events. The manager operating based on theories that are developed in one CMC may not always be the most effective way to manage her report.

3.4 Servant and Spiritual Leadership

The idea of servant leaders whose primary goal is to serve their followers rather than focus on organizational outcomes or effectiveness has been popular in recent years (van Dierendonck, 2011). Robert Greenleaf's (1998) work reintroduced the concept that was often the domain of faith, to a broader organizational audience. Over 40 different traits, attributes, and behaviors have been suggested to define servant leadership including the idea of being first among equals and being motivated by service, authenticity, humility, and empathy, all of which are not typically mentioned in leadership theories or Western conceptions of organizational leadership.

Another recent approach to leadership is spiritual leadership, which is rooted in vision, hope, faith, and altruistic love as key leadership attributes that engender a sense of wholeness, harmony, and well-being in followers and provide a balance between people, profit, and the planet (Chen & Li, 2013; Fry, 2003; Neubert, 2019). With a focus on followers' well-being, spiritual leadership shares common themes with servant leadership both with and without religious connotations (Fernando, 2011). Models of spiritual leadership incorporate several factors including integrity, honesty, humility, compassion, being a role model, having a vision and a calling, engaging in reflective practice, and being respectful of others (Fry, 2003; Reave, 2005).

3.4.1 Cross-cultural Applications. Servant leadership is a relatively new approach and needs considerably more empirical testing and development. Interestingly, although there is limited cross-cultural research about servant leadership, the idea of servant leaders exists in many cultures (e.g., Australia and Indonesia, Pekerti & Sendjaya, 2010) and many of the servant leadership concepts such as integrity, empathy, and humility are part of leadership characteristics in other cultures. For example, the themes of humility, accountability, and focus on followers are central to leadership ideals found in Iran and in other Indo-European cultures as you will read later in this chapter (Nahavandi & Krishnan, 2018). Additionally, a GLOBE study finds that some of constructs associated with servant leadership, namely moral authority and empowerment, are important across all cultures, while increased power distance was negatively related to the concept of servant leadership (Mittal & Dorfman, 2012).

There is limited research on spiritual leadership, but some studies have shown the positive organizational outcomes associated with the implementation of its principles (e.g., Fry & Cohen, 2009). Others have found applicability to several cultural settings including China (Baglione & Zimmerer, 2007; Chen & Li, 2013) and Turkey (Karadag, 2009). Some scholars suggest that introducing a spiritual viewpoint enhances other approaches that may lack an ethical and moral focus (Kanungo, 2001). One of the challenges, however, is the lack of a clear definition and the inclusion of a large number of factors that render the concept too broad. However, the idea of focusing on people's higher needs continues to make the approach appealing and warrants continued research.

Overall, although the recent approaches to leadership have given some consideration to cultural settings other than Europe and North America, the field of leadership continues to be Euro- and North America-centric. The work of GLOBE researchers we discuss next has provided some of the strongest and most reliable findings that indicate how we view leadership, and what we consider leadership and effectiveness are influenced by our CMC.

4. GLOBAL AND WORLDLY LEADERSHIP

LO 9.4 Appraise the global and worldly leadership approaches

In an attempt to address the specific challenges of leading organizations globally, several researchers have explored the type of attributes that may be needed for leaders who operate in global settings. The basic assumption is that leading in a global setting requires special attributes that are not addressed in most current theories of leadership. We present two such approaches next.

4.1 Global Leadership

The central idea behind the concept of global leadership is that there are unique and distinct attributes, skills, and competencies that leaders need when working in global and multicultural settings. Global leadership developed as businesses became more international and expatriate managers (see our discussion in Chapter 4) experienced increased complexity and the related unique challenges of working in cultures other than their own (Mendenhall et al., 2018). *Global leadership* is defined as follows:

The process and actions through which an individual influences a range of internal and external constituents from multiple national cultures and jurisdictions in a context characterized by significant levels of task and relationship complexity. (Mendenhall et al., 2018, p. 23)

4.1.1 Competencies of Global Leaders. As you can see, the definition is similar to the generic definition of leadership presented earlier in this chapter with the focus on groups and interpersonal influence. Global leadership suggests that because cultural diversity and working across different countries make the process of leading more complex, special competencies apply when the groups the leader works with are from diverse background. Researchers (e.g., Bueno & Tubbs, 2004; Jokinen, 2005; Osland, 2008) have identified more than fifty competencies that global leaders need. These are grouped into the following categories (Bird, 2018):

1. *Behavioral organizational acumen:* vision, strategy, business skills, managing communities

2. *Managing people and relationships:* valuing people, respect for other, cross-cultural communication, interpersonal skills

3. *Managing self:* global mindset, flexibility, resilience

4.1.2 Applying Global Leadership. There is no doubt that any leader, not just those working in global organizations, would benefit considerably from developing the over fifty competencies included in the global leadership approach. One could argue that in today's culturally diverse workplace, even leaders and managers who do not work across national boundaries must expand their ability to understand, communicate, and work with people from different cultures within their own country or organization.

It is clear that working in other cultures as expats creates unique challenges that need to be addressed (see Chapter 4 for a discussion of expats). The challenge of finding global leadership competencies is to some extent the circular nature of the concept. Global leadership requires a global mindset along with many of the competencies that would help any leader be effective and are therefore not specific to global leaders alone.

4.2 Worldly Leadership

Whereas globalization is concerned with the convergence of cultures, the idea of worldly leadership refers to paying attention to local differences. Accordingly, a *worldly leader* is a person who has wisdom and is experienced in life, has knowledge of various countries and cultures, and sees the world from a unitary and holistic perspective (Turnbull, Case, Edwards, Schedlitzki, & Simpson, 2012). Instead of proposing global leadership competencies, worldly leadership suggests taking an emic approach that pools leadership wisdom from across the world relying on non-Western indigenous knowledge from a variety of societies to provide alternative ways of thinking.

Building on Gosling and Mintzberg's (2003) distinction between global and worldly leadership, the concept of worldly leadership suggests that leaders must learn to pay attention to and respond to local differences, rather than learn specific competencies.

4.3 Evaluation

Global and worldly leadership have similar goals of addressing the challenges of managing and leading in a culturally diverse world. Global leadership relies on many of the current leadership and cross-cultural management theories. It does not address the fact that although the models and framework may have applications in other cultures, their development in one CMC, often without awareness or acknowledgment of the impact of the corresponding assumptions, values, and beliefs, may make them a poor fit in another culture.

Worldly leadership questions the application of Euro-centric leadership and management theories to other CMCs. With increased contact among cultures, the need to test current theories and to develop theories that stem from different cultures has never been greater. The GLOBE research about leadership we discuss next clearly indicates that views and ideals of leadership are not the same in different parts of the world and that cultural values shape leadership effectiveness and followers' expectations of their leaders.

5. IMPACT OF CULTURE ON LEADERSHIP: REVISITING GLOBE

LO 9.5 Elaborate on the leadership attributes proposed by GLOBE and different cultures' ideals of leadership

The GLOBE project that we introduced in Chapter 8 not only presented nine cultural dimensions and their impact on social and economic behaviors but also linked those to leadership by identifying universal leadership attributes and ideal leadership profiles for different cultures.

5.1 Leadership Attributes Across Cultures

While research on culture would indicate that leadership may be different in different cultures, are there still some leadership attributes that are universal? One of the contributions of the GLOBE project is the identification of leadership attributes across 62 countries and establishing which attributes or behaviors are more universal than others. Table 9.3 presents these results. The GLOBE researchers found that although some attributes are universally endorsed and considered desirable, and some are universally considered negative, several are contingent on the culture, meaning they are considered positive for some cultures but not for others (Den Hartog et al., 1999).

5.1.1 Universally Positive Leadership. According to GLOBE's study of 62 countries, there are some leadership attributes that most cultures find desirable (Den Hartog

WINDOW TO THE WORLD

Doing Business in Brazil

Brazil is the fifth largest country in the world, the third largest in the Americas, the largest economy, the most populous in South America, and one of the richest countries in the world in terms of natural resources. As opposed to the rest of Central and South America, which were under Spanish rule, Brazil was a Portuguese colony until 1822, with Portuguese still being the official language of the country. Its culture reflects its history with diverse population that is close to half mulatto (mixed white and black) and over 40% black with some Asians and a small percentage of remaining indigenous populations. The art and pleasure of working around rules, something Brazilians call *jeito*, or *jeitinho*, if the problem is small, is a national pastime and sometimes the only way to manage a highly bureaucratic country. Some basic tips are as follows:

- While somewhat individualistic, the family and clan are very important and nepotism is simply a fact of life and part of the obligation of taking care of those in your in-group.

- The culture is emotional where feelings matter, people show how they feel and communicate with passion with many hand gestures, frequent interruptions, people standing in close proximity to one another and often touching each other's arms and slapping backs.

- Expect delays and accept that everyone will be late; although as a guest, you should still be on time.

- This is food and coffee culture so be prepared to share and host lunches where business, if discussed, is left for the end.

- Football (*futebol* —and it is not called soccer) is a religion as Brazilians often call themselves the "the country of football" (*o país do futebol*). Argentina is the main rival, and its mention is likely to evoke passionate discourse.

Brazil is a favorite destination for investment and international business with many characteristics of a developed country while still having a low per capita GDP. It presents considerable diversity and contrasts. Learn as much Portuguese as you can and read up about the history and culture. Do not assume they speak Spanish; Brazil is a Latin country, but not Hispanic; Brazilians are proud of their unique identity in the Americas.

et al., 1999; see Table 9.3). Most people around the world would like leaders who are decisive and can provide vision and direction. They also expect some level of dynamism and the ability to bring people together in teams to solve problems. While ethical values are generally culture-contingent, having integrity and being trustworthy, honest, and fair are attributes that people universally consider positive in their leader. Depending on our culture, we may be more or less transparent or tolerate corruption to varying degrees, but our ideals of leadership involve integrity regardless of culture.

Table 9.3	Cross-Cultural Attributes of Leadership	
Universally Positive	**Culturally Contingent**	**Universally Negative**
Decisiveness	Enthusiasm	Ruthlessness
Trustworthiness and honesty	Risk-taking	Egocentrism
Dynamism	Sincerity	Being a loner
Fairness	Ambition	Noncooperation
Team building	Sensitivity	Dictatorial
Having a vision and a plan	Compassion	Lack of clarity
Intelligence	Communication style	Irritability
Administrative skills	Extent of egalitarianism	
Win-win problem-solver	Evasive	
	Cunning	

Sources: Based on information in Den Hartog et al. (1999) and House et al. (2004).

5.1.2 Culture-Contingent Leadership. Interestingly, the term charisma, which, as you read earlier in this chapter is central to many of the current popular approaches to leadership, evokes mixed reactions in different cultures. Additionally, although having a vision is considered positive in all cultures, how that vision should be presented and communicated differs across countries. For example, Chinese leaders are seen as effective if they communicate their vision in a nonaggressive and soft-spoken manner, whereas Indians prefer a bold and assertive expression (Den Hartog et al., 1999). US Americans and the British highly value charisma, and Middle Easterners place less importance on this characteristic from their leader. Nordic cultures are less favorable toward self-protective leadership behaviors where leaders focus on safety, protection, and face saving, whereas Southern Asians accept it more readily (House et al., 2004).

Followers universally value communication and dislike lack of clarity, but the style of communication, meaning how direct and forceful the leader is for instance, is more culture-specific. For example, in 2004, Cambodians expressed considerable enthusiasm at the ascendance of their new king, Norodom Sihamoni, valuing his modesty and soft-spoken manner (Sullivan, 2004). As the country faces continued political upheaval where the king has lost much of his power, Sihamoni's gentleness is considered to be a symbol of Cambodia (Gray, 2011). Furthermore, risk-taking, which is highly valued in the United States as a leadership attribute, is considerably less appreciated in cultures that are more uncertainty-avoidant and where caution is more prized.

5.1.3 Universally Negative Leadership. Not surprisingly, being malevolent and irritable are universally undesirable, whereas being ambitious, elitist, and humanistic are culturally contingent, meaning desirable in some, but not all, cultures (Dorfman, Javidan, Hanges, Dastmalchian, & House, 2012). It is important to note that being ruthless and dictatorial are universally unacceptable leadership attributes, even in cultures with higher power distance where leaders are given more power. As indicated in our discussion of GLOBE findings in Chapter 8, many individuals in different cultures desire less power distance and more egalitarian leadership than is actually practiced in their organizations (House, Dorfman, Javidan, Hanges, & Sully de Luque, 2014).

5.2 Impact of Culture: Culturally Endorsed Leadership Theories

One of the most significant findings from GLOBE is that culture impacts, but does not predict, leadership behaviors through people's expectations—what researchers call *culturally endorsed leadership theories* or *CLTs*. These statistically derived CLTs are the summary of the leadership attributes, skills, and abilities that people believe contribute to effective leadership (Dorfman et al., 2012; House et al., 2004). The idea of CLTs draws from *implicit theories* of leadership which suggest that people have a set of beliefs and expectations regarding leadership and that these beliefs influence what they look for in a leader and what they consider effective (Lord & Maher, 1991).

5.2.1 Six CLTs. GLOBE's research shows that culture influences the development and content of such implicit leadership theories so people from different cultures have different ideals and expectations of leaders and leadership. GLOBE research indicates that not only different cultures have different CLTs that prescribe what leaders should be and do, but that leaders who are perceived to behave in accordance with their cultures' CLT are considered most effective (Dorfman et al., 2012). GLOBE's six CLTs, which are based on what people believe leaders *should* be or do, are as follows:

- *Charismatic and value based:* Leadership based on the ability to inspire and motivate followers through core values and high-performance expectations

- *Team oriented:* Leadership focused on team building and developing a common goal

- *Participative:* Leadership based on involving followers in decision-making

- *Humane oriented:* Leadership based on consideration for followers through compassion and generosity

- *Autonomous:* Leadership based on independence and individualism

- *Self-protective:* Leadership focused on safety and security of individuals and groups through self-enhancement and face-saving

5.2.2 CLTs by Country Clusters. The GLOBE studies then identified leadership profiles for various country clusters (for a review of country clusters see Figure 8.3 in

LOVE THIS

Country Clusters	CLT[a]
Confucian Asia South Korea, Hong Kong, Singapore, Taiwan, China, and Japan	Self-protective; team-oriented; humane-oriented; charismatic
Southern Asia Philippines, Indonesia, Thailand, Malaysia, India, and Iran	Self-protective; charismatic; humane-oriented; team-oriented; autonomous
Latin America Venezuela, Guatemala, Costa Rica, Colombia, El Salvador, Argentina, Ecuador, Mexico, Bolivia, and Brazil	Charismatic; team-oriented; self-protective; participative
Nordic Europe Denmark, Sweden and Finland	Charismatic; participative; team-oriented; autonomous
Anglo US, Canada, Ireland, England, South Africa (white), New Zealand, and Australia	Charismatic; participative; humane-oriented; team-oriented
Germanic Europe Austria, Germany, Switzerland (German), and The Netherlands	Autonomous; charismatic; participative; humane-oriented
Latin Europe Italy, Spain, Israel, France, Portugal, and Switzerland (French)	Charismatic; team-oriented; participative; self-protective
Eastern Europe Kazakhstan, Slovenia, Georgia, Hungary, Albania, Poland, Greece, and Russia	Autonomous; self-protective; charismatic; team-oriented
Africa South Africa (black), Zimbabwe, Namibia, Zambia, and Nigeria	Humane-oriented; charismatic; team-oriented; participative
Middle East Morocco, Kuwait, Turkey, Egypt, and Qatar	Self-protective; humane-oriented; autonomous; charismatic

[a]The CLT profiles are listed in order of importance.

Sources: Based on information in House et al. (2004) and Dorfman et al. (2012).

Chapter 8). Table 9.4 summarizes these cultural leadership profiles, based on people's ideals rather than actual attributes or behaviors.

For instance, as indicated in Table 9.4, people in the Confucian Asian cluster, which includes South Korea, Hong Kong, Singapore, Taiwan, China, and Japan, believe that, ideally, leaders should be self-protective, team-oriented, humane, and charismatic. Nordic Europeans (Denmark, Sweden, and Finland) value leaders who are charismatic and value-based first, followed by those who are participative, team-oriented, and autonomous, whereas Middle Easterners' ideal leaders are self-protective, humane-oriented, autonomous, and charismatic. Leaders who act according to their country's CLT are considered more effective (Dorfman et al., 2012). Referring back to the *First Person* anecdote, based on GLOBE findings, the Middle-Eastern followers' CLT did not include participation, whereas the leader, being from the Anglo cluster, considered participation to be important.

GLOBE studies provide comprehensive information that establishes the impact of culture on people's ideal of leadership. The research clearly shows that effective leadership is in the eye of the beholder: what makes a leader effective in one culture is not the same in other cultures. People within a cultural group will have a leadership ideal, a CLT that reflects what they consider appropriate and desirable. That CLT will be different for different people strongly reinforcing the CJI concept. There is no objectively better or worse approach to leadership; what works depends on the CMC of leaders and followers. Because of the extensive data and research, GLOBE presents prototypes that can be used as a starting point for understanding leadership differences across cultures.

The research we presented here, so far, has applied Western, mostly US-based theories to other cultural contexts. In other words, they have relied on an etic approach. We are increasingly seeing more emic views that approach leadership not from the outside or as compared to Western approaches, but more from within other cultures. These approaches, rather than studying how concepts from one culture apply to another or comparing cultures, focus on describing and understanding leadership approaches in various cultures; we present several such models next.

6. LEADERSHIP IN NON-WESTERN CULTURES

LO 9.6 Examine three non-Western leadership approaches

In the foreword to their book *Global and Culturally Diverse Leaders and Leadership*, researchers Jean Lau Chin, Joseph Trimble, and Joseph Garcia (2018) state:

> *Traditional western models of leadership may be less and less relevant for societies that are increasingly diverse and global. As our societies become more diverse, more*

diverse leaders with a variety of styles are more relevant and appropriate; it is vital that the citizenry not only tolerate, but appreciate the contributions that diverse leaders can provide. (p. xiv)

Their statement echoes what we have extensively discussed in previous chapters of this book: the world is diverse and global, and the approaches developed from one CMC do not necessarily work or apply to others.

6.1 Leadership and the Culture Paradox

We have mentioned the culture paradox throughout this book: the rules that work in one small world do not always apply to a larger world. Therefore, you cannot simply assume that leadership theories that were developed in one cultural context would apply to all cultures. By one estimate, more than 90% of leadership theories that are currently in use in business and organizations and being actively studied and taught around the world were developed not only in the West but also in the United States (House & Aditya, 1997). In recent years, some leadership researchers have noted this shortcoming.

6.1.1 Euro/Western-Centric Leadership Theories. The approaches to leadership we have reviewed in this chapter have distinct Euro-centric and North American and male-focused cultural roots. They were developed almost in their entirety in Western contexts, and they inevitably reflect the CMC of the researchers and participants with their corresponding lenses and perspectives (for a detailed discussion of these challenges see Ayman & Korabik, 2010; Chin & Trimble, 2015; Chin et al., 2018; Eagly & Chin, 2010; Turnbull et al., 2012). Although many have been tested in other cultures, and, in some cases, have shown predicted results, they are applying the rules from one context (a small world) to another (etic approach) and make the often-unstated assumption that their definition and approaches to leadership are universal and culture neutral.

For example, the idea of the leader being a single and powerful person in charge of others, or the assumption that change is always needed and would eventually be welcome, or the idea that task and relationship are two separate entities are all tacit assumptions in our current leadership theories, and they are all the result of particular CMCs. Similarly, the preoccupation with improving the individual and self-actualization that are common in leadership in the United States (Jones, 2006) are rooted in a particular CMC. They are all the product of a small world and may not apply to a larger context.

6.1.2 Calls for a More Emic Approach. As suggested by worldly leadership, recognizing and understanding other cultural perspectives on leadership is a step in the right direction. Several non-European leadership approaches are beginning to gain wider audiences as non-European and non-Western countries are establishing economic strength. We consider a few of these perspectives next with the goal of describing and understanding them and their context, not to apply them to other cultures.

6.2 Community and Interdependence: Confucianism and Ubuntu

As we have discussed in earlier chapters, the concept of individualism-collectivism is one of the fundamental and essential dimensions that differentiates among cultures. Leadership theories that are developed in individualistic cultures will inexorably focus on the individual rather than the collective. What does leadership look like from a more collectivistic point of view? How does changing that focus change what leaders do and how they lead and what followers expect and consider effective?

One way to answer these questions is to explore leadership principles and practices in cultures that have strong collectivistic traditions. We focus on two such concepts first. We consider Confucianism, which is dominant in China and has influenced other countries in the GLOBE Confucian cluster, and Ubuntu which has been described as an African leadership approach, keeping in mind that Africa is highly culturally diverse and far from homogeneous (Iwowo, 2012). Together these regions represent approximately 38% of the world's population; for comparison, the United States includes 4% of the world's population.

6.2.1 Confucianism. Confucianism (developed by Kongzi who was given the name Confucius later by Jesuit missionaries) is a moral and political doctrine and philosophy that has guided China and many other Asian cultures since its presentation by Confucius around 500 BC. The GLOBE Confucian Asia cluster together represents over 21% of the world's population, with China alone including approximately 19%. Confucianism is a highly collectivistic view of relationships among people, with a focus on social order, mutual respect, and kindness. It is based on three Fundamental Bonds that are the basis of social relationships and society, and five Constant Virtues that are the values that guide behavior and are needed to live a proper life (Knapp, 2009). The three Bonds are as follows:

- The bond between parents and children (father and son as described by Confucius)

- The bond between lord and retainer

- The bond between husband and wife.

These bonds extend to other relationships and clarify not only a hierarchy between people with more and less power but also obligation between them. Accordingly, fathers or lords are superior to their children and subordinates who would owe them obedience and loyalty. However, in exchange, those in higher positions have the obligation to care for and protect those below them and those who have less power. The relationships constitute two inherently connected parts that make up a whole, yin and yang (Knapp, 2009).

Table 9.5 Confucianism's Five Constant Virtues

Principle (Chinese)	Description
Benevolence *(ren or jen)* *The base of all other virtues*	Kindness, humaneness, altruism—not being able to tolerate others' suffering and helping all living things; extending what is good in ourselves to others
Righteousness *(yi)*	Honesty, duty, obligation—doing what's proper to help others and supporting social order; involves thinking and rational action; showing moral integrity and self-restraint
Propriety *(li)*	Appropriateness, politeness, gracious behavior—acting according to established norms and making things right; showing loyalty and respect; one of the ways we can express our benevolence
Wisdom *(zhi or chih)*	Knowledge and insight—the way one can judge right from wrong; being astute and able to read and understand situations and people
Trustworthiness *(xin)*	Sincerity, integrity—staying true to one's word; having credibility and being dependable; actions must match words

Sources: Based on information in Elkington and Tuleja (2018) and Knapp (2009).

The five Virtues that are considered inherent to human beings and part of their energy and guide all human behaviors (Knapp, 2009) are presented in Table 9.5.

As you can see, the Confucian Bonds and the Virtues present a striking contrast to individualistic values that drive European and US American views of society and relationships. Instead of the focus on the individual, represented, for example, by the famous Cartesian philosophy of "I think, therefore I am," in the Confucian view, the person only exists in relationship to society (Elkington & Tuleja, 2018). This collective-centric approach has significant implications for leadership.

According to Confucian philosophy, the role of the leader is fundamentally that of a benevolent caretaker who is willing to sacrifice personal self-interest in order to create mutual benefit and maintain the social order. The Hofstede research on value orientations shows China as high on collectivism and power distance. It is further considered a tight culture where adherence to rules is important, vertical collectivism dominates, and self-sacrifice for the group is expected. Additionally, the GLOBE Confucian Asian cluster's CLT includes self-protection, team-, and humane orientation. All of these cultural values, as described from a Western perspective, are consistent with Confucian principles.

Very few studies have taken an emic approach and considered leadership from a Chinese perspective. However, the few that have taken that approach have supported the highly collectivistic view of leadership with the Chinese considering having interpersonal skills as a primary factor for leadership and giving further consideration to virtue, personal morality, integrity, and serving as a role model for others, followed by having a strategic vision (e.g., Ling, Chia, & Fang, 2000). Additionally, research aimed at assessing the meaning and application of concepts such as authentic leadership with Chinese leaders shows that self-disclosure is not considered desirable as it may lead to loss of face and diminishment of power (Aponte-Moreno & Koulouris, 2018). Some recent studies suggest that less traditional and more globally driven regions in China may be less connected to the Confucian principles, although those principles are still endorsed (Solansky, Gupta, & Wang, 2017).

6.2.2 Ubuntu. Ubuntu is an African concept that translates as "I am here because you are." While there is almost no Africa-focused theory of leadership, and there is considerable cultural diversity within Africa, Ubuntu is often used as a pan-African generic leadership concept. Archbishop Desmond Tutu has described it as follows:

> *It is the essence of being human, it is part of the gift that Africa will give the world. It embraces hospitality, caring about others, being able to go the extra mile for the sake of others. We believe that a person is a person through another person, that my humanity is caught up bound up, inextricably with yours. (as cited in Iwowo, 2012, p. 59)*

Ubuntu represents a highly interdependent view of societies where not only the collective is important and primary, but individuals are tightly and inseparably connected, and where

- Consideration of one individual is not conceivable without others.

- Mutual beneficence, where a person can only win when the collective does as well, is at the core of Ubuntu (Elkington & Tuleja, 2018).

- The individual does not exist without others and is only a person through others (du Plooy, 2014).

The principles of Ubuntu involve a collective identity, mutual dependence and respect, compassion, conformity to group, generosity toward others, and overall a sense of unity (Elkington & Tuleja, 2018; Mbigi, 2005) as depicted in Figure 9.4. Applying Ubuntu to leadership would move leadership from the development of individuals to the development of social capital in a community and connecting

Figure 9.4 Ubuntu Principles

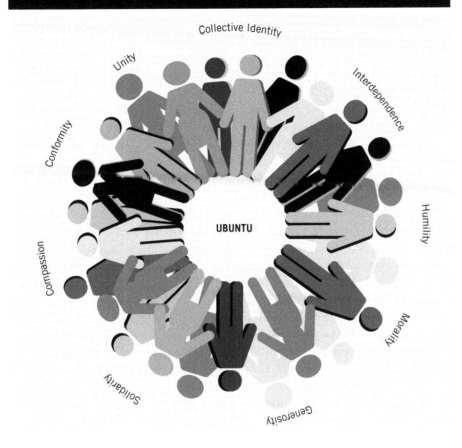

leadership with the community. Through Ubuntu, the actions such as self-care and self-development that Euro- and individualistic approaches consider essential to the long-term success of leaders are considered important because they contribute to the well-being of the collective (Bolden & Kirk, 2012). When the lens changes from the individual to the collective, although many actions leaders take to be effective may appear to be the same, their intention and meaning change with a focus on the well-being and success of the group, thus the group's CMC.

Confucianism and Ubuntu share the theme of the collective and interdependence as the core of social order and interaction. They are starkly different from the Western, individualistic, and Cartesian views where a person's existence is not because others are, but because that person as an individual "thinks."

6.3 Action, Integrity, and Accountability: Indo-European Leadership

Another example of a unique leadership approach is evident in many of the highly successful and profitable Indian conglomerates that have fueled the country's exponential economic development. This Indo-European Leadership (IEL) style is distinct from both Western and Eastern approaches with an emphasis on action, integrity, and accountability (Nahavandi & Krishnan, 2018). India alone represents 18% of the world's population.

The practice of IEL is exemplified in the case of the employees of the Taj Mahal Palace hotel in Mumbai when it came under a terrorist attack that left dozens dead and hundreds wounded on November 26, 2008. The exemplary and selfless conduct of the hotel staff during the attack is credited with saving many lives as it drew the attention of management experts (Deshpandé & Raina, 2011). The staff, many of whom were recruited from small villages because of the traditional values they would bring to work, had further been trained to focus both on people and profit. The Tata group that is among the world's largest conglomerates and the hotel's parent company is known for a distinct leadership and management style that puts employees first, conducts extensive training, is vigilant about maintaining a strong reputation for integrity, implements a long-term strategy, and emphasizes corporate social responsibility, while delivering high profit (Capelli, Singh, Singh, & Useem, 2015).

IEL has roots in the two ancient countries of Iran and India that share many Indo-European geographical, linguistic, and cultural roots and are classified in the same South Asian country cluster by GLOBE. Both countries also have old religious traditions, Zoroastrianism in Iran and Hinduism in India, that further impact IEL's unique character. Although collectivistic, India and Iran are ranked in the middle of the range by Hofstede, and show higher in-group collectivism rather than the institutional collectivism of countries in the Confucian Asian cluster. IEL is based on the principles summarized in Table 9.6.

Some of IEL's principles are present in other cultures. For example, both Ubuntu and Confucian traditions emphasize humility and caring for others. Similarly, moderation is valued in many cultural traditions with temperance and the *golden middle* being part of Taoism and Confucianism and ancient Greek philosophy. In IEL, the focus on integrity, compassion, moderation, and humility is complemented by a strong action orientation aimed at serving others. IEL leaders do not lead from behind; they are considered central and essential, not just part of the collective. Examples of IEL are evident in several Indian companies such as Wipro, Infosys, and Aravind Eye Care. Aravind's founder Govindappa Venkataswamy established the company to combat blindness due to cataracts and they provide free treatment to patients who cannot pay, along with high quality and still affordable care for the rest (Mehta & Shenoy, 2011). With a clear focus on service and social good, profit, efficient operations, and caring human resource practices (Govindarajan, 2012), Aravind represents many of the elements of IEL.

Table 9.6 Indo-European Leadership (IEL) Principles

IFI Principle (Hindi—Persian)	Description and Application
Integrity *(Inaandari—Sedaghat)*	The indispensable principle of IEL is moral character, honesty, and maintenance of a good reputation, which are all essential to effective leadership.
Action orientation *(Kayr anmukh—Amal garai)*	The need for leaders to be both present and decisive. IEL ascribes a central role to leaders as both agents of change and maintaining a healthy status quo.
Moderation *(Sanyam or Santoolan—Miyaneh ravi)*	Showing restraint and temperance and avoiding extremes and rash decisions and actions is the path to effective leadership.
Accountability *(Zimadaari or Javvabdehee—Pasokhgooee)*	The leaders' power is balanced by their accountability to those they lead and to a higher power.
Kindness *(Dayaaluta or Mehrabani—Mehrabani)*	Being kind, caring for others, and advocating for the weak are cornerstones of effective leadership.
Humility *(Vinamrata or Namrata—Forootani)*	Hubris, arrogance, and overconfidence are undesirable. Leaders must remain accessible to those they lead using their power to serve them.

Sources: Nahavandi (2012) and Nahavandi and Krishnan (2018).

6.4 The Larger Context

The countries we have included in our discussion in this section constitute close to 60% of the world's population. Even without including other highly populous countries such as Indonesia and Malaysia, which are also collectivistic, it is clear that the world is more collectivistic than individualistic and not WEIRD. Relying on theories developed in CMCs for approximately 12% of the world population (US, EU countries, Canada, and Australia combined) to describe, explain, and predict behaviors and practices for the rest of the world is unwise, at best.

Concepts such as Ubuntu, Confucianism, and IEL help expand our perspectives and horizon. Each is based on the respective culture's key values and assumptions. Some of their practices and recommendations may translate well to other cultural settings, some may not. They are effective because they fit the CMC of the people who practice them and are affected by them. Modern business organizations in China and India, particularly, are demonstrating how culturally fitting practices can be integrated with profit and Western capitalism while still addressing deep-rooted cultural values.

There is no question that current views and theories of leadership can benefit from consideration of culture. Teaching and training business leaders to be more global and worldly are fundamentally about making them aware of their CMCs and how it impacts their thinking and actions. The rich and extensive theory and research about leadership has much to add to that development. Whether European, North American, or from other parts of the world where our leadership theories have seldom been applied and tested, managers and leaders can learn from that research. However, accepting them without understanding the CMC in which they were developed and the CMC of the leaders, followers, and organizations in which they may be transferred and practiced is fraught with challenges, and may cause serious missteps.

Leaders and leadership are universal phenomena. When groups form, people are likely to need one or more persons, or some other mechanism to organize and integrate activities and help direct them by keeping the group members cohesive to achieve the goals. The fact that this process is needed everywhere does not mean that how it is applied is the same everywhere. To a great extent, what keeps people motivated and focused is culture-specific (we will discuss this topic more in Chapter 10); what goals are valued is culture-specific; and what processes work best is culture-specific (more on this in Chapter 11). We can learn and borrow from any leadership model, but we must maintain a CM that considers culture in how we make decisions and how we implement them.

FIRST PERSON REVISITED

The manager in our *First Person* example is facing what cross-cultural researchers are increasingly discovering. There are few, if any, rules regarding how to lead people well that are universal. The manager is leading based on his CMC; he believes he has established his credibility, then presents a problem to his team and seeks their help thereby empowering them to participate. The team members are operating based on their own CMC, which involves ideas of leaders as powerful and all-knowing rather than a person who seeks and needs help and consults with followers. People's expectations regarding who a leader is and what an effective leader should do vary from one culture to another. In this case, in spite of the manager's careful efforts to present himself as both competent and an expert, while also showing humility in seeking help, something that is likely to be both desirable and effective in the United States and some other countries, backfire in a culture where there is high power distance and a desire to avoid uncertainty, and where the image of an effective leader is one who has all the answers.

APPLYING WHAT YOU LEARNED: LEADERSHIP BASICS

Leadership inevitably involves social interaction. With increased diversity within many organizations and countries, facing cross-cultural challenges is not an uncommon occurrence. As you have learned in this chapter, many of the theories and models of leadership we teach are either not easily applicable in non-European settings or they have not been well validated outside of the CMC in which they were developed. Notwithstanding, they can still be very useful tools to improve your leadership capabilities and skills.

1. Familiarize yourself with as many theories and models as you can; they are tools to help you improve yourself and can provide guidance in many different situations. Some models will be more appealing, and some less appealing to you; learn about as many of them as you can through personal development or organizational training. While any knowledge is useful, be a critical consumer.

2. You should have solid awareness of your CMC-based assumptions, values, beliefs, and behaviors by now. Review those often to assure that you continue being aware of your own cultural point of view.

3. If you share the CMC in which the theories you are learning about have been developed, you are more likely to find them "logical" and "helpful." For example, transparency and sharing your values, which is part of authentic leadership, will be more or less comfortable depending on your CMC.

4. Remind yourself that while theories are often prescriptive and recommend a certain "best approach," they do not consider culture. What works in one CMC does not always work in another.

5. If you do not share the CMC in which the theories you are learning have been developed, consider how differences in culture may play a role regarding how well you could implement the model's recommendation. For example, are you comfortable asking for your followers' help?

6. You may not know the CMC of your team members and followers (and please don't simply assume), but you can safely assume that not everyone comes from the same place, so as you lead your team include culture as one of the factors you consider when making leadership decisions—i.e., activate your CM! In some cases, it will matter, in others it won't. And in yet others, it may matter, but organizational factors will override those concerns.

Having a CM does not mean that all your decisions will be based on culture. It does mean that you should consider culture as one of the many variables that you must take into account when you lead.

MANAGERIAL CHALLENGE: RELUCTANT OR UNQUALIFIED?

You have been leading your department of 40–50 people for 3 years and have been promoted to the next level. One of your last tasks as department manager is to recommend your replacement. You know most of the department members well, but because of some structural changes, about a third of them are relatively new and you have not had extensive contact with all of them. You think there are about 10 people who have the right experience and performance to be considered for your position. You decide to ask each of them to informally "apply" for the position. You send a brief email to everyone in the department providing them with a tentative timetable for your transition to the next level and the appointment of a new manager and end your email with:

> *If you are interested in being considered for the manager position, please send me a brief statement to tell me why you think you are the most qualified for this position. I will take your statements into consideration in my recommendation to the higher ups.*

A week later, you have twelve statements in your inbox. You consider only five of them to be actually qualified for the position, but you are surprised that at least four maybe five of the people you considered good potentials have not "applied." Interestingly, all five are either Asian or female.

1. What do you think is going on?

2. What are the factors that may be contributing to people either applying or not applying?

3. Considering possible cultural factors, how could you have handled the situation differently?

4. What can you do now?

SELF-ASSESSMENT 9.1: CHARACTERISTICS OF LEADERS

Think about leaders that you admire or simply people you consider to be effective. Consider not only people with formal titles such as a supervisor or boss and known figures such as historical and political figures but also others who may play a leadership role such as community and faith leaders, teachers, and professors, or other people you may have worked with that have demonstrated leadership and helped move your team forward.

Who are some effective leaders?

_____

_____

Now take a minute to think about leaders who have not been effective, or those you do not respect.

Who are some ineffective leaders?

_____

_____

While keeping people in those two groups in mind, list 5–7 desirable and 5–7 undesirable characteristics of leaders.

Desirable Characteristics of Leaders	Undesirable Characteristics of Leaders
1.	1.
2.	2.
3.	3.
4.	4.
5.	5.
6.	6.
7.	7.

Review your list and consider the following:

1. What are some common themes in your two lists?

2. To what extent are the items in the list necessary for effective or ineffective leadership? In other words, can someone be an effective leader by demonstrating

only three of the items in your first list? Or would a person need all the items in the undesirable column to be considered ineffective?

3. Which one of the items in your list do you consider more essential than others?

4. Your answers are an indication of your personal ideals for leadership. What are the sources of that definition? Where and when did you develop it?

5. What role do you think your culture might play in your list?

SELF-ASSESSMENT 9.2: LEADERSHIP IDEALS

The twelve statements below each describes an attribute/behavior/style of leadership.

For each of the statements, indicate the degree to which you think it is a required, essential, or necessary characteristic/attribute of good leadership. A rating of 4 would indicate that you believe that what is described is absolutely essential for good leadership and that one could not lead well without that attribute. A rating of 1 would indicate that the attribute is not necessary and that one could lead well without it. There are no right or wrong answers; you are simply indicating your beliefs.

1 = not at all essential; 2 = not really essential; 3 = somewhat essential; 4 = absolutely essential.

1.	Leaders must be able to inspire their followers.	1	2	3	(4)
2.	Leaders must care about their followers.	1	2	3	(4)
3.	Leaders must encourage their followers to participate in decision-making.	1	2	3	(4)
4.	Leaders must encourage teamwork.	1	2	3	(4)
5.	Leaders must be compassionate.	1	2	3	(4)
6.	Leaders must have a close emotional connection to their followers.	1	2	(3)	4
7.	Leaders must be able to stand alone when necessary.	1	2	(3)	4
8.	Leaders must protect themselves.	1	2	(3)	4
9.	Leaders must emphasize independence and individuality for themselves and their followers.	1	2	(3)	4
10.	Leaders must invite input from followers before making decisions.	1	2	3	(4)
11.	Leaders must emphasize cohesion and common purpose.	1	2	3	(4)
12.	Leaders must guard and cultivate their image.	1	2	(3)	4

16
12
28

Scoring

Charismatic leadership:

Add up your rating on items 1 and 6: _23_ ✓

Team oriented:

Add up your rating on items 4 and 11: _28_ ✓

Participative:

Add up your rating on items 3 and 10: _28_ ✓

Humane oriented:

Add up your rating on items 2 and 5: _~~Now~~ 8_

Autonomous:

Add up your rating on items 7 and 9: _6_

Self-protective:

Add up your rating on items 8 and 12: _6_

[handwritten, right margin:] Anglo / charismatic / participative / team oriented / humane-oriented

Interpretation

Each of the scores above correspond to one of the CLTs identified by GLOBE. Consider where you have higher scores. Those would indicate what you consider ideal leadership attributes—what a leader should be or do. According to GLOBE research presented earlier in this chapter, people from different cultures have different ideals for leadership. Review Table 9.4 and consider the following in interpreting your scores:

1. To what extent do your leadership ideals match the cultural cluster to which you belong? For example, people from Nordic Europe believe that ideal leaders should be charismatic, participative, team-oriented, and autonomous.

2. If you belong in more than one cultural cluster, to what extent do your ideals match those different clusters?

3. To what extent do you have ideals of leadership that do not match GLOBE findings? What explains those differences?

[handwritten, left margin:] my family is norwegian so I see parts of this being nordic and the way I was raised

[handwritten, lower right:] autonomous is my lowest ranking.

EXERCISE 9.1: UNDERSTANDING LEADERSHIP THROUGH PROVERBS

Objective: This exercise helps you apply the knowledge you have acquired.

Instructions: Consider the proverbs listed below. The first set is from the United States. The second set is from several different countries.

In your groups discuss the following:

1. What do these proverbs mean?
2. What do they each tell us about the culture? Refer back to the cultural values you have learned.
3. What do they each tell us about leadership in those cultures?
4. Which proverbs are your favorites? Why?
5. Which ones do you disagree with the most? Why?

United States

Proverb	Implications for Leadership
Actions speak louder than words.	
Strike while the iron is hot.	
Time is money.	
God helps those who help themselves.	

From Other Cultures

Proverb	Implications for Leadership
Rain can soak a leopard's skin, but it does not wash away its spots (Africa).	
One does not make the wind, but is blown by it (Asian cultures).	
Flies don't enter in closed mouths (Mexican).	

(Continued)

Proverb	Implications for Leadership
Order is half of life (Germany).	
When spider webs unite, they can tie up a lion (Ethiopia).	
Whatever you do, think about it seven times (Philippines).	
Don't be the first bird that comes out of the forest (China).	
Sometimes you ride the horse; sometimes you carry the saddle (Iran).	
We will be known forever by the tracks we leave (Native American—Lakota).	
Tree that grows bent will never get straight again (Mexico).	
A young tree is easy to straighten, but when it's big it is difficult (Philippines).	
One finger cannot lift a pebble (Hopi).	
Force, no matter how concealed, begets resistance (Lakota).	
Too many opinions sink the boat (Greece).	
Die rather than disgrace yourself (Japan).	
Extend your feet only as far as your blanket (Chaldean-Iraqi).	
When the winds of change blow, some build wall, while others build windmills (China).	

EXERCISE 9.2: THE WORLD AS A VILLAGE

Objective: This exercise helps you apply the knowledge you have acquired.

Instructions:

Individual Work

Watch the following video: *If the world was only 100 people.*

https://www.youtube.com/watch?v=A3nllBT9ACg

Group Work

In groups of 3–5, with all members having done the individual preparation, discuss the following questions:

1. Which of facts you read or heard surprised you the most? Why?

2. How can you use this information to inform what you know about leadership and how you practice leadership?

3. To what extent is this information relevant to how you may lead in a diverse world?

4. How does this information affect your CM?

CASE STUDY: FROM HERO TO INTERNATIONAL FUGITIVE: CARLOS GHOSN'S JOURNEY

The rise and fall of Carlos Ghosn, the former CEO of Nissan-Renault-Mitsubishi who in 2019 became an international fugitive, may be unbelievable if it was part of a movie. But, truth is stranger than fiction.

Ghosn, a French–Lebanese–Brazilian, French-educated engineer and executive came to international prominence when at the age 45, in 1999, after having helped French car maker Renault execute a successful turnaround, he was put in charge of the merger with the Japanese car maker Nissan. At that time, Nissan was nearly bankrupt having declared a ¥ 684.4 billion of net operating loss for the FY1999 (Nakae, 2005). Because of low margins, especially in the United States, high purchasing costs and underutilization of assets, the company's debt level had reached $22 billion. Nissan desperately needed to find a global strategic partner both for financing and to infuse new management practices (Millikin & Fu, 2005). In 1999, Louis Schweitzer, CEO of Renault, and Yoshikazu Hanawa, CEO of Nissan, signed an agreement called the Renault–Nissan Alliance. Under the terms of the agreement, Renault received 36.8% of Nissan shares, and Nissan received $5.4 billion from Renault (Nakae, 2005), and Ghosn was appointed as the Chief Operating Officer of Nissan to lead the implementation of the strategic alliance. Most analysts were convinced that the merger was bound to fail because of structural, financial, and cultural obstacles. John Casesa, top auto analyst at Merrill Lynch during that time, stated as he advised Ghosn to rent rather than buy a house in Tokyo: "The widely held consensus was that he would fail, that Nissan wasn't worth saving and it couldn't be done" (Chozick & Rich, 2018).

Ghosn was undeterred. Ignoring the predictions of top analysts, he confidently and arrogantly undertook major changes announcing a revitalization plan, embracing the idea that cultural differences, as long as they were managed and channeled correctly, would provide the impetus to create synergies (Stahl & Brannen, 2013). Ghosn's hands-on approach included literally walking around the entire company wearing a white jumpsuit, introducing himself to every employee in person, and shaking hands. Instead of hiring outside consultants, he personally undertook the task of mobilizing employees by seeking their recommendations and comments (Millikin & Fu, 2005). To implement his plan and make Nissan profitable again, a committee that included the CEO of Renault and Nissan and five vice presidents of each organization was built to champion joint strategies and synergies (Gill, 2012). Various teams made binding recommendations aimed at challenging existing practices and developing a new corporate culture based on Japan's national culture (Millikin & Fu, 2005). Ghosn also invested in cross-cultural training for more than 1,150 Renault employees and 400 Nissan employees (Pooley, 2005) to integrate the team-oriented and indirect Japanese with the confrontational individualistic French. He also closed factories, fired long time suppliers, and laid off 14% of the workforce (Chozick & Rich, 2018). Japanese life-long team-focused seniority-based HR practices were challenged by introducing performance-based incentive systems to hold individual employees accountable for mistakes and accomplishments. With targeted new hires and the 21,000 lay-offs, Ghosn was hoping to slowly change long-held traditions (Gill, 2012). He also took on the traditional Japanese Keiretsu system of networks of suppliers and financial institutions that were an inherent part of Nissan. Ghosn believed the system was responsible for inefficient coordination and cost controls that brought Nissan's buying costs 20–25% higher than Renault's (Gill, 2012; Millikin & Fu, 2005).

Ghosn seemed to have done the impossible. By March 2002, 1 year ahead of schedule, Nissan had cut the production costs by 20%, halted market share erosion, and launched a small car that took in third place among best-selling cars at the end of 2002 (Gill, 2012; Millikin & Fu, 2005). As the first CEO to lead two Global Fortune 500 companies simultaneously, Ghosn also achieved national hero status in Japan with people emulating his style, seeking his autograph, having a manga comic book about him, and receiving a medal from Emperor Akihito in 2004 (Chozick & Rich, 2018).

His actions, success, arrogance, and flamboyant style also created considerable resentment in a country that values modesty and humility. His $16.9 million salary (11 times that of the chairman of Toyota), many homes, planes, business trips, parties (including renting the Palace of Versailles for his wedding reception), and apparently personally targeted marketing campaigns and promotions, all paid for by Nissan, irked many, while his autocratic style silenced his internal critiques. Former Nissan employee, Yuichi Ishino states: "He was a person who was above the clouds. No one dared to say anything that would confront his opinions" (Chozick & Rich, 2018). The structures Ghosn put in place are believed to have created a weak board and powerless internal watchdogs and encouraged internal rivalries, with every part of the organization depending directly on him, all but obliterating any checks and balances on his power (Tabuchi, 2019). Some suggest that he lacked the actual, or at least the appearance of, modesty that is expected from leaders in Japan and showed too much hubris (Buruma, 2020). Many Japanese policymakers and business people distrusted the foreign outsider who was challenging Japanese practices, comparing him to MacArthur, the US general and architect of the Japanese defeat in World War II. People working for Nissan suspected that Ghosn was trying to impose French practices on their company (Tabuchi, 2019). All the while, Ghosn was making the case that he was underpaid by comparing his salary to that of his global counterparts (GM's Mary Barra has a $21.96 million salary), while both the Japanese and French government and public were rankled by his extravagance and demands.

On November 19, 2018, Carlos Ghosn and a Nissan board member who was accused of helping him were arrested in Tokyo hours apart, both charged with financial wrong-doings including hiding and underreporting earnings, breach of trust, and misappropriation of company funds. He was also later rearrested a couple more times on related charges. Some have pointed out that many other Japanese executives have committed similar offenses without facing such harsh consequences. However, Ghosn's actions were seen as aimed toward his personal benefit rather than at helping his company prosper. As, Jesper Koll, an economist who has worked in Japan for many years, stated: "The one thing that Japan does not want and would never tolerate is personal greed" (Chozick & Rich, 2018). On December 2018, while out on $15 million bail awaiting trial in Japan, Carlos Ghosn escaped reportedly by hiding in a musical instrument case and was smuggled out of the country, landing in Lebanon, a country that has celebrated his success by putting his face on a postage stamp, becoming an international fugitive, all the while loudly proclaiming his innocence and citing the unfairness of his treatment in the hands of Japanese authorities (Weir & Potter, 2020).

Questions

1. What are the cultural factors involved in this case?

2. Using cross-cultural leadership concepts from this chapter, how well does Ghosn leadership fit with the Japanese culture? What are the key challenges?

3. How do you evaluate Ghosn's performance in his turnaround of Nissan?

Sources

Buruma, I. (2020). Carlos Ghosn was too big not to fail in Japan. *The New York Times*, February 5. Retrieved from https://www.nytimes.com/2018/12/30/business/carlos-ghosn-nissan.html. Accessed on February 6, 2020.

Chozick, A., & Rich, M. (2018). The rise and fall of Carlos Ghosn. *The New York Times*, December 30. Retrieved from https://www.nytimes.com/2020/02/05/opinion/carlos-ghosn-japan.html. Accessed on February 2, 2020.

Gill, C. (2012). The role of leadership in successful international mergers and acquisitions: Why Renault-Nissan succeeded and DaimlerChrysler-Mitsubishi failed. *Human Resource Management*, 51(3), 433–456.

Millikin, J. P., & Fu, D. (2005). The global leadership of Carlos Ghosn at Nissan. *Thunderbird International Business Review*, 47(1), 121–137.

Nakae, K. (2005). *Cultural change: A comparative study of the change efforts of Douglas MacArthur and Carlos Ghosn in Japan* (Doctoral dissertation). Massachusetts Institute of Technology, Cambridge, MA.

Pooley, R. (2005). When cultures collide. *Management Services, 49*(1), 28–31.

Stahl, G. K., & Brannen, M. Y. (2013). Building cross-cultural leadership competence: An interview with Carlos Ghosn. *Academy of Management Learning & Education, 12*(3), 494–502.

Tabuchi, H. (2019). Inside the tensions at Carlos Ghosn's Nissan. *The New York Times*, March 28. Retrieved from https://www.nytimes.com/2019/03/28/business/nissan-carlos-ghosn.html. Accessed on February 2, 2020.

Weir, K., & Potter, M. (2020). Timeline: From arrest to flight – Key dates in the Ghosn affair. *Reuters*, January 8. Retrieved from https://www.reuters.com/article/us-nissan-ghosn-timeline/timeline-from-arrest-to-flight-key-dates-in-the-ghosn-affair-idUSKBN1Z71R7. Accessed on February 2, 2020.

CHAPTER TEN

MOTIVATING PEOPLE AND LEADING MULTICULTURAL TEAMS

FIRST PERSON

Lost in Boston

I have been working for a global Canadian insurance company for several years, primarily out of Montreal with many short-term assignments in various parts of the world, mostly in North Africa and Southern Europe. My parents were born and raised in Morocco and both went to school in France. I was born when they lived in Spain and we eventually moved to Mexico when my mother got a great job with her company; they are now retired. I got my MBA in a university in Montreal and I speak Arabic, French, and Spanish fluently and manage well in English. I really like my job and particularly enjoy the travel and getting to meet people from all over the world. A couple of years ago, I was assigned as the marketing lead for the launch of one of our new products and had to move to Boston for the duration of the project, reporting to our US regional VP, Lauren. I had never lived in the United States for an extended period of time, so I looked forward to an interesting assignment and the opportunity to explore New England. The team that I worked with was as multinational as they come with only the VP located in her own country. I was the only Canadian; we had a couple Filipino and Vietnamese team members, a woman from India, someone from Spain, a German, a French, and another American who worked out of Mexico City. We had a 6-month deadline for our first deliverable and with the talent and experience on the team, it should have been easy. It was not…It took us 3 weeks to find the time for our first video call and although we had all communicated through email, nothing got done until we could actually see one another. That first meeting was disappointing. It was later in the

Learning Objectives

10.1 Discuss the meaning of work across cultures.

10.2 Elaborate on the definition, antecedents, and consequences of motivation and engagement.

10.3 Detail approaches to motivation including the content and process theories.

10.4 Define key elements of multicultural teams.

10.5 Present various types of multicultural teams.

10.6 Elaborate on challenges and tools for leading multicultural teams.

evening for Lauren, me, and our US Mexico member; the rest were either barely waking up and still at home, or at work mid-morning. Some of us were tired; others still sleepy, and a few were full of energy having just had their mid-morning tea or coffee! Everyone spoke English, but not equally well and when they did, there were so many accents that, it was really hard to understand each other. One of our first decisions was for Lauren and I to look into various tech tools the company had to help our virtual meetings. These tools helped and our other meetings started getting a bit smoother as we broke into subgroups that had an easier time finding a meeting time. On some occasions, some of us actually traveled to do some face-to-face work. However, it was clear that one or more us was frustrated about something during every call. Aside from all those communication problems, I was having a very hard time adjusting to Boston and working with Lauren. She was professional and friendly, but matter-of-fact and completely bottom-line oriented. I didn't know Boston, and was feeling uncharacteristically homesick and lonely. It was the first time I was reporting to another woman and was really looking forward to getting some mentoring and help to meet some of the other women executives in the company and in Boston. But, none of that happened. We occasionally had lunch, take-out dinners, and drinks at the office waiting for the late video meetings, but that was it; she never had me over or even showed any interest in me as a person. All our interactions were focused on the project. She gave me regular direct, positive feedback about my performance, which I appreciated and always inquired if I needed anything at work, but nothing else. Those 6 months in Boston were some of the loneliest and worst of my career. I started feeling anxious about going to the office and barely contributed to the project. The only highlights were several trips I took to Mexico and Vietnam to connect with team members. I have continued to stay in touch with them and they have helped me on other projects after I left Boston. We managed to get the project off on time, but the quality was not what it should have been and I have avoided Boston, where we have a substantial operation ever since.

—Canadian in Boston

What drives you to action? Why do you work hard? What does work mean to you? What does being engaged and motivated look like? How do people with different CMCs who may have fundamentally different answers to these questions work together to achieve common goals? What can managers do to support both individuals and teams to help them perform? These are key motivation challenges that managers face in any setting and that get amplified when working across cultures. The *First Person* anecdote illustrates the difficulties virtual teams face and how someone may lose motivation when a manager does not address an employee's needs.

In the previous chapters, you learned that what people value and need is, to a great extent, influenced by their culture. Similarly, what we look for at work; what we expect of our bosses, coworkers, and teammates; and what motivates us to stay engaged are all influenced by our culture. The Canadian manager in our *First Person* example comes from a collectivistic culture and seeks interpersonal contact and long-term connection; her manager is focused on accomplishing a single project. What motivates each of them is different. In this chapter, we explore the concept of motivation in a cultural context and consider the various motivation theories that can be implemented to engage people at work. We also look at the challenges of teams in a multicultural context.

1. FIRST THINGS FIRST: WHAT DOES "WORK" MEAN?

LO 10.1 Discuss the meaning of work across cultures

Social psychologist Hazel Rose Markus (2016) states: "Motivation is shaped by the multiple intersection of cultures, those of national origin but also those of gender, race, ethnicity, class, religion, workplace, sexual orientation, etc. that people engage each day and across their lives" (p. 161). It is not surprising then that culture impacts what motivates people. As we will discuss in this chapter, and we have previously mentioned, it is not that the models and approaches that we use are wrong or inaccurate. The problem is that the large majority of theories and models of management do not fully consider culture. They are developed based on research in WEIRD (Western, Educated, Industrialized, Rich, and Democratic) settings and applied to other contexts that are not WEIRD (Markus, 2016).

1.1 Definition and Meaning of Work

Work is universal; regardless of culture and other contexts, people around the world work. The reasons why people work vary across cultures. For many, work is the primary means of interacting with others outside of their family. Work is, in some cases, closely tied to people's identity. We spend a lot of time at work, and in some cultures, social interactions and friendships often reside in the workplace (England & Harpaz, 1990). Those who stop working, either because of firing, layoffs, or retirement, often report negative feelings related to their identity and self-worth (Rudolph, 1998; Sennett, 1998). But not everyone sees work the same way.

A US-American manager working in Italy had a not uncommon firsthand experience with cultural differences in motivation and the perceived importance of work. She was working with a team of Italians and preparing a presentation to their manager and a group of potential clients. The team had been highly cooperative and effective in collecting the information needed and on putting together their presentation. On the day of the presentation, which was set for 2 p.m., the US manager had a quick lunch and went to the room where the presentation was scheduled around 1 p.m. To her surprise, she was the only team member present. As she started pulling up her presentation and checking the media, she encountered several technology problems: the presentation slides appeared fuzzy, the sound was less than clear, and, as she walked around the room practicing her speech, she noticed that people sitting in the back would have trouble both seeing and hearing the presentation. The clock was ticking with only 30 minutes to 2, and still neither the team members nor the manager had shown up. Her attempts to reach the IT department for help were fruitless and the offices around the presentation room were all deserted. Anxiety and panic were fast taking hold, as the US manager was seeing her work and that of her team going to waste because of technical difficulty. She was also worried about the reaction of her manager and being blamed for lack of preparation.

Finally, a few minutes before 2, her team members showed up, casually chatting. When asked why they are so late, they were all surprised since it was just 2 and they explained that they had come back from a wonderful lunch and were disappointed that she had not joined them. Their manager showed up a few minutes after 2, also returning from lunch, and few participants started streaming in. Eventually, the IT person was found (having returned from lunch) and resolved the problems quickly and the presentation went under way almost 30 minutes late. No one, except the US-American manager, seemed the least bit concerned and they all took the opportunity to tease her about taking things too seriously.

As the example indicates, the US-American manager focuses on work and the tasks she is assigned, with a strong sense of time urgency motivating her behavior, and her panic. Her Italian coworkers, her managers, and the participants in her presentation have considerably less focus on time and immediate task accomplishments. The respective cultural values and CMC of each individual are driving their behavior.

1.1.1 Meaning and Purpose of Work. Some researchers suggest that people are happiest and most fulfilled when their work provides opportunities to learn and be challenged (Seligman, 2002). Work is the source of joy, fulfillment, and satisfaction, as well as stress, disappointment, and anger (Ardichvili & Kuchinke, 2009). But does work mean the same thing in all cultures? Do people work for the same reasons? The US models of motivation and engagement are based on the assumptions that the individual and fulfilment of individual needs and aspirations are at the center of motivation. However, in a majority of other countries and cultures, motivation is not based on the satisfaction of individual needs, but rather on realizing the most good for the collective.

Research conducted by an international research team (Meaning of Work—MOW, 1981) and other researchers (England & Harpez, 1990) considered the possible differences in the meaning and purpose of work in several industrialized countries. The

Table 10.1 Ranking of Work Goals Across Countries

Why Do You Work?	Belgium	UK	Germany	Israel	Japan	Netherlands	US
Interesting work	1	1	3	1	2	2	1
Income	2	2	1	3	5	5	2
Contact with people	5	4	4	2	6	3	7
Opportunity	7	8	9	5	7	9	5
Promotions	10	11	10	8	11	11	10
Autonomy	4	10	8	4	3	1	8
Good work hours	9	5	6	7	8	8	9
Variety	6	7	6	11	9	4	6
Job security	3	3	2	10	4	7	3
Fit with job	8	6	5	6	1	6	4
Working conditions	11	9	11	9	10	10	11

Sources: Based on information in MOW (1981, 1987).

results show that, in all countries, work is significant and important not only as a necessity and means to survival but also as a means of drawing meaning and satisfaction from life. Respondents in the seven countries studied agreed on three out of eleven purposes of work (see Table 10.1). Across the board, people hope for interesting work, income, and contact with others. However, the commonalities stop there.

For example, income or pay is less of a reason for working for the Japanese and the Dutch, whereas it is important for people in the other countries. Similarly, autonomy is a primary factor for people in only four of the countries, including, not surprisingly, the Dutch (a horizontal individualist culture where being independent from others is valued). The Japanese are the only ones for whom fit with the job is the primary goal at work, something that can partially be explained with the high degree of collectivism in the culture.

1.2 Centrality of Work

MOW researchers (1981, 1987) further considered the degree to which work is considered central and some of the norms related to work. Not surprisingly, how important work is to people differs across the countries in their sample. Work is less central in the United Kingdom and Germany and most central in Japan and Israel. Other researchers have gone further and considered whether people define work differently (England & Harpaz, 1990). They found that for most people in their study of six countries, work is not defined as something that is unpleasant or something where someone tells you what to do, but the definition generally includes getting money for doing something (England & Harpaz, 1990). However, participants in their research did not agree on other factors. For example, for Belgians, the definition of work involves a feeling of belonging while for the Dutch and Israelis contributing to society is part of the definition.

Overall, the research about the meaning of work shows that the large majority of people across different countries would continue working even if they had no financial need and that, generally, people do not consider work to be unpleasant (England & Harpaz, 1990). However, cultural differences do exist, calling for managers to apply a Cultural Mindset (CM) and include culture when considering how to motivate their employees.

2. MOTIVATION AND ENGAGEMENT: ANTECEDENTS AND CONSEQUENCES

LO 10.2 Elaborate on the definition, antecedents, and consequences of motivation and engagement

Understanding what motivates people is essential for organizational performance. As a result, motivation has been a central part of management. We will first define motivation, look at its role in performance and the key factors that comprise it, and then review key approaches and models that managers can use to keep their employees motivated and engaged.

2.1 Definitions

Motivation is a state of mind, a desire, and energy that translates into action. Motivation is what drives people to action. The topic has been central to management because it is one of the factors that impact performance. *Engagement* is related to motivation, but it is defined as the rational and emotional commitment people have to do their work and sense of ownership that can drive performance and innovation. People may be engaged in a task because they are required to do so or because they do not want to let their team members down, but still not be personally motivated to do that task. Conversely, a person may be highly motivated and driven, but because of various organizational factors, such as lack of opportunity or trust, or poor leadership, not be engaged. Motivation and engagement are closely related, but not equivalent.

2.2 Motivation and Performance

Performance in any setting is a function of three key elements:

- A person's personal characteristics, including abilities and skills

- The opportunity to perform, meaning having chances to work and use those abilities and skills

- The motivation to perform, the desire to perform

Organizations evaluate and hire employees based on their abilities; managers can then provide opportunities for them to demonstrate those skills; and finally, the person's motivation is the other leg of the three-legged stool. All three elements are necessary to have good performance. While abilities are stable, motivation is not. It is dynamic and changes, and therefore, managers can impact their employees' motivations through their actions. The fact that managers can have an impact on employees' motivation is one of the reasons we study motivation.

Consider that when selecting a person for a foreign assignment, a manager can take into account a number of personal traits and abilities such as flexibility, curiosity, and openness to change. Once the right people, the ones with the desired abilities and skills are selected, the manager can then provide opportunities by offering training and support before, during, and after the assignment. The candidates' personal interest and motivation to take up a foreign assignment, and to perform is the final factor that plays a critical part in whether they will succeed. As we reviewed in Chapter 4, many expats who may have been carefully selected, received opportunities through the organization, and may have had initial enthusiasm and high motivation to perform, often lose their motivation to continue in their foreign assignments based on various cultural and family-related factors. Their motivation is key to performance.

2.3 Three Factors in Motivation

Three factors determine whether a person is motivated (see Figure 10.1):

- The person's or employee's characteristics

- The job the person is doing

- The organization in which the person works

Figure 10.1   Three Factors in Motivation

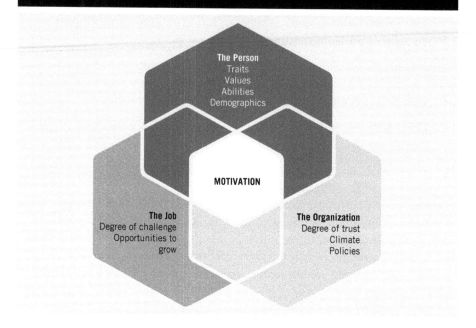

The various motivation models that we review in the next section address one or more of these factors.

2.3.1 The Person. First, motivation is related to the *person and individual differences* or characteristics which include personality traits, abilities, values, and demographic factors. For example, being a highly proactive person is likely to lead to having more initiative when undertaking various tasks. Similarly, traits such as introversion-extraversion or demographic factors such as gender or age will impact the types of opportunities and situations a person is interested in. Values, which are closely linked to culture, are further likely to influence what a person is motivated to do.

For example, if on the one hand, you value individual achievement, you are more likely to be motivated to demonstrate your achievements. On the other hand, if you value the collective, your actions will be more directed at helping the group succeed. In our *First Person* anecdote, the Canadian manager values interpersonal connections and consideration of long-term career goals. The US manager in Italy values the task first and foremost, whereas her Italian colleagues have a balanced focus on enjoyment of life. Who the person is and what he or she may value is one of the factors in motivation.

2.3.2 The Job. The second factor in motivation is the *actual job* that people do. If a job is interesting or challenging, people are more likely to be motivated to perform it, while a repetitive task, or one that presents overwhelming and impossible challenges, is less likely to motivate people. It is important to keep in mind that what is considered motivating and challenging is, to some extent, related to individual characteristics. In other words, what one person may consider interesting and challenging may be different from what piques another person's interest. Conversely, one person may lose interest quickly when doing a routine task, while another may be able to stay engaged. While managers cannot change a person's individual characteristics, they are more likely to be able to change the tasks and jobs that their employees do in order to keep them motivated and engaged.

2.3.3 The Organization. Finally, the *organization itself* plays a role in motivation. An organization that provides the climate and opportunities that fit a person's interests, values, and needs will positively impact motivation. It is again important to note that, while there may be some universally desirable organizational practices, for example fairness and consistency, whether a practice and policy is considered desirable and likely to motivate people is contingent upon the individuals and their CMC. For example, some will be highly motivated by financial and other tangible rewards that an organization offers, while others will seek other outcomes such as opportunities to grow or to develop a social network.

The example in the *First Person* anecdote shows that our Canadian manager is interested in growth and making connections to advance her career, while her manager is focused on the immediate task at hand. Additionally, personal factors of being new to Boston and lonely are impacting the manager's motivation. While Lauren, the manager, may not be able to change what her employee values and needs, or the virtual nature of their interactions with coworkers, she could make changes in the tasks and the job to help keep her employee engaged.

The three factors depicted in Figure 10.1 all play a role in whether a person is motivated. While one factor may be more or less important in different times, the highest motivation will result when all three factors are considered.

2.4 Work Engagement Around the World

In recent years, substantial attention has been given to engagement rather than motivation as several surveys have shown that employees around the world tend to lack the engagement that is likely to lead to high organizational performance. A Gallup survey of 142 countries provides some disheartening results (State of the Global Workplace, 2017). Worldwide, although approximately one in three respondents state that they have a "good job," only 13% of the employees surveyed indicate that they are engaged. Sixty-three percent state that they are not engaged, and 24% state that they are disengaged.

In country and regional comparisons, East Asia, dominated by China, had the lowest engagement with 6% and the Middle East and North Africa had the highest levels of disengagement. Only 10% of Western European employees indicate being engaged as compared to 33% in the United States and 27% in Latin America (State of the Global Workplace, 2017). The Gallup survey suggests that routine jobs and lack of concern for employees are the primary causes of disengagement worldwide. Conversely, factors such as positive relationships, recognition, and opportunities for development help boost engagement, with managerial and knowledge-based work leading to higher engagement. In addition to engagement being related to positive psychological factors for employees, the Gallup survey finds that it is associated with higher productivity, profitability, sales and customer metrics, lower turnover and absenteeism, and fewer quality-related problems.

Although the Gallup survey is only one indicator, and it has a distinctively Western point of view, the results suggest that the challenge of motivating and engaging employees is universal, although methods on how to achieve the goal may need to be much more culture-specific.

3. APPROACHES TO MOTIVATION

> **LO 10.3 Detail approaches to motivation including the content and process theories**

We just learned that motivation is a function of the person, the job, and the organization. Therefore any effective approach to motivation should consider as many of these factors as possible. There are two general approaches one can take to understanding and managing motivation:

- One is to look at the content, namely *what* motivates people

- The other is to look at the process, specifically *how* to motivate people.

We will present the content and process theories and close this section with an integrative roadmap that combines the various approaches to address the three factors in motivation: the person, the job, and the organization.

3.1 Content Theories

Content theories attempt to answer the question of what motivates people by focusing on human needs. In other words, they suggest that we are motivated to do something because of our unsatisfied needs. The foundation of such approaches is the well-known model developed by Abraham Maslow and his *Needs Hierarchy*.

3.1.1 Maslow's Needs Hierarchy. Maslow argues that people are motivated to satisfy unmet needs. He divides human needs along a pyramid with physiological needs such as need for food and water as the base and higher level needs such as relationships or achievement toward the top. As each level of needs is satisfied, they no longer are sources of motivation and people move up the hierarchy toward safety, then higher level needs of love and belonging, then esteem and self-image, culminating in self-actualization. Maslow (1943) assumes that, first, the pyramid of needs is fundamentally the same for everyone; second, that most people's basic needs are satisfied most of the time; and third, that higher level needs are often unsatisfied. His approach is primarily considering the individual factor of motivation.

3.1.2 Herzberg's Two-Factor Theory. Frederick Herzberg proposed another content approach to motivation called the two-factor theory. It is also based on a person's needs as the source of motivation, but takes a broader approach by considering the key role of the job people do. Herzberg (2003) suggests that the factors that lead to dissatisfaction and those that lead to motivation are on two separate fields (see Figure 10.2). When lower level needs, which Herzberg labels *hygiene factors* and are related to extrinsic rewards such as pay or working conditions, are not satisfied, employees will be dissatisfied. However, addressing those hygiene factors does not lead to motivation since when they are satisfied, they lead to a neutral state.

Motivators, which are intrinsic rewards such as the job itself, achievement, recognition, challenge, and growth, are what managers must focus on to motivate their employees. Although hygiene factors cannot motivate people, they must be satisfied before people are ready to be motivated. In other words, motivation requires a two-factor approach that first satisfies lower level hygiene needs, then allows for addressing higher level motivational factors.

3.1.3 Content Theories, the Three Factors in Motivation. Both of these content theories, by focusing on needs, primarily consider the person in motivation (see Figure 10.1). By including the work itself as a primary source of motivation, Herzberg makes a considerable contribution to our understanding of motivation as something within a person that is triggered by challenge and growth, rather than simple extrinsic rewards.

Although Maslow's needs hierarchy is probably one of the most recognizable approaches to motivation, there is little research to support the existence of the hierarchy, the order in which he has proposed the pyramid, or the idea of prepotency which suggests that we have to satisfy lower levels before we can move up to higher levels (Steers, Porter, & Bigley, 1996). Additionally, the self-actualization concept, in spite of its popularity, is ill-defined and the model does not take cultural differences

Figure 10.2 Herzberg's Two-Factor Theory

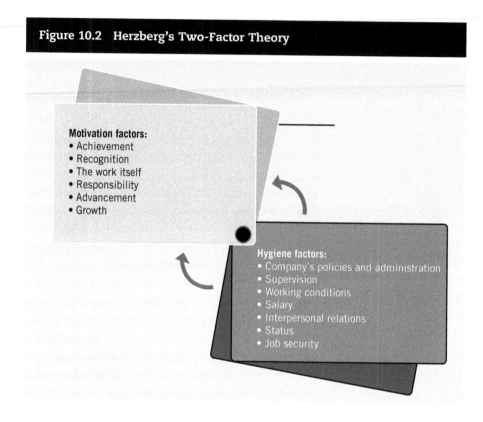

Motivation factors:
- Achievement
- Recognition
- The work itself
- Responsibility
- Advancement
- Growth

Hygiene factors:
- Company's policies and administration
- Supervision
- Working conditions
- Salary
- Interpersonal relations
- Status
- Job security

into account. Specifically, self-actualization is, by definition, a concept based on an individualistic CMC with a focus on people achieving their highest personal potential. Similarly, although some of Herzberg's concepts have been tested in other cultures, the assumptions behind his approach are also deeply rooted in the Western CMC with a focus on individuals.

3.1.4 Culture and Content Theories. Based on the information and examples presented at the beginning of this chapter on the meaning of work across cultures and the knowledge of value differences across cultures, it is clear that not every culture values the same thing and therefore, beyond sharing biological human needs, not all people order their needs the same way and value the same outcomes and rewards. For example, the US-American manager who works in Italy in our example is motivated by getting her job done and impressing her manager, while her Italian teammates are placing enjoyment of lunch and each others' company first.

The need theories of motivation have a strong "one best way" undertone that does not translate easily to consideration of cultural differences in today's global work environment. For example, Herzberg's model relegates factors such as status, job security, and interpersonal relationships to hygiene factors, elevating personal achievement, growth, and recognition to factors that can motivate employees. Such an approach does not recognize well-established differences in cross-cultural values. For instance, in collectivistic cultures, group harmony and interpersonal relationships are essential. In those cultures, managers cannot focus on personal achievement alone. Specifically, research shows, that, although there are no differences in actual performance between the two groups, Asian Americans are driven to work hard by consideration of parental and community expectations, whereas for European Americans, self-image is the driver (Fu & Markus, 2014). Furthermore, as an indicator of the importance of the collective, Chinese students rely more on advice from others than do Americans (Guan et al., 2015). This fundamental difference between individualistic and collectivistic cultures in regards to the importance of others and the collective as opposed to the self is only one of the many cultural factors that need consideration when managing and leading organizations across cultures.

3.2 Process Theories

Instead of focusing primarily on the content of what motivates people and individual needs, several other approaches to motivation concentrate on the process by which managers can help their employees increase their motivation—the *how* as well as the *what*. Expectancy theory, goal setting, equity theory, and the job design model all address the process of motivation by considering individual characteristics, the job people do, and organizational factors to varying degrees.

3.2.1 Expectancy Theory. Expectancy theory holds that people will be motivated when they believe and expect that their effort (E) will result in performance (a link called expectancy), and that the performance (P) will be instrumental in yielding desired outcomes (O; a link called instrumentality; Vroom, 1964). Expectancy is a cognitive approach that suggests that people's perception of events matters as much as actual events. Referring back to our Italian team example, the US-American manager believes that her efforts related to working hard, being prepared, and being on time are key to performance and to her manager's evaluation of her. She is therefore motivated to show up early and concerned about the time. Her Italian coworkers do not consider their performance on the presentation tied to being early and on time and are more motivated by the time spent with colleagues.

In another example, according to expectancy theory, for students to be motivated, they must believe and expect that studying for their exams (which requires effort; E to P expectancy link) will lead to high performance on the tests. The performance on the test then must lead to a high grade in the course (P to O instrumental link). If students do not see how their effort is linked to performance or that their performance does not get them the outcome (the grade they want), they will not be motivated to study. Additionally, they must value getting a good grade. The job of an instructor, or a manager in case of organizational settings, is to assure that students (or employees) are confident that the paths from working hard and putting in effort to actual outcomes are as clear as possible, and that the outcome that results from performance is something that they value.

Expectancy theory is concerned with how people think about motivation; what they think happens as a result of their effort and performance, as well as what outcomes they need or value. In order to motivate people, managers would have to consider needs, but also the job the person does and organizational factors that support or detract from performance. Therefore, the expectancy theory allows for addressing all three factors in motivation.

3.2.2 Goal Setting. The goal setting approach similarly considers how people think about their goals and focuses on how managers can help set goals that will motivate employees. The approach is based on extensive research that shows that having well designed and appropriately challenging goals can be motivating (Locke, 1978). The common practice referred to as SMART (Specific, Measurable, Achievable, Reasonable, Timetable) is based on that research and recommends that in order to be motivating, a goal must be clear and specific, achievable based on people's abilities, reasonable for the individuals, and have a set timeframe. In other words, simply saying "I will do better" would be poor goal setting, whereas saying "on my next sales call, I will apply the two principles I learned and aim at increasing my sales by 10 percent" would be an appropriate and motivating goal.

Goal setting principles suggest that managers implement SMART goals and further recommend active participation of employees in setting goals in order to increase engagement and motivation. In order to implement goal setting, managers would have to consider the person's needs and individual characteristics, namely what is an appropriate goal, but also consider the task or the job the person is doing.

3.2.3 Equity Theory. Equity theory is based on the notion that how people perceive a situation or event impacts their motivation (Adams & Freedman, 1976). It proposes that people regularly, and often subconsciously, evaluate how much effort (input) they put into their job and what outcomes (output) they receive. They also pick others they consider to be reasonably similar to them and compare their inputs and outputs to theirs. This input–output analysis and comparison with others yield a belief regarding how equitably and fairly they are treated. When people perceive inequity, they will react to restore balance by taking one or more of the actions presented in Table 10.2.

Consider the case of female university faculty who suspected that their salaries and rate of promotion (output/outcomes) were lower than their male counterparts' (comparison persons). They had many examples of male faculty who were hired with the same qualifications in the same time periods (inputs) as female faculty and had data

Table 10.2 Balancing Out Inequity

Reaction	Example
Increase outputs/outcomes	Asking for a raise or a promotion
Decrease input/efforts	Working fewer hours; holding back ideas and contributions; disengaging from work
Decrease outputs/outcomes	Refusing a raise or promotion
Increase inputs/effort	Working harder; learning new skills that support the job
Pick a different comparison person	Changing who you use as a comparison person; selecting someone who appears more similar to you in terms of effort and outcome
Increase other people's input/effort	Sabotaging other people's work; actively or passively refusing to help and support others to make them work harder
Decrease other people's output/outcome	Complaining or taking other actions that would prevent others from receiving rewards such as raises or promotions
Quit	Leaving the organization or transferring to another team or department

Source: Based on information in Adams and Freedman (1976).

regarding research and teaching productivity (input/effort). Because the university was private, actual salary data were not publicly available. Based on their suspicion, the women complained to the provost and university president, who first downplayed their concerns and insisted that their perceptions were not correct. As their discussion to address the problem with the university administration dragged on, several of the female faculty accepted better-paid positions in other universities. Many others reduced their workload by resigning from task forces and committees that they had volunteered to join and refused any additional work that was not clearly part of their job requirement (reduced their input/effort), actions that caused a reduction in their input and more work to shift to other faculty, increasing their input instead.

The women faculty also actively and loudly complained, involving the faculty senate, seeking support from student government, and taking their fight to local and national newspapers. After 2 years of arguments and debates, the university administration agreed to conduct a study and eventually set aside a substantial portion of general faculty yearly raises specifically to address gender equity. While many women faculty were satisfied with the outcome, because they did not have access to formal information about salaries, several suspected that the problem was worse than expected and was not fully addressed. Meanwhile, several senior male faculty members who had long tenure and whose salaries had fallen behind that of younger new hires raised concerns regarding the inequity of addressing just one type of salary disparity.

This case presents all the elements of the equity theory of motivation. When the women faculty perceived inequity, they became motivated to correct it through a number of actions. Unfortunately, the consequence of perceived or real inequity is often decreased organizational contributions. Although limited to perceptions of equity as the source of motivation, equity theory allows for consideration of individual, job, and organizational factors, depending on the areas that are involved in perceptions of equity.

3.2.4 The Job Design Framework. The job design model of motivation proposes that motivation is a function of the fit between people and the job they do (Garg & Rastogi, 2006; Hackman, Oldham, & Suttle, 1997). The model identifies five core job characteristics that can be used to describe any job and be combined to assess the degree to which it has the potential to motivate. These characteristics are:

- *Skills variety* refers to the number of different skills a person must apply when doing their job. For example, the job of a nurse or a manager requires a number of different skills, as opposed to a person who works in an Amazon warehouse facilities and prepares orders for shipping.

- *Task identity* refers to the degree to which a person identifies with his or her job. A carpenter who builds custom-made furniture or an artist both closely identify with their creation. Conversely, a clerk who is part of the large group of people who stack shelves in a store is less likely to identify with the task.

- *Task significance* refers to the overall significance of the job the person does. People whose jobs have high task significance believe that what they do matters to the organization, or the community, even the world.

- *Autonomy* refers to how much autonomy a person has in day-to-day activities. A person who has a high autonomy job can make many independent decisions regarding how to accomplish tasks.

- *Feedback* refers to whether a job provides direct feedback regarding performance. For example, salespeople can tell whether they have done a good job when the customer signs an order; they do not need to get feedback from their manager.

These five job characteristics determine how motivating a job can be. When all these factors are high, a job is inherently challenging and has the potential to motivate people. The motivating potential of a job then relates to critical psychological states

Figure 10.3   Job Design Model

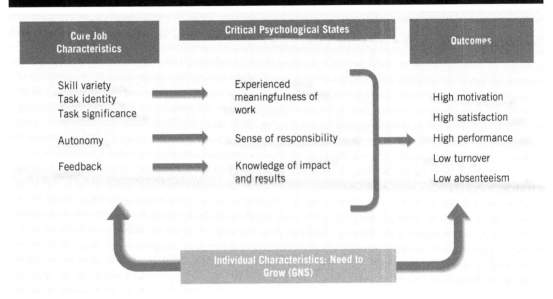

Sources: Based on information in Hackman et al. (1997) and Garg and Rastogi (2006).

(see Figure 10.3). A job with high motivating potential provides the people who do that job with a sense of meaningfulness, responsibility, and knowledge of how what they do impact others and results. Research supports the assertion that jobs that have the potential to motivate are associated with critical psychological states and are likely to lead to positive outcomes such as motivation, satisfaction, and performance (Garg & Rastogi, 2006; Hackman et al., 1997; see Figure 10.3).

Additionally, the job design model considers individual characteristics such that when there is a match between how much people need to grow (growth need strength—GNS) and the degree of challenge a job provides, people will be satisfied, energized, and motivated to perform (see Table 10.3). Conversely, when there is a mismatch between the person's need and the job at hand, motivation and performance will be low and absenteeism and turnover are likely to increase.

The primary task for managers is then to assure that there is fit between employees and the job they do. As opposed to Herzberg's two-factor theory that suggests that all jobs must be enriched and challenging to motivate people, the central contingency approach of job design allows for a nuanced approach that considers what a person needs. In other words, a job that may appear simple, routine, and boring to one person may be perfect and appropriately motivating to another who either has lower need for growth, or because of various situational factors such as going to

Table 10.3 Matching Individual Needs and Jobs

		Motivating Potential of a Job	
		Low	**High**
Individual Need to Grow	High	Mismatch • Simple job • Person who needs growth and challenge • Likely negative outcomes • Change needed	Match • Challenging job • Person who needs growth and challenge • Likely positive outcomes • Monitor and maintain
	Low	Match • Simple job • Person who has low need for growth and challenge • Likely positive outcomes • Monitor and maintain	Mismatch • Challenging job • Person who has low need for growth and challenge • Likely negative outcomes • Change needed

Source: Based on information in Hackman et al. (1997).

school while working full-time or other community and family responsibilities and challenges, is not looking for challenge and growth from their job.

More than any of the other approaches, the job design model fully considers both individual characteristics and needs and the job as motivating factors.

3.2.5 Culture and Process Theories. As is the case of the content theories of motivation, there is limited research of how culture impacts the implementation of process theories of motivation in non-Western cultural settings. However, by taking a cognitive approach and focusing on the process of how people think, rather than only on what they value, process theories can be applied to different cultural contexts more easily. Cognitive processes are not as culture-specific as needs and values are. Therefore, regardless of culture, a manager could consider whether an employee's efforts lead to performance, whether that performance garners outcomes that are valued by that employee, whether the goals are appropriate for the employee, or whether the job is a good fit for the person.

The principles of goal setting have not been extensively tested in non-Western settings. It is clear that what would be considered an appropriate goal may depend on the person's CMC. For example, in short-term-oriented cultures, such as the United States, short time windows are often recommended with regular and frequent checks to monitor progress on goals. Such short-term orientation is less likely to be appropriate in cultures that have a much longer time orientation.

Equity theory, which also takes a cognitive approach, can potentially be applied to different cultural contexts. However, there is little research on its applicability to non-Western cultures. Based on information on cultural value differences, one could assume that what people consider input and output and who they choose to compare themselves to are culturally determined.

Similarly, while job design has not been extensively applied to non-Western cultural settings, the contingency nature of the model allows for consideration of culture. Rather than suggesting that one type of job fits everyone, by including individual needs, there is room for taking cultural values into account. For example, cultural values related to performance orientation or tolerance for ambiguity are both likely to impact which types of job characteristics an individual may prefer. Someone with a strong performance orientation and high tolerance for ambiguity would likely be motivated by a job that provides variety and autonomy with direct feedback. Similarly, in tight cultures, employees may not expect or be uncomfortable with too much autonomy on their job and may prefer clear direction and expectations.

3.3 An Integrative Approach to Motivation

The process models, because they consider how people think and the processes that lead to motivation, are more amenable to applications across different CMCs. Using the elements of Expectancy Theory as a framework Figure 10.4 presents an integrative approach to motivation that includes both content and process approaches and provides

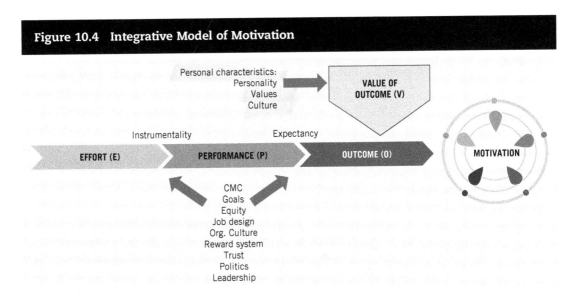

Figure 10.4   Integrative Model of Motivation

a comprehensive roadmap to address all three factors in motivation: the person, the job, and the organization. The model outlines various factors that may impact the E to P to O process and the V of outcomes, presented by expectancy theory allowing for the integration of people's culture-as-meta-context (CMC) in a variety of ways.

For example, individual needs and values that are influenced by culture impact what outcomes a person may value. In more individualistic, performance-oriented, and short-term cultures such as the United States and Western Europe, extrinsic rewards that are delivered quickly (e.g., yearly raises or quick promotions) will most likely be valued. However, in collectivistic cultures that have long-term focus such as Japan or Egypt, valued outcomes and rewards would involve long-tenure, more gradual promotions and recognition from team members.

3.4 The Integrative Approach and the Cultural Mindset

Since the cognitive models focus on how people think, their CMC is likely to provide both the context for interpreting situations and a guide for behavior. Therefore, it is likely to impact both the E to P and the P to O linkages. For example, what you consider effort and how you expect your performance to translate into outcomes is influenced by your CMC, as demonstrated in the Italian team example and in our *First Person* anecdote. Additionally, how goals are set, the design of the job, leadership, organizational culture, and trust, as well as perceptions of equity which are job and organizational factors, all play a role in whether people perceive that their efforts will lead to performance that gets them to outcomes that they value.

The motivation approaches we presented in this chapter were developed in a US-American CMC often relying on data from "WEIRD" (Western, Educated, Industrialized, Rich, and Democratic) participants. They can provide guidelines and recommendations for managers to understand how to motivate their employees. However, even within a single cultural context, they do not apply equally well to all employees; people are complex. When managers work across cultures with employees who operate from a different CMC, the broad application of concepts developed in one CMC to another become even more problematic, once more demonstrating the paradox that rules from one world do not always work in another. Simply applying models without consideration of culture is likely to create misunderstanding and confusion.

3.4.1 Considering Culture When Motivating People. Managers must be vigilant not to assume that what motivates or demotivates them or others who are similar to them will have the same impact on those who may have different assumptions, values, beliefs, and practices. This cultural self-awareness is a critical part of having a CM. Managers who have a CM must consider culture when they address individual, job, and organizational factors, and the steps outlined in the integrative model. Having

[handwritten margin note: ↑ good for essay ☆]

cultural knowledge about cultural differences as well as various theories and models, and curiosity (both also CM factors) further supports being able to address motivation with a pluralistic rather than ethnocentric or parochial mindset.

Consider how a manager in a telecom company in Northern Arizona in the United States attempted to build motivation of his department members. The manager, who was Anglo-American from the midwestern United States and a gregarious and extraverted person, often used public recognition either through a simple "let's cheer for our colleague who just reached a milestone" to plaques and awards to publicly celebrate his team's accomplishments. He had learned through his business classes and through personal experience that good managers must reward their employees in public and "punish" them in private, something he rarely did. He was always bragging about his team to other managers and holding up good performance of one or another employee any chance he got. He was very surprised to find out that his team's turnover was considerably higher than everyone else's in the plant. After much soul-searching, discussions with HR, and questioning his team members about possible causes, he finally discovered that a major factor was his insistence on public recognition. Because of the location of his plant near the Native American Navajo reservation, many employees and managers were Navajos, for whom sticking out from their group and appearing to be better than others is uncomfortable and even shameful. They were therefore quietly withdrawing from the group to avoid the embarrassment of being held up as an example for their peers. It became very clear that what motivated the manager and many others he had worked with in the past did not work for the cultural group he was managing in Northern Arizona.

Derek Irvine, vice president of Globoforce, suggests:

> The rewards must be 100 percent street level local. "Think global, thank local." It's so easy to say but the challenge is in the execution. Here's where many companies make a mistake. They think recognition comes in a box and can be shipped anywhere. But it's a personal moment that will vary vastly whether we are in Singapore or Sydney or San Francisco. (Pyrillis, 2011)

Motivating and working with individual employees can be challenging and effectively managing multicultural groups poses yet another level of challenge.

4. LEADING MULTICULTURAL TEAMS

LO 10.4 Define key elements of multicultural teams

Organizations are made of people who work together in structured and systematic ways to achieve common goals. People who work in groups of various sizes are the foundation of organizations. While understanding the individual characteristics of those individuals is important, when they organize themselves in groups, those groups become more than the simple sum of individual members; they take on a life of their own. In other words, knowing each individual within a group does not, in and of itself, allow you to understand and predict how a group will behave; you have to understand the group dynamics and how it functions. Although the words groups and teams are often used interchangeably, as we will do in this chapter, there are some differences that are worth noting.

4.1 Definitions

Groups are defined as two or more people who work together on a common goal. *Teams* are mature groups where members have complementary skills, are committed to common goals and to one another, share leadership, and hold one another accountable (Katzenbach & Smith, 2005). The two share some common characteristics. Both groups and teams develop certain stated and unstated rules and norms that guide their actions and implement either formal or informal hierarchies that establish leaders and followers. Both groups and teams also assign roles to different individuals. While the terms are often used interchangeably, they are not the same.

4.2 From Groups to Teams

Groups become teams when their activities and processes are clearly focused and purposeful and members actively work on improving internal processes to maintain the team's effectiveness. For groups to develop into teams, they typically have to go through the stages described in Table 10.4 and reach some level of maturity. In other words, simply putting together a number of people and assigning them a task does not guarantee that they will be able to do their job well. Groups need time to become effective and function as a team. Members go through an orientation period where everyone is figuring out what working in the group entails. Most groups face some sort of conflict as members disagree regarding norms, leadership, or other activities. Some groups may disband as a result of such conflicts; others resolve them and move to the next stages where they start developing common understanding and common ground. Having done so, they can finally perform well and can function as a team, rather than simply a group.

Although the five stages of development are not extensively researched and their order may change from one group to another, they are highly popular in management training. One of the key contributions of this stage model of groups and teams is to provide a general roadmap that suggests that groups are likely to take some time to become effective and productive and that some conflict is typical and to be expected. The stages are not linear, rather groups may go back and forth between the various

Table 10.4 Stages of Group Development

Stage (Typical Focus)	Description
Forming (Orientation)	Initial stage during which the members get acquainted and learn about one another. They discuss and set some general rules and norms and may identify a leader, or rely on assigned leader. Members at this stage often have the illusion that the group is cohesive.
Storming (Power struggles)	As the members establish goals and priorities and formalize rules, norms, and roles, disagreement is likely to occur leading to conflict. One of the typical sources of conflict at this stage is over leadership.
Norming (Cooperation)	As the group resolves its conflict, the members implicitly or explicitly agree on rules, norms, roles, and leadership and move toward goal accomplishment. Groups that reach this stage often have a sense of energy and cohesion.
Performing (Synergy)	Groups that resolve their differences and accomplish goals are now mature and able to perform consistently on delivering goals and resolving conflict constructively when they occur. This is the most task-productive stage for a group.
Adjourning (Closure)	When groups have completed their task and accomplished their goals, or if they fail to resolve their disagreement, they may adjourn or disband temporarily or permanently.

Sources: Based on information in Tuckman and Jensen (1977) and Tuckman (2001).

stages, as members turn over and new ones join, new tasks, challenges, and conflicts arise and get resolved. Managers should therefore provide the groups they form to accomplish a task with some time and resources to allow them to reach maturity. Simply putting a group of people together, as we often do for class assignments, no matter how able and skilled they are, does not create a group, and is not likely to lead to the development of a mature team.

4.3 Key Challenges of Groups and Teams

Whether they are mature or not, people who collaborate in groups and teams must address two key challenges:

- *Task*: they must organize and accomplish their tasks

- *Manage relationships:* they must address interpersonal processes.

How groups develop and progress through these stages and how they address the key challenges that arise is likely to be impacted by culture. In culturally homogeneous groups where members are from the same or similar cultural backgrounds, disagreement will be based on personality, style, or functional area. Such differences will exist in heterogeneous group with culturally diverse members, and be further complicated by cultural differences in language, values, norms, and beliefs which add a layer of complexity. Additionally, the degree to which they emphasize task or relationship may also depend on the cultural values of the members.

4.3.1 Culture in Teams. In heterogeneous groups and teams, where members have different cultural values, disagreements related to how to complete the task or resolve interpersonal differences will have deeper roots related to assumptions and values and the CMC of the group members. For example, in high power distance, vertical, and ascriptive cultures, the conflict over leadership is likely to be resolved more quickly by relying on either the formally assigned leader, or by designating the person with the highest perceived status to be the leader. In more egalitarian, horizontal, and performance-oriented cultures, members are prone to debate and argue to establish their credibility before they select a leader. Similarly, in tight cultures, the stated and unstated rules for behavior are likely to be established and followed. Values relating to time (short- or long-term goals), gender expectations, and degree of participation are all similarly likely to impact group processes. The importance and priority given to task over relationship management will further be influenced by cultural values of individualism-collectivism and other values such as performance orientation, being-doing, and masculinity-femininity.

A MBA class that combined US-American managers and visiting Mexican managers working on several team projects illustrates these challenges. The teams were preestablished with several US-American and Mexican teams. All students were highly motivated managers with years of experience in a variety of industries, yet their approaches to team projects were drastically different. Based on traditions of the program, the first task for the teams was to draft and sign a team contract that outlined norms, specifically those that addressed equal contributions, freeloaders, and ways to handle conflict. The Mexican managers were quite surprised at the need to engage in this exercise. Their members quickly selected their team leaders based on seniority, and the leader set rules with input from the team members; that designated leader handled most of the conflicts with a top-down approach that was accepted by the team. The US teams took considerable time to craft their team contracts, a process that was used as a way of developing cohesion. They argued over leadership as several team members vied to lead each team and members took some time to argue over and establish their norms.

The US teams set up clear and complicated rules for handling noncontributing members, as the issue of freeloaders was on members' minds who insisted on equal contribution. The Mexican group members were less worried about equal contribution; as long as everybody contributed what they could, contributions were considered fair. For example, some team members only helped with the presentations and did not write the paper, but they were still given equal credit. The US teams insisted on all members working equally on all stages of the projects. The teams were given the option of forming new ones in subsequent projects. Most of the US managers expressed the desire to switch groups; Mexican managers indicated a preference for staying in their established teams.

In this example, the eventual products of the groups were equal; the way the team members approached their work and their group dynamics were different. One approach was not better than the other; culture-just-is (CJI). Each cultural group reached the goals successfully operating based their own CMC. The fact that the groups were culturally homogeneous further assisted in that process.

5. DEGREES OF MULTICULTURALISM IN TEAMS

LO 10.5 Present various types of multicultural teams

Teams are characterized by collaboration and interdependence to achieve common goals where members have sustained commitment to one another, the success of the team, and their goal and they share leadership to varying degrees. The teams described in the previous example were homogeneous. The members all came from broadly similar cultural groups. There is no doubt that there were regional, group, and other professional differences among the members, but they all shared a nationality. It is increasingly unlikely for managers and employees to work in culturally homogeneous groups. Even within national boundaries, ethnic, gender, religious, and other group-level cultural differences are likely to add to the complexity of managing teams effectively.

In our discussion of diversity in Chapter 5, we presented research regarding the benefits and challenges of having groups with diverse membership. Overall, we know that working with people from diverse backgrounds, whether it is cultural diversity or other characteristics, is more likely to engender conflict and require more effort to build cohesion. However, there is also considerable evidence that diversity is essential for creativity and problem-solving, particularly in complex situations (see Chapter 5 Section "Diversity in Groups"). We consider next the different levels of multiculturalism in teams.

5.1 Token Teams

Organizations create groups with varying levels of diversity. Starting from the now increasingly rare homogeneous group, many organizations appear to make at least a symbolic gesture and infuse diversity by introducing one or a few diverse members (Kanter, 1977). International management expert Nancy Adler calls these *token teams* (Adler & Gundersen, 2008) where all members have the same background with one token, or a few, members from another cultural background. Fans of the HBO hit series *Insecure* have observed the central character, Issa (played by Issa Rae), a young black woman, who is the token minority in a nonprofit organization aimed at helping minority youth. She struggles as her unique and diverse perspective is neither sought nor valued. However, she is the sole representative of a group that the organization serves and her presence is therefore essential to providing it with apparent legitimacy. Although organizations are becoming more diverse, many members of minority groups and women continue to experience being the token member in their teams.

A recent panel at Vanderbilt University discussed the impact of tokenism with participants stating that although many organizations have good intentions, tokenism can be draining for employees and does not provide the full benefit of diversity (Sherrer, 2018). A 2019 review of the research about the extent and impact of tokenism by Marla Watkins and her colleagues (Watkins, Simmons, & Humphress, 2019) indicates that token members become highly salient and visible and experience considerable stress and pressure to perform that often impacts them negatively. These researchers also suggest that in more collectivistic cultures and those with lower power distance, the negative effects of tokenism can be reduced.

5.2 Bicultural and Multicultural Teams

Organizations are increasingly made up of *bicultural* and *multicultural* teams that include more than one member from different cultures. Joint ventures, business alliances, reliance on many global partners in supply chains and customers from different cultures, as well as diversity within countries requires working in multicultural teams with members from one or multiple cultures.

The Canadian manager in the *First Person* anecdote is working with such a multicultural team. Similarly, Lisa Wardell, CEO of Adtalem Global Education, has created highly diverse boards and leadership teams:

> *Currently, Adtalem's board is 37 percent African-American, 37 percent female and 62 percent diverse in gender and ethnicity. My leadership team went from being nominally diverse to 40 percent female and 73 percent diverse in gender and ethnicity. Adtalem is now more representative of our 18,000 global colleagues and the students we serve. (Wardell, 2018b)*

The diverse multicultural teams are a reality in all sectors, from education, to government, to nonprofit, health, or business.

5.3 Virtual Teams

With globalization and advances in technology, many multicultural teams that are composed of knowledge workers from across the globe now collaborate in a virtual environment where they meet synchronously or even asynchronously using multiple media with different degrees of personal contact. "Virtual collaboration occurs when people who are not colocated use communication technologies to work together and facilitate getting the job done. In sum, virtual collaboration is the process through which virtual teams get work done" (Nemiro, Beyerlein, Bradely, & Beyerlein, 2008, p. 2). These teams have been called Global Virtual teams (GVTs), multicultural distributed teams, transnational teams, or multinational teams, all characterized by cultural diversity, geographical dispersion, and electronic communication (Jimenez, Boehe, Taras, & Caprar, 2017). The 2020 COVID-19 pandemic put a particular highlight in the challenges and benefits of these virtual teams. Diverse coworkers who used to meet face-to-face were suddenly and unexpectedly facing the additional challenges of working together virtually (Frisch & Greene, 2020).

5.3.1 Challenges of Virtual Teams. In addition to the typical challenges that any team might face (e.g., leadership and building trust), virtual teams face a number of additional challenges (Ferrazzi, 2014):

Sue Freedman (2008), president and founder of the consulting firm Knowledge Work Global, states that GVTs face the triple challenges presented by distance, language, and culture. She suggests several cultural values may play a key role in virtual teams including collectivism, directness, task, risk tolerance, and hierarchy.

Consider the case of several Indian managers who were paired with their Silicon Valley counterparts in a team to plan out a major structural change from waterfall to agile practices for the Indian operation of their company. All team members spoke English, and each of the groups included members who had familiarity with the other culture: the US group included several Indian-born programmers and the Indian group included a couple of US educated MBAs. Although there was some reluctance and resistance to make the change to agile operations, all of the team members were experienced and committed. According to the US team members, the phone and video conferences were too slow and involved too much chitchat. The Indians found the timeframe for the switchover to be unrealistically fast, while the US members were confident it could be done. The Indians often cringed at what appeared to be demands and nasty criticisms from their US counterparts while the US team was frustrated for not knowing where the Indians stood on the issues or even the progress. Although there was no formal leader in the team, it was clear that the Indians would not make decisions without their most senior engineer present, a situation that caused problems because he was often either late or absent due to other major responsibilities. His absence caused delays as the Indian team members avoided action items.

Both groups needed specific recommendations and clarity regarding the task, but Indians found the US members to be "sloppy and overly optimistic" while the US group found the Indian team members to need too much direction. Their arguments almost turned into a shouting match when the US group asked to table a particular issue and the Indian members eagerly agreed and jumped into discussing the topic. Cooler heads prevailed when one of the Indian-born US team members reminded everyone that "tabling" has opposite meanings in US and British English. Additionally, both groups were frustrated by the almost 12-hour time difference; when one group started to work, the other was typically gone for the day, leaving some critical requests unanswered for hours. The leads of both groups complained that even if all the challenges were resolved, they never could get away, as they often had to address work issues late at night and on weekends to try to lessen the problems associated with the time difference. The GVT described here faced a challenging task that was exacerbated by distance, language, and culture (see Table 10.5 for a summary).

Being virtual requires even more effort and careful attention to the structural, interpersonal, and procedural elements of the team. As research on group diversity has shown, there are many advantages to these GVTs and even the time and geographical dispersion can boost productivity, since part of the team is working all the time.

Table 10.5 Opportunities and Challenges of GVTs

Opportunities	Challenges
• Greater diversity of perspectives and opinions	• Location, time, and distance
• Greater number of alternatives	• Culture and language differences
• Potential for constructive conflict	• Loss of rich communication and exchange that can build trust and cohesion
• Innovation and creativity	• Greater potential for impact of biases
• Reduced risk of groupthink	• Work–life balance
• Nonstop work and increased productivity	• Need for specialized skills and training
• Higher autonomy and satisfaction	• Increased possibility of distractions and multitasking • Feeling isolated and left out; lack of meaningful social interaction

Sources: Based on information in Freedman (2008) and Jimenez et al. (2017).

GVTs, like all other teams, provide the potential for creativity, innovation, and high performance associated with diverse opinions and perspectives and having part of the team always being productive. Furthermore, because of constructive conflict, the risk of groupthink, which is defined as poor decision-making due to a desire to maintain cohesion, is reduced.

5.3.2 Supporting Global Virtual Teams. Some research shows that because of the complexity they face, at least half of GVTs do not meet their goals (Zakaria, Amelinckx, & Wilemon, 2004). GVTs require considerable specialized training for team leaders and team members and there are many guidelines for supporting GVTs (e.g., Harwood, 2008; Hosseini, Chileshe, Zuo, & Baroudi, 2020; Peters & Manz, 2008). For example, just because members are not in the same location does not mean that the team should skip over social processes that help its members develop trust and cohesion. The tendency is to jump into action to get the task done, something that may backfire in the long run as members hesitate on relying on people they don't know well. Spending some time early on developing relationships and a sense of team and establishing some common norms can be extremely helpful. Many who are working remotely because of the pandemic have experienced that need to maintain social connections. Specific recommendations include (e.g., Aghina, Handscomb, Ludolph, West, & Yip, 2019; Demirel, 2020; Ferrazzi, 2014; Frisch & Greene, 2020):

- *Careful selection* of team members who are interesting in and willing to cooperate and who already have or are interested in developing a CM.

- *Taking time to get acquainted.* Set aside a first (or very early) meeting to socialize and allow team members to share some personal information and get to know other team members. This process simulates how face-to-face teams naturally start when first formed.

- *Establishing a team vision* that includes both task and relationship goals and roles. Discussions should go beyond the assigned task or project and include conversations regarding team identity, values, and performance.

- *Addressing the team structure* by discussing leadership, individual roles and responsibilities, norms of interaction, and communication and reporting structures and norms (i.e., who should talk to whom and when; what is acceptable and what is not)

- *Addressing task structure* by setting meeting times, rules, and goals, identifying key resources and learning and training needs, setting timelines, identifying milestones, and establishing interim deliverables.

- *Some face-to-face meetings:* Finding opportunities for the whole team or subgroups to meet face-to-face.

- *Celebration and appreciation:* Finding opportunities for celebration and member appreciation. Discuss what will happen when the team adjourns.

- *Good meeting practices:* Running meeting well by having a clear agenda, managing individual participation, using appropriate technology, among other practices is particularly important in GVT meetings.

The triple challenge of location, time, and distance is ever-present and cultural and language differences are likely to intensify those challenges. Without face-to-face interaction, team members miss many key opportunities to build cohesion and trust.

6. LEADING MULTICULTURAL TEAMS EFFECTIVELY

LO 10.6 Elaborate on challenges and tools for leading multicultural teams

Whether face-to-face or virtual, members of multicultural teams, and their managers cannot succeed without careful consideration of how to run a team effectively and without including culture in their preparation and implementation, planning, and developing a CM. Figure 10.5 presents some of the key factors in managing multicultural teams (GVT or face-to-face). In addition to having a CM that involves

Figure 10.5 Factors in the Success of Multicultural Teams

Cultural Mindset (Awareness, Knowledge, Skills)

Legitimate Use of Teams

Cultural Mentors and Brokers

Effective Multicultural Team

Careful Member Selection

Psychological safety and Conflict Management

Appropriate Team Structure

cultural self-awareness, knowledge, and consideration of culture, it is critical to assure that there is a real and legitimate reason to have individuals work in the team and that team members are aware of the consequences of not collaborating (Harwood, 2008). Individuals and homogeneous teams can be both more effective and more efficient when facing routine and simple situations; teams are needed in complex environments. Careful selection of members to assure that they have the necessary technical skills as well as the open-mindedness and flexibility to deal with complexity and uncertainty is also important.

6.1 General Conditions for Success

Based on interviews with over 500 leaders for his *New York Times* column the "Corner Office," Adam Bryant (2020) developed some key pointers for managing a successful team. These include:

- Appropriate team member selection

- Clear mission and goals

- Developing trust and strong communication

- Managing team size and processes

- Strong planning and rules

- Careful development and nurturing of a team culture and norms

These practical pointers are all echoed in research findings (e.g., Aghina et al., 2019; Frontiera & Leidl, 2012; Govindarajan & Terwilliger, 2012). As any person who works on a team would tell you, developing trust both supports and results from effective team management. Angie Hicks, founder of Angie's List, states:

> I've realized you just have to take extra care and make time to talk to people. I've realized that you need to over-communicate. When you're working with people, even if you think you've said something, maybe you need to say it two or three more times. (Bryant, 2012a)

Factors that help build trust include acting with integrity and fairness, competence and hard work, mutual respect, and celebrating success (Nahavandi, 2015). Ken Rees, president and CEO of Think Finance, a company that develops financial products, emphasizes the importance of recognition:

> It's easy to get focused on the fact that you're not where you want to be, as opposed to all that you've accomplished. So taking a moment to talk about good news, just keeps

things more upbeat than they otherwise would be. For a lot of CEOs, I think, we're so focused on where we need to be that we don't necessarily have the fun we need to have along the way. (Bryant, 2012b)

6.2 Addressing Culture in Multicultural Teams

The complexity introduced by having team members from different cultures adds particular challenges for managers and leaders of multicultural teams. Suzi Pomerantz of Innovative Leadership International LLC recommends:

Managers of cross-cultural teams must listen in order to understand the cultural distinctions and contexts of their people. Identify the unspoken obstacles to alignment, and create opportunities to build bridges between individuals who may have biases or invisible obstacles based on lack of cultural awareness. Be curious, create safety, and empower each team member to create alignment. (Forbes Coaches Council, 2016)

There is considerable research and specific practical advice regarding leading multicultural teams (e.g., Glikson & Erez, in press; Pittampalli, 2019; Reynolds & Lewis, 2018; Zander, Mockaitis, & Butler, 2012). The research integrates information about culture and teams to guide managers to address a difficult challenge.

6.2.1 The THINK–KNOW–DO Roadmap: Self-Awareness. Having a CM where managers and team members keep culture in mind when making decisions and working with the team is an essential step. Applying the THINK–KNOW–DO (TKD) roadmap that helps reinforce and develop a CM provides further practical guidelines to manage culture. Specifically, team members must first work on developing self-awareness regarding:

1. Their cultural identities and the corresponding CMC

2. The assumptions, values, and beliefs that shape their thinking and biases and guide their behavior

3. The impact they have on others, something that has been called the external self-awareness (Porter, 2019).

4. Their views of culture (i.e., parochial, ethnocentric, pluralistic) and how it impacts how they interact with others

This self-awareness is the first step in the TKD roadmap and particularly essential in working with multicultural teams where it is easy to focus on culture as something that matters for "other" team members, rather than something that all members have.

Addressing such team challenges Dieter Reuther, transformation facilitator at Team Dynamics Boston, says:

> *Being a German in the U.S., I know it myself, some things are just different, and you struggle with them if you work with other people. Somebody might just always be too close or be in your face and you don't like that. Or, some words just have different meanings [that can lead to misunderstanding]. (Moran, 2016)*

6.2.2 The THINK–KNOW–DO Roadmap: Cultural Knowledge. Maybe the simplest component of the TKD in teams is acquiring knowledge about various cultures. Since team membership is relatively stable and members know who their team members are, they can access relevant information about specific cultures through formal and informal training. Their actions have to reflect awareness of their own CMC and what they have learned about their team members. While relying on various models of culture and their associated cultural prototypes, it is important to remember to not overgeneralize and use the opportunity to ask questions to better understand how their team members relate to others and how they work.

6.2.3 The THINK–KNOW–DO Roadmap: Cultural Skills. Finally, team members must work on acquiring and reinforcing various cross-cultural skills needed to address cultural differences appropriately and effectively. These include language skills, communication skills, conflict management, and so forth as well working on meta-cognitive skills that encourage team members to reflect on their interactions with other team members to build on their successes and address their mistakes.

6.2.4 The Role of Team Leaders. While all team members must take on responsibility for having an effective team, team leaders and managers have particular roles to play in creating and maintaining a culture of trust and safety. Researcher Alison Reynolds of UK's Ashridge Business School and her colleague David Lewis, from the London Business School emphasize the importance of creating a balance between diversity and psychological safety. They define psychological safety as "the belief that one will not be punished or humiliated for speaking up with ideas, questions, concerns, or mistakes" (Reynolds & Lewis, 2018). They suggest that the combination of high diversity and psychological safety is ideal in creating a culture where teams can be creative and generative, and engage and experiment without fear of failure.

Kristin Behfar, professor at the University of Virginia, further emphasizes avoiding artificial divisions which can be created when some, but not all members, speak a certain language or when some countries, typically the United States, are given a higher status (Black, 2017). The importance of careful member selection once again comes into focus. Selecting team members who are culturally curious, and have a growth mindset, and the ability to self-monitor (all CM factors) can be helpful. Providing these carefully selected team members with cultural training to help them develop their CM is imperative.

Team leaders can further designate certain team members with strong CM as cultural mentors or brokers to help facilitate interactions (Jang, 2018). These brokers are people who may be familiar with several of the cultural groups represented by the team members and are skilled at translating and interpreting various practices and behaviors to help members understand one another. Reinforcing the importance of training and knowledge of cultural differences, Barbara Safani, of Career Solvers, recommends taking a contingency view: "Managers of cross-cultural teams may be trying too hard to treat everyone the same rather than uncovering what motivates employees in different cultures...Customize your management style to address cultural differences" (Forbes Coaches Council, 2016).

Figure 10.5 summarizes the factors that can support the success of multicultural teams, which include setting up appropriate team structures that address roles, equalizing power, specifying norms for behavior and those related to tasks and responsibility, as well as more complex issues such as encouraging psychological safety, and addressing conflict and biases. As recommended by extensive research on groups and teams, it is essential that they be formed and used when facing complex problems that could benefit from diverse perspectives. As members are picked, every member should be reminded to avoid groupings that are unrelated to task. For example, it is important to encourage team members to work across cultural groups rather than only in their own cultural bubbles. Even though it may be challenging, multicultural teams must address their language and cultural differences while avoiding stereotypes. Team members must monitor themselves and be vigilant of team dynamics.

Much of the research and practical advice about both motivating employees and leading teams has been developed in the CMC of Western management and leadership. For example, researchers often recommend that trust develops when members are open and vulnerable, communicate openly, and adhere closely to timelines (Peters & Manz, 2008). As you are well aware by now, these actions are not part of all cultures and may be easier or more difficult depending on a person's CMC. Motivation is complex in any setting. Leading teams is challenging even when all team members are from similar backgrounds. People are complex, and teams have a life of their own regardless of culture. However, given the multicultural nature of our organizations and interactions, culture will inevitably complicate and enrich the situation. Fundamental differences regarding what drives people's behavior, whether people are autonomous and independent or strive to be that way, or whether they should and want to rely on the group deeply impact motivation and interaction with others. Managers with a CM must take these cultural differences into consideration and not operate based on the automatic assumptions of their own CMC.

WINDOW TO THE WORLD

Doing Business in Africa

In spite of the size of the African continent (second largest land continent; the United States, China, India, Europe, and Japan all fit within Africa; see Figure 10.6), its large population (17% of the world population), its considerable natural resources and business potential, there is limited research about African management, culture, and leadership available in the West. There is a tendency to talk about Africa as a whole, rather than considering each of the 54

Figure 10.6 Relative Size of the African Continent

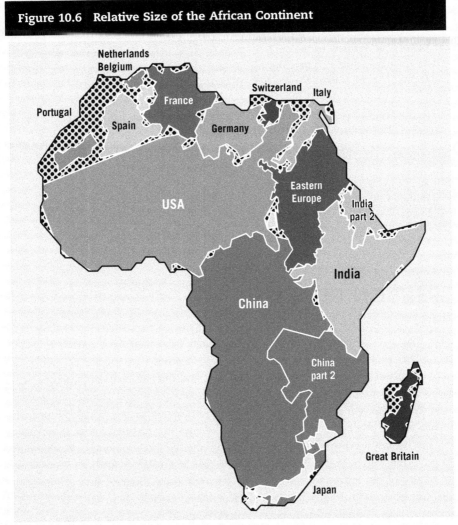

Sources: Fischetti, Mark. "Africa Is Way Bigger Than You Think." Scientific American. June 16, 2015; Desjardins, Jeff. "Mapped: Visualizing the True Size of Africa." Visual Capitalist. February 19, 2020.

countries and many diverse cultures that comprise it. Africa includes highly culturally diverse countries (e.g., Papua New Guinea, Tanzania, and the Republic of Congo), with over 2,000 languages and some of the world's most ancient civilizations (e.g., Egypt, Kingdom of Aksum, and Carthage). It is also the youngest continent with 60% of the population under the age of 25 years. The deep scars left by colonialism continue to define and shape the continent and how it is perceived by Africans themselves and by outsiders. Ethnic and cultural differences, whether rooted in ancient local history or fanned by colonial powers, are deep and meaningful. Therefore, making general statements about a whole continent is difficult and often misleading, requiring careful consideration of local cultures and traditions. However, a few general observations that can be used as a starting point are supported by research:

- Most of Africa, possibly with the exception of areas dominated by Europeans, is high-context and collectivistic

- Community and relationships matter and are essential to interacting successfully with others. As the leadership principle of Ubuntu that we reviewed in Chapter 9 indicates, the individual and collective are closely intertwined, where there is no "I" without "We."

- Partially related to high collectivism is a strong humane orientation where kindness, generosity, and caring for others are highly valued.

Given the lack of information available about Africa, it is essential to conduct careful research about the regions, countries, and cultures that one will be visiting. Correspondingly, getting local cultural mentors is essential to avoiding cultural faux pas that may be caused by lack of knowledge or deep-seated and often subconscious assumptions rooted in colonialism.

FIRST PERSON REVISITED

The Canadian manager in the *First Person* anecdote has lost her motivation and has disengaged from the project to which she has been assigned. The work itself continues to be interesting and she is connecting with her coworkers in spite of the challenges of virtual meetings, but her boss is not providing what she needs to grow and stay engaged. Leadership and the culture of the organization have become major factors in demotivating her, as her needs are not satisfied. Cultural differences in how each person approaches work and what

they expect from their work appears to also be a factor. Her boss is professional, highly task focused, and unemotional; the manager seeks personal connection and contact. As a result, her efforts are not leading to high performance and she does not feel that her performance is getting the desired outcomes. Furthermore, being part of a GVT is further creating challenges of time and distance, although members were able to resolve those through increased interaction and face-to-face meetings.

APPLYING WHAT YOU LEARNED: HOW TO RECOVER FROM A CULTURAL MISTAKE

Even the most culturally aware and skilled people who have a well-developed CM are likely to make a cultural faux pas from time to time. We ask a wrong question, make an inappropriate hand gesture, stand too close, or tap the wrong person on the arm. When we make such mistakes with people we are not likely to see again, there is often little we can do beyond apologizing. However, when you work in multicultural teams where you will have longer-term relationships with other team members, it is essential that you handle your mistakes well and take appropriate steps to recover from them. Here are some things you can do:

1. Don't overreact or even react too quickly—take a deep breath and assess the situation. Is the mistake small and could be treated with some self-deprecating humor? Or is it more serious and could offend the other person? If the mistake has serious consequences, an immediate simple apology should be delivered first.

2. If needed, follow up with more formal actions. Find out how apologies are delivered in the other person's culture. Rely on your team's cultural mentor (if there is one), or do your research, or ask another team member. For example, East Asians apologize often and accept apologies easily considering them as a way of establishing harmony and preventing further damage to a relationship. US-Americans see apologies as an admission of personal responsibility. Make sure your apology is not another cultural faux pas.

3. When reviewing, or ruminating over, the situation, reframe your mistake as a learning opportunity—do not dwell on what you did wrong or obsess over the event. Instead, review what happened and shift quickly to reflect on what you have learned and how you can use the information in the future. This self-reflection is key to developing meta-cognition and learning.

4. Stop ruminating and stop the "closed mindset" voice from kicking in. Distinguish between ruminating and problem-solving. Focus on the latter and on future solutions.

5. Consider discussing the situation with other team members, getting feedback, and maybe using the opportunity for the whole team to learn.

6. Keep you sense of humor! Depending on the situation and the cultural groups with whom you are interacting, you may not want to use humor, but you can always laugh at yourself when reflecting on the event or with your friends and colleagues.

Sources: Boyes (2019), Hahn and Molinsky (2018), and Maddux, Kim, Okumura, and Brett (2012).

CULTURAL MANAGERIAL CHALLENGE: WHO GETS THE PROJECT?

Your department includes 15 members, all of whom have been with you for at least a year. Although the department is generally cohesive and performs well, you are grooming four "stars" for promotion because you believe they are the best performers. You just landed a new account with a lot of potential, a tight deadline, and the need for considerable grooming and development. The success not only will give the person in charge of the project a lot of visibility, but also could affect your career in the company. Everyone in the department is aware of the importance of the project, and several people, including your four "stars," have volunteered to take it on. In particular, one of the members with the most tenure and experience (but not one of the four stars) is pushing to get the project. Given the project's importance, you want it to be handled well and without too much direction from you.

As you are about to delegate the project to your top star, you receive a call from the human resources director telling you that one of the department members filed an informal complaint against you, accusing you of favoritism. The director can't tell you the name yet, but wanted you to be aware of potential problems and that HR would be conducting informal fact-finding interviews.

1. Who will you assign to the project?

2. How do you assess the motivation of each team member?

3. What information do you need about team members' CM to be confident about your choice?

4. What are the implications of your decisions?

SELF-ASSESSMENT 10.1: WHAT MOTIVATES YOU?

This self-assessment helps you identify the factors that motivate you. Review the statements below and select eight items that best represent factors that motivate you at the present time.

1. A positive working relationship with my boss
2. Good pay
3. Autonomy on the job
4. Getting praise for doing my job well
5. Interesting and challenging work
6. Having coworkers I enjoy working with
7. Having clear guidelines regarding performance
8. Clear job description and responsibilities
9. A chance for promotion
10. A nice office
11. Being respected by others
12. Generous benefits (e.g., health care, retirements, etc.) *pay – hygiene*
13. Fair performance evaluation processes
14. Doing important and significant work
15. Generous time off
16. Serving the public and my community
17. Regular work hours
18. Being in the "in-group" and having inside information
19. Opportunity to learn and grow — *clear guidelines for performance*
20. Job security and stable employment *m/h*

List of eight items that motivate you:

1. _____
2. _____
3. _____
4. _____
5. _____

6. _____

7. _____

8. _____

Review your list by using material you have read in this chapter, particularly using Herzberg's Two-Factor Model:

1. Classify the factors you have selected into hygiene and motivation factors (see Figure 10.2).

2. Identify any patterns in the list you have selected.

3. Consider the role your cultural background may play in the items you selected.

4. Consider whether this list was different in the past, going back 1–2 years. What has changed? What has remained the same?

Source: Based on Herzberg's Two-Factor theory.

depended on the job

do you think these motivators have impacted team work?

SELF-ASSESSMENT 10.2: ARE YOU A TEAM LEADER?

Indicate the degree to which you agree with each of the statements using the scale provided here:

1 = Strongly disagree

2 = Somewhat disagree

3 = Neither agree nor disagree

4 = Somewhat agree

5 = Strongly agree

_____ 1. I enjoy helping others get their job done.

_____ 2. Managing others is a full-time job in and of itself.

_____ 3. I am good at negotiating for resources.

_____ 4. People often come to me to help them with interpersonal conflicts.

_____ 5. I tend to be uncomfortable when I am not fully involved in the task that my group is doing.

_____ 6. It is hard for me to provide people with positive feedback.

_____ 7. I understand organizational politics well.

_____ 8. I get nervous when I do not have expertise at a task that my group is performing.

_____ 9. An effective leader needs to have full involvement with all his or her team's activities.

_____ 10. I am skilled at goal setting.

Scoring Key: Reverse score for items 2, 5, 6, 8, and 9 (e.g., 1 = 5, 5 = 1). Add your score on all items. Maximum possible score is 50. The higher the score, the more team leadership skills you have.

Total: _____

Interpretation

Consider your score and take the opportunity to reflect on your areas of strengths and improvement to help you lead teams better.

EXERCISE 10.1: HOW DO YOU DEFINE WORK?

Objective: This exercise develops your knowledge of motivation and its connection to CMC.

Instructions:

Working does not have the same meaning and value in all cultures. When do you consider an activity as working?

Individual Work

Choose 4 of the following items that you consider to be central to defining what work is for you.

Work is when:

1. You do something regularly in a specific place.

2. Someone tells you what to do.

3. The activity is physically strenuous.

4. You do something to contribute to society.

5. You do something that gives you a feeling of belonging to a group.

6. The activity is mentally strenuous.

7. The activity occurs regularly at a certain time (for instance from 8 until 5).

8. Your activity or task adds value.

9. The activity is not pleasant.

10. You get money for doing an activity

11. You have to account or report to someone else.

12. You have to do a certain activity on a regular basis.

13. Others profit by it.

Group Work

Compare your list with others in your group and address the following:

1. What are common elements in your definitions?

2. What role does gender differences play in how people define work?

3. What role do other cultural differences play?

After the discussions, are you able to come up with a common definition of work that can satisfy all the group members?

Sources: Based on information in England and Harpaz (1990) and MOW International Research Team (1981, 1987).

EXERCISE 10.2: DIFFERENCES IN NEEDS

Objective: This exercise develops your knowledge of motivation and its connection to CMC.

Instructions:

Individual Work

Complete Self-Assessment 10.1.

Group Work

In groups of 4–5 members:

1. Take turns to share your list.

2. As a group, review any differences.

3. Assuming that your group is a team working together in an organization, discuss the implications of any differences in your members' selected motivational factors for:

   a. how the team may work together

   b. its leadership

   c. its performance

   d. how you may address the differences in what motivates team members

Presentation

Prepare a 5-minute presentation that summarizes your findings and conclusions.

CASE STUDY: LINCOLN ELECTRIC GOES GLOBAL

The research and first draft of this case were prepared by Tuba Pagda.

The Lincoln Electric Company is a US-based manufacturer of welding and cutting products and supplies founded in 1895 in Cleveland, Ohio. With $3 billion 2018 revenue, Lincoln has 11,000 employees worldwide with 60 manufacturing facilities in 19 countries ("Proxy Statement," 2019). In addition to its continued success in its industry, Lincoln has become famous for its unique and much-debated incentive system that has been the subject of numerous books, articles, news stories, and business cases.

When James Lincoln took over the control of the company in 1929, he strongly believed that ordinary people could achieve extraordinary results if they are appropriately motivated. To that end, he introduced a production and performance-based incentive system that remains largely unchanged to this date. With a normal 45–57-hour work week, the Lincoln workers are primarily paid for the number of the units they produce with no vacation, no paid sick leave, and no seniority-based job security (Solman, 2011). The company reserves one-third of its earning for profit sharing programs based on performance and, during times of economic downturn, it reduces work hours, but does not lay off its workers. Frank Koller who wrote a book about Lincoln Electric says that the company opted for employment security over income security:

> The idea of employment security is that you will always have employment, but that, in tough times, because the company is not doing so well, your income is going to decline, and that, in good time, it will increase again. (Solman, 2011)

This incentive system based on performance, defined as quantity and quality of work, dependability, and cooperation with others requires considerable hard work and flexibility as workers are asked to work different schedules and hours based on production needs. However, for those willing to work hard, it yields steady income and in some cases, even a six-figure salary (Steers, Sanchez-Runde, & Nardon, 2010).

To address increased global demand and counter growing competition in the 1980s and 1990s, Lincoln expanded its operations overseas through a variety of purchases and joint ventures in Japan, Venezuela, Norway, and the United Kingdom among other countries. An interesting example was the case of Germany. In the late 1980s, believing that it was hard to establish any foothold in the important German market, Lincoln purchased Messer, a small manufacturing company, for $70 million and appointed its VP of engineering, John Gonzalez, as the managing director of the

German operations. Similar to other Lincoln executives and board members, Gonzalez was a Lincoln insider, having come up through the ranks and had no significant international experience.

He decided not to relocate to Germany and managed the joint venture from the United States (Hastings, 1999) while German managers were left in place to continue to manage the day-to-day operations. One of the major changes to Messer was the implementation of the highly-prized Lincoln pay-for-performance incentive program (Hastings, 1999). However, inspite of high level of skill and a reputation for quality, the German workers did not accept the incentive system well. The highly-regulated and much shorter 35-hour work week, based on income security, did not match well with the long and flexible work hours based on the "do what it takes for as long as it takes to produce" Lincoln approach (Steers et al., 2010). Workers found the incentive system inhumane and exploitative compared to the German systems that allow for shorter guaranteed hours, benefits, and time for leisure (Steers et al., 2010). The Lincoln system put work, productivity, and flexibility fueled by the opportunity to make money first; Germans preferred the reliability of a stable income. While Lincoln products were selling well all over Europe, Lincoln-style management was not, with Germany being just one example. According to Donald Hastings, many of their European operations were promising high productivity but falling far short of their targets and: "There was absolutely no fire in their bellies to correct the problem of declining sales" (Hastings, 1999).

Years later, looking back on Lincoln's international journey, Donald Hastings, former CEO and Chairman of the Board at the Lincoln Electric Company, observed:

> We had long boasted that our unique culture and incentive system—along with the dedicated, skilled workforce that the company had built over the decades—were the primary sources of Lincoln's competitive advantage. We had assumed that the incentive system and culture could be transferred abroad, and the workforce could be quickly replicated.... The incentive system is transferable to some countries—especially in countries settled by immigrants, where hard work and upward mobility are ingrained parts of the culture. But in many other places, it won't easily take root. It is especially difficult to install it in a factory that has different work practices and traditions. (Hastings, 1999)

Facing an economic downtown that further compounded the challenges in European operations, Lincoln sold the Messer plant and ended several other joint ventures in Europe. However, it also added outside members with international experience to its leadership team, a factor that allowed it to manage non-US operations much more effectively while still relying on the considerable productivity and hard work that its unique company culture and incentive system support. Later forays into international ventures were more successful. For example, Lincoln has successfully implemented the incentive system in Mexico, where in spite of powerful unions and early resistance, the system was implemented gradually, through pilot programs with a few workers who earned considerably more than others (Ahlstrom & Bruton, 2009). Within 2 years, all 175 employees, convinced by their colleagues' success, willingly agreed to adopt the piecework pay-for-performance system (Hastings, 1999).

Questions

1. What elements of various motivation models are used by Lincoln Electric to motivate its workforce?

2. To what extent does the Lincoln incentive systems reflect US-American cultural values?

3. What are the causes and sources of the obstacles Lincoln faced in Germany?

4. Why was implementation more successful in Mexico?

5. Which aspect of CM did Lincoln leadership demonstrate when it first entered the international markets? How did those change and evolve?

Sources

Ahlstrom, D., & Bruton, G. D. (2009). *International management: Strategy and culture in the emerging world.* Mason, OH: South-Western-Cengage.

Hastings, D. F. (1999). Lincoln Electric's harsh lessons from international expansion. *Harvard Business Review*, May–June. Retrieved from https://hbr.org/1999/05/lincoln-electrics-harsh-lessons-from-international-expansion. Accessed on February 5, 2020.

Proxy statement. (2019). *Lincoln Electric.* Retrieved from https://ir.lincolnelectric.com/static-files/b49dcff8-9571-4c05-8469-82545797c622. Accessed on February 3, 2020.

Siegel, J. I., & Larson, B. Z. (2009). Labor market institutions and global strategic adaptation: Evidence from Lincoln Electric. *Management Science*, 55(9), 1527–1546.

Solman, P. (2011). Cleveland manufacturer welds together job security, profit. *PBS News Hour*, July 13. Retrieved from https://www.pbs.org/newshour/show/cleveland-company-welds-job-security-with-profits#transcript. Accessed on February 3, 2020.

Steers, R. M., Sanchez-Runde, C. J., & Nardon, L. (2010). *Management across cultures: Challenges and strategies.* Cambridge, UK: Cambridge University Press.

CHAPTER ELEVEN

MANAGING ORGANIZATIONAL STRATEGIC FORCES AND PROCESSES

FIRST PERSON

How Can I Not Help My Kin?

One of my responsibilities as associate dean of a college in a large state US university was to oversee the student disciplinary process that addressed violations of the honor code and infractions such as plagiarism, cheating, and inappropriate behaviors inside and outside of class. I convened a committee of faculty, students, and staff who heard the cases, interviewed all concerned, and made recommendations regarding how to address the infractions. The university and college both had a standard honor code that all students signed that mentioned cheating, plagiarizing, deceit, fabrication of information, inappropriately collaborating and aiding others, and falsifying academic records. Many of the cases we addressed were relatively routine. Younger students were adjusting to the academic culture and beginning to understand the full meaning of plagiarism; graduate students were learning the boundaries of research; stressed students acted out in class; and so forth. The committee members were often generous and tried to use the situations as learning and teaching opportunities. One particular case made an impression on many of us. A senior Afghani political science and public policy double major was caught collaborating with another younger Afghani student. He had shared his paper with the other student and helped his friend write parts of his paper. They both fully admitted to what was considered inappropriate collaboration under the university honor code. The younger student was very quiet and barely made eye contact with us, leaving his friend to explain and plead their case. The older student who was a senior in excellent standing and was planning to continue his education to get a masters degree in

Learning Objectives

11.1 Explain the critical role of enacting the environment and managing the internal strategic forces that impact organizations.

11.2 Elaborate on organizational structure and its link to national cultures.

11.3 Detail the components and options in organizational structure.

11.4 Appraise the impact of culture on organizational culture and structure.

11.5 Review the role of culture in the process of decision-making and views of ethics.

11.6 Contrast conflict management styles and strategies.

11.7 Elaborate on the challenges and opportunities of cross-cultural negotiations.

Public Administration before returning home to help rebuild his country, had lengthy conversations with me prior to and after the committee meeting. He switched back and forth between English and Dari since he knew that I spoke Farsi. "*Khanoom Doctor*, we know about the Honor Code; we understand what it means and we both signed it. But it's just a piece of paper that sets some bureaucratic rules. My friend is like my brother; our families know each other; we are *ghom-o-khish* (kin). He just came here a couple of years ago. He is having a hard time; he is all alone; I'm all he has and he works hard. But his English is not as good as mine. He needs help. I have recommended he get a tutor, but that has not worked out. He signed up for an appointment at the writing center, but he was late twice and lost his place. He is embarrassed that he has to get help from strangers. He is shy and I can do the same work a tutor does; and I care more and can give him more than 30 minutes, which is all they give him. How can I not reach out? How can I let him fail? What is the harm in helping him? We did not intend to lie or cheat. He is trying and is learning. What kind of person would not help someone who is trying so hard and needs help? How can I not help my kin? You have power; you are the *raiss* (boss); you are in charge; *Khanoom Jan* (dear lady) you understand us; you know why this is important. Just help us out."

–*Afsaneh Nahavandi, PhD*

The *First Person* scenario presents an ethical dilemma partially caused by cultural differences regarding what is considered to be right and wrong, what criteria should be used to make a decision, and the importance of organizational procedures. Should the rules of an organization take precedence over personal needs? Should rules and processes be adjusted to fit the demands of the situation or should they be applied equally to everyone? Are intentions important when evaluating the ethics of an action? The answers to these questions and the resolutions of the case may be simple and evident to some of you, although different people may come up with completely different answers; yet others may find the questions highly complicated without any simple answers. Making decisions in organizations is often a difficult process. Managers rarely have all the information they need, and they seldom see the situation the same way. Organizations set up systems that may either help or hinder those processes. In this chapter, we take a broader organizational perspective and consider how managers create a fit between their organization and its environment by implementing a THINK–KNOW–DO (TKD) roadmap. We look at the factors that provide the context outside and inside the organization, specifically organizational culture and structure, and shape how managers make decisions, resolve conflict, and negotiate agreements. We will consider the environment and the strategic forces that impact behavior in organizations and detail some of the processes managers use in the course of their activities.

1. THE ORGANIZATIONAL ENVIRONMENT AND CONTEXTUAL FACTORS

LO 11.1 Explain the critical role of enacting the environment and managing the internal strategic forces that impact organizations

Organizations are systems made up of people and groups who organize and collaborate together to accomplish their goals. They are impacted by internal strategic elements and external environmental forces and events. It is crucial to recognize that organizations do not function in a vacuum; instead, they dynamically, formally, and informally interact with their environment.

1.1 Organizations as Open Systems

Organizations are *open systems* of interrelated parts that are coherently interconnected and continually interact with one another and with their environment to address the challenges they face (see Figure 11.1). As open systems, organizations take and receive various inputs from their environment either in the form of resources (e.g., human or financial resources, information, technology) or demands (e.g., legal or political mandates, customer and citizen expectations). The inputs pass through the organizational systems and are converted to outputs (e.g., products, services, ideas). The outputs then flow into the environment, where they may affect customers, clients, citizens, other organizations, or society at large. How these various groups respond to the outputs from the organization becomes the feedback the organization uses to determine its future actions.

1.1.1 Characteristics of Open Systems. This cycle is continuous as long as an organization continues to exist. Looking at organizations as open systems means that we recognize that they must be aware of their environment and must interact with it. Because the parts of a system are interconnected, the only way to fully understand an organization is to consider each part *and* the interrelationships among them. Additionally, organizations as systems have the following characteristics:

- Systems are made up of interconnected parts that work together.
- Systems are dynamic and intentional.
- Systems are adaptable in response to internal and external pressures.

While most decisions managers make are focused on one or a few elements of the organizational system, they must be aware that organizations operate as systems and that no decision, action, or behavior occurs in isolation.

Figure 11.1   The Open System Model

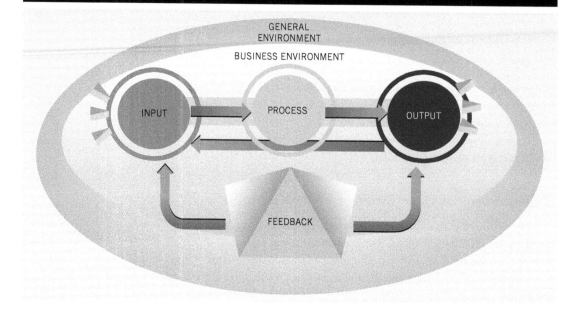

When Apple designed the iPhone, the initial focus was on making calls easier and faster. However, soon Apple realized that video calls, playing music, and thousands of other uses can be fit into this device. This "Aha" moment that led to the creation of our current smartphones came when tens of thousands of other entrepreneurs designed apps that customers were interested in using, leading Apple to take in new input, change its processes, and deliver new products. The smartphone that you use today is a perfect example of how the organization as an open system interacts with the environment and both influences it and is influenced by it.

1.2 The Environment

The *environment* of an organization is defined as all external factors that have the potential to affect the organization. The environment is divided into two separate but related groups of *general* and *business* environment, both of which are impacted by the culture-as-meta-context (CMC).

1.2.1 The General and Business Environment. The general environment is the broad context in which an organization operates and includes cultural, social, historical, political, and other general environmental sectors that present the backdrop for the organization. The business environment includes sectors that more directly impact an organization including the economy, competitors, customers, regulations, technology, and so forth. The delineation between the general and business environment is not hard, and some of the sectors may be part of both. Additionally, not all aspects of the general or business environment affect all organizations to the same extent or at the same time.

One of the key tasks of managers, especially those at higher levels of the organization, is to accurately define or *enact* their firm's environment (Weick, 1988). The enactment process defines the environment of an organization and delineates what the organization needs to focus on and address and what can be ignored or at least put on hold. For example, demographics and social trends are highly relevant for social media companies, but less important for a company that makes packaging for commercial shipping. Both companies may be in the same geographic area but they have different environments. Geopolitical events that affect global fluctuations in oil prices are key to oil companies and transportation firms, but less critical for an art gallery or a nonprofit with a mission to house homeless youth.

The environment is objectively the same for all organizations; however, each firm subjectively enacts its own environment based on its mission and goals. Given the global nature of business and cultural diversity, we have been arguing in this book that CMC is a crucial environmental factor for all organizations.

1.2.2 Environmental Uncertainty. Considerable research going back many years shows that understanding and managing environmental uncertainty is essential to organizational performance (e.g., Burns & Stalker, 1961; Cyert & March, 1963; Mintzberg, 1978; Simon, 1972; Teece & Leih, 2016). Uncertainty is a powerful force that impacts organizations, and it is the result of managers not having enough information to know what decisions would support their organization's performance (Alvarez, Afuah, & Gibson, 2018). Increasingly the environment is described as *VUCA*, an acronym used by the US military that refers to volatility, uncertainty, complexity, and ambiguity.

A manager's assumptions and values related to uncertainty avoidance and tolerance for ambiguity and risk are likely to impact the way they view their environment. What appears highly complex and uncertain, and therefore threatening, to one person may be considered more routine to another. A Singaporean or Swedish manager who are both tolerant of uncertainty would interpret events as less VUCA than Greeks or Russians who are more uncertainty avoidant. Additionally, as we have presented in the cases and examples throughout the book, organizations and managers that fail to fully consider the cultural environment can face dire consequences. For example, famous marketing failures point to products being rejected through feedback from the environment:

- The Chevy Nova, which was highly successful in the United States, did not do well in Spanish-speaking countries, where the name of the car translates into no-go (*no va*).

- The Honda Jazz, marketed as the Honda *Fitta*, had little success in Scandinavia where the name is a vulgar term.

- The Ikea desk called *Fartfull* did not sell well in English-speaking countries.

- The Italian mineral water *Traficante* found poor reception in Spanish-speaking countries where the name translates into drug dealer.

- Umbro, the UK sports apparel company, pulled its sneakers called Zyklon when consumers complained that it was the name of the gas used in Nazi gas chambers.

- Nike received thousands of petitions to withdraw a sneaker it was marketing in the Middle East with design on the sole that resembled the word *Allah* (God) in the Arabic script.

These relatively simple examples related to language and cultural differences are instances of the environment rejecting a product. They show how the environment interacts with an organization and the power it has to affect it. In every case, the firms involved not only had to correct their mistakes, but they also had to change their strategies and processes and address the public relations that impacted their reputation and their ability to do business successfully in those contexts. Change in one part of the system affected the whole system. The open system approach emphasizes the relationship between an organization and its environment and the interaction of the internal organizational elements. By viewing organizations as open systems, managers can avoid the tendency to see problems as independent and isolated events.

1.3 Organizational Strategic Forces

In addition to understanding and enacting the environment, managers must also consider other forces that operate inside the organization. Internally, organizations are impacted by a combination of strategic forces that shape decisions and actions (see Figure 11.2). These include (Malekzadeh, 2019):

- Organizational or corporate culture

- Organizational structure and design

- Organizational processes

- Leadership at all levels

The job of top managers is to juggle these forces to assure that they support and complement one another to address environmental challenges and uncertainty. We

Figure 11.2 Organizational Strategic Forces

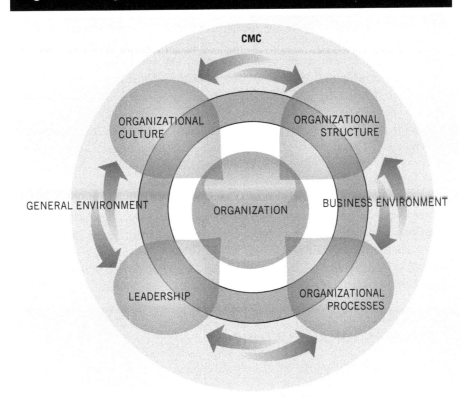

Source: Adapted from Malekzadeh (2019).

have discussed leadership in depth in Chapter 9. In this chapter we consider other strategic forces, focusing on those most closely impacted by culture, and provide information to help managers and leaders understand how to address each of the forces.

1.3.1 Defining the Strategic Forces. *Organizational* (or corporate or company) *culture* is defined as a system of learned assumptions, beliefs, values, and behaviors shared by members of an organization that makes the organization unique and is transmitted to new members, allowing the organization to make sense of its environment and guide its employees' behaviors. This definition mirrors the definition of national and group culture.

Organizational structure refers to how people are organized to get their work done. It includes a number of components that combine to indicate how a firm organizes its human resources. *Organizational processes* refer to various activities that are undertaken to accomplish the tasks. We focus on those most likely to be impacted by culture, including decision-making, conflict management, and negotiations.

1.3.2 Fit Among Strategic Forces. As depicted in Figure 11.2, the strategic forces interact to impact the organization. Ideally, they all fit well together to support organizational performance. For example, in 2004, Shell Oil was facing a major crisis brought on by dwindling oil reserves and compounded by a change in leadership. To address the challenge, the new CEO, Jeroen van der Veer, undertook major changes that included the structure and many processes, resulting in a more effective company (Arnold, 2015). Similarly, when in response to the financial crisis of 2008, EU regulators forced British RBS Group to sell its insurance business, the new separate organization reviewed and changed every aspect of its operation to create a new streamlined stand-alone business (Arnold, 2015). The success in both cases was due to addressing multiple internal systems all at once to fit the environmental changes.

While each force is important, not all are relevant to the same extent all the time. For example, leadership may become more prominent when major leadership changes are in process; or the structure will take center stage when an organization is undergoing strategic redirection that requires restructuring. The rest of this chapter considers each of the strategic forces and the impact of culture in detail.

2. ORGANIZATIONAL CULTURE

LO 11.2 Elaborate on organizational structure and its link to national cultures

The culture of an organization both determines and is manifested in the relationship employees have with their organization, how the organization structures itself, and how it operates. It impacts how business is done and how things operate. For many years, researchers have considered the impact of national culture on organizational culture and practices proposing that companies carry a certain administrative heritage that is influenced by their founders and the cultural traditions of their country of origin and operation (Bartlett & Ghoshal, 1987). GLOBE's findings further established national differences in leadership that shapes organizational culture.

2.1 Organizational Culture Basics

We have discussed national, regional, and group culture; organizational culture is yet another level of culture. The similarities with the definition of culture are clear (see Chapter 1; Table 1.2). The culture of an organization is one of the essential internal forces that shapes and guides both organizational decisions and actions and employee behavior. It acts as the organization's meta-context. While national, regional, and group culture have pervasive and long-lasting impact on individuals, organizational culture tends to be limited to behaviors that take place during work and are more temporary and short-lived as employees and managers move from one organization to another. However, given some length of time, all organizations develop a certain culture that helps them define themselves, and help employees interpret events in their environments, and guide their behaviors.

2.1.1 Components of Organizational Culture. Edgar Schein's well-known model of organizational culture matches the components of national culture and the representation of culture as an iceberg (see Chapter 1; Table 1.3) with surface levels artifacts and behaviors, deeper values, and often hidden basic assumptions (Schein, 2017). Strong, distinct, and recognizable organizational cultures are often celebrated and envied.

For example, at Zappos, the online shoe and apparel retailer, founder Tony Hsieh prides himself on a service-oriented, informal, and friendly culture (Kashyap, 2018). The company cultivates and maintains its culture through careful hiring going as far as offering new hires $2,000 to quit after the first week if they feel that the job is not a good fit for them. Extensive team building with company funds allocated to develop and maintain culture and a focus on skills development and objective performance evaluation to discourage subjective decision-making further help maintain the culture (Patel, 2015). Similarly, ProofHub, a company that offers project-management solutions, has a strong culture based on collaboration across its many departments and employees. The company's founder and CEO states: "We encourage team members to work both hard and smart. Everyone uses ProofHub to manage work, communicate, collaborate. And, it makes way for transparent work culture" (Kashyap, 2018).

The list of strong distinctive organizational cultures includes upstarts such as Warby Parker, tech and social media companies (Google and Twitter), and more traditional firms such as Southwest Airlines or REI. The latter provides its employees with generous benefits and encourages them to give "life to their purpose" by connecting with the core business and encouraging contributions to create a sense of ownership and engagement (Patel, 2015). Other firms such as Meltwater, a Swedish technology company, that emphasizes fun, personal development, and respect, build their culture on helping employees achieve their personal best (Arruda, 2017).

2.2 Purpose and Impact of Organizational Culture

A strong company culture serves a number of purposes:

- It sets the overall context and tone for the organization.

- It clarifies expectations regarding acceptable behaviors.

- It provides guidelines for decision-making.

While employees have legal contracts with their employers that specify job descriptions and outcomes (e.g., salary and benefits), the organizational culture manifests itself in unstated expectations employees have regarding how they will work and how they will be treated.

2.2.1 The Psychological Contract. The informal expectations regarding the exchange between an organization and its employees have been labeled the *psychological contract* (Rousseau, 1989). Whereas the formal employment contract is a legal document that clarifies job responsibilities and remuneration, the psychological contract is informal and includes factors such as relationship with supervisors, the hierarchy within an organization, degree of formality and of autonomy, and what is valued and rewarded. It relates to the culture of the organization and is influenced by people's CMCs, which guide their interpretation of events and their behavior. As we discussed in Chapter 10, culture impacts how people view work and what they value in their work. Culture is also likely to influence how employees view their psychological contract with their organization.

For example, some employees expect a long-term relationship with their employer where there are not only monetary obligations and exchanges but also opportunities for social involvement. Others may see the exchange with their employer as purely transactional with no relational expectations, so that the psychological contract closely follows the legal one. Researchers have found that such expectations are consistent with a country's cultural profile (Ravlin, Liao, Morrell, Au, & Thomas, 2012; Thomas et al., 2010). For example, a culture's power distance and tight-loose values are likely to influence to what extent and how employees can express their disagreement with their supervisor. In high power distance and tight cultures, employees are much less likely to openly disagree with their boss, complain about their actions, or expect to participate in decision-making. In contrast, in looser and more individualistic cultures, partly in response to employee expectations, leaders tend to be more facilitative (Ashkanasy, 2002).

2.2.2 National Differences in Expectations. The informal psychological contracts are both a reflection of and contributors to the culture of an organization. Several large-scale surveys of people around the world indicate that although everyone seeks growth opportunities (Grunewald, 2014), there are regional differences regarding what people expect from their work (Kolowich, 2015). For example, Latin and North Americans, Australians and New Zealanders, Europeans, and Middle Easterners all prize work–life balance more than those in the Asia Pacific region, while organizational culture and having good colleagues is more important for North and Latin Americans than other cultural groups. These expectations are reflected both in organizational practices and social policy. For example, France and several other European countries have set boundaries regarding the extent to which employers can expect their employees to stay connected through email and other means when they are not at work. HubSpot's cofounder states: "Just like attracting customers is much easier with a great product, attracting amazing people is much easier with a great culture" (Kolowich, 2015).

Through assumptions, values, and beliefs, a corporate culture can either support or detract from employee engagement and performance and contribute to overall firm performance. The fit between a firm's environment and its culture, structure, and processes where the various internal elements combine to make the company competitive is essential for success. The examples we presented above all show that fit between strategic elements. In a company like Zappos, Google, or Southwest Airlines, the strong corporate culture supports the goals and strategies of the organization. However, a strong culture can also become an impediment to performance when behaviors, values, and assumptions support unethical or illegal activities.

2.2.3 Toxic Organizational Cultures. Recent examples of toxic corporate culture include Uber, under founder Travis Kalanick, where a corporate culture that was focused on the drive for performance and competition encouraged a combative attitude that pitted employees against one another, and ignored harassment and bullying inside the organization (Isaac, 2017) and reports of sexual assaults and serious accidents during rides (Siddiqui, 2019). While complaints from riders and drivers and accusations of isolation, abuse, and sexual harassment mounted, Kalanick refused to see the cultural problems, instead insisting on better public relations (Newcomer & Stone, 2018). As is often the case, the founder's personality and style are reflected in the culture of the organization. Uber was no exception where Kalanick's reputed ruthlessness and machismo were blamed for the development of a toxic culture. Mark Cuban, one of Uber's major investors, states that Kalanick's strength and weakness is that "… he will run through a wall to accomplish his goals" (Kleinman, 2017).

WeWork provides another example of the impact and potential for toxicity of corporate culture. In 2019, WeWork, once a promising upstart company that leased office space, imploded with its estimated $47 billion market valuation reduced to $7 billion (Chozick, 2019). The firm was built on its founder's, Adam Neumann, charisma and a frenetic culture where work and play melded into each other. Neuman bragged that businesses and people came to WeWork for the energy and culture, encouraged employees and potential investors to drink alcohol and smoke pot at work or around a campfire at fraternity and boys' club-like events in the woods where he lectured about his own version of self-help spirituality, all with the goal of building a unique company culture (Holmes, 2019). Although WeWork experienced exponential growth, at some point being the largest occupier of office space in London, New York, and Washington, the strong, but excessive corporate culture that was promoted by the founder and supported the firm's initial growth eventually contributed to the company's downfall and left many employees feeling abused and harassed (Bort, 2019).

As these dramatic examples show, the strength of the culture of a company can work against the organization when it does not fit with the environment and does not support the mission, goals, and strategies that are necessary for success. The US business press and general management teachings often show a preference for a particular type of organizational culture, one that is informal, open, participative, empowering, and employee-focused with flat hierarchies and relatively equal power throughout the organization. However, it is important to note that the only *good* organizational culture is one that fits with the other strategic forces and with the environment and the predominant national culture. The importance of fit is noticeably demonstrated in mergers and acquisitions, particularly when they involve companies from two different national cultures.

2.3 Organizational Culture Clashes

A strong culture that fits with other strategic forces can support the success of an organization and can also become toxic; it can also become an obstacle when the organization faces changes. Examples of mergers and acquisitions that have failed because of clashes between both national and corporate cultures go back many years with considerable research devoted to the topic (e.g., Chatterjee, Lubatkin, Schweiger, & Weber, 1992; Gelfand, Gordon, Li, Choi, & Prokopowicz, 2018; Graebner, Heimeriks, Nguyen, & Vaara, 2016; Nahavandi & Malekzadeh, 1988).

2.3.1 The Renault–Volvo Case. The 1993 merger between French automaker Renault and Swedish Volvo is a case in point. The planned merger started officially in 1990 when Volvo approached Renault to form a strategic alliance focused on sharing research and development and cooperation on boards. The planned merger ended three years later when a revolt from Volvo's manager and opposition from shareholders and several members of the board led to the resignation of Volvo's CEO and two board members and the withdrawal from the merger (Stevenson, 1993). With a potential $5 billion windfall, the business case for the merger was clear. Both companies were financially healthy and could benefit from the markets and resources that the other offered. Although many technical, financial, and operational obstacles presented themselves making the alliance and the planned merger difficult, cultural and managerial differences were blamed for its eventual failure. The two companies had clearly different cultures and managerial approaches. Volvo's core values were safety and engineering with a decentralized and informal management style. Renault focused on styling and cost management and had a distinctly centralized and formal culture (Bruner & Spekman, 1998).

Both corporate cultures reflected the national cultures of their countries of origin. Swedish managers cited that they were more comfortable working with Germans and Brits than they were with the French and other managers from Southern Europe

(Bruner & Spekman, 1998). There were also concerns at the national level in Sweden, about the loss of a national industrial gem, their beloved Volvo (Zhu, 2014). While the two companies had made many plans to address business differences, they could not address cultural ones.

2.3.2 Tight and Loose Cultures. Other examples include the merger between Daimler Benz and Chrysler in 1998 where technical and business potential was hampered by cultural differences with Benz's formal and hierarchical culture clashing with Chrysler's looser and more entrepreneurial style (Zhu, 2014). The merger of Sprint and Nextel where the former's bureaucratic culture clashed with latter's customer-focused approach is another example (Dumont, 2019).

Michelle Gelfand et al. (2018) have applied the concept of tight and loose cultures (see Chapter 8) to organizations to explain the challenges that many companies face when trying to forge alliances. They suggest that cultural incongruity significantly impacts the performance of organizational alliances (Gelfand, 2018). Amazon's 2017 acquisition of Whole Foods provides an illustration. Prior to the merger, Whole Foods was celebrated for its highly participative team-based and decentralized organizational culture and structure where employees who were known for their initiative and high satisfaction made decisions on the spot to address customer needs (Gelfand et al., 2018). Amazon, on the other hand, is data-driven, highly rule-bound, and top-down. In other words, Whole Foods' company culture is loose, whereas Amazon prides itself on being tight.

2.3.3 Acculturation and Merging Organizational Cultures. As is the case with national cultures and how people acculturate to one another (see Chapter 4 for a discussion of acculturation), the similarity between two cultures is less important than the two organizations agreeing on how they will undertake their relationship and resolve the conflict that arise from their contact (Nahavandi & Malekzadeh, 1988). In other words, the cultures of the two organizations do not need to be similar; instead managers in a merger need to agree on how their two cultures will interact and acculturate. For example, in the case of Amazon and Whole Foods, the fact that they are different does not matter if both agree that each would retain its unique culture (i.e., acculturate through separation), which would mean that the more powerful Amazon would allow Whole Foods to continue to operate as it had before. Alternatively, the two could agree that some changes would be made with Whole Foods adopting some of Amazon's efficient business practices and Amazon implementing some of Whole Foods' participative management techniques (i.e., integration). Various mergers provide evidence of the important role of organizational culture.

While it may appear that some organizational cultures are "better," some may appeal more to some people than others, as is the case with national and group culture, organizational culture-just-is—CJI. Managers can follow the TKD roadmap and fit the external factors and other organizational elements such as structure to support effectiveness of the culture of their organization.

3. ORGANIZATIONAL STRUCTURE

Where the culture of an organization addresses collective assumptions, values, and behaviors, the structure relates to how people are organized to get work done.

3.1 Components of Structure

Various components comprise the structure of an organization and combine to organize people to do their work (see Table 11.1 for components of structure). While each of the components is listed separately, they are related where, for instance, most centralized organizations are also formal and standardized, while being decentralized is

Table 11.1 Components of Organizational Structure	
Centralization	The extent to which decisions are made at the top or throughout other levels of an organization. In centralized organizations, a few people at the top make most of the decisions.
Formalization	The number of written and specific documentation relating to organizational processes. A formal organization clearly describes how employees should perform many of their activities and tasks.
Specialization	The degree to which each individual, team, or department performs narrow and unique tasks. High specialization means that individuals perform specific and limited tasks.
Standardization	The degree to which similar activities are performed in the same way. In standardized organizations, all individuals who perform similar tasks perform them the same way.
Span of control	The number of people who report to each supervisor or manager. A large span of control means that managers have many employees who report to them.
Departmentation	The way organizations are divided into divisions, departments, groups, or teams to perform their task.

often associated with less formality, less specialization, and less standardization. For example, bureaucracies are characterized by formality, centralization, standardization, specialization, and clear departments, and where leadership is based on reference to rules with little room for flexibility (Merz, 2011).

3.1.1 Options in Structures. The structure of an organization is often represented through an organizational chart that depicts departmentation and reporting relationship. There are a wide number of options regarding organizational structures and they are connected to the other strategic forces and to the environment of the organization, so that managers must consider all these factors and how they fit as they design the structure of their organization.

For example, Whole Foods, at least prior to being acquired by Amazon, was a decentralized and informal organization. The company founder and CEO, John Mackey, who was described as an "anarchist" rather than a manager, would roam the stores and interact freely with employees and customers (Fishman, 2004). Employees organized into small teams made many of the decisions including who to hire, what products to display, and how to distribute raises after they conducted their own performance reviews (Fishman, 2004). Contrast that structure with Amazon where employees are tightly controlled with highly standardized work. A recent report for instance indicated that Amazon's tight and demanding schedules caused serious lapses in safety (Ingram & Kent, 2019) with lack of flexibility and formalization contributing to a toxic and abusive work environment (DeMers, 2018; Kantor & Streitfeld, 2015).

In addition to the tight-loose culture concept mentioned above, another way to describe the structural differences between the two organizations is the concept of mechanistic vs. organic. Amazon is more *mechanistic* (or more bureaucratic) and functions based on standardized processes, leadership is based on rules, and employee performance is closely measured and monitored (Kantor & Streitfeld, 2015). Conversely, Whole Foods is more *organic*, where rules are more flexible and less formal with decentralized team leadership. It is clear that size is closely related with structure.

3.1.2 The Impact of Size. The larger an organization, the more likely it is to include more bureaucratic elements (Hickson & Pugh, 1995). Organizational size is therefore one factor that impacts how organizations structure their human resources. Many other factors influence structure leading to a contingency approach regarding structure, where both external environmental factors and internal elements such as size, organizational culture, leadership, as well as corporate strategy and technology all play a role in the structure (Child, 1974). For example, classical research in organization theory suggests that in low complexity environment where change is slow, organizations tend to function well bureaucratically, whereas when complexity and change increase, they lean toward more organic and flexible structures (Burns & Stalker, 1961; Duncan, 1972; Lawrence & Lorsch, 1967).

4. THE IMPACT OF NATIONAL CULTURE ON ORGANIZATIONAL CULTURE AND STRUCTURE

LO 11.4 Appraise the impact of culture on organizational culture and structure

Although there is relatively limited research regarding the impact of national cultural differences on both organizational cultures and structures with most of the studies focusing instead on the size and environmental complexity, some research has considered how cross-cultural differences impact organizations (e.g., Peng, 2002). It is logical to assume that some of the key cultural values such as power distance and uncertainty avoidance, as well as degree of individualism or collectivism that impact how people prefer to work and interact in organizations, would impact the culture and structure of organizations. For example, Israeli firms operate in more organic ways with informality and an egalitarian focus, while Korean companies are highly mechanistic with military-like socialization processes to on-board their employees. A Samsung employee states: "You have to fall in line … If you don't, the peer pressure's unbearable. If you can't follow a specific directive, you can't stay at the firm" (Gelfand, 2018, p. 145).

4.1 Trompenaars's Organizational Types

We reviewed Fons Trompenaars's model for culture in Chapter 8. He and his colleague Charles Hampden-Turner further provide a complex model that integrates national and organizational culture with structure to help managers understand the interrelationship of these elements (Trompenaars & Hampden-Turner, 2012). Implementing a contingency view of organizations, they suggest that there is no one best way to structure and manage organizations (2012). Instead, they propose that cross-cultural organizations can be classified based on two dimensions:

- Whether the organization is *egalitarian* or *hierarchical*

- Whether the organization is oriented toward the *people* or *tasks*

When combined, these dimensions yield four general cross-cultural organizations types: *incubator*, *guided missile*, *family*, and *Eiffel Tower* (Figure 11.3). The four general types combine national and organizational structures and cultures.

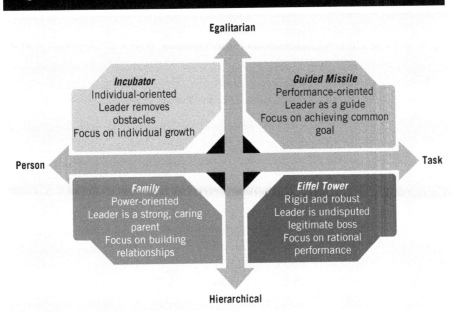

Figure 11.3   Trompenaars's Cross-Cultural Organizational Types

Egalitarian

Incubator
Individual-oriented
Leader removes
obstacles
Focus on individual growth

Guided Missile
Performance-oriented
Leader as a guide
Focus on achieving common
goal

Person

Task

Family
Power-oriented
Leader is a strong, caring
parent
Focus on building
relationships

Eiffel Tower
Rigid and robust
Leader is undisputed
legitimate boss
Focus on rational
performance

Hierarchical

4.1.1 Egalitarian Organizations: Incubators and Guided Missiles. Incubator cultures are egalitarian, decentralized, and focused on taking care of individual needs. Examples of incubator cultures can be found in many start-ups and high-technology firms in the United States and Great Britain (Trompenaars & Hampden-Turner, 2012). In these cultures, professionals are given considerable latitude to do their jobs, and leaders emerge from the group rather than being assigned. Additionally, management is based on competence and expertise with managers being responsible to provide resources, manage conflict, and remove obstacles.

Many Israeli start-up organizations also fall within this type with highly egalitarian cultures and informal rules. Dan Senor and Saul Singer, who have chronicled the growth of these organizations, when describing the Israeli culture, state:

> *in the way university students speak with their professors, employees challenge their bosses, sergeants question their general, and clerks second-guess governmental ministers. To Israelis, however, this isn't* Chutzpah, *it's the normal mode of being and employees who question and challenge their supervisors. (Gelfand, 2018, p. 143)*

The *guided missile* is also an egalitarian culture, but the focus is on task completion rather than individual needs. As a result, the organizational culture is impersonal and, as indicated by its name, entirely directed toward accomplishing the job. Trompenaars uses the US National Aeronautics and Space Administration (NASA) as an example of the guided missile. In NASA and other guided-missile organizations, management is based on expertise, where power tends to be decentralized with little standardization and strong expectations for employee participation. People work in teams of professionals with equal status, and performance is the primary criterion for effectiveness.

4.1.2 Hierarchical Organizations: Families and Eiffel Towers. The *family* and *Eiffel Tower* cultures both are hierarchical with centralized power. Whereas the Eiffel Tower is focused on the task, the family takes care of individuals. As its name indicates, the family organizational type functions like a traditional family with little formalization and standardization, but where the manager is a powerful parental figure, who is responsible for the welfare of all members. Trompenaars suggests that family organizational cultures are found in Greece, Italy, Singapore, South Korea, and Japan. The Eiffel Tower is hierarchical and task focused. Consistent with the name—the Eiffel Tower—many French organizations have such a culture, characterized by a steep, stable, and rigid structures with high specialization and standardization and formal tasks. Additionally, Trompenaars suggests that this type of culture and structure is present in many German organizations where the focus is on performance through order and obedience of legal and legitimate authority and where power is centralized and managers have a high degree of responsibility and are accountable for their employees' work.

Trompenaars's work on cross-cultural organizational types provides a unique integration of national and organizational culture with structure of organizations. Examples of distinct organizational structures in several countries provide another window into the interrelationship of national culture and organizational culture and structure.

4.2 Unique Organizational Forms: The Case of China, Japan, and Korea

As is the case with other management theories, concepts related to organizational structure and culture have been developed in Western countries that have predominant individualistic values. With the growth of Asian economies, several countries in that region of the world which are characterized by collectivistic cultural values provide examples of organizational forms that reflect those values. Not surprisingly, the family type of organization is the primary form of organizations.

4.2.1 Chinese Businesses. The dominant principle of Chinese businesses is reliance on relationships as represented by the concept of *guanxi* which is defined as relationships that operate at the personal, business, and governmental levels by creating mutual obligations (Bian, 2019; Wenderoth, 2018). Extensive research about guanxi and its role in various relationships points to its importance in business success in China (for a review see Luo, Huang, & Wang, 2011). Business relationships in China, both inside companies and between them and the government, are deeply socially embedded so that cultivation and maintenance of relationships is key to achieving goals (Guo & Miller, 2010; Peng & Luo, 2000). Chinese cultural values are further evident in Chinese-owned businesses outside of China. Many of these family-owned businesses operate with the same principles with a high degree of paternalism, hierarchy, and focus on relationships and obligations.

The influence of Confucian ideals of order and interdependence are evident in Chinese companies that operate as families where the leader is granted the power and respect associated with a parental, often father, figure. Organizational activities are aimed at creating a sense of togetherness and bonding among employees. In the current economy, Chinese business have become highly entrepreneurial and risk-taking (Ngai, 2018). Jobs in these organizations are not clearly defined and integrate great flexibility with expectations that employees will do what is needed in order to help the business succeed and maintain group harmony. Employees often work long hours beyond the typical nine-to-five structure common in many Western countries. Face saving, indirect communication, respect of authority, and careful conflict management are crucial and considered essential to success. These organizational characteristics and processes reflect the primary Chinese cultural values of collectivism, power distance, and high context and contribute to an organizational structure and culture that are unique to Chinese organizations. Similar values manifest themselves in Japanese organizations with a high focus on collaboration.

4.2.2 Japanese Keiretsus. The Japanese economy is dominated by large *keiretsus* (translated into a system or grouping) such as Mitsubishi and Mitsui that are family-owned conglomerates made up of webs of various companies, a complex network of business relationships, and mutual shareholding among these companies. The origin of these keiretsus are *zaibatsus* formed during the economic growth of the 19th century and disbanded by the United States after World War II (Pae, 2019). Keiretsus are structured around a financial institution and a trading company all with strong family ties, although increasingly run by professional managers. These groupings have no direct or formal connection with the government, but they work in very close coordination and cooperation with it and with one another to support the long-term economic goals of the country. The structure of the keiretsus and their extensive cross-collaboration is considered to have played a key role in the postwar development of Japan and in helping it become the economic power it is today (Aoki & Lennerfors, 2013).

The keiretsus' most distinctive element is the intense formal and informal collaboration among its members. For example, Toyota closely cooperates with its suppliers and vendors, providing them physical space and educational and training opportunities (Aoki & Lennerfors, 2013). Operating as a family, with leadership held at various levels by powerful father figures, these Japanese conglomerates are personal and hierarchical and reward long-term orientation and relationships and where employees derive their motivation from working with their coworkers and pleasing their superiors with their performance (Trompenaars & Hampden-Turner, 2012). The case of Carlos Ghosn in Chapter 9 demonstrates the staying power of these networks, as Ghosn's attempts to create more efficient relationships were met with considerable resistance. Not surprisingly, the keiretsus reflect the key elements of Japanese culture: institutional collectivism, high-power distance, high-context, and diffuse relationships.

4.2.3 Korean Chaebols. Large industrial conglomerates called *chaebols* (translates into wealth clan) that include such well-known names as Samsung, LG, and Hyundai are family-controlled companies that are the engines of the booming South Korean economy. They started emerging after the Japanese occupation of Korea and are modeled after the Japanese *zaibatsus*. Their dominance of the economy started in the 1960s, driven by what was called guided capitalism with close connections and interdependence with the government, a factor that allowed them to play a key role in the economic boom of the 1980s. In addition to business interests, chaebols are involved in politics, with many of their prominent members holding various elected or appointed offices, a relationship that has raised numerous ethical and legal concerns (Tejada, 2017). For example, the head of the Samsung group, the largest chaebol that controls approximately 18% of the Korean economy, was jailed in 2017 for bribery and corruption and released soon thereafter with a reduced sentence (Pae, 2019). These large conglomerates are a ubiquitous part of South Korean lives and touch every aspect of daily activities through products, services, and infrastructure. As suggested by Bia Lee, a South Korean student: "People think products of a big company have better quality" (Premack, 2017).

Chaebols are built on neo-Confucian values of order and family with highly paternalistic leadership that acts as stern and loving father figures. Decision-making is highly centralized with formalized work and personal relationships, promotions based on tenure and age where loyalty to the organization is highly prized, and reinforcement of traditional gender roles (Yoon, 2018). The structure and culture of these conglomerates fit closely into Trompenaars's family type of organizations and reflect the Korean culture's strong institutional collectivism, high power distance, and ascriptive and diffuse cultural values. As a family, Chaebols impact not only their employees' professional lives but also their personal lives. While their unchecked power has become a problem in recent years, this organizational culture and structure fit well and closely mirror the values of a highly homogenous culture.

The examples of how organizational cultures and structures manifest in these three cultures, although they have many differences (see Froese, 2013), are all high on institutional collectivism, have high power distance, and are high-context, provide an insight into the impact of CMC on organizations. In other countries that share similar values, for example India, these values have been found to be the core of the structure of many firms (Capelli, Singh, Singh, & Useem, 2015). These examples indicate that many of the components of structure that are common and considered desirable in the United States and other Western countries and are often used as the basis for understanding organizational forms are less critical in collectivistic cultures. Instead, organizational relationships are defined by interconnection and collaboration and respect for authority, values that guide the way people are organized to get their work done.

As they enact their environment and attempt to create and maintain and sustain a structure and culture that address environmental challenges and fit the CMC, managers engage in a variety of organizational process we consider next.

5. ORGANIZATIONAL PROCESSES

LO 11.5 Review the role of culture in the process of decision-making and views of ethics

All organizational activities start with managerial decisions. Managers must enact their environment; select, support, or discontinue products and services; set goals and strategies to achieve them; assess external partners for joint ventures, mergers and acquisitions; hire, promote, motivate, and fire employees; adjust or set structures; allocate resources to implement their strategies; and so forth. Throughout, they must address conflicts and negotiate agreements to enhance organizational performance.

5.1 Decision-Making

The many decisions managers make fall into two broad categories:

- Some of the decisions are *programmed*, meaning they are expected, are routine, and have established processes and procedures attached to them. For example, routine hiring and replacement of employees are programmed decisions with set processes and procedures in place for managers to follow.

- Other decisions are *nonprogrammed*, meaning they are unexpected and outside of typical activities with no clear guidelines for managers on how to proceed. Replacing CEOs who have been forced to resign after a scandal or ethical violation is a nonprogrammed decision. In these cases, organizations need to carefully address unknown and unpredictable consequences of the CEOs' transgressions and select new executives with a particular focus on addressing potential problems. While there may be guidelines and help, these decisions are not programmed.

In addition to the nature of the problem, which may be run-of-the-mill or unusual, having knowledge, education, and training can turn what could be an unknown and extraordinary decision into a more routine situation. The more experience and knowledge managers have, the less unprogrammed problems will seem to them.

5.1.1 Decisions in Unfamiliar Cultural Contexts. Making decisions in unfamiliar cultural settings is, by definition, unprogrammed because our own cultural rules and criteria do not apply. Even simple decisions that are routine in a manager's own cultural context, such as hiring employees, can become nonprogrammed and much more complex when the manager does not have the knowledge of the laws, traditions, and values associated with hiring a new employee. In the United States and many other Western countries, the hiring process is highly regimented and formal to avoid bias and provide fairness in the selection process. In many other countries, for example in China, relationships, networks, and contacts take priority over formal rules, turning a routine decision into a nonroutine one for outsiders.

The world's worst industrial disaster occurred in December of 1984 in Bhopal India when a poisonous gas spewed from a US-owned Union Carbide (UC) pesticide plant and exposed over 500,000 people to a highly toxic substance that spread to a large geographic area, causing a death toll estimated to range from the official 8,000 to 15,000, to considerably higher numbers reported by the local population. Hundreds of thousands suffered injuries that continue to affect people in the area even today. UC paid $470 million in 1989 (approximately $900 million in 2019 dollars) to settle the claims stemming from the disaster and was able to deny any further liability. The US courts dismissed additional claims and referred them to Indian courts that eventually sentenced several Indian managers to a few years of prison for negligence in 2010; they were promptly released on bail. Even more than thirty years later, the disaster is still unfolding with thousands continuing to suffer from ongoing pollution and contamination of the poisonous gas that has never been cleaned up (Mandavilli, 2018).

The causes of the disaster, as is the case of any industrial accident, are highly complex ranging from poor training and poor maintenance to human error, and indifferent and callous management in India and the United States. In addition, many layers of cultural challenges have played a role in this disaster (Shrivastava, 1987). Class and economic differences impacted people in the community in 1984 and continue to do so, creating social and cultural conflicts at multiple levels. Those with financial and social means got away and received medical help; those without have suffered dire consequences. The plant workers, who were mostly uneducated and from lower castes, were, by and large, ignored and dismissed. The United States blamed local Indian managers for their poor implementation of safety measures and lack of understanding of the culture of technology and shifted the blame to the Indian government's lack of enforcement (Shrivastava, 1987). Indians blamed the exploitative American company for using its might to dodge responsibility. A few victims received some compensation, as is the local tradition, but their lack of knowledge regarding the company, which they often equated with the United States, and the US court system prevented them from seeking significant redress. The local magistrate, Mohan Tiwari, who handled the case stated: "The tragedy was caused by the synergy of the very worst of American and Indian cultures. An American corporation cynically used a third world country to escape from the increasingly strict safety standards imposed at home," adding that local authorities' callous indifference further exacerbated a terrible tragedy ("Bhopal Tragedy," 2010).

The terrible Bhopal tragedy provides an example of a nonprogrammed decision made even more complex by cross-cultural interactions. Handling an environmental crisis of this magnitude is nothing if not unprogrammed; doing so in a different cultural context exacerbated the challenges. Regardless of the type of decision and the cultural context, the goal of any manager is to make the best decision possible and avoid mistakes by using all the information and resources that are available at the time.

5.1.2 Process of Decision-Making. Whether programmed or nonprogrammed, managers can follow a rational process to help them in decision-making to assure fewer mistakes and better decisions (see Figure 11.4). The rational decision-making steps in Figure 11.4 do not always occur in order, and managers do not always have the ability or opportunity to implement each fully. However, aiming to recognize and define the problem clearly, seeking information and generating alternatives, systematically evaluating them, and selecting possible solutions are appropriate steps for any decision. Ideally, managers would conduct their information search and evaluation objectively and consider every possible aspect of the situation.

5.1.3 Biases in Decision-Making. Considerable research and many personal accounts from managers can attest that decision-making is fraught with biases and mistakes. The perceptual processes with the associated biases and heuristics we discussed in detail in Chapter 3 play a considerable role in our decision-making. What we choose to pay attention to, how we organize, and how we interpret information all connect directly to the process of rational decision-making (see Figure 3.3 in Chapter 3). What one person may consider a problem may not catch the attention of another; individuals organize and retrieve information in different ways; and how each of us makes attributions for the cause of behavior and events depends on a number of factors and determine how we generate and evaluate alternatives and what we decide to do and implement.

Figure 11.4   Steps in Rational Decision-Making

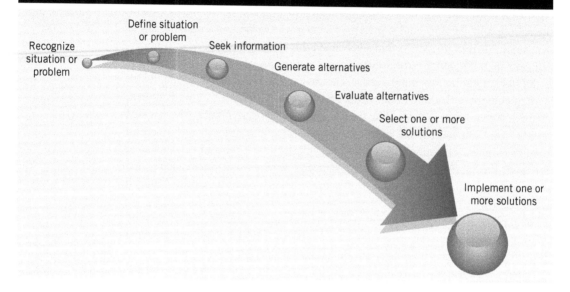

As we discussed in Chapter 3, human beings, regardless of their cultural background, are cognitive misers who are limited in how much information they can process and therefore aim to be as efficient as possible. We use various strategies, or heuristics, to simplify complex situations and achieve these efficiencies. The use of heuristics and biases (see Tables 3.1 and 3.2) are therefore an integral part of the decision-making process. Our System I (see Table 3.3) handles routine and programmed decisions quickly and efficiently. However, when we recognize that decisions are nonprogrammed, we must activate a slower and more deliberate System II that leads us to carefully weigh information before we reach a decision. The desire to avoid biases and mistakes is at the root of imposing the rational, step-by-step, and systematic decision-making process depicted in Figure 11.3.

5.1.4 Role of Culture in Decision-Making. The role of culture in decision-making can be considered in two ways:

- First, people with different cultural values approach decision-making in different ways.

- Second, when we cross cultural barriers and interact with people who have a CMC that is different from ours, we need to slow down our decision-making processes because decisions are likely to be nonprogrammed.

Table 11.2 outlines some of the cultural contingencies that may play a role in each stage of decision-making. It is likely that managers from different cultures recognize and define problems in different ways, seek different types of information, use different methods and sources to generate alternatives, and select final solutions and implement them through different means.

For example, managers from a *being* culture or those that have a submissive view of nature, are less likely to recognize a problem or address it as quickly as those from a *doing* culture, who tend to aim to dominate nature. The delay in production or delivery from suppliers will be addressed more quickly and directly by a German manager as compared to an Emirati or Mexican supervisor. Similarly, persons from emotional cultures will rely on context-rich information, while those from rational cultures will need hard data before they can make a decision.

Who is involved in the generation and evaluation of alternatives and the final decision-making are further affected by cultural norms and values regarding participation, collectivism, and power distance, which all affect whether the manager seeks input from employees or feels comfortable making the decision alone. Orientation to time and degree of uncertainty avoidance further play a role in how quickly a problem is recognized, when alternatives are evaluated, and the timing of the final implementation of a possible solution. What is perceived to be an urgent matter to people from one cultural group may appear to be of little consequence to another, leading to different approaches to decision-making.

Table 11.2 Impact of Culture in Stages of Decision-Making

Stage of Decision-Making	Cultural Contingencies
Recognition	Being-Doing; Relationship to environment
Definition	Uncertainty avoidance; Human nature
Information seeking	Neutral-Affective
Alternative generation	Time orientation; Relationship to environment; Being-Doing; Individualism-Collectivism
Alternative evaluation	Individualism-Collectivism; Time orientation; Communication context
Solution selection	Individualism-Collectivism; Tolerance for ambiguity; Power distance; Performance orientation; Tight-loose
Implementation	Time orientation; Being-Doing; Tight-loose

Many firms in the United States rely on so-called personality measures such as the Myers–Briggs Type Inventory (MBTI) to help their employees understand different decision styles. Notwithstanding the popularity of such tools despite their total lack of validity and reliability (Grant, 2013), they help people in teams and organizations realize that different people approach decision-making in different, but equally valid, ways. In a similar fashion and based on more reliable research and information, cultural values and CMC help us interpret events and guide our behaviors and therefore have considerable impact in how we make decisions. Having knowledge of other cultures and having a CM can make nonprogrammed cross-cultural decisions more accurate.

5.2 Ethics of Decision-Making

One of the basic and essential yardsticks by which we judge decisions is whether they are ethical. *Ethics* are moral standards and principles based on written and unwritten codes that guide a person's behavior. Ethics involve what is fundamentally good for people and societies, not just what is legal, thereby going beyond what is established by law.

5.2.1 Ethics and Culture: Relativism and Universalism. Ethics are inexorably tied to culture as they are connected with assumptions, values, and beliefs that people hold. When managers cross cultural boundaries, the ethical challenges they face become even more complex. Should they abide by their own ethical values and those of their company or follow the rules of their host country? Should they invest in countries that violate their personal and their own culture's ethical and moral codes, for example in the case of unequal treatment of women or LGBTQ individuals, persecution of political dissenters, or violation of environmental health and safety standards? These are complex questions with no easy answers.

Consider the *First Person* vignette in this chapter where the ethical standards and approaches of the US university and those of the Afghan students were at odds. In the US culture and most large organizations, decisions are based on standards that theoretically and ideally apply to all equally (universal value). For the Afghan students, there are different rules when dealing with members of one's clan and when helping friends, than when working with strangers (particular value). With family, a code of ethics is just a "piece of paper" that has little value when compared to relationships. The difference in ethical codes is one perspective for understanding and evaluating the opening case: should the rules be applied equally to everyone in all circumstances or should various contingencies be considered?

In Chapter 4, we discussed the concept of cultural relativism (Brown, 2008; Dall & Boas, 1887) that suggests that although truth exists, it is relative to a cultural context (Booth, 2001). Such a view advocates that cultures should be evaluated and assessed within their own context rather than based on absolute standards. It further suggests that what is ethical and moral depends on the cultural context. In other words, different cultural groups consider different decisions and actions to be either ethical or objectionable and there is no singular truth that can guide behavior.

Relativism in ethics is consistent with cultural pluralism that proposes that all cultures have values and norms that guide people's thinking and behaviors and that one cannot use standards from one culture to evaluate or judge another. Conversely, a universal approach to ethics suggests that some universal principles apply to all people regardless of culture or other contingencies. In other words, certain actions are wrong, unethical, and immoral regardless of the context and circumstances. Universalism is often associated with an ethnocentric view of culture (see Table 4.2 in Chapter 4) whereby standards from one culture are considered superior and applied to other cultures, what some have called ethical imperialism (Donaldson, 2016). On the one hand, applying the universal ethical principles to the Afghan students would mean that their behaviors are unethical and inappropriate and are considered cheating based on the university's honor code. On the other hand, applying relativistic standards would lead to the conclusions that their behaviors are appropriate given their cultural values and their intentions and therefore should not be considered cheating.

5.2.2 Applying Relativism and Universalism. Relativistic and universal approaches to culture each present advantages and challenges. Critics of relativism suggest that ethics is more than what a group or a majority of people agree is right and that certain actions and decisions are fundamentally wrong and immoral. In contrast, opponents of universalism point to the importance of context and the fact that applying universal rules inevitably and necessarily assumes that one group's moral codes are superior and represent the "truth" (Donaldson, 2016). For example, to many Westerners, the Chinese concept of *guanxi* which involves building relationships and creating mutual obligation through various means, including exchange of gifts, is tantamount to bribery and therefore unethical. Furthermore, US laws, through the Foreign Corrupt Act, strictly prohibit directly or indirectly offering anything of value to any foreign official with the intent of influencing their decisions or actions, thereby requiring US businesses to apply the US's ethical principles in other countries, making guanxi problematic when working in China. Application of universal standards of ethics leads many executives to consider various strategies such as building the cost of avoiding bribery into their plans, or staying away from areas where business practices clearly conflict with their ethical and legal mandates (Montero, 2018).

Most countries around the world have anticorruption and antibribery laws and are signatories to international agreements related to anticorruption such as the 2003 UN Convention against corruption (https://www.unodc.org/unodc/en/treaties/CAC/). However, according to a World Bank report, approximately one-third of businesses around the world engage in some form of bribery (Montero, 2018). In recent years, many demonstrations, uprisings, and civil society movements around the world, including the Arab Spring of 2010 and demonstrations in Lebanon, Iraq, and Chile in 2019, were at least partially motivated by anticorruption sentiments. The GLOBE findings further indicate that integrity is a universally desirable leadership characteristic; people from all cultures want their leaders to behave with integrity. These facts point to some common and possibly universal aspirations for ethical behavior. However, aspirational values and what people desire and what is actual practice do not always match. Additionally, people's perception and interpretation of what constitutes ethics, corruption, and fairness differ greatly across cultures. Nonetheless, organizations such as Transparency International provide regular corruption indices that rate most of the countries in the world (Transparency International, 2019). In the latest survey, Denmark, New Zealand, Finland, Singapore, Sweden, and Switzerland are ranked among the least corrupt, while Somalia, Syria, South Sudan, Yemen, and North Korea are ranked as the most corrupt. Table 11.3 presents the rankings for the world's largest countries and top economies.

5.2.3 Approaches to Ethics. In addition to the idea of universalism vs. relativism, researchers and philosophers have developed a number of approaches and perspectives

Table 11.3 Country Rankings on Corruption	
Country	**Ranking Among 180 Countries[a]**
Canada	9
Germany	11
UK	11
Japan	18
US	22
Indonesia	38
India	78
China	87
Brazil	105
Pakistan	117
Russia	138

[a]A lower score indicates less corruption.
Source: CPI Index (2018).

to describe and explain differences in ethical views. Some key views and their implications for organizations are summarized in Table 11.4. Views on ethics range from focus on making decisions based on helping as many people as possible (teleological) to application of moral principles and duty (deontological), to fairness and justice, and respect for individual autonomy.

The perspectives are inevitably tied to CMC; culture impacts ethics. Professor Mary Gentile of the Darden School of Business recounts the reactions of Indian entrepreneurs to her ethics lecture. One executive summarized the groups' reaction:

Madam, we are very happy to have you here and we are happy to listen to what you have to say about ethics and values in the workplace. But this is India, and we are entrepreneurs—we can't even get a driver's license without paying a bribe. (Gentile, 2016)

As a result of facing similar reactions around the world, Gentile recommends taking the cultural context into consideration and acknowledging the validity of different points of views. Business and ethical practices are not culturally neutral as they reflect the values of the cultures where they were created. For example, three out of the four ethics perspectives presented in Table 11.4 are rooted in individualistic values with focus on personal duty, individual rights, and autonomy, all concepts that are less crucial in collectivistic societies.

The teleological-utilitarian perspective is the only perspective that considers the good of the collective over individual welfare. Researchers have given considerable attention to cultural differences in ethics (for example, a 2014 special issue of the *Journal of Business Ethics* was dedicated to ethics and culture) and have consistently demonstrated the impact of culture both at the national and group levels. For example, in collectivistic and higher power distance cultures such as China or Korea, ethical decisions are based on what is good for the collective rather than the individual (e.g., Garcia, Mendez, Ellis, & Gautney, 2014) or based on hierarchical relationships (Moon, Uskul, & Weick, 2017). Relying on GLOBE dimensions, some research suggests that values of performance orientation and assertiveness are associated with a higher tolerance of ethical violations (Parboteeah, Bronson, & Cullen, 2005). Other scholars (e.g., Dalton & Ortegren, 2011; Fredricks, Tilley, & Pauknerova, 2014; Holtbrügge, Baron, & Friedmann, 2015) have found that men are less sensitive to questionable ethical behaviors and corporate ethical lapses. In an extensive study of over 2,700 men and women in over 25 countries Chung-wen Chen and his colleagues found that male managers were more willing to justify business-related unethical behaviors than female managers and that the difference increased in collectivistic and performance-oriented cultures (Chen et al., 2016). These gender differences are generally explained in terms of more communal and relationship-oriented values

Table 11.4 Perspectives on Ethics

Perspective	Description	Organizational Implication
Teleological Utilitarian Beneficence	The view suggests that decisions and actions should be judged and evaluated based on their consequences, not their intentions. Emphasis is on "doing good" above all for as many people as possible. An action is moral and ethical if it creates the greatest good for the largest number of people and inflicts the least harm. Consequently, the rights of the collective (the largest number of people) may supersede those of individuals. The highest benefit must guide decisions regardless of situational constraints. (associated with Aristotle, Thomas Hobbs, John Stuart Mill, Friedrich Nietzsche, and Jean Paul Sartre).	Policies, procedures, and managerial actions that help the largest number of people will be implemented without regard for individual rights. Managers must weigh benefits and losses and make decisions that provide the highest benefit for the most people.
Deontological	The view states that people should be guided and act in accordance to their moral values, duties, and obligations regardless of the consequences, allowing individuals to be highly consistent from one situation to another. The view is agent-centered, focusing on the person's intention and duty to act when required. Acts are judged based on their moral value regardless of their consequences on people or social welfare. (associated with Immanuel Kant; basis for many religious views of ethics).	Organizational policies, procedures, and managerial actions encourage individuals to make decisions based on their own moral principles. Organizations support individual growth and moral development to allow them to make better decisions.
Justice Moral rights	The view focuses on being fair to those involved by providing equal, impartial, and fair treatment to all. It assumes that all people have an equal right to fair treatment without any discrimination based on any criteria. The view emphasizes individual rights.	Organizational policies, procedures, and managerial actions are applied to all employees consistently regardless of who they are and their position in the organization.
Respect for autonomy	The view recommends that decisions must focus on respecting people's right to be autonomous and make their own decisions. Accordingly, individuals are best positioned to decide what is best for them.	Organizations and managers must provide maximum autonomy, flexibility, and empowerment to allow individuals to pursue their aspirations.

WINDOW TO THE WORLD

Doing Business in China

According to a recent book by Yanjie Bian (2019), *guanxi* is how China works. The complex and mutual network of relationships that define *guanxi* is how individuals, organizations, and governments interact to achieve their goals. In the collectivistic, indirect, long-term-oriented, high-power distance, and high-context culture of China, who you know matters more than what you know. The massive population, fast-paced growth, and booming economy characterized by agility and many opportunities of doing business in China present both an irresistible and challenging environment for outsiders. Before considering some specific pointers, remember that in China, relationships—*guanxi*—are everything. They are slow to develop and establish and require attention and maintenance, but once in place are likely to be strong and long-lasting. *Guanxi* creates special relationships and favoritism at the personal, organizational, and governmental levels. Whether you consider that a fair system or not, if you want to succeed in China, take time to get to know your partners and establish solid friendships and networks. Additionally:

- Be aware of political and social structures. Even with the growth of private enterprises, business and government (and politics) are closely interconnected.

- In addition to cultural values that we have discussed throughout this book, be aware of more surface-level manifestations of culture that are substantial and important in Chinese culture. These include such things as significance of colors, calendar dates and numbers, and room arrangements and directions, among others.

- Be mindful on how you handle some precarious topics such as Tibet and the Dalai Lama, Taiwan independence, Uyghur Muslims and human rights, treatment of animals and the Falun Gong, all of which may seem innocuous to outsiders, but can be major triggers in interactions with the Chinese.

- Punctuality, courtesy, formality, and respect for elders and the hierarchy are all very important. Be on time, be polite, and dress conservatively.

- Humility is valued and appreciated; don't brag, exaggerate, or overpromise.

- There are extensive and precise rituals related to gift-giving, which should never appear to be a bribe. Learn about those traditions and follow them.

- Elaborate meals, especially banquets to celebrate high-status people, are common and include many complicated rituals and rules. Learn about them so that you can show your hosts respect and avoid faux pas that may jeopardize your relationships.

- Join Chinese social media (WeChat, QQ, and Weibo), but keep your participation simple and avoid controversial topics.

- Learn as much Mandarin as you can; it is the language of government and business. While many business people speak English, any effort you make to speak Mandarin will be appreciated.

- Find a reliable translator and cultural coach to help you, even if you know the culture and speak the language.

(Continued)

China is an old and complex culture with deep-rooted traditions. Take the time to prepare for your interaction by reading about China's rich history and learning about the details of business etiquette. There are many resources easily available on the Web, and enlisting the help of a cultural coach and translator is highly recommended.

typically held by women. Whether at the national or group level, cultural values play a role in what factors managers consider when making decisions.

Because of the extensive global collaboration and the exponential growth of international business, the challenge of negotiating across cultures has received extensive attention and there is sizeable research-based and practical information available regarding specific conflict management and negotiation styles of people in different cultures. In this section, we review general information about the impact of culture on conflict management and negotiations to allow for more effective managerial practices.

6. MANAGING CONFLICT

LO 11.6 Contrast conflict management styles and strategies

One of the inescapable by-products of cross-cultural interaction and acculturation is conflict. Although conflict occurs in culturally homogeneous groups and organizations, cultural differences in and of themselves can be a source of conflict as people with different CMCs approach problems with different assumptions and use different values and rules to determine how to interact with others and how to make decisions. Many typical cross-national activities that businesses undertake such as cross-national mergers, joint ventures, licensing, and working with suppliers and distributors involve some level of disagreement and conflict and require negotiations to reach mutually beneficial agreements. Managing conflict is challenging for most managers even without the added complexity of cultural differences.

6.1 Definition and Impact of Conflict

Conflict occurs when people disagree over significant issues, thereby creating friction. It is an ongoing rather than a singular occurrence that involves opposing interests, beliefs, or feelings that are acknowledged by the parties and that prevents them from accomplishing their goals. Although conflict can be dysfunctional and destructive if poorly handled, it can also lead to creativity and innovation when managed properly. It is important the managers understand the possible benefits of conflict and make the distinction between conflict and competition, which is a rivalry where there are necessarily winners and losers, a factor that is not automatically part of conflict.

6.1.1 Conflict and Performance. Figure 11.5 presents the relationship between conflict and motivation and performance. Too little conflict can lead to complacency and lack of motivation and energy, while excessive conflict engenders in-fighting, distorted perceptions, and lack of cooperation; both extremes impact performance negatively. The sweet spot is somewhere in the middle where some level of conflict is optimal to stimulate and challenge employees and motivate them to be creative without creating dysfunction. The challenge, however, is that people do not agree on where that sweet spot is and what is the optimal level of conflict.

6.1.2 Conflict and Culture. Cultural values are one of the factors that impact how comfortable people are with conflict and how they manage it. What a German or Swede consider moderate conflict may be intolerably high for a Thai or Japanese

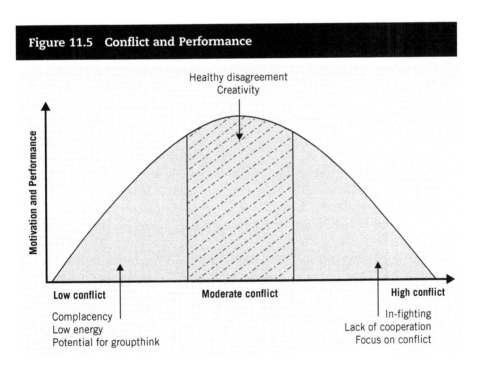

Figure 11.5   Conflict and Performance

who are more indirect and collectivistic. The harmony-focused and cooperative approach of many Latin Americans, Asians, Africans, or Middle Easterners, who are indirect and collective, may be perceived as a waste of time and too compliant to North Americans or Western Europeans with individualistic values and direct communication styles. Additionally, gender differences may also play a role as women, particularly when they are in low-power situations, have been found to be more accommodating and less direct (e.g., Nelson, Bronstein, Shacham, & Ben-Ari, 2015) and less interested in conflict (e.g., Schneider, Holman, Diekman, & McAndrew, 2015).

6.2 Conflict Management Styles and Strategies

Research on individual conflict management styles has established four generic styles of conflict management (see Figure 11.6) that are determined by degree of assertiveness or concern for self and cooperativeness or concern for others (Rahim, 2017). The resulting four styles are applied in a contingency framework where each can be effective depending on the situation.

6.2.1 Selecting a Style of Conflict Management. When parties have equal power and there is time to work out the issues involved in the conflict, collaboration is an appropriate strategy. Conversely, it may be advantageous to avoid a conflict if the issues at hand are either not important or unlikely to be resolved, for example when conflicts are related to beliefs. Forcing a resolution through competition may be the only workable alternative when a decision is needed and the parties cannot agree; and managers may appropriately use accommodation when they are trying to build a relationship, the issue is not important to them, and there is likely to be an ongoing exchange. Compromise may appear to be an ideal approach that allows all parties to achieve some, but not all, of their goals. However, although an acceptable agreement is reached through give and take, the solution reached by compromise is, by definition, less than optimal. Each of these styles of conflict resolution is effective in certain settings, and those who manage conflict effectively are able to use each style in different situations. Specifically, they should consider:

- *How important the issue is to those involved in the conflict and to the organization:* Some issues may matter to individuals but not be important for organizational performance; in other cases, the opposite may be true.

- *The power of the parties involved in the conflict, including your own:* Equal power in terms of title, rank, and status, or any other factors that may impact power, will make cooperation or compromise more appropriate.

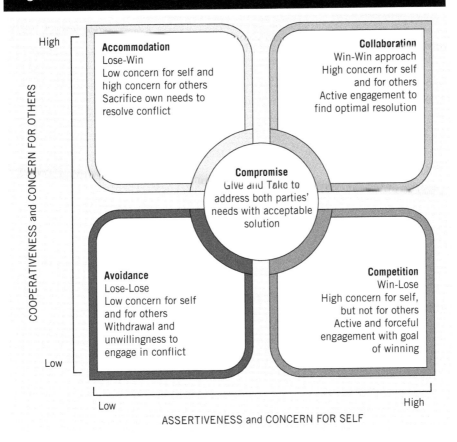

Figure 11.6   Conflict Management Styles

COOPERATIVENESS and CONCERN FOR OTHERS

High

Accommodation
Lose-Win
Low concern for self and
high concern for others
Sacrifice own needs to
resolve conflict

Collaboration
Win-Win approach
High concern for self
and for others
Active engagement to
find optimal resolution

Compromise
Give and Take to
address both parties'
needs with acceptable
solution

Avoidance
Lose-Lose
Low concern for self
and for others
Withdrawal and
unwillingness to
engage in conflict

Competition
Win-Lose
High concern for self,
but not for others
Active and forceful
engagement with goal
of winning

Low

Low   High

ASSERTIVENESS and CONCERN FOR SELF

- *Time availability:* Resolving issues through collaboration and compromise is time consuming, whereas the other styles are more efficient.

- *Need for long-term resolutions:* Long-term interactions call for approaches that satisfy all those involved without creating winners and losers.

6.2.2 Culture and Conflict Management Styles. While the five styles are based on individual differences, the application to cultural values is evident. When working across cultures or in diverse groups, managers must include culture as one of the factors they consider before they select a style. A person's culture may make you more likely to lean toward one style over another.

For example, the French are generally more assertive and direct than Costa Ricans or Iranians. US-Americans are usually competitive as they are often socialized in win-at-all-cost environments through sports and other events since early childhood. In contrast, the necessity and desirability to please parents and elders is drilled into Japanese and Indian children from an early age allowing for more willingness to avoid conflict or accommodate others.

Individualistic and direct cultures are more likely to value more assertive approaches, and collectivistic and indirect cultures are likely to lean toward high cooperativeness. A 2016 study of over 1,500 individuals from ten different cultures conducted by Marjaana Gunkel and her colleagues found that people who are uncertainty avoidant and have long-term orientation tend to prefer compromising, obliging, and integrating styles of conflict management and that those who are collectivistic avoid a dominating style (Gunkel, Schlaegel, & Taras, 2016).

6.3 Managing Conflict

While it might be easy to focus on ways to reduce conflict, it is important for managers to keep in mind that both too little and too much conflict can result in poor performance (see Figure 11.5 and the discussion earlier). Therefore, managers must develop a repertoire of techniques to manage, rather than only reduce conflict.

6.3.1 Reducing and Preventing Conflict. Table 11.5 summarizes approaches to managing conflict that can prevent and reduce as well as increase conflict:

- *Attitudinal approaches* aim to change attitudes, beliefs, and feelings for a more long-term solution.

- *Behavioral approaches* are short term and target immediate behaviors.

As managers consider culture along with the other factors such as time and power, they have many options to keep the conflict in their team, department, or organization at the optimal level that would benefit performance.

6.3.2 How to Increase Conflict. Managers may also face situations where their team or departments are highly cohesive with little conflict or disagreement, a condition that may lead to complacency, lack of creativity, or even dysfunctional processes such as groupthink. In some cases, the cultural makeup of the group may require intentionally increasing conflict to be able to match the members' sense of what constitutes "optimal" conflict. For example, an Emirati manager who prefers less conflict but

Table 11.5   Conflict Management Strategies

		Use When …	Consequences
Attitudinal Strategies	*Team building and organizational development*	• Conflict is complex • Issues are significant • Long-lasting resolution is needed • There is time • Resources are available	• Lasting change • Sources of conflict are addressed • Skill development • In-group cohesion • Costly and time consuming
	Rotating employees to other teams or departments with whom there is conflict	• There is interteam or interdepartment conflict • Issues are significant • There is time • There is organizational flexibility	• Increased empathy for others • Skill development that supports flexible work assignment • Better task cooperation • Lasting impact • Cross-organization cohesion • Costly and time consuming
	Rewarding cooperation through formal and informal means	• Resources are available • Conflict is caused by competition over scarce resources (e.g., promotions or raises)	• Possible long-term impact • Source of conflict is not always addressed • Requires continued access to resources
	Competition with other group inside or outside the organization (e.g., common enemy)	• Competition supports organizational mission and goals	• Increased in-group cohesion • Source of conflict is not addressed • Conflict can reemerge • Hard feelings toward other groups • Us-vs-them attitude

(Continued)

Table 11.5 Conflict Management Strategies (Continued)

		Use When …	Consequences
Behavioral Strategies	*Enforcement of rules*	• Issues are trivial • Immediate resolution is needed	• Quick results • Sources of conflict is not addressed • No long-lasting resolution • Conflict likely to reemerge
	Separation (e.g., moving people to different offices or department)	• Conflicting parties are not interdependent and do not have to work together directly • There is physical space to move people • There are alternative positions available	• Quick results • May increase conflict and resentment • No long-lasting resolution • Sources of conflict are not addressed • Conflict likely to reemerge • Challenging when parties need to work together
	Clear tasks	• Conflict is related to the task rather than interpersonal issues • Tasks can be clarified	• Quick results • Limited to each specific situation

whose employees are Western and Northern Europeans may find that their desire for debate, challenge and lively discussion is not satisfied by seeking harmony in the group. Accordingly, that manager, and others who may be facing similar situations can increase conflict by implementing one of the following strategies:

- *Introduce change:* Assign new, less routine tasks; bring in new members; change processes; change structures and reporting lines; change leadership; bring together people who do not typically work together.

- *Increase task ambiguity:* Assign unknown or new tasks without providing clear guidelines or training to force group members to debate and argue.

- *Create interdependence:* Assign tasks where people need to rely on one another to complete their assignment.

- *Introduce competition:* Set up competition inside the group to stimulate the group members.

The ideal level of conflict is one where employees are stimulated to be creative and innovative without feeling overwhelmed by disagreements and friction that may prevent them from performing their job. Managers with a CM are able to achieve the right level of conflict for their teams and departments by using the TKD roadmap. They gain awareness of their own culture and its CMC and that of others; they acquire knowledge regarding the impact of culture and then implement various organizational processes that address the cultural values of their organization and their employees.

7. NEGOTIATING ACROSS CULTURES

LO 11.7 Elaborate on the challenges and opportunities of cross-cultural negotiations

When working with partners around the world, and in many cases in their own country, managers spend much of their time negotiating with people who have different values, communication styles, and goals. All international business endeavors fall under complex international laws, and laws of two or more countries, and are impacted by the CMC of the parties involved. Negotiation involves communication, conflict resolution, decision-making, and persuasion, all of which vary across cultures. As is the case with conflict, negotiating in any setting is difficult and requires considerable skill and practice. Cross-cultural negotiations are even more intricate, as culture adds a layer of richness and complexity that challenges even highly skilled negotiators. As a result, negotiating across cultures often leads to less desirable outcomes when compared to similar situations within the same culture (Shonk, 2019). Implementation of the TKD roadmap requires managers to know when and how to stop their automatic, well-practiced, and habitually highly effective tactics (System I) and slow down to operate under a much more deliberate System II (see Chapter 3 for a discussion of System I and II). They have to learn when to slow down and what to pay attention to and learn many new negotiating skills and behaviors.

Negotiation is considered a multiphase process that starts with investigation and planning, then presentation of interests and positions. The third phase is bargaining, which is what most people consider the actual negotiation, and the final phase involves closing the process. In most cases, long-term business partners are involved in ongoing negotiations as they reach an agreement on one issue and start the process over another.

7.1 Reasons for Failure in Negotiations

Table 11.6 outlines typical reasons why cross-cultural negotiations fail. Some of the factors are common causes of failure in any negotiation; others are unique to cross-cultural interactions. Lack of preparation is one of the key reasons why negotiators fail. Preparing by gathering data about the topic under negotiation and who the negotiating partners is particularly important when working across cultures. Additionally, while negotiation experts always emphasize the need to build relationships (Fisher & Ury, 2011), in many collectivistic cultures such relationship building is even more critical.

A particularly important issue when negotiating across cultures is being aware of one's own perspective, including one's ego, and understanding how one's CMC engenders a perspective that may not be shared by those with a different CMC. In other words, the rules from your world may not apply to other worlds. What appears simple or of little importance to you may be highly complex and significant for people from another culture. The negotiation style that works in your culture may not be effective in another, and so forth. Finally, when considering the importance of culture, cultural knowledge of prototypes should be a starting point, but not used as the basis to overgeneralize and stereotype.

7.1.1 Interrelated Challenges. The factors summarized in Table 11.6 are often interrelated. For example, when negotiators have little cultural knowledge, they are likely to rely on their own CMC, become overconfident, or use stereotypes instead of acquiring and using more complex information. Lack of preparation about various aspects of the negotiation process as well the culture and approach of the negotiating partners is also a central factor. For example, Asian negotiators are known for using a less direct approach, showing little emotion, relying on long periods of silence, especially when they have the upper hand, insisting on clarifying details and

Table 11.6 Typical Reasons for Failure of Cross-Cultural Negotiations

Lack of preparation	Preparation is one of the most important aspects of any negotiation. It becomes even more important when working across cultures where it should include research about the other party's CMC. Many of the problems in negotiation stem from lack of preparation and can be addressed by more thorough preparation.
Not building relationships	Negotiation is between people. While the task and outcome are important, it is first and foremost an interpersonal process. Taking time to build a relationship is therefore essential in any negotiation and particularly important when working with people from collectivistic cultures.
Overconfidence and ego	Arrogance and overestimating one's abilities can lead to lack of preparation and disregarding the other party's needs or strengths. Overconfidence can further be damaging when working with people from cultures that value more indirect and subtle approaches.
Focus on short-term wins	Winning at all costs and looking for the short term rather than looking beyond the immediate outcome is likely to lead to the lack of development of a relationship. This can be a particular problem when dealing with partners from collectivistic and long-term-oriented cultures.
Using own CMC as the only lens	Interpreting the situation using your own culture is a fundamental problem in cross-cultural negotiations. It can lead to using the wrong framework for understanding the other party and set up inappropriate and unrealistic expectations regarding the process and the outcome of the negotiation.
Reliance on stereotypes	Making broad and overly simplistic assumptions about the other person based on stereotypes rather than research and more in-depth knowledge is bound to lead to mistakes. This is often related to lack of preparation and overconfidence.

Sources: Partially based on information in Fisher and Ury (2011) and Shonk (2019).

maintaining harmony. Conversely, Latin Americans are expressive, argumentative, impulsive and passionate, and often impatient with details. Both cultural groups share in the desire to establish long-term relationships and the essential value of saving face. As opposed to these two groups, US-American negotiators are notoriously direct and impersonal, focused on the outcome rather than relationships, and are often impatient and short-term-oriented.

In addition to national culture, group culture and particularly gender has an impact on negotiations, as we discussed in Chapter 5 in detail. Each group's style reflects their cultural assumptions, values, and beliefs, their CMC, and CJI, and one is not better than the other. Effective negotiators are aware of their own CMC and its role in their style of negotiation and take the time to gain knowledge regarding the other party's culture before they engage in negotiation. In other words, they use the TKD approach. They are aware of the role of CMC, have knowledge of cultural differences, and use appropriate strategies to reach an agreement.

7.2 Approaches to Negotiation

Negotiations experts have identified two general approaches to negotiation:

- *Distributive* negotiations are zero-sum with winners and losers.

- *Integrative* strategies are intended to develop outcomes that satisfy both parties and allow for a win-win outcome.

While there are situations when each approach may be appropriate, the general tendency when approaching negotiation is to create a win-win outcome where both parties are able to walk away having satisfied some of their goals.

7.2.1 Five Negotiating Strategies. The styles of conflict management we discussed in the previous section are mirrored in negotiation strategies where the degree to which the relationship and the outcome are important yields five strategies (see Figure 11.7). When the relationship is important, negotiators should rely on either *trusting collaboration*, which aims at an integrative approach with a win-win outcome, or *open collaboration*, where they may yield to maintain the relationship. If the relationship has low importance, either *active avoidance* or *firm competition* can be used. Additionally, negotiators should consider how important the outcome of the negotiation is to them. Collaboration and competition will both help them achieve the task outcome, while open subordination and avoidance will not.

7.2.2 Selecting a Negotiation Strategy. While most experts would recommend a win-win strategy integrative when negotiating long-term agreements that involve substantial issues, there are circumstances where the other four strategies can be used successfully. For example, active avoidance may be needed to delay negotiations until a more appropriate time; competition may be the best option when a quick win is key without a desire to engage further; subordination may help build a long-term relationship by allowing the other party to prevail; and compromise on some issues may set the stage for future agreements.

Below are some other actions that negotiation experts such as Roger Fisher and William Ury (2011), the authors of the best-selling negotiation book and program *Getting to Yes*, recommend. Keep in mind that their perspective is US-American and that it may not apply to other cultures. For example, in collectivistic

Figure 11.7   Negotiation Strategies

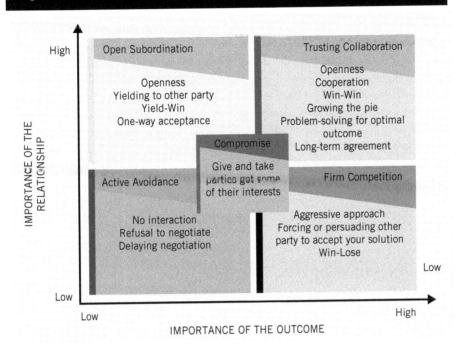

cultures with a diffuse view of relationships, separation of people and issues is neither easy nor desirable. Similarly, insistence on specific objective criteria and standards as the basis for the outcome and keeping emotions in check are less applicable in cultures that are more emotional and less performance-oriented. Nonetheless, their advice provides good preparation for negotiations and has been well tested and highly successful when applied in culturally appropriate contexts such as North America and Europe.

- Separate the people and the problem.

- Focus on interests rather than positions and work on understanding the former.

- Generate many options and delay making the final decision.

- Base the agreement on objective criteria and standards.

- Keep your emotions in check and remain calm and dispassionate.

Organizations operate within environments that are increasingly turbulent where in today's global and interconnected world cultural differences play a key role. While they must balance the strategic forces of leadership, organizational culture, structure, and various processes, effective leaders and managers are those with a Cultural Mindset who are able to include culture in their decision-making and actions. They can rely on a TKD roadmap to develop and enhance their Cultural Mindset. They must become aware of culture and its role in people's thinking and organizational processes; they need to rely on knowledge about cultures to understand, describe, and predict their impact; and develop the skills to manage their organizations while considering the role of culture. Culture and leaders' CMCs impact how they enact their environment and create and maintain organizational cultures and structures that provide the setting for other organizational processes.

FIRST PERSON REVISITED

The Afghani students in the *First Person* anecdote were acting based on their CMC. While aware of the fact that they were in a different context, the rules dictated by their CMC, their "small world" took precedence because they were facing fundamental ethical and moral challenges related to their relationship and responsibility to each other and what they considered humane and appropriate treatment. Furthermore, within their cultural context, rules apply differently to in- and out-group members and to the associate dean, whom they considered an in-group member because of her cultural background, thereby appealing to her to act according to their sets of rules. Whether their behavior is ethical or not and the decision that must be made clearly depend on the CMC. What would work in one CMC does not work in another.

APPLYING WHAT YOU LEARNED: ADDRESSING ETHICAL DILEMMAS

One of the challenges of addressing ethical dilemmas, particularly when working across cultures, is that there are no easy answers. No matter which position you take, you are likely to face questions and disagreements. Should you apply universal principles or take a relativistic view? If you are using universal principles, how do you know that they are universal? Do you consider the consequences of the decision or do what is right regardless? These are not easy questions to answer and there are no simple solutions. Here are some guidelines that may help in most situations:

1. Reflect on your own ethical perspectives and values and be clear on what your principles are and why; and be consistent! (The THINK part of the TKD)

2. Be ready to explain your position without defensiveness:

   a. Are you focusing on consequences? The most good for the highest number of people?

   b. Are you relying on universal standards or at least those you consider universal and that you can comfortably apply?

   c. Are you doing no harm and caring for people to the highest degree possible?

3. Rely on your organization's code of ethics if one is available

4. Invite as many people as you can to the table to contribute information and ideas and keep discussions going to get continued commitment from those around you. Don't fight this alone. (The KNOW part of the TKD)

5. Don't approach the dilemma as an "either-or" decision, but rather take an integrative approach and take an "AND" attitude. (The DO part of the TKD)

6. Finally, do not expect perfection. You are likely to make mistakes. Use them as learning opportunities for yourself and your team and help those who may be affected adversely address the challenges your decision may have created.

MANAGERIAL CHALLENGE: WHOSE CULTURE IS IT ANYWAY?

You have been appointed as the manager of a department that has been highly successful and has been consistently ranked as one of the best for its contributions to the firm's bottom line. As a result of its success, several of the members have been promoted up to other positions and you are joining them along with five new members who are coming in from both inside and outside the company. With these newcomers, almost half of the department is new. You quickly realize that part of the success of the group is due to a very strong and cohesive culture that is highly competitive, aggressive, cutthroat, and in some cases acts as a separate entity. The "old-timers" are direct, very critical, and often arrogant and dismissive. You and the new members are more cooperative, low-key, willing to work with others throughout the company, and therefore find the group's culture abrasive at times. You are aware that the department's success is partly due to its culture and that you are the newcomers, but your morale and motivation and that of the other new members are affected by the culture.

1. How would you approach the situation?

2. Who should define the culture of the department?

3. Should you work on changing the culture?

4. How do you achieve your goal?

SELF-ASSESSMENT 11.1: YOUR CONFLICT MANAGEMENT STYLE

We all have a preferred or dominant style of conflict management.

Assess Your Style

Copies of the Rahim Conflict Management Style Inventory are accessible at the URL listed below. You can select the most appropriate version for you and complete the inventory: http://www.semisrc.org/uploads/9/5/4/7/9547971/rocii_conflict_questionnaire__2_.pdf.

Record Your Scores

Enter each of your scores in the figure below.

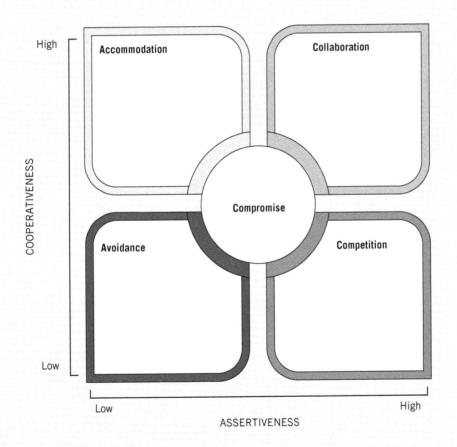

Further Assessment

- Do the scores match with your perception and recollection of how you react to conflict?

- Provide specific situations that represent your two dominant styles:

Example 1:

Example 2:

- Which style is your least dominant? In other words, which style do you use least often, or not at all?

SELF-ASSESSMENT 11.2: YOUR NEGOTIATION STYLE

Indicate your agreement or disagreement with each of the following statements by checking the appropriate box. Please keep in mind that there are no right or wrong answers.

		Disagree	Agree
1.	The only good outcome of the negotiation is when I get what I want.	☐	☐
2.	Negotiation is about finding creative solutions and growing the pie.	☐	☐
3.	I dislike negotiating no matter the setting.	☐	☐
4.	Everybody should leave the negotiating table with something.	☐	☐
5.	I like to let the other person make their offer first to see how I can address what they want.	☐	☐
6.	I share information openly.	☐	☐
7.	No one ever gets all they want; we all have to give up something.	☐	☐
8.	The goal of negotiating is to get what I came in for.	☐	☐
9.	I am likely to take a comment back or try to soften it if I realize that it hurt someone's feelings.	☐	☐
10.	The best option is to aim for the middle ground for both parties.	☐	☐
11.	I focus on what I need; let the other person worry about what they need.	☐	☐
12.	You have to concede some things to get what you want.	☐	☐
13.	I prefer to not negotiate or let someone else do it for me.	☐	☐
14.	There are always creative ways to satisfy all parties; we just have to dig and find them.	☐	☐
15.	I worry a lot about what the other party may think of me.	☐	☐
16.	The real win is when the other person gets less than me.	☐	☐
17.	I am always willing to compromise to reach a solution.	☐	☐

(Continued)

		Disagree	Agree
18.	Everyone's concerns need to be heard and hashed out.	☐	☐
19.	I avoid conflict by keeping my disagreements to myself.	☐	☐
20.	There is no point trying to change people's mind.	☐	☐
21.	I stay firm so that I don't look weak.	☐	☐
22.	I exchange information as much as I can so we can solve the problem together.	☐	☐
23.	I always look for the middle ground.	☐	☐
24.	If the other party's position is really important to them, I am willing to give up my own.	☐	☐
25.	I let the other person get what they want so that they are not upset.	☐	☐
26.	Negotiation is an opportunity to win.	☐	☐
27.	I worry about the other party feeling pressured and getting upset.	☐	☐
28.	I prefer to avoid negotiating altogether.	☐	☐
29.	Conflict is stressful, so I do my best to stay out of it.	☐	☐
30.	The best way is to hear everyone's concerns.	☐	☐

Scoring

For each of the following styles, give yourself a point if you have agreed with the questions listed.

Trusting Collaboration
Questions: 2:_____ 6:_____ 15:_____ 19:_____ 23: _____ 30: _____

Total: _____

Firm Competition
Questions: 1:_____ 8:_____ 11:_____ 16:_____ 21:_____ 26:_____

Total: _____

Open Subordination
Questions: 5:_____ 9:_____ 15:_____ 24:_____ 25:_____ 27:_____

Total: _____

Active Avoidance
Questions: 3:_____ 13:_____ 19:_____ 20:_____ 28:_____ 29:_____

Compromise
Questions: 4:_____ 7:_____ 10:_____ 12:_____ 17:_____ 23:_____

Total: _____

Interpretation

You may have high scores in more than one style, or only in one or two areas. As you consider your scores reflect on the following themes:

1. How effective have you been in negotiations in the past?

2. In which way has your negotiation style contributed to the outcome? Why or why not?

3. Is your preferred style (as indicated by your score) aspirational or is it actually indicative of how you approach negotiations? If not, why?

4. What role does your CMC play in your preferences as indicated in this self-assessment?

5. What can you learn from this self-assessment to use in your next negotiation?

EXERCISE 11.1: ETHICAL DILEMMAS

Objective: This exercise helps develop knowledge and skills regarding the role of culture in ethics.

The following two cases were contributed by Dr. Juan Roche.

Instructions:

Individual Preparation

Read each of the following cases and draft a brief answer to the questions.

Case 1: The Expensive Rolex. A team of representatives from Nabisco was negotiating a deal in Saudi Arabia. After agreeing with Nabisco's local partner on a new manufacturing facility in Saudi Arabia, the Saudi partner presented the head of the Nabisco team with a gold Rolex watch as a thank-you present. In the Middle East, it is customary to exchange presents that are usually in proportion to the value of the business that is conducted, after you have closed a deal or finished a new project. This was a big project, so the expensive watch was not an outrageous gift, by Saudi standards. However, accepting such a gift was against Nabisco company policy and illegal according to US law. Rejecting the gift would be an outright insult to the Saudi partners and would jeopardize future relationships.

1. What are the ethical considerations?

2. If you were the manager receiving the gold Rolex, how would you deal with this issue?

3. Consider the role your CMC plays in your position.

Case 2: The Intermediaries. To do business in Russia, it is necessary to hire intermediaries who act as go-betweens between the foreign firm and the Russian entity. This practice is especially important if you are a small or medium size business that may have less clout than a big multinational corporation. For example, you can't distribute your products unless you go through a third party; you can't buy raw materials unless you hire an outside broker; and you can't obtain government permits unless you hire a mediator. This practice is not only inefficient and adds to the overall cost of doing business. It is also tantamount to bribery, which makes it unethical by some culture's standards, and illegal based on US law. The extra cost of doing business is simply a bribe or toll that you have to unnecessarily pay.

1. What are the ethical considerations?

2. If you are the head of a business that only sells $30 million worth of product a year in Russia, what would you do?

3. Consider the role your CMC plays in your position.

Group Activity

In groups of 3–5 members:

1. Review each group member's reaction to the cases considering the role of culture in each person's position.

2. Develop a group argument for each case. Your group's response should include:

    a. Your decision and its potential cultural roots

    b. A clarification of the principles from the chapter that you are using in your argument

    c. An evaluation of the possible consequences, benefits, and disadvantages of your decision

3. Prepare a 5-minute presentation of your decision to share with the class.

CASE STUDY: THE MACADAMIA NUT SCANDAL IN FIRST-CLASS

On December 5, 2014, a passenger in the first-class cabin of Korean Air (KA) flight 86 from New York City's John F. Kennedy to Incheon, South Korea, started what became known at the *nut rage incident* or *nut-gate scandal*, when she violently expressed her displeasure at the way she was served macadamia nuts while the plane was taxiing to take off (Jeong & Berlinger, 2018). The offending flight attendant, Mr. Kim Do-hee, made the mistake of handing the passenger the nuts in a packet rather than in a porcelain bowl (Kwon, 2019) causing her to call in the crew chief Mr. Park Chang-jin, allegedly making both of them kneel in front of her to apologize, hitting them with a pamphlet, and demanding that they be removed from the plane immediately. The plane was taxied back to the gate to honor her demands, causing a 20-minute delay, while 250 other passengers waited onboard (Sang-Hun, 2014, 2017).

There are some disagreements about the events, but what is described above was confirmed by several other passengers and witnesses (Kwon, 2019). KA issued an apology to all passengers for the delay, and initially justified the macadamia-loving passenger's actions by stating that serving nuts in the package was indeed against KA first-class service standards. The Korean ministry of Land, Infrastructure and Transport initiated an investigation, although Mr. Kim, the flight attendant, who was fired, stated that he was pressured at least a dozen times by several government officials investigating the case, two of whom were former KA employees, to revise his account of the incident (Choi, 2014). Mr. Kim refused and, both he and Mr. Park went public with their side of the incident, gaining support from several passengers who corroborated their version of the event.

The unfortunate incident would have been attributed to yet another drunk entitled passenger abusing the flight crew. However, this passenger happened to be Cho Huan-ah, aka Heather Cho, vice president of KA, and daughter of the airline's CEO and chairman Lee Myung-hee, considered the matriarch of KA (Kwon, 2019). The Cho family owns the Hanjin Group, the chaebol that owns KA. Soon after the nut rage event, records of previous similar ones that had been covered up by KA came to light. Ms. Lee Myung-hee and Heather Cho's sister, Cho Hyun-min, also a KA executive, had been accused of physically abusing their staff on various occasions. A spokesperson for the Hanjin Group admitted that some of the abuse accusations were true and issued apologies (Kwon, 2019). Cho's brother, Won-tae, was also investigated for pushing an elderly woman in 2015 (Taylor, 2014b).

Ms. Heather Cho, who first denied, then downplayed the whole incident, was eventually forced to resign her vice-president position in KA, but retained other executive level positions in the airline's network of companies (Reuters in Seoul, 2015). As she was being formally investigated by the Aviation and Railway Board for interfering with a flight, during some meetings she attended, she finally promised to apologize, claimed she had visited the crew members' house, but not finding them, had left letters of apology. As public furor over this, and many other similar incidents, mounted, the Korean public became highly skeptical that Ms. Cho would ever have to face the consequences of her actions. Ms. Cho was eventually indicted and charged, served several months in prison for a lighter charge, before being acquitted of the more serious charge of altering a flight path, and immediately released (Sang-Hun, 2017).

Mr. Kim, who has accused KA of intimidation (Sang-Hun, 2014), stated that these abuses are so common that KA has a 70-page manual specifically dedicated to how to handle abuse from powerful people. "They tell you at the training: when they hit you, pretend as if it didn't happen and do not act perturbed," Kim added (Kwon, 2019). Mr. Park, the crew chief, who was demoted after he testified against Ms. Cho, filed a lawsuit against KA. Although the court ruled that his demotion was legal, he was awarded $18,000 in compensation for coercion and assault (Jeong & Berlinger, 2018). During the initial investigation, he claims that KA executives were present and participated in the questioning by the government to assure that he did not deviate from their version of events (Sung-Hun, 2014).

Mr. Park, who become a public voice against disrespect and abuse of underlings by powerful people, something common enough to have its own name (*gapjil*), says:

> *Because our livelihood hangs on it, we must keep our mouths shut … Most Korean people have the same experience as me, because our society is divided by wealth, … We are told just to endure and if we get attacked, just keep quiet … My father always told me to be diligent and follow the rules of the country and if I did that, the country would protect me, but I realized there is no system to support regular people like me. (Boroweic, 2018)*

My case illustrates how those who say no to economic power in South Korea come under a systematic attack from their organization (Sang-Hun, 2017).

Gapjil which includes powerful people, such as managers, educators, and politicians demanding complete obedience and physically and verbally punishing those who they perceive are beneath them, often with complete impunity (Lee & May, 2018), is such a common occurrence that there is a *Gapjil 911* hotline that documents and advises the victims. Hotline representatives report that one of their busiest times is following the university entrance exam, when young students desperate for earning tuition are particularly vulnerable to abuse (Boroweic, 2018). Describing the power of Mr. Lee Kun-hee and other South Korean executives, one Samsung insider stated: "The word of the owner is like the word of the emperor, the word of God, and it can't be refuted in any way" (Taylor, 2014b).

Yet, the resolution of the nut rage case provides a small victory for many in South Korea. Ms. Cho's public apology, and her dismissal and being called foolish by her father, although aimed at appeasing the public, also reflects a common Korean value of a sense of burden and deep sorrow, called *han*, which is partially blamed for an epidemic of suicides in the country (Taylor, 2014a).

Questions

1. Discuss the events of the case in relation to the chaebol structure in South Korea.

2. How is conflict handled in this case?

3. What role does culture play in the events presented in this case?

4. How does your culture influence your interpretation of the case?

Sources

Boroweic, S. (2018). McDonald's "gapjil" indcident illustrates bullying culture. *Asia Times*, November 24. Retrieved from https://asiatimes.com/2018/11/mcdonalds-gapjil-incident-illustrates-bullying-culture/. Accessed on May 5, 2020.

Choi, J. S. (2014). Transport ministry must submit to independent probe. *The Chonunilbo (English edition)*, December 23. Retrieved from http://english.chosun.com/site/data/html_dir/2014/12/23/2014122301831.html. Accessed on May 7, 2020.

Jeong, S., & Berlinger, J. (2018). Korean Air "nut rage" scandal: Flight attendant awarded $18,000 settlement. *CNN*, December 20. Retrieved from https://www.cnn.com/2018/12/19/asia/korea-air-nut-rage-settlement-intl/index.html. Accessed on May 5, 2020.

Kwon, J. (2019). Culture of abuse and violence at the heart of some of South Korea's biggest companies. *CNN World*, February 21. Retrieved from https://www.cnn.com/2019/02/21/asia/south-korea-nut-rage-abuse-intl/index.html. Accessed on May 5, 2020.

Lee, S. H., & May, T. (2018). Go home, South Korea tell workers, as stress takes its toll. *The New York Times*, July 28. Retrieved from https://www.nytimes.com/2018/07/28/world/asia/south-korea-overwork-workweek.html. Accessed on May 5, 2020.

Reuters in Seoul. (2015). Korean Air chairman's daughter denies conspiring in nut-rage coverup. Retrieved from https://www.theguardian.com/world/2015/jan/19/korean-air-chairman-daughter-heather-cho-denies-conspiring-nut-rage-coverup. Accessed on May 7, 2020.

Sang-Hsu, C. (2018). Sister of Korean "nut rage" heiress accused of throwing her own tantrum. *The New York Times*, April 13, 2018. Retrieved from https://www.nytimes.com/2018/04/13/world/asia/nut-rage-sister-korean-air.html. Accessed on August 4, 2020.

Sang-Hun, C. (2014). Flight attendant kicked off Korean Air flight alleges cover-up. *The New York Times*, December 18. Retrieved from https://www.nytimes.com/2014/12/19/world/asia/steward-kicked-off-korean-air-flight-accuses-airline-and-south-korea-of-attempting-cover-up.html?_r=0. Accessed on May 7, 2020.

Sang-Hun, C. (2017). "Nut rage" whistle-blower says Korean Air retaliated against him. *The New York Times*, November 20. Retrieved from https://www.nytimes.com/2017/11/20/world/asia/south-korea-korean-air-whistle-blower-nuts-daughter.html. Accessed on May 7, 2020.

Taylor, A. (2014a). South Korea's ferry tragedy touches on the country's suicide epidemic. *The Washington Post*, April 18. Retrieved from https://www.washingtonpost.com/news/worldviews/wp/2014/04/18/south-koreas-ferry-tragedy-touches-on-countrys-suicide-epidemic/?arc404=true. Accessed on May 7, 2020.

Taylor, A. (2014b). Why 'nut-rage' is such a big deal in South Korea. *The Washington Post*, December 12. Retrieved from https://www.washingtonpost.com/news/worldviews/wp/2014/12/12/why-nut-gate-is-such-a-big-deal-in-south-korea/?arc404=true. Accessed on May 7, 2020.

CHAPTER TWELVE

CROSSING THE THRESHOLD: DEVELOPING A CULTURAL MINDSET

We live in a complex and multicultural world where people are increasingly interconnected. We may have more opportunities to travel around the world and interact and work with people from different cultures than our parents and ancestors did, and we may know more about people and events around the globe. However, these opportunities to interact with others have not changed a key fact. People in different parts of the world still have unique cultures that provide them with a sense of identity, values, and beliefs and validation regarding their approach to solving their everyday and existential challenges. Our cultures are the meta-contexts (CMC) that guide our thinking and behavior and provide the filter and framework through which we interpret and understand the world. There is considerable diversity in cultures, and they shape every aspect of our personal and professional lives. Culture matters and it cannot be ignored.

This book has aimed at developing your Cultural Mindset (CM) by:

- Increasing your self-awareness of your cultural identities and their impact on your worldview

- Expanding your knowledge regarding culture and providing you with a vocabulary to be able to understand, describe, and predict cultural differences

- Growing your managerial toolbox and developing the skills that are essential in managing diverse people and global organizations.

In this last chapter, we provide a review of the key themes of the book and the factors that make up a CM, and present a summary of how you can develop and expand your CM by applying the THINK–KNOW–DO (TKD) roadmap.

Learning Objectives

12.1 Review the critical themes of cross-cultural management.

12.2 Explain the Cultural Mindset (CM) and its ten factors.

12.3 Detail specific actions to implementing the THINK–KNOW–DO (TKD) roadmap to a CM.

12.4 Present concluding thoughts to the topic of cross-cultural management.

1. CRITICAL THEMES

We started this book with the paradox that states that what works well in one context or culture does not necessarily work in another. In other words, the rules of one small world do not apply to all worlds. This paradox has been the guiding theme of the book. You cannot assume that what works for you, feels right to you, and is your ideal will also apply to other people. In addition to individual differences that make each of us unique, we have cultural assumptions, values, and beliefs that provide us with unique and equally valid perspectives and frames of reference. To be effective in a culturally diverse and global world, managers must understand and be able to describe cultural differences and predict how they will impact people and organizations.

1.1 The Importance and Impact of Culture

Given that we no longer have the choice or option not to interact with other worlds, the culture paradox takes on particular importance. We live in a multicultural world where there are over 10,000 cultures. Additionally, people belong to countless group-level cultures such as gender, ethnicities, generational groups, and sexual orientation. Even if you stay in your own neighborhood, city, or country, you will encounter people who are different from you on one or more cultural dimensions.

We have defined culture as:

A complex system of long-lasting and dynamic learned assumptions, beliefs, values, and behaviors shared by members of a group that makes the group unique and that is transmitted from one person to another, allows the group to interpret and make sense of the world, and guides its members' behaviors.

This definition applies to culture at all levels: national, regional, group, and even at the organizational level. Remember that although deeply engrained, culture is learned and has no biological or genetic roots. As you think about the complexity, staying power, and dynamism of culture, you must also keep in mind that the visible parts of culture are only the tip of the iceberg.

Having read this book, you now know that many visible manifestations of culture have deeper hidden roots in beliefs, values, and assumptions that may not be conscious and accessible. For the same reason, while we can learn a lot about other cultures, unless you are a member of a cultural group, or become deeply and significantly immersed in a culture, you never can fully understand a culture other than your own. Nonetheless, culture as a significant software that provides us with frameworks for understanding ourselves, others, and the world around us deserves attention.

1.2 Culture-as-Meta-Context

A critical theme of this book is that culture creates a meta-context (CMC) that provides you with a worldview, lens, or perspective through which you see the world. Accordingly, one of the goals is to increase your awareness regarding the role and importance of culture in shaping your and other people's thinking and behavior. Specifically:

- *We all have culture.* Culture is not something that others have; we all are part of one or more cultural groups and culture impacts everyone.

- *Culture is ever-present.* Because it is engrained and deep-rooted and affects our thinking and behavior, it is always in the background and has the potential to play a key role in any situation. Therefore, today's managers must keep culture in the back of their mind as they interact with people and make decisions for their team, department, and organizations.

- *Culture is one of many critical factors.* Culture is not the only or always the most important element that managers must consider to be effective. There are clearly many other factors they must keep in mind and implement in their organizations. Managers must understand when and how culture is significant.

1.3 Culture-Just-Is

Another theme of the book is the culture-just-is (CJI) concept. CJI refers to the fact that all cultures develop and exist to allow people to address the environmental challenges they face. Although some cultures may have been more successful at addressing challenges in some cases, cultures are neither inherently good or bad, strong or weak, worthy or unworthy. They simply are CJI.

CJI is one of the most challenging ideas for many people and one that is often resisted. Our tendency to evaluate cultures, and to consider some, often our own, either superior or to be the "norm," is deeply engrained and hard to change. Even people who are multicultural and have a pluralistic view of culture have some trouble with fully accepting that all cultures are equally valid as a way for people to address their environmental challenges. There are always one or two examples about something in another culture they find distasteful, offensive, or intolerable. Too much or too little gender equality, a justice system that is too harsh or too lenient, too much or too little care for animals or the environment, too much or too little directness and ability to address issues….The list is long and often predictable.

It is inevitable that we will come across some assumptions, values, beliefs, or practices of other cultures that are so contrary to our own that we cannot accept them. However,

- CJI means acknowledging that people have developed different assumptions, values, beliefs, and practices to address the environmental challenges that they have faced; their culture reflects that simple fact.

- CJI does not mean that you like or accept all values from all cultures.

- CJI means that what others do may not be the way you do things, but it is valid and effective for them, as yours is for you.

- CJI means that you can accept that what others do works for them and still not consider it acceptable for you.

- CJI means that you can be proud of your own culture and also respect others.

Being able to accept other cultures just for what they are and try to understand and describe rather than evaluate them is a critical part of having a CM.

1.4 It's in Your Mind: The Cognitive Approach

Before we learn to behave appropriately in different cultural settings, we have to learn to think differently. The focus on how we think and the cognitive approach to culture is another theme of the book. By focusing on the CM, we emphasize that how we think is the source of behavior. Our mindset predisposes us to see the world in a certain way; it provides us with a frame of reference and filters what we see and how we interpret information. By developing a CM, you have a new way of thinking where culture is fully considered. We have taken particular care to examine the cognitive processes that we use to perceive and interpret the world. Being aware of the heuristics we use, the biases that subconsciously influence our perceptions and decisions, and the automatic and deliberate Systems I and II that we employ to make decisions is essential to gaining awareness of how your culture impacts your thinking.

A new way of thinking is not an easy process. However, it is considerably more achievable than trying to learn how to behave in over 10,000 cultures. Changing your mindset and developing a CM, where you take culture, your own and that of others, into consideration is possible with motivation, practice, and reflection. Educators have for many years known the importance of meta-cognition. Thinking about what you are learning and how you are thinking solidifies and enhances learning.

1.5 A Word of Caution: The Dangers of Overgeneralizing

Along with the importance of culture, another critical theme is to be aware of the dangers of oversimplifying and overgeneralizing information about culture. While cultural frameworks and models provide valuable information to understand, describe, and predict cultural differences, managers must be aware of their limits. People cannot simply be reduced to a few characteristics of the cultural groups to which they belong; they are much more complex than that. People's cultural identity, or identities, is just one part of who they are. Some fit the cultural prototypes well; others do not.

The frameworks and vocabulary you have acquired are excellent starting points to understand cultural prototypes. They are tools for preparation when interacting with people from different cultures. They do not replace the information that can be gathered from face-to-face sustained interaction or immersion into other cultures, whenever possible.

2. THE CULTURAL MINDSET

LO 12.2 Explain the Cultural Mindset (CM) and its ten factors

It is inescapable then, that people from other cultures coexist with us; their culture, just like our own, CJI, and it influences them as much as ours influences us. Therefore, in order to manage effectively in this multicultural world, we must actively consider culture as a factor when assessing ourselves and other people and situations, and when making decisions and acting on them. We have defined CM as

> ...a way of thinking and a frame of mind or reference that considers culture as a factor when assessing yourself and other people and situations, and when making decisions and acting on them. Having a CM means that you are aware of your own cultural backgrounds and the fact that culture-just-is and that it provides a meta-context.

We must have a CM, so that

- We are aware of the "small" world rules that consciously and subconsciously govern our thinking and behavior;

- We actively choose to acquire knowledge about other worlds; and

- We choose to learn to interact and work effectively across many worlds.

2.1 The Ten Cultural Mindset Factors

As detailed in Chapter 2, the CM includes ten factors that you must address (see Figure 12.1):

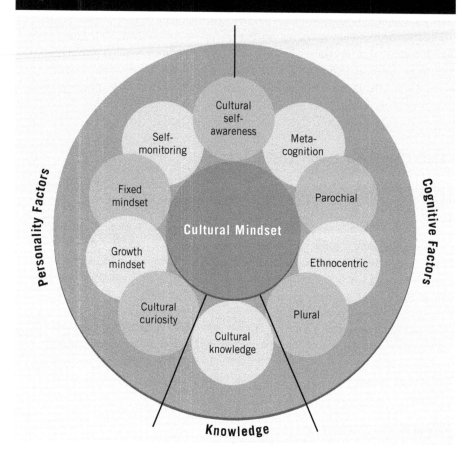

Figure 12.1 Ten CM Factors

- *Cognition:* Self-awareness, three views of culture (parochial, ethnocentric, pluralistic), and meta-cognition

- *Knowledge:* cultural knowledge

- *Behaviors:* Fixed and growth mindsets, cultural curiosity, and self-monitoring

The various chapters in the book have provided you with in-depth information about each of the factors. CM is not something you are born with; it is something you can learn. Although some of the factors that make up a CM are personality-based (e.g., self-monitoring and fixed-growth mindset; see Figure 12.3), many others such as cultural knowledge, views of culture, meta-cognition, and self-awareness are not. It is therefore possible to learn and grow, even in the case of personality factors.

We next detail steps to develop or expand your CM.

3. HOW TO GET THERE: IMPLEMENTING THE TKD ROADMAP

The basic roadmap to developing a CM is the TDK model. The chapters of the book have followed this roadmap by addressing cognition, knowledge, and behaviors (see Figure 12.2). The TKD roadmap allows you to develop, grow, and engage your CM and cross the threshold to become conscious and mindful regarding culture, and become effective when crossing cultural thresholds.

Engaging in the cultural discovery journey can be overwhelming; there is so much to learn and so many opportunities for mistakes. Many other approaches that help you become more effective in cross-cultural interactions and managing

Figure 12.2 The Roadmap to CM: Think–Know–Do

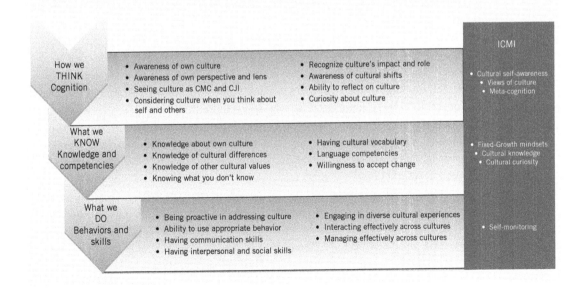

people across cultures focus on providing you knowledge of other cultures or teaching you specific behaviors that work in specific cultures. They focus on informative learning aimed at changing *what* you know—a worthy and necessary endeavor. However, through the TKD roadmap to developing your CM, we address *how* you know, a process called transformative learning, as well as *what* you need to learn.

3.1 Choosing Your Attitude: Deciding to Learn and Grow

Having a CM, being aware of culture, and its impact on us and others is something we can learn. Just as culture is not a biological, but rather a socially learned factor that impacts every aspect of our lives, having a CM is also not a personality trait or part of our biology. As managers in a global and diverse world, we must choose to consider culture and engage in learning that will allow us to do so effectively and efficiently. However, just because it can be learned, it does not mean that it is easy and accessible.

Learning is the process of acquiring new knowledge or behavior, or modifying what we know or do. It involves a relatively permanent change to that knowledge or behavior. Figure 12.3 illustrates the factors that influence learning: motivation, readiness, and ability. For our purposes, ability is the least relevant since developing a CM does not require any particular ability. Motivation and readiness are individual choices. If you have made the decision that you would like to be more effective working across cultures and would like to develop your CM, then you are motivated and ready to learn.

Learning anything requires perseverance, practice, and repetition. You cannot change a habit or behavior, acquire new skills and competencies, or develop new practices without experimentation, repetition, and failure. For learning to be truly impactful, you have to know how to learn and reflect on your own process of learning and growing. You can then learn the *what* and acquire the information that you need. The shift that occurs when you develop your CM and become aware of the role and importance of culture in your own and others' thinking and behavior is transformational; once you cross that threshold, you cannot unlearn CM; you cannot not see the impact of culture any longer.

Finally, learning further involves acquiring a new vocabulary that helps you understand and explain events and people in new and more accurate ways. In choosing to develop a CM, we must then choose to engage in learning about culture, its various dimensions, and its impact. As managers, learning truly occurs when we are able to apply what we have learned to help our teams and organizations.

Remember that understanding how we think and what impacts our thinking are essential to developing a CM.

Figure 12.3 Factors That Influence Learning

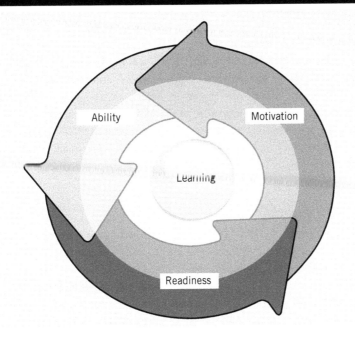

3.2 Self-Awareness of Our Own Culture

Awareness of your own culture is essential in understanding your own perspective and CMC and how they may impact your thinking and behavior. You have completed several self-assessments and exercises that have guided you in self-examining your cultural identity and its corresponding assumptions, values, and beliefs. You have also acquired a vocabulary to describe your own culture. These activities serve two purposes. First, they help deepen your cultural self-awareness, and second, and equally important, they provide you with opportunities to practice and become more proficient at meta-cognition, which involves thinking about your own thinking. The cultural self-awareness and meta-cognition are fundamental starting points to developing a CM.

3.3 Understanding Cognitive Processes and Biases

You should be able to integrate material in Chapter 3 to understand how the perception process, the heuristics and biases you rely on, whether they are based on your cultural background or other factors, and your System I and System II thinking provide the filters through which you see, understand, and interpret the world. The goal is for you to be aware when your automatic System I, which is both effective and efficient in your own culture, is operating, and then be able to activate a more deliberate System II when crossing cultures.

Without being aware of your own culture, you will not be able to know the filters that operate. Therefore, the cultural self-awareness and self-examination and perceptual processes are closely tied together. Your culture, as your software, will automatically kick in, unless you are aware of it and are able to suspend it to be more deliberate in assessing situations, something that is essential to effective cross-cultural interactions. You need to be able to know the rules of your small world to assess whether they can be applied to other worlds and avoid unconscious bias.

3.4 Your Views of Culture

Another factor in the THINK part of the roadmap is views of culture. Beliefs and feelings about your in-group and those who are in your out-groups and your view of your culture in relation to others have a strong impact on the potential success of your cross-cultural interactions. Feelings of pride and belonging regarding our own culture are both essential and desirable. However, strong beliefs regarding the superiority of one's own culture provide a lens that will make effective and harmonious interactions with those from other cultures challenging. The plural view of culture, where we value both our own and other cultures, is the basis for managing well in a global environment.

Finally, through the ICMI, discussions in various chapters, and end of chapter material, you have gained or increased your awareness regarding some of the personality characteristics that may support or hinder your cultural journey. Having cultural curiosity and a growth mindset and being a high self-monitor (all ICMI factors) will facilitate the development of a CM. Conversely, if you have low cultural curiosity and a fixed mindset that lead to avoiding experimentation and possible failure and are low on self-monitoring, which means that you either do not read environmental cues or do not use them to adjust your behavior, you are likely to face some difficulty in your CM journey. However, personality characteristics do not dictate behavior; rather, they create zones of comfort. Learning and growth occur when we push the boundaries of those zones. With motivation to learn and practice, change, and growth are achievable.

3.5 Cultural Knowledge: Frameworks and a New Vocabulary

There is no question that knowledge about other cultures is essential. You may already have acquired information about other cultures through your personal and professional experiences. You may have friends from many different cultures; may have traveled as a tourist; or may have lived and worked in other countries and cultures. You may also have curiosity about other cultures, which has led you to read diverse literature, listen to music from around the world, eat new foods, and so forth. Some of the knowledge you have may be at the surface level, while other knowledge may go deeper.

Everything you have read in this book has increased your knowledge of culture, its impact, and how to manage better across cultures. For example, knowledge of acculturation processes and strategies discussed in Chapter 3 can help manage inevitable conflict and stress that expats experience. However, the chapters in Parts III and IV have more specifically helped you acquire an extensive vocabulary to understand, describe, explain, and predict cultural differences based on reliable research that can be applied to all cultures. Specifically, you can rely on the information about diversity, gender, and any of the cultural values and dimensions to talk about culture in a more intelligent and thoughtful manner.

Effectively addressing the needs of a diverse workforce and being able to motivate and lead people from different cultural groups is an essential part of any manager's job. Understanding the challenges, opportunities, and benefits associated with cultural diversity and their sources, causes, and consequences not only contributes to managerial and organizational effectiveness but also fulfills broader imperatives related to social justice and corporate social responsibility. Being able to create an engaging and inclusive workforce is no longer a debatable issue. The demographic and social changes around the world, including an aging population, and increasing migration and diversity, require managers to have knowledge of the various issues related to diversity and be able to address them effectively. Women and members of underrepresented groups are the growing part of the labor force around the world; organizations that welcome them and create an environment that engenders feelings of inclusivity and belonging will be more effective and more successful.

Chapters 7 and 8 have presented the extensive research related to understanding cross-cultural values in management and leadership. That information is again essential to allowing managers to understand, describe, and predict how their coworkers, employees, business associates, and negotiating partners from different cultures may perceive various situations and react to them. The broad cultural values and dimensions, including individualism-collectivism, power distance, communication styles, and uncertainty avoidance among others, provide an excellent starting point for cross-cultural interactions. Throughout the book, through cases, examples, and various anecdotes, you also have acquired knowledge about specific countries and cultures. While these do not even scratch the surface in presenting the over 10,000 cultures from around the world, they are a starting point to pique your curiosity. Knowledge of cultural differences and having a vocabulary to fully understand and explain them are key to developing a CM.

3.6 Integrating Culture Into Management Practice

The final part of the TKD roadmap involves integrating and using all the knowledge about self and cultural differences to be a more effective manager. Part V of the book considers key management topics including leadership, motivation, managing teams, organizational structures, and processes such as decision-making and managing conflict and negotiations from a cross-cultural perspective. The information from previous chapters is integrated to help you lead and manage more effectively. As in previous parts of the book, new knowledge, this time from management theory and practice, is introduced.

The focus in the final part is on how to implement that knowledge to manage and lead better. It is important for you to keep in mind that research and theories of management have been developed and tested in traditionally Western contexts. You know by now that simple and wholesale translation and application to manage people who, in some cases, have drastically different assumptions, values, and beliefs can be problematic. People from different cultures have different ideals and expectations of leaders, value different elements of their work, are motivated by many different factors, value teamwork to different degrees, use different approaches to decision-making and ethics, perceive and manage conflict differently, and have different negotiating styles. Applying your knowledge of cultural differences while also being fully aware of your own cultural perspective when implementing various management theories can only support your success.

4. FINAL THOUGHTS ABOUT CROSS-CULTURAL MANAGEMENT

LO 12.4 Present concluding thoughts to the topic of cross-cultural management

With an increasingly interconnected world and global organizations that employ diverse workers, have complex global supply chains, and sell products and services to the four corners of the world, being able to manage culture is basic and indispensable. Today's managers must have the ability to manage people who are different from them and lead organizations that have global reach and impact. The underlying theme of this book, and a fundamental paradox we all face, is that what works in our small world, in our CMC, is not likely to work everywhere. We therefore need to first be aware of the rules that govern our thinking behavior so that we do not automatically and thoughtlessly cross cultural boundaries. We then need to have knowledge about the world around us. Culture impacts us and it impacts everyone else; it matters. Finally, we must learn to adapt our management and leadership theories and practices to address cultural differences.

Your challenge and your journey start with being interested and motivated to learn about the world around you. Because the goal is not to learn something about over 10,000 cultures, an impossible feat, but rather to implement a new way of thinking that can be activated any time you encounter a different culture, the journey need not be overwhelming. You now have the tools to undertake this journey, can plan your next steps systematically, and cross the cultural threshold to a CM.

FINAL EXERCISE: YOUR PERSONAL TKD PLAN

This final exercise is designed to help you identify areas of your CM that you need to address and design a plan to improve your CM. Your goal is to engage in some version of this process on a regular basis. After you plan, you implement changes, then review the outcomes leading to new plans. This Plan-Do-Review process is used in many organizations to encourage goal-setting, taking responsibility, solving problems, and ensuring continuous improvement.

1. Your Commitment

Before you undertake any planning, reflect on your level of commitment. How motivated are you in developing your CM? What is your level of commitment and what are your goals? Based on that reflection, draft a cultural mission statement for yourself that includes the following elements: your end goal, the reasons why, and your level of commitment.

For example, you can start your mission statement by filling in the information below.

My overall goal regarding developing a CM is...........

This is important to me because ....

Growth in my CM will allow me to ....

Growth in my CM will allow my team/organizations to ....

My level of commitment to this endeavor is ....

Review and revise your CM mission on an occasional basis.

2. Review

You have completed a number of self-assessments while reading this book, including the ICMI. Take the time to pull together all the information from those self-assessments and review the results. Use the list below as a summary.

- Your overall ICMI score and score in each factor (Self-Assessments 2.1; 4.1)

- Your cultural background (Self-Assessments 1.1, 2.1, 3.1, 8.1, 8.2, and 8.3)

- Your key values (Self-Assessments 1.2 and 7.2; Exercises 2.1, 7.2, 10.1, and 10.2)

- Your biases and the stereotypes you hold (Self-Assessments 5.1 and 5.2; Exercise 6.1)

- Other personality or abilities (Self-Assessments 2.1, 6.1, 7.1, 9.1, 9.2, 10.1, 10.2, 11.1, and 11.2)

- Your overall knowledge of culture. You can use you ICMI cultural knowledge-factor score as a starting point

3. Identify Areas of Strength

Based on your review of the various information you have gathered about yourself, your experiences while reading this book, and other personal and professional experiences that may be related to CM, identify your top 5–7 areas strength. What are you good at? What can you do well? What do you know well?

1. _____

2. _____

3. _____

4. _____

5. _____

6. _____

7. _____

4. Identify Weaknesses/Areas of Opportunity

Based on your review of the various information you have gathered about yourself, your experiences while reading this book, and other personal and professional experiences that may be related to CM, identify 5–7 areas that present a challenge. What are some key weaknesses? What is hardest for you to learn/do? What are you least motivated to learn/do?

1. _____

2. _____

3. _____

4. _____

5. _____

6. _____

7. _____

5. Reflect on Your Destination

Using the TKD roadmap reflect on what you would like to or need to address and adjust your mission accordingly if needed.

6. Set SMART Goals

Using all the information you have gathered from this exercise so far, identify short-term and long-term goals; you may also choose to further create midterm goals or any time frame that you prefer. As you now know, your CMC may affect your goal-setting time frame. You should refer back to your mission statement and revise it if necessary. While long-term goals may be more generic and less precise, similar to short-term goals, they should follow the SMART guidelines; meaning they should be specific, measurable, achievable, reasonable, and have a time frame. Use your strengths and weaknesses to assess the degree to which the goals are achievable and reasonable. For example, if your general cultural knowledge is low, it would not be reasonable to achieve a high level of knowledge through a short-term goal.

Short-Term Goals (1–3 Months)	Long-Term Goals (6 Months to 1 Year)
1.	1.
2.	2.
3.	3.
4.	4.
5.	5.

7. Strategies: How Will You Get There?

Now that you have a series of goals, for each of them identify strategies to achieve them. For example, if your goal is to increase your cultural knowledge, strategies might include taking a course, attending cultural festivals, reading literature, watching films, travelling, and so forth. The worksheet below is just a suggestion to get you started.

Goal 1: _____

Strategies, time frame, and resources:

1. _____
2. _____
3. _____
4. _____

Goal 2: _____

Strategies, time frame, and resources:

1. _____
2. _____
3. _____
4. _____

Goal 3: _____

Strategies, time frame, and resources:

1. _____
2. _____
3. _____
4. _____

8. Do....

Implement your various strategies and keep track of your progress. Take small steps and do not get overwhelmed or discouraged. Consider mistakes to be a learning opportunity (growth mindset) and keep your sense of humor. Achieving your goals and developing a CM is a journey; expect successes and failures and learn from both. Enjoy the process; the outcome is worth it!

9. Review

Set yourself a timeline to review your progress and assess whether your strategies are having the right impact, or whether your goals are appropriate. At this point, depending on your level of commitment and your motivation, you can start the cycle back with new goals, and so forth, and continue to develop and refine your CM.

APPENDIX

APPENDIX A: THE DEVELOPMENT OF THE ICMI

In the Spring of 2016, after years of teaching culture and management using the concept of cultural mindset as a base, I offered a PhD seminar that brought together 16–18 students from a variety of disciplines who had an interest in culture and cross-cultural leadership.

I presented to them my approach to culture and tasked us with developing a theory-based assessment that would capture the complexity of the concept. Our work drew from a number of disciplines including:

- Cross-cultural management (e.g., Hofstede and GLOBE)

- Dweck's work on fixed-growth mindset (2016)

- Mezirow's work on transformative learning (2000)

- Kegan and Lahey's writings on change (2009)

- The extensive research in cognitive psychology on biases and heuristics (e.g., Fiske & Taylor, 2017; Kahneman, 2011)

- Cross-cultural psychology and anthropology research on cultural viewpoints

- The many scholarly and practitioner articles, books, and websites on cultural competence and literacy (e.g., Javidan's *The Global Mindset*, Liverpool's Cultural Intelligence, and IDI)

- The self-monitoring concept (Snyder, 1974)

- Research on Third Culture Kids (TCK; e.g., Pollock, Van Reken, & Pollock, 2017)

Many in the group had done some work in each of the areas or had had some training with the various tools. Having a cross-disciplinary group brought considerable richness and complexity to the concept as it quickly became obvious that the concept of culture is addressed in a wide variety of disciplines. We also realized, as I had hoped, that the strongly cognitive approach I had used and was proposing was unique and could provide considerable value added.

After developing the original questions (the first ICMI) based on our research, a factor analysis reduced the number of questions and substantially supported our theory-based groupings. Since then, I have further tested and refined the assessment to yield the version that is provided with this book.

The work of the original team in that 2016 seminar, almost all of whom have finished their PhD at this book's writing, was invaluable in moving the project along. Here are their names in alphabetical order:

- Ebtesam Alteneiji, PhD
- Jeff Bourgeois, PhD
- Christopher Brown, PhD
- Robert Gonzales
- Elissa Haddad, PhD
- Kim Hunt, PhD

- David Hunt
- Yang Jiang, PhD
- Bharat Mohan, PhD
- Derek Olson, PhD
- Jeff Sloan
- Crystal Trull, PhD
- Stephanie Van Dellen, PhD
- Ryosuke (Reo) Watanabe

I am very grateful for their contributions, their energy, and their passion.

APPENDIX B: SAMPLE OF US IMMIGRATION POLICIES AND PRACTICES

Event, Policy, or Law	Description and Examples
1780–1802 Naturalization laws	Naturalization requirements included 5 years of residency in the country, good moral character, and applicants being "free white persons" favoring northern and western European immigrants
1855 Women's citizenship tied to their husband	Women's immigration status was tied to that of their husband continuing to deny citizenship to non-white and enslaved women
1870 Naturalization Act	Following the 14th Amendment and the emancipation of slaves, the act extends citizenship only to "aliens of African nativity and to person of African descent" still excluding all other non-white groups
1882 Chinese Exclusion Act	The first ever US law restricting immigration to the United States imposed a 10-year absolute ban on immigration of Chinese into the United States and barring courts from naturalizing any Chinese person (repealed in 1943) The law was in reaction to the large number of Chinese immigrants who built the railroads in the Western United States and established many businesses
1907 Expatriation Act	Allowed for revoking the citizenship of women who married noncitizens The 19th Amendment that gave women the right to vote in 1920 moderated some of these laws

(Continued)

Event, Policy, or Law	Description and Examples
1913 Alien Land Laws	Law passed in California targeting Asian immigrants and prohibiting them from owning or leasing land
1924 Native American Birthright	"All non-citizen Indians born within the territorial limits of the United States be, and they are hereby, declared to be citizens of the United States"
	Although the 14th Amendment of the US constitution clarified citizenship for all born or naturalized in the United States in 1886, it did not apply to the original and indigenous population of the continent who were granted "citizenship" in 1924
1924 Asian Exclusion Act	Prevented immigration from Asia and set quotas for immigrants from the Eastern Hemisphere
1920s—Court cases denying citizenship to "non-whites" using geographical boundaries that established certain zones barred and mentioning certain races, including "Hebrew"	Examples: <ul><li>1922—Takao Ozawa, born in Japan, was denied citizenship on the grounds that he was not a white person</li><li>1923—Bhagat Singh, born in India, was denied citizenship because he was not white, although he was Caucasian</li><li>John Mohammed Ali, born in Arabia, had his citizenship canceled, based on his dark skin</li><li>Feroz Din, born in Afghanistan, was denied naturalization because he was neither white nor of African descent</li><li>Parsees from Northern India were not eligible for citizenship because they were natives of the Asiatic barred zone</li></ul>
1924 Johnson–Reed Act	Creates first quota system favoring immigrants and northern and western Europe or "inferior" races of Asian and southern and eastern Europe
1952 McCarran–Walter Act	Upheld national origin quotas
Japanese Internment during World War II 1942–1945	After the Japanese attack on Pearl Harbor, over 110,000 American citizens of Japanese ancestry, particularly those living on the Pacific Coast, were incarcerated in internment camps in the interior of the United States
	The United States formally apologized in 1988 and disbursed over $1.6 billion reparations to those who were interned and their families
1965 Nationality Act	Abolished national and annual quotas based on race and national origin

Sources: Partially adapted from Go Deeper (2003), Smith (2002a, 2002b), and Taparata (2016).

APPENDIX C: BRIEF TIMELINE OF EVENTS AND MILESTONES RELATED TO SLAVERY AND CIVIL RIGHTS IN THE UNITED STATES

Landmark Events and Milestones	Description and Examples
1619—First African slaves brought to America	20 African slaves were brought by Dutch sailors to Jamestown
1776—American Revolution	Slavery was legal and practiced in all 13 colonies
1777—First slavery ban	Vermont becomes the first state to legally ban slavery
1808—Prohibition on importation of slaves	Congress prohibited the importation of slaves (not slavery), although illegal smuggling continued
1819—Canada	Canada frees all black residents of Canada
1829—Mexico	Mexico abolishes slavery
1857—Africans denied US citizenship	Africans, whether free or slaves, were legally denied US citizenship
1859—Last slave ship	The Clotilde is the last ship to bring slaves into the United States in Alabama
1861–1865 Civil War	War between the North (Union) and the South (Confederacy) with slavery as the immediate cause
1863—Emancipation Proclamation	Abraham Lincoln signed an executive order that designated all enslaved Africans as free
1865—13th Amendment	Abolishment of the legal institution of slavery and involuntary servitude in the United States
1868—14th Amendment	Grants citizenship and equal protection to African Americans
1870—15th Amendment	Grants the right to vote to African Americans
1896—Segregation and Jim Crow laws	Southern states enact segregation laws under the "separate but equal" doctrine that were legally practiced until the 1960s and 1970s
1934—Beginning of redlining	The Federal government's low-cost loans and housing programs specifically excludes African Americans, starting the redlining practices that prevented many from owning homes and segregated them in specific neighborhoods

(Continued)

Landmark Events and Milestones	Description and Examples
1954—Brown vs. Board of Education	Supreme Court's unanimous landmark ruling against the "separate but equal" doctrine in education, allowing desegregation of schools
1955—Montgomery Bus Boycott and start of Civil Rights movement	Rosa Park arrested for refusing to give up her seat in a bus to a white man, marking the start of the Civil Rights movement Boycotts, sit-ins, Freedom rides, civil disobedience, desegregation of schools and universities, violence and bombings
1963—March on Washington	Dr. King's "I have a dream" speech
Freedom summer in 1964	
1964—Civil Rights Act	Passage of the Civil Rights Act gave the Federal government broad power to fight racism and discrimination—establishment of the Equal Employment Opportunity Commission (EEOC)
March from Selma to Montgomery 1965	
1965—Voting Rights Act	Attempts to overcome barriers to African Americans voting
1967—End of miscegenation laws	The US Supreme court ends all laws prohibiting interracial marriages between whites and non-whites
1968—Fair Housing Act Assassination of Dr. King	Attempt to address discrimination in housing April 4th—Dr. King's assassination
1995—Last state to ratify the 13th Amendment	Mississippi became the last state to ratify the 13th Amendment that abolished slavery in the United States

Sources: Adapted from information in Black History Milestones (2019), Go Deeper (2003), and History of Slavery (n.d.).

GLOSSARY

Abstract vs. concrete. Refers to a communication style whereby people communicate either through data, concepts, and theories *or* through examples, stories, and metaphors

Accommodation—second stage of CM development. Stage where people are beginning to use cultural information and knowledge

Acculturation. The process by which two cultural groups that have come in continuous and direct contact resolve the inevitable conflicts and challenges that arise from their contact resulting in changes in one or both groups

Acculturation strategies. Strategies related to how we interact with and acculturate to other cultures to resolve the inevitable conflicts that arise when different cultures interact

Acculturative stress. The physiological, psychological, and behavioral reactions to the conflict that results from sustained contact with another culture

Achievement cultures. Cultures where personal achievement and expertise are valued, the basis of status, and used to evaluate people

Affective cultures. Cultures where emotions are expressed freely and their display is considered appropriate and desirable

Allies. Nonprejudiced individuals who are open-minded and tolerant and are willing to advocate for others

Allocentric. Individuals who behave like people from collectivistic cultures

Anomie or anomy. The absence of cultural norms that engenders many social ills such as delinquency, crime and lawlessness, and personal distress

Ascriptive cultures. Cultures where relationships and connections are the basis of evaluation and social standing

Assertiveness. The degree to which individuals are assertive, direct, and confrontational

Assimilation (or accommodation). Acculturation strategy that occurs when one group gives up most of its cultural elements and adopts the assumptions, values, beliefs, and practices of the other

Assumptions. Cultural expectations, suppositions, and conventions that are accepted and taken for granted without the need for proof

Attention stage of perception. The first stage of social perception where some cues catch your attention while others do not, as there is no way that we can pay attention to everything

Attitudinal approach to conflict management. Aims to change attitudes, beliefs, and feelings for a more long-term solution

Attribution. The process of inferring the cause of behavior and meaning and deciding why people act the way they do or attributing a cause to behavior

Authentic leadership. Leadership approach that highlights the leader's self-awareness, consistent values, and transparency

Automatic processing. Partially or fully subconscious cognitive processes that operate without our full knowledge to process information

Awareness—first stage of CM development. Stage where people become aware and notice cultural elements and their impact

Behavior era of Leadership. Research about leadership trait from the mid-1940s to late 1970s that focused on behaviors of effective leaders

Behavioral approaches to conflict management. Approaches that are short term–oriented and target immediate behaviors

Behaviors. Visible components; things we do; how we act and interact with others; visible elements of culture

Being. A cultural value dimension that refers to people having internal motivation and focusing on doing what is best in the moment

Beliefs. Convictions and ideas about what is true; *the way things are*

Belonging—diversity. Organizational policies and procedures that aim at creating a sense security and support with acceptance, inclusion for all cultural groups to form and maintain lasting, positive, and significant relationships

Benevolent sexism. Putting women on a pedestal along with a desire to protect them

Biases. Systematic and often subconscious errors in thinking

Bicultural and multicultural teams. Groups or teams that include more than one member from different cultures

Binary and non binary gender. Considering only two genders of male or female as opposed to seeing gender as a continuum with male and female as the only two options among many

Business environment. Sectors outside the organization that more directly impact it such as the economy, competitors, customers, regulations, and technology

Centralization. One of the components of structure; the extent to which decisions are made at the top or throughout other levels of an organization

Chaebols. Korean groupings or clans that are family-controlled networks of interrelated companies

Charismatic leadership. Leadership based on the leader's unique personality traits that engender a strong emotional connection with followers

Chronically accessible concepts. Characteristics that are easily accessible, often triggered subconsciously, and applied when assessing ourselves or others

Closure. A cognitive process we use to fill in missing information to understand a situation

Cognitive approach to culture. An approach to culture that focuses on people as thinkers who seek to consistently make sense of their world

Cognitive miser. Because people are biologically limited in how much information they can process, they try to be as parsimonious and efficient as possible. As a result, the goal of the social perception process is to be first efficient

Collectivism (COL). A cultural value that refers to the extent to which family, clan, or society is the source of identity. The collective has priority over individuals with an emphasis on conformity and social obligation

Colonialism. One country fully or partially controlling others

Communication style. A combination of various factors that differentiate how people communicate including degree of directness, linearity, abstraction, task, and intellectual approaches

Conflict. Disagreement over significant issues that creates friction

Confucian-based leadership. A leadership approach based on Confucian philosophy that emphasizes social order and relationships with others, with the leader being a benevolent caretaker willing to sacrifice personal self-interest for mutual benefit

Contact-conflict-resolution. The three stages of acculturation

Content theories of motivation. A group of theories that attempt to answer the question of *what* motivates people by focusing on human needs; they suggest that we are motivated to do something because of our unsatisfied needs

Contingency era of Leadership. Approach to leadership that focuses on understanding both the leader and the leadership situation whereby different leadership styles are predicted to be effective in different situations

Country clusters. Groups of countries that based on the GLOBE project share similar cultural characteristics

Cultural curiosity. One of the ten Cultural Mindset (CM) factors. Interest in learning about culture, one's own and that of others; seeking cultural experiences; willingness to engage with different cultures.

Cultural diversity. The variety of human structures, beliefs systems, and strategies for adapting to situations that exist within different groups

Cultural iceberg. Metaphor used to describe culture that refers to only behaviors and artifacts of culture being visible, whereas the majority of culture made up of assumptions, values, and beliefs are hidden and not easily accessible

Cultural identity. Identity typically related to membership in racial, ethnic, or geographical groups, but can also be related to other factors including gender, sexual orientation, class, religion, or other groups that a person considers significant

Cultural knowledge. One of the ten Cultural Mindset (CM) factors. Having information about other cultures' values, history, organizational systems, etc.; knowledge of world events outside of one's culture and country

Cultural lens. A filter based on cultural assumptions that help us process and interpret information

Cultural Mindset (CM). A way of thinking and a frame of mind or reference that considers culture as a factor when assessing yourself and other people and situations and when making decisions and acting on them. Having a CM means that you are aware of your own cultural backgrounds and the fact that culture-just-is and that it provides a meta-context

Cultural Mindset (CM) as threshold. A conceptual gateway that once crossed opens up new and previously inaccessible ways of thinking that can transform people

and help them understand and interpret the world in radically different ways

Cultural prototypes. General models of the typical qualities that a group of people share based on research about that culture

Cultural self-awareness. One of the ten Cultural Mindset (CM) factors. Having knowledge of your own culture(s), assumptions, values, and beliefs and their implications for how you think and behave

Culturally Endorsed Leadership Theories (CLT). Based on GLOBE research, a finding that culture impacts, but does not predict, leadership behaviors through people's expectations and that leaders who behave according to their culture's CLT are more likely to be considered effective

Culture. A complex system of long-lasting and dynamic learned assumptions, beliefs, values, and behaviors shared by members of a group that makes the group unique and that is transmitted from one person to another, allows the group to interpret and make sense of the world, and guides its members' behaviors

Culture shock. Distress experienced during short-term contact with an unfamiliar cultural setting

Culture-as-meta-context (CMC). The ever-present background, lens, and perspective that shape how members of a cultural group think and perceive the world; and a guide to their actions and behaviors

Culture-just-is (CJI). The idea that one culture is not objectively better than another. All cultures have developed and exist to help a group address challenges they face and provide them with a meta-context that allows them to interpret their world and function

Deculturation (or marginalization). An acculturation strategy that occurs when one culture gives up its cultural elements without adopting any of the other group's culture; a systematic destruction of a culture by forcing members to give up their assumptions, values, beliefs, and practices

Deliberate processing. A cognitive process where deliberate decisions are based on careful consideration and evaluation of information

Deontological perspective of ethics. A view of ethics that states that people should be guided and act in accordance with their moral values, duties, and obligations regardless of the consequences, allowing individuals to be highly consistent from one situation to another

Departmentation. One of the components of structure; the way organizations are divided into divisions, departments, groups, or teams to perform their task

Diffuse cultures. Cultures where relationships apply to different contexts, communication is indirect and evasive, and saving face is important

Direct vs. indirect. A communication style whereby people are either blunt, clear, specific, and explicit *or* subtle, vague, general, and implicit

Discrimination. Unfair and differential behaviors and actions toward individuals based on their membership in certain groups

Diversity and inclusion (D&I). Organizational policies and procedures aimed at increasing cultural diversity and including various groups fully in the organization

Doing. A cultural value dimension that refers to people having external motivation and doing what is approved by others placed on manage

Double bind. An impossible situation where no matter what women do, they are not considered leadership material. When they take on female gender roles, they are not considered capable of leading; when they take on male gender roles, they are disliked

Eiffel Tower. One of Trompenaars's organizational types; organizations that are hierarchical with centralized power and focus on the task, formalization, and standardization

Emic approach. A way of studying culture that relies on the description of the culture provided by members of that culture rather than imposing an outsider's framework

Engagement. The rational and emotional commitment people have to do their work and sense of ownership that can drive performance and innovation

Equality vs. equity. Treating everyone the same as opposed to treating each person differently to help them succeed

Essentialism. An assumption that the same characteristics are shared by all members of a group and that people's essence can be captured by that characteristic; one of the criticisms of how culture is used and researched

Ethics. Moral standards and principles based on written and unwritten codes that guide a person's behavior

Ethnicity. Culture of a group within a particular geographic region

Ethnocentrism. One of the ten Cultural Mindset (CM) factors. The belief that one's country, culture, ethnic group, tribe, or way of life (and even organization) is unique, predominant, and superior to others. It includes both a sense of pride and superiority

Ethno-nationality. Ethnic groups based on nationality

Etic approach. A way of studying culture that relies on outsiders' description, using information gathered by outsiders who observe the culture and collect data through various means

Expatriates (expats). Individuals who choose to live and work in a country other than their own for an extended period of time

Family. One of Trompenaars's organizational types; organizations that are hierarchical with powerful parental figures, centralized power and focus on taking care of individuals, little formalization and standardization

Fixed mindset. One of the ten Cultural Mindset (CM) factors. Belief that people have limited talents and abilities to learn and grow and are therefore unable to change substantially

Formalization. One of the components of structure; the number of written and specific documentation relating to organizational procedures

Future orientation. The extent to which people invest in the future and engage in future-oriented behaviors and are willing to delay gratification; one of the GLOBE dimensions

Gender. Socially constructed and dynamic characteristics of women and men that vary from one society to another

Gender as master status. Views of gender that dominate our perceptions of others and are effortlessly and often subconsciously available and frequently used

Gender egalitarianism. The extent of gender role differentiation and promotion of gender equity; one of the GLOBE dimensions

Gender stereotypes. Expectations regarding how people do and should act based on their membership in specific gender groups

General environment. The broad external context in which an organization operates and includes cultural, social, historical, political, and other general environment sectors that present the backdrop for the organization

Glass ceiling. The invisible social and organizational barriers that hold women and members of under-represented groups back and prevent them from reaching top level

Glass cliff. A situation where women and members of under represented groups are picked for leadership roles that have a usually high risk of failure

Global leadership. A leadership approach that suggests that leading in a global context requires unique and distinct attributes, skills, and competencies

Global virtual teams. Multicultural distributed teams, transnational teams, or multinational teams, all characterized by cultural diversity, geographical dispersion, and electronic communication

Globalization. The extent to which cultures, societies, and economies are interconnected and integrated

GLOBE. Global Leadership and Organizational Behavior Effectiveness. Extensive research project about cultural values and leadership conducted in 62 countries

Goal-oriented semi-automatic processes. Cognitive processes that are both automatic and partially motivated by specific conscious goals. Culture is such a process that operates both automatically and actively to make decisions

Groups. Two or more people who work together on a common goal

Growth mindset. One of the ten Cultural Mindset (CM) factors. Belief that people can change and grow, meaning that time and experience allows people to develop

Guanxi. Chinese term defined as relationships that operate at the personal, business, and governmental levels by creating mutual obligations

Guided missile. One of Trompenaars's organizational types; organizations that are egalitarian with focus on task completion rather than individual needs

Harmony. A cultural value dimension that refers to people believing they can and should manage the environment and live in balance with nature

Hegemonic myth. Widely held assumptions and beliefs about girls being vulnerable and dependent, while boys are considered to be strong and independent. These beliefs translate into clearly gendered values that drive to wanting to protect girls

Heuristics. Efficient shortcuts, methods, strategies, or rules of thumb that are used to derive a solution

Hierarchy. A cultural value dimension that refers to people accepting inequality where some have more power than others

High context. A way to describe how people communicate. Those who come from high context cultures rely on the context and pay attention to and use information that they have either internalized or is present in the environment to communicate. Part of Hall's communication context framework

Homogeneous vs. diverse groups. Groups made up of members who are similar on several primary and secondary dimensions as opposed to groups that have a diverse membership

Horizontal cultures. Cultures where equality is emphasized and there are few power differences

Humane orientation. The degree to which a culture values fairness, generosity, kindness, and caring for others; one of GLOBE's unique dimensions

Hygiene and Motivating Factors. Key elements of Herzberg's two-factor theory of motivation. Hygiene factors are those related to extrinsic rewards such as pay or working conditions; motivators are intrinsic rewards such as the job itself, achievement, recognition, challenge, and growth are what managers must focus on to motivate their employees

Idiocentric. Individuals who behave like people from individualistic cultures

Implicit leadership theories. Leadership theories that suggest that people have a set of beliefs and expectations regarding leadership and that these beliefs influence what they look for in a leader and what they consider effective

Impostor syndrome—impostorism. Inability to internalize and accept credit for one's success and accomplishments and attributing one's success to factors outside of one's ability; belief that success is not earned or deserved

Incubator. One of Trompenaars's organizational types; organizations that are egalitarian, decentralized, and focus on taking care of individual needs

Individualism (IND). The extent to which individuals or a closely knit social structure, such as the extended family, is the basis for social systems. Cultural value where individuals have priority and are independent and separate from the group or collective

Indo-European Leadership (IEL). A leadership approach originating in India and Iran with a focus on integrity, accountability, and moderation and where effective leaders are kind and humble while also being action-oriented

In-group. The group to which we belong, with members who are similar to us and whose welfare concerns us. It is the basis of our cultural identity

In-group collectivism. The degree to which individuals express pride in and cohesion with their family or organizations; one of GLOBE's unique dimensions

Institutional bias. Biases based on race or sex or other dimensions that are embedded in the fabric of society and organizations and that systematically disadvantage certain groups

Institutional collectivism. The degree to which a culture values and practices collective action and collective distribution of resources; one of GLOBE's unique dimensions

Institutional sexism. Gender inequity and discrimination that are embedded in the fabric of society and organizations and that systematically disadvantage women and other members of non male gender groups

Integration (or synergy). An acculturation strategy that occurs when both groups want to maintain their cultural elements and are also motivated to interact and are interested in adopting some of each other's assumptions, values, beliefs, and practices

Integration—third stage of CM development. Being able to integrate cultural information and knowledge into various aspects of one's life

Intellectual vs. emotional. A communication style whereby people either stick to objective and logical arguments or convey feelings, emotions, and subjective impressions as part of their message

Interpretation and inference stage of perception. The third stage of social perception where we interpret the information we have organized and decide the cause of behavior or make attributions

Intersectionality. Considering the combination and connection of many cultural group factors rather than focusing on each separately

Keiretsus. Japanese groupings that are family-owned conglomerates made up of webs of various companies and a complex network of business relationships, and mutual shareholding among these companies

Leadership gap. Having a disproportionate number of white males in leadership of organization, thereby creating a gap between eligible number of women and minority groups who could lead and those who are actually in leadership positions

Levels of culture. Three general levels at which culture operates: national, regional, and group

Linear vs. circular. A communication style whereby people either make a straight connection between points *or* start at one point, taking a detour and then going back

Loose cultures. Cultures where few norms and rules are enforced and people tolerate deviation from social norms

Low context. A way to describe how people communicate. Those who come from low context cultures rely focus on explicit and specific verbal and written messages to understand people and situations and to communicate with others. Part of Hall's communication context framework

Masculinity-Femininity. A cultural value that refers to the extent to which assertiveness and independence from others is valued. Masculinity leads to high gender role differentiation, focus on independence, ambition, and material goods; femininity is focused on caring for others and quality of life

Master status. Individual characteristics, group membership, or social positions that are the primary identifying characteristics of an individual and overshadow all others

Mastery. A cultural value dimension that refers to people believing that they can and should have control over the environment

Mechanistic organizations. A form of organizational structure where functions are based on standardized processes, leadership is based on rules, and employee performance is closely measured and monitored

Meta-cognition. One of the ten Cultural Mindset (CM) factors. Ability to think and reflect about one's own thinking; understanding one's own thinking, how it operates and its impact

Mindset. The sum total of activated cognitive procedures tied to a particular task

Monochronic (M-Time). A way of describing how cultures perceive time. People from monochronic cultures see time as linear, tangible, finite, measurable, and valuable with events ordered in manageable sequences. Part of Hall's communication context framework

Motivated tactician. Refers to how people process information as engaged thinkers who both consciously and subconsciously look for strategies to make sense of the world

Motivation. A state of mind, a desire, and energy that drive people to act; one of the three elements of performance

Multiculturalism. The coexistence of equal and diverse cultures where cultures are assumed to contribute equivalent value

Nationality. Cultural groups based on the country of citizenship

Neocharismatic era of leadership. Current approaches to leadership that focus on the emotional connection between leaders and followers with an emphasis on inspiration

Neutral cultures. Cultures where emotions are avoided and their display is not considered desirable

Nonprogrammed decisions. Decisions that are unexpected and outside of typical activities with no clear guidelines for managers on how to proceed

Open systems. View of organizations as being made up of interrelated parts that are coherently interconnected and continually interact with one another and with their environment to address the challenges they face

Organic organizations. A form of organizational structure where rules are more flexible and less formal with decentralized team leadership. It is clear that size is closely related with structure

Organization stage of perception. The second stage of social perception where we organize information into manageable chunks. We often use schemas at this stage

Organizational (corporate, company) culture. A system of learned assumptions, beliefs, values, and behaviors shared by members of an organization that makes the organization unique and is transmitted to new members, allows the organization to make sense of its environment, and guides its employees' behaviors

Organizational processes. One of the strategic forces in organizations that refers to various activities that are undertaken to accomplish the tasks including decision-making, conflict management, and negotiations

Organizational strategic forces. Key forces that operate inside an organization and require managers' attention; they include organizational culture, structure processes, and leadership

Organizational structure. One of the strategic forces in organizations that refers to how people are organized to get their work done. It includes a number of components that combine to indicate how a firm organizes its human resources

Out-group. The group to which we do not belong and that we perceive as different and distant from us

Overgeneralization. Reducing a whole complex culture, group, or individuals to a few simple characteristics; one of the criticisms of research about culture

Parochial view. One of the ten Cultural Mindset (CM) factors. A narrow view of culture that only considers one's own culture, with little interest in other cultures and a belief that culture is not important. Having a strong attraction to one's in-group and being centered on one's own community, region, religion, or culture (and even organization)

Particular cultures. Cultures where principles and rules change depending on the person and relationships among people

Pay gap. A differential between the pay of people in similar jobs; used in reference to women and under-represented groups earning less than men for similar work

Perceptual filters. Filters that we use to process information that allow some information to pass unnoticed while other information is selected for examination

Performance orientation. The degree to which a culture values and encourages performance and excellence; one of GLOBE's unique dimensions

Pluralism. One of the ten Cultural Mindset (CM) factors. A view of culture that considers all cultures to be of equal value with a high interest in other cultures

Polychronic (P-Time). A way of describing how cultures perceive time. People from polychronic cultures see time as flexible and nonlinear with many actions occurring at once and events and activities are not ordered linearly. Part of Hall's communication context framework

Positive leadership. Leadership that emphasizes individual strengths in helping people achieve their highest potential through an affirmative bias and optimism

Post colonialism. Recognition of the continued impact of colonialism on the groups who were colonized and on the relationship between them and the colonizers

Post liminal—last stage of CM development. Final stage of CM development where people are both conscious and mindful of culture at all times

Power distance. The extent to which people accept and expect unequal distribution of power. In higher power distance cultures, there is a wider gap between the powerful and the powerless

Power double bind. A situation where when women assert power, they are disliked and not respected, but when they do not assert power, they are ignored, often unable to lead in organizational settings

Prejudice. An emotional response to and judgment of a social group and its members based on stereotypes and other preconceptions and biases

Primary dimensions of diversity. Group memberships that are typically visible and less subject to change and include race, ethnicity, gender, sexual orientation, age, and physical ability; also called endowed traits

Process theories of motivation. A group of theories of motivation that concentrate on how people come to be motivated and the processes involved in motivation

Programmed decisions. Decisions that are expected, routine, and have established processes and procedures attached to them

PsyCap-psychological capital. Positive psychological states, confidence, positive attributions, perseverance, and resilience that can be triggered by applying positive leadership

Psychological contract. The informal expectations regarding the exchange between an organization and its employees

Psychological safety. The belief that one will not be punished or humiliated for speaking up with ideas, questions, concerns, or mistakes

Race. A socially constructed concept that is developed and used to describe differences in the physical appearance of people

Reentry. The process by which expatriates return back home and re-engage with their own culture

Relationship (consideration) behaviors. Key leadership behaviors, specifically defined during the behavior era, that are related to taking care of followers and the relationship between the leader and followers

Relativistic view of ethics. A view of ethics that suggests that all cultures have values and norms that guide people's thinking and behaviors and that one cannot use standards from one culture to evaluate or judge another

Reverse culture shock. Distress experienced in interaction with one's own culture when returning home after an extended period of time

Salience. Stimuli that stand out because they are novel, unusual, or different, pass through the filters, and get our attention in the first stage of social perception

Saving face. Refers to one aspect of communication style present in some cultures where people have a strong desire to avoid embarrassment and humiliation and maintain one's own and others' dignity and reputation

Schemas. Mental models and patterns about situations and events that are used, often in the organization stage of perception, to organize and understand information

Secondary dimensions of diversity. Group memberships that can usually be changed and include factors such as nationality, religion, income, education, marital status, as well as several others; also called acquired traits

Self-categorization. The process by which people identify themselves as belonging to particular groups

Self-monitoring. One of the ten Cultural Mindset (CM) factors. Ability to read the cues from the environment and adjust behavior accordingly

Separation (or segregation or domination). One of the acculturation strategies that occur when a group keeps most of its cultural elements without adopting any of the other culture's

Servant leadership. Leadership based on the leader focusing primarily on serving the needs of followers with the leader being considered first among equals and being motivated by service, authenticity, humility, and empathy

Sexual harassment. Unwelcome sexual advances and other activities of a sexual nature that interferes with one's work and is considered a form of workplace discrimination

Social perception process. The process of gathering, selecting, and interpreting information about others

Sophisticated stereotypes. Generalizations about people based on research and theoretically sound concepts rather than limited personal experiences

Span of control. One of the components of structure; the number of people who report to each supervisor or manager

Specialization. One of the components of structure; the degree to which each individual, team, or department performs narrow and unique tasks

Specific cultures. Cultures where relationships are specific to particular tasks, and communication is direct and purposeful

Spiritual leadership. Leadership rooted in vision, hope, faith, and altruistic love as key leadership attributes that engender a sense of wholeness, harmony, and well-being in followers

Stages of CM development. CM develops through three stages of awareness, accommodation, integration, and the final post liminal stage

Stages of group/team development. Five stages that groups go through to become effective teams; they include forming, storming, norming, performing, and adjourning

Standardization. One of the components of structure; the degree to which similar activities are performed in the same way

Striving. A cultural value dimension that refers to people focusing on personal development

Submission. A cultural value dimension that refers to people believing that nature and the environment control them

System I. Information processing that operates automatically and is based on well-practiced and deeply ingrained assumptions, values, beliefs, and knowledge

System II. Information processing that involves deliberate, thoughtful, intentional, and effortful processing of information

Task (structuring) behaviors. Key leadership behaviors, specifically defined during the behavior era, that are related to how the task is accomplished

Task vs. people. A communication style whereby people express themselves either by focusing on ideas, outcomes, and results *or* by focusing on people and relationships

Teams. Mature groups where members have complementary skills, are committed to common goals and to one another, share leadership, and hold one another accountable

Teleological perspective of ethics. A view of ethics that suggests that decisions and actions should be judged and evaluated based on their consequences, not their intentions

Think leader–think male. The belief and expectation that leadership and management by and large equate with male, often white male, stereotypes

THINK–KNOW–DO roadmap or model. The three-step roadmap to developing a Cultural Mindset. First stage involves cognition and being aware of culture and its impact on self and others. Second stage involves developing knowledge of culture. Third stage involves acquiring the behaviors and skills required to act appropriately

Tight cultures. Cultures where people enforce and abide by norms and there is little tolerance for and acceptance of deviation from those norms

Token teams. Groups or teams where all members have the same background with one token or a few members from another cultural background

Trait era of leadership. Early research approaches to leadership between the late 1800s to mid-1940s that focused on personal traits and attributes of leaders with the assumption that leaders are born and not made

Transactional leadership. Leadership based on an exchange between the leader and the follower

Transformational leadership. Leadership aimed at large-scale change and based on an emotional connection between leaders and followers that involves inspiration, empowerment, and individual consideration

Tribalism. Loyalty to one's in-group or tribe with a strong sense of superiority and associated with a strong Us-vs-Them attitude where the out-group is seen as a threat and treated with hostility

Triple challenge of GVT. The typical challenges of global virtual teams that include distance, language, and culture

Ubuntu leadership. An African concept characterized by "I am here because you are" associated with a leadership approach focused on the collective, mutual benefits, and interconnections among people

Uncertainty avoidance. A cultural value that refers to the extent to which people feel threatened by ambiguous situations. High uncertainty avoidance leads to low tolerance for uncertainty and an attempt to avoid ambiguity

Unconscious or implicit bias. Perceptions of others that are activated without our conscious knowledge and operate automatically and outside of our control before we become aware of them

Universal cultures. Cultures where universal principles and rules apply to everyone equally

Universal leadership attributes. Leadership attributes that have been found by GLOBE researchers to be considered universally desirable

Universal view of ethics. A view of ethics that suggests that some universal principles apply to all people regardless of culture or other contingencies

Us-vs-Them. A dualistic view of in-groups and out-groups where in-group members are seen as positive and those in the out-groups are perceived negatively

Values. Stable, long-lasting beliefs and preferences about what is worthwhile and desirable

Vertical cultures. Cultures where hierarchy is emphasized and individuals are not considered equals

Virtual teams. Groups or teams where members are not co-located and use communication technologies to work together

VUCA—volatile, uncertain, complex, ambiguous. Characteristics of environments that create uncertainty

Work-life balance. The equilibrium between work and other factors; often a factor in women's inability to succeed in organizations

Worldly leadership. An emic approach to leadership that suggests that effective leadership in a diverse world requires leaders who have wisdom and experience with knowledge of various countries and who do not apply concepts from one culture to the other

REFERENCES

#79 Huawei. (2018). *Forbes*. Retrieved from https://www.forbes.com/companies/huawei/#12e8e8025d26. Accessed on May 17, 2019.

A class divided. (1985). *Frontline*, March 26. Retrieved from https://www.pbs.org/video/frontline-class-divided/. Accessed on August 4, 2019.

AAA statement on "Race". (1998). American Anthropological Association, May 17. Retrieved from https://www.americananthro.org/ConnectWithAAA/Content.aspx?ItemNumber=2583. Accessed on May 25, 2019.

Abbott, H. (2018). Five businesses that have nailed the creative culture. *Virgin*, July 5. Retrieved from https://www.virgin.com/entrepreneur/five-businesses-have-nailed-creative-culture. Accessed on September 21, 2019.

ABD (Alliance for Board Diversity). (2018). *Missing pieces report: The 2018 board diversity census of women and minorities on Fortune 500 boards*. Retrieved from https://theabd.org. Accessed on June 9, 2019.

About Nutella. (2019). Retrieved from https://www.nutella.com/en/uk/ferrero-group. Accessed on May 17, 2019.

Abrams, A. (2018). Yes, impostor syndrome is real: Here's how to deal with it. *Time*, June 20. Retrieved from https://time.com/5312483/how-to-deal-with-impostor-syndrome/. Accessed on June 11, 2019.

Abrams, D., & Hogg, M. (2006). *Social identifications: A social psychology of intergroup relations and group processes*. London: Routledge.

Adair, W. L., Taylor, M. S., & Tinsley, C. H. (2009). Starting out on the right foot: Negotiation schemas when cultures collide. *Negotiation and Conflict Management Research*, 2(2), 138–163.

Adams, J. S., & Freedman, S. (1976). Equity theory revisited: Comments and annotated bibliography. *Advances in Experimental Social Psychology*, 9, 43–90.

Adler, N., & Gundersen, A. (2008). *International dimensions of organizational behavior* (5th ed.). Mason, OH: Thomson/South-Western.

Agarwal, P. (2019). Belonging in a workplace: A new approach to diversity and inclusivity. *Forbes*, August 26. Retrieved from https://www.forbes.com/sites/pragyaagarwaleurope/2019/08/26/belonging-in-the-workplace-a-new-approach-to-diversity-and-inclusivity/#654306087a66. Accessed on January 29, 2020.

Aghina, W., Handscomb, C., Ludolph, J., West, D., & Yip, A. (2019). How to select and develop individuals for successful agile teams: A practical guide. *McKinsey & Company*. Retrieved from https://www.contextisleading.nl/wp-content/uploads/2019/08/How-to-select-and-develop-individuals-for-successful-agile-teams.pdf. Accessed on May 4, 2020.

Aguilar, L. A. (2013). The important role of immigrants in our economy. U.S. Securities and Exchange Commission, May 18. Retrieved from https://www.sec.gov/news/speech/2013-spch051813laahtm. Accessed on August 17, 2019.

Ahler, D. J., & Sood, G. (2018). The parties in our heads: Misconceptions about party composition and their consequences. *The Journal of Politics*, 8(3), 964–981. doi:10.1086/697253

Aizenman, N., & Gharib, M. (2019). American with no medical training ran center for malnourished Ugandan kids. 105 died. *All Things Considered*, August 9. Retrieved from https://www.npr.org/sections/goatsandsoda/2019/08/09/749005287/american-with-no-medical-training-ran-center-for-malnourished-ugandan-kids-105-d. Accessed on August 10, 2019.

Altman, A. (2016). The year of hygge, the Danish obsession with getting cozy. *The New Yorker*, December 18. Retrieved from https://www.newyorker.com/culture/culture-desk/the-year-of-hygge-the-danish-obsession-with-getting-cozy. Accessed on April 6, 2020.

Alvarez, S., Afuah, A., & Gibson, C. (2018). Should management theories take uncertainty seriously? *Academy of Management Review*, 43(2), 169–172.

Amanatullah, E. T., & Morris, M. W. (2010). Negotiating gender roles: Gender differences in assertive negotiating are mediated by women's fear of backlash and attenuated when negotiating on behalf of others. *Journal of Personality and Social Psychology*, 98(1), 256–267.

Ambrose, K. (2019). How these women entrepreneurs learned to battle impostor syndrome. *Fast Company*, July 6. Retrieved from https://www.fastcompany.com/90372812/how-these-women-entrepreneurs-learned-to-battle-impostor-syndrome. Accessed on January 29, 2020.

American time use survey. (2017). U.S. Bureau of Labor Statistics. Retrieved from https://www.bls.gov/news.release/pdf/atus.pdf. Accessed on June 8, 2019.

Amin, S. (2000). *Capitalism in the age of globalization: The management of contemporary society*. London: Zed Books.

Amodio, D. (2014). The neuroscience of prejudice and stereotyping. *Nature Reviews of Neuroscience*, 15, 670–682.

Anand, R., & Winter, M. F. (2008). A retrospective view of corporate diversity training from 1964 to the present. *Academy of Management Learning and Education*, 7(3), 356–372.

Anders, A. (2013). The dangers of growing Russian parochialism. *The Moscow Times*, October 15.

Retrieved from https://www.themoscowtimes.com/2013/10/15/the-dangers-of-growing-russian-parochialism-a28626. Accessed on July 29, 2019.

Anderson, C. (1997). Values-based management. *Academy of Management Executive*, 11(4), 25–46.

Anderson, C., Spataro, S. E., & Flynn, F. J. (2008). Personality and organizational determinants of influence. *Journal of Applied Psychology*, 93(3), 702–710.

Andrews, S. (2020). Why women don't always support other women. *Forbes*, January 21. Retrieved from https://www.forbes.com/sites/forbescoachescouncil/2020/01/21/why-women-dont-always-support-other-women/#1855831e3b05. Accessed on August 2, 2020.

Antonakis, J., Day, D. V., & Schyns, B. (2012). Leadership and individual differences: At the cusp of a renaissance. *The Leadership Quarterly*, 23, 643–650.

Aoki, K., & Lennerfors, T. T. (2013). The new, improved keiretsu. *Harvard Business Review*, September. Retrieved from https://hbr.org/2013/09/the-new-improved-keiretsu. Accessed on November 19, 2019.

Aponte-Moreno, M., & Koulouris, K. (2018). Indo-European leadership (IEL): A non-western leadership perspective. In J. L. Chin, J. E. Trimble, & J. E. Garcia (Eds.), *Global and culturally diverse leaders and leadership: New dimensions, opportunities, and challenges for business, industry, education and society*. A Volume in the ILA Building Leadership Bridges (BLB) Series (pp.

41–81). Bingley, UK: Emerald Publishing Limited.

Appiah, K. A. (2006). *Cosmopolitanism: Ethics in a world of strangers*. New York, NY: W. W. Norton.

Ardichvili, A., & Kuchinke, K. P. (2009). International perspective on the meaning of work and working: Current research and theory. *Advances in Developing Human Resources*, 11(2), 155–167.

Argyris, C., & Schon, D. (1974). *Theories in practice*. San Francisco, CA: Jossey-Bass.

Arnold, P. (2015). The 5 greatest examples of change management in business history. Chartered Management Institute, July 20. Retrieved from https://www.managers.org.uk/insights/news/2015/july/the-5-greatest-examples-of-change-management-in-business-history. Accessed on December 11, 2019.

Arruda, W. (2017). 5 great companies that get the corporate culture right. *Forbes*, August 17. Retrieved from https://www.forbes.com/sites/williamarruda/2017/08/17/5-great-companies-that-get-corporate-culture-right/#2c3f0f731582. Accessed on November 14, 2019.

Ashikali, T., & Groeneveld, S. (2013). Diversity management in public organizations and its effect on employees' affective commitment: The role of transformation leadership and the inclusiveness of the organizational culture. *Review of Public Personnel Administration*, 35(2), 146–168.

Ashkanasy, N. M. (2002). Leadership in the Asian century: Lessons from GLOBE. *International*

Journal of Organisational Behaviour, 5(3), 150–163.

Atcheson, S. (2018). Allyship – The key to unlocking the power of diversity. *Forbes*, November 30. Retrieved from https://www.forbes.com/sites/shereeatcheson/2018/11/30/allyship-the-key-to-unlocking-the-power-of-diversity/#182ea73949c6. Accessed on August 30, 2019.

Avolio, B. J., & Gardner, W. L. (2005). Authentic leadership development: Getting to the root of positive forms of leadership. *The Leadership Quarterly*, 16, 315–338.

Ayman, R., & Chemers, M. M. (1983). Relationship of supervisory behavior ratings to work group effectiveness and subordinate satisfaction. *Journal of Applied Psychology*, 68, 338–341.

Ayman, R., & Korabik, K. (2010). Leadership: Why gender and culture matter. *American Psychologist*, 65(3), 157–170.

Babcock, L., & Laschever, S. (2003). *Women don't ask: Negotiation and the gender divide*. Princeton, NJ: Princeton University Press.

Babcock, L., Recalde, M. P., Vesterlund, L., & Weingard, L. (2017). Gender differences in accepting and receiving requests for task with low promotability. *American Economic Review*, 107(3), 714–747.

Badger, E., & Miller, C. C. (2018). Americans love families. American policies don't. *The New York Times*, June 24. Retrieved from https://www.nytimes.com/2018/06/24/upshot/americans-love-families-american-policies-dont.html. Accessed on June 11, 2019.

Badgett, M. V. L., & Folbre, N. (2003). Job gendering: Occupational choice and the labor market. *Industrial Relations: A Journal of Economy & Society*, 42(2), 270–298. doi:10.1111/1468-232X.00290

Bagarino, C. (2018). 7 ways Japanese baseball is different from American baseball. *Culture Trip*, March 1. Retrieved from https://theculturetrip.com/asia/japan/articles/7-ways-japanese-baseball-is-different-from-american-baseball/. Accessed on September 15, 2019.

Baglione, S., & Zimmerer, T. (2007). Spirituality, values and leadership beliefs and practices: An empirical study of U.S. and Chinese business leaders. *International Journal of Business Strategy*, 7(2), 32–40.

Bajarin, T. (2019). A distracted, divided U.S. is no match for China's long-term plans for domination. *Fast Company*, May 9. Retrieved from https://www.fastcompany.com/90346943/china-long-term-domination-plan-can-beat-a-divided-america. Accessed on September 14, 2019.

Baker, L., & Brown, A. L. (1984). Metacognitive skills and reading. In P. D. Pearson, M. Kamil, R. Barr, & P. Mosenthal (Eds.), *Handbook of reading research* (Vol. 1, pp. 353–394). New York, NY: Longman.

Barbra Streisand: Library Archives. (1992). Retrieved from http://barbra-archives.com/bjs_library/90s/elle-women-speech.html. Accessed on June 12, 2019.

Barta, T., Kleiner, M., & Neuman, T. (2012). Is there a payoff from top-team diversity? *McKinsey Quarterly*, April. Retrieved from http://www.mckinsey.com/insights/organization/is_there_a_payoff_from_top-team_diversity. Accessed on Accessed on July 7, 2014.

Bartlett, C. A., & Ghoshal, S. (1987). Managing across borders: New strategic requirements. *MIT Sloan Management Review*, 28(4). Retrieved from https://my.uopeople.edu/pluginfile.php/57436/mod_book/chapter/38890/BUS2207U1Text4.pdf. Accessed on May 22, 2019.

Bartsch, M., Brandt, A., & Steinvorth, D. (2010). Turkish immigration to Germany: A sorry history of self-deception and wasted opportunity. *Der Spiegel* [Online], September 7. Retrieved from https://www.spiegel.de/international/germany/turkish-immigration-to-germany-a-sorry-history-of-self-deception-and-wasted-opportunities-a-716067.html. Accessed on August 17, 2019.

Bass, B. M. (1960). *Leadership, psychology, and organizational behavior*. New York, NY: Harper & Row.

Bass, B. M. (1985). *Leadership and performance beyond expectations*. New York, NY: Free Press.

Bass, B. M. (1990a). *Bass and Stogdill's handbook of leadership* (3rd ed.). New York, NY: Free Press.

Bass, B. M. (1990b). From transactional to transformational leadership: Learning to share the vision. *Organizational Dynamics*, 18(3), 19–31.

Bass, B. M. (1997). Does the transactional-transformational leadership paradigm transcend organizational and national boundaries? *American Psychologist*, 52(3), 130–139.

Bass, B. M., & Avolio, B. J. (1990). The implications of transactional and transformational leadership for individual, team and organizational development. *Research in Organizational Change and Development*, 4, 231–272.

Bass, B. M., & Avolio, B. J. (1993). Transformational leadership: A response to critiques. In M. M. Chemers & R. Ayman (Eds.), *Leadership theory and research: Perspectives and directions* (pp. 49–80). San Diego, CA: Academic Press.

Basu, S., Zuo, X., Lou, C., Acharya, R., & Lundgren, R. (2017). Learning to be gendered: Gender socialization in early adolescence among urban poor in Delhi, India and Shanghai, China. *Journal of Adolescent Health*, 61(4), S24–S29. doi:10.1016/j.jadohealth.2017.03.012

Becker, S. W., & Eagly, A. H. (2004). The heroism of men and women. *American Psychologist*, 59(3), 163–178.

Becker, T. (1997). *Traditional American Indian leadership: A comparison with U.S. governance*. Retrieved from http://www.navajocourts.org/Harmonization/Traditional%20American%20Indian%20Leadership.pdf. Accessed on October 10, 2019.

Beckett, L. (2019). More than 175 killed worldwide in the last eight years in white nationalist-linked attacks. *The Guardian*, August 4. Retrieved from https://www.theguardian.com/us-news/2019/aug/04/mass-shootings-white-nationalism-linked-attacks-worldwide. Accessed on August 16, 2019.

Befu, H. (2001). *Hegemony of homogeneity: An anthropological analysis of Nihonjinron*. Melbourne, Aus: Trans Pacific Press.

Benhold, K. (2020). A German exception? Why the country's coronavirus death rate is low. *The New York Times*, April 4. Retrieved from https://www.nytimes.com/2020/04/04/world/europe/germany-coronavirus-death-rate.html. Accessed on April 24, 2020.

Benmamoun, M., Kalliny, M., Chun, W., & Kim, S. H. (2018). The impact of manager's animosity and ethnocentrism on multinational enterprise (MNE) international entry-mode decisions. *Thunderbird International Business Review*, 61(2), 413–423.

Bennett, M. (1996). Men's and women's self-estimates of intelligence. *Journal of Social Psychology*, 136(3), 411–412.

Bennett, M., Sani, F., Hopkins, N., Agostini, L., & Malucchi, L. (2000). Children's gender categorization: An investigation of automatic processing. *Journal of Developmental Psychology*, 18, 97–102.

Bennett, M. J. (1986). A developmental approach to training for intercultural sensitivity. *International Journal of Intercultural Relations*, 10(2), 179–195.

Bennett, M. J. (1993). Towards ethnorelativism: A developmental model of intercultural sensitivity. In R. M. Paige (Ed.), *Education for the intercultural experience* (pp. 21–71). Yarmouth, ME: Intercultural Press.

Benson, J., & Dvesdow, S. (2003). Discovery mindset: A decision-making model for discovery and collaboration, *Management Decision*, 41(10), 997–1005. doi:10.1108/00251740310509526

Berger, M. (2019). Women in Japan were told not to wear glasses to work. Their response has been fiery. *The Washington Post*, November 8. Retrieved from https://www.washingtonpost.com/world/2019/11/08/women-japan-were-told-not-wear-glasses-work-their-response-has-been-fiery/. Accessed on January 29, 2020.

Bernstein, L. (2019). NIH director will no longer speak at all-male science panels. *The Washington Post*, June 12. Retrieved from https://www.washingtonpost.com/health/nih-director-will-no-longer-speak-on-all-male-science-panels/2019/06/12/fe3b6386-8d2c-11e9-adf3-f70f78c156e8_story.html?utm_term=.e61610945b9c. Accessed on June 14, 2019.

Berrey, E. (2015). *The enigma of diversity: The language of race and limits of racial justice*. Chicago, IL: University of Chicago Press.

Berry, J. W. (1997). Immigration, acculturation, and adaptation. *Applied Psychology: An International Review*, 46(1), 5–34.

Berry, J. W. (2005). Acculturation: Living successfully in two cultures. *International Journal of Intercultural Relations*, 29(6), 697–712.

Berry, J. W., Poortinga, Y. H., Segall, M. H., & Dasen, P. R. (1992). *Cross-cultural psychology: Research and applications*. Cambridge, UK: Cambridge University Press.

Berry, J. W., Kim, U., Minde, T., & Mok, D. (1987). Comparative studies of acculturative stress. *International Migration Review*, 21(3), 491–511.

Berzonsky, M. D. (2011). A social-cognitive perspective on identity construction. In S. Schwartz, K. Luyckx, & V. Vignoles (Eds.), *Handbook of identity theory and research* (pp. 55–76). New York, NY: Springer.

Bhawuk, D. P. S., Landis, D., & Lo, K. D. (2016). Intercultural training. In D. L. Sam & J. W. Berry (Eds.), *The Cambridge handbook of acculturation psychology* (pp. 504–524). Cambridge, UK: Cambridge University Press.

Bhopal tragedy due to worst of American, Indian cultures. (2010). *Rediff.com*, June 9. Retrieved from https://www.rediff.com/news/report/bhopal-tragedy-due-to-worst-of-american-indian-cultures/20100609.htm. Accessed on December 5, 2019.

Bhutan's Gross National Happiness Index. (2019). Oxford Poverty & Human Development Initiative. Retrieved from https://ophi.org.uk/policy/national-policy/gross-national-happiness-index/. Accessed on May 26, 2019.

Bian, Y. (2019). *Guanxi: How China works*. Cambridge, UK: Polity Press.

Bird, A. (2018). Mapping the content domain of the global leadership competencies. In M. E. Mendenhall, J. S. Osland, A. Bird, G. R. Oddou, M. J. Stevens, M. L. Maznevski, & G. K. Stahl (Eds.), *Global leadership: Research, practice and development* (pp. 119–142). New York, NY: Routledge.

Bishu, S. G., & Alkadry, M. G. (2017). A systematic review of the gender pay gap and factors that predict it. *Administration and Society*, 49(1), 65–104. doi: 10.1177/0095399716636928

Bisoux, T. (2008). The instant messenger. *BizEd*, 7(January–February), 16–20.

Bittman, M., England, P., Sayer, L., Folbre, N., & Matheson, G. (2003). When does gender trump money? Bargaining time in household work. *American Journal of Sociology*, 109(1), 186–214.

Black, C. (2017). Advice from the trenches: How to lead multicultural teams. *UVA-Darden Ideas to Action*, May 2. Retrieved from https://ideas.darden.virginia.edu/advice-from-the-trenches-how-to-lead-multicultural-teams. Accessed on August 3, 2020.

Black history milestones. (2019). *History*. June 6. Retrieved from https://www.history.com/topics/black-history/black-history-milestones. Accessed on August 16, 2019.

Black, S., & Gregersen, H. B. (2016). The right way to manage expats. In *HBR's 10 must read on managing across cultures* (pp. 139–155). Boston, MA: Harvard Business Review Press.

Blair, I. V., Judd, C. M. & Chapleau, K. M. (2004). The influence of Afrocentric facial features on criminal sentencing. *Psychological Science*, 15, 674–679.

Blakemore, E. (2019). How Hong Kong's complex history explains its current crisis with China. *National Geographic*, August 7. Retrieved from https://www.nationalgeographic.com/culture/topics/reference/hong-kong-history-explain-relationship-china/. Accessed on August 10, 2019.

Blanding, M. (2018). In America, immigrants really do get the job done. *Forbes*, August 1. Retrieved from https://www.forbes.com/sites/hbsworkingknowledge/2018/08/01/in-america-immigrants-really-do-get-the-job-done/#2de3d76f1935. Accessed on August 2, 2020.

Blight, K. (2019). Why re-onboarding new parent employees is vital to your organization's growth. *Adapt – Sprout Social*, March 26. Retrieved from https://sproutsocial.com/adapt/new-parent-employees/. Accessed on June 12, 2019.

Blomstrom, D. (2019). Why a culture of "us vs. them" is deadly. *Forbes*, February 6. Retrieved from https://www.forbes.com/sites/duenablomstrom1/2019/02/06/why-a-culture-of-us-vs-them-is-deadly/#1d37b0f87520. Accessed on July 27, 2019.

BLS Reports. (2018). *Labor force characteristics by race and ethnicity, 2017*. Retrieved from https://www.bls.gov/opub/reports/race-and-ethnicity/2017/pdf/home.pdf. Accessed on August 21, 2019.

Blum, R. W., Mmari, K., & Moreau, C. (2017). It begins at 10: How gender expectations shape early adolescence around the world. *Journal of Adolescent Health*, 60(4), S3–S4. doi:10.1016/j.jadohealth.2017.07.009

Bogen, M. (2019). All the ways hiring algorithms can introduce bias. *Harvard Business Review*, May 9. Retrieved from https://hbr.org/2019/05/all-the-ways-hiring-algorithms-can-introduce-bias. Accessed on August 23, 2019.

Bok, S. (2002). *Common values*. Columbia, MO: University of Missouri Press.

Bolden, R., & Kirk, P. (2012). Leadership development as a catalyst for change. In S. Turnbull, P. Case, G. Edwards, D. Schedlitzki, & P. Simpson (Eds.), *Worldly leadership: Alternative wisdoms for a complex world* (pp. 32–51). New York, NY: Palgrave Macmillan.

Bono, J. E., & Ilies, R. (2006). Charisma, positive emotion and mood contagion. *The Leadership Quarterly*, 17, 317–334.

Booth, W. C. (2001). Relativism, pluralism, and skepticism (philosophical perspective): Cultural concerns. In N. J. Smelser & P. B. Baltes (Eds.), *International encyclopedia of the social and behavioral sciences* (pp. 13018–13023). Amsterdam: Elsevier.

Boroditsky, L. (2017). How language shapes the way we think. *TED*, November. Retrieved from https://www.ted.com/talks/lera_boroditsky_how_language_shapes_the_way_we_think?utm_campaign=social&utm_medium=referral&utm_source=facebook.com&utm_content=talk&utm_term=social-science#t-573395. Accessed on July 10, 2019.

Bort, J. (2019). A former WeWork executive who made $300,000 and is now suing. *Business Insider*, September 20. Retrieved from https://www.businessinsider.com/wework-vp-lawsuit-discrimination-cultish-culture-2019-9. Accessed on November 14, 2019.

Bostock, B. (2020). Germany has a remarkably low coronavirus death rate – Thanks largely to mass testing, but also culture, luck, and an impressive healthcare system. *Business Insider*, March 28. Retrieved from https: //www.businessinsider.com/germany-why-coronavirus-death-rate-lower-italy-spain-test-healthcare-2020-3. Accessed on April 27, 2020.

Bourke, J., van Berkel, A., Garr, S., & Wong, J. (2017). Diversity and inclusion: The reality gap. *Deloitte Insights*, February 27. Retrieved from https://www2.deloitte.com/us/en/insights/focus/human-capital-trends/2017/diversity-and-inclusion-at-the-workplace.html. Accessed on August 24, 2019.

Bowles, H. R., Babcock, L., & Lai, L. (2007). Social incentives for gender differences in propensity to initiate negotiations: Sometimes it hurts to ask. *Organizational Behavior and Human Decision Processes*, 103, 84–103.

Boyes, A. (2019). How to stop obsessing over your mistakes. *Harvard Business Review*, April 12. Retrieved from https://hbr.org/2019/02/how-to-stop-obsessing-over-your-mistakes. Accessed on November 7, 2019.

Boykoff, P. (2019). Japan's day care crisis is turning working moms into activists. *CNN*, July 7. Retrieved from https://flipboard.com/@CNN/japan-s-day-care-crisis-is-turning-working-moms-into-activists/a-WCFRrCA5TfiwrQT0LMyTXw%3Aa%3A129384039-5ac6463ba7/cnn.com. Accessed on January 29, 2020.

Brannon, S. M., & Gawronski, B. (2018). Does contextualized attitude change depend on individual differences in response to belief incongruent information? *Journal of Experimental Social Psychology*, 78, 148–161. doi: 10.1016/j.jesp.2018.03.015

Bransford, J. D., Brown, A. L., & Cocking, R. R. (Eds.). (2000). *How people learn*. Washington, DC: National Academy Press. Retrieved from https://www.nap.edu/read/9853/chapter/1. Accessed on July 14, 2019.

Braun, S., Peus, C., Weisweiler, S., & Frey, D. (2013). Transformational leadership, job satisfaction and team performance: A multilevel mediation model of trust. *The Leadership Quarterly*, 24, 270–283.

Brett, J., Behfar, K., & Kern, M. C. (2006). Managing multicultural teams. *Harvard Business Review*, November. Retrieved from https://hbr.org/2006/11/managing-multicultural-teams. Accessed on September 13, 2019.

Brewer, P., & Venaik, S. (2011). Individualism–collectivism in Hofstede and GLOBE. *Journal of Business Studies*, 42(3), 436–445.

Brill, A. (2010). Saving face. *Psychology Today*, November 29. Retrieved from https://www.psychologytoday.com/us/blog/chronic-healing/201011/saving-face. Accessed on September 12, 2019.

Brown, M. F. (2008). Cultural relativism 2.0. *Current Anthropology*, 49(3), 363–383. doi:10.1086/529261

Bruner, R., & Spekman, R. (1998). The dark side of alliances: Lessons from Volvo–Renault. *European Management Journal*, 16(2), 136–150. Retrieved from http://www.hbs.edu/faculty/Publication%20Files/The%20Dark%20Side%20of%20Alliances_95819048-0ced-40f4-97e0-875f6df79423.pdf. Accessed on November 15, 2019.

Brunswik. (1955). Representative design and probabilistic theory in a functional psychology. *Psychological Review, 62,* 193–217.

Bryant, A. (2009). No doubt women are better managers. *The New York Times,* July 26. Retrieved from http://www.nytimes.com/2009/07/26/business/26corner.html. Accessed on August 2, 2020.

Bryant, A. (2012a). Let everyone swim, but make sure you're in the pool. *The New York Times,* June. Retrieved from http://www.nytimes.com/2012/06/24/business/angies-list-co-founder-reviews-management-style.html. Accessed on May 4, 2020.

Bryant, A. (2012b). How to become a bus driver, not a bulldozer. *The New York Times,* October 6. Retrieved from https://www.nytimes.com/2012/10/07/business/ken-rees-of-think-finance-on-leading-a-growing-company.html. Accessed on August 3, 2020.

Bryant, A. (2020). How to build a successful team. *The New York Times.* Retrieved from https://www.nytimes.com/guides/business/manage-a-successful-team. Accessed on May 4, 2020.

Bryman, A. (2011). Research methods in the study of leadership. In A. Bryman, D. Collinson, K. Grint, B. Jackson, & M. Uhl-Bien (Eds.), *The SAGE handbook of leadership* (pp. 15–28). Thousand Oaks, CA: SAGE.

Buckenmeyer, C. (2009). No Japanese work for leadership? *Japan Intercultural Consulting,* May 25. Retrieved from https://www.japanintercultural.com/en/news/default.aspx?newsid=21. Accessed on October 10, 2019.

Bueno, C. M., & Tubbs, S. L. (2004). Identifying global leadership competencies: An exploratory study. *Journal of American Academy of Business,* 5(1/2), 80–87.

Burke, A. (2017). 10 facts about American women in the workforce. *Brookings Institution.* Retrieved from https://www.brookings.edu/blog/brookings-now/2017/12/05/10-facts-about-american-women-in-the-workforce/. Accessed on June 4, 2019.

Burns, T., & Stalker, C. M. (1961). *The management of innovation.* London, UK: Tavistock.

Buser, T., Niederle, M., & Oosterbeek, H. (2014). Gender, competitiveness and career choices. *Quarterly Journal of Economics,* 129(3), 1409–1447.

Caligiuri, P. (2012). When Unilever bought Ben & Jerry's: A story of CEO adaptability. *Fast Company,* August 14. Retrieved from https://www.fastcompany.com/3000398/when-unilever-bought-ben-jerrys-story-ceo-adaptability. Accessed on September 1, 2019.

Caligiuri, P. M., & Day, D. V. (2000). Effect of self-monitoring on technical, contextual, and assignment specific performance: A study of cross-national work performance ratings. *Group and Organization Management,* 25(2), 154–174. doi:10.1177/1059601100252004

Cameron, D. (2011). PM's speech at Munich security conference. *The National Archives,* February 5. Retrieved from https://web archive.nationalarchives.gov.uk/20130102224134 and http://www.number10.gov.uk/news/pms-speech-at-munich-security-conference/. Accessed on July 31, 2019.

Cameron, K. (2008). *Positive leadership.* San Francisco, CA: Berrett-Koehler.

Cameron, K., Dutton, J. E., & Quinn, R. E. (Eds.). (2003). *Positive organizational scholarship: Foundations of a new discipline.* San Francisco, CA: Berrett-Koehler.

Campbell, P. D. (2017). Those are our Eiffel Towers, our pyramids: Why Standing Rock is about much more than oil. *The Guardian,* May 15. Retrieved from https://www.theguardian.com/science/2017/may/15/those-are-our-eiffel-towers-our-pyramids-why-standing-rock-is-about-much-more-than-oil. Accessed on September 15, 2019.

Canada at 175. (2019). *Deloitte.* Retrieved from https://www.canada175.ca/sites/default/files/download/files/inclusion_aoda_en_0.pdf. Accessed on April 13, 2020.

Capelli, P., Singh, H., Singh, J. V., & Useem, M. (2015). Indian business leadership: Broad mission and creative value. *The Leadership Quarterly,* 26, 7–12.

Caprino, K. (2015). Gender bias is real: Women's perceived competency drops significantly when judged as being forceful. *Forbes,* August 25. Retrieved from https://www.forbes.com/sites/kathycaprino/2015/08/25/gender-bias-is-real-womens-perceived-competency-drops-significantly-when-judged-as-being-forceful/#72c97

6772d85. Accessed on August 2, 2020.

Carbado, D. W., & Gulati, M. (2013). *Acting white? Rethinking race in "post-racial" America.* Oxford, UK: Oxford University Press.

Cardon, P. W. (2008). A critique of Hall's contexting model: A meta-analysis of literature on intercultural business and technical communication. *Journal of Business and Technical Communication,* 22(4), 399–428.

Carli, L. L. (1999). Gender, interpersonal power, and social influence. *Journal of Social Issues,* 55, 81–99.

Carlyle, T. (1907). *Heroes and hero worship.* Boston, MA: Adams Media.

Carpenter, S. (2000). Effects of cultural tightness and collectivism on self-concept and causal attributions. *Cross-Cultural Research,* 34, 38–56.

Cartwright, D. C. (1965). Influence, leadership, control. In J. G. March (Ed.), *Handbook of organizations* (pp. 1–47). Chicago, IL: Rand McNally.

Catalyst-Double-Bind. (2018). Infographic: The double-bind dilemma for women in leadership. *Catalyst,* August 2. Retrieved from https://www.catalyst.org/research/infographic-the-double-bind-dilemma-for-women-in-leadership/. Accessed on December 6, 2020.

Cha, V. (2020). South Korea offers a lesson in best practices. *Foreign Affairs,* April 10. Retrieved from https://www.foreignaffairs.com/articles/united-states/2020-04-10/south-korea-offers-lesson-best-practices. Accessed on April 27, 2020.

Chaiken, S., & Trope, Y. (Eds.). (1999). *Dual-process theories in social psychology.* New York, NY: Guilford Press.

Chalabi, M. (2018). What is white culture exactly? Here's what the stats say. *The Guardian,* February 26. Retrieved from https://www.theguardian.com/world/2018/feb/26/white-culture-statistics-vegetables-alcohol. Accessed on December 17, 2019.

Chandrashekar, R. (2017). I learned to stop giving cultural ignorance a pass. *HuffPost,* August 3. Retrieved from https://www.huffpost.com/entry/navigating-the-american-dream_b_59813d60e4b02be325be0224. Accessed on July 28, 2019.

Chatterjee, S., Lubatkin, M. H., Schweiger, D. M., & Weber, Y. (1992). Cultural differences and shareholder value in related mergers: Linking equity and human capital. *Strategic Management Journal,* 13(5), 319–334.

Chemers, M. M. (1969). Cross-cultural training as a means for improving situational favorableness. *Human Relations,* 22, 531–546.

Chen, C., Tuliao, V. K., Cullen, J. B., & Chang, Y. Y. (2016). Does gender influence managers' ethics? A cross-cultural analysis. *Business Ethics: A European Review,* 25(4), 345–362.

Chen, C. Y., & Li, C. I. (2013). Assessing the spiritual leadership effectiveness: The contribution of follower's self-concept and preliminary test for moderation of culture and managerial position. *The Leadership Quarterly,* 24, 240–255.

Chhokar, J. S., Brodbeck, F. C., & House, R. J. (Eds.). (2007). *Culture and leadership across the world: The GLOBE book of in-depth studies of 25 societies.* Mahwah, NJ: Lawrence Erlbaum.

Child, J. (1974). What determines organizational performance? The universals vs. the it all depends. *Organizational Dynamics,* 3(1), 2–18.

Chin, J. L., & Trimble, J. E. (2015). *Diversity and leadership.* Thousand Oaks, CA: SAGE.

Chin, J. L., Trimble, J. E., & Garcia, J. E. (2018). *Global and culturally diverse leaders and leadership.* Bingley, UK: Emerald Publishing Limited.

China power project. (2019). Center for Strategic and International Studies. Retrieved from https://chinapower.csis.org/china-belt-and-road-initiative/. Accessed on September 14, 2019.

Chira, S., & Milord, B. (2017). "Is there a man I can talk to?": Stories of sexism in the workplace. *The New York Times,* June 20. Retrieved from https://www.nytimes.com/2017/06/20/business/women-react-to-sexism-in-the-workplace.html. Accessed on June 8, 2019.

Chozick, A. (2109). Adam Neumann and the art of failing up. *The New York Times,* November 8. Retrieved from https://www.nytimes.com/2019/11/02/business/adam-neumann-wework-exit-package.html. Accessed on November 14, 2019.

Chrisafis, A. (2015). 'Nothing changed': 10 years after French riots, banlieues remain in crisis. *The Guardian,* October 22. Retrieved from https://www.theguardian.com/world/2015/oct/22/nothings-changed-10-years

-after-french-riots-banlieues-remain-in-crisis. Accessed on August 19, 2019.

Chuang, R. (2003). A postmodern critique of cross-cultural and intercultural communication research: Contesting essentialism, positivist dualism, and eurocentricity. In W. J. Starosta & G.-M. Chen (Eds.), *Ferment in the intercultural field: Axiology/value/praxis* (pp. 24–53). Thousand Oaks, CA: SAGE.

CIA World Factbook—India. (2019). Retrieved from https://www.cia.gov/-library/publications/the-world-factbook/geos/in.html. Accessed on August 20, 2019.

Cilluffo, A., & Cohn, D. (2019). 6 demographic trends shaping the U.S. and the world in 2019. *Pew Research Center-Fact Tank*, April 11. Retrieved from https://www.pewresearch.org/fact-tank/2019/04/11/6-demographic-trends-shaping-the-u-s-and-the-world-in-2019/. Accessed on August 13, 2019.

Civettini, N. H. W. (2007). Similarity and group performance. *Social Psychology Quarterly*, 70(3), 262–271.

Clance, R. R., & Imes, S. A. (1978). The impostor phenomenon in high achieving women: Dynamics and therapeutic intervention. *Psychotherapy: Theory Research and Practice*, 15(3), 241–247. doi: 10.1037/h0086006

Cloninger, R., Svarkic, D., & Prusbeck, T. R. (1993). Psychobiological model of temperament and character. *Archives of General Psychiatry*, 50, 975–990.

Coates, T. N. (2015). There is no post-racial America. *The Atlantic*, July/August. Retrieved from https://www.theatlantic.com/magazine/archive/2015/07/post-racial-society-distant-dream/395255/. Accessed on April 13, 2020.

Cohn, J. (2014). I'm insanely jealous of Sweden's work-family policies. You should be, too. *The New Republic*, June 22. Retrieved from https://newrepublic.com/article/118294/us-should-copy-sweden-and-denmarks-work-family-policies. Accessed on June 11, 2019.

Combs, G. M., & Luthans, F. (2007). Diversity training: Analysis of the impact of self-efficacy. *Human Resource Development Quarterly*, 18(1), 91–120.

Conger, J. A., & Kanungo, R. N. (1998). *Charismatic leadership in organizations*. Thousand Oaks, CA: SAGE.

Cook, A., & Glass, C. (2013). Above the glass ceiling: When are women and racial/ethnic minorities promoted to CEO. *Strategic Management Journal*, 35, 1080–1089.

Corrigan, T. (2019). Ambassador Mandela's chauvisnism makes South Africa look tacky. *News24*, June 19. Retrieved from https://www.news24.com/Columnists/GuestColumn/ambassador-mandelas-chauvinism-makes-south-africa-look-tacky-20190619. Accessed on July 30, 2019.

Cowley, S. (2018). Nike will raise wages for thousands after outcry over inequality. *The New York Times*, July 23. Retrieved from https://www.nytimes.com/2018/07/23/business/nike-wages-raises.html?module=inline. Accessed on June 8, 2019.

Cox, T. H., Jr. (2000). *Creating the multicultural organization: A strategy for capturing the power of diversity*. San Francisco, CA: Jossey-Bass.

Cozma, I. (2011). How are individual and collectivism measured? *Romanian Journal of Applied Psychology*, 13(1), 11–17.

CPI index. (2018). Transparency International. Retrieved from https://www.transparency.org/cpi2018. Accessed on December 4, 2019.

Craig, C. S., & Douglas, S. P. (2006). Beyond national culture: Implications of cultural dynamics for consumer research. *International Marketing Review*, 23, 322–342.

Craig, W. (2018). 10 ways to enhance company innovation in your employees. *Forbes*, November 13. Retrieved from https://www.forbes.com/sites/williamcraig/2018/11/13/10-ways-to-encourage-company-innovation-in-your-employees/#3823e5333a22. Accessed on September 21, 2019.

Crenshaw, K. (1989). Demarginalizing the intersection of race and sex: A black feminist critique of antidiscrimination doctrine, feminist theory and antiracist politics. *University of Chicago Legal Forum*, 1989(1), Article 8. Retrieved from http://chicagounbound.uchicago.edu/uclf/vol1989/iss1/8

Creswell, J., Draper, K., & Abrams, R. (2018). At Nike, revolt led by women leads to exodus of make executives. *The New York Times*, April 28. Retrieved from https://www.nytimes.com/2018/04/28/business/nike-women.html?module=inline. Accessed on June 8, 2019.

C.S-W. (2017). Gender equality on MBA programmes: Slow progress. *The Economist*, December 5.

Retrieved from https://www.eco nomist.com/whichmba/gender-equality-mba-programmes-slow-progress. Accessed on June 4, 2019.

Cuddy, A. (2015). *Presence: Bringing your boldest self to your biggest challenges*, New York, NY: Little, Brown and Company.

Cuddy, A. J. C., Fiske, S. T., & Glick, P. (2004). When professionals become mothers, warmth doesn't cut the ice. *Journal of Social Issues*, 60, 701–718.

Cullinan, R. (2018). In collaborative work cultures, women carry more of the weight. *Harvard Business Review*, July 24. Retrieved from https://hbr.org/2018/07/in-collaborative-work-cultures-women-carry-more-of-the-weight. Accessed on June 2, 2019.

Cyert, R., & March, J. (1963). *A behavioral theory of the firm*. Englewood Cliffs, NJ: Prentice Hall.

Dabbs, J. M., & Dabbs, M. G. (2000). *Heroes, rogues and lovers: On testosterone and behavior*. New York, NY: McGraw-Hill.

Dall, W. H., & Boas, F. (1887). Museums of ethnology and their classification. *Science*, 9(228), 587–589.

Dalton, D., & Ortegren, M. (2011). Gender differences in ethics research: The importance of controlling for the social desirability response bias. *Journal of Business Ethics*, 103(1), 73–93.

Danzinger, P. (2018). 9 demographic trends shaping retail's future. *Forbes*, September 6. Retrieved from https://www.forbes.com/sites/pamdanziger/2018/09/06/9-demographic-trends-shaping-retails-future/#2632d5507b00. Accessed on August 14, 2019.

Das, A. (2019). U.S. women's soccer team sues U.S. Soccer for gender discrimination. *The New York Times*, March 8. Retrieved from https://www.nytimes.com/2019/03/08/sports/womens-soccer-team-lawsuit-gender-discrimination.html. Accessed on June 14, 2019.

Dastagir, A. (2017). Gender stereotypes are destroying girls, and they're killing boys. *USA Today*, September 21. Retrieved from https://www.usatoday.com/story/news/2017/09/21/gender-stereotypes-destroying-girls-and-theyre-killing-boys/688317001/. Accessed on May 31, 2019.

Dastin, J. (2018). Amazon scraps secret AI recruiting tool that showed bias against women. *Reuters*, October 9. Retrieved from https://www.reuters.com/article/us-amazon-com-jobs-automation-insight/amazon-scraps-secret-ai-recruiting-tool-that-showed-bias-against-women-idUSKCN1MK08G. Accessed on August 23, 2019.

Davis, K. M., & Gardner, W. L. (2012). Charisma under crisis revisited: Presidential leadership, perceived leader effectiveness, and contextual influences. *The Leadership Quarterly*, 23, 918–933.

Davis, M. (2018). Can perceived schema expectations affect retrieval accuracy? *Journal of Social and Psychological Sciences*, 11(1), 15–38.

Davis-Young, K. (2019). For many Native Americans, embracing LGBT members is a return to the past. *The Washington Post*, March 29. Retrieved from https://www.washingtonpost.com/national/for-many-native-am ericans-embracing-lgbt-mem bers-is-a-return-to-the-past/2019/03/29/24d1e6c6-4f2c-11e9-88-a1-ed346f0ec94f_story.html. Accessed on April 15, 2020.

Day, J. C. (2019). *Among the educated, women earn 74 cents for every dollar men make*. US Census Bureau. Retrieved from https://www.census.gov/library/stories/2019/05/college-degree-widens-gender-earnings-gap.html. Accessed on September 21, 2020.

De, S., Gelfand, M. J., Nau, D., & Roos, P. (2015). The inevitability of ethnocentrism revisited: Ethnocentrism diminishes as mobility increases. *Nature – Scientific Reports*, 5, Article 17963. Retrieved from https://www.nature.com/articles/srep17963. Accessed on July 27, 2019.

De Brigard, F., Brady, T. F., Ruzic, L., & Schacter, D. L. (2016). Tracking the emergence of memories: A category-learning paradigm to explore schema-driven recognition. *Memory & Cognition*, 45(1), 105–120.

de Janasz, S., & Cabrera, B. (2018). How women can get what they want in negotiation. *Harvard Business Review*, August 17. Retrieved from https://hbr.org/2018/08/how-women-can-get-what-they-want-in-a-negotiation. Accessed on June 11, 2019.

De Pillis, E., Kernochan, R., Meilich, O., Prosser, E., & Whiting, V. (2008). Are managerial gender stereotypes universal? *Cross Cultural Management: An International Journal*, 15, 94–102.

de Tocqueville, A. (2000). *Democracy in America*. Chicago, IL: Univerisity of Chicago Press.

Demby, G. (2015). 'Diversity' is rightly criticized as an empty buzzword. So how can we make it work. *NPR: Code Switch*, November 5. Retrieved from https://www.npr.org/sections/codeswitch/2015/11/05/453187130/diversity-is-rightly-criticized-as-an-empty-buzzword-so-how-can-we-make-it-work. Accessed on April 13, 2020.

DeMers, J. (2018). Amazon's allegedly harsh work culture has made headlines: Here's what you can learn. *Entrepreneur.com*, May 7. Retrieved from https://www.entrepreneur.com/article/312942. Accessed on November 15, 2019.

Demirel, D. (2020). How can the coordination of the processes be achieved in virtual teams?: Implications for virtual organizations. *International Journal of Networking and Virtual Organisations*, 22(3), 301–322.

Den Hartog, D. N., House, R. J., Hanges, P. J., Ruiz-Quintanilla, S. A., & Dorfman, P. W. (1999). Culture-specific and cross-culturally generalizable implicit leadership theories: Are attributes of charismatic/transformation leadership universally endorsed? *Leadership Quarterly*, 10, 219–256.

Deshpandé, R. & Raina, A. (2011). The ordinary heroes of the Taj. *Harvard Business Review*.

Desilver, D. (2018). Women scarce at the top of U.S. business and in the jobs that lead there. *Pew Research Center*, April 30. Retrieved from https://www.pewresearch.org/fact-tank/2018/04/30/women-scarce-at-top-of-u-s-business-and-in-the-jobs-that-lead-there/. Accessed on June 9, 2019.

Devillard, S., de Zelicourt, A., Kossoff, C., & Sancier-Sultan, S. (2017). Reinventing the workplace for greater gender diversity. *McKinsey & Company*, January. Retrieved from https://www.mckinsey.com/featured-insights/gender-equality/reinventing-the-workplace-for-greater-gender-diversity. Accessed on September 2, 2019.

Diab, A. (2016). 5 flexible work strategies and companies that use them. *Fast Company*, March 30. Retrieved from https://www.fastcompany.com/3058344/5-flexible-work-strategies-and-the-companies-who-use-them. Accessed on June 12, 2019.

Digest of education statistics. (2013). National Center for Education Statistics. Retrieved from https://nces.ed.gov/programs/digest/d13/tables/dt13_203.50.asp. Accessed on June 4, 2019.

Digest of education statistics. (2017). National Center for Education Statistics. Retrieved from https://nces.ed.gov/programs/digest/d17/tables/dt17_324.20.asp. Accessed on June 4, 2019.

Dilts, E. (2019). Top U.S. CEOs say companies should put social responsibility above profit. *Reuters*, August 19. Retrieved from https://www.reuters.com/article/us-jp-morgan-business-roundtable/top-u-s-ceos-say-companies-should-put-social-responsibility-above-profit-idUSKCN1V91EK. Accessed on August 29, 2019.

DiMaggio, P. (1997). Culture and cognition. *Annual Review of Sociology*. 23, 263–287. doi: 10.1146/annurev.soc.23.1.263

Dishman. (2017). The hidden gender gap among MBA graduates. *Fast Company*. Retrieved from https://www.fastcompany.com/40447757/the-hidden-gender-gap-among-mba-graduates. Accessed on June 4, 2019.

DiStefano, J. J., & Maznevski, M. L. (2000). Creating value with diversity teams in global management. *Organizational Dynamics*, 29(1), 45–63.

Dobbin, F., & Kalev, A. (2016). Why diversity programs fail. *Harvard Business Review*, July–August. Retrieved from https://hbr.org/2016/07/why-diversity-programs-fail. Accessed on April 13, 2020.

Donaldson, T. (2016). Values in tension: Ethics away from home. In *HBR's 10 must read on managing across cultures* (pp. 85–102). Boston, MA: Harvard Business Review Press.

Donnelly, G. (2018). The number of Black CEOs at Fortune 500 companies is at its lowest since 2002. *Fortune*, February 28. Retrieved from http://fortune.com/2018/02/28/black-history-month-black-ceos-fortune-500/. Accessed on June 9, 2019.

Dorfman, P., Javidan, M., Hanges, P., Dastmalchian, A., & House, R. J. (2012). Globe: A twenty year journey into the intriguing world of culture and leadership. *Journal of World Business*, 47, 504–518.

Dose, J. J. (1997). Work values: An integrative framework and illustrative application to organizational socialization. *Journal of*

Occupational and Organizational Psychology, 70, 219–240.

Dover, T. L., Major, B., & Kaiser, C. R. (2016). Diversity policies rarely make companies fairer, and they feel threatening to white men. *Harvard Business Review*, January 4. Retrieved from https://hbr.org/2016/01/diversity-policies-dont-help-women-or-minorities-and-they-make-white-men-feel-threatened. Accessed on April 13, 2020.

du Plooy, B. (2014). Ubuntu and the recent phenomenon of the charter for compassion. *South African Review of Sociology*, 45(1), 83–100.

Dubner, S. J. (2018). Extra: Carol Bartz full interview. *Freakonomics*, ep. 327. Retrieved from http://freakonomics.com/podcast/carol-bartz/. Accessed on June 10, 2019.

Dujarric, R. (2015). Behind Japanese parochialism. *The Japan Times*, November 17. Retrieved from https://www.japantimes.co.jp/opinion/2015/11/17/commentary/japan-commentary/behind-japanese-parochialism/#.XT-ecfZKglI. Accessed on July 29, 2019.

Dumont, M. (2019). 4 biggest merger and acquisition disasters. *Investopia*, June 25. Retrieved from https://www.investopedia.com/articles/financial-theory/08/merger-acquisition-disasters.asp. Accessed on November 15, 2019.

Dumphy, S. M. (2004). Demonstrating the value of diversity for improved decision making: The "wuzzle-puzzle" exercise. *Journal of Business Ethics*, 53, 325–331.

Duncan, P., & Holder, J. (2017). Revealed: Britain's most powerful elite is 97% white. *The Guardian*, September 24. Retrieved from https://en.wikipedia.org/wiki/History_of_colonialism#cite_note-67. Accessed on August 15, 2019.

Duncan, R. B. (1972). Characteristics of organizational environments and perceived environmental uncertainty. *Administrative Science Quarterly*, 17(3), 313–327.

Dunlop, W. L., & Beauchamp, M. R. (2011). Does similarity make a difference? Predicting cohesion and attendance behaviors within exercise group settings. *Group Dynamics: Theory, Research, and Practice*, 15(3), 258–266.

Dunn, M. W., Dastoor, B., & Sims, R. L. (2012). Transformational leadership and organizational commitment: A cross-cultural perspective. *Journal of Multidisciplinary Research*, 4(1), 45–59.

Durkheim, E. (1893–1984). *The division of labor in society*. New York, NY: Free Press.

Dutt, K., Pfaff, D. L., Bernstein, A. F., Dillard, J. S., & Block, C. J. (2016). Gender differences in recommendation letters for postdoctoral fellowships in geoscience. *Nature Geoscience*, 9, 805–808.

Dweck, C. M. (2016). *Mindset: The new psychology of success*. New York, NY: Ballantine Books.

Dyble, M., Salali, G. D., Chaudhary, N., Page, A., Smith, D., Thompson, J., … Migliano, A. B. (2015). Sex equality can explain the unique social structure of hunter-gatherer bands. *Science*, 348(6237), 796–798.

Eagly, A. H., & Chin, J. L. (2010). Diversity and leadership in a changing world. *American Psychologist*, 65(3), 216–224.

Eagly, A. H., Johannesen-Schmidt, M. C., & van Engen, M. L. (2003). Transformational, transactional, and laissez-faire leadership styles: A meta-analysis comparing women and men. *Psychological Bulletin*, 129, 569–591.

Eagly, A. H., & Karau, S. J. (2002). Role congruity theory of prejudice toward female leaders. *Psychological Review*, 109, 573–598. doi:10.1037/0033-295X.109.3.573

Eagly, A. H., Karau, S. J., & Makhijani, M. (1995). Gender and the effectiveness of leaders: A meta-analysis. *Psychological Bulletin*, 117, 125–145.

Eagly, A. H., & Steffen, V. J. (1986). Gender and aggressive behavior: A meta-analytic review of the social psychological literature. *Psychological Bulletin*, 100, 309–330.

Earley, P. C., & Ang, S. (2003). *Cultural intelligence: Individual interactions across cultures*. Palo Alto, CA: Stanford University Press.

Earley, P. C., & Mosakowski, E. (2016). Cultural intelligence. In *HBR's 10 must read on managing across cultures* (pp. 1–16). Boston, MA: Harvard Business Review Press.

Eberhardt, J. L., Dasgupta, N. & Banaszynski, T. L. (2003). Believing is seeing: The effects of racial labels and implicit beliefs on face perception. *Personality and Social Psychology Bulletin*, 29, 360–370.

Eckert, P., & McConnell-Ginet, S. (2003). *Language and gender*. Cambridge, UK: Cambridge University Press.

Educational attainment in the United States. (2017). United

States Census Bureau. Retrieved from https://www.census.gov/data/tables/2017/demo/education-attainment/cps-detailed-tables.html. Accessed on June 4, 2019.

EEOC. (2019). EEOC releases fiscal year 2018 enforcement and litigation data [Press release]. U.S. Equal Employment Opportunity Commission, April 10. Retrieved from https://www.eeoc.gov/eeoc/newsroom/release/4-10-19.cfm. Accessed on August 29, 2019.

Eisenbeiss, S. A., van Knippenberg, D., & Boerner, S. (2008). Transformational leadership and team innovation: Integrating team climate principles. *Journal of Applied Psychology*, 93(6), 1438–1446.

ELI, Inc. (2020). How to avoid a "diversity backlash" at your company. *ELI*, February 7. Retrieved from https://www.eliinc.com/how-to-avoid-a-diversity-backlash-at-your-company/. Accessed on April 12, 2020.

Eligon, J. (2018). Hate crimes increase for the third consecutive year, FBI reports. *The New York Times*, November 13. Retrieved from https://www.nytimes.com/2018/11/13/us/hate-crimes-fbi-2017.html. Accessed on August 16, 2019.

Elkington, R., & Tuleja, E. A. (2018). How the communal philosophies of Ubuntu in Africa and Confucius thought in China might enrich Western notions of leadership. In J. L. Chin, J. E. Trimble, & J. E. Garcia (Eds.), *Global and culturally diverse leaders and leadership: New dimensions,* opportunities, and challenges for business, industry, education and society. A Volume in the ILA Building Leadership Bridges (BLB) Series (pp. 63–81). Bingley, UK: Emerald Publishing Limited.

Elkins, T. H., & Bisson, T. N. (2019). France. *Encyclopaedia Britannica*, August 14. Retrieved from https://www.britannica.com/place/France/Population-structure. Accessed on August 16, 2019.

Ellemers, N. (2018). Gender stereotypes. *Annual Review of Psychology*, 69, 275–298. doi: 10.1146/annurev-psych-122216-011719

Ellevest Team. (2018). Ellevest launches 2018 money census. *Ellevest*, January 17. Retrieved from https://www.ellevest.com/magazine/news/ellevest-launches-2018-money-census-report. Accessed on June 7, 2019.

Employment. (2020). Employment contracts & policies. *DLA Piper*. Retrieved from https://www.dlapiperintelligence.com/goingglobal/employment/index.html?t=06-employment-contracts. Accessed on April 24, 2020.

England, G. W., & Harpaz, I. (1990). How working is defined: National context and demographic organizational role influences. *Journal of Organizational Behavior*, 11, 253–266.

Eriksson, T., Mao, L., & Villeval, M. C. (2017). Saving face and group identity. *Experimental Economics*, 20(3), 622–647. doi: 10.1007/s10683-016-9502-3

Esser, J. K. (1998). Alive and well after 25 years: A review of groupthink research. *Organizational Behavior and Human Decision Processes*, 73(2/3), 116–141.

Estow, S., Jamieson, J. P., & Yates, J. R. (2007). Self-monitoring and mimicry of positive and negative social behaviors. *Journal of Research in Personality*, 41, 425–433.

Fabregat, E., & Kperogi, F. A. (2019). White norm, black deviation: Class, race and resistance in America's 'post-racial' media discourse. *Howard Journal of Communication*, 30(3), 265–283.

Facts over time – Women in the labor force. (2017). Women's Bureau-United States Department of Labor. Retrieved from https://www.dol.gov/wb/stats/NEWSTATS/facts/women_lf.htm#CivilianLFSex. Accessed on June 4, 2019.

Fajardo, S. (2017). Why Toronto is the most multicultural city in the world. *Narcity*. Retrieved from https://www.narcity.com/ca/on/toronto/lifestyle/why-toronto-is-the-most-multicultural-city-in-the-world. Accessed on August 5, 2019.

Fanon, F. (1952). *Black skin, white masks*. New York, NY: Grove Press.

Fantini, A., & Tirmizi, A. (2006). *Exploring and assessing intercultural competence* (Paper 1). World Learning Publications. Retrieved from http://digitalcollections.sit.edu/worldlearning_publications/1

Farber, M. (2017). 3 reason why the gender pay gap still exists. *Fortune*, April 3. Retrieved from http://fortune.com/2017/04/03/equal-pay-day-2017-wage-gap/. Accessed on June 7, 2019.

Farley, R. (2018). Detroit fifty years after the Kerner report: What has changed, what has not, and why. *The Russel Sage Foundation Journal of Social Sciences*, 4(6), 206–241.

Faupel, A., Scheuerman, H. L., Parris, C. L., & Werum, R. (2019). Hate crimes are on the rise. *The Washington Post*, August 13. Retrieved from https://www.washingtonpost.com/politics/2019/08/13/hate-crimes-are-rise-what-does-it-take-get-state-governments-respond/?noredirect=on. Accessed on August 16, 2019.

Feldman, M. W., Lewontin, R. C., & King, M. C. (2003). Race: A genetic melting-pot. *Nature*, 424, 374. doi:10.1038/424374a

Feng, J. B., Liu, L. A., & Jians, C. (2019). Parochialism and implications for Chinese firm's globalization. *Management and Organization Review*, 15, 705–736. doi:10.1017/mor.2019.12

Fenson, Z. (2020). Women's invisible labor is keeping America going. *The Week*, April 8. Retrieved from https://theweek.com/articles/907054/womens-invisible-labor-keeping-america-going. Accessed on April 17, 2020.

Fenwick, G. D., & Neal, D. J. (2002). Effect of gender composition on group performance. *Gender, Work, & Organization*, 8(2), 205–225.

Fernando, M. (2011). Spirituality and leadership. In A. Bryman, D. Collinson, K. Grint, B. Jackson, & M. Uhl-Bien (Eds.), *SAGE handbook of leadership* (pp. 483–494). Thousand Oaks, CA: SAGE.

Ferrazzi, K. (2014). Getting virtual teams right. *Harvard Business Review*, December. Retrieved from https://hbr.org/2014/12/getting-virtual-teams-right. Accessed on May 4, 2020.

Ferrel, J. (2014). Richard Branson: Foster diversity not division. *Live Mint*, March 3. Retrieved from https://www.livemint.com/Opinion/HIVNbMGl3oJuyVh174F1FI/Richard-Branson–Foster-diversity-not-division.html. Accessed on August 11, 2019.

Fessler, D. M. T., Barrett, H. C., Kanovsky, M., Stich, S., Holbrook, C., … Laurence, S. (2015). Moral parochialism and contextual contingency across seven societies. *Proceedings Royal Society B*, 282, 20150907. doi:10.1098/rspb.2015.0907

Fiedler, F. E. (1967). *A theory of leadership effectiveness*. New York, NY: McGraw-Hill.

Fiedler, F. E., & Chemers, M. M. (1974). *Leadership and effective management*. Glenview, IL: Scott Foresman.

Fine, C. (2013). Neurosexism in functional neuroimaging: From scanner to pseudo-science to psyche. In M. K. Ryan & N. R. Branscombe (Eds.), *The SAGE handbook of gender and psychology* (pp. 45–60). Thousand Oaks, CA: SAGE.

Finkelstein, S., & Hambrick, D. C. (1996). *Strategic leadership: Top executives and their effects on organizations*. Minneapolis, MN: West.

Fisher, M. (2013). These are the best and worst countries to be elderly. *The Washington Post*, October 3. Retrieved from https://www.washingtonpost.com/news/worldviews/wp/2013/10/03/these-are-the-best-and-worst-countries-to-be-elderly/?utm_term=.d3e4a8a63305. Accessed on June 11, 2019.

Fisher, R., & Ury, W. (2011). *Getting to yes: Negotiating agreement without giving in*. New York, NY: Penguin Books.

Fishman, C. (2004). The anarchist's cookbook. *Fast Company*, July, pp. 70–78. Retrieved from https://www.fastcompany.com/50426/anarchists-cookbook. Accessed on November 16, 2019.

Fiske, S. T., & Taylor, S. E. (2017). *Social cognition: From brains to culture*. Thousand Oaks, CA: SAGE.

Fitzsimmons, S. R. (2013). Multicultural employees: A framework for understanding how they contribute to organizations. *Academy of Management Review*, 38(4), 525–549.

Fixmer-Oraiz, N., & Wood, J. T. (2019). *Gendered lives: Communication, gender, and culture* (13th ed.). Boston, MA: Cengage Learning.

Flavell, J. H. (1985). *Cognitive development*. Englewood Cliffs, NJ: Prentice Hall.

Fleishman, E. A. (1953). The measurement of leadership attitudes in industry. *Journal of Applied Psychology*, 37, 153–158.

Flitter, E. (2019). This is what racism sounds like in the banking industry. *The New York Times*, December 11. Retrieved from https://www.nytimes.com/2019/12/11/business/jpmorgan-banking-racism.html. Accessed on January 29, 2020.

Folbre, N. (2012). Should women care less? Intrinsic motivation and gender inequality. *BJIR: An International Journal of Employee Relations*, 50(4), 597–619. doi:10.1111/bjir.12000

Fondrevay, J. (2018). After a merger, don't let "us vs. them" thinking ruin the company. *Harvard Business Review*, May 21. Retrieved from https://hbr.org/2018/05/after-a-merger-dont-let-us-vs-them-thinking-ruin-the-company. Accessed on July 27, 2019.

Forbes Coaches Council. (2016). Nine ways managers can support multicultural teams. *Forbes*, June 3. Retrieved from https://www.forbes.com/sites/forbescoachescouncil/2016/06/03/nine-ways-managers-can-best-support-multicultural-teams/#76d3f28a2e67. Accessed on November 7, 2019.

Foronda, C., Baptiste, D.-L., Reinholdt, M. M., & Ousman, K. (2016). Cultural humility: A concept analysis. *Journal of Transcultural Nursing*, 27(3), 210–217.

Fortune Editors. (2013). The 50 greatest business rivalries of all time. *Fortune*, March 21. Retrieved from https://fortune.com/2013/03/21/the-50-greatest-business-rivalries-of-all-time/. Accessed on July 28, 2019.

Fotsch, B., & Case, J. (2016). The sad legacy of us vs. them. *Forbes*, September 6. Retrieved from https://www.forbes.com/sites/fotschcase/2016/09/06/the-sad-legacy-of-us-vs-them/#123d1e134b35. Accessed on July 27, 2019.

Fredricks, S. M., Tilley, E., & Pauknerova, D. (2014). Limited gender differences in ethical decision making between demographics in the USA and New Zealand. *Gender in Management: An International Journal*, 29(3), 126–147.

Freedman, S. (2008). Combating confusion: Virtual teams that cross borders. In J. Nemiro, M. Beyerlein, L. Bradley, & S. Beyerlein (Eds.), *The handbook of high-performance virtual teams* (pp. 367–390). San Francisco, CA: Jossey-Bass.

French, R. P., II. (2017). The fuzziness of mindsets: Divergent conceptualizations and characterizations of mindset theory and praxis. *International Journal of Organizational Analysis*, 24(4), 673–691. doi: 10.1108/IJOA-09-2014-0797

Friedman, U. (2018). Trust is collapsing in America. *The Atlantic*, January 21. Retrieved from https://www.theatlantic.com/international/archive/2018/01/trust-trump-america-world/550964/. Accessed on September 10, 2019.

Frisch, B., & Greene, C. (2020). What it takes to run a great virtual meeting. *Harvard Business Review*, March 6. Retrieved from https://hbr.org/2020/03/what-it-takes-to-run-a-great-virtual-meeting. Accessed on May 4, 2020.

Froese, F. J. (2013). Work values of the next generation of business leaders in Shanghai, Tokyo, and Seoul. *Asia Pacific Journal of Management*, 30(1), 297–315.

Frontiera, J. & Leidl, D. (2012). *Team turnarounds: A playbook for transforming underperforming teams*. San Francisco, CA: Wiley.

Frum, D. (2018). Competing visions of Islam will shape Europe in the 21st century. *The Atlantic*, May 2. Retrieved from https://www.theatlantic.com/international/archive/2018/05/akbar-ahmed-islam-europe/559391/. Accessed on August 20, 2019.

Fry, L. W. (2003). Toward a theory of spiritual leadership. *The Leadership Quarterly*, 14, 693–727.

Fry, L. & Cohen, M.P. (2009). Spiritual leadership as a paradigm for organizational transformation and recovery from extended work hours cultures. *Journal of Business Ethics*, 84(2), 265–278.

Fu, A. S. & Markus, H. R. (2014). My mother and me: Why tiger mothers motivate Asian Americans but not European Americans. *Personality and Social Psychology Bulletin*, 40(8), 739–749.

Fuegen, K., Biernat, M., Haines, E., & Deaux, K. (2004). Mothers and fathers in the workplace: How gender and parental status influences judgement of job-related competence. *Journal of Social Issues*, 60(4), 737–754.

Fukuyama, F. (2020). The thing that determines a country's resistance to the coronavirus. *The Atlantic*, March 30. Retrieved from https://www.theatlantic.com/ideas/archive/2020/03/thing-determines-how-well-countries-respond-coronavirus/609025/. Accessed on April 24, 2020.

Fusaro, K. (2009). 10 etiquette rules for a happy hostess. *Women's Day*, June 23. Retrieved from https://www.womansday.com/relationships/family-friends/advice/a3929/10-etiquette-rules-for-a-happy-hostess-78711/. Accessed on August 6, 2019.

Galinsky, A. (2017). What drives us to speak up? *NPR: TED Radio Hour*, April 7. Retrieved from https://www.npr.org/templates/transcript/transcript.php?storyId=522857511. Accessed on June 10, 2019.

Galinsky, A. (2018). *Are gender differences just power differences in disguise? Ideas and Insights – Columbia Business School*, March 13. Retrieved from https://www8.gsb.columbia.edu/articles/ideas-work/are-gender-differences-just-power-differences-disguise. Accessed on June 10, 2019.

Galton, R. (1869). *Hereditary genius*. New York, NY: Appleton.

Galston, W. A. (2018). *Anti pluralism: The populist threat to liberal democracy*. New Haven, CT: Yale University Press.

Garcia, F., Mendez, D., Ellis, C., & Gautney, C. (2014). Cross-cultural values and ethics differences and similarities between the US and Asian countries. *Journal of Technology Management in China*, 9(3), 303–322.

Gardner, W. L., Coglier, G. C., Davis, K. M., & Dickens, M. P. (2011). Authentic leadership: A review of the literature and research agenda. *The Leadership Quarterly*, 22, 1120–1145.

Garg, P., & Rastogi, R. (2006). New model of job design: Motivation employees' performance. *Journal of Management Development*, 25(6), 572–587.

Geertz, C. (1973). *The interpretation of cultures* (p. 44). New York, NY: Harper Collins/Basic Books.

Gelfand, M. J. (2018). *Rule maker, rule breakers: How tight and loose cultures wire our world*. New York, NY: Scribner.

Gelfand, M. J., Gordon, S., Li, C., Choi, V., & Prokopowicz, P. (2018). One reason mergers fail: The two cultures aren't compatible. *Harvard Business Review*, October 2. Retrieved from https://hbr.org/2018/10/one-reason-mergers-fail-the-two-cultures-arent-compatible. Accessed on September 25, 2019.

Gelfand, M. J., Leslie, L. M., & Fehr, R. (2008). To prosper organizational psychology should ... adopt a global perspective. *Journal of Organizational Behavior*, 29, 493–517.

Gelfand, M. J., Raver, J. L., Nishii, L. H., Leslie, L. M., Lun, J., Lim, B. C., … Yamaguchi, S. (2011). *Differences between tight and loose cultures: A 33 nation study*. Ithaca, NY: Cornell University, ILR. Retrieved from https://digitalcommons.ilr.cornell.edu/articles/1287

Gentile, M. C. (2016). Talking ethics across cultures. *Harvard Business Review*, December 23. Retrieved from https://hbr.org/2016/12/talking-about-ethics-across-cultures. Accessed on December 5, 2019.

Gerhart, B. (2008). Cross cultural management research: Assumptions, evidence, and suggested directions. *International Journal of Cross-Cultural Management*, 8, 259–274.

Gezen, L., & Kottak, C. (2014). *Culture* (2nd ed.). New York, NY: McGraw-Hill.

Gigerenzer, G., & Gaissmaier, W. (2011). Heuristic decision making. *Annual Review of Psychology*, 62, 451–482. doi:10.1146/annurev-psych-120709-145346

Gino, F., & Wood Brooks, A. (2015). Explaining gender differences at the top. *Harvard Business Review*, September 23. Retrieved from https://hbr.org/2015/09/explaining-gender-differences-at-the-top. Accessed on June 2, 2019.

GLAAAD. (2020). GLAAD media reference guide – Transgender. Retrieved from https://www.glaad.org/reference/transgender. Accessed on August 2, 2020.

Glaman, J. M., Jones, A. P., & Rozelle, R. M. (1996). The effects of co-worker similarity on the emergence of affect in work teams. *Group and Organizational Studies*, 21(2), 192.

Glick, P., Fiske, S. T., Mladinic, A., Saiz, J., Abrams, D., Masser, B., … Lopez, W. L. (2000). Beyond prejudice as simple antipathy: Hostile and benevolent sexism across cultures. *Journal of Personality and Social Psychology*, 79(5), 763–775. doi:10.1037/0022-3514.79.5.763

Glikson, E., & Erez, M. (in press). The emergence of a communication climate in global virtual teams. *Journal of World Business*. Retrieved from https://reader.elsevier.com/reader/sd/pii/S1090951617308787?token=D846009A2674E173066C00428129DD4A2959CC07A477342539C6BE47836FACBD40948A65BF15D5F42FF3F679E7305876. Accessed on November 7, 2019.

Global diversity and inclusion: Fostering innovation through a diverse workforce. (2011). *Forbes*. Retrieved from https://i.forbesimg.com/forbesinsights/StudyPDFs/Innovation_Through_Diversity.pdf. Accessed on August 2, 2020.

Global gender gap report. (2018). Retrieved from http://www3.weforum.org/docs/WEF_GGGR_2018.pdf. Accessed on August 18, 2019.

Go Deeper. (2003). Race: The power of an illusion. *PBS*. Retrieved from https://www.pbs.org/race/000_About/002_03_

d-godeeper.htm. Accessed on August 16, 2019.

Goldin, C., & Katz, L. F. (2002). The power of the pill: Oral contraceptives and women's career and marriage decisions. *DASH – Digital Access to Scholarship at Harvard*. Retrieved from https://dash.harvard.edu/bitstream/handle/1/2624453/Goldin_PowerPill.pdf?sequence=4_1. Accessed on August 2, 2020.

Golden, J. (2018). Nike accused of fostering hostile workplace in new gender discrimination lawsuit. *CNBC*, August 11. Retrieved from https://www.cnbc.com/2018/08/10/ex-nike-employees-sue-over-gender-discrimination-hostile-workplace.html. Accessed on June 8, 2019.

Goldin, C. (2014). A grand gender convergence: Its last chapter. *American Economic Review*, 104(4), 1091–1119. Retrieved from http://scholar.harvard.edu/files/goldin/files/goldin_aeapress_2014_1.pdf

Gollwitzer, P. M. (1990). Action phases and mind-sets. In T. E. Higgins & R. M. Sorrentino (Eds.), *Handbook of motivation and cognition: Foundations of social behavior* (Vol. 2, pp. 53–92). New York, NY: Gilford Press.

Gollwitzer, P. M. (2012). Mindset theory of action phases. In P. A. M. Van Lange, A. W. Kruglanski, & E. T. Higgins (Eds.), *Handbook of theories of social psychology* (Vol. 1, pp. 526–545). Thousand Oaks, CA: SAGE. Retrieved from http://kops.uni-konstanz.de/bitstream/handle/123456789/17990/gollwitzer_mindset_theory.pdf?sequence=1&isAllowed=y

Gollwitzer, P. M., & Bayer, U. C. (1999). Deliberative versus implemental mindsets in the control of action. In S. Chaiken & Y. Trope (Eds.), *Dual-process theories in social psychology* (pp. 403–422). New York, NY: Guilford Press.

Golshan, T. (2019). How the US women's soccer team 13-0 World Cup win against Thailand became about pay equity. *Vox*, June 11. Retrieved from https://www.vox.com/culture/2019/6/11/18661914/women-soccer-team-world-cup-win-thail and-pay-gap. Accessed on June 14, 2019.

Gompers, P., & Kovvali, S. (2018). The other diversity dividend. *Harvard Business Review*, July–August. Retrieved from https://hbr.org/2018/07/the-other-diversity-dividend. Accessed on August 21, 2019.

Goncalo, J. A., & Staw, B. M. (2006). Individualism-collectivism and group creativity. *Organizational Behavior and Human Decision Processes*, 100(1), 96–109.

Gonzàles, M. J., & Cortina, C. (2019). Do women have fewer opportunities to be hired? *Social Observatory of "La Caixa"*. Retrieved from https://observatoriosociallacaixa.org/en/-/mujeres-oportunidades-contratadas. Accessed on August 2, 2020.

Gosling, J., & Mintzberg, H. (2003). The five minds of a manager. *Harvard Business Review*, 81(11), 54–63. Retrieved from https://hbr.org/2003/11/the-five-minds-of-a-manager. Accessed on October 14, 2019.

Govindarajan, V. (2012). Profitable audacity: One company's success story. *Harvard Business Review*, January 25. Retrieved from https://hbr.org/2012/01/profitable-audacity-one-companys-success-story. Accessed on October 14, 2019.

Govindarajan, V., & Terwilliger, J. (2012). Yes, you can brainstorm without groupthink. *Harvard Business Review*, June 25. Retrieved from https://hbr.org/2012/07/yes-you-can-brainstorm-without. Accessed on September 25, 2020.

Graebner, M. E., Heimeriks, K. H., Nguyen, Q., & Vaara, E. (2016). The process of post-merger integration: A review and agenda for future research. *Academy of Management Annals*, 11(1), 1–32.

Graen, G. B. (2006). In the eye of the beholder: Cross-cultural lesson in leadership from project GLOBE: A response viewed from the third culture bonding (TCB) model of cross-cultural leadership. *The Academy of Management Perspective*, 20(4), 95–101.

Graen, G. B., & Uhl-Bien, M. (1995). Relationship-based approach to leadership: Development of the leader-member exchange (LMX) theory of leadership over 25 years: Applying a multi-level multi-domain perspective. *The Leadership Quarterly*, 6, 219–247.

Graf, N. (2018). Sexual harassment at work in the era of #MeToo. *Pew Research Center*, April 4. Retrieved from https://www.pewsocialtrends.org/2018/04/04/sexual-harassment-at-work-in-the-era-of-metoo/. Accessed on June 8, 2019.

Gramlich, J. (2019). Young Americans are less trusting of other people – and key institutions – than their elders. *Pew Research Center*, August 6. Retrieved from https://www.pewresearch.org/fact-tank/2019/08/06/young-americans-are-less-trusting-of-other-people-and-key-institutions-than-their-elders/. Accessed on September 10, 2019.

Grant, A. (2013). Goodbye to MBTI, the fat that won't die. *LinkedIn*, September 17. Retrieved from https://www.linkedin.com/pulse/20130917155206-69244073-say-goodbye-to-mbti-the-fad-that-won-t-die. Accessed on December 5, 2019.

Graves, L. (2014). Who will take care of the elderly? *The Atlantic*, September 12. Retrieved from https://www.theatlantic.com/business/archive/2014/09/who-will-take-care-of-americas-elderly/380147/. Accessed on June 8, 2019.

Gray, D. D. (2011). Cambodia's king a 'prisoner' in his palace. *Asia-Pacific – NBC News*, May 29. Retrieved from http://www.nbcnews.com/id/43209362/ns/world_news-asia_pacific/t/cambodias-king-prisoner-his-palace/#.XZ9ya_ZKhuU. Accessed on October 10, 2019.

Gray, J. (2004). *Men are from Mars, women are from Venus*. New York, NY: HarperCollins.

Greenfield, R. (2016). How to make flexible work schedules a reality. *Bloomberg Business*, January 21. Retrieved from https://www.bloomberg.com/news/articles/2016-01-21/how-to-make-flexible-work-schedules-a-reality. Accessed on June 12, 2019.

Greenleaf, R. K. (1998). *The power of servant leadership*. San Francisco, CA: Berrett-Koehler.

Grosz, E. (1995). *Space, time and perversion: Essay on the politics of bodies*. New York, NY: Routledge.

Grunewald, M. (2014). Why more employees are considering leaving their companies. *LinkedIn – Talent Blog*, March 18. Retrieved from https://business.linkedin.com/talent-solutions/blog/2014/03/internal-mobility-exit-survey. Accessed on December 11, 2019.

Guan, Y., Chen, S. X., Levin, N., Bond, M. H., Luo, N., Xu, J., … Xue, H. (2015). Differences in career decision-making profiles between American and Chinese university students: The relative strength of mediating mechanisms across cultures. *Journal of Cross-Cultural Psychology*, 46, 856–872.

Gudykunst, W. B. (2009). Uncertainty reduction and predictability of behavior in low- and high-context cultures: An exploratory study. *Communication Quarterly*, 31(1), 49–55. doi:10.1080/01463378309369485

Gunkel, M., Schlaegel, C., & Taras, V. (2016). Cultural values, emotional intelligence, and conflict handling styles: A global study. *Journal of World Business*, 51(4), 568–585.

Guo, C., & Miller, J. K. (2010). *Guanxi* dynamics and entrepreneurial firm creation and development in China. *Management and Organization Review*, 6(2), 267–291.

Gupta, A. K., & Govindarajan, V. (2002). Cultivating a global mindset. *Academy of Management Executive*, 16(1), 116–126. doi:10.5465/ame.2002.6640211

Guzman, Z. (2018). This chart shows how far behind America is in paid time off compared to the rest of the world. *CNBC Make It*, August 15. Retrieved from https://www.cnbc.com/2018/08/15/statista-how-far-behind-us-is-in-paid-time-off-compared-to-the-world.html. Accessed on April 24, 2020.

Hackett, C., Conner, P., & Stonawski, M. (2017). Europe's growing Muslim population. *Pew Research Center*, November 29. Retrieved from https://www.pewforum.org/2017/11/29/europes-growing-muslim-population/. Accessed on August 20, 2019.

Hackman, J. R., Oldham, R. G., & Suttle, J. L. (1997). *Improving life at work: Behavioral science approaches to organizational change*. Santa Monica, CA: Goodyear.

Hahn, M., & Molinsky, A. (2018). How to recover from a cultural faux pas. *Harvard Business Review*, April 12. Retrieved from https://hbr.org/2018/04/how-to-recover-from-a-cultural-faux-pas. Accessed on November 7, 2019.

Haken, B. T. (2018). How to move people past an "us versus them" mindset at work. *Talent Culture*, February 15. Retrieved from https://talentculture.com/how-to-move-people-past-an-us-versus-them-mindset-at-work/. Accessed on July 27, 2019.

Halevy, N., Bornstein, G., & Sagiv, L. (2008). "In-group love" and "out-group hate" as motives for individual participation in intergroup conflict: A new game paradigm. *Psychological Science*, 19(4), 405–411.

Hall, E. T. (1976). *Beyond culture.* Garden City, NY: Anchor Press/Doubleday.

Hall, E. T. (1992). *An anthropology of everyday life.* New York, NY: Doubleday.

Halpin, A. W., & Winer, B. J. (1957). A factorial study of the leader behavior descriptions. In R. M. Stogdill & A. E. Coons (Eds.), *Leader behavior: Its description and measurement.* Columbus: The Ohio State University, Bureau of Business Research

Hambrick, D. C., Cho, T. S., & Chen, M. (1996). The influence of top management team heterogeneity on firms' competitive moves. *Administrative Science Quarterly*, 41, 659–684.

Hammet, G. (2018). 3 steps Ray Dalio uses radical transparency to build a billion-dollar company. *Inc*, May 23. Retrieved from https://www.inc.com/gene-hammett/3-steps-ray-dalio-uses-radical-transparency-to-build-a-billion-dollar-company.html. Accessed on June 12, 2019.

Hammond, R. A., & Axelrod, R. (2006). The evolution of ethnocentrism. *Journal of Conflict Resolution*, 50(6), 926–936. doi:10.1177/0022002706293470

Hannah-Jones, N. (2016). The end of the postracial myth. *The New York Times*, November 15. Retrieved from https://www.nytimes.com/interactive/2016/11/20/magazine/donald-trumps-america-iowa-race.html. Accessed on April 13, 2020.

Harnois, C. E., & Bastos, J. L. (2018). Discrimination, harassment and gendered health inequalities: Do perceptions of workplace mistreatment contribute to the gender gap in self-reported health? *Journal of Health and Social Behavior*, 59(2), 283–299.

Harrington, J. (2019). Wouldn't you like 30 mandated days off? Here are the countries with the most vacation days. *USA Today*, July 23. Retrieved from https://www.usatoday.com/story/money/2019/07/23/paid-time-off-countries-with-the-most-vacation-days-brazil-france/39702323/. Accessed on April 24, 2020.

Harrington, J. R., & Gelfand, M. J. (2014). Tightness-looseness across the 50 United States. *Proceedings of the National Academy of Sciences – PNAS*, 111(22), 7990–7995. doi:10.1073/pnas.1317937111

Harrison, D., & Oh, S. (2019). Women working longer hours, sleeping less, as they juggle commitments. *The Wall Street Journal*, June 19. Retrieved from https://www.wsj.com/articles/women-working-longer-hours-sleeping-less-labor-department-finds-11560980344. Accessed on January 29, 2020.

Harrison, J. K., Chadwick, M., & Scales, M. (1996). The relationship between cross-cultural adjustment and the personality variables of self-efficacy and self-monitoring. *International Journal of Intercultural Relations*, 20(2), 167–188. doi:10.1016/0147-1767(95)00039-9

Hart, A. (2017). Goodbye Hygge, hello Langom: The secret of Swedish contentment. *The Telegraph*, January 16. Retrieved from https://www.telegraph.co.uk/health-fitness/mind/goodbye-hygge-hello-lagom-secret-swedish-contentment/. Accessed on April 6, 2020.

Hart, W. B. (1999). Interdisciplinary influences in the study of intercultural relations: A citation analysis of the *International Journal of Intercultural Relations*. *International Journal of Intercultural Relations*, 23, 575–589.

Hartocollis, A. (2019). Harvard won a key affirmative action battle. But the war's not over. *The New York Times*, October 2. Retrieved from https://www.nytimes.com/2019/10/02/us/harvard-admissions-lawsuit.html. Accessed on August 2, 2020.

Harwood, G. G. (2008). Design principles for successful virtual teams. In J. Nemiro, M. Beyerlein, L. Bradely, & S. Beyerlein (Eds.), *The handbook of high-performance virtual teams: A toolkit for collaborating across boundaries* (pp. 59–83). San Francisco, CA: Jossey-Bass. Retrieved from http://citeseerx.ist.psu.edu/viewdoc/download?doi=10.1.1.470.3868&rep=rep1&type=pdf. Accessed on November 5, 2019.

Hazareesingh, S. (2015). *Think: An affectionate portrait of an intellectual people.* New York, NY: Basic Books.

Headland, T. N., Pike, K. L., & Harris, M. (1990). *Emics and etics: The insider/outsider debate.* Thousand Oaks, CA: SAGE.

Heider, F. (1958). *The psychology of interpersonal relations.* New York, NY: Wiley.

Hekman, D. R., Johnson, S. K., Foo, M., & Yang, W. (2007). Does diversity-valuing behavior result in diminished performance ratings for non-White and female leaders? *Academy of Management Journal*, 60(2), 771–797.

Hemphill, J. K., & Coons, A. E. (1957). Development of the leader behavior description questionnaire. In R. M. Stogdill, & A. E. Coons (Eds.), *Leader behavior: Its description and measurement*. Columbus, OH: The Ohio State University, Bureau of Business Research.

Henderson, J. K. (2005). Language diversity in international management teams. *International Studies of Management and Organization*, 35, 66–82.

Henrich, J., Heine, S. J., & Norenzayan, A. (2010). Most people are not WEIRD. *Nature*, 466, 29.

Herrera, J. I. (2015). The challenge of cultural diversity in Mexico through the official recognition of legal pluralism. *The Age of Human Rights Journal*, 4, 60–80.

Herskovits, M. (1948). *Man and his works: The science of cultural anthropology*. New York, NY: Alfred A. Knopf.

Herzberg, F. (2003). One more time: How do you motivate employees? *Harvard Business Review*, January. Retrieved from https://hbr.org/2003/01/one-more-time-how-do-you-motivate-employees. Accessed on October 31, 2019.

Hickson, D. J., & Pugh, D. S. (1995). *Management worldwide: The impact of society culture on organizations around the globe*. London, UK: Penguin Books.

Higgins, E. T., King, G. A., & Mavin, G. H. (1982). Individual construct accessibility and subjective impressions and recall. *Journal of Personality and Social Psychology*, 84, 1140–1153.

Hill, J. (2019). They gave America 13 goals – And got a lecture in return. *The Atlantic*, June 13. Retrieved from https://www.theatlantic.com/ideas/archive/2019/06/the-us-womens-soccer-team-deserves-to-celebrate/591625/. Accessed on August 2, 2020.

Hills, M. D. (2002). Kluckhohn and Strodtbeck's values orientation theory. *Online Readings in Psychology and Culture*, 4(4). Retrieved from https://scholarworks.gvsu.edu/orpc/vol4/iss4/3/. Accessed on September 27, 2020.

History of slavery. (n.d.). National Geographic. Retrieved from https://www.nationalgeographic.org/interactive/slavery-united-states/. Accessed on August 16, 2019.

HK vs. China GDP: A sobering reality. (2017). *Ejinsight*, June 9. Retrieved from http://www.ejinsight.com/20170609-hk-versus-china-gdp-a-sobering-reality/. Accessed on August 10, 2019.

Hoffman, K. M., Trawalter, S., Axt, J. R., & Oliver, M. N. (2016). Racial bias in pain sessment and treatment recommendations, and false beliefs about biological differences between black and whites. *PNAS*, 113(16), 4296–4301. Retrieved from https://www.pnas.org/content/pnas/113/16/4296.full.pdf. Accessed on August 23, 2019.

Hofstede, G. (1996). Riding the waves of commerce: A test of the Trompenaars' "model" of national culture differences. *International Journal of Intercultural Relations*, 20(2), 189–198. doi:10.1016/0147-1767(96)00003-X

Hofstede, G. (2002). *Culture's consequences: International differences in work-related values* (2nd ed.). Thousand Oaks, CA: SAGE.

Hofstede, G., & Bond, M. H. (1984). Hofstede's cultural dimensions: An independent validation using Rokeach's value survey. *Journal of Cross-Cultural Psychology*, 15, 417–503.

Hofstede, G., & Bond, M. H. (1988). The Confucius connection: From cultural roots to economic growth. *Organizational Dynamics*, 16(4), 5–21. doi:10.1016/0090-2616(88)90009-5

Hofstede, G., Hofstede, G. J., & Minkow, M. (2010). *Cultures and organizations: Software of the mind*. New York, NY: McGraw-Hill.

Hogan, H. W. (1978). IQ estimates of males and females. *The Journal of Social Psychology*, 106(1), 137–138.

Hogg, M. A., & Terry, D. I. (2000). Social identity and self-categorization processes in organizational contexts. *Academy of Management Review*, 25(1), 121–140.

Holger, D. (2019). Companies falter in making diversity and inclusion a C-suite job. *The Wall Street Journal*, October 26. Retrieved from https://www.wsj.com/articles/companies-falter-in-making-diversity-and-inclusion-a-c-suite-job-11572091208. Accessed on January 29, 2020.

Holmes, A. (2015). Has diversity lost its meaning? *The New York Times*, October 27. Retrieved from https://www.nytimes.com/2015/11/01/magazine/has-diver

sity-lost-its-meaning.html?_r=0. Accessed on April 13, 2020.

Holmes, H. (2019). WeWork's corporate drinking culture seems incredibly stressful. *The Observer*, June 10. Retrieved from https://observer.com/2019 /06/wework-corporate-drinking-culture/. Accessed on November 14, 2019.

Holopainen, J., & Björkman, I. (2005). The personal characteristics of the successful expatriate: A critical review of the literature and an empirical investigation. *Personnel Review*, 34(1), 37–50.

Holtbrügge, D., Baron, A., & Friedmann, C. B. (2015). Personal attributes, organizational conditions, and ethical attitudes: A social cognitive approach. *Business Ethics: A European Review*, 24(3), 264–281.

Holtbrügge, D., & Berning, S. C. (2017). Email communication styles across cultures. In Y. Y. Kim (Ed.), *The international encyclopedia of intercultural communication* (pp. 1–5). Hoboken, NJ: Wiley. doi:10.1002/9781118783665.ieicc0246

Homans, G. C. (1950). *The human group*. New York, NY: Harcourt, Brace.

Hong, H. J. & Doz, Y. (2013). L'Oréal masters multiculturalism. *Harvard Business Review*, June. Retrieved from https://hbr.org/2013/06/loreal-masters-multiculturalism. Accessed on September 7, 2020.

Hong, L., & Page, S. E. (2004, November 16). Groups of diverse problem solvers can outperform groups of high-ability problem solvers. *PNAS*, 101(46), 16385–16389.

Hosseini, M. R., Chileshe, N., Zuo, J., & Baroudi, B. (2020). A conceptual framework for member selection in global virtual teams (GVTs). *Entrepreneurship Vision, 2020*, 400–411.

Hours of training per employee. (2019). *Statista*. Retrieved from https://www.statista.com/statistics/795813/hours-of-training-per-employee-by-company-size-us/. Accessed on September 10, 2019.

House, R. J. (1971). A path-goal theory of leader effectiveness. *Administrative Science Quarterly*, 16, 321–339.

House, R. J., & Aditya, R. N. (1997). The social scientific study of leadership: Quo vadis? *Journal of Management*, 23, 409–473.

House, R. J., Dorfman, P. W., Javidan, M., Hanges, P. J., & Sully de Luque, M. F. (2014). *Strategic leadership across cultures*. Thousand Oaks, CA: SAGE.

House, R. J., Hanges, P. J., Javidan, M., Dorfman, P. W., & Gupta, V. (2004). *Culture, leadership, and organizations: The GLOBE study of 62 countries*. Thousand Oaks, CA: SAGE.

House, R. J., & Javidan, M. (2004). Introduction. In R. J. House, P. J. Hanges, M. Javidan, P. W. Dorfman, & V. Gupta (Eds.), *Culture, leadership, and organizations: The GLOBE study of 62 countries* (pp. 9–28). Thousand Oaks, CA: SAGE.

House, R. J., & Shamir, B. (1993). Toward the integration of transformational, charismatic and visionary leadership. In M. M. Chemers & R. Ayman (Eds.), *Leadership theory and*

research: Perspective and directions (pp. 81–107). New York, NY: Academic Press.

How's Microsoft's marriage with LinkedIn working out? (2018). *CBS News*, February 1 Retrieved from https://www.cbsnews.com/news/microsoft-linkedin-how-marriage-is-working-out/. Accessed on September 1, 2019.

Howard, J. A. (2000). Social psychology of identities. *Annual Review of Sociology*, 26(1), 367–393. doi:10.1146/annurev.soc.26.1.367

Howell, J. M. (1988). Two faces of charisma: Socialized and personalized leadership in organizations. In J. Conger & R. Kanungo (Eds.), *Charismatic leadership: The illusive factor in organizational effectiveness* (pp. 213–236). San Francisco, CA: Jossey-Bass.

Howell, J. M., & Avolio, B. J. (1992). The ethics of charismatic leadership: Submission or liberation. *Academy of Management Executive*, 6(2), 43–54.

Hsu, T. (2018). Ex-employees Sue Nike, alleging gender discrimination. *The New York Times*, August 10. Retrieved from https://www.nytimes.com/2018/08/10/business/nike-discrimination-class-action-lawsuit.html. Accessed on June 8, 2019.

Human Rights Watch-World Reports. (2019). Retrieved from https://www.hrw.org/world-report/2019. Accessed on August 19, 2019.

Hunt, V., Layton, D., & Prince, S. (2015). Why diversity matters. *McKinsey & Company*. Retrieved from https://www.mckinsey.com/~/media/McKinsey/Business%20Functions/Organization

/Our%20Insights/Why%20dive rsity%20matters/Why%20divers ity%20matters.ashx. Accessed on August 21, 2019.

Hunt, V., Prince, S., Dixon-Fyle, S., & Yee, L. (2018). Delivering through diversity. *McKinsey & Company*. Retrieved from https://www.ifsskillnet.ie/wp-con tent/uploads/2019/01/Delivering -Through-Diversity.pdf. Accessed on August 21, 2019.

Hunzaker, M. B. F. (2016). Cultural sentiments and schema-consistency bias in information transmission. *American Sociological Review*, 81(6), 1223–1250. doi: 10.1177/0003122416671742

Hyde, J. (2014). Gender similarities and differences. *Annual Review of Psychology*, 65, 373–398. doi: 10.1146/annurev-psych-010213-115057

Ibarra, H., & Obodaru, O. (2009). Women and the vision thing. *Harvard Business Review*, January 2009. Retrieved from https://hbr.org/2009/01/women-and-the-vision-thing. Accessed on June 2, 2019.

IES-NCES. (2017). Fast facts. National Center for Education Statistics. Retrieved from https: //nces.ed.gov/fastfacts/display.asp ?id=72. Accessed on June 4, 2019.

Ilies, R., Nahrgang, J. D., & Morgeson, F. P. (2007). Leader-member exchange and citizenship behaviors: A meta-analysis. *Journal of Applied Psychology*, 92, 269–277.

Ingelhart, R., & Welzel, C. (2005). *The human development sequence*. Cambridge, UK: Cambridge University Press.

Ingram, D., & Kent, J. L. (2019). Inside Amazon's delivery push: Employees and drivers say an overworked system is lax on safety as packages pile up. *NBC News*, November 27. Retrieved from https://www.nbcnews.com /tech/tech-news/inside-amazon-s-delivery-push-employees-drive rs-say-overworked-system-n1087 661. Accessed on December 9, 2019.

Isaac, M. (2017). Inside Uber's aggressive unrestrained workplace culture. *The New York Times*, February 22. Retrieved from https://www.nytimes.com/ 2017/02/22/technology/uber-workplace-culture.html. Accessed on November 14, 2019.

Isajiw, W. W. (1993). Definition and dimensions of ethnicity: A theoretical framework. In Statistics Canada & U.S. Bureau of the Census (Eds.), *Challenges of measuring an ethnic world: Science, politics and reality: Proceedings of the Joint Canada-United States conference on the measurement of ethnicity, April 1–3, 1992* (pp. 407–427). Washington, DC: U.S. Government Printing Office.

Ito, T. A., & Urland, G. R. (2003). Race and gender and the brain: Electrocortical measures of attention to the race and gender of multiply categorizable individuals. *Journal of Personality and Social Psychology*, 85(4), 616–626.

Iwowo, V. (2012). The internationalization of leadership development. In S. Turnbull, P. Case, G. Edwards, D. Schedlitzki, & P. Simpson (Eds.), *Worldly leadership: Alternative wisdoms for a complex world* (pp. 52–67). New York, NY: Palgrave Macmillan.

Jackson, K. T. (2000). The polycentric character of business ethics decision making in international contexts. *Journal of Business Ethics*, 23(1), 123–143.

Jackson, S. (2019). It will be 257 years before women have equal pay, gender gap report says. *NBC News*, December 17. Retrieved from https://www. nbcnews.com/news/world/it-will-be-257-years-women-have-equal-pay-new-n1103481. Accessed on January 29, 2020.

Jameel, M., & Yerardi, J. (2019). Workplace discrimination is illegal. But our data shows it's still a huge problem. *Vox*, February 28. Retrieved from https://www.vox.com/policy-and-politics/2019/2/28/18241973/ workplace-discrimination-cpi-investigation-eeoc. Accessed on June 8, 2019.

James, W. (1880). Great men, great thoughts, and their environment. *Atlantic Monthly*, 46, 441–459.

Jana, T., & Diaz Mejias, A. (2018). *Erasing institutional bias: How to create systemic change for organizational inclusion*. Oakland, CA: Berrett-Koehler.

Jang, S. (2018). The most creative teams have a specific type of cultural diversity. *Harvard Business Review*, July 24. Retrieved from https://hbr.org/2018/07/ the-most-creative-teams-have-a-specific-type-of-cultural-diversity. Accessed on November 7, 2019.

Janis, I. (1971). *Groupthink*. Boston, MA: Houghton Mifflin.

Jarman, J., Balckburn, R. M., & Racko, G. (2012). The dimensions of occupational gender segregation in industrial countries. *Sociology*, 46(6), 1003–1019. doi:10.1177/0038038511 435063

Javidan, M., & Hauser, M. (2004). The linkage between GLOBE findings and other cross-cultural information. In R. J. House, P. J Hanges, M. Javidan, P. W. Dorfman, & V. Gupta (Eds.), *Culture, leadership, and organizations: The GLOBE study of 62 countries* (pp. 102–121). Thousand Oaks, CA: SAGE.

Javidan, M., House, R. J., & Dorfman, P. W. (2004). Nontechnical summary of GLOBE findings. In R. J. House, P. J. Hanges, M. Javidan, P. W. Dorfman, & V. Gupta (Eds.), *Culture, leadership, and organizations: The GLOBE study of 62 countries* (pp. 29–48). Thousand Oaks, CA: SAGE.

Javidan, M., & Walker, J. L. (2013). *Developing your global mindset: The handbook for successful global leaders.* Edina, MN: Beaver's Pond Press.

Jazeel, T. (2012). Postcolonialism: Orientalism and the geographic imagination. *Geography*, 92(1), 4–11.

Jg, L., Hafenbrack, A. C., Eastwick, P. W., Wang, D. J., Maddux, W. W., & Galinsky, A. D. (2017). "Going out" of the box: Close intercultural friendships and romantic relationships spark creativity, workplace innovation, and entrepreneurship. *Journal of Applied Psychology*, 102(7), 1091–1108. doi:10.1037/apl0000212

Jiang, Y. (2019). Seeking mirrors: Representation and identity at Asian Pacific Islanders film festivals. *Digital USD – Dissertations.* Retrieved from https://digital.sandiego.edu/dissertations/151/. Accessed on May 25, 2019.

Jimenez, A., Boehe, D. M., Taras, V., & Caprar, D. V. (2017). Working across boundaries: Current and future perspective on global virtual teams. *Journal of International Management*, 23, 341–349.

Johnston, B. (1995). *The Manitous: The supernatural world of the Ojibway.* New York, NY: HarperCollins.

Jokinen, T. (2005). Global leadership competencies: A review and discussion. *Journal of European Industrial Training*, 29(3), 199–216.

Jones, E. E., & Davis, K. K. (1965). From acts to dispositions: The attribution process in person perception. In L. Berkowitz (Ed.), *Advances in experimental social psychology* (Vol. 2, pp. 220–266). New York, NY: Academic Press.

Jones, E. L. (2006). *Cultures merging: A history and economic critique of culture.* Princeton, NJ: Princeton University Press.

Joo, M., Terzina, K. A., Cross, S. E., Yamaguchi, N., & Ohbuchi, K. (2019). How does culture shape conceptions of forgiveness? Evidence from Japan and the United States. *Journal of Cross-Cultural Psychology*, 50(2), 676–702. doi:10.1177/0022022119845502

Joshi, A., Son, J., & Roh, H. (2015). When can women close the gap? A meta-analytic test of sex differences in performance rewards. *Academy of Management Journal*, 51.

Judge, T. A., Piccolo, R. F., & Ilies, R. (2004). The forgotten ones? The validity of consideration and initiation of structure in leadership research. *Journal of Applied Psychology*, 89(1), 36–51.

Kahneman, D. (2011). *Thinking fast and slow.* New York, NY: Farrar, Straus and Giroux.

Kahneman, D., & Frederick, S. (2002). Representativeness revisited: Attribute substitution in intuitive judgment. In T. Gilovich, D. Griffin, & D. Kahneman (Eds.), *Heuristics and biases: The psychology of intuitive judgement* (pp. 49–81). New York, NY: Cambridge University Press.

Kang, S. K., DeCelles, K. A., Tilcsik, A., & Jun, S. (2016). Whitened resumes: Race and self-presentation in the labor market. *Administrative Science Quarterly*, 61(3), 469–502.

Kanter, R. M. (1977). *Men and women of the corporation.* New York, NY: Basic Books.

Kantor, J., & Streitfeld, D. (2015). Inside Amazon: Wrestling big ideas in a bruising workplace. *The New York Times*, August 15. Retrieved from https://www.nytimes.com/2015/08/16/technology/inside-amazon-wrestling-big-ideas-in-a-bruising-workplace.html. Accessed on November 15, 2019.

Kanungo, R. N. (2001). Ethical values of transitional and transformational leaders. *Canadian Journal of Administrative Sciences*, 18(4), 257–265.

Karakitapoğlu-Aygün, Z., & Gumusluoglu, L. (2012). The bright and dark sides of leadership: Transformational vs. non-transformational leadership in a non-Western context. *Leadership*, 9(1), 107–133.

Karadag, E. (2009). Spiritual leadership and organizational culture: A study of structural equation modeling. *Educational Sciences: Theory and Practice*, 9(3), 1391–1405.

Kashyap, V. (2018). 8 companies with enviable company cultures.

ProofHub, May 10. Retrieved from https://www.proofhub.com/articles/8-companies-with-enviable-company-cultures. Accessed on November 14, 2019.

Katty, K., & Shipman, C. (2014, May). The confidence gap. *The Atlantic*, 331(4), 55–66.

Katz, D., & Kahn, R. L. (1966). *The social psychology of organizations*. New York, NY: Wiley.

Katzenbach, J., & Smith, D. (2005). The discipline of teams. *Harvard Business Review*, August. Retrieved from https://hbr.org/2005/07/the-discipline-of-teams. Accessed on November 2, 2019.

Kegan, R., & Lahey, L. L. (2009). *Immunity to change: How to overcome it and unlock the potential in yourself and your organization*. Boston, MA: Harvard Business Review Press.

Keller, J. (2015). What makes Americans so optimistic? *The Atlantic*, March 25. Retrieved from https://www.theatlantic.com/politics/archive/2015/03/the-american-ethic-and-the-spirit-of-optimism/388538/. Accessed on May 25, 2019.

Kenny, C., & Jaluka, T. (2018). Assessing the gender gap at nonprofits in global development. Center for Global Development, March 5. Retrieved from https://www.cgdev.org/blog/assessing-gender-gap-nonprofits-global-development. Accessed on June 9, 2019.

Kim, J., & Kim, J. (2020). We've observed how South Korea and the U.S. have handled coronavirus – and the differences are clear. *The Independent*, March 19. Retrieved from https://www.independent.co.uk/voices/coronavirus-usa-south-korea-testing-trump-covid-19-cure-vaccine-a9411796.html. Accessed on April 27, 2020.

Kittler, M. G., Rygl, D., & MacKinnon, A. (2011). Beyond culture or beyond control? Reviewing the use of Hall's high-/low-context concept. *International Journal of Cross-Cultural Management*, 11(1), 63–82.

Klein, J. G. (2002). Us versus them, or us versus everyone? Delineating consumer aversion to foreign goods. *Journal of International Business Studies*, 33(2), 345–363. doi:10.1057/palgrave.jibs.8491020

Kleinman, Z. (2017). Uber: The scandals that drove Travis Kalanick out. *BBC News*, June 21. Retrieved from https://www.bbc.com/news/technology-40352868. Accessed on November 14, 2019.

Klement, P. (2018). Web design around the world – McDonald's using the power of power distance. *GFluence*, August 8. Retrieved from https://gfluence.com/web-design-around-the-world-mcdonalds-using-the-power-of-power-distance/. Accessed on September 19, 2019.

Kluckhohn, F. R., & Strodtbeck, F. L. (1961). *Variations in value orientations*. Evanston, IL: Row, Peterson.

Knapp, K. N. (2009). Three fundamental bonds and five constant virtues. In L. Cheng (Ed.), *The Berkshire encyclopedia of China* (pp. 2252–2255). Great Barrington, MA: Berkshire. Retrieved from http://chinaconnectu.com/wp-content/pdf/ThreeFundamentalBondsandFiveConstantVirtues.pdf. Accessed on October 19, 2019.

Koening, A. M., Eagly, A. H., Mitchell, A. A., & Ristikari, T. (2011). Are leader stereotypes masculine? A meta-analysis of three research paradigms. *Psychological Bulletin*, 137(4), 616–642. doi:10.1037/a0023557

Koffka. (1935). *Principles of Gestalt psychology*. Routledge.

Koithan, M., & Farrell, C. (2010). Indigenous Native American healing traditions. *Journal of Nurse Practitioners*, 6(6), 477–478. doi:10.1016/j.nurpra.2010.03.016

Koll, J. (2018). Japan, savings superpower of the world. *The Japan Times*, September 2. Retrieved from https://www.japantimes.co.jp/opinion/2018/09/02/commentary/japan-commentary/japan-savings-superpower-world/#.XOm43S-ZNPU. Accessed on May 25, 2019.

Kolowich, L. (2015). Job expectations around the world: What do people care about the most? *HubSpot*, February 1. Retrieved from https://blog.hubspot.com/marketing/job-priorities-international. Accessed on December 11, 2019.

Kotkin, J. (2010). The changing demographics of America. *The Smithsonian.com*, August. Retrieved from https://www.smithsonianmag.com/travel/the-changing-demographics-of-america-538284/. Accessed on August 14, 2019.

Kottak, C. (2006). *Mirror for humanity*. New York, NY: McGraw-Hill.

Kovach, R. (2017). How tribalism hurts companies, and what to do about it. *Harvard Business Review*, July 26. Retrieved from https://hbr.org/2017/07/how-tribalism-hurts-companies-and-what-to-do-about-it. Accessed on July 27, 2019.

Krech, D., & Crutchfield, R. S. (1948). *Theory and problems of social psychology*. New York, NY: McGraw-Hill.

Krempholtz, E. (2019). Some Native Americans recognized not two, not three...but five genders. Buzzworthy. Retrieved from https://www.buzzworthy.com/native-americans-five-genders/. Accessed on April 14, 2020.

Krishnan, A., & Berry, J. W. (1992). Acculturative stress and acculturation attitudes among Indian immigrants to the United States. *Psychology and Developing Societies*, 4(2), 187–212. doi:10.1177/097133369200400206

Kroeber, A. L., & Kluchhohn, C. (1952). Culture: A critical review of concepts and definitions (Papers of the Peabody Museum of American Archeology and Ethnology). Harvard University, XLVII(1). Retrieved from http://www.pseudology.org/Psyhology/CultureCriticalReview1952a.pdf. Accessed on May 17, 2019.

Krook, J. (n.d.). Lifetime employment in Japan: Casual work, part-time work and women under equal opportunity law. *New Intrigue*. Retrieved from https://newintrigue.com/2017/02/24/lifetime-employment-in-japan-casual-work-part-time-work-and-women-under-equal-opportunity-law/. Accessed on September 13, 2019.

Kujala, J., & Pietilainen, T. (2007). Developing moral principles and scenarios in the light of diversity: An extension to the multidimensional ethics scale. *Journal of Business Ethics*, 70, 141–150.

Labor force, female. (2019). The World Bank, April. Retrieved from https://data.worldbank.org/indicator/SL.TLF.TOTL.FE.ZS. Accessed on June 8, 2019.

Labor projections to 2024. (2015). Bureau of Labor Statistics-Monthly Labor Review, December. Retrieved from https://www.bls.gov/opub/mlr/2015/article/labor-force-projections-to-2024.htm. Accessed on August 14, 2019.

LaGuarde, C. (2010). Women, power, and the challenge of financial crisis. *The New York Times*, May 10. Retrieved from http://www.nytimes.com/2010/05/11/opinion/11iht-edlagarde.html?_r=1. Accessed on August 2, 2020.

Larmer, B. (2018). Why does Japan make it so hard for working women to succeed? *The New York Times*, October 17. Retrieved from https://www.nytimes.com/2018/10/17/magazine/why-does-japan-make-it-so-hard-for-working-women-to-succeed.html. Accessed on August 19, 2019.

Larson, E. (2017). New research: Diversity + inclusion = better decision making at work. *Forbes*, September. Retrieved from https://www.forbes.com/sites/eriklarson/2017/09/21/new-research-diversity-inclusion-better-decision-making-at-work/#19d1065d4cbf. Accessed on August 21, 2019.

Laurent, A. (1983). The cultural diversity of Western conceptions of management. *International Studies of Management and Organizations*, 13(1/2), 75–96. Retrieved from https://www.jstor.org/stable/40396954?seq=1#page_scan_tab_contents

Lawrence, C. (n.d.). Diversity backlash is real. Here's how to avoid it. *Deloitte Canada*. Retrieved from https://www.canada175.ca/en/blog/diversity-backlash-real-heres-how-avoid-it. Accessed on April 12, 2020.

Lawrence, P., & Lorsch, J. (1967). Differentiation and integration in complex organizations. *Administrative Science Quarterly*, 12, 1–47.

Lee, H. L. (2017). Singapore's approach to diversity has created a distinctive identity across ethnic groups. *The Straits Times*, May 19. Retrieved from https://www.straitstimes.com/politics/singapolitics/pm-whether-chinese-malay-or-indian-a-singaporean-can-spot-a-fellow-citizen. Accessed on January 3, 2020.

Lee, W. N., & Choi, S. M. (2005). The role of horizontal and vertical individualism and collectivism in online consumers' responses toward persuasive communication on the web. *Journal of Computer-Mediated Communication*, 11(1), 317–336. Retrieved from https://academic.oup.com/jcmc/article/11/1/317/4616669. Accessed on October 1, 2019.

Leslie, S. J., Cimpian, A., Meyer, M., & Freeland, E. (2015). Expectations of brilliance underlie gender distributions across academic disciplines. *Science*, 347(6219), 262–265. doi:10.1126/science.1261375

Levine, R. A., & Campbell, D. T. (1972). *Ethnocentrism*. New York, NY: Wiley.

Lewin, K., & Lippit, R. (1938). An experimental approach to the study of autocracy and democracy: A preliminary note. *Sociometry*, 1, 292–300.

Lewin, K., Lippit, R., & White, R. K. (1939). Patterns of aggressive behavior in experimentally created social climates. *Journal of Social Psychology*, 10, 271–301.

Li, N. N. (2012). Seven secrets to success as an expat executive. *Forbes*, March 12. Retrieved from https://www.forbes.com/sites/85broads/2012/03/12/seven-secrets-to-success-as-an-expat-executive/#361521f8b359. Accessed on August 8, 2019.

Liang, S. G., & Chi, S. S. (2013). Transformational leadership and follower task performance: The role of susceptibility to positive emotions and follower positive emotions. *Journal of Business Psychology*, 28(1), 17–29.

Lim, T. S., & Urakami, J. (2019). Cross-cultural comparison of German and Japanese mobile messenger communication. In J. Kantola, S. Nazir, & T. Barath (Eds.), *Advances in human factors, business management and society*. AHFE 2018: Advances in Intelligent Systems and Computing (Vol. 783). Cham: Springer.

Ling, W., Chia, R., & Fang, L. (2000). Chinese implicit leadership theory. *The Journal of Social Psychology*, 140(6), 729–739.

Lippard, L. (1998). *The lure of the local: Senses of place in a multicentered society*. New York, NY: The New Press.

Liptak, A. (2017). A Google employee wrote an anti-diversity 'manifesto' that's going viral inside the company. *The Verge*, August 5. Retrieved from https://www.theverge.com/2017/8/5/16101978/google-employee-wrote-anti-diversity-manifesto. Accessed on July 31, 2019.

Littrell, L. N., Salas, E., & Hess, K. P. (2006). Expatriate preparation: A critical analysis of 25 years of cross-cultural training research. *Human Resource Development Review*, 5(3), 355–388. doi:10.1177/1534484306290106

Liu, M. (2016). Verbal communication styles and culture. *Communication*, November. Retrieved from https://oxfordre.com/communication/view/10.1093/acrefore/9780190228613.001.0001/acrefore-9780190228613-e-162. Accessed on September 12, 2019.

Livermore, D. (2011). *The cultural intelligence difference*. New York, NY: AMACOM Division of American Management Association.

Locke, E. A. (1978). The ubiquity of the technique of goal setting in theories of and approaches to employee motivation. *The Academy of Management Review*, 3(3), 594–601.

Lord, R., & Maher, K. J. (1991). *Leadership and information processing: Linking perception and performance*. Boston, MA: Unwin Hyman.

Lorenzo, R., & Reeves, M. (2018). How and where diversity drives financial performance. *Harvard Business Review*, January 30. Retrieved from https://hbr.org/2018/01/how-and-where-diversity-drives-financial-performance. Accessed on August 21, 2019.

Luby, M. (2017). Why are Australians so laid back. *BBC Travel*, June 12. Retrieved from http://www.bbc.com/travel/story/20170607-why-are-australians-so-laid-back. Accessed on September 26, 2019.

Luo, Y., Huang, Y., & Wang, S. L. (2011). *Guanxi* and organizational performance: A meta-analysis. *Management and Organization Review*, 8(1), 139–172. Retrieved from https://www.cambridge.org/core/services/aop-cambridge-core/content/view/01809BBE18130E83F8DFEF078DF13640/S1740877600002783a.pdf/guanxi_and_organizational_performance_a_metaanalysis.pdf. Accessed on November 19, 2019.

Ma, A. (2018). China has started ranking citizens with a creepy "social credit" system – Here's what you can do wrong, and the embarrassing, demeaning ways they can punish you. *Business Insider*, October 9. Retrieved from https://www.businessinsider.com/china-social-credit-system-punishments-and-rewards-explained-2018-4. Accessed on August 3, 2020.

MacLeish, W. (1995). *The day before America: Changing the nature of a continent*. New York, NY: Houghton Mifflin.

MacLellan, L. (2019). The countries with the most Starbucks locations. *Quartz*, January 30. Retrieved from https://qz.com/1536009/the-countries-with-the-most-starbucks-locations/. Accessed on May 17, 2019.

MacNell, L., Driscoll, A., & Hunt, A. N. (2015). What's in a name: Exposing gender bias in student ratings of teaching. *Innovative Higher Education*, 40(4), 291–303.

Macrae, C. N., Hook, B. M., Milne, A. B., Rowe, A. C., & Mason, M. F. (2002). Are you looking at me? Eye gaze and person perception. *Psychological Science*, 13, 77–87.

Maddux, W., Kim, P. H., Okumura, T., & Brett, J. (2012). Why "I'm sorry" doesn't always translate. *Harvard Business Review*, June. Retrieved from https://hbr.org/2012/06/-why-im-sorry-doesnt-always-translate. Accessed on November 7, 2019.

Malekzadch, A. R. (2019) *Organizational strategic forces*. Working paper.

Malik, K. (2007). Against multiculturalism. *New Humanist*, May 31. Retrieved from https://newhumanist.org.uk/articles/523/against-multiculturalism. Accessed on July 31, 2019.

Managing international assignments. (2017). Society for Human Resource Management, May 1. Retrieved from https://www.shrm.org/resourcesandtools/tools-and-samples/toolkits/pages/cms_010358.aspx. Accessed on August 8, 2019.

Mandavilli, A. (2018). The world's worst industrial disaster is still unfolding. *The Atlantic*, July 10. Retrieved from https://www.theatlantic.com/science/archive/2018/07/the-worlds-worst-industrial-disaster-is-still-unfolding/560726/. Accessed on December 5, 2019.

Markus, H. R. (2016). What moves people to action? Culture and motivation. *Current Opinion in Psychology*, 8, 161–166.

Martinez, M. (2020). California study tracks hate crimes against Asian Americans amid COVID-19 outbreak. *KCRA News 3*, April 10. Retrieved from https://www.kcra.com/article/california-study-tracks-hate-crimes-against-asian-americans-amid-covid-19-outbreak/32100956#. Accessed on April 12, 2020.

Maseland, R., & van Hoorn, A. (2010). Value and marginal preferences in international business. *Journal of International Business Studies*, 41, 1325–1329.

Maslow, A. (1943). A theory of human motivation. *Psychological Review*, 50, 370–396.

Mason, M. F., Tatkow, E. P., & Macrae, C. N. (2005). The look of love: Gaze shifts and person perception. *Psychological Science*, 16, 236–239.

Mayne, D. (2019). How to be a well-mannered guest. *The Spruce*, March 2. Retrieved from https://www.thespruce.com/how-to-be-a-well-mannered-guest-1216525. Accessed on August 6, 2019.

Maznevski, M. L., DiStefano, J. J., Gomez, C. B., Noorderhaven, N. G., & Wu, P. C. (2002). Cultural dimensions at the individual level of analysis: The cultural orientations framework. *International Journal of Cross-Cultural Management*, 2(3), 275–295.

Mbigi, L. (2005). *Ubuntu: The spirit of African transformation man agreement*. Randburg: Knowledge Resources.

McCabe, J., Fairchild, E., Grauerholz, L., Perscosolido, B. A., & Tope, D. (2011). Gender in twentieth-century children's books: Patterns of disparity in titles and central characters. *Gender & Society*, 25(1), 197–226.

McClintock, A. (1992). The angel of progress: Pitfall of the term "postcolonialism". *Social Text*, 31–32, 84–98.

McDaniel, A. E. (2008). Measuring gender egalitarianism: The attitudinal difference between men and women. *International Journal of Sociology*, 38(1), 58–80.

McDermott, B. (2016). SAP's CEO on being the American head of a German multinational. *Harvard Business Review*, November. Retrieved from https://hbr.org/2016/11/saps-ceo-on-being-the-american-head-of-a-german-multinational. Accessed on September 13, 2019.

McDonald, M. L., Keeves, G. D., & Westphal, J. D. (2018). One step forward, one step back: White male top manager organizational identification and helping behavior toward other executives following the appointment of a female or racial minority CEO. *Academy of Management Journal*, 61(2), 405–439. doi:10.5465/amj.2016.0358

McGirt, E. (2018). The Asian glass ceiling. *Fortune*, June 4. Retrieved from https://fortune.com/2018/06/04/raceahead-asian-glass-ceiling/. Accessed on August 22, 2019.

McGonagle, J. (2017). Ethnicity in France: Representing diversity [Blog post]. *OUPblog*, July 14. Retrieved from https://blog.oup.com/2017/07/representing-diversity-france/. Accessed on August 18, 2019.

McGregor, J. (2015). There are more men on corporate boards named John, Robert, William or James than there are women on boards altogether. *The Washington Post*, February 25. Retrieved from https://www.

washingtonpost.com/news/on-leadership/wp/2015/02/25/there-are-more-men-on-corporate-boards-named-john-robert-william-or-james-than-there-are-women-altogether/. Accessed on August 21, 2019.

McGregor, J. (2018). Even among Harvard MBAs, few black women ever reach corporate America's top rungs. *The Washington Post*, February 20. Retrieved from https://www.washingtonpost.com/news/on-leadership/wp/2018/02/20/even-among-harvard-mbas-few-black-women-ever-reach-corporate-americas-top-rungs/. Accessed on August 23, 2019.

McGregor, J., & Siegel, R. (2018). Why there are still so few minority women CEOs. *The Washington Post*, August 9. Retrieved from https://www.washingtonpost.com/business/2018/08/09/why-there-are-still-so-few-minority-women-ceos/. Accessed on August 23, 2019.

McGregor Burns, J. M. (1978). *Leadership*. New York, NY: Harper & Row.

McIntosh, P. (1989). Unpacking the invisible knapsack. National SEED project on inclusion curriculum. Wellesley Centers for Women. Retrieved from https://nationalseedproject.org/images/documents/Knapsack_plus_Notes-Peggy_McIntosh.pdf. Accessed on July 13, 2019.

Mealy, M., Stephan, W., & Urrutia, I. C. (2007). The acceptability of lies: A comparison of Ecuadorian and Euro-Americans. *International Journal of Intercultural Relations*, 31(6), 689–702.

Meena, K. (2015). Diversity dimensions of India and their organization challenges: An analysis. *Journal of Business and Management*, 17(7), 77–90.

Mehta, P. K., & Shenoy, S. (2011). *Infinite vision: How Aravind became the world's greatest business case*. San Francisco, CA: Berrett-Koehler.

Mello, A. S., & Ruckes, M. E. (2006). Team composition. *Journal of Business*, 79(3), 1019–1039.

Mendenhall, M. E., Osland, J. S., Bird, A., Oddou, G. R., Stevens, M. J., Maznevski, M. L., & Stahl, G. K. (Eds.). (2018). *Global leadership: Research, practice and development*. New York, NY: Routledge.

Menendez, A. (2019). *The likeability trap: How to break free and succeed as you are*. New York, NY: Harper Business.

Menon, T. (2018). *The secret to great opportunities? The person you haven't met yet. TED-Ideas worth spreading*. Retrieved from https://www.ted.com/talks/tanya_menon_the_secret_to_great_opportunities_the_person_you_haven_t_met_yet. Accessed September 19, 2020.

Merz, F. (2011). *Max Weber's theory of bureaucracy and its negative consequences*. Norderstedt, Ger: Druck und Bindung Books.

Metzl, J. M. (2019). It's time to talk about being white in America. *The Washington Post*, April 29. Retrieved from https://www.washingtonpost.com/opinions/its-time-to-talk-about-being-white-in-america/2019/04/29/20aed83a-6a9b-11e9-be3a-33217240a539_story.html. Accessed on December 17, 2019.

Meyer, E. (2014). *The culture map: Breaking through the invisible boundaries of global business*. New York, NY: Public Affairs.

Meyer, E. (2015). When culture does not translate. *Harvard Business Review*, October. Retrieved from https://hbr.org/2015/10/when-culture-doesnttranslate. Accessed on September 13, 2019.

Meyer, J. H. F., & Land, R. (2003). Threshold concepts and troublesome knowledge: Linkages to thinking and practising within the disciplines. In C. Rust (Ed.), *Improving student learning: Theory and practice – 10 years on: Proceedings of the 2002 10th International Symposium Improving Student Learning* (pp. 412–424). Oxford, UK: Centre for Staff and Learning Development.

Meyer, J. H. F., & Land, R. (2006). Threshold concepts and troublesome knowledge: Issues of liminality. In J. H. F. Meyer & R. Land (Eds.), *Overcoming barriers to student understanding: Threshold concepts and troublesome knowledge* (pp. 19–32). London, UK: Routledge.

Mezirow, J. (2000). *Learning as transformation: Critical perspectives on a theory in progress*. San Francisco, CA: Jossey-Bass.

Miller, C. C. (2014). Pay gap is because of gender, not jobs. *The New York Times*, April 23. Retrieved from https://www.nytimes.com/2014/04/24/upshot/the-pay-gap-is-because-of-gender-not-jobs.html?module=inline. Accessed on June 7, 2019.

Miller, C. C. (2015). Stressed, tired, rushed: A portrait of the modern family. *The New York Times*, November 4. Retrieved from https://www.nytimes.com/2015/

11/05/upshot/stressed-tired-rush ed-a-portrait-of-the-modern-fam ily.html?module=inline. Accessed on June 7, 2019.

Miller, C. C. (2017). The gender pay gap is largely because of motherhood. *The New York Times*, May 13. Retrieved from https://www.nytimes.com/2017/ 05/13/upshot/the-gender-pay-gap -is-largely-because-of-mother hood.html. Accessed on June 7, 2019.

Miller, D. (2018a). Vice Media sued by former employee alleging systematic pay suspends 2 top executives after sexual miscon-duct reports. *Los Angeles Times*, February 13. Retrieved from https://www.latimes.com/business /hollywood/la-fi-ct-vice-media-lawsuit-20180213-story.html. Accessed on February 9, 2020.

Miller, G. E. (2018b). A personal saving rate country comparison. *20somethingfinance.com*. Retrieved from https://20somethingfinance. com/a-personal-savings-rate-by-country-comparison/. Accessed on May 25, 2019.

Miller, C. C. (2019). Why women, but not men, are judged for a messy house. *The New York Times*, June 11. Retrieved from https://www.nytimes.com/2019/ 06/11/upshot/why-women-but-not-men-are-judged-for-a-messy-house.html. Accessed on January 6, 2020.

Minkov, M., Dutt, P., Schachner, M., Morales, O., Sanchez, C., Jandosova, J., ... Mudd, B. (2017). A revision of Hofstede's individualism-collectivism dimension. *Cross-Cultural and Strategic Management*, 24(3), 386–404.

Mintzberg, H. (1978). Patterns in strategy formation. *Management Science*, 24, 934–948.

Mintzberg, H., & Caldwell, C. (2017). Leadership, "communi-tyship," and "the good folk". *International Journal of Public Leadership*, 13(1), 5–8.

MIRAE Assets. (2018). Consumption growth: Investing in today's emerging markets. Retrieved from http://www.mira easset.com/upload/insights/thou ght-leadership/Mirae_Asset_Con sumption_Growth_-_Investing_ in_Todays_Emerging_Markets_ 201803.pdf. Accessed on December 28, 2019.

Miss Japan won by half Indian Priyanka Yoshikawa. (2016). *BBC News*, September 8. Retrieved from https://www.bbc .com/news/world-asia-37283518. Accessed on August 23, 2019.

Misumi, J., & Peterson, M. F. (1985). The performance-maintenance (PM) theory of leadership: Review of a Japanese research program. *Administrative Science Quarterly*, 30, 198–223.

Mitsuhashi, Y. (2017). Ikigai: A Japanese concept to improve work and life. *BBC Worklife*, August 7. Retrieved from https: //www.bbc.com/worklife/article /20170807-ikigai-a-japanese-con cept-to-improve-work-and-life. Accessed on September 14, 2019.

Mittal, R., & Dorfman, P. W. (2012). Servant leadership across cultures. *Journal of World Business*, 47, 555–570.

Miyamoto, Y., & Kitayama, S. (2002). Cultural variation in cor-respondence bias: The critical role of attitude diagnosticity of

socially constrained behavior. *Journal of Personality and Social Psychology*, 83, 1239–1248.

Mlambo-Ngcuka, P. (2018). UN women applauds historic advances towards gender parity in the Mexican congress. *UN Women*, July. Retrieved from https://www.unwomen.org/en/ news/stories/2018/7/statement-ed-phumzile-womens-political-participation-mexico. Accessed on August 18, 2019.

Molinsky, A. (2013). *Global dexter-ity*. Boston, MA: Harvard Uni-versity Press.

Montero, D. (2018). How man-agers should respond when bribes are business as usual. *Harvard Business Review*, November 16. Retrieved from https://hbr.org/2018/11/how-ma nagers-should-respond-when-bri bes-are-business-as-usual. Acce-ssed on December 5, 2019.

Monterroza, M. (2017). People of color talk about the times they "code switched". *Vice*, August 17. Retrieved from https://www.vi ce.com/en_ca/article/bjjjvm/peo ple-of-colour-talk-about-the-tim es-they-code-switched. Accessed on August 23, 2019.

Moon, C., Uskul, A. K., & Weick, M. (2017). On culture, ethics and hierarchy: How cultural variations in hierarchical rela-tions are manifested in the code of ethics of British and Korean organizations. *Journal of Applied Social Psychology*, 48(1), 15–27.

Mor Barak, M. (2014). *Managing diversity* (3rd ed.). Thousand Oaks, CA: SAGE.

Moran, G. (2016). 5 essentials to managing multicultural teams.

Fast Company, March 22. Retrieved from https://www. fastcompany.com/3058037/5-ess entials-to-managing-multicultural -teams. Accessed on November 7, 2019.

Morehead, G., Neck, C., & West, M. (1998). The tendency toward defective decision making within self-managing teams: The relevance of groupthink for the 21st century. *Organizational Behavior and Human Decision Processes*, 73(2/3), 327–351.

Moreland, R. L., Levine, J. M., & Wingert, M. L. (2009). Creating the ideal group: Composition effects at work. In E. Witte & J. A. Davis (Eds.), *Understanding group behavior. Vol. 2: Small groups processes and interpersonal relations* (pp. 11–35). Mahwah, NJ: Lawrence Erlbaum.

Morling, B., & Masuda, T. (2012). Social cognition in real worlds: Cultural psychology and social cognition. In S. T. Fiske & C. N. Macrae (Eds.), *SAGE handbook of social cognition* (pp. 429–450). Thousand Oaks, CA: SAGE.

Morris, M. (2016). Standard white: Dismantling white normality. *California Law Review*, 104, 949–978. Retrieved from https: //scholarship.law.berkeley.edu/ cgi/viewcontent.cgi?article=43 28&context=californialawreview. Accessed on December 17, 2019.

Morrison, T., & Conaway, W. A. (2006). *Kiss, bow or shake hands*. Avon, MA: Adams Media.

Mossman, A. (2016). Global assignment policies and practices survey. *KPMG*. Retrieved from https://assets.kpmg.com/content/dam/kpmg/xx/pdf/2016/10 /global-assignment-policies-and-practices-survey-2016.pdf. Accessed on August 8, 2019.

MOW International Research Team. (1981). The meaning of working. In G. Dlugos & K. Weiermair (Eds.), *Management under differing value system: Political, social and economical perspectives in a changing world* (pp. 565–630). Berlin: Walter de Gruyter.

MOW International Research Team. (1987). *The meaning of working*. London: Academic Press.

Multiculturalism: What does it mean? (2011). BBC News, February 7. Retrieved from https://www.bbc.com/news/magazine-12381027. Accessed on July 31, 2019.

Murat, L., & Perreau, B. (2016). *Diversity: America vs. France* [Blog post]. Stanford University Press, November 8. Retrieved from https://stanfordpress.typepad.com/blog/2016/11/diversity-america-vs-france.html. Accessed on August 18, 2019.

Naffsinger, P. A. (1995). Face among the Arabs. *CIA Library*, September 18. Retrieved from https://www.cia.gov/library/center-for-the-study-of-intelligence/-kent-csi/vol8no3/html/v08i3a05 p_0001.htm. Accessed on September 12, 2019.

Nahavandi, A. (2012). Iranian mystical leadership: Lessons for contemporary leaders. In G. P. Prastacos, F. Wang, & K. E. Soderquist (Eds.), *Leadership through the classics: Learning management and leadership from ancient East and West philosophy* (pp. 191–204). New York, NY: Springer-Verlag.

Nahavandi, A. (2015). *The art and science of leadership*. Upper Saddle River, NJ: Pearson.

Nahavandi, A. (2017). Threshold concepts and culture-as-meta-context. *Journal of Management Education*, 40(6), 794–816.

Nahavandi, A., & Aranda, E. (1994). Restructuring teams for the re-engineered organization. *Academy of Management Executive*, 8(4), 58–68.

Nahavandi, A., & Corbett, L. (2018). Leaping into public leadership. *International Journal of Public Leadership*, 14(4), 218–231.

Nahavandi, A., & Krishnan, H. (2018). Indo-European leadership (IEL): A non-western leadership perspective. In J. L. Chin, J. E. Trimble, & J. E. Garcia (Eds.), *Global and culturally diverse leaders and leadership: New dimensions, opportunities, and challenges for business, industry, education and society*. A Volume in the ILA Building Leadership Bridges (BLB) Series (pp. 105–123). Bingley, UK: Emerald Publishing Limited.

Nahavandi, A., & Malekzadeh, A. R. (1988). Acculturation in mergers and acquisitions. *Academy of Management Review*, 13(1), 79–90.

Naithani, P., & Jha, A. N. (2015). Challenges faced by expatriate workers in Gulf Cooperation Council countries. *International Journal of Business and Management*, 5(1), 98–104.

Nania, R. (2018). Power imbalances, 'myths' make sexual harassment pervasive at work. *WTOP*, October 24. Retrieved from https://wtop.com/living/2018/10

/power-imbalances-myths-make-sexual-harassment-pervasive-at-work/. Accessed on June 8, 2019.

Nardon, L. (2017). *Working in a multicultural world: A guide to developing intercultural competence*. Toronto, Canada: University of Toronto Press.

Nash, C. (2002). Cultural geography: Postcolonial cultural geographies. *Progress in Human Geography*, 26(2), 219–230.

Nathan, M., & Lee, N. (2015). Cultural diversity, innovation, and entrepreneurship: Firm level evidence from London. *Economic Geography*, 89(4), 367–394.

Neate, R. (2018). Global pay gap will take 202 years to close, says World Economic Forum. *The Guardian*, December 18. Retrieved from https://www.theguardian.com/world/2018/dec/18/global-gender-pay-gap-will-take-202-years-to-close-says-world-economic-forum. Accessed on June 7, 2019.

Neeley, T. (2017). How to successfully work across countries, languages and cultures. *Harvard Business Review*, August 29. Retrieved from https://hbr.org/2017/08/how-to-successfully-work-across-countries-languages-and-cultures. Accessed on August 5, 2019.

Nelson, M. R., & Shavitt, S. (2002). Horizontal and vertical individualism and achievement values. *Journal of Cross-Cultural Psychology*, 33(2), 439–458.

Nelson, N., Bronstein, I., Shacham, R., & Ben-Ari, R. (2015). The power to oblige: Power, gender, negotiation behaviors, and their consequences. *International Association for Conflict Management*, 8(1), 1–24.

Nemiro, J., Beyerlein, M., Bradely, L., & Beyerlein, S. (Eds.). (2008). *The handbook of high-performance virtual teams: A toolkit for collaborating across boundaries*. San Francisco, CA: Jossey-Bass. Retrieved from http://citeseerx.ist.psu.edu/viewdoc/download?doi=10.1.1.470.3868&rep=rep1&type=pdf. Accessed on November 5, 2019.

Neubert, M. J. (2019). With or without spirit: Implications for scholarship and leadership. *Academy of Management Perspectives*, 33(3), 253–263. doi:10.5465/amp.2016.0172

Newcomer, E., & Stone, B. (2018). The fall of Travis Kalanick was a lot weirder and darker than you thought. *Bloomberg Business*, January 18. Retrieved from https://www.bloomberg.com/news/features/2018-01-18/the-fall-of-travis-kalanick-was-a-lot-weirder-and-darker-than-you-thought. Accessed on November 14, 2019.

Newkirk, V. R., II. (2017). The myth of reverse discrimination. *The Atlantic*, August 5. Retrieved from https://www.theatlantic.com/education/archive/2017/08/myth-of-reverse-racism/535689/. Accessed on July 31, 2019.

Ngai, J. (2018). What you need to know about working for a Chinese company. *McKinsey & Company*. Retrieved from https://www.mckinsey.com/featured-insights/china/what-you-need-to-know-about-working-for-a-chinese-company. Accessed on November 19, 2019.

Ng, K. Y., Van Dyne, L., & Ang, S. (2009). From experience to experiential learning: Cultural intelligence as a learning capability for global leaders development. *Academy of Management Learning and Education*, 8(4), 511–526.

NGO Advisor. (2015). *Top 100 NGOs*. Retrieved from https://www.ngoadvisor.net/top100ngos/

Nittle, N. K. (2019). 5 big companies sued for racial discrimination. *ThoughtCo.* January 20. Retrieved from https://www.thoughtco.com/big-companies-sued-for-racial-discrimination-2834873. Accessed on August 23, 2019.

Niwa, S., & Maruno, S. (2010). Strategic aspects of cultural schema: A key for examining how cultural values are practices in real-life settings. *Journal of Social, Evolutionary, and Cultural Psychology*, 4(2), 79–91.

Noguchi, Y. (2018). More employers avoid legal minefield by not asking about pay history. *NPR: All Things Considered*. Retrieved from https://www.npr.org/2018/05/03/608126494/more-employers-avoid-legal-minefield-by-not-asking-about-pay-history. Accessed on June 12, 2019.

NoiseCat, J. B. (2017). The western idea of private property is flawed. Indigenous people have it right. *The Guardian*, March 27. Retrieved from https://www.theguardian.com/commentisfree/2017/mar/27/western-idea-private-property-flawed-indigenous-peoples-have-it-right. Accessed on September 15, 2019.

Noordin, F. (2018). Individualism-collectivism: A tale of two countries. *Problems and Perspectives in Management*, 7(2), 1–11. Retrieved from https://pdfs.semanticscholar.org/0ce9/90a1a09a98e0ac4af7082109c955a4f9bafd.pdf. Accessed on October 1, 2019.

Norman, R. T. (2018). What is Janteloven? *Scandinavian Standard*, December 29. Retrieved from http://www.scandinaviastandard.com/what-is-janteloven-the-law-of-jante/. Accessed on September 26, 2019.

NPR Staff. (2013). Breaking into the business world with "women-friendly" model. *Weekend Edition Sunday*, June 23. Retrieved from https://www.npr.org/2013/06/23/194683800/breaking-into-the-business-world-with-woman-friendly-model. Accessed on August 2, 2020.

Nussbaum, D. (2019). Tight and loose cultures: A conversation with Michele Gelfand. *Behavioral Scientist*, January 17. Retrieved from https://behavioralscientist.org/tight-and-loose-cultures-a-conversation-with-michele-gelfand/. Accessed on September 25, 2019.

O'Keefe, P. A., Dweck, C. S., & Walton, G. M. (2018). Implicit theory of interest: Finding your passion or developing it? *Psychological Science*, 29(10), 1653–1664. doi:10.1177/0956797618780643

O'Reilly, C. A., III, Caldwell, D. F., & Barnett, W. P. (1989). Work group demography, social integration and turnover. *Administrative Science Quarterly*, 34(1), 21–37.

O'Reilley, S. (2017). Britain has a sense of moral superiority most other countries don't feel. *The Irish Times*, October 5. Retrieved from https://www.irishtimes.com/culture/books/britain-has-a-sense-of-moral-superiority-most-other-countries-don-t-feel-1.3237161. Accessed on April 6, 2020.

Olson, E. (2019). Slow gains for women and minorities on board of big U.S. firms, study says. *The New York Times*, January 19. Retrieved from https://www.nytimes.com/2019/01/15/business/women-minorities-corporate-boards.html. Accessed on June 9, 2019.

Orr, L. M., & Hauser, W. J. (2008). A re-inquiry of Hofstede's cultural dimensions: A call for 21st century cross-cultural research. *Marketing Management Journal*, 18(2), 1–19.

Ortiz-Ospina, E., & Roser, M. (2018). Economic inequality by gender. *Our World in Data*. Retrieved from https://ourworldindata.org/economic-inequality-by-gender#differences-in-pay. Accessed on June 7, 2019.

Ortiz-Ospina, E., & Tzvetkova, S. (2017). Working women: Key facts and trends in female labor force participation. *Our World in Data*, October 16. Retrieved from https://ourworldindata.org/female-labor-force-participation-key-facts. Accessed on June 8, 2019.

Osland, J. S. (2008). The multi-disciplinary roots of global leadership. In M. E. Mendenhall, J. S. Osland, A. Bird, G. R. Oddou, & M. L. Maznevski (Eds.), *Global leadership: Research, practice and development* (pp. 18–33). Abingdon, UK: Routledge.

Osland, J. S., & Bird, A. (2000). Beyond sophisticated stereotyping: Cultural sensemaking in context. *Academy of Management Executive*, 14(1), 65–77.

Oyserman, D., Sorensen, N., Reber, R., & Chen, S. X. (2009). Connecting and separating mind-sets: Culture as situated cognition, *Journal of Personality and Social Psychology*, 97(2), 217–235. doi:10.1037/a0015850

P&G Diversity. (2015). P&G 2015 diversity & inclusion annual report: Enabling a culture of innovation & productivity. Retrieved from https://us.pg.com/diversity-and-inclusion/. Accessed on August 24, 2019.

Pae, P. (2019). South Korea's Chaebol. *Bloomberg*, August 29. Retrieved from https://www.bloomberg.com/quicktake/republic-samsung. Accessed on November 18, 2019.

Pagda, Z. (2019). *The case of Stefan in Egypt*. Personal communication, September.

Parboteeah, K. P., Bronson, J. W., & Cullen, J. B. (2005). Does national culture affect willingness to justify ethically suspect behaviors? A focus on the GLOBE culture scheme. *International Journal of Cross Cultural Management*, 5(2), 123–138.

Park, Y. S., & Kim, B. S. K. (2008). Asian and European American cultural values and communication styles among Asian American and European college students. *Cultural Diversity and Ethnic Minority Psychology*, 14(1), 47–56.

Parsons, T., & Shils, E. A. (1951). *Toward a general theory of action*. Cambridge, MA: Harvard University Press.

Patel, S. (2015). 10 examples of companies with fantastic cultures. *Entrepreneur.com*, August 6. Retrieved from https://www.entrepreneur.com/article/249174. Accessed on November 14, 2019.

Peck, E. (2017). Around the world, girls are taught the same limiting lesson. *Huffington Post*, September 20. Retrieved from https://www.huffpost.com/entry/gender-stereotypes-worldwide_n_59c15e88e4b087fdf5089cab?guccounter=1&guce_referrer=aHR0cHM6Ly93d3cuZ29vZ2xlLmNvbS8&guce_referrer_sig=AQAAABI4XpyTZqQmBJJkSS160YJdmcxV8hFKGcsqurdsnW7gjO9yXfmCxQSsEB957uJ9pflQQq1_s202x8aeKQoD08B0UteFCZRqh63lbwnJt1BBjo27f4TP3hD4T8Fsjz7PHglRb1O6CoCj4dgO1SXb-0RXM-WN4osHx1XVnHmNtlGN. Accessed on May 31, 2019.

Peck, E. (2019). Women at Ernst & Young instructed on how to dress, act nicely around men. *HuffPost*, October 21. Retrieved from https://www.huffpost.com/entry/women-ernst-young-how-to-dress-act-around-men_n_5da721eee4b002e33e78606a. Accessed on January 29, 2020.

Pekerti, A. A., & Sendjaya, S. (2010). Exploring servant leadership across cultures: Comparative study in Australia and Indonesia. *The International Journal of Human Resource Management*, 21(5), 754–780.

Pelto, P. (1968). The difference between "tight" and "loose" societies. *Transaction*, 5, 37–40.

Peng, M. W. (2002). Cultures, institutions, and strategic choices: Toward an institutional perspective on business strategy. In M. J. Gannon & K. L. Newman (Eds.), *Handbook of cross-cultural management* (pp. 52–66). Oxford, UK: Blackwell.

Peng, M. W., & Luo, Y. (2000). Managerial ties and organizational performance in a transition economy: The nature of a micro-macro link. *Academy of Management Journal*, 43(3), 486–501.

Peters, L. M. L., & Manz, C. C. (2008). Getting virtual teams right the first time: Key to successful collaboration in the virtual world. In J. Nemiro, M. Beyerlein, L. Bradely, & S. Beyerlein (Eds.), *The handbook of high-performance virtual teams: A toolkit for collaborating across boundaries* (pp. 105–129). San Francisco, CA: Jossey-Bass. Retrieved from http://citeseerx.ist.psu.edu/viewdoc/download?doi=10.1.1.470.3868&rep=rep1&type=pdf. Accessed on November 5, 2019.

Petit, P. (2007). The effects of age and family constraints on gender hiring discrimination: A field experiment in the French financial sector. *Labour Economics*, 14(3), 371–391.

Phillips, K. W. (2014). How diversity makes us smarter. *Scientific American*, October 2014. Retrieved from https://www.scientificamerican.com/article/how-diversity-makes-us-smarter/. Accessed on August 21, 2019.

Pittampalli, A. (2019). Why groups struggle to solve problems together. *Harvard Business Review*, November 7. Retrieved from https://hbr.org/2019/11/why-groups-struggle-to-solve-problems-together?ab=hero-main-text. Accessed on November 7, 2019.

Pollock, D. C., Van Reken, R. E., & Pollock, M. V. (2017). *Third culture kids: Growing up among worlds* (3rd ed.). London, UK: Nicholas Brealey Publishing.

Porter, J. (2019). To improve your team, first work on yourself. *Harvard Business Review*, January 29. Retrieved from https://hbr.org/2019/01/to-improve-your-team-first-work-on-yourself. Accessed on November 7, 2019.

Powell, G. N., Butterfield, D. A., & Parent, J. D. (2002). Gender and managerial stereotypes: Have the times changed? *Journal of Management*, 28, 177–193.

Premack, R. (2017). South Korea's conglomerates. *SAGE Business Researcher*. Retrieved from https://scholar.harvard.edu/files/frankel/files/skorea-conglomerates2017sage.pdf. Accessed on November 19, 2019.

Prentice, D. A., & Carranza, E. (2002). What women and men should be, shouldn't be, are allowed to be, and don't have to be: The contents of prescriptive gender stereotypes. *Psychology of Women Quarterly*. 26(4) 269–281. doi:10.1146/annurev-psych-010213-115057

Presse Canadienne. (2019). Quebecers say separatism is passé but worry about the future of French. *Montreal Gazette*, March 22. Retrieved from https://montrealgazette.com/news/local-news/quebecers-say-separatism-is-passe-but-worry-about-future-of-french-poll. Accessed on August 5, 2019.

Proudfoot, D., Kay, A. C., & Koval, C. Z. (2015). A gender bias in the attribution of creativity: Archival and experimental evidence for the perceived association between masculinity and creative thinking. *Psychological Science*, 26, 1751–1761. doi:10.1177/0956797615598739

Puyat, J. H. (2013). Is the influence of social support on mental health the same for immigrants and non-immigrants. *Journal of Immigrant and Minority Health*, 15(3), 598–605.

Pyramid: Women in S&P 500 companies. (2019). *Catalyst*, May 1. Retrieved from https://www.catalyst.org/research/women-in-sp-500-companies/. Accessed on June 7, 2019.

Pyrillis, R. (2011). Avoid culture shock when rewarding international employees. *Workforce*, August 23. Retrieved from https://www.workforce.com/2011/08/23/avoid-culture-shock-when-rewarding-international-employees/. Accessed on November 12, 2019.

Quick Take-US. (2018). Women in the workforce. *Catalyst*. Retrieved from https://www.catalyst.org/research/women-in-the-workforce-united-states/. Accessed on June 4, 2019.

Quick Take-Global. (2018). Women in management. *Catalyst*. Retrieved from https://www.catalyst.org/research/women-in-management/. Accessed on June 4, 2019.

Rabouin, D. (2019). Only 1 Fortune 500 company is headed by a woman of color. *Axios*, January 14. Retrieved from https://www.axios.com/fortune-500-no-women-of-color-ceos-3d42619c-967b-47d2-b94c-659527b22ee3.html. Accessed on June 10, 2019.

Radjou, N. (2009). Polycentric innovation: A new mandate for multinationals. *The Wall Street Journal*, November 9. Retrieved from https://www.wsj.com/articles/SB125774328035737917. Accessed on July 30, 2019.

Rahim, M. A. (2017). *Managing conflict in organizations*. London: Taylor & Francis.

Raising kids and running a household: How working parents share the load. (2015). Pew Research Center, November 4. Retrieved from https://www.pewsocialtrends.org/2015/11/04/raising-kids-and-running-a-household-how-working-parents-share-the-load/. Accessed on June 7, 2019.

Ramadurai, C. (2018). Cracking India's mystifying 'nod' code. *BBC Travel*. July 23. Retrieved from http://www.bbc.com/travel/story/20180722-cracking-indias-mystifying-nod-code. Accessed on May 26, 2019.

Ramamoorthy, N., & Carroll, S. J. (1998). Individualism/collectivism orientations and reactions toward alternative human resource management practices. *Human Relations*, 51(5), 571–588. doi:10.1023/A:1016954217602

Ramamoorthy, N., Gupta, A., Sardessai, R. M., & Flood, P. C. (2007). Individualism/collectivism and attitudes towards human rsources systems: A comparative study of American, Irish and Indian MBA students. *The International Journal of Human Resource Management*, 16(5), 852–869. doi:10.1080/09585190500083459

Ramasamy, B., & Yeung, M. C. H. (2016). Diversity and innovation. *Applied Economics Letters*, 23(14), 1037–1041. doi:10.1080/13504851.2015.1130785

Rampen, J. (2019). Backlash against diversity programmes shows the need for a re-think. *DiversityQ*, August 12. Retrieved from https://diversityq.com/backlash-against-diversity-programmes-shows-the-need-for-a-re-think-1507275/. Accessed on April 13, 2020.

Rappleye, E. (2019). Former Billings clinic CEO accused of 'almost daily' sexual harassment. *Becker's Hospital Review*. Retrieved from https://www.beckershospitalreview.com/hospital-management-administration/former-billings-clinic-ceo-accused-of-almost-daily-sexual-harassment.html. Accessed on June 8, 2019.

Rattansi, S. (2020). US protestors slam surveillance during COVID-19 crisis. *Al Jazeera*, April 25. Retrieved from https://www.aljazeera.com/news/2020/04/protesters-slam-surveillance-covid-19-crisis-200425160235593.html. Accessed on April 27, 2020.

Ravlin, E. C., Liao, Y., Morrell, D. L., Au, K., & Thomas, D. C. (2012). Collectivistic orientation and the psychological contract: Mediating effect of creditor ideology. *Journal of International Business Studies*, 43, 772–782.

Ray, T., Chaudhuri, A. R., & Sahai, K. (2017). *Whose education matters? An analysis of inter caste marriages in India* (Discussion paper 17-05). Indian Statistical Institute. Retrieved from https://www.isid.ac.in/~epu/wp-content/uploads/2017/09/dp17-05.pdf. Accessed on August 20, 2019.

Reave, L. (2005). Spiritual values and practices related to leadership effectiveness. *The Leadership Quarterly*, 16(5), 655–687.

Reay, D. (2017). Why German Turks are numerous, divided and bitter. *Handelsblatt Today*,

April 13. Retrieved from https://www.handelsblatt.com/today/handelsblatt-explains-why-german-turks-are-numerous-divided-and-bitter/23568860.html?ticket=ST-1718150-EALgWPg6tAqIKGu9LLHf-ap2. Accessed on August 17, 2019.

Redfield, R., Linton, R., & Herkovitz, M. (1936). Memorandum on the study of acculturation. *American Anthropologist*, 38, 149–152.

Reiger, T. (2011). Beware of parochial managers. *Gallup Business Journal*, May 26. Retrieved from https://news.gallup.com/businessjournal/147653/beware-parochial-managers.aspx. Accessed on July 28, 2019.

Reuben, E., Sapienza, P., & Zingales, L. (2014). Taste for competition and the gender gap among young business professionals. Retrieved from https://www.reuben.net/research/GenderGapCompetitiveness.pdf.

Reynolds, A., & Lewis, D. (2018). The two traits of the best problem-solving teams. *Harvard Business Review*, April 2. Retrieved from https://hbr.org/2018/04/the-two-traits-of-the-best-problem-solving-teams. Accessed on November 7, 2019.

Rhinesmith, S. H. (1992). Global mindset for global managers. *Training & Development*, 46(10), 63–68.

Richardson, D. S., & Hammock, G. S. (2007). Social context of human aggression: Are we paying too much attention to gender? *Aggression and Violent Behavior*, 12(4), 417–426. doi:10.1016/j.avb.2006.11.001

Rink, F., & Ellemers, N. (2010). Benefiting from deep-level diversity: How congruence between knowledge and decision rules improves team decision making and team perceptions. *Group Processes and Intergroup Relations*, 13(3), 345–359.

Ritzer, G. (2007). *Sociological theory* (7th ed.). New York, NY: McGraw-Hill.

Ro, S. (2015). Here's how much business S&P 500 companies do outside of the US. *Business Insider*, July 9. Retrieved from http://www.businessinsider.com/foreign-revenues-by-region-2015-7

Roberts, E. (2015). Expat life lessons: Your stories. *The Telegraph*, January 15. Retrieved from https://www.telegraph.co.uk/expat/expatlife/11344630/Expat-life-lessons-your-stories.html. Accessed on August 4, 2019.

Robins, N. (2012). *The corporation that changed the world: How the East India Company shaped the modern multinational*. London, UK: Pluto.

Roche, J. F. (2016). Clones in the MBA classroom: Understanding the relationship between culture and MBA students' attitudes towards socially responsible business leadership. Digital USD – Dissertations. Retrieved from https://digital.sandiego.edu/dissertations/23/. Accessed on May 25, 2019.

Rock, D., & Grant, H. (2016). Why diverse teams are smarter. *Harvard Business Review*, November 2016. Retrieved from https://hbr.org/2016/11/why-diverse-teams-are-smarter. Accessed on September 27, 2020.

Rokeach, M. (1973). *Understanding human value*. New York, NY: Free Press.

Romano, A., Balliet, D., Yamagishi, T., & Liu, J. H. (2017). Parochial trust and cooperation across 17 societies. *Proceedings of the National Academy of Sciences*, 114(48), 12702–12707. doi:10.1073/pnas.1712921114

Romero, S. (2007). When a mother country tells its kid, "shut up". *The New York Times*, November 25. Retrieved from https://www.nytimes.com/2007/11/25/weekinreview/25romero.html. Accessed on August 16, 2019.

Romero, S., & Gilbert, J. (2014). Why so many world cup fans dislike Argentina. *The New York Times*, June 10. Retrieved from https://www.nytimes.com/2014/06/11/upshot/why-so-many-world-cup-fans-dislike-argentina.html. Accessed on April 6, 2020.

Rousseau, D. M. (1989). Psychological and implied contracts in organizations. *Employee Responsibilities and Rights Journal*, 2, 121–139.

Rousseau, D. M., & Fried, Y. (2001). Location, location, location: Contextualizing organizational research. *Journal of Organizational Behavior*, 22, 1–13.

Rox, M. (2011). 11 simple rules of excellent houseguest etiquette. *Wise Bread*, May 27. Retrieved from https://www.wisebread.com/11-simple-rules-of-excellent-houseguest-etiquette. Accessed on August 6, 2019.

Rudman, L., & Glick, P. (2002). Prescriptive gender stereotypes and backlash toward agentic women. *Journal of Social Issues*, 57(4), 742–762. doi:10.1111/0022-4537.00239

Rudolph, B. (1998). *Disconnected: How six people from AT&T discovered the new meaning of work in a downsized corporate America.* New York, NY: Free Press.

Ruhm, C. J. (2011). Policies that assist parents with young children. *Future Child*, 21(2), 37–68. Retrieved from https://www.ncbi.nlm.nih.gov/pmc/articles/PMC3202345/. Accessed on June 11, 2019.

Ryan, M. K., & Haslam, S. A. (2007). The glass cliff: Exploring the dynamics surrounding the appointment of women to precarious leadership positions. *Academy of Management Review*, 32(2), 549–572. doi:10.5465/amr.2007.24351856

Saad, G., Cleveland, M., & Ho, L. (2015). Individualism-collectivism and the quantity versus quality dimension of individual and group creative performance. *Journal of Business Research*, 68(3), 578–586. doi:10.1016/j.jbusres.2014.09.004

Schmader, T., Whitehead, J., & Wysocki, V. H. (2007). A linguistic comparison of letter of recommendation for male and female chemistry and biochemistry job applicants. *Sex Roles*. 57, 509–514.

Saewyc, E. (2017). A global perspective on gender roles and identity. *Journal of Adolescent Health*, 61(4): S1–S2. doi:10.1016/j.jadohealth.2017.07.010

Said, E. (1978/1991). *Orientalism.* London, UK: Penguin.

Sakulku, J. (2011). The impostor phenomenon. *International Journal of Behavioral Sciences*, 6(1), 75–97. doi:10.14456/ijbs.2011.6

Salam, M. (2019). Womansplaining the pay gap. *The New York Times*, April 2. Retrieved from https://www.nytimes.com/2019/04/02/business/equal-pay-day.

html. Accessed on June 7, 2019.

SalesForce CEO on equality. (2017). *CNN Business*, November 13. Retrieved from https://www.youtube.com/watch?v=yZUQ5ZG8mco. Accessed on June 11, 2019.

Samnani, A., & Singh, P. (2013). When leaders victimize: The role of charismatic leaders in facilitating group pressure. *The Leadership Quarterly*, 24, 189–202.

Sandberg, S. (2013). *Lean in: Women, work and the will to lead.* New York, NY: Alfred A. Knopf.

Sanneh, K. (2017). The limits of "diversity". *The New Yorker*, October 2. Retrieved from https://www.newyorker.com/magazine/2017/10/09/the-limits-of-diversity. Accessed on April 13, 2020.

Santos, H. C., Varnum, M. E. W., & Grossman, I. (2017). Global increases in individualism. *Psychological Science*, 28(9), 1228–1239. doi:10.1177/0956797617700226

Saracer, B. E., Karacy-Aydin, G. Asarkaya, Ç., & Kabasakal, H. (2012). Linking the worldly mindset with an authentic leadership approach: An exploratory study in a middle Eastern context. In S. Turnbull, P. Case, G. Edwards, D. Schedlitzki, & P. Simpson (Eds.), *Worldly leadership: Alternative wisdoms for a complex world* (pp. 207–222). New York, NY: Palgrave Macmillan.

Sashkin, M. (2004). Transformational leadership approaches. In J. Antonakis, A. T. Cianciolo, & R. J. Sternberg (Eds.), *The*

nature of leadership (pp. 171–196). Thousand Oaks, CA: SAGE.

Savage, L. J. (1954). *The foundation of statistics.* New York, NY: Dover.

Scandura, T., & Dorfman, P. (2004). Leadership research in an international and cross-cultural context. *The Leadership Quarterly*, 15, 277–307.

Schedlitzki, D. (2012). National language and its importance for worldly leadership. In S. Turnbull, P. Case, G. Edwards, D. Schedlitzki, & P. Simpson (Eds.), *Worldly leadership: Alternative wisdoms for a complex world* (pp. 17–31). New York, NY: Palgrave Macmillan.

Schein, E. H. (2017). *Organizational culture and leadership.* San Francisco, CA: Wiley/Jossey-Bass.

Schlossberg, M. (2015). 26 crazy McDonald's items you can't get in America. *Business Insider*, July 1. Retrieved from https://www.businessinsider.com/mcdonalds-international-menu-items-2015-7. Accessed on September 1, 2019.

Schneider, M. C., Holman, M. R., Diekman, A. B., & McAndrew, T. (2015). Power, conflict, and community: How gendered views of political power influence women's political ambition. *Political Psychology*, 37(4), 515–531.

Schwantes, M. (2018). The CEO of Salesforce found out his female employees were paid less than men. His response is a priceless leadership lesson. *Inc.*, July 26. Retrieved from https://www.inc.com/marcel-schwantes/the-ceo-of-salesforce-found-out-female-employees-are-paid-less-than-men-his-response-is-a-priceless-leadership-lesson.html. Accessed on June 11, 2019.

Schwartz, A. Y., & Dawes, D. E. (2020). Racial inequality persists in health care, but this insurance plan is narrowing the gap. *MarketWatch*, January 21. Retrieved from https://www.marketwatch.com/story/racial-inequality-persists-in-health-care-but-this-insurance-plan-is-helping-2020-01-20. Accessed on January 29, 2020.

Schwartz, S. H. (1992). Universals in the content and structure of values: Theoretical advances and empirical tests in 20 countries. *Advances in Experimental Social Psychology*, 25, 1–65.

Sclafani, J. (2019). Can a woman sound presidential? *Scientific American*, February 6. Retrieved from https://blogs.scientificamerican.com/voices/can-a-woman-sound-presidential/. Accessed on August 31, 2019.

Seegert, L. (2017). U.S. ranks worse in elder care vs. other wealthy nations. *AHCJ-Covering Health*, November 15. Retrieved from https://healthjournalism.org/blog/2017/11/u-s-ranks-worse-in-elder-care-vs-other-wealthy-nations/. Accessed on June 11, 2019.

Seigel, R. (2020). Women outnumber men in the American workforce for only the second time. *The Washington Post*, January 10. Retrieved from https://www.washingtonpost.com/business/2020/01/10/january-2020-jobs-report/. Accessed on January 29, 2020.

Seligman, M. E. P. (2002). *Authentic happiness: Using the new positive psychology to realize your potential for lasting fulfillment*. New York, NY: Free Press.

Seligman, M. E. P., & Csikszentmihalyi, M. (2000). Positive psychology. *American Psychologist*, 55, 5–14.

Sennett, R. (1998). *The corrosion of character: The personal consequences of work in the new capitalism*. New York, NY: W.W. Norton & Company.

Sexual Harassment. (2019). U.S. Equal Opportunity Commission. Retrieved from https://www.eeoc.gov/eeoc/publications/fs-sex.cfm. Accessed on June 8, 2019.

Shah, A. K., & Oppenheimer, D. M. (2008). Heuristics made easy: An effort-reduction framework. *Psychological Bulletin*, 137, 207–222.

Shavitt, S., Lalwani, A., Zhang, J., & Torelli, C. (2006). The horizontal/vertical distinction in cross-cultural consumer research. *Journal of Consumer Psychology*, 16(4), 325–342.

Shavitt, S., Torelli, C. J., & Reimer, H. (2011a). Horizontal and vertical individualism and collectivism. In M. J. Gelfand, C. Chiu, & Y. Hong (Eds.), *Advances in culture and psychology* (Vol. 1). New York, NY: Oxford University Press.

Shavitt, S., Johnson, T. P., & Zhang, J. (2011b). Horizontal and vertical culture differences in the content of advertising appeal. *Journal of Consumer Marketing*, 23(3–4), 298–310.

Sherif, M., Harvey, O. J., White, B. J., Hood, W., & Sherif, C. W. (1961). *Intergroup conflict and cooperation: The Robbers Cave experiment*. Norman, OK: The University Book Exchange.

Sherrer, K. (2018). What is tokenism, and why does it matter in the workplace. Vanderbilt University-Owen Graduate School of Management, February 26. Retrieved from https://business.vanderbilt.edu/news/2018/02/26/tokenism-in-the-workplace/. Accessed on November 5, 2019.

Shonk, K. (2019). How to resolve cultural conflict: Overcoming cultural barriers at the negotiating table. Program on Negotiation – Harvard Law School, September 10. Retrieved from https://www.pon.harvard.edu/daily/conflict-resolution/a-cross-cultural-negotiation-example-how-to-overcome-cultural-barriers/. Accessed on December 8, 2019.

Shrivastava, P. (1987). A cultural analysis of conflicts in industrial disaster. *International Journal of Mass Emergencies and Disasters*, 5(3), 243–264. Retrieved from http://ijmed.org/articles/147/download/. Accessed on December 5, 2019.

Siddiqui, F. (2019). Uber discloses 3,000 reports of sexual assault on U.S. rides last year in its long-awaited safety study. *The Washington Post*, December 5. Retrieved from https://www.washingtonpost.com/technology/2019/12/05/uber-disclosed-sexual-assaults-us-rides-last-year-its-long-awaited-safety-report/?arc404=true. Accessed on December 9, 2019.

Simon, B., Hastedt, C., & Aufderheide, B. (1997). When self-categorization makes sense: The role of meaningful social categorization in minority and majority members' self-perception. *Journal of Personality* and *Social Psychology*, 73, 310–320.

Simon, H. A. (1972). Theories of bounded rationality. *Decision and Organization*, 1(1), 161–176.

Simon, H. A. (1979). Rational decision making in business organizations. *American Economic Review*, 69(4), 493–513.

Sincrope, C., Norris, J., & Watanabe, Y. (2007). Competence: A summary of theory, research and practice (technical report for the foreign language program evaluation project). *Second Language Studies*, 26(1), 1–58.

Singelis, T. M., Triandis, H. C., Bhawuk, D. P. S., & Gelfand, M. J. (1995). Horizontal and vertical dimensions of individualism and collectivism: A theoretical and measurement refinement. *Cross-Cultural Research*, 29(3), 240–275. doi: 10.1177/106939719502900302

Singer, P. (1969). Toward a re-evaluation of the concept of charisma with reference to India. *Journal of Social Research*, 12(2), 13–25.

Singletary, M. (2018). Michelle Obama is right. We can't have it all. *The Washington Post*, December 4. Retrieved from https://www.washingtonpost.com/business/2018/12/04/michelle-obama-is-right-we-cant-have-it-all/. Accessed on August 2, 2020.

Sivadas, E., Bruvold, N. T., & Nelson, M. R. (2008). A reduced version of the horizontal and vertical individualism and collectivism scale: A four-country assessment. *Journal of Business Research*, 61(3), 201–210. doi:10.1016/j.jbusres.2007.06.016

Six top online MBA programs with gender parity. (2018). *QS Top MBA*. Retrieved from https://www.topmba.com/programs/-distance-online-mba/six-top-online-mba-programs-gender-parity. Accessed on June 4, 2019.

Slater, J. (2019). A young Indian couple married for love. Then the bride's father hired assassins. *The Washington Post*, August 19. Retrieved from https://www.washingtonpost.com/world/asia_pacific/a-young-indian-couple-married-for-love-then-the-brides-father-hired-assassins/2019/08/19/3d1ce9a0-a1d0-11e9-a767-d7ab84aef3e9_story.html. Accessed on August 20, 2019.

Slaughter, A. M. (2012). Why women still can't have it all. *The Atlantic*, July -August. Retrieved from https://www.theatlantic.com/magazine/archive/2012/07/why-women-still-cant-have-it-all/309020/. Accessed on September 21, 2020.

Smith, M. L. (2002a). Race, nationality, and reality. *National Archives: Prologue Magazine*, 32(2). Retrieved from https://www.archives.gov/publications/prologue/2002/summer/immigration-law-1.html. Accessed on August 16, 2019.

Smith, M. L. (2002b). Race, nationality, and reality, Part 2. *National Archives: Prologue Magazine*, 32(2). Retrieved from https://www.archives.gov/publications/prologue/2002/summer/immigration-law-2.html. Accessed on August 16, 2019.

Smith, K. (2018). The dangers of parochialism in international relations. *E-International Relations*, August 30. Retrieved from https://www.e-ir.info/2018/08/30/the-dangers-of-parochialism-in-international-relations/. Accessed on July 29, 2019.

Smith, N. (2019). Japan begins experiment of opening to immigration. *Bloomberg*, May 22. Retrieved from https://www.bloomberg.com/opinion/articles/2019-05-22/japan-begins-experiment-of-opening-to-immigration. Accessed on August 17, 2019.

Smith, S., & Eckardt, A. (2018). Germans of Turkish descent struggle with identity, seek acceptance. *NBC News*, August 14. Retrieved from https://www.nbcnews.com/news/world/germans-turkish-descent-struggle-identity-seek-acceptance-n886961. Accessed on August 23, 2019.

Snyder, C. R., Lopez, S. J., & Pedrotti, J. T. (2011). *Positive psychology: The scientific and practical explorations of human strengths* (2nd ed.). Thousand Oaks, CA: SAGE.

Snyder, M. (1974). The self-monitoring of expressive behavior. *Journal of Personality and Social Psychology*, 30, 526–537.

Solansky, S., Gupta, V., & Wang, J. (2017). Ideal and Confucian implicit leadership profiles in China. *Leadership and Organization Development Journal*, 38(2), 164–177. doi:10.1108/LODJ-06-2015-0114

SØndergaard, M. (1994). Research note: Hofstede's consequences: A study of reviews, citations and replications. *Organization Studies*, 15(3), 447–456.

Spector, N. (2017). The hidden health effects of sexual harassment. *NBC News*, November 10. Retrieved from https://www.nbcnews.com/better/health/

hidden-health-effects-sexual-harassment-ncna810416. Accessed on June 8, 2019.

Spector, N. (2019). What is "niksen", the Dutch concept of doing nothing? And how does it work exactly? *NBC News*, July 30. Retrieved from https://www.nbcnews.com/better/lifestyle/what-niksen-dutch-concept-doing-nothing-how-does-it-work-ncna1036171. Accessed on April 6, 2020.

Spencer, J. (2012). Ways of being. *Philosophy Compass*, 7(12), 910–918.

St. John, I. (2012). *The making of the Raj: India under the East India company*. Santa Barbara, CA: Praeger.

Stahl, G. K., Maznevski, M. L., Voigt, A., & Jonsen, K. (2010). Unraveling the effects of cultural diversity in team: A meta-analysis of research on multicultural groups. *Journal of International Business Studies*, 41, 690–709.

Starbucks Stories. (2018). Starbuck to close all stores nationwide for racial-bias education on May 29. *Starbucks Stories and News*, April 17. Retrieved from https://stories.starbucks.com/press/2018/starbucks-to-close-stores-nationwide-for-racial-bias-education-may-29/. Accessed on April 12, 2020.

Starner, T. (2019). These will be the top HR challenges in 2020. *Human Resource Executive*, December 20. Retrieved from https://hrexecutive.com/these-are-the-top-hr-challenges-in-2020/. Accessed on April 12, 2020.

State of the global workplace. (2017). *Gallup*. Retrieved from https://www.gallup.de/183833/state-the-global-workplace.aspx. Accessed on October 30, 2019.

Stauffer, B. (2018). "Only men need apply": Gender discrimination in job advertisements in China. *Human Rights Watch*, April 2018. Retrieved from https://www.hrw.org/report/2018/04/23/only-men-need-apply/gender-discrimination-job-advertisements-china. Accessed on June 11, 2019.

Steel, E. (2017). At Vice, cutting-edge media and allegations of old-school sexual harassment. *The New York Times*, December 23. Retrieved from https://www.nytimes.com/2017/12/23/business/media/vice-sexual-harassment.html. Accessed on February 9, 2020.

Steers, R. M., Porter, L. W., & Bigley, G. A. (Eds.). (1996). *Motivation and leadership at work*. New York, NY: McGraw-Hill.

Steinlauf, R. (2019). Learn from my experience: 3 ways to ensure expat assignment success. *CEOWorld Magazine*, January 24. Retrieved from https://ceoworld.biz/2019/01/24/learn-from-my-experience-3-ways-to-ensure-expat-assignment-success/. Accessed on August 8, 2019.

Stern, C. (2018). The great divide. *Daily Mail*, May 8. Retrieved from https://www.dailymail.co.uk/femail/article-5700519/Women-spend-TWICE-time-chores-male-partners-husbands.html. Accessed on June 8, 2019.

Stevenson, R. W. (1993). Volvo abandons Renault merger. *The New York Times*, December 3. Retrieved from http://www.hbs.edu/faculty/Publication%20Files/The%20Dark%20Side%20of% 20Alliances_95819048-0ced-40f4-97e0-875f6df79423.pdf. Accessed on November 15, 2019.

Steward, E. (2018). Why struggling companies promote women: The class cliff explained. *Vox*, October 31. Retrieved from https://www.vox.com/2018/10/31/17960156/what-is-the-glass-cliff-women-ceos. Accessed on June 10, 2019.

Stiglitz, J. E. (2010). *Freefall: America, free markets, and the sinking of the world economy*. New York, NY: W. W. Norton.

Strauss, K., Griffin, M. A., & Rafferty, A. E. (2009). Proactivity directed toward the team and organization: The role of the leadership, commitment and role-breadth self-efficacy. *British Journal of Management*, 20(3), 279–290.

Su, R., Rounds, J., & Armstrong, P. I. (2009). Men and things, women and people: A meta-analysis of sex differences in interests. *Psychological Bulletin*, 135(6), 859–884.

Sullivan, M. (2004). Cambodia's new king ascends the throne. *All Things Considered*, October 29. Retrieved from https://www.npr.org/templates/story/story.php?storyId=4133660. Accessed on October 10, 2019.

Suneson, G. (2018). From AMC Network's Josh Sapan to Broadcom's Hock Tan: There are the highest paid CEOs of 2018. *USA Today*, December 21. Retrieved from https://www.usatoday.com/story/money/2018/12/21/highest-paid-ceos-2018/38756663/. Accessed on June 7, 2019.

Sushma, U. N. (2018). India Inc is now willing to pay more to fix its gender diversity problem. *Quartz India*, March 21. Retrieved from https://qz.com/india/1227834/gender-diversity-indian-companies-are-now-paying-more-to-hire-women/. Accessed on August 20, 2019.

Svendsen, G. L. H., & Svendsen, G. T. (2016). Homo voluntaries and rural idyll: Voluntary work, trust and solidarity in rural and urban areas. *Journal of Rural and Community Development*, 11(1), 56–72. Retrieved from https://journals.brandonu.ca/jrcd/article/view/1375/299. Accessed on April 22, 2020.

Swidler, A. (1986). Culture in action: Symbols and strategies. *American Sociological Review*, 51(1), 273–286.

Syrda, J. (2019). Spousal relative income and male psychological distress. *Personality and Social Psychology Bulletin*, 46(6), 976–992. Retrieved from https://journals.sagepub.com/doi/10.1177/0146167219883611. Accessed on January 6, 2020.

Szalai, G. (2015). MTV international channels go from "I Want" to "I am my MTV". *The Hollywood Reporter*, June 25. Retrieved from https://www.hollywoodreporter.com/news/mtv-international-channels-go-i-804789. Accessed on September 1, 2019.

Szkudlarek, B. (2010). Reentry—A review of the literature. *International Journal of Intercultural Relations*, 34(1), 1–21. doi:10.1016/j.ijintrel.2009.06.006

Tajfel, H., & Turner, J. (1986). The social identity theory of intergroup behavior. In S. Worchel & W. G. Austin (Eds.), *The psychology of intergroup relations* (pp. 7–24). Chicago, IL: Nelson.

Tannen, D. (1986). *That's not what I meant: How conversational style makes or break relationships*. New York, NY: Ballantine Books.

Tannen, D. (Ed.). (1993). *Gender and conversational interaction*. Oxford, NY: Oxford University Press.

Taparata, E. (2016). The US has come a long way since its first, highly restrictive naturalization law. *PRI-Justice*, July 4. Retrieved from https://www.pri.org/stories/2016-07-04/us-has-come-long-way-its-first-highly-restrictive-naturalization-law. Accessed on August 16, 2019.

Tata group business profile. (2019). Retrieved from https://www.tata.com/business/overview. Accessed on May 17, 2019.

Tavernise, S., & Oppel, R. A., Jr. (2020). Spit on, yelled at, attacked: Chinese-Americans fear for their safety. *The New York Times*, March 23. Retrieved from https://www.nytimes.com/2020/03/23/us/chinese-coronavirus-racist-attacks.html. Accessed on April 13, 2020.

Teece, D., & Leih, S. (2016). Uncertainty, innovation, and dynamic capabilities: An introduction. *California Management Review*, 58(4), 5–12.

Tejada, C. (2017). Money, power, family. *The New York Times*, February 17. Retrieved from https://www.nytimes.com/2017/02/17/business/south-korea-chaebol-samsung.html. Accessed on November 18, 2019.

Thaler, R. H., & Sunstein, C. R. (2009). *Nudge: Improving decisions about health, wealth, and happiness*. London, UK: Penguin Books.

The global gender gap report. (2018). World Economic Forum. Retrieved from http://www3.weforum.org/docs/WEF_GGGR_2018.pdf. Accessed on June 7, 2019.

The Indian nod: Explained [Video file]. (*n.d.*). YouTube. Retrieved from https://www.youtube.com/watch?v=0RaBxH_MKQI. Accessed on May 26, 2019.

The perils of parochialism. (2008). *The Economist*, November 8. Retrieved from https://www.economist.com/special-report/2008/11/08/the-perils-of-parochialism. Accessed on July 29, 2019.

The simple truth. (2018). AAUW. Retrieved from https://www.aauw.org/research/the-simple-truth-about-the-gender-pay-gap/. Accessed on June 7, 2019.

The training industry report. (2017). Retrieved from https://trainingmag.com/trgmag-article/2017-training-industry-report/. Accessed on September 10, 2019.

The training industry report. (2018). Retrieved from https://trainingmag.com/trgmag-article/2018-training-industry-report/. Accessed on September 10, 2019.

Thibaut, J. W., & Kelly, H. H. (1959). *The social psychology of groups*. New York, NY: Wiley.

Thite, M., Wilkinson, A., & Shah, D. (2011). Internationalization and HRM strategies across subsidiaries in multinational corporation from emerging economies – A conceptual framework. *Journal of World*

Business, 47(2), 251–258. doi: 10.1016/j.jwb.2011.04.012

Thomas, D. C., Fitzsimmons, S. R., Ravlin, E. C., Au, K. Y., Ekelund, B. Z., & Barzanty, C. (2010). Psychological contracts across cultures. *Organization Studies*, 31(12), 1–22.

Thorton, A. (2019). These countries have the most women in parliament. *World Economic Forum*, February 12. Retrieved from https://www.weforum.org/agenda/2019/02/chart-of-the-day-these-countries-have-the-most-women-in-parliament/. Accessed on June 9, 2019.

Tims, M., Bakker, A. B., & Xanthopoulou, D. (2011). Do transformational leaders enhance their followers' daily work engagement? *The Leadership Quarterly*, 22, 121–131.

Tipu, S. A. A., Ryan, J. C., & Fantazy, K. A. (2012). Transformational leadership in Pakistan: An examination of the relationship of transformational leadership to organizational culture and innovation propensity. *Journal of Management and Organization*, 18(4), 461–480.

Tomaney, J. (2012). Parochialism – A defence. *Progress in Human Geography*, 37(5), 658–672. doi: 10.1177/0309132512471235

Tony. (2018). Being an expat in Saudi Arabia. *ToughNickel*, December 21. Retrieved from https://toughnickel.com/finding-job/Being-an-Expat-in-Saudi-Arabia. Accessed on August 8, 2019.

Toossi, M. (2002). A century of change: The U.S. labor force, 1950–2050. *Monthly Labor Review*, May, pp. 15–28. Retrieved from https://www.bls.gov/opub/mlr/2002/05/art2full.pdf. Accessed on August 17, 2019.

Torchia, M., Calabró, A., & Morner, M. (2015). Board of directors' diversity, creativity and cognitive conflict. *International Studies of Management and Organization*, 45(1), 6–24. doi:10.1080/00208825.2015.1005992

Torelli, C. J., & Kaikati, A. M. (2009). Values as predictors of judgments and behaviors: The role of abstract and concrete mindsets. *Journal of Personality and Social Psychology*, 96(1), 231–247. doi:10.1037/a0013836

Transparency International. (2019). Retrieved from https://www.transparency.org/news/feature/cpi_2018_global_analysis. Accessed on December 4, 2019.

Treviño, L. J., Gomez-Mejia, L. R., Balkin, D. B., & Mixon, F. G. (2015). Meritocracies or masculinities? The differential allocation of named professorships by gender in the academy. *Journal of Management*, 44(3), 972–1000. doi:10.1177/0149206315599216

Triandis, H. C. (1989). Self and social behavior in differing cultural contexts. *Psychological Review*, 96, 506–520.

Triandis, H. C. (1995). *Individualism and collectivism*. Boulder, CO: Westview Press.

Triandis, H. C. (2004). The many dimensions of culture. *The Academy of Management Executive*, 18(4), 88–93.

Triandis, H. C., Carnevale, P., Gelfand, M. L., Robert, C., Wasti, S. A., Probst, T., … Chen, X.-P. (2001). Culture and deception in business negotiations: A multilevel analysis. *International Journal of Cross-Cultural Management*, 1(1), 73–90.

Triandis, H. C., & Gelfand, M. J. (1998). Converging measurement of horizontal and vertical individualism and collectivism. *Journal of Personality and Social Psychology*, 74(1), 118–128.

Trompenaars, F., & Hampden-Turner, C. (2012). *Riding the waves of culture: Understanding diversity in global business*. New York, NY: McGraw-Hill.

Tsai, J. (2016). How websites design differs in four corners of the world. *Website Magazine*, July 10. Retrieved from https://www.websitemagazine.com/blog/how-website-design-differs-in-four-corners-of-the-world. Accessed on December 6, 2020.

Tsurumi, R. (1982). American origins of Japanese productivity: The Hawthorne experiment rejected. *Pacific Basin Quarterly*, 7(Spring–Summer), 14–15.

Tuan, Y. F. (1977). *Space and place*. Minneapolis, MN: Minnesota University Press.

Tuckman, B., & Jensen, M. (1977). Stages of small group development revisited. *Groups and Organizational Studies*, 2, 419–427.

Tuckman, B. W. (2001). Developmental sequence in small groups. *Group Facilitation*, 3, 66–81.

Turnbull, S., Case, P., Edwards, G., Schedlitzki, D., & Simpson, P. (2012). *Worldly leadership: Alternative wisdoms for a complex world*. New York, NY: Palgrave Macmillan.

Turner, J. C., Hogg, M. A., Oakes, P. J., Reicher, S. D., & Wetherell, M. S. (1987). *Rediscovering the social group: A* self-categorization theory. Oxford: Basil Blackwell.

Turnley, W. H., & Bolino, M. C. (2001). Achieving desired images while avoiding undesired images: Exploring the role of self-monitoring in impression management. *Journal of Applied Psychology*, 86(2), 351–360.

Tversky, A., & Kahneman, D. (1974). Judgment under uncertainty: Heuristics and biases. *Science*, 185, 1124–1131.

Tweedie, S. (2016). Microsoft buys LinkedIn for $26.2 billion. *Business Insider*, June 13. Retrieved from https://www.businessinsider.com/microsoft-buys-linkedin-2016-6. Accessed on September 1, 2019.

Tylor, E. B. (1871/2016). *Primitive culture* (Vol. 1). Mineola, NY: Dover.

Tyrrell, I. (2016). What exactly is American exceptionalism. *The Week*, October 21. Retrieved from https://theweek.com/articles/654508/what-exactly-is-american-exceptionalism. Accessed on April 7, 2020.

Umaña-Taylor, A. J. (2011). Ethnic identity. In S. Schwartz, K. Luyckx, & V. Vignoles (Eds.), *Handbook of identity theory and research* (pp. 791–809). New York, NY: Springer.

UN Women. (2108a). *Facts and figures: Economic development*. Retrieved from http://www.unwomen.org/en/what-we-do/economic-empowerment/facts-and-figures. Accessed on June 4, 2019.

UN Women. (2018b). *Facts and figures: Peace and security*. Retrieved from http://www.unwomen.org/en/what-we-do/peace-and-security/facts-and-

figures#_Notes. Accessed on June 9, 2019.

Unger, J. (2011). Cultural identity and public health. In S. Schwartz, K. Luyckx, & V. Vignoles (Eds.), *Handbook of identity theory and research* (pp. 811–825). New York, NY: Springer.

Usinier, J. C., & Roulin, N. (2010). The influence of high- and low-context communication styles on the design, content and language of business-to-business web sites. *Journal of Business Communication*, 47(2), 189–227.

Uz, I. (2014). The index of cultural tightness and looseness among 68 countries. *Journal of Cross-Cultural Psychology*, 46, 319–335.

Van den Scott, L., & Van den Hoonard, D. (2016). The origins and evolution of Everett Hughes's concept: 'master status'. In R. Helmes-Hayes & M. Santoro (Eds.), *The Anthem companion to Everett Hughes* (pp. 173–192). New York, NY: Anthem Press.

van Dierendonck, D. (2011). Servant leadership: A review and synthesis. *Journal of Management*, 37(4), 1228–1261.

van Dijk, H., Meyer, B., van Engen, M., & Loyd, D. L. (2017). Microdynamics in diverse teams: A review and integration of the diversity and stereotyping literatures. *Academy of Management Annals*, 11(1), 517–557.

van Honk, J., Terburg, D., & Bos, P. A. (2011). Further notes on testosterone as a social hormone. *Trends Cognitive Sciences*, 15(7), 291–292. doi:10.1016/j.tics.2011.05.003

van Knippenberg, D., & Sitkin, S. B. (2013). A critical assessment

of charismatic-transformational leadership research: Back to the drawing board? *The Academy of Management Annals*, 7(1), 1–60.

Vega, T. (2019). The historical precedent for Trump's public charge rule. *The Takeaway*, August 15. Retrieved from https://www.wnycstudios.org/story/historical-precedent-trumps-public-charge-rule. Accessed on August 16, 2019.

Vega, W. A., & Rumbaut, R. G. (1991). Ethnic minorities and mental health. *Annual Review of Sociology*, 17, 351–383.

Verniers, C., & Vala, J. (2018). Justifying gender discrimination in the workplace: The mediating role of the motherhood myths. *PLOS One*, 13(7), e0201150. doi:10.1371/journal.pone.0190657

Vernon, P. E., & Allport, G. W. (1931). A test of personal values. *The Journal of Abnormal and Social Psychology*, 26(3), 231–248.

Vial, A. C., Napier, J. L., & Brescoll, V. L. (2016). A bed of thorns: Female leaders and the self-reinforcing cycle of illegitimacy. *The Leadership Quarterly*, 27, 400–414.

Virgin – About us. (2019). Retrieved from https://www.virgin.com/virgingroup/content/our-purpose-0. Accessed on August 11, 2019.

Vlachos, K. (2017). Making your expat assignment easier on your family. *Harvard Business Review*, March 10. Retrieved from https://hbr.org/2017/03/making-your-expat-assignment-easier-on-your-family. Accessed on August 4, 2019.

Vroom, V. H. (1964). *Work and motivation*. New York, NY: Wiley.

Vroom, V. H., & Jago, A. G. (1988). *The new leadership: Managing participation in organizations.* Upper Saddle River, NJ: Prentice Hall.

Wakabayashi, D. (2017). Google fires engineer who wrote memo questioning women in tech. *The New York Times*, August 7. Retrieved from https://www.nytimes.com/2017/08/07/business/google-women-engineer-fired-memo.html. Accessed on August 23, 2019

Walumbwa, F. O., & Lawler, J. J. (2003). Building effective organizations: Transformational leadership, collectivist orientation, work-related attitudes, and withdrawal behavior in three emerging economies. *International Journal of Human Resource Management*, 14, 1083–1101.

Walumbwa, F. O., Lawler, J. J., & Avolio, B. J. (2007). Leadership, individual differences, and work-related attitudes: A cross-cultural investigation. *Applied Psychology*, 56, 212–230.

Ward, C., Bochner, S., & Furnham, A. (2001). *The psychology of culture shock*. London: Routledge.

Wardell, L. (2018a). Diversity drives organization performance. *Chief Executive*, March 22. Retrieved from https://chief-executive.net/diversity-drives-organizational-performance/. Accessed on August 21, 2019.

Wardell, L. (2018b). Board diversity propels performance. *Corporate Board Member*. Retrieved from https://board-member.com/board-diversity-propels-performance/. Accessed on November 5, 2019.

Warner, J., Ellmann, N., & Boesch, D. (2018). The women's leadership gap. Center of American Progress, November 20. Retrieved from https://www.americanprogress.org/issues/women/reports/2018/11/20/461273/womens-leadership-gap-2/. Accessed on June 9, 2019.

Warner-Søderholm, G. (2012). Was the grass trampled when the two elephants fought? Measuring societal cultures: Project GLOBE vs. Hofstede. *Journal of International Doctoral Research*, 1(1). Retrieved from http://hdl.handle.net/11250/93918. Accessed on September 30, 2019.

Watkins, M. B., Simmons, A., & Humphress, E. (2019). It's not black and white: Toward a contingency perspective on the consequences of being a token. *Academy of Management Perspectives*, 33(3), 334–365. doi:10.5465/amp.2015.0154

Weber, L. (2018). White men challenge workplace diversity efforts. *The Wall Street Journal*, March 14. Retrieved from https://www.wsj.com/articles/white-men-challenge-workplace-diversity-efforts-1521036001. Accessed on April 13, 2020.

Weick, K. E. (1988). Enacted sensemaking in crisis situations. *Journal of Management Studies*, 25(4), 305–317.

Wenderoth, M. C. (2018). How a better understanding of Guanxi can improve your business in China. *Forbes*, May 16. Retrieved from https://www.forbes.com/sites/michaelcwenderoth/2018/05/16/how-a-better-understanding-of-guanxi-can-improve-your-business-in-china/#52d107f5d85b. Accessed on November 19, 2019.

Werman, M. (2019). Google's new Nigerian accent. *PRI: The World*, August 2. Retrieved from https://www.pri.org/file/2019-08-02/googles-new-nigerian-accent. Accessed on August 5, 2019.

Whack, E. H. (2018). Black men arrested at Starbucks settle for $1 each, and a promise of a $200K for young entrepreneurs program. *The Chicago Tribune*, May 2. Retrieved from https://www.chicagotribune.com/business/ct-biz-black-men-arrested-starbucks-settlement-20180502-story.html. Accessed on April 12, 2020.

What is India's caste system? (2019). *BBC News*, June 19. Retrieved from https://www.bbc.com/news/world-asia-india-35650616. Accessed on August 20, 2019.

What the average American CEO looks like. (2018). *BBC Worklife*. Retrieved from https://www.bbc.com/worklife/article/20180801-what-the-average-american-ceo-looks-like. Accessed on August 22, 2019.

Whelan, R. (2018). Women test Mexico's 'Macho' political culture with big electoral gains. *The Wall Street Journal*, July 12. Retrieved from https://www.wsj.com/articles/women-test-mexicos-macho-political-culture-with-big-electoral-gains-1531387800. Accessed on August 18, 2019.

Whitaker, W. (2018). A whole new world: Students with disability transition to postsecondary education. Digital USD –

Dissertations. Retrieved from https://digital.sandiego.edu/dissertations/107/. Accessed on August 4, 2019.

WHO. (2020). *Gender*. World Health Organization-Health Topics. Retrieved from https://www.who.int/health-topics/gender. Accessed on April 14, 2020.

Wijekoon, L. V., Sutton, T. M., Alvi, S. H., & Gopalikrishnan, V. (2018). India: Recent development will affect diversity in the workplace. *SHRM*, October 5. Retrieved from https://www.shrm.org/resourcesandtools/legal-and-compliance/employment-law/pages/global-india-diversity-developments.aspx. Accessed on August 20, 2019.

Williams, J. C., Berdahl, J. L., & Vandello, J. A. (2016). Beyond work-life "integration". *Annual Review of Psychology*, 67, 515–539. doi:10.1146/annurev-psych-122414-033710

Willis, J., & Todorov, A. (2006). First impressions: Making up your mind after a 100-ms exposure to a face. *Psychological Science*, 17(7), 592–598. doi:10.1111/j.1467-9280.2006.01750.x

Wilson, S. (2016). 5 strange Japanese office occurrences. *Japan Today*, August 14. Retrieved from https://japantoday.com/category/features/lifestyle/5-strange-japanese-office-occurrences. Accessed on September 15, 2019.

Witkin, H. A., & Berry, J. W. (1975). Psychological differentiation in cross-cultural perspective. *Journal of Cross-Cultural Psychology*, 6, 4–87.

Wittenberg-Cox, A. (2014). In search of a less sexist hiring process. *Harvard Business Review*, March 17. Retrieved from https://hbr.org/2014/03/in-search-of-a-less-sexist-hiring-process. Accessed on June 7, 2019.

Wolfers, J. (2015). Fewer women run big companies than men named John. *The New York Times*, March 2. Retrieved from https://www.nytimes.com/2015/03/03/upshot/fewer-women-run-big-companies-than-men-named-john.html?_r=0. Accessed on August 21, 2019.

Women and Hollywood. (2019). *Report: Black male directors made major gains in 2018, number of women plateaued again*. Retrieved from https://womenandhollywood.com/report-black-male-directors-made-major-gains-in-2018-number-of-women-plateaued-again/. Accessed on June 9, 2019.

Women in the Labor Force. (2010). Women's Bureau-US Department of Labor. Retrieved from https://www.dol.gov/wb/factsheets/qf-laborforce-10.htm. Accessed on June 4, 2019.

Women's invisible labor. (2019). *CISION PR Newswire*, March 4. Retrieved from https://www.prnewswire.com/news-releases/womens-invisible-labor-highlighted-in-new-smithsonian-exhibit-300806247.html. Accessed on April 14, 2020.

Wood, J. T. (2009). *Gendered lives: Communication, gender, and culture* (8th ed.). Boston, MA: Wadsworth Cengage Learning.

World Atlas. (2019). Retrieved from https://www.worldatlas.com/articles/most-ethnically-diverse-countries-in-the-world.html. Accessed on May 17, 2019.

World Atlas-India. (2019). Retrieved from https://www.worldatlas. com/webimage/countrys/asia/india/infacts.htm#page. Accessed on August 20, 2019.

World Atlas-Japan. (2019). Retrieved from https://www.worldatlas.com/articles/ethnic-groups-and-nationalities-in-japan.html. Accessed on August 19, 2019.

World Atlas-Mexico. (2019). Retrieved from https://www.worldatlas.com/articles/largest-ethnic-groups-in-mexico.html. Accessed on August 18, 2019.

Witte, F. M., Stratton, T. D., & Nora, M. L. (2006). Stories from the field: Students' description of gender discrimination and sexual harassment during medical school. *Academic Medicine*, July 81(7): 648–654.

Würtz, E. (2017). Intercultural communication on web sites: A cross-cultural analysis of web sites from high-context cultures and low-context cultures. *Journal of Computer-Mediated Communication*, 11(1), 274–299. doi:10.1111/j.1083-6101.2006.tb00313.x

Yam, P. C., Ng, G. T., Au, W. T., Tao, L., Lu, S., Leung, H., & Fung, J. M. Y. (2018). The effect of subgroup homogeneity of efficacy on contributions in public good dilemmas. *PLOS One*, July 31. Retrieved from https://journals.plos.org/plosone/article/metrics?id=10.1371/journal.pone.0201473. Accessed on August 21, 2019.

Yamagishi, T., Jin, N., & Kiyonari, T. (1999). Bounded generalized reciprocity. *Advances in Group Processes*, 16, 161–197.

Yamagishi, T., & Mifune, N. (2008). Does shared group membership promote altruism? Fear, greed, and reputation. *Rationality and Society*, 20(1), 5–30. doi: 10.1177/1043463107085442

Yamawaki, K. (2019). Is Japan becoming a country of immigration? *The Japan Times*, June 26. Retrieved from https://www.japantimes.co.jp/opinion/2019/06/26/commentary/japan-commentary/japan-becoming-country-immigration/#.XVh5-PZKiRs. Accessed on August 17, 2019.

Yammarino, F. J., Dubinsky, A. J., Comer, L. B., & Jolson, M. A. (1997). Women and transformational and contingency reward leadership: A multiple-levels-of-analysis perspective. *Academy of Management Journal*, 40, 205–222.

Yoon, S. J. (2018). The organisational culture of the chaebol and workplace inequality: Stunted mobility of Korean Chinese employees in a Beijing subsidiary. *Journal of Contemporary Asia*, 49(1), 78–103.

Youssef, C. M., & Luthans, F. (2012). Positive global leadership. *Journal of World Business*, 47, 539–547.

Youssef-Morgan, C. M., & Luthans, F. (2013). Positive leadership: Meaning and application across cultures. *Organizational Dynamics*, 42(2), 198–208.

Yu, C., Zuo, X., Blum, R. W., Tolman, D., Kagesten, A., Mnari, K., … Lou, C. (2017). Marching to a different drummer: A cross-cultural comparison of young adolescents who challenge gender norms. *Journal of Adolescent Health*, 61(4), S48–S54. doi:10.1016/j.jadohealth.2017.07.005

Zaharna, R. S. (1995). Understanding cultural preferences of Arab communication patterns. *Public Relations Review*, 21(3), 241–255. doi:10.1016/0363-8111(95)90024-1

Zakaria, N., Amelinckx, A., & Wilemon, D. (2004). Working together apart? Building knowledge sharing culture for global teams. *Creativity and Innovation Management*, 13(1), 15–29.

Zalis, S. (2018). Get what you want: The woman's guide to negotiation. *Forbes*, August 15. Retrieved from https://www.forbes.com/sites/shelleyzalis/2018/08/15/get-what-you-want-the-womans-guide-to-negotiation/#dc8ead365457. Accessed on June 11, 2019.

Zambas, J. (2018). The 15 highest paid CEOs in the world. *CareerAddict – Money & Success*. August 17. Retrieved from https://www.careeraddict.com/top-ceos. Accessed on June 7, 2019.

Zander, C. (2014). Even Scandinavia has a CEO gender gap. *The Wall Street Journal*, May 21. Retrieved from https://www.wsj.com/articles/how-sandvik-scania-are-addressing-the-ceo-gender-gap-1400712884. Accessed on August 22, 2019.

Zander, L., Mockaitis, A. I., & Butler, C. L. (2012). Leading global teams. *Journal of World Business*, 47(4), 592–603.

Zarya, V. (2018). The share of female CEOs in the Fortune 500 dropped by 25% in 2018. *Fortune*, May 21. Retrieved from http://fortune.com/2018/05/21/women-fortune-500-2018/. Accessed on June 9, 2019.

Zenger, J. (2018). The confidence gap in men and women: Why it matters and how to overcome it. *Forbes*, April 8. Retrieved from https://www.forbes.com/sites/jackzenger/2018/04/08/the-confidence-gap-in-men-and-women-why-it-matters-and-how-to-overcome-it/#670793de3bfa. Accessed on June 2, 2019.

Zhu, K. (2014). 3 failed mergers and what they reveal. *Axial*, January 23. Retrieved from https://www.axial.net/forum/3-failed-mergers-and-what-they-reveal/. Accessed on November 15, 2019.

INDEX

relativism, 144
self-assessment, 390–391
sources of, 22–23
stable, 10–11
as system, 9–10
theories, 474–475
transmitting, 11
values, 15–16, 80–81, 378–379
Culture-as-meta-context (CMC) (figure),
    4, 29, 58, 195, 247, 565
attention, 97
as background, 28–30
cultural identity, 116
cultural lens, 93
cultural self-awareness, 50, 51
as guide, 30
heuristics, 102
meta-cognition, 52
omnipresent, 30–31
THINK–KNOW–DO (TKD), 69
Culture-contingent leadership, 431
Culture-just-is (CJI) concept, 4, 31–32,
    58, 69, 195, 565–566
Culture paradox
emic approach, 435
Euro/Western-centric leadership
    theories, 435

Dai, W., 201
Dalio, R., 281
Damore, J., 228, 229
Decision-making, 525–526
biases, 527–528
ethics, 530–533
process, 527
stages (table), 529
unfamiliar cultural contexts, 526–527
Deculturation, 24, 159–160
DeVries, M. K., 166
Dimon, J., 191
Directness, 308–309
Diversity (table). *See also* Cultural
    diversity, 5, 6
Diversity and inclusion (D&I), 238–239
implementation, 228–230
stages of (figure), 225–227, 226
targeting, 230

Dominance, 158
Double bind (figure), 273–275, 273, 285
Dweck, C., 54
Dwyer, S. L., 274

Eagly, A., 275
Earley, C., 64
Edwards, T., 268
Egalitarian organizations, 520–521
Ellemers, N., 256, 257
Ellinghaus, U., 40
Elliot, J., 134
Endowed traits, 190
England, G. W., 499
English Only movement, 149, 156
Environmental uncertainty, 509–510
Equal Employment Opportunity
    Commission (EEOC), 208
Equality. *See also* Gender, 236–237
gender, 282
theory (table), 470–472, 471, 475
Essentialism, 25–26, 247
Ethics
approaches to, 532–533, 536
culture, 530–531
decision-making, 530–533
ethical dilemmas, 555–556
perspectives (table), 534
relativism, 530–532
universalism, 530–532
Ethnicity (table), 21–22, 36, 204
Ethnocentrism (table), 52, 137, 139
consequences of, 142–144
elements of, 142
Ethnorelativism, 144
Etiquette rules, 172
Euro/Western-centric leadership
    theories, 435
Exceptionalism, 130
Expatriates (table), 164, 165
acculturation, 168
education, 166
integration for, 167
selection, 166
separation for, 167–168
training, 166
Expectancy theory, 469–470

Milton Keynes UK
Ingram Content Group UK Ltd.
UKHW022320110324
439192UK00009B/675

9 781544 381503